TREATING COMPLEX TRAUMATIC
STRESS DISORDERS IN ADULTS

Also by Julian D. Ford and Christine A. Courtois

*Treating Complex Traumatic Stress Disorders
in Children and Adolescents:
Scientific Foundations and Therapeutic Models*
Edited by Julian D. Ford and Christine A. Courtois

*Treatment of Complex Trauma:
A Sequenced, Relationship-Based Approach*
Christine A. Courtois and Julian D. Ford

TREATING COMPLEX TRAUMATIC STRESS DISORDERS IN ADULTS

Scientific Foundations and Therapeutic Models

SECOND EDITION

edited by
JULIAN D. FORD
CHRISTINE A. COURTOIS

Foreword by Judith Lewis Herman
Afterword by Bessel A. van der Kolk

THE GUILFORD PRESS
New York   London

The authors have checked with sources believed to be reliable in their efforts
to provide information that is complete and generally in accord with the
standards of practice that are accepted at the time of publication. However,
in view of the possibility of human error or changes in behavioral, mental
health, or medical sciences, neither the authors, nor the editors and publisher,
nor any other party who has been involved in the preparation or publication
of this work warrants that the information contained herein is in every
respect accurate or complete, and they are not responsible for any errors or
omissions or the results obtained from the use of such information. Readers
are encouraged to confirm the information contained in this book with other
sources.

Library of Congress Cataloging-in-Publication Data

Names: Ford, Julian D., editor. | Courtois, Christine A., editor.
Title: Treating complex traumatic stress disorders in adults : scientific
  foundations and therapeutic models / edited by Julian D. Ford, Christine
  A. Courtois ; foreword by Judith Lewis Herman ; afterword by Bessel A.
  van der Kolk.
Other titles: Treating complex traumatic stress disorders.
Description: Second edition. | New York : The Guilford Press, [2020] |
  Revison of: Treating complex traumatic stress disorders / 2009. |
  Includes bibliographical references and index. |
Identifiers: LCCN 2019051296 | ISBN 9781462543625 (paperback) |
  ISBN 9781462542178 (hardcover)
Subjects: LCSH: Post-traumatic stress disorder. | Psychic trauma.
Classification: LCC RC552.P67 T763 2020 | DDC 616.85/21—dc23
LC record available at *https://lccn.loc.gov/2019051296*

In memory of Anne and Jim (J. F.) and Normand and Irene (C. C.),
who are our role models for resilience, integrity, and love.

To clients who have suffered the complicated
consequences of complex trauma and whose symptoms
have often been misunderstood and misdiagnosed,
often compounding their pain and ability to recover.
It is our hope that the material in this book assists in
unraveling the complicated aftereffects and leads to better
understanding and more effective treatment.

To therapists everywhere who seek to understand the
complexities presented by these clients and who guide
them on the often arduous path to healing and recovery.
We hope this book fills in the gaps that so many of
us have experienced in our training and professional
experience, and offers helpful guidance on the treatment
process and the variety of therapeutic approaches
that make a real difference.

About the Editors

Julian D. Ford, PhD, ABPP, a clinical psychologist, is Professor of Psychiatry at the University of Connecticut School of Medicine, where he is Director of the Center for Trauma Recovery and Juvenile Justice and the Center for the Treatment of Developmental Trauma Disorders. He is past president of the International Society for Traumatic Stress Studies, a Fellow of the American Psychological Association (APA), and Associate Editor of the *Journal of Trauma and Dissociation* and the *European Journal of Psychotraumatology*. Dr. Ford has published more than 250 articles and book chapters. His research focuses on developmental trauma disorder and the Trauma Affect Regulation: Guide for Education and Therapy (TARGET) therapeutic intervention.

Christine A. Courtois, PhD, ABPP, a counseling psychologist, is retired from clinical practice and now serves as a consultant/trainer on trauma psychology and treatment. She is a Fellow of the APA and the International Society for the Study of Trauma and Dissociation. Dr. Courtois is a past president of APA Division 56 (Trauma Psychology) and served as Chair of the APA's *Clinical Practice Guideline for the Treatment of Posttraumatic Stress Disorder in Adults*. She has received the Award for Distinguished Contributions to Independent Practice from the APA, the Sarah Haley Award for Clinical Excellence from the International Society for Traumatic Stress Studies, the Award for Distinguished Service and Contributions to the Profession of Psychology from the American Board of Professional Psychology, and the Lifetime Achievement Award from APA Division 56.

Contributors

Pamela C. Alexander, PhD, private practice, Natick, Massachusetts

Lynne E. Angus, PhD, Department of Psychology, York University, Toronto, Ontario, Canada

John Briere, PhD, Department of Psychiatry and the Behavioral Sciences, Keck School of Medicine, University of Southern California, Los Angeles, California

Laura S. Brown, PhD, ABPP, private practice, Seattle, Washington

James Caringi, MSW, PhD, College of Health Professions and Biomedical Sciences, University of Montana School of Social Work, Missoula, Montana

Kathleen M. Chard, PhD, Cincinnati VA Medical Center and Department of Psychiatry and Behavioral Neuroscience, University of Cincinnati, Cincinnati, Ohio

Marylene Cloitre, PhD, Institute for Trauma and Stress, NYU Child Study Center and Department of Psychiatry, NYU School of Medicine, New York, New York, and National Center for PTSD, Dissemination and Training Division, VA Palo Alto Health Care System, Menlo Park, California

Christine A. Courtois, PhD, ABPP, private practice, Bethany Beach, Delaware

Anke Ehlers, PhD, Centre for Anxiety Disorders and Trauma, Department of Experimental Psychology, University of Oxford, Oxford, United Kingdom

Thomas Elbert, PhD, Department of Psychology, University of Konstanz, Konstanz, Germany

Janina Fisher, PhD, private practice, Sensorimotor Psychotherapy Institute, Oakland, California

Edna B. Foa, PhD, Center for the Treatment and Study of Anxiety, Department of Psychiatry, Perelman School of Medicine, University of Pennsylvania, Philadelphia, Pennsylvania

Julian D. Ford, PhD, ABPP, Department of Psychiatry, University of Connecticut Health Center, Farmington, Connecticut

Berthold Gersons, MD, PhD, Department of Psychiatry, Amsterdam University Medical Center, University of Amsterdam, Amsterdam, and ARQ National Psychotrauma Center, Diemen, The Netherlands

Ellen T. Healy, PhD, Women's Health Sciences Division, National Center for PTSD, VA Boston Healthcare System, Boston, Massachusetts

Elizabeth A. Hembree, PhD, Mood and Anxiety Disorders Treatment and Research Program, Department of Psychiatry, Perelman School of Medicine, University of Pennsylvania, Philadelphia, Pennsylvania

Judith Lewis Herman, MD, Department of Psychiatry, Harvard University, Cambridge, Massachusetts

Denise Hien, PhD, ABPP, Center of Alcohol and Substance Use Studies, Graduate School of Applied and Professional Psychology, Rutgers, The State University of New Jersey, Piscataway, New Jersey

Christie Jackson, PhD, private practice, New York, New York

Deborah L. Korn, PsyD, private practice, Cambridge, Massachusetts

Lisa Caren Litt, PhD, Department of Psychology, The New School for Social Research, New York, New York

Teresa López-Castro, PhD, Department of Psychology, Colin Powell School for Civic and Global Leadership, City College of New York, New York, New York

Andrea Lopez-Yianilos, PsyD, New York State Psychiatric Institute, Department of Psychiatry, Columbia University College of Physicians and Surgeons, New York, New York

Ari Lowell, PhD, New York State Psychiatric Institute, Department of Psychiatry, Columbia University College of Physicians and Surgeons, New York, New York

John C. Markowitz, MD, New York State Psychiatric Institute, Department of Psychiatry, Columbia University College of Physicians and Surgeons, New York, New York

Colleen E. Martin, PhD, Trauma Recovery Center, Cincinnati VA Medical Center, Cincinnati, Ohio

DeAnna L. Mori, PhD, VA Boston Healthcare System and Department of Psychiatry, Boston University School of Medicine, Boston, Massachusetts

Hannah Murray, PhD, Centre for Anxiety Disorders and Trauma, Department of Experimental Psychology, University of Oxford, Oxford, United Kingdom

Frank Neuner, PhD, Department of Psychology, Bielefeld University, Bielefeld, Germany

Mirjam J. Nijdam, PhD, Department of Psychiatry, Amsterdam University Medical Center, University of Amsterdam, Amsterdam, and ARQ National Psychotrauma Center, Diemen, The Netherlands

Barbara L. Niles, PhD, Behavioral Science Division, National Center for PTSD, VA Boston Healthcare System and Department of Psychiatry, Boston University School of Medicine, Boston, Massachusetts

Kore Nissenson, PhD, private practice, New York, New York

Pat Ogden, PhD, Sensorimotor Psychotherapy Institute, Broomfield, Colorado

Sandra C. Paivio, PhD, private practice, Toronto, Ontario, Canada

Laurie Anne Pearlman, PhD, private practice, Holyoke, Massachusetts

Katy Robjant, DClinPsy, Department of Psychology, University of Konstanz, Konstanz, Germany

Lesia M. Ruglass, PhD, Center of Alcohol and Substance Use Studies, Graduate School of Applied and Professional Psychology, Rutgers, The State University of New Jersey, Piscataway, New Jersey

Maggie Schauer, PD Dr, Department of Psychology, University of Konstanz, Konstanz, Germany

Ulrich Schnyder, MD, Department of Psychiatry and Psychotherapy, University of Zurich, Zurich, Switzerland

Francine Shapiro, PhD(deceased), EMDR Institute, Watsonville, California

Geert E. Smid, MD, PhD, Arq National Psychotrauma Center, Diemen, and University of Humanistic Studies, Utrecht, The Netherlands

Stefanie F. Smith, PhD, Hanna Boys Center, Sonoma, California

Joseph Spinazzola, PhD, Foundation Trust, Melrose, Massachusetts, and School of Counseling, Richmont Graduate University, Atlanta Georgia

Kathy Steele, MN, CS, private practice, Atlanta, Georgia

Ashley R. Trautman, MSW, JD, College of Health Professions and Biomedical Sciences, University of Montana School of Social Work, Missoula, Montana

Onno van der Hart, PhD, Department of Clinical and Health Psychology, Utrecht University, Utrecht, The Netherlands

Bessel A. van der Kolk, MD, Department of Psychiatry, Boston University School of Medicine, Boston, and Trauma Research Foundation, Brookline, Massachusetts

Sarah Krill Williston, PhD, Behavioral Science Division, National Center for PTSD, VA Boston Healthcare System, Boston, Massachusetts

Foreword

JUDITH LEWIS HERMAN

Sometimes the whole is greater than the sum of its parts.

The beauty of the complex posttraumatic stress disorder (PTSD) concept is in its integrative nature. Rather than a simple list of symptoms, it is a coherent formulation of the consequences of prolonged and repeated trauma. The first time I proposed the concept (Herman, 1992a), it was an attempt to bring some kind of order to the bewildering array of clinical presentations in survivors who had endured long periods of abuse. The concept gained sufficient recognition that it was subjected to field trials in DSM-IV, the American Psychiatric Association's official diagnostic manual (American Psychiatric Association, 1994). I was privileged to be part of the PTSD Working Group for DSM-IV, and so had a chance to participate in these studies.

The data seemed promising: My co-investigators and I found that somatization, dissociation, and affect dysregulation, three cardinal symptoms of complex PTSD, were present particularly in survivors of childhood abuse, less commonly in those abused in adolescence or adulthood, and rarely in people who had endured a single acute trauma that was not of human design. Moreover, these three groups of symptoms were highly intercorrelated (van der Kolk et al., 1996). We thought this demonstration of the prevalence and internal consistency of the diagnosis would constitute a strong argument for its inclusion in the DSM, and the PTSD Working Group agreed. Unfortunately, we were overruled at higher levels. The argument against inclusion of a separate diagnosis, as I understood it, went something like this: "We can't include complex PTSD as part of the trauma spectrum, because it does not fit neatly under the category of anxiety disorders. It might fit equally well under dissociative disorders, or somatization disorders, or even personality disorders." Which was, of course, exactly the point.

Though relegated to the "associated features" of PTSD in DSM-IV, the concept of complex PTSD nevertheless took on a life of its own. I like to think that this was because it was congruent with a vast body of clinical observation and experience, and it helped clinicians make sense of what they were observing. It also helped patients make sense of themselves.

When it came time for the next edition of the DSM, the same arguments were repeated (Resick et al., 2012). Asked to consult to the PTSD committee for DSM-5, I proposed that the concept was both parsimonious and clinically useful. While complex PTSD shared features of many other diagnoses, I argued, failure to recognize it as a separate and coherent entity resulted in many practical clinical problems: multiple diagnoses, multiple treatment protocols, and polypharmacy (Herman, 2012). Instead of recognizing complex PTSD as a separate diagnostic entity, however, DSM-5, in its wisdom, simply expanded the basic definition of PTSD to include many of the features of complex PTSD (American Psychiatric Association, 2013). Fortunately, our international colleagues have approached the issue with greater clarity. Based on collaborative international research that clearly supported the validity of the concept (Hyland et al., 2017; Palic et al., 2016), the World Health Organization's (2018) *International Classification of Diseases*, 11th edition (ICD-11), finally recognized complex PTSD as a distinct entity.

These days, when I teach about complex PTSD, I always begin with the social ecology of prolonged and repeated interpersonal trauma. There are two main points to grasp here. The first is that such trauma is always embedded in a social structure that permits the abuse and exploitation of a subordinate group. The predominance of women among patients who meet criteria for complex PTSD starts to make sense when one understands the insidious pervasiveness of violence against women and girls (Tjaden & Thoennes, 1998; Breiding et al., 2014; World Health Organization, 2013). The second point is that such trauma is always relational. It takes place when the victim is in a state of captivity, under the control and domination of the perpetrator.

Violence is but one among an array of methods that a perpetrator uses to establish dominion over a victim. Others include use of threats, control of bodily functions, capricious enforcement of petty rules, and random intermittent rewards; isolating the victim; and forcing the victim to engage in activities that are degrading or immoral. These methods break down normal capacities for self-regulation, autonomy, and initiative; they humiliate the victim and undermine the victim's closest relationships. These methods are cross-cultural and international; they are used because they work (Amnesty International, 1973). The symptoms later observed in survivors often make sense when one understands the methods of coercion to which they have been subjected.

If the victim is a child, and the perpetrator, as is most commonly the case, is a parent, a close family member, or a primary role model, such as a teacher, coach, or religious leader, the absence of a protective parent or the presence of passive bystanders is felt as palpably as the presence of the perpetrator. Abuse is compounded by neglect, when others fail to notice or intervene. It seems increasingly clear that the pathological changes in relationship and identity seen in survivors reflect the disruptions in attachment that almost always attend childhood abuse. The "characterological" features of complex PTSD start to make sense if one imagines how a child might develop within a relational matrix in which the strong do as they please, the weak submit, caretakers seem willfully blind, and there is no one to turn to for protection.

What kind of "internal working models" (Bowlby, 1973) of self, other, and relationship would be likely to develop under such circumstances? This thought experiment turns out to be quite useful clinically. One begins to understand the survivor's malignant self-loathing, the deep mistrust of others, and the template for relational reenactments that the survivor carries into adult life. Forming a therapeutic alliance becomes somewhat easier if the clinician understands at the outset why the patient might be unable to imagine a relationship that is genuinely caring, freely chosen, fair to both parties, mutually attuned, and mutually rewarding. It becomes the therapist's task, then, to model, explain, and engage the patient in such a relationship, knowing that initially the patient will perceive this is as another likely setup for betrayal.

The past two decades have seen the flowering of clinical innovation in the psychotherapy field, with the development of many new evidence-informed treatment models addressing some of the core manifestations of complex PTSD. The wealth and diversity of therapeutic approaches are well represented in this comprehensive volume. We are still in a period of experimentation; it is far too early to make any kind of judgment about which treatment approaches might be the most effective for which patients. Nevertheless, some constants have emerged.

First, many authors cite the importance of recognizing areas of strength and resilience, even in the most severely traumatized individuals, as this will constitute the basis for forming a therapeutic alliance (Harvey & Tummala-Narra, 2007). One of the many advantages of group therapy for this population is that group members are called upon to give supportive feedback to one another, and in the process discover that they have something of genuine value to give (Mendelsohn, Zachary, & Harney, 2007). Couple and family systems therapies also provide opportunities for survivors to discover or build healthy relationships and new working models for trust and security within their most immediate relationships.

Second, there does seem to be a consensus about the central importance of developing a trusting and truly collaborative, rather than authoritarian, treatment relationship. Indeed, the strongest "evidence base" we have in the study of psychotherapy supports the central importance of the therapeutic alliance (Horvath, Del Re, Flükiger, & Symonds, 2011). Most authors also recognize that forming a stable, collaborative relationship is particularly challenging with a person who has been subjected to coercive control, because of the mistrustful survivor's tendency to engage the therapist in relational reenactments. The difficulties of maintaining a well-bounded therapeutic frame and the risks of vicarious traumatization are now well understood, as are the prescriptions for therapists' self-care and self-reflection.

Beyond the notion of collaboration or mutuality, many authors invoke some concept of an observing therapeutic alliance, that is, a relationship within which the patient develops an "observing ego," or the capacity to "mentalize" (Fonagy, Gergely, Jurist, & Target, 2002; Bateman & Fonagy, 2006). In mentalizing trauma, the aim is "to help patients think, feel, and talk about the experience so as to be able to have the experience in mind without being overwhelmed by it" (Allen, 2013, p. 202).

Finally, most current treatment approaches make use of a tripartite model of recovery stages (Herman, 1992b). The task of the first stage is to establish safety. That of the second stage is to come to terms with the trauma story. Finally, the task of the third stage is to repair and enlarge the survivor's social connections. This sequence has always seemed commonsensical to me, and apparently most of the authors in this volume have agreed.

Of course, these stages are not meant to be applied rigidly. In early recovery, for example, issues of safety and self-care always take priority, but this does not mean the subject of trauma should be avoided. On the contrary, patients in early recovery often benefit greatly from trauma-informed treatment. Acknowledging the trauma and naming its consequences begin the process of meaning making. Survivors come to understand, often for the first time, that their symptoms make sense in the context of a formative relationship of coercive control. This understanding is a powerful antidote to the feelings of malignant shame and stigma that afflict so many survivors. What one does *not* do in early recovery is any form of "exposure" therapy. Coming to terms with the grim details of the trauma story must await the development of a solid therapeutic alliance and some sort of secure base in the present from which the past can be safely approached. This is a task that requires more than a few scripted sessions.

The concept of stages can be applied to both group and individual psychotherapy. At the Victims of Violence Program (in the Department of Psychiatry at Cambridge Health Alliance), we have developed a wide array of time-limited groups. These range from an "entry-level" Stage 1 group, the Trauma Information Group, which has minimal screening requirements or demands for commitment (Herman et al., 2018), to a trauma-focused, Stage 2 group, the Trauma Recovery Group, which has careful screening requirements and demands a high level of commitment from group members (Herman & Schatzow, 1984; Mendelsohn et al., 2011). The former is a psychoeducational group with weekly topics and homework assignments similar to those described in this volume. The latter is a goal-focused group in which trauma narratives are shared, empathic feedback is cultivated, and survivors experience active mastery in affiliation with others.

We do not have a Stage 3 trauma group model, because we find that at this stage, the survivor no longer feels that his or her identity is defined by her trauma history. Furthermore, with an expanded capacity for relationship, the survivor will have gained confidence that mutual understanding and compassion are possible even with people who have not endured the same kinds of traumas. There is no need, therefore, to restrict group membership only to trauma survivors. If group therapy is indicated, a basic interpersonal psychotherapy group will be quite suitable.

In the Foreword to the first edition of this volume, 10 years ago, I expressed the hope that the future would bring more cooperative ventures integrating different treatment models. In this regard, I imagined that the congruence between features of complex PTSD and borderline personality disorder (BPD), first documented now almost 30 years ago (Herman, Perry, & van der Kolk, 1989; Ford & Courtois, 2014), might have increasing importance from a practical standpoint because of clinical advances in the treatment of BPD.

For example, in a remarkable 8-year follow up study of a randomized controlled trial, Bateman and Fonagy (2008) demonstrated that a psychodynamic, "mentalization"-based treatment program was much more successful than treatment as usual for patients with BPD. Their model called for 18 months of intensive day treatment, followed by 18 months of biweekly group psychotherapy. Certainly, this time frame seemed much more realistic to me than that of existing evidence-based treatment models for PTSD; therefore, I expressed the hope that we would soon develop similarly intensive, multimodal treatment models that might become the standard of care for complex PTSD.

Alas, this has not happened—yet. Rather, we have seen the proliferation of many brands of short-term therapy for classic PTSD, along with attempts to apply these models to complex PTSD. The limitations of this approach are well demonstrated in a meta-analysis by Dorrepaal et al. (2014), who further suggest that the next phase of research should focus on direct comparison of active treatment modalities. In practice, many of the models described in this book are designed for greater flexibility than their short-term research protocols might suggest, or they are techniques designed for integration into a relational, open-ended psychotherapy rather than a stand-alone model. Since it is not realistic to expect that practitioners will become expert in numerous different, specialized techniques, some researchers now suggest that we might be ready to shift our focus from studies of competing models to studies that elucidate the common features of effective therapies (Laska, Gurman, & Wampold, 2014).

But that is for the future. In the meantime, it makes sense to pause and reflect on how far the field has come in a quarter century, and to represent the state of current knowledge in the field of complex traumatic disorders. This is the task that these editors and authors have set for themselves. This volume captures the intellectual excitement of a field in rapid development—or perhaps I should say, of multiple fields, intersecting in surprising and unforeseen ways. It also captures the spirit and passionate commitment of the many contributing authors, researchers, and clinicians who have devoted their professional lives to the project of survivors' recovery.

References

Allen, J. G. (2013). *Restoring mentalizing in attachment relationships: Treating trauma with plain old therapy*. Washington, DC: American Psychiatric Press.

American Psychiatric Association. (1994). *Diagnostic and statistical manual of mental disorders* (4th ed.). Washington, DC: Author.

American Psychiatric Association. (2013). *Diagnostic and statistical manual of mental disorders* (5th ed.). Arlington, VA: Author.

Amnesty International. (1973). *Report on torture*. New York: Farrar, Straus & Giroux.

Bateman, A., & Fonagy, P. (2006). *Mentalization-based treatment for borderline personality disorder: A practical guide*. New York: Oxford University Press.

Bateman, A., & Fonagy, P. (2008). Eight-year follow up of patients treated for borderline personality disorder: Mentalization-based treatment vs. treatment as usual. *American Journal of Psychiatry, 165,* 631–638.

Bowlby, J. (1973). *Attachment and loss: Vol. 2. Separation: Anxiety and anger*. New York: Basic Books.

Breiding, M. J., Smith, S. G., Basile, K. C., Walters, M. L., Chen, J., & Merrick, M. T. (2014, September). Prevalence and characteristics of sexual violence, stalking, and intimate partner violence victimization—National Intimate Partner and Sexual Violence Survey, United States, 2011. *Morbidity and Mortality Weekly Report, Surveillance Summaries, 63*(8), 1–18.

Dorrepaal, E., Thomaes, K., Hoogendoorn, A. W., Veltman, D. J., Draijer, N., & van Balkom, A. J. (2014). Evidence-based treatment for adult women with child abuse-related Complex PTSD: A quantitative review. *European Journal of Psychotraumatology, 5,* Article 23613.

Fonagy, P., Gergely, G., Jurist, E. L., & Target, M. (2002). *Affect regulation, mentalization, and the development of the self*. New York: Other Press.

Ford, J. D., & Courtois, C. A. (2014). Complex PTSD, affect dysregulation, and borderline personality disorder. *Borderline Personality Disorder and Emotion Dysregulation, 1,* 9.

Harvey, M. R., & Tummala-Narra, P. (Eds.). (2007). *Sources and expressions of resilience in trauma survivors: Ecological theory, multicultural practice*. New York: Haworth.

Herman J. L. (1992a). Complex PTSD: A syndrome in survivors of prolonged and repeated trauma. *Journal of Traumatic Stress, 5,* 377–391.

Herman J. L. (1992b). *Trauma and recovery*. New York: Basic Books.

Herman, J. L. (2012). CPTSD is a distinct entity: Comment on Resick et al. *Journal of Traumatic Stress, 25,* 256–257.

Herman, J. L., Kallivayalil, D., Glass, L., Hamm, B., Brown, P., & Astrachan, T (2018). *Group trauma treatment in early recovery: Promoting safety and self-care*. New York: Guilford Press.

Herman, J. L., Perry, J. C., & van der Kolk, B. A. (1989). Childhood trauma in borderline personality disorder. *American Journal of Psychiatry, 146,* 490–495.

Herman, J. L., & Schatzow, E., (1984). Time-limited group therapy for women with a history of incest. *International Journal of Group Psychotherapy, 34,* 605–616.

Horvath, A.O., Del Re, A.C., Flükiger, C., & Symonds, D. (2011). Alliance in individual psychotherapy. In J. C. Norcross (Ed.), *Psychotherapy relationships that work: Evidence-based responsiveness* (pp. 25–69). New York: Oxford University Press.

Hyland, P., Shevlin, M., Elklit, A., Murphy, J., Vallieres, F., Garvert, D. W., & Cloitre, M. (2017). An assessment of the construct validity of the ICD-11 proposal for complex posttraumatic stress disorder. *Psychological Trauma: Theory, Research, Practice, and Policy, 9,* 1–9.

Laska, K. M., Gurman, A. S., & Wampold, B. E. (2014). Expanding the lens of evidence-based practice in psychotherapy: A common factors perspective. *Psychotherapy, 51,* 467–481.

Mendelsohn, M., Herman, J. L., Schatzow, E., Coco, M., Kallivayalil, D., & Levitan, J. (2011). *The Trauma Recovery Group: A guide for practitioners.* New York: Guilford Press.

Mendelsohn, M., Zachary, R., & Harney, P. (2007). Group therapy as an ecological bridge to new community for trauma survivors. In M. R. Harvey & P. Tummala-Narra (Eds.), *Sources and expressions of resilience in trauma survivors: Ecological theory, multicultural practice* (pp. 227–244). New York: Haworth.

Palic, S., Zerach, G., Shevilin, M, Zeligman, Z., Elkit, A., & Solomon Z. (2016). Evidence of complex posttraumatic stress disorder (CPTSD) across populations with prolonged trauma of varying interpersonal intensity and ages of exposure. *Psychiatry Research, 246*, 692–699.

Resick, P., Bovin, M., Calloway, A., Dick, A., King, M., Mitchell, K., & Wolf, E. J. (2012). A critical evaluation of the complex PTSD literature: Implications for DSM-5. *Journal of Traumatic Stress, 25*, 239–249.

Tjaden, P., & Thoennes, N. (1998, November). Prevalence, incidence, and consequences of violence against women: Findings from the National Violence against Women Survey. *National Institute of Justice and Center for Disease Control and Prevention: Research in Brief*, pp. 1–16. (NCJ 172837)

van der Kolk, B. A., Pelcovitz, D., Roth, S, Mandel, F., McFarlane, A., & Herman, J. L. (1996). Dissociation, affect dysregulation and somatization: The complexity of adaptation to trauma. *American Journal of Psychiatry, 153*(Festschrift Supplement), 83–93.

World Health Organization, Department of Reproductive Health and Research, London School of Hygiene and Tropical Medicine, & South African Medical Research Council. (2013). *Global and regional estimates of violence against women: Prevalence and health effects of intimate partner violence and non-partner sexual violence* (WHO ref. no. 978 92 4 156462 5). Geneva, Switzerland: World Health Organization.

Acknowledgments

We are most grateful to many colleagues—too many, unfortunately, to mention all by name. We are deeply appreciative of the insights and expertise contributed to this book by each of the chapter authors and by our Foreword and Afterword authors and mentors Judith Lewis Herman and Bessel A,van der Kolk. All were enthusiastic in joining this project and contributing their work, as well as admirably tolerant of our timelines, deadlines, and editing.

We want to especially thank our colleagues who have championed the issue of complex trauma and metamodel of complex traumatic stress disorders over the past 30 years and whose dedication and hard work in the past decade has so greatly informed this book. Many have generously served as the contributors for this book, while others have provided leadership and both intellectual and moral support to the professionals and the survivors who strive to prevent complex trauma and to heal and promote the recovery of all who have experienced its multifaceted consequences.

And for their dedicated work in advancing the science and treatment of complex traumatic stress disorders, we sincerely thank the leadership and members of the International Society for the Study of Trauma and Dissociation, the International Society for Traumatic Stress Studies and the growing number of other Traumatic Stress Societies around the world, Division 56 (Psychological Trauma) of the American Psychological Association, the National Child Traumatic Stress Network, the Academy on Violence and Abuse, and the American Professional Society on the Abuse of Children.

We also gratefully acknowledge the ongoing support from our family members and friends, and especially from our spouses (Judy and Tom). They have provided each of us with countless gifts of wisdom, patience, and encouragement that have added immeasurable meaning to our lives and have helped to make this book possible.

Contents

PART I. OVERVIEW

PART II. EVIDENCE-SUPPORTED INDIVIDUAL
TREATMENT MODALITIES AND MODELS

PART III. GROUP/CONJOINT THERAPY MODELS

TREATING COMPLEX TRAUMATIC STRESS DISORDERS IN ADULTS

PART I

OVERVIEW

Defining and Understanding Complex Trauma and Complex Traumatic Stress Disorders

JULIAN D. FORD
CHRISTINE A. COURTOIS

In this chapter, we first provide an overview of cutting-edge definition, theory, and research on complex trauma and complex traumatic stress disorders (CTSDs), then discuss the newly included diagnosis of complex posttraumatic stress disorder (CPTSD) in the latest edition of the *International Classification of Diseases* (ICD-11; World Health Organization, 2018) and the dissociative subtype of posttraumatic stress disorder (PTSD) in the fifth edition of the *Diagnostic and Statistical Manual of Mental Disorders* (DSM-5; American Psychiatric Association, 2013). We identify key developments and controversies in the definition of complex trauma, CTSDs, and the diagnosis of complex PTSD and evolving practice guidelines including the distinction between clinical and professional practice guidelines, and best practices and consensus-based guidelines, along with evidence-based treatment. We then preview the chapters that follow, describing how each uniquely, and the entire set collectively, offer a picture of how the CTSD treatment field is evolving and its likely direction in the next decade and beyond. We begin by defining complex trauma.

Complex Traumatic Stressors: Evolving Definitions of an Elusive Concept

Stressors are events that require adaptation on the part of the affected individual in order to protect against a threat, solve a problem, or take advantage of an opportunity—they may be experiences or events that are positive and growth producing (leading to *eustress*) or negative and growth-stunting and damaging events (leading to *distress*). *Traumatic stressors* "up the ante," so to speak. These are stressors—events, experiences, and exposures—that greatly exceed the individual's capacity to control, cope with, or withstand and that compromise the individual's psychophysiological equilibrium or stasis. Traumatic stressors have had many definitions over the past 150 years, but a recurrent theme is that they pose an imminent threat or actuality of death, or through other means cause fundamental and life-altering psychophysiological harm (*psychological trauma*) to the organism. Of note is that most of the definitions of traumatic stress refer to physical events personally experienced or witnessed (alone or in a group), and do not explicitly recognize emotional or psychological events and harms as traumatic per se, a stance that has been the subject of critique (DePrince et al., 2012). DSM-5 Criterion A describes traumatic stressors as "exposure to actual or threatened death, serious injury, or sexual violence" through direct experience, witnessing, learning about extreme harm to family or close friends, or experiencing repeated or extreme exposure to aversive details (American Psychiatric Association, 2013, p. 271). Additionally, although the consequences are acknowledged as possibly lifelong and extensive, traumatic exposure and experience do not receive much recognition in the DSM as being impacted or expressed by the victim's age/stage of development, except in the most general of ways (p. 279). A subtype of "PTSD in children age 6 years or younger" was included in this edition of the DSM; however, it is noteworthy that there is no separate diagnosis of PTSD in children after age 6.

Complex trauma refers to traumatic stressors with many additional complications. In our previous work, we identified several defining characteristics of *complex psychological trauma*: (1) interpersonal experiences and events that often involve relational betrayal; (2) repetitive, prolonged, pervasive, and in some cases, ongoing events; (3) involvement of direct attack, harm, and/or neglect and abandonment by caregivers or other adults who are responsible for responding to or protecting children and adolescents—this may extend to organizations and cultures that are disbelieving of the victim and deny the occurrence of the traumatic circumstance and so are unresponsive or that support or provide safe haven for perpetrators; (4) occurrence at developmentally vulnerable times in the victim's life, often beginning in early childhood (and sometimes in utero and in infancy); and (5) have great potential to compromise severely a child's physical and psychological maturation and development, and to undermine or even reverse important developmental attainments at any point in the lifespan (Courtois & Ford, 2019, p. 1; Ford & Courtois, 2014, p. 9). When abuse occurs in a family or other closed context or system (i.e., parish/synagogue/temple/ashram/mosque/church hierarchy; school, work, military command, team, or recreational setting) by a member of that group, escape is often difficult, if not impossible. Such a circumstance creates a condition of accessibility and captivity that makes recurrence and escalation much more likely. So, too, do intimidation tactics, including threats of abandonment or violence or other coercion that are used to pressure victims into silence and nondisclosure, a process that, when successful, further entraps them and renders them susceptible to additional abuse.

Although much of the emphasis in our previous books (and in this one as well) is on complex trauma that occurs over the course of childhood and adolescence, it is now recognized that this form of trauma can continue or begin in adulthood in forms such as sexual harassment and assault, domestic violence, refugee status, racial, cultural, religious, or gender/sexual identity and orientation-based violence and oppression, geographical displacement, kidnapping, war, torture, genocide, personal or cyberbullying, human trafficking, and sexual or other forms of captivity or slavery. Moreover, complex trauma often occurs across generations (labeled as intergenerational, historical, or colonialism), fueled by the lack of acknowledgment or resolution of previous trauma and loss as well as recurring abuse. Complex trauma may be further based on unique characteristics of the individual and primary group membership and associated power or lack thereof. These characteristics may include ethnicity, skin color and other distinguishing features, gender, sexual identity and orientation, class, age, ability, and economic status. Prejudice and discrimination based on these characteristics can lead to the oppression and mistreatment of entire families, clans, tribes, nations, and those who hold different religious, cultural, and political beliefs, among other factors (Kira et al., 2011) over the course of generations, creating conditions of *historical cumulative individual trauma, as well as group or societal trauma.*

Most often, complex trauma occurs in a repeated and layered fashion that causes a compounding of the need for ongoing psychobiological defenses that ultimately alter the body and mind of the survivor. Such recurring and layered events and their multifaceted aftermath are referred to as *polyvictimization.* An additional element of this tragic trajectory is that it often creates ongoing risk for revictimization. Ford (2017a) summarized the dimensions of complex trauma that distinguish it from other forms into five "I's," to which we add several more: *Intentional interpersonal* acts that are *inescapable* and cause *injury* that is potentially *irreparable.* Additionally, complex traumatic stressors are highly *intimate, intrusive,* and *invasive* of the body and the self of the *individual,* often involving *imminent threat,* the totality of which results in deformations of *identity* (including the capacity to *integrate one's identity and experience and maintain one's integrity*) and disrupting *interpersonal capacity for intimate and other relationships.*

The first two "I's" are *intentional interpersonal acts* that violate the rights and integrity of others with the intent of meeting a particular need (e.g., among others, domination, power, sex, affection, sadism) of the perpetrator (i.e., the "evil that men [and women] do"). When people harm other people, it constitutes a desecration of the basic social contract, a willful disregard for and disrespect of the safety, dignity, integrity, and well-being of other human beings. In addition to creating fear/terror in relation to the perpetrator(s) (which can result in the PTSD symptoms of intrusive reexperiencing, numbing, avoidance, and hypervigilance), such acts raise existential issues and call into question whether *anyone* can be trusted, whether there is *any* hope for the future, and whether there is something *fundamentally damaged or defective* about the survivor that made them[1] the target or victim of the trauma and possibly its cause (Herman, 1992a). Many CT survivors describe themselves, their existence, or their worlds as being a "void" or a "black hole filled with vileness." Moreover, when harm is perpetrated by individuals or institutions that should safeguard the welfare and rights of victim/survivors, this *betrayal* exacerbates the original betrayal involved in the trauma, causing additional fear and demoralization that can lead to a sense of shame and profound disconnection and alienation from self and others (Fisher, 2017; Smith & Freyd, 2014; see also Chapter 24).

When traumatic experiences actually are, or seem to be, *inescapable,* the sense of being *entrapped* and *helpless* can lead to a combination of conditioned defeat and learned helplessness in both children and adults (Hammack, Cooper, & Lezak, 2012). In extreme cases, such as when political or ethnic violence involves subjecting children (Gadeberg, Montgomery, Frederiksen, & Norredam, 2017) or adults (McDonnell, Robjant, & Katona, 2013) to captivity or torture, victims understandably can feel morally and mentally defeated and helpless to protect themselves, loved ones, and their community and institutions. Tragically, the core features of captivity and torture are not limited to these public forms of violence but also may occur in more disguised ways as a result of child abuse and domestic or intimate partner violence, and in single or repeated episodes of sexual assault, sexual harassment, or kidnapping. Much like the response of animals to inescapable danger when escape from a predator is impossible, human victims often go beyond the initial physiological fight-or-flight defensive response and move into a state of freeze and collapse (also known as *tonic immobility*—the body and mind shutting down) (Bovin et al., 2014, p. 721; Porges, 2011). This response, which appears to be an automatic self-protective reaction that occurs without conscious intent, ironically can later cause the victim to feel chronically guilty and ashamed for not having been better at fighting back or self-protection (Bovin et al., 2014), feelings that potentially set the stage for severe or complex PTSD symptoms.

The *irreparable injury* that is caused by *intentional and inescapable* acts of harm and *personal intrusion* primarily is psychological and spiritual (Walker, Courtois, & Aten, 2015), although certainly it causes physiological alteration and damage as well. *Moral injury* initially was thought to occur when a survivor committed acts in traumatic events that violated personal values, but it also has been found to be associated with being violated psychologically and spiritually by other person(s) (Hoffman, Liddell, Bryant, & Nickerson, 2018). Moral injury sustained as a result of one's own or others' actions often leads to guilt, shame, anger, and depression, as well as PTSD, but when injury results from the actions of others (i.e., especially when they involve betrayal of some sort and violate the terms of a relationship or an agreed-to commitment, duty,

---

[1] "They," "their," "them," and "themselves" have been used in this chapter and our other chapters (Chapters 2, 3, 4, 18, 19, 21, and the Epilogue) to represent nongendered pronouns.

or responsibility), the PTSD symptoms are often the most severe and complex. Moral injury caused by others' acts also tends to be associated with a sense of having been not only harmed but also essentially damaged in ways that seem *irreparable,* and this can lead to severe problems with feeling disillusioned with and alienated from others, alienated from self, grossly defective, and deserving of mistreatment and lack of assistance. Dissociation, self-harm, multiple forms of addiction, and suicidality can occur in response to these feelings (Ford & Gomez, 2015) and as means of self-management and tension reduction, and paradoxically as self-soothing and self-repair (Briere, 2019).

Although *intentional, inescapable, and irreparably injurious* acts occur both in public and in private, in either case they are *intimate, intrusive,* and *invasive,* since they violate the survivor's physical, psychological, and spiritual *integrity* and boundaries. Because complex trauma is the opposite of safe, respectful, mutual, and self-determined intimate encounters or relationships, it calls into question the safety, sanctity, and even the very possibility of being a unique and *integrated individual* who can be *intimately involved* with other human beings. When experiences involve psychological or physical (or both) domination, oppression, and intrusion, the sense of subjugation and exploitation intensifies the survivor's sense of *inescapable* and *irreparable injury,* often identified as self-alienation, that occurs in conjunction with problems of self-integration (Fisher, 2017; see also Chapter 24). This, in turn, leads to estrangement and withdrawal from contact with others, identified as other-alienation and involving profound mistrust (see Chapters 20 and 21). The result is severely dysregulated emotions and actions, potentially including depression, panic and other anxiety conditions and disorders, guilt, shame, anger and rage, addiction, disorders of eating or sexual involvement, psychosomatic or autoimmune illness, borderline personality disorder, psychosis, or suicidality. These are cardinal features and adaptations—not *disorders* but complex stress *reactions and expressions of distress/symptoms*—that are found in CTSDs.

CTSDs: Controversy and Innovation

Complex Traumatic Stress Reactions and Adaptations

The ongoing and repetitive exposure to and experiencing of complex traumatic stressors without relief typically result in stress reactions that are, in parallel form, more complex. The findings of child psychiatrist Lenore Terr, a pioneer researcher of childhood trauma, indicated a distinct pattern of response when the trauma was what she termed Type I (single event or very short term, usually of an *impersonal* nature and occurring quite suddenly and unexpectedly) as opposed to Type II (recurrent and prolonged/pervasive *interpersonal* trauma including physical/sexual and emotional intrusion that comes to be anticipated and dreaded) (Terr, 1991). While both types have the potential to cause symptoms of acute stress disorder (ASD) and PTSD in their aftermath, Type II has additional dimensions that cause reactions and symptoms above and beyond those of standard or classic PTSD. According to Terr, survivors of Type II trauma must find ways to emotionally and physically fend off or defend against repeated acts of aggression and intrusion, whether these occur regularly or on a more intermittent basis.

Ford (2005) labeled Type II trauma as "developmentally adverse interpersonal traumas" in recognition of their capacity to interfere with and interrupt the victim's healthy physical and psychological development. As we wrote in the first edition of this text, "Complex trauma often forces the child victim to substitute automatic (i.e., implicit or nonconscious defensive and) survival tactics for adaptive self-regulation, starting at the most basic level of physical reactions (e.g., intense states of hyperarousal/agitation or hypoarousal/immobility) and behavioral (e.g., aggressive or passive–avoidant response) that can become so automatic and habitual that the child's emotional and cognitive development are derailed or distorted" (Courtois & Ford, 2013, p. 14). Polyvagal theory (Porges, 2007) has given a psychophysiological explanation for the freeze and collapse that is often involved in repeated abuse, as has research findings that dissociation (i.e., escape where there is no escape; floating above and seeing it happen to him or her; "not me") is a quite common response in repeatedly abused children (Putnam, 2009). Furthermore, we noted that "in vulnerable children, complex trauma compromises attachment security, self-integrity, and ultimately self-regulation. Thus, it constitutes a threat not only to physical but also to psychological survival—to the development of the self and the capacity to regulate emotions" (Courtois & Ford, 2013, p. 14). This finding accords with a deformation of the developing self and loss of a sense of positive identity that occurs when PTSD gets intertwined with the child's physical and emotional maturation and developing personality (Herman, 1992a).

As discussed previously (Ford, 2009) and in more detail in Chapter 2, the immediate responses to stressors—whether traumatic or not—are *psychophysiological stress reactions* that mobilize the body to fight or flee and occur instantaneously, automatically, and out of conscious awareness (implicitly), directed by areas in the more primitive midbrain and lower brain that operate on reflex and habit and so do not require thought or reflection. However, as areas become activated in the brain's outer layer (cortex), cognitive processes enable the individual to ascertain the degree of danger and consciously (explicitly) and intentionally modify and redirect the automatic stress reactions (i.e., executive function). The classic example is the instinctual alarm response in reaction to seeing an object that looks like a snake and connotes imminent danger. The alarm system spontaneously activates, but when the perceptual information reaches the cortex and it determines that the "snake" is actually a stick, the alarm reaction downshifts and the body returns to its normal state. However, when the alarm reaction is the result of actual severe danger or harm (i.e., acute traumatic stressors, the instinctual reaction can dominate and override the reflective cognitive reappraisal), leading to extreme and potentially persistent and impairing stress reactions and an ASD (Bryant, 2017).

The severity, and especially the ongoing or ambient recurrence of complex or Type II trauma, can, as Terr (2000) noted, evoke stress reactions that are so powerful that they override or shut down any subsequent conscious or self-reflective stress response. These reactions often involve dissociation and a splitting of the self from the stressor that, over time, become an autonomic and automatic mechanism that initially or exclusively occurs in response to antici- pating and coping with ongoing threat. This type of response can generalize to other situations or stimuli that serve as triggers to the same response, even when the situation is neutral and benign rather than dangerous. Such responses are often observed in the clinical setting and can involve reexperiencing phe- nomena, hyperarousal and hypervigiliance on one hand, or hypoarousal, numbing, alexithymia, and dissociation on the other. The latter reactions can at times lead to physical and emotional shutdown and ultimately to collapse and inability to respond.

Thus, *complex traumatic stress reactions,* like other reactions to ordi- nary and traumatic stressors, involve states of heightened or diminished (i.e., hyper- or hypo-) arousal. This involves a sequence of responses of freeze, fight, flight, and immobility that was first identified in the study of animals caught in situations of inescapable danger. In the *fight* response, stress reactions mani- fest as aggression directed toward the source of the threat or the environment (e.g., fighting back, hitting, kicking, attacking, raging, screaming). In the *flight* response, the victim tries to physically escape the dangerous person or environ- ment through whatever means are available (e.g., making a run for it, calling for help). If fight and flight fail to resolve the danger or provide an escape, the *immobility* response involve physical collapse and a paralysis-like state. Like that of a captured animal about to be attacked and even killed, this response involves analgesia and anesthesia to lessen the pain and physical immobility that can appear to a predator as if the prey is severely injured or dead. The immobility response also involves a psychological shutdown, including feelings such as intense despair, defeat, resignation, and helplessness, and deperson- alization, derealization, and dissociative fragmentation of the self (e.g., "It's not happening, it's not happening to me, I'm not in the picture"; Ford, 2017a; Porges, 2011).

The repeated and escalating nature of traumatic circumstances that involve intentional harm by perpetrator(s) known to or related to a dependent, acces- sible, and vulnerable victim in a closed environment (i.e., ongoing incestuous abuse in a family, sexual harassment in the workplace, domestic violence in the home, torture in a prison) may result in an automatic overriding of the fight– flight phases of the stress response and feigned compliance and almost imme- diate immobilization. The victim may have learned that fight–flight is useless because it results in escalation of the danger rather than its cessation. This is especially the case if resistance or attempted escape enrages a perpetrator who views it as a challenge to their domination and control. Victimized individuals may also superficially comply (or feign compliance) with their perpetrators in an attempt to mollify them or decrease their dangerousness. It may also be more self-protective to go into a state of collapse and associated analgesia and anesthesia in order to blunt awareness and pain. CTSDs involve chronic and extreme reactions that are virtually identical to the immobility phase of the stress response, at times interspersed with hyperarousal symptoms. Both therefore represent unsuccessful attempts at fight or flight.

Complex Traumatic Stress Disorders

CTSDs in Adulthood

Complex PTSD (Herman, 1992a) or disorders of extreme stress not otherwise specified (DESNOS; van der Kolk, Roth, Pelcovitz, Sunday, & Spinazzola, 2005) were first proposed as psychiatric diagnoses more than 25 years ago. Since then, these and other models of adult CTSDs have spurred important advances in clinical research (Ben-Ezra et al., 2018; Cloitre, Garvert, Weiss, Carlson, & Bryant, 2014; Ford, 2015; Karatzias et al., 2017a, 2018; Krammer, Kleim, Simmen-Janevska, & Maercker, 2016; Murphy, Elklit, Dokkedahl, & Shevlin, 2018; Palic et al., 2016; Sachser, Keller, & Goldbeck, 2017; Van Dijke, Ford, Frank, & van der Hart, 2015; Van Dijke, Hopman, & Ford, 2018) and practice (Briere & Lanktree, 2012; Cloitre, 2015; Cloitre et al., 2011; Courtois & Ford, 2013; Ford & Courtois, 2014; Herman, 2012; Schnyder & Cloitre, 2015). Although still controversial as a diagnosis (Bryant, 2012; Goodman, 2012; Herman, 2012; Resick et al., 2012), CTSDs represent a psychobiologically based metamodel for psychopathology that overarches several main responses and diagnoses and is person centered (Jenness & McLaughlin, 2015) and adaptation and resilience focused (McLaughlin & Lambert, 2017).

A core construct has emerged to distinguish CTSDs/complex PTSD from PTSD and other psychiatric disorders: *disturbances of self-organization* (DSOs; Cloitre, Garvert, Brewin, et al., 2013; Shevlin et al., 2017, 2018) or what Herman (1992a) identified as *deformations of the self* and Smith and Freyd (2014) as betrayal-trauma from recurrent traumatic exposure and the need for the victim to mount extensive psychological defenses in response. This stands in contrast to the adaptations used to cope with fear resulting from a loss of safety due to external (and even extreme danger) that characterize PTSD responses. In contrast, DSOs involve developmental, maturational, and self-adaptations to cope with the confusion and demoralization resulting from repeated exposure to trauma and the associated recurrent loss of personal control. DSOs also entail the loss of an integrated and stable identity due to the internal emotional turmoil resulting from ongoing and inescapable interpersonal traumatic stress, usually with no recourse for protection and intervention. Both PTSD and DSOs are the results of attempts to cope with an existential threat, but whereas the driver for PTSD is the threat of physical destruction or death, DSOs are driven by the disruption of essential developmental relationships that poses a threat of profound relational loss or psychological disintegration of the self. DSOs have three core components that parallel but differ substantially from the core criteria for a diagnosis of PTSD, which are (1) intrusive reexperiencing; (2) numbing; (3) active avoidance and changes in beliefs and cognition in the interest of avoidance; and (4) physiological hyperarousal and hypervigilance. In contrast, DSOs involve (1) emotion dysregulation in the form of either extreme emotional turmoil (e.g., terror, rage, incapacitating shame) or profound emotional shutdown and alexithymia (e.g., pervasive feelings of emptiness, numbing, depersonalization, detachment, dissociation); (2) interpersonal dysregulation in the form of intensely conflictual, enmeshed, detached, or chaotic relationships; and (3) self-dysregulation, in the form of self-loathing, viewing oneself as irreparably damaged or contaminated, or the absence of self as a separate and unique individual.

In PTSD, emotional, mental, and relational turmoil occur as a byproduct of coping with fear/terror and complicate the other fear-related symptoms (Kaczkurkin et al., 2017). However, in DSOs, psychological and relational turmoil have become unmanageably extreme, such that the person's very psychophysiological integrity and identity are threatened, as is trust in the ability of others to be benign, caring, and nonexploitive. In DSOs, the sense of a coherent, acceptable self ("who I am"; "what makes me unique"; "what makes me worthwhile and worthy") is unstable, tenuous, and at times entirely undeveloped or lost, which tragically is an expectable result of repeated mistreatment and associated lack or response, soothing, or protection.

Thus, DSOs can be understood as a psychological and biological exacerbation and amplification of the externally focused fear that drives PTSD. However, in addition to fear, DSOs involve a blockage, disruption, or distortion of the victim's developmental trajectory. Caught in either an emotional maelstrom or a black hole, trapped in either victimizing/invalidating relationships or in a state of extreme relational isolation, it is understandable that complex trauma survivors would have difficulty in developing a coherent and authentic identity and sense of self. DSOs represent the dilemma experienced by many complex trauma survivors as a result of having been unable to develop the capacities for emotion regulation and interpersonal involvement that are the essential foundations for an integrated personality, accurate self-knowledge, and a sense of self-integrity. Despite all, many survivors of complex trauma who experience DSOs are remarkably resilient and courageous individuals faced with making emotional, relational, and physical survival a higher priority than their own personal development. The extremity of their struggle to come to terms with their emotions, relationships, and confusion about their identity reflects the enormity of the adversity they have survived, but it is not a measure of the capacities and potential they possess.

Although complex PTSD was not included as a discrete diagnosis in DSM-5 (American Psychiatric Association, 2013), neurological research that demonstrated biological, structural, and psychological differences in PTSD symptoms when they were complicated by severe dissociation (often due to chronic child abuse without relief) resulted in the inclusion for the first time of a dissociative subtype of PTSD (Frewen, Brown, Steuwe, & Lanius, 2015; Lanius, Brand, Vermetten, Frewen, & Spiegel, 2012; Nicholson et al., 2015, 2017; Steuwe, Lanius, & Frewen, 2012). The dissociative PTSD subtype is not a separate diagnosis but a variant of PTSD that includes additional clinically significant symptoms of depersonalization or derealization. The dissociative subtype tends to involve states of hypoarousal, in contrast to the hyperarousal that is more characteristic of classic PTSD. This psychophysiological shutdown or sequestering of emotions, thoughts, somatic reactions, and other persons may produce states of severe dysregulation of emotions (including *alexithymia*, the absence or nonrecognition of emotions), relationships, and identity that parallel the core features of complex PTSD. However, the two paradigms are not synonymous, because dissociative PTSD often involves only a state of profound biopsychosocial shutdown—without the extreme heightening of arousal and distress that also is a hallmark of complex PTSD.

More recently, complex PTSD has been included in the ICD-11 (World Health Organization, 2018), based on international research with a wide variety of populations that indicate DSO symptoms can be distinguished from symptoms of PTSD (Brewin et al., 2017; Hyland et al., 2017; Karatzias et al., 2016, 2017a, 2017b; Shevlin et al., 2017) and from the symptoms of self-disorganization that constitute borderline personality disorder (Cloitre, Garert, Weiss, Carlson, & Bryant, 2014; Ford & Courtois, 2014). The ICD-11 version of complex PTSD is both simpler and more complicated than the earlier complex PTSD/DESNOS models of adult CTSD. ICD-11 complex PTSD can be viewed as more parsimonious, including only six core symptoms (two each for the three features of emotion, interpersonal, and self-dysregulation, and not including the DESNOS features of dissociation, bodily dysregulation, or altered core beliefs and spirituality). On the other hand, ICD-11 complex PTSD adds the requirement of at least one symptom from each of the classic PTSD domains of intrusive reexperiencing, avoidance, and hyperarousal, *in addition to* the DSO symptoms.

Ford (2017a) identified several similarities and differences in a recent review of adult CTSDs. The prevalence of current CTSDs is comparable to that of PTSD in nonclinical (i.e., 1–5%) and psychiatric or other high-risk (16-45%) adult populations. CTSDs are characterized by a history of chronic exposure to interpersonal traumatic stressors (e.g., family or community physical or sexual violence or abuse), often (but not always, e.g., when adults experience domestic violence or other types of traumatic captivity or torture) beginning in childhood and exacerbated by neglect and nonprotection, and revictimization in adolescence and adulthood. Complex PTSD often co-occurs with PTSD and may occur separately, but it is associated with more severe psychiatric comorbidity (e.g., depression, anxiety and all types of phobias, addictive, or personality disorders) and psychosocial impairment (e.g., interpersonal conflict or isolation, relationship difficulties, educational or work problems and failure, self-harm or suicidality) than PTSD alone. Consistent with the ICD-11 complex PTSD formulation, dissociation and bodily dysregulation (i.e., somatization) occur often in conjunction with DSOs; however, DSOs equally can occur *without* dissociation or somatization. For example, profound neglect due to caregivers providing a child with minimal emotional responses and little if any help in identifying, modulating, and discriminating emotions, may lead to DSOs that are characterized by a sense of the self as empty and emotionless (Lowe et al., 2016). The risk of self-harm and revictimization also are elevated in complex PTSD, although this is primarily the case in a subgroup for whom extreme emotion and self-dysregulation is accompanied by severe dysphoria, dissociation, or addictive disorders and may be prompted when disregard and antipathy expressed by primary caretakers is reenacted by the victim, often unconsciously. Thus, adult CTSDs are indeed complex, with a variety of core and associated symptoms and impairments that vary for each person and require thorough individualized assessment and treatment planning.

CTSDs in Childhood: Risks for the Lifespan

Beginning as early as in utero or infancy/toddlerhood, exposure to complex traumatic stressors in childhood (especially with no preventive or therapeutic intervention or other relief or support) can lead to neurobiopsychosocial problems all along the lifespan (Briggs-Gowan et al., 2010), persisting or worsening in the elementary or middle school years (Briggs-Gowan, Carter, & Ford, 2012), in adolescence (Dierkhising, Ford, Branson, Grasso, & Lee, 2019; Ford, Elhai, Connor, & Frueh, 2010a; Grasso, Dierkhising, Branson, Ford, & Lee, 2016), and into middle and late adulthood (Horan & Widom, 2015a, 2015b; Young & Widom, 2014). A study with adolescents who were receiving treatment for persistent traumatic stress reactions identified those who had experienced complex traumatic stressors in one or more of three developmental epochs (Grasso, Dierkhising, et al., 2016): (1) early childhood (i.e., ages 0–6 years) primarily involved intrafamilial maltreatment (including neglect and emotional abuse) or physical violence associated with dangerous/impaired/addicted/absent/unresponsive caregivers, and parental/caretaker substance dependence and addictions are commonly involved, although not always; (2) in middle childhood (i.e., ages 7–12 years), extrafamilial sexual abuse and community/school violence (e.g., assault, in-person, and cyberbullying) increasingly were reported as contributors to complex trauma both apart from, and in combination with, past and ongoing intrafamilial maltreatment and violence; and (3) in adolescence complex trauma exposure became still more complex, increasingly involving sexual and physical assault and community/school violence in addition to/on top of family abuse and violence. Finkelhor (2008) labeled such a history as poly-victimization, describing this as a common as well as tragic layering of exposure to multiple types of trauma and adversity over many years and often an entire lifetime (often referred to as revictimization).

Although the specific nature of complex trauma exposure changed across the developmental epochs, youth who had been exposed to complex trauma in early childhood tended to experience additional (or continued and compounded) complex trauma exposure in middle childhood and adolescence (Dierkhising et al., 2019). Tellingly, youth who reported exposure to complex trauma *only* in early childhood (i.e., not in middle childhood or adolescence) were twice as likely to be described by a parent as having clinically significant emotional and behavioral problems, compared to those who had experienced other, more impersonal traumas (e.g., severe bereavement or accidents) but were never exposed to complex trauma in early life. This suggests that early attachment security and parents/caregivers who are responsive to the child's emotional needs may provide a form of inoculation to the development of later distress. And youth who reported experiencing complex trauma in all three developmental epochs, from birth and early childhood through adolescence, were twice as likely as other youths to have not only emotional and behavioral problems but also clinically significant PTSD and complex PTSD symptoms (Dierkhising et al., 2019).

So, by the time they reach early adulthood, those individuals who experienced complex trauma in early life are at risk for a range of severe emotional, relational, and behavioral problems. Unfortunately, many receive treatment that does not address their problems as traumatic in origin, particularly if mental health providers do not screen for a history of trauma or do not recognize its significance and its possible connection to symptoms when a trauma history is reported. Since it is only those who have had chronic exposure to complex trauma continuing throughout childhood and adolescence who are likely to develop classic PTSD symptoms that are possibly recognized as such, other symptoms may not be viewed as having any association with past trauma. Due to the temporal disconnection of symptoms from the traumatic stressor origins(s), both victims and clinicians may misunderstand or misattribute the origin and meaning of symptoms, making complex PTSD more difficult to recognize. Yet, clearly, more than PTSD is occurring for these adolescent and young adult survivors—problems with their developing identity and associated emotion dysregulation and conflict in or withdrawal from relationships and additional experiences of victimization may impede their success in school, work, and other life pursuits long into adulthood.

As noted earlier, although there is as yet no freestanding diagnosis for PTSD in children in any edition of the DSM, modifications to the PTSD diagnosis in the form of a subtype for young children were included in the latest revision in order to prevent children who present with only a few of the symptoms—but symptoms that are severe enough to cause serious impairment—from being excluded from PTSD treatment (Scheeringa, Myers, Putnam, & Zeanah, 2012). The "before age 6 subtype of PTSD," as the name implies, applies only to children age 6 years and younger and not to school-age children or adolescents. Its criteria include intrusive reexperiencing symptoms not only as they present verbally but also in reenactments of traumatic events in play. Only one symptom of either avoidance of reminders or emotional distress/numbing is required, since young children typically do not develop as many of these symptoms as do older children or adults.

In addition, as discussed, children and adolescents who experience complex trauma often have symptoms that persist into adulthood and extend beyond those of classic PTSD, which alone (and especially if unrecognized and unaddressed) can alter the course of a child's entire life. Moreover, complex traumatic stress reactions can lead children to receive multiple psychiatric diagnoses that can follow them in complicated and unique ways, causing symptoms and related stigma that damages their developing and possibly already fragile identities and relationships, and can be lifelong. Among the disorders that often are diagnosed in children who have complex trauma histories are reactive attachment disorder (RAD); generalized or phobic anxiety, panic, or obsessive–compulsive disorders; bipolar disorder, psychotic or dissociative disorders; eating, body image, or sexual disorders; disruptive behavior disorders (e.g., attention-deficit/hyperactivity disorder; oppositional defiant or conduct disorders), and traits of personality disorders (D'Andrea, Ford, Stolbach, Spinazzola, & van der Kolk, 2012). While childhood exposure to complex trauma and complex traumatic stress reactions may not be the sole, or even primary, cause of the additional symptoms of these disorders, when they contribute to and exacerbate the complex symptoms, standard treatments for those disorders may be ineffective or iatrogenic, since they do not remediate the unrecognized role of past trauma or CTSDs.

Unfortunately, such youth also may be identified as "antisocial," "aggressive," or "delinquent," and deemed unsuitable for therapeutic treatments despite having shown signs (often overlooked) of emotional distress related to complex trauma exposure earlier in their lives (Ford, Chapman, Connor, & Cruise, 2012). A study with psychiatrically and behaviorally impaired children revealed that a complex trauma history (physical or sexual abuse) was associated with reactive (but not proactive) aggression (Ford, Fraleigh, & Connor, 2010c) and low bodily reactivity to and a high threshold for physical pain (Ford, Fraleigh, Albert, & Connor, 2010b). This combination of aggression and reduced psychophysiological responsivity often leads youth to be labeled psychopathic, or "callous and unemotional." However, there is evidence that many may have developed a form of "acquired callousness," hypoarousal (i.e., shutting down physiologically), dissociation/detachment, and alexithymia as CTSD defenses rather than an intractable antisocial personality disorder (Bennett & Kerig, 2014; Porges, 2007).

Developmental Trauma Disorder

Despite the extensive evidence that children and adolescents who are exposed to complex trauma are at risk for potentially lifelong complex traumatic stress reactions, not until an expert group from the National Child Traumatic Stress Network was convened and generated data was there a call to action (D'Andrea et al., 2012) and a CTSD diagnosis for children formally proposed to the DSM-5 working group. Based on an international survey of child-serving clinicians (Ford et al., 2013) and a field trial study with a new structured interview

(Ford, Spinazzola, van der Kolk, & Grasso, 2018; Spinazzola, van der Kolk, & Ford, 2018; van der Kolk, Ford, & Spinazzola, 2019), developmental trauma disorder (DTD) was established as a framework of assessment and treatment planning with children who are dysregulated in three overarching domains: emotional; cognitive and behavioral; and identity and ability to relate to others (van der Kolk, 2005). The DTD dysregulation domains thus closely parallel (although not exactly duplicating), and may be the precursors of, the three domains of adult DSO/CTSDs, namely, complex PTSD.

The proposed structure for DTD that was validated in the field trial study is based on research on the development of self-regulation capacities and the adverse impact of exposure to complex trauma stressors in childhood (see Chapter 2). Since identity development occurs in the context of key relationships, those processes were included in a single DTD feature as opposed to separate distinct features in complex PTSD. Cognitive and behavioral self-control are in flux but highly interrelated in childhood; thus, they too comprise a single feature in DTD. The combination of emotion and bodily dysregulation as a single feature in DTD is consistent with the changes in children's bodies and emotions as they mature, and with the common finding that emotions often are expressed by children in behavior and symptoms rather than in words. Of note, although children and adolescents who showed dysregulation consistent with DTD in the interview study tended to have complex trauma histories involving multiple types of victimization in multiple life settings and relationships, DTD was best distinguished from PTSD by past exposure to both community and family violence and severely impaired primary caregivers and related attachment trauma (Spinazzola et al., 2018).

Although not accepted as a diagnosis in DSM-5 (Bremness & Polzin, 2014), DTD represents a promising clinical framework for identifying and guiding the treatment of CTSDs in children, not only to "unimpair" (and prevent the loss of) their childhood but also to avert future intergenerational transmission of CTSDs. In keeping with evidence that parents' own personal histories of trauma, neglect, and loss that are unresolved are associated with difficulties in providing secure attachment relationships for their own children (San Cristobal, Santelices, & Miranda Fuenzalida, 2017; van Ee, Kleber, & Jongmans, 2016), effective treatment for CTSDs with children and with parents (alone and together) may also prevent its transmission to future generations (Berthelot et al., 2015; Bowers & Yehuda, 2016).

Treatment Guidelines, Evidence-Based Treatment, and Clinical Best Practices Treatment Guidelines

Treatment guidelines, well-developed research-based scientific directives, are most associated with contemporary medical care. They offer the medical provider information on the efficacy and effectiveness of different treatments for different illnesses as a support for clinical decision making. In 2011, the

National Academies of Science Institute of Medicine (IOM) published a guide to treatment guidelines entitled *Clinical Guidelines We Can Trust*.[2] The report defined eight standards for developing trustworthy clinical practice guidelines, among them (1) transparency in both process and funding; (2) appointment of a multidisciplinary group of experts and public members and assessing and minimizing conflicts of interest; (3) use of a systematic review of evidence of comparative effectiveness research following standards set by the IOM; (4) provision of detailed and precise recommendations based on an appraisal of the quality, completeness, consistency, and gaps in both the research evidence and the input of values, opinion, theory, and clinical experience, along with ratings of potential benefits and harms; (5) provision of an opportunity for independent external review of draft guidelines; and (6) updating guidelines on a regular basis as new evidence is made available.

Due to a more limited research evidence base than that for many medical illnesses and treatments, treatment guidelines for psychology, psychiatry, and other mental health professions initially were largely based on expert consensus and available research findings. The increase in mental health research evidence in recent decades—developed with greater methodological rigor over time—has allowed adoption of IOM methodology and standards by the mental health professions, although this process has not been without difficulties. A primary challenge is that the evidence base in the mental health fields has been defined more broadly than that in medicine. Additionally, medical symptoms and illnesses tend to be more readily objectively defined than those in the psychological domain and are therefore more amenable to quantitative study as treatment outcomes.

In the early 2000s, the American Psychological Association convened a Task Force on Evidence-Based Practice, which stipulated that systematic evaluation of three criteria domains were necessary to justify rating a treatment as evidence based: (1) the best research evidence, (2) clinician expertise and judgment, and (3) client values and preferences (American Psychological Association, 2006). While mindful of the significance of research findings, treatment guidelines were viewed as requiring evidence that was not only solely and narrowly based on research but also included the perspectives of those involved in treatment, both clinicians and clients.

In 2015, the American Psychological Association followed up by publishing a document that defined and differentiated two main types of treatment guidelines: *clinical practice guidelines* (CPGs) and *professional practice guidelines* (PPGs). Both types of treatment guidelines serve three functions, specifically, to enable practitioners and professional organizations to (1) fulfill relevant legal, regulatory (and, we would add, funding/reimbursement) requirements, (2) provide services that are beneficial and safe to the public, and (3) deliver services based on the best available professional expertise and scientific

---

[2] *www.nationalacademies.org/hmd/reports/2011/clinical-practice-guidelines-we-can-trust/standards.aspx*

knowledge as to their efficacy and safety (American Psychological Association, 2015).

CPGs most closely resemble the medical field's treatment guidelines and emphasize the selection of evidence-based treatments based on research evidence derived from randomized clinical trial (RCT) research studies following the standards promulgated by the IOM in 2011.[3] In contrast, PPGs are based on reviews of the clinical and research literature *and* surveys of clinicians' or reviews of authoritative writing of those determined to be experts in the particular treatment under investigation *and* client preferences and values. Key features of this type of guideline are "to educate, to facilitate competence . . . , and to assist the practitioner in the provision of high-quality psychological services by providing well-supported practical guidance and education in a particular practice area" (American Psychological Association, 2015, p. 824).

As applied to the treatment of PTSD, the earliest guidelines were produced throughout the 2000s (Bernardy & Friedman, 2012; Foa et al., 1999; Foa, Keane, Friedman, & Cohen, 2009; Forbes et al., 2010; Stein et al., 2009; Ursano et al., 2004). The earliest PTSD treatment guidelines were of necessity consensus-based PPGs rather than CPGs, as efficacy research was just being undertaken and a research base had not yet fully developed. In the past decade, however, treatment guidelines for PTSD have become more methodologically sophisticated, tending to adopt the IOM standards. There are now at least 10 PTSD CPGs, including for adult PTSD by the American Psychological Association[4] and the National Institute for Health and Clinical Excellence (NICE),[5] as well as revised and updated guidelines from the Phoenix Australian Centre for Posttraumatic Mental Health[6] and the U.S. Department of Department of Defense/Veterans Affairs.[7] The International Society for Traumatic Stress Studies published PTSD clinical practice guidelines for children and adults, first in 2000 and now updated in 2009 (Foa, Keane, Friedman, & Cohen, 2009) and in 2019, with the latter based on the IOM methodology.[8] While all of these guidelines are specific to the symptoms of classic PTSD, several mention their application to complex PTSD (but with no specific guidance for CTSD treatment).

Evidence-Based Treatments

In identifying evidence-based treatments for PTSD, CPGs have adhered to IOM standards for research reviews that are transparent, systematic, and based on

---

[3] *www.nationalacademies.org/hmd/Reports/2011/Clinical-Practice-Guidelines-We-Can-Trust.aspx*

[4] *www.apa.org/ptsd-guideline/ptsd.pdf*

[5] *www.nice.org.uk/guidance/gid-ng10013/documents/draft-guideline-2*

[6] *https://phoenixaustralia.org/resources/ptsd-guidelines*

[7] *www.healthquality.va.gov/guidelines/mh/ptsd/vadodptsdcpgfinal012418.pdf*

[8] *www.istss.org/getattachment/treating-trauma/new-istss-prevention-and-treatment-guidelines/istss_preventiontreatmentguidelines_fnl.pdf.aspx*

independent peer review. However, public and client input has been obtained only in relation to general principles of collaborative and ethically sound treatment, and these are presented either as an addendum to the research-based specific recommendation of evidence-based treatments or not at all. By using evidence solely from research studies to identify evidence-based treatments and privileging results from rigorously controlled RCTs that are critically evaluated to meet certain research standards, the guidelines strengthen the scientific (internal) validity of their evidence-based treatment recommendations.

Yet because research was not sufficiently specific and of the highest methodological quality, and the preferences of a wide variety of public members and clients were not solicited in formulating evidence-based treatment recommendations, the crucial question of when and for whom different evidence-based treatment models or their components are recommended remains unanswered. The available PTSD CPGs consistently and explicitly caution (e.g., American Psychological Association, 2017, PTSD Guideline, p. 76) that the evidence is not yet available to recommend which treatments work best for which clients. Thus, the guidelines select evidence-based treatments that research suggest are effective, either explicitly stating or implying that "one size" (i.e., any effective evidence-based treatment for PTSD) is expected to fit all. However, this stance that has been sharply questioned for PTSD treatment, and especially as applied to CTSDs (Cloitre, 2015; Courtois, 2010; Courtois & Brown, 2019).

Drawing from these available treatment guidelines, across the civilian and military adult populations, the following three evidence-based treatments for psychotherapy for adult PTSD have been consistently strongly recommended as frontline treatments: prolonged exposure, cognitive processing therapy; and cognitive therapy. Four other evidence-based treatments are consistently recommended as well: eye movement desensitization and reprocessing therapy, narrative exposure therapy, and brief eclectic psychotherapy for PTSD and some forms of pharmacotherapy for adults with PTSD. These are described in detail as applied to CTSDs and complex PTSD in this book.

Current Best Practices for CTSD Psychotherapy

As noted earlier, until recently, the treatment of CTSDs in adults has been guided by complex trauma-based adaptations of clinician-formulated *best practices* and research-driven evidence-based treatment models for psychotherapy in general and for PTSD therapy specifically. Judith Herman's (1992b) prescient book *Trauma and Recovery* provided a synthesis of best practices for complex PTSD treatment based on the experience of complex trauma survivors and the writings of therapists over the course of the prior century, especially the treatment approach developed by French neurologist Pierre Janet (van der Kolk & van der Hart, 1989). Its cornerstone is a sequenced, three-phase framework that begins with a pretreatment assessment. Phase 1 explicitly focuses on the client's personal, relational, and environmental safety (i.e., safety to and from self and others); provides education about the nature and impact of traumatic stressors over time and the process of recovery from traumatic stress disorders; develops or upgrades needed skills such as emotion regulation, self-reflection, and life skills; addresses comorbidities such as addictions, depression, anxiety, and self-injury/suicidality; and deliberately works on establishing a collaborative therapeutic relationship and alliance. As needed, based on the client's ability to function and symptom picture, Phase 2 involves a guided therapeutic exploration of the client's memories and emotions related to past experience(s) with traumatic stressors, and reflective processing as to their meaning (Harvey, 1996) including the impact that those experience(s) have had in relation to the client's self and life (i.e., trauma processing; Ford, 2018). Phase 3 concludes the treatment by helping the client to translate the knowledge and skills acquired in earlier phases into day-to-day life, shifting the focus from recovery from CTSD symptoms to the achievement of a life, lifestyle, relationships, and accomplishments that are personally meaningful and fulfilling.

The three-phase approach to complex PTSD psychotherapy has been elaborated in subsequent descriptions of best practices for CTSD treatment (Courtois & Ford, 2013; Courtois, Ford, & Cloitre, 2009). In the mid-2000s, The International Society for Traumatic Stress Studies (ISTSS) commissioned a Task Force on Complex Trauma, whose aim was to produce a consensus-based set of professional practice guidelines for adult complex PTSD based on an international survey of identified expert clinicians (half of whom were specialists in treatment of classic forms of PTSD and the other half who specialized in complex PTSD (Cloitre et al., 2011). Most (84%) of the 50 respondents from both the PTSD and complex PTSD domains endorsed a phased approach to complex PTSD treatment and suggested that interventions should be individualized and tailored to the needs of individual clients and target specific (and often idiosyncratic) problematic symptoms and circumstances, as well as personal/relational strengths and resilience (Cloitre et al., 2011).

Based on the survey and a review of nine research studies of complex PTSD psychotherapy outcomes, Best Practice Recommendations for the Treatment of Complex PTSD[9] were published in 2012. The guidelines explicitly recognized that treatment of complex PTSD may exceed the time allocated for completion by the standard evidence-based, trauma-focused treatments for PTSD. A Phase 1 of approximately 6 months was recommended to stabilize and prepare the complex PTSD client for trauma processing in Phase 2, in order to ensure personal, interpersonal, and environmental safety, and to teach or strengthen life skills and those needed for emotional self-regulation (Ford, Courtois, Steele, van der Hart, & Nijenhuis, 2005) and initiate a therapeutic alliance (Ford, 2013). For Phase 2 trauma processing, at least 3–6 months were recommended, in which unresolved aspects of trauma memories were reviewed and reappraised, in order to "integrate [them] into an adaptive representation of self, relationships, and world" (p. 5). Finally, a Phase 3 of 6–12 months was

---

[9]*www.istss.org/istss_main/media/documents/istss-expert-consensus-guidelines-for-complex-ptsd-updated-060315.pdf*

recommended, with weekly sessions gradually titrated to less frequent contacts, to ensure "consolidation of treatment gains to facilitate the transition . . . to greater engagement in relationships, work or education, and community life" (pp. 5–6).

These 2012 ISTSS recommendations were entitled "Consensus Guidelines," because they were not based on a definitive research review (due to the small number of relevant studies), and did not include direct input from the public/clients and other professionals. Recently, more than 25 expert classic PTSD clinical researchers, including several of the PTSD experts from the 2011 survey, published a rebuttal that challenged the need for and the evidence to support this three-phase psychotherapy model (De Jongh et al., 2016). They cited the research supporting the efficacy of various cognitive-behavioral therapies (CBTs) that were applied as early as the first session in research studies of PTSD treatment without the formal Phase 1 period of preparation and stabilization. They also called into question whether therapists who adopted a phased treatment approach avoided engaging their clients in trauma processing due to their own personal avoidance/fears, thereby unnecessarily delaying or failing to provide evidence-based treatments and prolonging their treatment. Their critique was challenged as failing to consider the need to individualize PTSD treatment (Cloitre, 2015) and as prematurely rejecting potentially effective therapeutic approaches that are trauma-focused but do not require immediate intensive processing of trauma memories (Ford, 2017b). It has also been challenged by many practitioners experienced in the treatment of clients with CTSDs, particularly those who are highly dissociative and the most dysregulated, as creating an iatrogenic danger for decompensation when applied without first attending to safety, skill building, and self-regulation. However, partly in response to that critique, the most recent ISTSS PTSD treatment guidelines declined to include best practice recommendations for complex PTSD treatment (of children or adults), instead providing narrative descriptions of the gaps in, and need for, systematic research on methods and outcomes of PTSD treatment with adults and children (see below).

Concurrently with the development of the ISTSS Complex PTSD Consensus Guidelines, in 2012, the Australian organization Adults Surviving Child Abuse (ASCA) (now renamed Blue Knot Foundation) published best practice recommendations for professionals, treatment program staff, and advocates working with adult survivors of childhood abuse.[10] Although entitled "practice guidelines," this document represents a synthesis of best practices derived from the experience of clinicians and clients with CTSDs, including comprehensive published recommendations (Courtois & Ford, 2013; Courtois et al., 2009). The ASCA guidelines recommend a three-phase model with several specific goals: (1) enhance affect regulation, (2) facilitate the acquisition or restoration of self- and relational capacities that were disrupted or never developed due to

---

[10] *www.recoveryonpurpose.com/upload/asca_practice%20guidelines%20for%20the%20 treatment%20of%20complex%20trauma.pdf*

coping with the impact of complex trauma, (3) facilitate reappraisal of symptoms as adaptive reactions, (4) explain the normative bodily adaptations that occur in reaction to complex trauma, (5) encourage establishment or strengthening of support networks, (6) facilitate awareness and resolution of attachment insecurity and shame, and (7) facilitate awareness and modulation of extreme arousal states, dissociation, and sensorimotor expression of emotions.

A more recent review of the literature on the treatment of CTSDs (including the dissociative disorders) has resulted in several best practice recommendations that are in line with those of the Australian ASCA (Courtois & Ford, 2019). Treatment for CTSDs should not be limited to static interventions but instead should be based on systematic assessment and treatment planning (Briere & Scott, 2015). Methods and algorithms for deploying, sequencing, and evaluating strategies for selecting and sequencing treatment goals and interventions are currently under development (Grasso, Ford, & Lindhiem, 2016; Layne, 2011).

Uniquely, the ASCA guidelines also provide recommendations for

> trauma-informed care and service delivery . . . targeted at *organizations and their workforces* . . . [e.g.,] community managed mental health and human service sectors (drug and alcohol, sexual assault, child protection, housing, supported accommodation, refugee services, disability, advocacy, aged care, indigenous, . . . GBLTQI . . . private practice counselling, psychotherapy psychology, and psychiatry . . . primary and allied health care services . . . public and private hospitals . . . criminal justice . . . emergency . . . legal . . . policing . . . education, [and] employment [services]. (p. xxxiii, emphasis in original)

General principles of trauma-informed approaches to services for adult survivors of CT have been published,[11] but the ASCA guidelines are the most extensive and specific recommendations for policy, procedures, and extratherapeutic interactions with clients with CTSD who are receiving services. The ASCA trauma-informed care (TIC) service recommendations are also based on a synthesis of prior published principles (Bloom, 2013; Fallot & Harris, 2008) (i.e., trauma screening, safety, trustworthiness, choice, collaboration, empowerment, safe environment) that are mapped explicitly onto practitioner and organizational practices.

Two additional PPGs have been published more recently, one by the National Institute for Health and Care Excellence in the United Kingdom, and a comprehensive update of the Australian guidelines by the Blue Knot Foundation, published along with other documents outlining the treatment of complex trauma and the special issues related to traumatic memory and dissociation.[12] The United Kingdom document[13] most resembles the findings of the previously published PPGs while the Blue Knot document is more far-reaching and incor-

---

[11] *https://store.samhsa.gov/shin/content/sma14-4884/sma14-4884.pdf*

[12] *www.blueknot.org.au/resources/Publications/Practice-Guidelines*

[13] *www.nice.org.uk/guidance/ng116*

porates a great deal of new data from neuroscience and attachment research and what is termed the "neurobiological revolution in psychotherapy." The Blue Knot guideline espouses the use of body-based (or "bottom-up") techniques in recognition of the implicit encoding of traumatic stress in the body, rather than relying only on "top down" or cognitive-behavioral and psychodynamic approaches. The Blue Knot guidelines emphasize helping clients pay specific attention to their experience (both physiological and psychological) and learning emotion identification and means of modulation designed to disrupt autonomic entrenched survival mechanisms and defensive operations. They state it this way: "Many therapists still focus on a client's thoughts, feelings and beliefs without paying sufficient attention to their *experience*. This is not logical as physiological experience precedes reflection and subjectivity . . . and failure to acknowledge this in treatment can have destabilizing effects." (p. 3). They therefore emphasize the salience of the body and encourage greater use of body and brain-based treatments.

Moreover, the Blue Knot guidelines return attention to the issue of traumatic memory, especially the role of implicit (subcortical) memory and its difference from conscious, explicit memory. Both forms of memory are important in trauma memory processing (Ford, 2018), and several approaches to psychotherapy for complex traumatic stress disorders directly address implicit, body-based sensations and emotions (see Chapters 23–26). The Blue Knot guidelines challenge some of the more established recommendations for the treatment of complex traumatic stress disorders, encouraging therapists to be flexible, focused on the client's experience, and to "think outside the box." This body/brain-based approach stands in contrast to most current practice guidelines and evidence-based treatments for classic PTSD.

Adapting Evidence-Based Treatments for PTSD to Complex PTSD: What's a Therapist to Do?

Since the early 1990s, paralleling the development of CTSD psychotherapy best practices, several evidence-based treatments for adult PTSD (Bisson, Roberts, Andrew, Cooper, & Lewis, 2013; Cusack et al., 2016) have shown promise in treating adolescents and adults with childhood sexual or physical abuse histories (Chard, 2005; Cohen et al., 2016; Foa, McLean, Capaldi, & Rosenfield, 2013; McDonagh et al., 2005; O'Callaghan, McMullen, Shannon, Rafferty, & Black, 2013; Resick, Nishith, & Griffin, 2003; Resick, Suvak, & Wells, 2014; Steuwe et al., 2016). The issues involved in these applications were the subject of our previous books (Courtois & Ford, 2009, 2013; Ford & Courtois, 2013), where we explicitly suggested that caution was warranted in approaching trauma memory processing (TMP) too quickly with these clients due to what is often their emotional and environment instability, multiple presenting problems and comorbidities, severe difficulties with dissociation, and limitations in the ability to maintain safety or to manage their emotions or their actions.

We also discussed differential application based on client readiness and attachment history, as well as therapist training. We still believe that caution is warranted due to evidence of increased rates of premature termination by individuals with childhood abuse histories in these evidence-based treatments, particularly in the trauma processing phase (McDonagh et al., 2005; Resick et al., 2014). However, we do agree that when TMP is decided as a treatment strategy it optimally should occur as soon as is feasible, according to the client's readiness and willingness and based on choice of treatment. A novel framework for TMP has been proposed, in which the intentional recall of trauma memories in therapy is understood as paradoxically facilitating the capacity to intentionally suppress intrusions of trauma memories and thereby escape the vicious cycle in which intrusive reexperiencing is perpetuated by self-defeating attempt to avoid (Ford, 2018). TMP thus involves developing and purposefully employing the necessary cognitive and emotion regulation capacities to choose to pay attention to trauma memories in order to find self-relevant meaning in them (Harvey, 1996). This is the exact opposite of a futile attempt to avoid paying attention to trauma memories or reminders—a strategy that backfires by increasing the intrusive reexperiencing of trauma memories instead of facilitating recovery from them. From this perspective, TMP can serve as a vehicle not merely for reducing PTSD-related avoidance but moreover for enhancing the very self-capacities that are disorganized or diminished in DSOs and CTSDs.

As described in several chapters in this book, adaptations to evidence-based treatments for PTSD that facilitate safe and effective therapeutic trauma processing when CTSDs complicate their implementation have been proposed, developed, and researched (Chard, 2005; Harned, Korslund, & Linehan, 2014). Moreover, recent studies showing that interpersonal psychotherapy (IPT; Chapter 16) and present-centered therapy (PCT; Foa et al., 2018) achieve comparable outcomes to prolonged exposure in reducing PTSD symptoms have important implications. They suggest that *intensive review of trauma memories is not necessary in all cases, and that other forms of trauma-focused or present-centered, client-centered, and interpersonal forms of treatment that do not require intensive trauma memory processing may be equally effective as evidence-based treatments for adult PTSD* (Ford, 2017b; Hoge & Chard, 2018; Markowitz et al., 2015). Therapists and clients with CTSDs thus have choices regarding how to proceed and what strategies to use, based on ongoing clinical assessment, clinical judgment, and clients' goals, preferences, and resources.

Practice Guidelines for PTSD Psychotherapy: Applicable to CTSDs?

As noted earlier and described in more detail in subsequent chapters in this book, there is evidence that *adaptations of evidence-based treatments for PTSD may be safe and effective for clients with CTSDs, especially when applied after a period or phase of assessment and stabilization and the development of the treatment relationship, including an alliance between therapist and client.* However, there also is evidence that many clients with CTSDs have been screened out of the research studies testing those therapies (e.g., due to suicidality, self-harm, addiction, or severe affective lability or personality disturbance) (Spinazzola, Blaustein, & van der Kolk, 2005). Other clients with CTSDs do not benefit from evidence-based treatments for PTSD—or find the form or intensity of treatment sufficiently distressing to choose to "vote with their feet" by discontinuing treatment before achieving meaningful improvement. The research evidence also is almost exclusively based on treatment that is delivered for, at most, 4–5 months (i.e., 12–20 or fewer sessions), which is only half the length of time described by expert clinicians as optimal for Phases 1 and 2 of complex PTSD therapy (i.e., 9–12 months) (Cloitre et al., 2011). While these estimates are approximate and not research-based, even if Phase 1 was truncated or entirely eliminated as recommended by some (De Jongh et al., 2016), the third phase of integration of treatment gains into day-to-day life, relationships, and functioning is not addressed—or at best is left to a few sessions at the end of formal treatment or in posttherapy booster/check-in sessions. Current clinical practice guidelines for PTSD treatment generally do not provide clinicians with guidance about how to conduct therapy when clients either do not agree to follow an evidence-based treatment protocol for PTSD or do not benefit from it, or how to help clients with CTSDs integrate treatment gains into sustained positive changes in their day-to-day lives—let alone how to prevent or manage severe impairments or crises related to extreme states of bodily, affective, relational, or identity distress or confusion.

To address these shortcomings, the 2017 American Psychological Association PTSD Guideline (pp. 80–83) included input from community members and clinicians in practice, and the Veterans Administration/Department of Defense PTSD Guidelines incorporated client focus group input. In contrast to the guidelines' recommendations of prepackaged evidence-based treatments, both laypersons and clinicians recommended a personalized approach to psychotherapy that is determined in the context of a culturally sensitive and collaborative therapeutic alliance by the client (and supporters) with a clinician who has specialized skill in treating PTSD with clients of similar background and clinical characteristics. Rather than any single evidence-based treatment, the preferred course was a variety of approaches to treatment, with a thoughtful and fully informed discussion of the process and pros and cons of different approaches, in order to fully inform client choice. Correspondingly, the use of PTSD practice guidelines in real-world clinical practice is inconsistent at best. For example, in contracted or direct services for military veterans with PTSD, evidence-based treatments are used by only half of all practitioners, and typically with little or no formal training or adherence to the protocols (Finley et al., 2019; Hepner et al., 2018).

Other PTSD practice guidelines are either silent regarding complex trauma and CTSDs or cite the unavailability of research to determine the safety and effectiveness of PTSD evidence-based treatments for this population. The 2018 NICE PTSD Guideline is an exception, cogently stating that treatment for "people with additional needs, including those with complex PTSD" (p. 17) should directly address dissociation and emotion dysregulation. The NICE guidelines also recommend providing sufficient treatment duration to support these clients in fully engaging and developing a sense of trust, as well as increasing "the number of trauma-focused therapy sessions according to the person's needs" and making provisions to support "return to everyday activities and ongoing symptom management."

In response to these and related concerns, the American Psychological Association recently convened a working group to develop a "Professional Practice Guideline on Key Considerations in the Treatment of PTSD/Trauma." The work group is in the process of developing recommendations for clinicians in practice that is designed to complement the 2017 American Psychological Association *Clinical Practice Guideline for PTSD in Adults* evidence-based recommendations with information on responsible client-centered PTSD psychotherapy, including management of the many challenges that often accompany this treatment population. Most telling of all, this work group will articulate the importance of therapist empathy, congruence, and positive regard, and a therapeutic alliance based on collaborative treatment planning and evaluation by the client and therapist as partners (Elliott, Bohart, Watson, & Murphy, 2018; Eubanks, Muran, & Safran, 2018; Farber, Suzuki, & Lynch, 2018; Flückiger, Del Re, Wampold, & Horvath, 2018; Friedlander, Escudero, Welmers-van de Poll, & Heatherington, 2018; Gelso, Kivlighan, & Markin, 2018; Karver, De Nadai, Monahan, & Shirk, 2018; Nienhuis et al., 2018).

In summary, although the research evidence base for models of PTSD psychotherapy has grown sufficiently in the past decade to warrant major updates in clinical practice guidelines, there continues to be insufficient outcome research on CTSD psychotherapy to support the designation of evidence-based treatments or the recommendation of practice guidelines. Notably, despite admirable efforts to adapt PTSD evidence-based treatments across cultures and populations (Chen, Olin, Stirman, & Kaysen, 2017; Schnyder et al., 2016), even the most comprehensive PTSD clinical practice guidelines cannot recommend how best to individualize treatment to clients with different PTSD symptoms, comorbidities, personal characteristics, life experiences, and preferences, or in different cultural, community, or family contexts that also attends to client preference and therapist training. Thus, at this point, we believe the real-world delivery of evidence-based treatments and practice guidelines for both PTSD and CTSDs still rest upon the "standard of care" foundation provided by expert clinicians' best practices. These continue to evolve with emerging research findings from the neurosciences and other fields and the resultant development of innovative clinical approaches. Of note, some of these (most of which are body based such as acupuncture, thought field therapy, mantra-based meditation, and yoga) have a preliminary evidence base and a designation as emerging (Metcalf et al., 2016; see Chapter 26).

The remainder of this book is devoted to a summary of the most up-to-date best practices for CTSD psychotherapy and their basis in neurobiopsychosocial clinical research and theory, followed by detailed descriptions of specific approaches to CTSD psychotherapy that are adaptations of PTSD evidence-based treatments or innovative approaches designed specifically for the treatment of CTSDs.

To bring closure to the book's review of best practices and evidence-based treatment models for CTSDs, a concluding chapter identifies past and new challenges facing the complex trauma/CTSD field. The book closes with an evocative and inspiring Afterword by Bessel van der Kolk, in which this key pioneer in the traumatic stress and CTSD field provides a cogent reprise of the past and an illuminating glimpse into the future of our field. In summary, we aim to chart a course forward for the next decade of innovation in clinical practice and research on complex trauma and recovery, so that in 10 years we have much good news to report in a third edition of this book. In the meantime, we invite you to join us in learning about the advances that have taken place in the past decade. We hope that they provide insights that you can apply to your work and studies with the resilient survivors of complex trauma whom you—and we, too—are honored to learn from and to serve.

References

American Psychiatric Association. (2013). *Diagnostic and statistical manual of mental disorders* (5th ed.). Arlington, VA: Author.

American Psychological Association (2006). Evidence-based practice in psychology. *American Psychologist, 61*(4), 271–285.

American Psychological Association. (2015). Professional practice guidelines: Guidance for developers and users. *American Psychologist, 70*(9), 823–831.

American Psychological Association. (2017). *Clinical practice guidelines for the treatment of PTSD*. Washington, DC: Author.

Ben-Ezra, M., Karatzias, T., Hyland, P., Brewin, C. R., Cloitre, M., Bisson, J. I., . . . Shevlin, M. (2018). Posttraumatic stress disorder (PTSD) and complex PTSD (CPTSD) as per ICD-11 proposals: A population study in Israel. *Depression and Anxiety, 35*(3), 264–274.

Bennett, D. C., & Kerig, P. K. (2014). Investigating the construct of trauma-related acquired callousness among delinquent youth: Differences in emotion processing. *Journal of Traumatic Stress, 27*(4), 415–422.

Bernardy, N. C., & Friedman, M. J. (2012). 2010 VA/DOD Clinical Practice Guideline for Management of Post-Traumatic Stress: How busy clinicians can best adopt updated recommendations. *Journal of Rehabilitation Research and Development, 49*(5), vii–viii.

Berthelot, N., Ensink, K., Bernazzani, O., Normandin, L., Luyten, P., & Fonagy, P. (2015). Intergenerational transmission of attachment in abused and neglected mothers: The role of trauma-specific reflective functioning. *Infant Mental Health Journal, 36*(2), 200–212.

Bisson, J. I., Roberts, N. P., Andrew, M., Cooper, R., & Lewis, C. (2013). Psychological therapies for chronic post-traumatic stress disorder (PTSD) in adults. *Cochrane Database Systematic Reviews, 12*, CD003388.

Bloom, S. L. (2013). The Sanctuary model. In J. D. Ford & C. A. Courtois (Eds.), *Treating complex traumatic stress disorders in children and adolescents: Scientific foundations and therapeutic models* (pp. 277–294). New York: Guilford Press.

Bovin, M. J., Dodson, T. S., Smith, B. N., Gregor, K., Marx, B. P., & Pineles, S. L. (2014). Does guilt mediate the association between tonic immobility and posttraumatic stress disorder symptoms in female trauma survivors? *Journal of Traumatic Stress, 27*(6), 721–724.

Bowers, M. E., & Yehuda, R. (2016). Intergenerational transmission of stress in humans. *Neuropsychopharmacology, 41*(1), 232–244.

Bremness, A., & Polzin, W. (2014). Commentary: Developmental trauma disorder: A missed opportunity in DSM V. *Journal of the Canadian Academy of Child and Adolescent Psychiatry, 23*(2), 142–145.

Brewin, C. R., Cloitre, M., Hyland, P., Shevlin, M., Maercker, A., Bryant, R. A., . . . Reed, G. M. (2017). A review of current evidence regarding the ICD-11 proposals for diagnosing PTSD and complex PTSD. *Clinical Psychology Review, 58,* 1–15.

Briere, J. N. (2019). *Treating risky and compulsive behavior in trauma survivors.* New York: Guilford Press.

Briere, J. N., & Lanktree, C. B. (2012). *Treating complex trauma in adolescents and young adults.* Los Angeles: SAGE.

Briere, J. N., & Scott, C. (2015). Complex trauma in adolescents and adults: Effects and treatment. *Psychiatric Clinics of North America, 38*(3), 515–527.

Briggs-Gowan, M. J., Carter, A. S., Clark, R., Augustyn, M., McCarthy, K. J., & Ford, J. D. (2010). Exposure to potentially traumatic events in early childhood: Differential links to emergent psychopathology. *Journal of Child Psychology and Psychiatry and Allied Disciplines, 51*(10), 1132–1140.

Briggs-Gowan, M. J., Carter, A. S., & Ford, J. D. (2012). Parsing the effects violence exposure in early childhood: Modeling developmental pathways. *Journal of Pediatric Psychology, 37*(1), 11–22.

Bryant, R. A. (2012). Simplifying complex PTSD: Comment on Resick et al. (2012) [Comment]. *Journal of Traumatic Stress, 25*(3), 252–253; discussion 260–253.

Bryant, R. A. (2017). Acute stress disorder. *Current Opinion in Psychology, 14,* 127–131.

Chard, K. M. (2005). An evaluation of cognitive processing therapy for the treatment of posttraumatic stress disorder related to childhood sexual abuse. *Journal of Consulting Clinical Psychology, 73*(5), 965–971.

Chen, J. A., Olin, C. C., Stirman, S. W., & Kaysen, D. (2017). The role of context in the implementation of trauma-focused treatments: Effectiveness research and implementation in higher and lower income settings. *Current Opinion in Psychology, 14,* 61–66.

Cloitre, M. (2015). The "one size fits all" approach to trauma treatment: Should we be satisfied? *European Journal of Psychotraumatology, 6,* 27344.

Cloitre, M., Courtois, C. A., Charuvastra, A., Carapezza, R., Stolbach, B. C., & Green, B. L. (2011). Treatment of complex PTSD: Results of the ISTSS expert clinician survey on best practices. *Journal of Traumatic Stress, 24*(6), 615–627.

Cloitre, M., Garvert, D. W., Brewin, C. R., Bryant, R. A., & Maercker, A. (2013, May 15). Evidence for proposed ICD-11 PTSD and complex PTSD: A latent profile analysis. *European Journal of Psychotraumatology, 4.*

Cloitre, M., Garvert, D. W., Weiss, B., Carlson, E. B., & Bryant, R. A. (2014, September 15). Distinguishing PTSD, complex PTSD, and borderline personality disorder: A latent class analysis. *European Journal of Psychotraumatology, 5.*

Cohen, J. A., Mannarino, A. P., Jankowski, K., Rosenberg, S., Kodya, S., & Wolford, G. L., II. (2016). A randomized implementation study of trauma-focused cognitive behavioral therapy for adjudicated teens in residential treatment facilities. *Child Maltreatment, 21*(2), 156–167.

Courtois, C. A. (2010). *Healing the incest wound: Adult survivors in therapy* (2nd ed.). New York: Norton.

Courtois, C. A., & Ford, J. D. (Eds.) (2009). *Treating complex traumatic stress disorders: An evidence-based guide.* New York: Guilford Press.

Courtois, C. A., & Ford, J. D. (2013). *Treating complex trauma: A sequenced relationship-based approach.* New York: Guilford Press.

Courtois, C. A., & Ford, J. D. (2019). Sequenced relationship-based treatment for complex traumatic stress disorders. In R. Benjamin, J. Haliburn, & S. King (Eds.), *Humanising mental health care in Australia: A guide to trauma-informed approaches* (pp. 211–222). New York: Routledge.

Courtois, C. A., Ford, J. D., & Cloitre, M. (2009). Best practices in psychotherapy for adults. In C. A. Courtois & J. D. Ford (Eds.), *Treating complex traumatic stress disorders: An evidence-based guide* (pp. 82–103). New York: Guilford Press.

Cusack, K., Jonas, D. E., Forneris, C. A., Wines, C., Sonis, J., Middleton, J. C., . . . Gaynes, B. N. (2016). Psychological treatments for adults with posttraumatic stress disorder: A systematic review and meta-analysis. *Clinical Psychology Review, 43*(1), 128–141.

D'Andrea, W., Ford, J., Stolbach, B., Spinazzola, J., & van der Kolk, B. A. (2012). Understanding interpersonal trauma in children: Why we need a developmentally appropriate trauma diagnosis. *American Journal of Orthopsychiatry, 82*(2), 187–200.

De Jongh, A., Resick, P. A., Zoellner, L. A., van Minnen, A., Lee, C. W., Monson, C. M., . . . Bicanic, I. A. (2016). Critical analysis of the current treatment guidelines for complex PTSD in adults. *Depression and Anxiety, 33*(5), 359–369.

DePrince, A. P., Brown, L. S., Cheit, R. E., Freyd, J. J., Gold, S. N., Pezdek, K., & Quina, K. (2012). Motivated forgetting and misremembering: Perspectives from betrayal trauma theory. *Nebraska Symposium on Motivation, 58,* 193–242.

Dierkhising, C. B., Ford, J. D., Branson, C., Grasso, D. J., & Lee, R. (2019). Developmental timing of polyvictimization: Continuity, change, and association with adverse outcomes in adolescence. *Child Abuse and Neglect, 87,* 40–50.

Elliott, R., Bohart, A. C., Watson, J. C., & Murphy, D. (2018). Therapist empathy and client outcome: An updated meta-analysis. *Psychotherapy, 55*(4), 399–410.

Eubanks, C. F., Muran, J. C., & Safran, J. D. (2018). Alliance rupture repair: A meta-analysis. *Psychotherapy, 55*(4), 508–519.

Fallot, R., & Harris, M. (2008). Trauma-informed services. In G. Reyes, J. D. Elhai, & J. Ford (Eds.), *The encyclopedia of psychological trauma* (pp. 660–662). Hoboken, NJ: Wiley.

Farber, B. A., Suzuki, J. Y., & Lynch, D. A. (2018). Positive regard and psychotherapy outcome: A meta-analytic review. *Psychotherapy, 55*(4), 411–423.

Finkelhor, D. (2008). *Childhood victimization: Violence, crime, and abuse in the lives of young people.* New York: Oxford University Press.

Finley, E. P., Mader, M., Haro, E. K., Noel, P. H., Bernardy, N., Rosen, C. S., . . . Pugh, M. J. V. (2019). Use of guideline-recommended treatments for PTSD among community-based providers in Texas and Vermont: Implications for the Veterans Choice Program. *Journal of Behavioral Health Services and Research, 46*(2), 217–233.

Fisher, J. (2017). *Healing the fragmented selves of trauma survivors: Overcoming internal self-alienation.* New York: Routledge, Taylor & Francis.

Flückiger, C., Del Re, A. C., Wampold, B. E., & Horvath, A. O. (2018). The alliance in adult psychotherapy: A meta-analytic synthesis. *Psychotherapy, 55*(4), 316–340.

Foa, E. B., Davidson, J. R. T., Frances, A., Culpepper, L., Ross, R. J., & Ross, D. (1999). The expert consensus guideline series: Treatment of posttraumatic stress disorder. *Journal of Clinical Psychiatry, 60*(16), 4–76.

Foa, E. B., Keane, T. M., Friedman, M. J., & Cohen, J. (Eds.). (2009). *Effective treatments for PTSD: Practice guidelines from the International Society for Traumatic Stress Studies.* New York: Guilford Press.

Foa, E. B., McLean, C. P., Capaldi, S., & Rosenfield, D. (2013). Prolonged exposure vs supportive counseling for sexual abuse-related PTSD in adolescent girls: A randomized clinical trial. *Journal of the American Medical Association, 310*(24), 2650–2657.

Foa, E. B., McLean, C. P., Zang, Y., Rosenfield, D., Yadin, E., Yarvis, J. S., . . . STRONG STAR Consortium. (2018). Effect of prolonged exposure therapy delivered over 2 weeks vs 8 weeks vs present-centered therapy on PTSD symptom severity in military personnel: A randomized clinical trial. *Journal of the American Medical Association, 319*(4), 354–364.

Forbes, D., Creamer, M., Bisson, J. I., Cohen, J. A., Crow, B. E., Foa, E. B., . . . Ursano, R. J.

(2010). A guide to guidelines for the treatment of PTSD and related conditions. *Journal of Traumatic Stress, 23*(5), 537–552.

Ford, J. D. (2005). Treatment implications of altered neurobiology, affect regulation and information processing following child maltreatment. *Psychiatric Annals, 35*, 410–419.

Ford, J. D. (2009). Neurobiological and developmental research: Clinical implications. In C. A. Courtois & J. D. Ford (Eds.), *Treating complex traumatic stress disorders: An evidence-based guide* (pp. 31–58). New York: Guilford Press.

Ford, J. D. (2013). Enhancing emotional regulation with complex trauma survivors. In D. Murphy & S. Joseph (Eds.), *Trauma and the therapeutic relationship* (pp. 58–77). New York: Palgrave Macmillan.

Ford, J. D. (2015). Complex PTSD: Research directions for nosology/assessment, treatment, and public health. *European Journal of Psychotraumatology, 6,* 27584.

Ford, J. D. (2017a). Complex trauma and complex PTSD. In J. Cook, S. Gold, & C. Dalenberg (Eds.), *Handbook of trauma psychology* (Vol. 1, pp. 322–349). Washington, DC: American Psychological Association.

Ford, J. D. (2017b). Emotion regulation and skills-based interventions. In J. Cook, S. Gold, & C. Dalenberg (Eds.), *Handbook of trauma psychology* (Vol. 2, pp. 227–252). Washington, DC: American Psychological Association.

Ford, J. D. (2018). Trauma memory processing in PTSD psychotherapy: A unifying framework. *Journal of Traumatic Stress, 31,* 933–942.

Ford, J. D., Chapman, J. C., Connor, D. F., & Cruise, K. R. (2012). Complex trauma and aggression in secure juvenile justice settings. *Criminal Justice and Behavior, 39*(5), 695–724.

Ford, J. D., & Courtois, C. A. (Eds.) (2013). *Treating complex stress disorders in children and adolescents.* New York: Guilford Press.

Ford, J. D., & Courtois, C. A. (2014). Complex PTSD, affect dysregulation, and borderline personality disorder. *Borderline Personality Disorder and Emotion Dysregulation, 1,* 9.

Ford, J. D., Courtois, C. A., Steele, K., van der Hart, O., & Nijenhuis, E. R. (2005). Treatment of complex posttraumatic self-dysregulation. *Journal of Traumatic Stress, 18*(5), 437–447.

Ford, J. D., Elhai, J. D., Connor, D. F., & Frueh, B. C. (2010a). Poly-victimization and risk of posttraumatic, depressive, and substance use disorders and involvement in delinquency in a national sample of adolescents. *Journal of Adolescent Health, 46*(6), 545–552.

Ford, J. D., Fraleigh, L. A., Albert, D. B., & Connor, D. F. (2010b). Child abuse and autonomic nervous system hyporesponsivity among psychiatrically impaired children. *Child Abuse and Neglect, 34,* 507–515.

Ford, J. D., Fraleigh, L. A., & Connor, D. F. (2010c). Child abuse and aggression among psychiatrically impaired children. *Journal of Clinical Child and Adolescent Psychology, 39*(1), 25–34.

Ford, J. D., & Gomez, J. M. (2015). The relationship of psychological trauma and dissociative and posttraumatic stress disorders to nonsuicidal self-injury and suicidality: A review. *Journal of Trauma and Dissociation, 16*(3), 232–271.

Ford, J. D., Grasso, D., Greene, C., Levine, J., Spinazzola, J., & van der Kolk, B. (2013). Clinical significance of a proposed developmental trauma disorder diagnosis: Results of an international survey of clinicians. *Journal of Clinical Psychiatry, 74*(8), 841–849.

Ford, J. D., Spinazzola, J., van der Kolk, B., & Grasso, D. (2018). Toward an empirically based developmental trauma disorder diagnosis for children: Factor structure, item characteristics, reliability, and validity of the Developmental Trauma Disorder Semi-Structured Interview (DTD-SI). *Journal of Clinical Psychiatry, 79*(5), e1–e9.

Frewen, P. A., Brown, M. F., Steuwe, C., & Lanius, R. A. (2015). Latent profile analysis and principal axis factoring of the DSM-5 dissociative subtype. *European Journal of Psychotraumatology, 6,* 26406.

Friedlander, M. L., Escudero, V., Welmers-van de Poll, M. J., & Heatherington, L. (2018). Meta-analysis of the alliance–outcome relation in couple and family therapy. *Psychotherapy, 55*(4), 356–371.

Gadeberg, A. K., Montgomery, E., Frederiksen, H. W., & Norredam, M. (2017). Assessing trauma and mental health in refugee children and youth: A systematic review of validated screening and measurement tools. *European Journal of Public Health, 27*(3), 439–446.

Gelso, C. J., Kivlighan, D. M., & Markin, R. D. (2018). The real relationship and its role in psychotherapy outcome: A meta-analysis. *Psychotherapy, 55*(4), 434–444.

Goodman, M. (2012). Complex PTSD is on the trauma spectrum: Comment on Resick et al. (2012). *Journal of Traumatic Stress, 25*(3), 254–255; discussion 253–60.

Grasso, D. J., Dierkhising, C. B., Branson, C. E., Ford, J. D., & Lee, R. (2016). Developmental patterns of adverse childhood experiences and current symptoms and impairment in youth referred for trauma-specific services. *Journal of Abnormal Child Psychology, 44*(5), 871–886.

Grasso, D. J., Ford, J. D., & Lindhiem, O. (2016). A patient-centered decision-support tool informed by history of interpersonal violence: "Will this treatment work for me?" *Journal of Interpersonal Violence, 31*(3), 465–480.

Hammack, S. E., Cooper, M. A., & Lezak, K. R. (2012). Overlapping neurobiology of learned helplessness and conditioned defeat: Implications for PTSD and mood disorders. *Neuropharmacology, 62*(2), 565–575.

Harned, M. S., Korslund, K. E., & Linehan, M. M. (2014). A pilot randomized controlled trial of dialectical behavior therapy with and without the dialectical behavior therapy prolonged exposure protocol for suicidal and self-injuring women with borderline personality disorder and PTSD. *Behaviour Research and Therapy, 55*, 7–17.

Harvey, M. (1996). An ecological view of psychological trauma and trauma recovery. *Journal of Traumatic Stress, 9*, 3–23.

Hepner, K. A., Farris, C., Farmer, C. M., Iyiewuare, P. O., Tanielian, T., Wilks, A., . . . Pincus, H. A. (2018). Delivering clinical practice guideline-concordant care for PTSD and major depression in military treatment facilities. *RAND Health Quarterly, 7*(3), 3.

Herman, J. L. (1992a). Complex PTSD: A syndrome in survivors of prolonged and repeated trauma. *Journal of Traumatic Stress, 5*(3), 377–391.

Herman, J. L. (1992b). *Trauma and recovery*. New York: Basic Books.

Herman, J. L. (2012). CPTSD is a distinct entity: Comment on Resick et al. (2012). *Journal of Traumatic Stress, 25*(3), 256–257.

Hoffman, J., Liddell, B., Bryant, R. A., & Nickerson, A. (2018). The relationship between moral injury appraisals, trauma exposure, and mental health in refugees. *Depression and Anxiety, 35*(11), 1030–1039.

Hoge, C. W., & Chard, K. M. (2018). A window into the evolution of trauma-focused psychotherapies for Posttraumatic Stress Disorder. *Journal of the American Medical Association, 319*(4), 343–345.

Horan, J. M., & Widom, C. S. (2015a). Cumulative childhood risk and adult functioning in abused and neglected children grown up. *Development and Psychopathology, 27*(3), 927–941.

Horan, J. M., & Widom, C. S. (2015b). From childhood maltreatment to allostatic load in adulthood: The role of social support. *Child Maltreatment, 20*(4), 229–239.

Hyland, P., Shevlin, M., Brewin, C. R., Cloitre, M., Downes, A. J., Jumbe, S., . . . Roberts, N. P. (2017). Validation of post-traumatic stress disorder (PTSD) and complex PTSD using the International Trauma Questionnaire. *Acta Psychiatrica Scandinavica, 136*(3), 313–322.

Jenness, J. L., & McLaughlin, K. A. (2015). Towards a person-centered approach to the developmental psychopathology of trauma. *Social Psychiatry and Psychiatric Epidemiology, 50*(8), 1219–1221.

Kaczkurkin, A. N., Zang, Y., Gay, N. G., Peterson, A. L., Yarvis, J. S., Borah, E. V., . . . Consortium, S. S. (2017). Cognitive emotion regulation strategies associated with the DSM-5 posttraumatic stress disorder criteria. *Journal of Traumatic Stress, 30*(4), 343–350.

Karatzias, T., Cloitre, M., Maercker, A., Kazlauskas, E., Shevlin, M., Hyland, P., . . . Brewin, C. R. (2017a). PTSD and complex PTSD: ICD-11 updates on concept and measurement in the UK, USA, Germany and Lithuania. *European Journal of Psychotraumatology, 8*(Suppl. 7), 1418103.

Karatzias, T., Shevlin, M., Fyvie, C., Hyland, P., Efthymiadou, E., Wilson, D., . . . Cloitre, M. (2016). An initial psychometric assessment of an ICD-11 based measure of PTSD and complex PTSD (ICD-TQ): Evidence of construct validity. *Journal of Anxiety Disorders, 44,* 73–79.

Karatzias, T., Shevlin, M., Fyvie, C., Hyland, P., Efthymiadou, E., Wilson, D., . . . Cloitre, M. (2017b). Evidence of distinct profiles of posttraumatic stress disorder (PTSD) and complex posttraumatic stress disorder (CPTSD) based on the new ICD-11 Trauma Questionnaire (ICD-TQ). *Journal of Affective Disorders, 207,* 181–187.

Karatzias, T., Shevlin, M., Hyland, P., Brewin, C. R., Cloitre, M., Bradley, A., . . . Roberts, N. P. (2018). The role of negative cognitions, emotion regulation strategies, and attachment style in complex post-traumatic stress disorder: Implications for new and existing therapies. *British Journal of Clinical Psychology, 57*(2), 177–185.

Karver, M. S., De Nadai, A. S., Monahan, M., & Shirk, S. R. (2018). Meta-analysis of the prospective relation between alliance and outcome in child and adolescent psychotherapy. *Psychotherapy, 55*(4), 341–355.

Kira, I., Templin, T., Lewandowski, L., Ramaswamy, V., Bulent, O., Abu-Mediane, S., . . . Alamia, H. (2011). Cumulative tertiary appraisal of traumatic events across cultures: Two studies. *Journal of Loss and Trauma, 16*(1), 43–66.

Krammer, S., Kleim, B., Simmen-Janevska, K., & Maercker, A. (2016). Childhood trauma and complex posttraumatic stress disorder symptoms in older adults: A study of direct effects and social-interpersonal factors as potential mediators. *Journal of Trauma and Dissociation, 17*(5), 593–607.

Lanius, R. A., Brand, B., Vermetten, E., Frewen, P. A., & Spiegel, D. (2012). The dissociative subtype of posttraumatic stress disorder: Rationale, clinical and neurobiological evidence, and implications. *Depression and Anxiety, 29*(8), 701–708.

Layne, C. M. (2011). Developing interventions for trauma-exposed children: A comment on progress to date, and 3 recommendations for further advancing the field. *Archives of Pediatrics and Adolescent Medicine, 165*(1), 89–90.

Lowe, S. R., Quinn, J. W., Richards, C. A., Pothen, J., Rundle, A., Galea, S., . . . Bradley, B. (2016). Childhood trauma and neighborhood-level crime interact in predicting adult posttraumatic stress and major depression symptoms. *Child Abuse and Neglect, 51,* 212–222.

Markowitz, J. C., Petkova, E., Neria, Y., Van Meter, P. E., Zho, Y., Hembree, E., . . . Marshall, R. D. (2015). Is exposure necessary?: A randomized clinical trial of Interpersonal Psychotherapy for PTSD. *American Journal of Psychiatry, 172*(5), 430–440.

McDonagh, A., Friedman, M., McHugo, G., Ford, J. D., Sengupta, A., Mueser, K., . . . Descamps, M. (2005). Randomized trial of cognitive-behavioral therapy for chronic posttraumatic stress disorder in adult female survivors of childhood sexual abuse. *Journal of Consulting and Clinical Psychology, 73*(3), 515–524.

McDonnell, M., Robjant, K., & Katona, C. (2013). Complex posttraumatic stress disorder and survivors of human rights violations. *Current Opinion in Psychiatry, 26*(1), 1–6.

McLaughlin, K. A., & Lambert, H. K. (2017). Child trauma exposure and psychopathology: Mechanisms of risk and resilience. *Current Opinion in Psychology, 14,* 29–34.

Metcalf, O., Varker, T., Forbes, D., Phelps, A., Dell, L., DiBattista, A., . . . O'Donnell, M. (2016). Efficacy of fifteen emerging interventions for the treatment of posttraumatic stress disorder: A systematic review. *Journal of Traumatic Stress, 29*(1), 88–92.

Murphy, S., Elklit, A., Dokkedahl, S., & Shevlin, M. (2018, April 10). Testing competing factor models of the latent structure of post-traumatic stress disorder and complex post-traumatic stress disorder according to ICD-11. *European Journal of Psychotraumatology, 9*(1), 1457393.

Nicholson, A. A., Densmore, M., Frewen, P. A., Theberge, J., Neufeld, R. W., McKinnon, M. C., & Lanius, R. A. (2015). The dissociative subtype of posttraumatic stress disorder: Unique Resting-state functional connectivity of basolateral and centromedial amygdala complexes. *Neuropsychopharmacology, 40*(10), 2317–2326.

Nicholson, A. A., Friston, K. J., Zeidman, P., Harricharan, S., McKinnon, M. C., Densmore, M., . . . Lanius, R. A. (2017). Dynamic causal modeling in PTSD and its dissociative subtype: Bottom-up versus top-down processing within fear and emotion regulation circuitry. *Human Brain Mapping, 38*(11), 5551–5561.

Nienhuis, J. B., Owen, J., Valentine, J. C., Winkeljohn Black, S., Halford, T. C., Parazak, S. E., . . . Hilsenroth, M. (2018). Therapeutic alliance, empathy, and genuineness in individual adult psychotherapy: A meta-analytic review. *Psychotherapy Research, 28*(4), 593–605.

O'Callaghan, P., McMullen, J., Shannon, C., Rafferty, H., & Black, A. (2013). A randomized controlled trial of trauma-focused cognitive behavioral therapy for sexually exploited, war-affected Congolese girls. *Journal of the American Academy of Child and Adolescent Psychiatry, 52*(4), 359–369.

Palic, S., Zerach, G., Shevlin, M., Zeligman, Z., Elklit, A., & Solomon, Z. (2016). Evidence of complex posttraumatic stress disorder (CPTSD) across populations with prolonged trauma of varying interpersonal intensity and ages of exposure. *Psychiatry Research, 246*, 692–699.

Porges, S. W. (2007). The polyvagal perspective. *Biological Psychology, 74*(2), 116–143.

Porges, S. W. (2011). *The polyvagal theory: Neurophysiological foundations of emotions, attachment, communication, and self-regulation.* New York: Norton.

Putnam, F. W. (2009). Taking the measure of dissociation. *Journal of Trauma and Dissociation, 10*(3), 233–236.

Resick, P. A., Bovin, M. J., Calloway, A. L., Dick, A. M., King, M. W., Mitchell, K. S., . . . Wolf, E. J. (2012). A critical evaluation of the complex PTSD literature: Implications for DSM-5. *Journal of Traumatic Stress, 25*(3), 241–251.

Resick, P. A., Nishith, P., & Griffin, M. G. (2003). How well does cognitive-behavioral therapy treat symptoms of complex PTSD?: An examination of child sexual abuse survivors within a clinical trial. *CNS Spectrums, 8*(5), 340–355.

Resick, P. A., Suvak, M. K., & Wells, S. Y. (2014). The impact of childhood abuse among women with assault-related PTSD receiving short-term cognitive-behavioral therapy. *Journal of Traumatic Stress, 27*(5), 558–567.

Sachser, C., Keller, F., & Goldbeck, L. (2017). Complex PTSD as proposed for ICD-11: Validation of a new disorder in children and adolescents and their response to trauma-focused cognitive behavioral therapy. *Journal of Child Psychology and Psychiatry, 58*(2), 160–168.

San Cristobal, P., Santelices, M. P., & Miranda Fuenzalida, D. A. (2017). Manifestation of trauma: The effect of early traumatic experiences and adult attachment on parental reflective functioning. *Frontiers in Psychology, 8*, 449.

Scheeringa, M. S., Myers, L., Putnam, F. W., & Zeanah, C. H. (2012). Diagnosing PTSD in early childhood: An empirical assessment of four approaches. *Journal of Traumatic Stress, 25*(4), 359–367.

Schnyder, U., Bryant, R. A., Ehlers, A., Foa, E. B., Hasan, A., Mwiti, G., . . . Yule, W. (2016). Culture-sensitive psychotraumatology. *European Journal of Psychotraumatology, 7*, 31179.

Schnyder, U., & Cloitre, M. (Eds.). (2015). *Evidence based treatments for trauma-related psychological disorders.* Zurich, Switzerland: Springer.

Schnyder, U., Ehlers, A., Elbert, T., Foa, E. B., Gersons, B. P., Resick, P. A., . . . Cloitre, M. (2015, August 14). Psychotherapies for PTSD: What do they have in common? *European Journal of Psychotraumatology, 6*, 28186.

Shevlin, M., Hyland, P., Karatzias, T., Fyvie, C., Roberts, N., Bisson, J. I., . . . Cloitre, M. (2017). Alternative models of disorders of traumatic stress based on the new ICD-11 proposals. *Acta Psychiatrica Scandinavica, 135*(5), 419–428.

Shevlin, M., Hyland, P., Roberts, N. P., Bisson, J. I., Brewin, C. R., & Cloitre, M. (2018, January 17). A psychometric assessment of disturbances in self-organization symptom indicators for ICD-11 complex PTSD using the International Trauma Questionnaire. *European Journal of Psychotraumatology, 9*(1), 1419749.

Smith, C. P., & Freyd, J. J. (2014). Institutional betrayal. *American Psychologist, 69*(6), 575–587.

Spinazzola, J., Blaustein, M., & van der Kolk, B. A. (2005). Posttraumatic stress disorder treatment outcome research: The study of unrepresentative samples? *Journal of Traumatic Stress, 18*(5), 425–436.

Spinazzola, J., van der Kolk, B., & Ford, J. D. (2018). When nowhere is safe: Trauma history antecedents of posttraumatic stress disorder and developmental trauma disorder in childhood *Journal of Traumatic Stress, 31*(5), 631–642.

Stein, D. J., Cloitre, M., Nemeroff, C. B., Nutt, D. J., Seedat, S., Shalev, A. Y., . . . Zohar, J. (2009). Cape Town consensus on posttraumatic stress disorder. *CNS Spectrums, 14*(1, Suppl. 1), 52–58.

Steuwe, C., Lanius, R. A., & Frewen, P. A. (2012). Evidence for a dissociative subtype of PTSD by latent profile and confirmatory factor analyses in a civilian sample. *Depression and Anxiety, 29*(8), 689–700.

Steuwe, C., Rullkotter, N., Ertl, V., Berg, M., Neuner, F., Beblo, T., & Driessen, M. (2016). Effectiveness and feasibility of narrative exposure therapy (NET) in patients with borderline personality disorder and posttraumatic stress disorder—a pilot study. *BMC Psychiatry, 16*, 254.

Terr, L. (1991). Childhood traumas: An outline and overview. *American Journal of Psychiatry, 148*(1), 10–20.

Ursano, R. J., Bell, C., Eth, S., Friedman, M., Norwood, A., Pfefferbaum, B., . . . PTSD Steering Committee on Practice Guidelines. (2004). Practice guideline for the treatment of patients with acute stress disorder and posttraumatic stress disorder. *American Journal of Psychiatry, 161*(11 Suppl.), 3–31.

van der Kolk, B. A. (2005). Developmental trauma disorder: Toward a rational diagnosis for children with complex trauma histories. *Psychiatric Annals, 35*(5), 401–408.

van der Kolk, B. A., Ford, J. D., & Spinazzola, J. (2019). Toward an empirically-based developmental trauma disorder (DTD) diagnosis for children: 3. Psychiatric comorbidity of DTD and posttraumatic stress disorder (PTSD). *European Journal of Psychotraumatology, 10*(1), 1562841.

van der Kolk, B. A., Roth, S., Pelcovitz, D., Sunday, S., & Spinazzola, J. (2005). Disorders of extreme stress: The empirical foundation of a complex adaptation to trauma. *Journal of Traumatic Stress, 18*(5), 389–399.

van der Kolk, B. A., & van der Hart, O. (1989). Pierre Janet and the breakdown of adaptation in psychological trauma. *American Journal of Psychiatry, 146*(12), 1530–1540.

Van Dijke, A., Ford, J. D., Frank, L. E., & van der Hart, O. (2015). Association of childhood complex trauma and dissociation with complex posttraumatic stress disorder symptoms in adulthood. *Journal of Trauma and Dissociation, 16*(4), 428–441.

Van Dijke, A., Hopman, J. A. B., & Ford, J. D. (2018, January 23). Affect dysregulation, psychoform dissociation, and adult relational fears mediate the relationship between childhood trauma and complex posttraumatic stress disorder independent of the symptoms of borderline personality disorder. *European Journal of Psychotraumatology, 9*(1), 1400878.

van Ee, E., Kleber, R. J., & Jongmans, M. J. (2016). Relational patterns between caregivers with PTSD and their nonexposed children: A review. *Trauma Violence and Abuse, 17*(2), 186–203.

Walker, D. F., Courtois, C. A., & Aten, J. D. (Eds.). (2015). *Spiritually oriented psychotherapy for trauma*. Washington, DC: American Psychological Association.

World Health Organization. (2018). *International classification of diseases* (11th ed.). Geneva, Switzerland: Author.

Young, J. C., & Widom, C. S. (2014). Long-term effects of child abuse and neglect on emotion processing in adulthood. *Child Abuse and Neglect, 38*(8), 1369–1381.

CHAPTER 2

Developmental Neurobiology

JULIAN D. FORD

This chapter updates and extends the developmental neurobiology formulation of complex traumatic stress disorders (CTSDs) presented in the first edition of this text (Ford, 2009), based on advances in the past decade in research on developmental neurobiology and neuroimaging, in addition to new findings on traumatic stress symptomics (i.e., patterns of interrelationships among traumatic stress symptoms). The overarching theme is the continuation of a *paradigm shift* from traditional views of traumatic stress symptoms as *psychopathology* (i.e., maladaptive reactions or deficits in adaptive capacities) to a focus on *adaptive capacities* and *resilience*. Traumatic stress symptoms increasingly are viewed instead as *survival-based* adaptations that draw on, and can greatly alter, the brain and body's self-regulation capacities.

Why and how could an adaptive response to stress or adversity become a source of distress and impairment? When survival and security are severely and repeatedly threatened—the hallmark of complex trauma—protective/defensive systems in the brain become dominant and essentially hijack the rest of the brain and the body. The brain's functioning shifts into survival mode (involving the brainstem, the amygdala, and other midbrain structures), for a time diminishing or shutting down areas in the brain that coordinate conscious thinking, the thinking/judging/learning parts of the brain (the prefrontal areas of the cortex). Optimally, those executive areas in the brain come back online if the danger passes but, in the aftermath of complex trauma, the executive areas in the brain often stay largely offline and the brain's functioning is chronically driven by the survival/defensive areas (Ford, 2009). The *learning brain* is the organization of systems within the brain that enables humans to develop freely and explore the world in pursuit of personally meaningful knowledge, and to achieve core life goals (e.g., relationships, learning, skills, creativity,

35

and accomplishment) and a positive and coherent or consistent sense of self/identity. When the *survival brain* remains dominant in the long-term aftermath of exposure to complex trauma (including, but not limited to, when complex trauma continues chronically or reoccurs episodically), the learning brain's operations are interrupted or taken offline, resulting in emotional lability or shutdown and impulsive or avoidant thinking and behavior that are the hallmarks of CTSDs. Simultaneously, the body's physical resources are depleted or exhausted as a result of staying in a perpetual state of defensive mobilization—what has been described as *allostatic load* (McEwen, 2017)—leading to susceptibility to illness, injury, and a vicious cycle of escalating exposure to additional complex trauma and to symptoms of CTSDs. Persistent reliance on the *survival brain* and nonconscious reflex responses can result in a paradoxical decrease in capacity for self-protection. Like an addiction that physiologically alters the brain and its functioning, a brain stuck in survival mode can become second nature and automatic, as other modes of self-regulation fall away. Individuals experiencing CTSDs are entrapped by and at the mercy of a brain that is either highly reactive (hyperaroused), numbed, slowed or dissociative (hypoaroused), or both (i.e., a survival brain). It is this dilemma of being trapped in survival mode, and not a lack of intelligence, willpower, or character, that leads to CTSDs.

Recovery from CTSDs first and foremost requires a condition of emotional and environmental safety, so that the individual can downshift from a state of hyper- or hypoarousal to an alert but more relaxed state. As this occurs, in the psychobiological shift that can follow, the *learning brain* begins to be restored to ascendancy over the *survival brain*. CTSD treatment focuses on assisting the complex trauma survivor disengage the *survival brain* while accessing, reengaging, and strengthening the *learning brain* in order to restore the executive functions necessary for affective/cognitive self-regulation. The goal is not to "fix" or eliminate the *survival brain,* as it oversees the automatic and nonconscious physically based reactions necessary to respond to danger, but to restore and strengthen other brain capacities that enable the survivor to restore and sustain the *learning brain*. To do this, the clinician and the complex trauma survivor must be able to understand and recognize the operations and goals of both the *survival brain* and the *learning brain*. Therefore, this chapter describes advances in the past decade in developmental neurobiology, neuroimaging, and symptomics that provide insights regarding the role of the two brain modalities in CTSDs, and in treatment and recovery. This provides a framework for evaluating the best practices and evidence-based and emerging treatment models for CTSDs presented in the rest of the book.

Adaptation to Stress: A Shared Foundation for the Learning Brain and the Survival Brain

In contrast to the traditional emphasis on pathology (deficits, regression, degeneration), the adaptive psychobiological theories propose that psychological and physical symptoms and impairment occur when *adaptive* biopsycho-social capacities become maladaptive "symptoms." Some key history serves as background for an update on the emerging science of trauma and the brain. The *learning brain* and the *survival brain* formulation of adaptation to complex trauma and subsequent CTSDs fits within the tradition of adaptive psychology articulated a century or more ago by Pierre Janet (van der Kolk & van der Hart, 1989) and Adolph Meyer (Wortis, 1986):

> Adolph Meyer . . . preferred to rely upon the ability of the trained clinician to analyse the biosocial factors in the life of the "whole person" that contributed to the psychological and behavioural "reactions" that constituted all known mental disorders. (Noll, 1999, p. 146)

Hans Selye's (1951) stress-related model of medical and psychosomatic illness, what he termed the *general adaptation syndrome,* extended Meyer's work by explicitly linking the body, brain, and mind within an adaptive psychobiology framework. In studies of the human stress response, Selye found that the body becomes aroused in numerous ways in response to *average stress* and that once it lessens, the body returns to a state of *homeostasis* from which it started. In contrast, in response to *traumatic stressors* involving danger and insecurity, especially when experienced repeatedly or continuously, the body eventually reaches a point at which its stress response capacities are exceeded, resulting in *allostasis* (McEwen, 2017). Allostasis is now understood to be a "dis-ease" state, in which the body does not return to a condition of homeostasis but stays chronically aroused and therefore prone to exhaustion, breakdown, and illness. Rather than originating in some deficiency in the individual, stress-related disorders can be viewed as resulting from neurological and psychobiological alterations that are adaptive in the short term but overwhelm the body's capacities and lead to allostasis in the long run.

From this perspective, CTSDs can be understood as unintended consequences of the diversion of the brain's (and body's) adaptive capacities away from healthy development and learning to a more primal goal of surviving "prolonged and repeated trauma" (Herman, 1992, p. 377). The transformation of an innate *learning brain* into an altered *survival brain* in reaction to exposure to complex trauma (Ford, 2009) thus represents a biological trade-off between coping/survival and facilitation of growth, learning, self-development, healing, and rejuvenation. The trade-off has profound downstream costs (i.e., allostasis). Without safety from ongoing threats to survival, there can only be limited growth and well-being, and survival requires fundamentally different biological adaptations in the brain and body that can inadvertently further undermine growth and well-being. Complex trauma does not change the brain and body's overarching adaptive capacities and goal—to regulate bodily processes so as to achieve optimal outcomes. What changes is that survival displaces the health, well-being, and growth as the body's focal outcome and *raison d'être.*

Complex trauma is inherently unpredictable, uncontrollable, and aversive; therefore, it elicits correspondingly complex survival and functional adaptations (Courtois, 2004). What distinguishes posttraumatic survival-focused coping (and the *survival brain*) from health-focused growth and development (and the *learning brain*), is what Selye (1954) described as an "alarm reaction" that occurs when the brain and body's "innate alarm system" (Lanius et al., 2017) has been activated. This is the classic stress response that unfolds sequentially in four stages: freeze, fight, flight, and tonic immobility (Fragkaki, Stins, Roelofs, Jongedijk, & Hagenaars, 2016; Porges, 2007). The survival brain is not less intelligent than the learning brain; instead, it represents a pattern of connectivity within the brain that is what we would call, colloquially, "street smart"—exceptionally intelligent in dealing with danger, but at the cost of depleting the mental and physical resources available to handle life goals. In order to understand how the survival brain functions, and how it can displace the learning brain when people are faced with traumatic threats, it is helpful to understand the essential stress response.

From Adaptive Acute Stress Responses to Chronic CTSDs

Freeze reactions are the first step in the body's response to stressors, involving a rapid orienting response in order to scan the environment for stressors and for portals to solutions or paths to escape. While freezing, the body stills and inhibits overt action (i.e., the "deer in the headlights" phenomenon) and mobilizes physiologically for action (i.e., heart pounding, muscles tensing, rapid respiration, release of stress hormones). This combination of vigilance, delayed action, and physiological arousal is highly effective in stressful situations that require carefully selected responses executed with precision in order to overcome challenges or threats.

However, if the preparation provided by freezing does not prevent or resolve danger that is life threatening or life altering (i.e., traumatic) and these conditions continue or escalate, freeze reactions can become a chronic state rather than temporary adaptation. Persistent freeze responses (often involving dissociation—see Chapter 6 for definitions) are highly likely when traumatic stressors are complex, because experiencing or witnessing intentional injury caused by other human beings places the survivor in a position of having to defend against the very individuals (or groups, organizations, or societies) that should be a source of protection rather than the agents of harm. Dissociation of physical and emotional awareness may be what allow the individual to tolerate the intolerable or to escape the inescapable. Under those conditions, persistent freeze responses may be adaptive for survival but can become maladaptive when they persist because of the allostatic load they place on the body and the resultant strain caused to the individual's health, well-being, and relationships.

Chronic freeze reactions are evident in several posttraumatic stress disorder (PTSD) symptoms, including pervasive fear or anxiety and a corresponding preoccupation with past or future threats (e.g., hypervigilance, blame of self or others, rumination), intrusive reexperiencing (i.e., recurrent involuntary trauma memories, dreams, or flashbacks), altered beliefs and expectancies (e.g., viewing the world, people, and relationships as untrustworthy, exploitive, and dangerous), and states of chronic hyperarousal. In the complex PTSD domain, freeze responses can be seen as additionally contributing to the dysregulation of emotion (e.g., inability to recover from states of intense fear, guilt, or shame), attention (e.g., preoccupation with either detecting or avoiding threat), behavior (e.g., self-harm in order to contain and not be overwhelmed by physical, emotional, or existential/spiritual pain), relatedness (e.g., social isolation or emotional detachment; traumatic grief; revictimization), and self/identity (e.g., dissociative self-fragmentation; viewing oneself as damaged or deficient and therefore as untrustworthy and in need of constant internal or external bolstering).

Fight reactions are defensive attempts to overcome threats of harm by aggressively attacking or combating adversaries. Fight reactions involve a further surge in bodily arousal initiated by the brain's innate alarm system (Lanius et al., 2017), and proportionately forceful actions directed to overcome, protect against, or gain control over stressors and perpetrators. When stressors involve traumatic harm or threat, the intensity of fight reactions escalates proportionally in order to counteract the danger and immobilize or neutralize perpetrators. Intense fight reactions are evident in several PTSD and CTSD symptoms that involve psychobiological states of hyperarousal and intense anger, irritability, or reactive aggression.

Flight reactions are attempts to escape or avoid stressors that cannot be resolved or overcome either by careful assessment and delaying impulsive action (i.e., freezing) or by aggressively changing the environment or overcoming a source of problems (i.e., fighting). Flight reactions involve an escalation of physical arousal similar to fight reactions, but behaviorally they differ substantially, with flight involving arousal to escape or move away from or reduce exposure to sources of threat or danger that cannot be overcome or eliminated with direct action. Flight reactions therefore tend to occur after bodily resources and strength already have been depleted by the mobilization (i.e., freeze) and aggression (i.e., fight) phases of the stress response. As such, similar to fight reactions, flight responses require intense bursts of energy that cannot be sustained for lengthy periods of time without either severely reducing the individual's biological and psychological reserves or compromising bodily and psychological health (e.g., stress-related medical illnesses or behavioral health problems). Flight reactions also leave the stressor(s) and the agent(s) responsible for the stressor(s) unchanged, often resulting in vicious cycles in which attempts to escape or avoid stressors place the individual paradoxically at greater risk for subsequent exposure to the same or similar stressors.

PTSD and CTSD symptoms involving avoidance of reminders or memories of traumatic experiences, emotional numbing, and dissociation are classic flight reactions. Self-harm may also be a flight reaction when the intent is to reduce or contain intense distress or to end the danger. The escape occurs biologically (e.g., analgesia, anesthesia) or psychologically (e.g., alexithymia, derealization), or both, and physically when the individual's self-harm is acute or a suicide attempt results in loss of consciousness, coma, or death. Attempts to take flight, paradoxically, can intensify rather than ameliorate distress (e.g., due to escalating anxiety, depression, and intrusive memories of past traumas) and lead to rather than prevent revictimization (e.g., due to addictions or exploitation by perpetrators).

Prolonged and repeated exposure to entrapping, complex trauma can result in an involuntary state of physical and psychological paralysis or collapse (i.e., tonic immobility [TI], the ultimate stage of the stress response). However, TI may also occur during or after a single incident of intentional interpersonal injury that is inescapable and irreparably harmful (e.g., violent sexual assault, torture, or kidnapping). TI is less common than freeze, fight, or flight, and occurs as an innate defense when necessary to divert a predatory attacker by signaling capitulation and/or acting to conserve a small reserve of physical resources in the event that escape becomes possible (Marx, Forsyth, Gallup, Fuse, & Lexington, 2008). TI involves reactions that closely parallel PTSD's dissociative subtype and several CTSD symptoms: (1) negative variants of both somatoform (e.g., paralysis, blindness) and psychoform (e.g., depersonalization, derealization, fugue states, psychogenic amnesia) dissociation (Van Dijke, Ford, Frank, & van der Hart, 2015); (2) altered core beliefs reflecting despair and hopelessness; (3) involuntary avoidance responses; (4) extreme emotional numbing and alexithymia; (5) extreme detachment from relationships; (6) severe shame and guilt (Bovin et al., 2014); and (7) difficulty initiating or completing goal-directed behavior. TI essentially is a state of involuntary physical collapse and submission that may enable a person exposed to complex trauma to survive (Porges, 2007), but at the cost of a sense of helplessness and defeat that can lead adaptive immobilization to become maladaptive paralysis.

Thus, the symptoms of PTSD and CTSD can be understood as survival adaptations based on the classic freeze, fight, flight, and TI reactions. They become symptoms because they exact a heavy cost, including biological exhaustion and illness, psychosocial distress and impairment, and, ultimately and tragically, vulnerability to retraumatization. Resilience and recovery therefore depend on the individual restoring enough physical and emotional safety to allow the body and brain to shift from survival mode to a more neutral mode that allows the resumption of a learning, no-longer-on-high-alert mode. Resilience in the wake of complex trauma does not necessarily mean that biological stress/alarm reactions or psychological distress are totally absent. Instead, posttraumatic resilience involves the capacity to carry on and to achieve a productive life and meaningful relationships, even in the face of some lingering symptoms related to the allostatic load of the stress response. Such resilience, in turn, can bolster additional strength and resilience in what appears to be a virtuous cycle (Wingo et al., 2017).

Therefore, CTSDs are the outcome of competing demands on the brain and body produced by survival-focused stress reactivity leading the *learning brain* to be supplanted by a *survival brain* that operates primarily by locking into a chronic repetition of the freeze, fight, flight, and TI stress reactions. A brain stuck in survival mode cannot develop the core adaptive capacities that comprise health, growth, learning, and resilience (i.e., self-regulation, a coherent sense of self, physical, and meaningful accomplishments and relationships). In order to understand how complex trauma can fundamentally derail psychobiological health and development, it is important to begin by reviewing how the learning brain develops and provides a biological basis for self-regulation.

The Developing Learning Brain and the Emergence of Self-Regulation

In early childhood, the brain and body mature, and attachments with caregivers and other life experiences provide new learning that results in increasingly complex capacities for self-regulation. Self-regulation involves several adaptive processes: (1) *attentional flexibility*, the ability to disengage, shift, and reengage with a new focus of attention (Calcott & Berkman, 2014, 2015); (2) *inhibitory control*, the ability to withhold or reduce nonoptimal behavior or cognition (Cassotti, Agogue, Camarda, Houde, & Borst, 2016); (3) *effortful control*, the ability to intentionally focus attention and engage in goal-directed problem solving, planning, and behavior (Pallini et al., 2018); (4) *working memory*, the ability to hold new information available while drawing conclusions and making decisions, as well as to form long-term memories and retrieve them when needed (Yaple & Arsalidou, 2018); (5) *emotion regulation*, the ability to recognize emotions, modulate their intensity (i.e., arousal level) and valence (i.e., perceived positivity–negativity), and engage actively in attributing meaning to them and (when negative valence) coping or reparative behavior (Webb, Miles, & Sheeran, 2012); and (6) *mindfulness*, the ability to be aware of internal physiological, emotional, and mental states with nonjudgmental acceptance (Kaunhoven & Dorjee, 2017; Marusak et al., 2018).

The attainment of the capacity to self-regulate in childhood, initially through coregulation by a parent or other primary caregiver, provides a foundation for the evolution of additional adaptive capacities over the lifespan (Loizzo, 2009; Mullen & Hall, 2015). Self-regulation subsequently facilitates achieving personal and relational goals by enabling the child to identify and acquire the resources necessary to support and implement effective, sustained action plans based on accurate cost–benefit projections, while also preserving personal and relational safety and health by detecting immediate dangers (Harkness, Reynolds, & Lilienfeld, 2014).

In other words, the development of self-regulation involves acquiring and strengthening the psychobiological capacities necessary to achieve not only safety (i.e., the domain of the *survival brain*) but also autonomy, physical growth and health, an increasingly elaborated and coherent identity and sense of self, and relationships with caregivers, family, and peers, academic and avocational achievements (i.e., the domains of the *learning brain*). In early childhood, the brain develops networks or systems that comprise pathways within and between centers that oversee the specific physical and psychological operations necessary for self-regulation. The brain's centers, pathways, and systems/networks are distinct yet interconnected. In infancy, brain development is spurred and guided largely by innate growth processes (i.e., maturation) and input from the external environment (Lewis, 2005). However, from the earliest days of life, self-regulation gradually supersedes these innate and external forces as the child actively translates life experiences into intentional thought and emotion, and increasingly self-aware perceptions and behavior— the building blocks of self-regulation, as well as the sculpting of brain systems that expand and strengthen self-regulation. The capacities for self-regulation emerge in early childhood from "scaffolded interactions" in which caregivers physically (e.g., by holding or feeding) and behaviorally (e.g., by facial and vocal expressions; motoric interactions; changes in ambient temperature, sound, and light) model regulatory activities and encourage the infant/toddler to join in coregulation (McClelland & Cameron, 2011, p. 31). The development of self-regulation proceeds through several levels (Goldsmith, Pollak, & Davidson, 2008).

Self-Regulation Level 1: Arousal Modulation and Attentional Flexibility (the Brainstem)

Three levels have been identified in the hierarchy of the brain's systems (MacLean, 1985), each of which corresponds to a set of self-regulation capacities. Level 1 is the brainstem, which is located at the base of the brain and top of the spinal column. The brainstem integrates sensory inputs from the body and environment, and regulates bodily arousal states via the body's autonomic and vagal nervous systems and the corticosteroids produced in the hypothalamic–pituitary–adrenal axis (Geva & Feldman, 2008; Porges, 2007). Arousal modulation provides the infant with the ability to achieve the first level of self-regulation, attentional flexibility. In order to be able to shift attention flexibly in response to outer and inner stimuli, the infant must be able to maintain a level of physiological and brain arousal that is sufficient to mobilize attention but not so intense that attention becomes interrupted or confused. If arousal modulation is not well established by 4 months of age, the infant tends to be reactive to internal arousal states and to have difficulty in regulating attention (Geva & Feldman, 2008). Children whose parents are emotionally supportive and consistent, and whose families have socioeconomic advantages, tend to develop both a strong foundation of arousal modulation and good attentional flexibility by age 4 years (Berthelsen, Hayes, White, & Williams, 2017). The toddler develops increasing brainstem integrity and connections between the brainstem and higher-level brain systems, as well as more complex sensory integration and arousal modulation capacities. This relational or interpersonal foundation enables the child to begin to develop early forms of other key self-regulation capacities (i.e., inhibitory control, effortful control, working memory, and emotion coregulation with primary caregivers) in the first 3 years postpartum (Geva & Feldman, 2008).

Self-Regulation Level 2: Attentional Flexibility and Emergent Self-Control (the Midbrain)

The midbrain is located just above the brainstem, in the center of the brain. In infancy and toddlerhood, midbrain centers associated with vigilance (the basal ganglia) and selective focusing of attention (the superior colliculus in concert with the parietal cortex) become selectively sensitive or insensitive to (and activated or deactivated by) change in environmental circumstances (Coubard, 2015). This extends the child's capacities for attentional flexibility, particularly if caregivers are available, physically and emotionally, to provide a base of safety and security. Caregivers also model and support the balancing of automatic attentional vigilance capacities with the self-directed intentional use of attention, to enable the child to be actively immersed in learning (Bosmans, De Raedt, & Braet, 2007). This is the emergence of the *learning brain,* as the child becomes able to selectively attend to stimuli of interest rather than simply "going with the flow" of external and internal events. Intentional shifting of attention provides the foundation for the development of *inhibitory control* (i.e., the ability to choose not to think or act) and *effortful control* (i.e., the ability to choose what to think and how to act). *Working memory* also begins to emerge in toddlerhood as the midbrain neurons and pathways are increasingly interconnected in integrated centers (e.g., hippocampus) that can be activated in order to set and achieve goals (rather than reflexively reacting to inner and outer stimuli). During this early childhood epoch, the relative influence of the environment (i.e., learning) on children's inhibitory control capacities also increases dramatically compared to that of inborn maturation (i.e., genetics). Learning accounts for 94% of the variability in inhibitory control by age 3, versus 62% at age 2 (Gagne & Saudino, 2016).

Between ages 2 and 4 years, children learn to inhibit reactions by self-distraction and self-calming. The importance of this development of learned inhibitory control capacities is illustrated by findings in a study of children from economically disadvantaged backgrounds, in which toddlers who developed self-distraction capacities were able to handle frustration without problematic anger by age 4 and had low levels of externalizing behavior problems at age 5 (Bendezu et al., 2018). Moreover, the children whose parents modeled ways to use language in their interactions were best able to achieve inhibitory control and positive behavioral outcomes (Benedezu et al., 2018). By school age, children can use inhibitory control to tolerate frustration and disappointment in learning, with peers, and with adults who request compliance and set limits (Blair & Raver, 2015). Inhibitory control also is a foundation for creativity across the lifespan (Cassotti et al., 2016).

Infants and toddlers also develop a repertoire of primitive emotion regulation skills, initially through coregulation with primary caregivers in the second and third years postpartum, and with increasing autonomy thereafter. By age 3 years, toddlers are able to engage in a number of tactics to delay reflexive reactions when frustrated or disappointed, including self-soothing, seeking soothing from caregiver(s), calmly seeking information, or distracting by either shifting attention elsewhere temporarily or becoming immersed in an alternative activity (Cole, Bendezu, Ram, & Chow, 2017). By age 5 years, children develop emotion regulation skills involving assertive engagement in problem solving when confronted with frustration or disappointment. By the early elementary school years, this cognitive approach to emotion regulation enhances the child's active engagement in learning (Berthelsen et al., 2017) and social competence (Penela, Walker, Degnan, Fox, & Henderson, 2015). These emotion regulation capacities are especially important for children who are temperamentally shy, inhibited, and dysphoric as toddlers (Penela et al., 2015) or those who have a propensity for impulsivity and dysphoria (Cole et al., 2017).

As a result of the development of emotion regulation capacities in early childhood, "by school age children are usually able to tolerate the difficulties of learning new material, to delay and inhibit selfish responses in order to get along with others, to comply with adult directions and prohibitions even if they conflict with their goals, and to control impulsive action even if frustrated or disappointed" (Cole et al., 2017, p. 685). Self-regulation capacities for intentional attention shifting, inhibitory control, working memory, and effortful control thus provide a basis for the school-age child to cope with, modulate, and recover from emotional distress (i.e., emotion regulation), as well as intentionally respond to challenges and opportunities rather than reacting impulsively or dysphorically (i.e., self-control).

However, if caregiver protection, modeling, and coregulation are not consistently available in early childhood (Schore, 2000), and the child is exposed to traumatic stressors or complex trauma, their attention will become selectively focused on threat (Fonzo et al., 2016) rather than on creative opportunities and interests (i.e., the *survival brain*). As a result, the development of other self-regulation capacities such as inhibitory and effortful control, working memory, and emotion regulation becomes organized around the avoidance of harm rather than on achievement, enjoyment, relatedness, and identify formation. A fundamental attentional bias toward threat developed in early life can make the *survival brain* dominant rather than coequal with or subsumed by the *learning brain,* placing the child on a trajectory (Briggs-Gowan, Carter, & Ford, 2012) that can lead to lifelong problems with traumatic stress reactions (Fani et al., 2012; Felmingham, Rennie, Manor, & Bryant, 2011; Iacoviello et al., 2014).

Self-Regulation Level 3: Attentional Control, Effortful Control, and Emotion Regulation Provide a Foundation for the Emergence of Mindful Self-Regulation (the Cortex)

The third system in the brain is actually several networks that have their primary centers in the outer layers of the brain, the cortex. Although the brain's cortex is growing both in size and interconnections throughout infancy and early and middle childhood, a key transitional period occurs late in preadolescence and in early adolescence, when neuronal growth decelerates and the number of neurons in the brain's cortex *declines* (i.e., reduced volume and thickness) compared to earlier in life (Foulkes & Blakemore, 2018). The adolescent brain continues to develop connective paths linking brain centers (i.e., white matter), within the cortical and hippocampal areas associated with effortful control and emotion regulation, hormonal changes related to puberty (Sisk, 2017), resulting in neurons and their interconnections being pruned, sculpted, and sealed over (myelinated) (Tamnes, Bos, van de Kamp, Peters, & Crone, 2018; Wierenga et al., 2014). Inhibitory control and working memory, which were intertwined before age 10, can by adolescence be activated separately when and as needed (Shing, Lindenberger, Diamond, Li, & Davidson, 2010). Thus, youth can restrain impulsive reactions even when working memory (i.e., the ability to hold and utilize past learning along with new information) is not available, and can draw on working memory as a guide to thoughtful action when having difficulty inhibiting reactive impulses.

As brain networks involving the cortex develop, children and teens increasingly are able to intentionally pay attention to and utilize abstract concepts (e.g., self-relevant memories and mental imagery), as well as concrete sensory phenomena (e.g., environmental stimuli, bodily sensations), and thus to reflect on and remember the personal relevance and meaning of life experiences (Luckmann, Jacobs, & Sack, 2014). The ability to learn from experience by recalling not only the events but also one's own personal commitments and goals, enables the adolescent to use memory to plan for the future (i.e., prospective memory) (Cona, Scarpazza, Sartori, Moscovitch, & Bisiacchi, 2015) and exert self-control rather than reacting without a plan and depending on solely on the control of external rules and influences. As a result, working memory becomes more abstract, episodic memory becomes a more coherent self-focused narrative, and thinking and emotion processing/regulation become based on a more integrated understanding of self in relation to the external world (Harding, Yucel, Harrison, Pantelis, & Breakspear, 2015). These capacities support the emergence in preadolescence of *mindfulness*—nonjudgmental awareness and acceptance of one's own and other persons' thoughts, emotions, and ways of thinking and feeling (Kaunhoven & Dorjee, 2017; Marchand, 2014; Marusak et al., 2018).

In adolescence, several brain centers are still growing and maturing rather than slimming down and becoming highly efficient, including areas associated with attention (i.e., basal ganglia) and stress reactivity (i.e., amygdala), which continue to increase in volume and thickness through adolescence into early adulthood (Foulkes & Blakemore, 2018; Wierenga et al., 2014). Compared to adults, adolescents tend to be more driven by immediate rewards, the influence of peers, and fears of social exclusion, and correspondingly less able to recognize and utilize other people's informational and emotional input when making decisions (Morris, Squeglia, Jacobus, & Silk, 2018; Mueller, Cromheeke, Siugzdaite, & Nicolas Boehler, 2017). They have higher levels of brain activation than adults in response to actual or anticipated rewards in subcortical areas (e.g., striatum, insula) associated with impulsivity and emotionally driven behavior but lower levels of activation in areas involved in executive functions and emotion regulation (i.e., frontal and parietal cortices) (Casey, Getz, & Galvan, 2008; Silverman, Jedd, & Luciana, 2015). In response to situations eliciting disappointment or regret, teens also show less activation than do young adults in brain areas associated with felt emotion (i.e., insula), appraisal of one's own and others' emotions and intentions, and inhibition (Hansen, Thayer, Feldstein Ewing, Sabbineni, & Bryan, 2018) of risky (e.g., sexual) (Rodrigo, Padron, de Vega, & Ferstl, 2018) behavior. Youth, in comparison to adults, also show more impulsive (i.e., amygdala) yet affectively blunted (i.e., striatum) responses to negative emotional experiences in social contexts, as well as increased connectivity between the striatum and prefrontal cortex (which may represent an attempt to inhibit impulsivity and increase relational connection) (Fareri et al., 2015).

Thus, although adolescents' effortful control and emotion regulation capacities are growing stronger, more flexible, and more differentiated (i.e., more available to be deployed separately in order to handle complex relational, learning, and performance challenges), they continue to be challenged when attempting emotion regulation and mindfulness. Overall, childhood and adolescence are periods of notable immaturity and also maturation by the brain and body, which provide a foundation for experience-dependent learning that leads to major increases in the complexity and effectiveness of the adolescent's self-regulation abilities. Their learning brain develops progressively more sophisticated and interconnected centers and systems to support several emerging capacities for self-regulation: flexible shifting and focusing of attention (i.e., attentional control), inhibiting impulsive reactions (i.e., inhibitory control), planning and carrying out goal-directed actions (i.e., effortful control), integrating new information with prior learning (i.e., working memory), and maintaining emotional balance (i.e., emotion regulation). These capacities of the *learning brain* enable the youth to enter adulthood with a strong base of knowledge, psychological and physical health and resilience, and interpersonal connectedness and support. However, in adolescence, as well as earlier in childhood, exposure to complex trauma can shift the brain away from learning and toward survival, strengthening the networks and connections that comprise the *survival brain* and the body's inner alarm system—resulting in CTSDs.

Complex Trauma and the Ascendance of the Survival Brain

Childhood and adolescence are developmental periods in which experiences with people who serve as models, helpers, guides, comforters, competitors, and sources of validation and security are particularly catalytic for healthy brain and self-development. Complex trauma during transitional periods in which major lasting changes in personality and self-regulation occur often involves social interactions that teach the child or adolescent to focus on danger and survival rather than on trust and learning. If exposure to complex trauma shifts the brain's trajectory of development away from creative learning and exploration toward defensive states geared to promote survival, the child's biological and psychological capacities for self-regulation may be stunted or largely lost. Neural networks in the brain can become correspondingly fixed and difficult to change as a result of adverse experience-based biologically entrenched expectations of danger that lead to preoccupation with detecting and defending against threats in all walks of life (Luby, Barch, Whalen, Tillman, & Belden, 2017; Miller, Chen, & Parker, 2011). In shifting from a learning brain to a survival brain, neural pathways thus may become excessively and prematurely consolidated into a structure geared mainly toward monitoring and/or avoiding threat (Naim et al., 2015; Pine et al., 2005).

Moreover, children exposed to complex trauma are prone to heightened levels of immune system inflammatory defenses (Miller et al., 2011) and biobehavioral irritability (Salum et al., 2017) that place them at further risk for both psychological and biological health problems and psychosocial impairment at the time and later (Luby et al., 2017; Pagliaccio, Pine, Barch, Luby, & Leibenluft, 2018). Furthermore, by early adolescence, areas in the brain associated with face processing tend to be underactivated when children become preoccupied with detecting and avoiding danger, potentially leading them to have severe relational difficulties due to not being able to recognize the cues that communicate other persons' emotions and intentions (Sylvester, Petersen, Luby, & Barch, 2017). Thus, paradoxically, when the *survival brain* is dominant, rather than protecting the youth, this can be hazardous to health and relationships.

To understand what happens when a child's *learning brain* is subsumed by a *survival brain* in response to complex trauma, it is instructive to consider an important marker of generalized impairment in a wide range of self-regulation capacities in childhood: irritability. Children's extent of exposure to adversity is correlated with their level of irritability and, intriguingly, both are associated with higher levels of cortical thickness in brain areas related to key self-regulation capacities (i.e., attention and executive control, interpersonal information processing, reward–loss processing; Pagliaccio et al., 2018). Cortical thickness tends to peak in early childhood (Lyall et al., 2015; Porter, Collins, Muetzel, Lim, & Luciana, 2011), and subsequent thinning has been shown to be associated with language and executive function capacities that "likely reflect maturation toward adult-like cortical organization and processing" (Porter, Collins, Muetzel, Lim, & Luciana, 2011, p. 1865). Correspondingly, greater cortical thickness has been found to be related to deficits in both executive function and language skills in childhood and adulthood (Brito, Piccolo, Noble, & Pediatric Imaging, Neurocognition, and Genetics Study, 2017). To further complicate matters, children exposed to early life adversity have been found to have deficits in late school age or pre-adolescence in the size and differentiation of a key area in the prefrontal cortex, the inferior frontal gyrus (Luby et al., 2018). This area has been shown to play a key role in accurately understanding and reappraising other persons' emotions and intentions (Dal Monte et al., 2014; Grecucci, Giorgetta, Bonini, & Sanfey, 2013), as well in learning emotionally significant lessons and retaining this knowledge in working memory when biologically underaroused (i.e., a state of biological and emotional detachment that is common in adolescence) (Becker et al., 2013).

In this way, childhood exposure to complex trauma may contribute to, or exacerbate, delays in brain development (i.e., lesser gains in cortical consolidation and efficiency, as represented by lesser amounts of cortical pruning and thinning), which could undermine the development of self-regulation capacities and (especially if the child is subject to continuing traumas/adversities) replacing it with maladaptive survival-based coping (e.g., attentional bias toward threat and emotion dysregulation in the form of irritability). Neuroimaging studies document an association of exposure to complex trauma in childhood with underdevelopment of neural capacities and pathways required for inhibitory and effortful control, working memory, and reflective self-awareness (Teicher & Samson, 2016). Such deficits in the development of key capacities for self-regulation can reduce the youth's curiosity, resulting in a tendency to react reflexively to life experiences with relatively automatic, chaotic, and fixated perceptions, thoughts, and action: In other words, survival-adaptive experience-expectant reactivity comes to take precedence over experience-dependent learning (Lewis, 2005).

As a result, rather than inhibiting immediate impulses and seeking and being guided by reflective self-awareness, the child who has experienced (or currently is experiencing) complex trauma is likely to be preoccupied (i.e., intrusive reexperiencing) with anticipating (i.e., hypervigilance) and reacting based on aggression, avoidance, or to simply go "offline" (i.e., fight, flight, or dissociation). Although developed in the face of threat or danger, it extends to life experiences and relationships associated with emotional, interpersonal, or physical challenge, uncertainty, or vulnerability. Threat avoidance and mitigation thus can become the dominant form of attentional focusing, behavioral inhibition, goal-directed action, and working memory for the child who is faced with complex trauma. Children's strategies for avoiding or mitigating threats are highly resourceful and creative, but consistent with their still-developing self-regulation capacities, they tend to be immature and often self-defeating. These may include worry, rumination, perseverative behavior, attempts at self-soothing, defiance, school avoidance, social withdrawal, substance use, self-harm, or risky or delinquent behavior. The intent of behaviors of these types is to reduce a sense of vulnerability, powerlessness, and hopelessness by avoiding or minimizing awareness of extreme states of anxiety, dysphoria, and high and low levels of physiological arousal. This can result in a hyperamplification of stress and reward pathways in the brain that already normatively are in a high state of activation or readiness. Hyperactivation of those brain circuits can cause what Lewis describes as "sudden changes in global neural patterning, causing a rapid switch in appraisals" (2005, p. 262)—that is, a shift from the *learning brain* to the *survival brain*.

Memories that could otherwise be integrated into the youth's evolving life narrative and sense of self may instead become fragmented and intrusive as a result of being infused with overwhelming distress or emotional emptiness. Actions that otherwise would seem reckless may be appraised as the best or only way to cope with persistent harm or danger (e.g., assuming that injury is inevitable, it is better to "bring it on" than wait passively as a victim, as captured in the colloquial expression that *the best defense is a good offense*). The cascade of negative consequences that follow (e.g., severe academic problems or expulsion from school, repeated contacts with law enforcement and the courts, rejection or severe conflict in peer relationships) tend to be circularly appraised as evidence that the world is indeed hostile, people (including oneself) cannot be trusted, and the best defense against being a powerless victim is to never let down one's guard, or to crawl into a shell of emotional and physical withdrawal and shut out the world. So what began as survival-adaptive neural and behavioral responses to complex trauma may become chronic biological, emotional, mental, and interpersonal hypervigilance, avoidance, and dissociation based on the belief that nowhere and no one is safe (Spinazzola, van der Kolk, & Ford, 2018)—in other words, the *survival brain* replaces the *learning brain*.

Consistent with this view, Grasso, Dierkhising, Branson, Ford, and Lee (2016) found that adolescents who had been exposed to complex trauma in middle childhood (e.g., sexual abuse or polyvictimization) were more likely to have severe internalizing and PTSD avoidance symptoms than youth who also experienced traumas in middle childhood, but of a lesser degree of complexity (e.g., life-threatening accidents, community violence)—but *not* more likely to have severe externalizing behavior problems. However, youth who had experienced complex trauma *in adolescence* were at risk for severe externalizing and hyperarousal problems, as well as internalizing and PTSD avoidance symptoms (Grasso et al., 2016). Thus, the defensive adaptations undertaken by the survival brain may change over the course of childhood, most evident initially as freeze and flight reactions (i.e., internalizing and avoidance symptoms) that subsequently expand with the addition of fight reactions (i.e., externalizing and hyperarousal), and ultimately immobilization (i.e., isolation, severe depression, suicidality).

By middle childhood or adolescence, children exposed to complex trauma may be diagnosed with a plethora of psychiatric and behavioral disorders (e.g., bipolar, dissociative, disruptive behavior, substance use, reactive attachment, intermittent explosive, and borderline personality disorders). Children exposed to complex trauma whose attachment bonds with primary caregivers also are compromised are at particularly high risk for such polydiagnosis (van der Kolk, Ford, & Spinazzola, 2019). This has been described as developmental trauma disorder, the childhood form of chronic PTSD, complex PTSD, and CTSDs (Ford, Spinazzola, van der Kolk, & Grasso, 2018).

Origins of the Survival Brain:
(Epi)Genetics and Neuroimaging Research

How does the *survival brain* emerge in the wake of complex trauma? Evolving research on genetics and brain imaging offers some intriguing clues. There are, as yet, no identified definitive genetic risk factors for PTSD (Sheerin, Lind, Bountress, Nugent, & Amstadter, 2017), let alone for CTSDs. However, recent studies suggest that there may be genes that, when activated by exposure to traumatic stressors, lead to the emergence of symptoms consistent with PTSD (and also CTSDs). While some children may be genetically predisposed to shift from a *learning brain* to a *survival brain* when exposed to trauma, the mechanism(s) underlying this shift may be *epi*genetic rather than genetic. *Epigenetics* refers to changes in genes that occur as a result of when life experiences. Potential epigenetic pathways that may lead to PTSD or CTSDs involve genes associated with anticipating and coping with threat: fear and stress reactivity (Lowe et al., 2015; Watkins et al., 2016), dopamine-related addictive processing (Li et al., 2016), and immune/inflammatory reactions and accelerated cell aging and death (Mellon, Gautam, Hammamieh, Jett, & Wolkowitz, 2018). Thus, complex trauma may "turn on" genes that specifically incline the brain to shift into survival mode and the body to hyper- or hypoarousal (McEwen, 2017).

Brain imaging research has identified brain systems that may account for the possible epigenetic changes whereby exposure to complex trauma results in the ascendance of the survival brain. Two overarching brain networks play key roles in both the learning brain and the survival brain. The first is the task-positive network (TPN), which enables us to cope with stressors and to achieve our life goals. The TPN comprises three primary subnetworks: The first is responsible for focusing attention (AN; attention network); the second oversees the stress response (SN; salience network); and the third is the executive system (EN; executive network) that enables us to use our emotions and mental capacities to self-regulate and achieve our higher goals. The survival brain involves either a hyperactivation or shutdown of both the AN and the SN, which is precisely what has been observed in brain imaging studies with children or adults who have been exposed to complex trauma and are experiencing symptoms of PTSD/CTSDs (Teicher & Samson, 2016). By contrast, the learning brain involves the activation of EN structures in the prefrontal cortex and related areas that enable us to be aware of, regulate, and effectively express our emotions in relationships and in other important life pursuits (e.g., school, work, recreation, creative activities). Consistent with the view that recovery from PTSD/CTSDs involves a shift from the survival brain to the learning brain, successful treatment of those disorders has been found to be associated with EN activation and dominance (Ford, 2018).

The default mode network (DMN), the second crucial brain system involved in both the survival brain and the learning brain, is an array of brain structures that extend across the entire brain, overlapping or connecting with several parts of the TPN. When the DMN is activated, the individual is able to engage in complex integrative thought independent of current circumstances, including creating and retrieving thoughts and memories that give meaning to life and define a person's core identity (Mak et al., 2017; Margulies et al., 2016; Miller et al., 2016). The DMN is active when the TPN goes off-line (Wang et al., 2018), including active disengagement from the external environment in order to deeply reflect on personally meaningful issues, memories, or plans, as well as more passive states of daydreaming or "mind wandering" (Poerio et al., 2017). As Margulies and colleagues (2016, p. 12578) conclude:

> The DMN is important, because it permits cognitive processing . . . independent of the here and now. This capacity is adaptive, because it permits . . . original and creative thoughts to emerge. . . . Beyond supporting states of creativity and planning, the DMN has also been implicated in almost all psychiatric conditions, indicating that there may be costs as well as benefits from the capacity to apprehend the world as it might be rather than seeing it as it is right now.

When the brain is in *learning* mode, the DMN and EN work in tandem and usually are anticorrelated (i.e., when one network is dominant, the other is quiescent). However, they also can be simultaneously active and are collaborative when the individual is pursuing a long-term self-relevant goal (Margulies & Smallwood, 2017). On the other hand, in psychiatric disorders, the brain operates largely in *survival* mode, with the DMN and EN becoming disconnected—leading to a preoccupation with intrusive internal stimuli such as delusional thought and dysphoric rumination (Whitfield-Gabrieli & Ford, 2012).

Consistent with this view, adults with PTSD have heightened activation of the SN but reduced activation in the DMN (Koch et al., 2016), and reduced connectivity between the EN and DMN (Clausen et al., 2017). These "altered resting-state connectivity and activity patterns could represent neurobiological correlates of increased salience processing and hypervigilance (SN), at the cost of awareness of internal thoughts and autobiographical memory (DMN)" (Koch et al., 2016, p. 592), as well as "deficiencies in recruiting . . . frontal regions associated with executive control, thus impairing the ability to acutely regulate the DMN and switch from an internal focus to a goal-directed state" (Clausen et al., 2017, p. 433). PTSD also is associated with altered connections within the DMN that could help to account for hypervigilance and intrusive reexperiencing (Leech & Sharp, 2014; Cavanna, 2007; Miller et al., 2017).

Other brain areas that show patterns of increased or decreased activation and interconnectivity in PTSD include those involved in monitoring homeostasis (e.g., the insula, which also is responsible for shifts in dominance between the EN and DMN), modulating arousal (e.g., the locus coeruleus), processing and orienting to sensory information (e.g., the thalamus and superior colliculus), subconscious integration of sensory input with behavior and conscious awareness (e.g., the cerebellum), and social cognition (e.g., the medial prefrontal cortex and junction of the temporal and parietal lobes) (Lanius et al., 2017). Connectivity between these areas both in resting state and when consciously or subconsciously processing threat stimuli has been described as the "innate alarm system" (Lanius et al., 2017). The innate alarm system focuses on external threats (i.e., the survival brain) and takes conscious awareness of self-state (both bodily and emotion) and self-relevant or relational goals offline (i.e., the learning brain). of the meaning of both specific stimuli and one's self in context (Lanius, Frewen, Tursich, Jetly, & McKinnon, 2015; Lanius et al., 2017).

In summary, the alterations in brain systems relevant to CTSDs (Akiki, Averill, & Abdallah, 2017; Lanius et al., 2015) involve the ascendance of the *survival brain*: a bias toward anticipating threat and heightened activation of the innate alarm system (SN). Simultaneously, the *learning brain's* capacities for reflective self-awareness and executive function are sidelined due to diminished activation in, and connectivity between, the DMN and EN. The *learning brain* also may become co-opted by the *survival brain* in the service of avoiding awareness of threat or distress—notably when the SN controls and heightens activation of the DMN and EN, such that the person experiences severe dissociation and a fragmentation of self.

Symptomics as a Window on CTSDs

CTSDs are challenging for genetics and neuroimaging researchers, because the symptoms are multifaceted and occur across multiple biopsychosocial domains in different combinations rather than as a single homogeneous illness condition. Considering PTSD alone, there are an estimated over 600,000 potential combinations of the disorder's 20 core symptoms that could qualify for this diagnosis (Stein, 2018). One approach to resolve this dilemma is the identification of subtypes of PTSD based on "intermediate phenotypes" (IPs), which are defined as "specific brain-based pathophysiological mechanism(s) leading to 'altered' brain function and specific . . . PTSD symptoms" (Liberzon, 2018, p. 797). Liberzon has postulated several IPs that may constitute PTSD subtypes, including (1) abnormal fear learning (FL) that centers on excessive activation and insufficient inhibition of the amygdala (Krabbe, Grundemann, & Luthi, 2018); (2) reduced emotion regulation and executive function (ER/EF) due to insufficient activation and connectivity in the prefrontal cortex (PFC); (3) exaggerated threat detection (TD) due to hyperconnectivity of structures in the SN, such as the amygdala; and (4) deficient contextual processing (CP; i.e., awareness of the relevant external circumstances) that centers on the hippocampus and its connections to the PFC. Taken together, these IPs could account for the core features of the *survival brain* and the symptoms of CTSDs: persistent fear, intrusive reexperiencing, and avoidance (FL), survival-focused hypervigilance (TD), emotion dysregulation (EC/ER), and disturbances of self-organization and relationships (CP). These alterations in brain networks are accompanied by parallel complex alterations in the body's stress response systems (Deslauriers et al., 2018), including brain chemistry (Nees, Witt, & Flor, 2018); the hypothalamic–pituitary–adrenal axis and glucocorticoids (Daskalakis, Provost, Hunter, & Guffanti, 2018; Nees et al., 2018; Girgenti & Duman, 2018); sex-based hormones (Ramikie & Ressler, 2018); and, locus coeruleus-mediated hyper- and hypoactivation of the sympathetic and parasympathetic branches of the autonomic nervous system (Daskalakis et al., 2018; Mellon et al., 2018; Naegeli et al., 2018; Nees et al., 2018), and metabolic and immune systems (Girgenti & Duman, 2018; Mellon et al., 2018).

Paralleling the search for genetic profiles or signatures of diseases (i.e., genomics), other studies are mapping neural interconnections (or networks) that link to CT/CTSD-related symptoms—an approach referred to as *symptomics* (Armour, Fried, & Olff, 2017b). Symptomics using network statistical analyses with adult trauma survivors have identified three relatively distinct subsets of symptoms that are centrally located among the full set of PTSD symptoms (Armour, Fried, Deserno, Tsai, & Pietrzak, 2017a; Mitchell et al., 2017): (1) fear circuitry (e.g., intrusive reexperiencing, avoidance); (2) survival defense (e.g., hyperarousal, hypervigilance); and (3) defeat and demoralization, which may include emotional numbing (Armour et al., 2017a; Birkeland & Heir, 2017), dysphoria (McNally et al., 2015), depression (Choi, Batchelder, Ehlinger, Safren, & O'Cleirigh, 2017), or self-blame (Armour et al., 2017a). Fear circuitry symptoms are central in the acute phase of adult PTSD; as PTSD became more chronic, clusters of survival defense and defeat/demoralization symptoms are more emergent (Bryant et al., 2017). With traumatized children, network studies reveal that fear circuitry symptoms (e.g., nightmares, flashbacks, trauma-related rumination) are interconnected (Russell, Neill, Carrion, & Weems, 2017) and connected to dissociative symptoms (Saxe et al., 2016). Less is known about the brain circuitry involved in survival defense and defeat reactions by traumatized children, but high levels of trauma-related fear are likely to lead to activation of those systems—and to the emergence of CTSDs.

Recent symptomics/network studies also have included CTSD symptoms with survivors of complex trauma. A study with adult survivors of childhood maltreatment revealed that chronic anger was not specifically related to any type of maltreatment, but when it was manifested in the form of angry rumination about past events, it was highly associated with several types of maltreatment and especially strongly with emotional abuse (Gluck, Knefel, & Lueger-Schuster, 2017). PTSD symptoms also were closely associated with a history of emotional abuse but not with angry rumination or anger—supporting a distinction between PTSD and CTSDs, with the latter involving disturbances of self-organization consistent with chronic anger and angry rumination (consistent with a state of survival defense and demoralization; i.e., the survival brain). A study of adult survivors of childhood sexual abuse revealed that physiological and emotional reactivity to abuse reminders were the primary drivers of other PTSD symptoms, with abuse-related dreams (potentially indirectly reflecting hypervigilance or attempts at trauma mastery) and anhedonia (possibly reflecting defeat and demoralization) centrally located among the PTSD symptoms (McNally, Heeren, & Robinaugh, 2017). These findings suggest that CTSDs involve chronic fear-related bodily and emotional reactivity (both while asleep and awake), as well as severe self- and relational dysregulation. This can be understood as the result of a combination of chronic threat processing (i.e., the *survival brain*) with diminished reflective self-awareness, identity development, and goal-oriented executive functions (i.e., the *learning brain*).

Conclusion

According to this formulation, psychotherapy for CTSDs involves the activation and strengthening of the learning brain as a means of counterbalancing and reducing the dominance of the survival brain. This begins in Phase 1 with a focus on enhancing awareness of the survival brain while ensuring safety, providing psychoeducation, teaching self-regulation skills, and the development of a therapeutic alliance. In Phase 2, trauma processing engages the learning brain in a reexamination of memories of past traumas and their reenactment in current symptoms, with a focus on validating the personal meaning of the experiences (i.e., an emphasis on learning from the experiences rather than mere survival) (Ford, 2018; Ford, Courtois, Steele, van der Hart, & Nijenhuis, 2005). In Phase 3, this shift from the survival brain to the learning brain is extended into all domains of daily life by systematically enhancing quality of life and well-being. Thus, across all of the modalities of psychotherapy for CTSDs that are described in this book, the key unifying theme is that treatment involves restoring trauma survivors' ability to access and be guided by the learning brain, as a fundamental shift from being controlled by the survival brain.

References

Akiki, T. J., Averill, C. L., & Abdallah, C. G. (2017). A network-based neurobiological model of PTSD: Evidence from structural and functional neuroimaging studies. *Current Psychiatry Reports, 19*(11), 81.

Armour, C., Fried, E. I., Deserno, M. K., Tsai, J., & Pietrzak, R. H. (2017a). A network analysis of DSM-5 posttraumatic stress disorder symptoms and correlates in U.S. military veterans. *Journal of Anxiety Disorders, 45,* 49–59.

Armour, C., Fried, E. I., & Olff, M. (2017b, December 8). PTSD symptomics: Network analyses in the field of psychotraumatology. *European Journal of Psychotraumatology, 8*(Suppl. 3).

Becker, B., Androsch, L., Jahn, R. T., Alich, T., Striepens, N., Markett, S., . . . Hurlemann, R. (2013). Inferior frontal gyrus preserves working memory and emotional learning under conditions of impaired noradrenergic signaling. *Frontiers in Behavioral Neuroscience, 7,* 197.

Bendezu, J. J., Cole, P. M., Tan, P. Z., Armstrong, L. M., Reitz, E. B., & Wolf, R. M. (2018). Child language and parenting antecedents and externalizing outcomes of emotion regulation pathways across early childhood: A person-centered approach. *Development and Psychopathology, 30*(4), 1253–1268.

Berthelsen, D., Hayes, N., White, S. L. J., & Williams, K. E. (2017). Executive function in adolescence: Associations with child and family risk factors and self-regulation in early childhood. *Frontiers in Psychology, 8,* 903.

Birkeland, M. S., & Heir, T. (2017, June 2). Making connections: Exploring the centrality of posttraumatic stress symptoms and covariates after a terrorist attack. *European Journal of Psychotraumatology, 8*(Suppl. 3).

Blair, C., & Raver, C. C. (2015). School readiness and self-regulation: A developmental psychobiological approach. *Annual Review of Psychology, 66,* 711–731.

Bosmans, G., De Raedt, R., & Braet, C. (2007). The invisible bonds: Does the secure base script of attachment influence children's attention toward their mother? *Journal of Clinical Child and Adolescent Psychology, 36*(4), 557–567.

Bovin, M. J., Dodson, T. S., Smith, B. N., Gregor, K., Marx, B. P., & Pineles, S. L. (2014). Does guilt mediate the association between tonic immobility and posttraumatic stress disorder symptoms in female trauma survivors? *Journal of Traumatic Stress, 27*(6), 721–724.

Briggs-Gowan, M. J., Carter, A. S., & Ford, J. D. (2012). Parsing the effects violence exposure in early childhood: Modeling developmental pathways. *Journal of Pediatric Psychology, 37*(1), 11–22.

Brito, N. H., Piccolo, L. R., Noble, K. G., & the Pediatric Imaging, Neurogenetic, and Imaging Study. (2017). Associations between cortical thickness and neurocognitive skills during childhood vary by family socioeconomic factors. *Brain and Cognition, 116,* 54–62.

Bryant, R. A., Creamer, M., O'Donnell, M., Forbes, D., McFarlane, A. C., Silove, D., & Hadzi-Pavlovic, D. (2017). Acute and chronic posttraumatic stress symptoms in the emergence of posttraumatic stress disorder: A network analysis. *JAMA Psychiatry, 74*(2), 135–142.

Calcott, R. D., & Berkman, E. T. (2014). Attentional flexibility during approach and avoidance motivational states: the role of context in shifts of attentional breadth. *Journal of Experimental Psychology: General, 143*(3), 1393–1408.

Calcott, R. D., & Berkman, E. T. (2015). Neural correlates of attentional flexibility during approach and avoidance motivation. *PLOS ONE, 10*(5), e0127203.

Casey, B. J., Getz, S., & Galvan, A. (2008). The adolescent brain. *Developmental Review, 28*(1), 62–77.

Cassotti, M., Agogue, M., Camarda, A., Houde, O., & Borst, G. (2016). Inhibitory control as a core process of creative problem solving and idea generation from childhood to adulthood. *New Directions for Child and Adolescent Development, 2016*(151), 61–72.

Cavanna, A. E. (2007). The precuneus and consciousness. *CNS Spectrums, 12*(7), 545–552.

Choi, K. W., Batchelder, A. W., Ehlinger, P. P., Safren, S. A., & O'Cleirigh, C. (2017). Applying network analysis to psychological comorbidity and health behavior: Depression, PTSD, and sexual risk in sexual minority men with trauma histories. *Journal of Consulting and Clinical Psychology, 85*(12), 1158–1170.

Clausen, A. N., Francisco, A. J., Thelen, J., Bruce, J., Martin, L. E., McDowd, J., . . . Aupperle, R. L. (2017). PTSD and cognitive symptoms relate to inhibition-related prefrontal activation and functional connectivity. *Depression and Anxiety, 34*(5), 427–436.

Cole, P. M., Bendezu, J. J., Ram, N., & Chow, S. M. (2017). Dynamical systems modeling of early childhood self-regulation. *Emotion, 17*(4), 684–699.

Cona, G., Scarpazza, C., Sartori, G., Moscovitch, M., & Bisiacchi, P. S. (2015). Neural bases of prospective memory: A meta-analysis and the "Attention to Delayed Intention" (AtoDI) model. *Neuroscience and Biobehavioral Reviews, 52,* 21–37.

Coubard, O. A. (2015). Attention is complex: Causes and effects. *Frontiers in Psychology, 6,* 246.

Courtois, C. A. (2004). Complex trauma, complex reactions: Assessment and treatment. *Psychotherapy: Theory, Research, Practice, Training, 41*(4), 412–425.

Courtois, C. A., & Ford, J. D. (Eds.). (2009). *Treating complex traumatic stress disorders: An evidence-based guide.* New York: Guilford Press.

Dal Monte, O., Schintu, S., Pardini, M., Berti, A., Wassermann, E. M., Grafman, J., & Krueger, F. (2014). The left inferior frontal gyrus is crucial for reading the mind in the eyes: Brain lesion evidence. *Cortex, 58,* 9–17.

Daskalakis, N. P., Provost, A. C., Hunter, R. G., & Guffanti, G. (2018). Noncoding RNAs: Stress, glucocorticoids, and posttraumatic stress disorder. *Biological Psychiatry, 83,* 849–865.

Deslauriers, J., Acheson, D. T., Maihofer, A. X., Nievergelt, C. M., Baker, D. G., Geyer, M. A., . . . the Marine Resiliency Study. (2018). COMT val158met polymorphism links to altered fear conditioning and extinction are modulated by PTSD and childhood trauma. *Depression and Anxiety, 35*(1), 32–42.

Fani, N., Tone, E. B., Phifer, J., Norrholm, S. D., Bradley, B., Ressler, K. J., . . . Jovanovic, T. (2012). Attention bias toward threat is associated with exaggerated fear expression and impaired extinction in PTSD. *Psychological Medicine, 42*(3), 533–543.

Fareri, D. S., Gabard-Durnam, L., Goff, B., Flannery, J., Gee, D. G., Lumian, D. S., . . . Tottenham, N. (2015). Normative development of ventral striatal resting state connectivity in humans. *NeuroImage, 118,* 422–437.

Felmingham, K. L., Rennie, C., Manor, B., & Bryant, R. A. (2011). Eye tracking and physiological reactivity to threatening stimuli in posttraumatic stress disorder. *Journal of Anxiety Disorders, 25*(5), 668–673.

Fonzo, G. A., Ramsawh, H. J., Flagan, T. M., Simmons, A. N., Sullivan, S. G., Allard, C. B., . . . Stein, M. B. (2016). Early life stress and the anxious brain: Evidence for a neural mechanism linking childhood emotional maltreatment to anxiety in adulthood. *Psychological Medicine, 46*(5), 1037–1054.

Ford, J. D. (2009). Neurobiological and developmental research: Clinical implications. In C. A. Courtois & J. D. Ford (Eds.), *Treating complex traumatic stress disorders: An evidence-based guide* (p. 31–58). New York: Guilford Press.

Ford, J. D. (2018). Trauma memory processing in PTSD psychotherapy: A unifying framework. *Journal of Traumatic Stress, 31*(6), 933–942.

Ford, J. D., Courtois, C. A., Steele, K., van der Hart, O., & Nijenhuis, E. R. (2005). Treatment of complex posttraumatic self-dysregulation. *Journal of Traumatic Stress, 18*(5), 437–447.

Ford, J. D., Spinazzola, J., van der Kolk, B., & Grasso, D. (2018). Toward an empirically based developmental trauma disorder diagnosis for children: Factor structure, item characteristics, reliability, and validity of the Developmental Trauma Disorder Semi-Structured Interview (DTD-SI). *Journal of Clinical Psychiatry, 79*(5), e1–e9.

Foulkes, L., & Blakemore, S. J. (2018). Studying individual differences in human adolescent brain development. *Nature Neuroscience, 21*(3), 315–323.

Fragkaki, I., Stins, J., Roelofs, K., Jongedijk, R. A., & Hagenaars, M. A. (2016). Tonic immobility differentiates stress responses in PTSD. *Brain and Behavior, 6*(11), e00546.

Gagne, J. R., & Saudino, K. J. (2016). The development of inhibitory control in early childhood: A twin study from 2–3 years. *Developmental Psychology, 52*(3), 391–399.

Geva, R., & Feldman, R. (2008). A neurobiological model for the effects of early brainstem functioning on the development of behavior and emotion regulation in infants: Implications for prenatal and perinatal risk. *Journal of Child Psychology and Psychiatry, 49*(10), 1031–1041.

Girgenti, M. J., & Duman, R. S. (2018). Transcriptome alterations in posttraumatic stress Disorder. *Biological Psychiatry, 83*(10), 840–848.

Glück, T. M., Knefel, M., & Lueger-Schuster, B. (2017, September 19). A network analysis of anger, shame, proposed ICD-11 post-traumatic stress disorder, and different types of childhood trauma in foster care settings in a sample of adult survivors. *European Journal of Psychotraumatology, 8*(Suppl. 3).

Goldsmith, H. H., Pollak, S. D., & Davidson, R. J. (2008). Developmental neuroscience perspectives on emotion regulation. *Child Development Perspectives, 2*(3), 132–140.

Grasso, D. J., Dierkhising, C. B., Branson, C. E., Ford, J. D., & Lee, R. (2016). Developmental patterns of adverse childhood experiences and current symptoms and impairment in youth referred for trauma-specific services. *Journal of Abnormal Child Psychology, 44*(5), 871–886.

Grecucci, A., Giorgetta, C., Bonini, N., & Sanfey, A. G. (2013). Reappraising social emotions: The role of inferior frontal gyrus, temporo-parietal junction and insula in interpersonal emotion regulation. *Frontiers in Human Neuroscience, 7*, 523.

Hansen, N. S., Thayer, R. E., Feldstein Ewing, S. W., Sabbineni, A., & Bryan, A. D. (2018). Neural correlates of risky sex and response inhibition in high-risk adolescents. *Journal of Research on Adolescence, 28*(1), 56–69.

Harding, I. H., Yucel, M., Harrison, B. J., Pantelis, C., & Breakspear, M. (2015). Effective connectivity within the frontoparietal control network differentiates cognitive control and working memory. *NeuroImage, 106*, 144–153.

Harkness, A. R., Reynolds, S. M., & Lilienfeld, S. O. (2014). A review of systems for psychology and psychiatry: Adaptive systems, personality psychopathology five (PSY-5), and the DSM-5. *Journal of Personality Assessment, 96*(2), 121–139.

Herman, J. L. (1992). Complex PTSD: A syndrome in survivors of prolonged and repeated trauma. *Journal of Traumatic Stress, 5*(3), 377–391.

Iacoviello, B. M., Wu, G., Abend, R., Murrough, J. W., Feder, A., Fruchter, E., . . . Charney, D. S. (2014). Attention bias variability and symptoms of posttraumatic stress disorder. *Journal of Traumatic Stress, 27*(2), 232–239.

Kaunhoven, R. J., & Dorjee, D. (2017). How does mindfulness modulate self-regulation in pre-adolescent children?: An integrative neurocognitive review. *Neuroscience and Biobehavioral Reviews, 74*(Pt. A), 163–184.

Koch, S. B., van Zuiden, M., Nawijn, L., Frijling, J. L., Veltman, D. J., & Olff, M. (2016). Aberrant resting-state brain activity in posttraumatic stress disorder: A meta-analysis and systematic review. *Depression and Anxiety, 33*(7), 592–605.

Krabbe, S., Grundemann, J., & Luthi, A. (2018). Amygdala inhibitory circuits regulate associative fear conditioning. *Biological Psychiatry, 83*(10), 800–809.

Lanius, R. A., Frewen, P. A., Tursich, M., Jetly, R., & McKinnon, M. C. (2015, March 31). Restoring large-scale brain networks in PTSD and related disorders: A proposal for neuroscientifically-informed treatment interventions. *European Journal of Psychotraumatology, 6*.

Lanius, R. A., Rabellino, D., Boyd, J. E., Harricharan, S., Frewen, P. A., & McKinnon, M. C. (2017). The innate alarm system in PTSD: Conscious and subconscious processing of threat. *Current Opinion in Psychology, 14*, 109–115.

Leech, R., & Sharp, D. J. (2014). The role of the posterior cingulate cortex in cognition and disease. *Brain, 137*(Pt. 1), 12–32.

Lewis, M. D. (2005). Self-organizing individual differences in brain development. *Developmental Review, 25*, 252–277.

Li, L., Bao, Y., He, S., Wang, G., Guan, Y., Ma, D., . . . Yang, J. (2016). The association between genetic variants in the dopaminergic system and posttraumatic stress disorder: A meta-analysis. *Medicine, 95*(11), e3074.

Liberzon, I. (2018). Searching for intermediate phenotypes in posttraumatic stress disorder. *Biological Psychiatry, 83*(10), 797–799.

Loizzo, J. (2009). Optimizing learning and quality of life throughout the lifespan: A global framework for research and application. *Annals of the New York Academy of Sciences, 1172*, 186–198.

Lowe, S. R., Meyers, J. L., Galea, S., Aiello, A. E., Uddin, M., Wildman, D. E., & Koenen, K. C. (2015). RORA and posttraumatic stress trajectories: Main effects and interactions with childhood physical abuse history. *Brain and Behavior, 5*(4), e00323.

Luby, J. L., Barch, D., Whalen, D., Tillman, R., & Belden, A. (2017). Association between early life adversity and risk for poor emotional and physical health in adolescence: A putative mechanistic neurodevelopmental pathway. *JAMA Pediatrics, 171*(12), 1168–1175.

Luckmann, H. C., Jacobs, H. I., & Sack, A. T. (2014). The cross-functional role of frontoparietal regions in cognition: Internal attention as the overarching mechanism. *Progress in Neurobiology, 116*, 66–86.

Lyall, A. E., Shi, F., Geng, X., Woolson, S., Li, G., Wang, L., . . . Gilmore, J. H. (2015). Dynamic development of regional cortical thickness and surface area in early childhood. *Cerebral Cortex, 25*(8), 2204–2212.

MacLean, P. D. (1985). Evolutionary psychiatry and the triune brain. *Psychological Medicine, 15*(2), 219–221.

Mak, L. E., Minuzzi, L., MacQueen, G., Hall, G., Kennedy, S. H., & Milev, R. (2017). The Default Mode Network in healthy individuals: A systematic review and meta-analysis. *Brain Connectivity, 7*(1), 25–33.

Marchand, W. R. (2014). Neural mechanisms of mindfulness and meditation: Evidence from neuroimaging studies [Review]. *World Journal of Radiology, 6*(7), 471–479.

Margulies, D. S., Ghosh, S. S., Goulas, A., Falkiewicz, M., Huntenburg, J. M., Langs, G., . . . Smallwood, J. (2016). Situating the default-mode network along a principal gradient of macroscale cortical organization. *Proceedings of the National Academy of Sciences of the USA, 113*(44), 12574–12579.

Margulies, D. S., & Smallwood, J. (2017). Converging evidence for the role of transmodal cortex in cognition. *Proceedings of the National Academy of Sciences of the USA, 114*(48), 12641–12643.

Marusak, H. A., Elrahal, F., Peters, C. A., Kundu, P., Lombardo, M. V., Calhoun, V. D., . . . Rabinak, C. A. (2018). Mindfulness and dynamic functional neural connectivity in children and adolescents. *Behavioural Brain Research, 336*, 211–218.

Marx, B. P., Forsyth, J. P., Gallup, G. G., Fuse, T., & Lexington, J. M. (2008). Tonic immobility as an evolved predator defense: Implications for sexual assault survivors. *Clinical Psychology: Science and Practice, 15*(1), 74–90.

McClelland, M. M., & Cameron, C. E. (2011). Self-regulation and academic achievement in elementary school children. *New Directions in Child and Adolescent Development, 2011*(133), 29–44.

McEwen, B. S. (2017). Allostasis and the epigenetics of brain and body health over the life course: The brain on stress. *JAMA Psychiatry, 74*(6), 551–552.

McNally, R. J., Heeren, A., & Robinaugh, D. J. (2017, July 15). A Bayesian network analysis of posttraumatic stress disorder symptoms in adults reporting childhood sexual abuse. *European Journal of Psychotraumatology, 8*(Suppl. 3).

McNally, R. J., Robinaugh, D. J., Wu, G., Wang, L., Deserno, M. K., & Borsboom, D. (2015). Mental disorders as causal systems: A network approach to posttraumatic stress disorder. *Clinical Psychological Science, 3*, 836–849.

Mellon, S. H., Gautam, A., Hammamieh, R., Jett, M., & Wolkowitz, O. M. (2018). Metabolism, metabolomics, and inflammation in posttraumatic stress disorder. *Biological Psychiatry, 83*, 866–875.

Miller, D. R., Hayes, S. M., Hayes, J. P., Spielberg, J. M., Lafleche, G., & Verfaellie, M. (2017). Default mode network subsystems are differentially disrupted in posttraumatic stress disorder. *Biological Psychiatry: Cognitive Neuroscience and Neuroimaging, 2*(4), 363–371.

Miller, G. E., Chen, E., & Parker, K. J. (2011). Psychological stress in childhood and susceptibility to the chronic diseases of aging: Moving toward a model of behavioral and biological mechanisms. *Psychological Bulletin, 137*(6), 959–997.

Miller, M. W., Sperbeck, E., Robinson, M. E., Sadeh, N., Wolf, E. J., Hayes, J. P., . . . McGlinchey, R. (2016). 5-HT2A gene variants moderate the association between PTSD and reduced Default Mode Network connectivity. *Frontiers in Neuroscience, 10,* 299.

Mitchell, K. S., Wolf, E. J., Bovin, M. J., Lee, L. O., Green, J. D., Rosen, R. C., . . . Marx, B. P. (2017). Network models of DSM-5 posttraumatic stress disorder: Implications for ICD-11. *Journal of Abnormal Psychology, 126*(3), 355–366.

Morris, A. S., Squeglia, L. M., Jacobus, J., & Silk, J. S. (2018). Adolescent brain development: Implications for understanding risk and resilience processes through neuroimaging research. *Journal of Research on Adolescence, 28*(1), 4–9.

Mueller, S. C., Cromheeke, S., Siugzdaite, R., & Nicolas Boehler, C. (2017). Evidence for the triadic model of adolescent brain development: Cognitive load and task-relevance of emotion differentially affect adolescents and adults. *Developmental Cognitive Neuroscience, 26,* 91–100.

Mullen, S. P., & Hall, P. A. (2015). Physical activity, self-regulation, and executive control across the lifespan. *Frontiers in Human Neuroscience, 9,* 614.

Naegeli, C., Zeffiro, T., Piccirelli, M., Jaillard, A., Weilenmann, A., Hassanpour, K., . . . Mueller-Pfeiffer, C. (2018). Locus coeruleus activity mediates hyperresponsiveness in posttraumatic stress disorder. *Biological Psychiatry, 83*(3), 254–262.

Naim, R., Abend, R., Wald, I., Eldar, S., Levi, O., Fruchter, E., . . . Bar-Haim, Y. (2015). Threat-related attention bias variability and posttraumatic stress. *American Journal of Psychiatry, 172*(12), 1242–1250.

Nees, F., Witt, S. H., & Flor, H. (2018). Neurogenetic approaches to stress and fear in humans as pathophysiological mechanisms for posttraumatic stress disorder [Review]. *Biological Psychiatry, 83,* 810–820.

Noll, R. (1999). Styles of psychiatric practice, 1906–1925: Clinical evaluation of the same patient by James Jackson Putnam, Adolph Meyer, August Hoch, Emil Kraepelin and Smith Ely Jelliffe. *History of Psychiatry, 10*(38, Pt. 2), 145–189.

Pagliaccio, D., Pine, D. S., Barch, D. M., Luby, J. L., & Leibenluft, E. (2018). Irritability rrajectories, cortical thickness, and clinical outcomes in a sample enriched for preschool depression. *Journal of the American Academy of Child and Adolescent Psychiatry, 57*(5), 336–342.

Pallini, S., Chirumbolo, A., Morelli, M., Baiocco, R., Laghi, F., & Eisenberg, N. (2018). The relation of attachment security status to effortful self-regulation: A meta-analysis. *Psychological Bulletin, 144*(5), 501–531.

Penela, E. C., Walker, O. L., Degnan, K. A., Fox, N. A., & Henderson, H. A. (2015). Early behavioral inhibition and emotion regulation: Pathways toward social competence in middle childhood. *Child Development, 86*(4), 1227–1240.

Pine, D. S., Mogg, K., Bradley, B. P., Montgomery, L., Monk, C. S., McClure, E., . . . Kaufman, J. (2005). Attention bias to threat in maltreated children: Implications for vulnerability to stress-related psychopathology. *American Journal of Psychiatry, 162*(2), 291–296.

Poerio, G. L., Sormaz, M., Wang, H. T., Margulies, D., Jefferies, E., & Smallwood, J. (2017). The role of the default mode network in component processes underlying the wandering mind. *Social Cognitive and Affective Neuroscience, 12*(7), 1047–1062.

Porges, S. W. (2007). The polyvagal perspective. *Biological Psychology, 74*(2), 116–143.

Porter, J. N., Collins, P. F., Muetzel, R. L., Lim, K. O., & Luciana, M. (2011). Associations between cortical thickness and verbal fluency in childhood, adolescence, and young adulthood. *NeuroImage, 55*(4), 1865–1877.

Ramikie, T. S., & Ressler, K. J. (2018). Mechanisms of sex differences in fear and posttraumatic stress disorder. *Biological Psychiatry, 83*(10), 876–885.

Rodrigo, M. J., Padron, I., de Vega, M., & Ferstl, E. (2018). Neural substrates of counterfactual emotions after risky decisions in late adolescents and young adults. *Journal of Research on Adolescence, 28*(1), 70–86.

Russell, J. D., Neill, E. L., Carrion, V. G., & Weems, C. F. (2017). The network structure of posttraumatic stress symptoms in children and adolescents exposed to disasters. *Journal of the American Academy of Child and Adolescent Psychiatry, 56*(8), 669–677.

Salum, G. A., Mogg, K., Bradley, B. P., Stringaris, A., Gadelha, A., Pan, P. M., . . . Leibenluft, E. (2017). Association between irritability and bias in attention orienting to threat in children and adolescents. *Journal of Child Psychology and Psychiatry, 58*(5), 595–602.

Saxe, G. N., Statnikov, A., Fenyo, D., Ren, J., Li, Z., Prasad, M., . . . Aliferis, C. (2016). A complex systems approach to causal discovery in psychiatry. *PLOS ONE, 11*(3), e0151174.

Schore, A. N. (2000). Attachment and the regulation of the right brain. *Attachment and Human Development, 2*(1), 23–47.

Selye, H. (1951). The general adaptation syndrome and the diseases of adaptation. *American Journal of Medicine, 10*(5), 549–555.

Selye, H. (1954). The alarm reaction, the general adaptation syndrome, and the role of stress and of the adaptive hormones in dental medicine. *Oral Surgery, Oral Medicine, and Oral Pathology, 7*(4), 355–367.

Sheerin, C. M., Lind, M. J., Bountress, K. E., Nugent, N. R., & Amstadter, A. B. (2017). The genetics and epigenetics of PTSD: Overview, recent advances, and future directions. *Current Opinion in Psychology, 14*, 5–11.

Shing, Y. L., Lindenberger, U., Diamond, A., Li, S. C., & Davidson, M. C. (2010). Memory maintenance and inhibitory control differentiate from early childhood to adolescence. *Developmental Neuropsychology, 35*(6), 679–697.

Silverman, M. H., Jedd, K., & Luciana, M. (2015). Neural networks involved in adolescent reward processing: An activation likelihood estimation meta-analysis of functional neuroimaging studies. *NeuroImage, 122*, 427–439.

Sisk, C. L. (2017). Development: Pubertal hormones meet the adolescent brain. *Current Biology, 27*(14), R706–R708.

Spinazzola, J., van der Kolk, B., & Ford, J. D. (2018). When nowhere is safe: Trauma history antecedents of posttraumatic stress disorder and developmental trauma disorder in childhood. *Journal of Traumatic Stress, 31*(5), 631–642.

Stein, M. B. (2018). Genomics of posttraumatic stress disorder: Sequencing stress and modeling misfortune. *Biological Psychiatry, 83*(10), 795–796.

Sylvester, C. M., Petersen, S. E., Luby, J. L., & Barch, D. M. (2017). Face processing in adolescents with positive and negative threat bias. *Psychological Medicine, 47*(5), 800–809.

Tamnes, C. K., Bos, M. G. N., van de Kamp, F. C., Peters, S., & Crone, E. A. (2018). Longitudinal development of hippocampal subregions from childhood to adulthood. *Developmental Cognitive Neuroscience, 30*, 212–222.

Teicher, M. H., & Samson, J. A. (2016). Annual Research Review: Enduring neurobiological effects of childhood abuse and neglect. *Journal of Child Psychology and Psychiatry and Allied Disciplines, 57*(3), 241–266.

van der Kolk, B., Ford, J. D., & Spinazzola, J. (2019). Comorbidity of developmental trauma disorder (DTD) and post-traumatic stress disorder: Findings from the DTD field trial. *European Journal of Psychotraumatology, 10*(1), 1562841.

van der Kolk, B. A., & van der Hart, O. (1989). Pierre Janet and the breakdown of adaptation in psychological trauma. *American Journal of Psychiatry, 146*(12), 1530–1540.

Van Dijke, A., Ford, J. D., Frank, L. E., & van der Hart, O. (2015). Association of childhood complex trauma and dissociation with complex posttraumatic stress disorder symptoms in adulthood. *Journal of Trauma and Dissociation, 16*(4), 428–441.

Wang, H. T., Bzdok, D., Margulies, D., Craddock, C., Milham, M., Jefferies, E., & Smallwood, J. (2018). Patterns of thought: Population variation in the associations between large-scale network organisation and self-reported experiences at rest. *NeuroImage, 176*, 518–527.

Watkins, L. E., Han, S., Harpaz-Rotem, I., Mota, N. P., Southwick, S. M., Krystal, J. H., . . .

Pietrzak, R. H. (2016). FKBP5 polymorphisms, childhood abuse, and PTSD symptoms: Results from the National Health and Resilience in Veterans Study. *Psychoneuroendocrinology, 69,* 98–105.

Webb, T. L., Miles, E., & Sheeran, P. (2012). Dealing with feeling: A meta-analysis of the effectiveness of strategies derived from the process model of emotion regulation. *Psychological Bulletin, 138*(4), 775–808.

Whitfield-Gabrieli, S., & Ford, J. M. (2012). Default mode network activity and connectivity in psychopathology. *Annual Review of Clinical Psychology, 8,* 49–76.

Wierenga, L., Langen, M., Ambrosino, S., van Dijk, S., Oranje, B., & Durston, S. (2014). Typical development of basal ganglia, hippocampus, amygdala and cerebellum from age 7 to 24. *NeuroImage, 96,* 67–72.

Wingo, A. P., Briscione, M., Norrholm, S. D., Jovanovic, T., McCullough, S. A., Skelton, K., & Bradley, B. (2017). Psychological resilience is associated with more intact social functioning in veterans with post-traumatic stress disorder and depression. *Psychiatry Research, 249,* 206–211.

Wortis, J. (1986). Adolph Meyer: Some recollections and impressions. *British Journal of Psychiatry, 149,* 677–681.

Yaple, Z., & Arsalidou, M. (2018). N-back working memory task: Meta-analysis of normative fMRI studies with children. *Child Development, 89*(6), 2010–2022.

CHAPTER 3

Best Practices in Psychotherapy for Adults

CHRISTINE A. COURTOIS
JULIAN D. FORD
MARYLENE CLOITRE
ULRICH SCHNYDER

Our purpose in this chapter is to update the best practice recommendations for the treatment of complex traumatic stress disorders (CTSDs) presented a decade ago (Courtois, Ford, & Cloitre, 2009). The current recommendations are based on a synthesis of the (1) evidence-based practice guidelines for posttraumatic stress disorder (PTSD; American Psychological Association, 2017; Forbes et al., 2010; Hamblen et al., 2019; International Society for Traumatic Stress Studies, 2019; Phoenix Australia–Center for Posttraumatic Mental Health, 2013; U.S. Department of Veterans Affairs and Department of Defense, 2017), (2) consensus and evidence-based guidelines for complex PTSD (Blue Knot Foundation, 2017, 2019; International Society for Traumatic Stress Studies, 2012, 2018a, 2018b; McFetridge et al., 2017; Stravopolous & Keselman, 2012), and (3) those for dissociative disorders (International Society for the Study of Trauma and Dissociation, 2011), all of which were published in the past decade. In addition, in accord with the American Psychological Association's criteria for guideline development and evaluation (American Psychological Association, 2002) and its definition of components of evidence-based treatment (American Psychological Association, 2006), clinicians' real-world observations and clinical judgments and patients' values, preferences, and experiences are taken into account in all recommendations (Cook, Rehman, Bufka, Dinnen, & Courtois, 2011; Simiola, Neilson, Thompson, & Cook, 2015).

Complex Psychological Trauma, Complex Reactions, Complex Treatment

Complex Psychological Trauma

As noted throughout this text, *complex psychological trauma* typically refers to experiences that (1) involve repetitive or prolonged exposure to, or experience of, multiple traumatic stressors (2) involve harm or abandonment by caregivers or ostensibly responsible adults, some of whom hold a fiduciary duty, and (3) occur at developmentally vulnerable times or transitions in the person's life, especially (but not exclusively) over the course of childhood, and therefore become intertwined with and incorporated within the person's biopsychosocial development. It is now acknowledged that complex psychological trauma can occur de novo in adulthood or it may layer upon previous childhood experiences of complex psychological trauma (Ford, 2017). For example, domestic violence, prolonged incarceration, torture, genocide, human trafficking, forced separation of asylum-seeking or refugee families, all forms of slavery, hate-based violence, and other forms of systematic oppression, dehumanization, exploitation, and degradation may expose individuals, families, and entire communities or populations to complex psychological trauma at different points across the lifespan or across the individual's entire lifespan.

Complex Traumatic Stress Reactions

The psychological, emotional, and social consequences of complex traumatic events begin as biological adaptations in reaction to the threat to physical and psychological survival posed by complex trauma (see Chapter 2). These survival adaptations tend to be rapid and extreme, and as such can sharply alter the individual's physical and psychological homeostasis (i.e., the balance of biological and psychological systems that is essential to health). When that inner balance is severely disrupted by the kinds of extreme physical and psychological injury and fear/terror caused by complex trauma, homeostasis may be replaced by compensatory adaptations that throw bodily and psychological systems out of their normal alignment and create a state of chronic stress and exhaustion that has been described as allostasis (McEwen, 2017). Physiologically this can result in severe illness, and psychologically it can lead to severe and debilitating anxiety, dysphoria, and both lability and dissociation of emotions in relationships and in the core sense of self, all responses to complex stress.

Complex traumatic stress reactions begin as adaptive efforts under conditions of adversity, but when they persist over time, they go awry and overtax the body and mind rather than serving their intended protective function. The result—CTSDs—is a wide variety of symptoms that are due to the psychobiological misalignment and exhaustion that occur when a person primarily is functioning biologically and psychologically in survival mode (see Chapter 2 for elaboration). When the body and mind perceive threat to be the norm, survival and defense against threat are constant priorities, and normal healthy psychobiological development—which is based on adaptations to maintain or restore homeostasis as the individual matures—is replaced by hypervigilance and hyperarousal based on allostasis. Prolonged states of hypervigilance and hyperarousal are simply unsustainable, however; thus, survival mode can devolve into chronic states of biological and psychological shutdown (e.g., dissociation, numbing, recklessness, passive revictimization, despair). Victims and survivors can alternate between these two states, moving from activation and hyperarousal to shutdown when the danger, fear/terror, and arousal continue unabated. Clinicians must appreciate that shutdown is a state of high arousal indicative of overload and does not mean the stress response is absent. Dissociation and other mechanisms may mask the symptoms. For example, shutdown has been shown to be related to the vagal nervous system (Porges, 2011), which may cause a physiological immobilization and collapse of the organism to occur when traumatic stress is ongoing, escalating, and inescapable.

Complex Treatment

The treatment of CTSDs is predicated on assisting persons who are trapped in survival mode to make a fundamental shift to healthy modes of attaining both biological and psychological homeostasis and of repairing trauma-related states through the cultivation of new experiences (Fisher, 2017). Given the involvedness and variety of complex traumatic stress reactions and CTSD symptoms, treatment is inevitably and inherently correspondingly complex. However, by focusing on the core dilemma underlying CTSDs—chronic entrapment in survival mode and lack of personal agency—it is possible for practitioners not to become "lost in the weeds" (the often overwhelming multiplicity of specific symptoms) but instead to guide complex trauma survivors in deploying their adaptive psychological and biological capacities to life goals beyond mere survival.

Treatment of CTSDs, therefore, rests on a foundation that includes the necessity of the practitioner demonstrating in actions, as well as words, that each individual, and their identity and personal development, has an essential intrinsic value. This requires a rigorous adherence to the highest standards of humanism and professionalism, which are readily endorsed in principle but often are very difficult to follow when working with those who have had to resort to any means necessary—including harming themselves and others (usually inadvertently, but at times frankly intentionally)—in order to ward off actual or perceived radical threats to their survival (which, in some cases, may be ongoing). It is important for the therapist to discern whether the patient is still in unsafe circumstances or surroundings and to place preliminary emphasis on ways to achieve some degree of safety and to engage in methods of self-protection. That said, it may take patients a very long time to be able to disclose experiences and conditions of ongoing abuse and threat. Many continue to be actively coerced into silence and secrecy, or they may continue to believe they (and often their loved ones) remain under significant threat, even when that is no longer the case (e.g., the perpetrator and others are dead or otherwise incapacitated or incarcerated).

In addition to compassion and professionalism, the treatment of CTSDs also requires a firm dedication to the scientific attitude. This includes relying on scientific evidence in selecting and implementing therapeutic interventions (i.e., evidence-based and informed treatment) while maintaining an ongoing awareness of theoretical developments and treatment innovations in the field. However, more fundamentally, the scientific attitude is one of rigorously and continuously applied empiricism: seeking and being guided by accurate and valid immediate evidence that one's interaction with the patient is leading to therapeutic benefit. This is not to say that CTSD treatment is a steady and unbroken arc of success, but rather to highlight that, in the midst of the turmoil and upheaval that accompanies chronic survival adaptations, the therapist is responsible for maintaining steady and consistent support that assists the patient incrementally to restore healthy development and functioning. The scientific attitude is an unswerving focus on tracking the course toward health, not a rote reliance on preset technical rules or interventions. Technically sound and sophisticated rules and interventions are potentially valuable means, but the end is facilitating the patient to have experiences that allow a life that is more than mere survival.

Philosophical Foundations for the Treatment of CTSDs

Based on the principles of humanism, professionalism, and science, there are several key philosophical foundations for the treatment of CTSDs (Courtois, 1999; Courtois et al., 2009). These foundations include (1) respect for the individual and empowering them based on their personal strengths and capacities; (2) fostering and sustaining a therapeutic alliance; (3) providing evidence-based and informed treatment within the framework of trauma-informed care and incorporating approaches that are developing based on neuroscientific advances (e.g., "bottom-up" body-based approaches along with those that are "top down" cognitive and talk based; and (4) ensuring that treatment is provided with expertise based on professional training, qualifications, and ongoing attention on the part of the therapist to emotional and physical health status, self-monitoring of transference and countertransference and other personal issues, and the utilization of supervision and consultation.

Respect for the Individual

Treatment of CTSDs is organized around recognition of the *primacy and uniqueness of the individual* and the *right to self-determination based on informed autonomous choice*. Each person's complex trauma history and complex traumatic stress reactions are unique, as are personal strengths, aspirations, competencies, values, relationships, and life circumstances. Treatment of CTSDs therefore is never a "one size fits all" approach (Cloitre, 2015; Courtois, 1999), one of the pitfalls of an exclusive focus on evidence-based treatments (Courtois & Brown, 2019) or the inflexible application of treatment phases or techniques. Rather, each patient is assessed, and treatment is planned differentially, according to the specific needs and preferences of the individual that can vary considerably and in idiosyncratic ways. Needs and preferences may also vary over time with the emergence of previously hidden issues and resources over the course of treatment, sometimes due to treatment progress (Courtois, 2004). This therapy takes a phenomenological/contextual approach, which means that the therapist focuses simultaneously on the patient's internal experience and on external contexts as well (see Chapters 2, 4, 7, and 24). A "whole person" philosophy prevails: Although symptoms, deficits, and distress are reasons for seeking treatment and generally become targets for intervention, the client's uniqueness, strengths, resources, resilience, personalized needs, and values are identified and reinforced. Enhancing posttraumatic growth (Nijdam et al., 2018) and resilience (Jenness & McLaughlin, 2015; McEwen, 2017) and developing opportunities for competency and mastery that counter powerlessness, defined on an individual basis and according to the patient's capacities, resources, and autonomous choices, are fundamental goals of CTSD treatment.

Therapists treating CTSDs also recognize that the individual has authority over the meaning and interpretation of their personal life history, current needs and preferences, and goals for the future (Harvey, 1996). The therapist functions as an active, empathic, and responsive listener and guide to enable the patient to voice openly, explore and analyze, and therapeutically work through feelings of grief, anger, guilt, shame, or other emotions that may have been long avoided/suppressed/dissociated or forbidden. The therapist must have an attitude of positive regard and openness (Farber, Suzuki, & Lynch, 2018) that provides the patient with genuine emotional validation and conveys that they are "seen," "felt," and appreciated. This compassionate attitude is important not just to reassure the patient and build or support self-esteem, but specifically to counter the invalidation (and often the antipathy and disrespect) that is endemic in experiences of complex trauma (Herman, 1992). An attitude of respect for the individual also encourages emotional self-reflection that is then extended to reflection on self-in-relationship that is an essential aspect of shifting out of survival mode and restoring healthy functioning and development (Chapter 2). In this work, the client must address issues of personal and relational betrayal that is so often part of complex trauma. The client may also have difficulty accepting the positive regard of others, even as it is craved and needed, one of the relational dilemmas that are part of this treatment.

Strengths-Based Empowerment

The therapist treating CTSDs also strives to create a relationship that is as egalitarian and collaborative as possible, but this too may be difficult for the survivor patient to understand and accept. The therapist is invested by society, and usually also by the patient, with authority based on professional knowledge and expertise. Patients seek guidance from the therapist based on the therapist's presumed stature as an expert. This context creates a power and status differential in which the therapist apparently has greater strengths and authority than the patient. However, the patient brings to the treatment not only problems and questions but also personal, relational, and cultural strengths—knowledge and expertise—that are an essential complement to the therapist's professional and technical knowledge and expertise. Experiencing complex trauma and living in survival mode often make these patients' strengths opaque or invisible to themselves and to others in their lives: The symptoms and impairment caused by chronic complex traumatic stress reactions can become so prominent that the person's underlying strengths go unnoticed. Moreover, it is often the case that survivors feel like imposters and may be unable to accept their strengths or talents as legitimately their own. Or, strengths have been pejoratively redefined as faults or deficits by emotionally abusive or inadvertently misguided people (e.g., a determined pursuit of relational connection might be redefined as dependence or neediness, or as a severe deficit in self-reliance and autonomy).

Empowering patients with complex trauma histories therefore begins with the therapist's purposeful search for, and recognition and validation of capabilities and areas of resourcefulness. Over time and with persistent but sensitive therapeutic mirroring of their admirable qualities, abilities, and values, the goal is for patients to be able to tolerate and ultimately to accept and value their own strengths and self-worth. This is difficult for many with complex trauma histories, because they have had little or no validation as a result of the traumatic circumstances they have endured and/or the pervasive misunderstanding of their survival adaptations as pathology or weakness. Or they may have received validation but only in combination with coercion, devaluation, and other forms of victimization, and not in the context of a caring relationship. Or, yet again, they may have received authentic validation from key people in their lives, only to lose it when separated from or betrayed by those persons as a result of traumatic events or losses (e.g., additional abuse, violence, break-ups, death) or impairment (e.g., mental health or criminal or legal problems) in the other persons' lives. Thus, many patients with CTSDs find acknowledging their own strengths deeply painful, not only because of an inability to appreciate their own positive attributes but due to traumatic injury or loss that they have come to associate with receiving any form of validation. Providing recognition and validation of patients' core strengths in the face of a strong sense of defectiveness or "negative specialness" is therefore a delicate therapeutic process. It involves helping them to develop skills and competencies that result in experiences of attainment and to work through the traumatic associations (including memories, as well as emotional distress and beliefs) that have made validation a source of pain rather than affirmation.

While continuing to recognize and mirror core strengths, the therapist builds on that foundation by helping the patient to exert autonomy and rely on their own personal knowledge, expertise, and authority, while they work together on the patient's goals. Importantly, the therapist conveys an openness to the patient's questioning of authority (including that of the therapist) and supports the patient's ultimate authority over their life, memories, and therapeutic engagement and progress. Moreover, the therapist is careful to maintain appropriate boundaries and limitations and is responsible for scrupulously avoiding dual relationships and situations of any kind in which the patient might be subject to intentional or inadvertent pressure, coercion, or exploitation. Treatment should be based on a planned and systematic (not *laissez-faire*) shared strategy that utilizes effective treatment approaches and practices, and is organized around a careful assessment (that is best considered as ongoing since different issues and symptoms emerge or remit over the course of treatment and require flexibility regarding the treatment plan on the part of the therapist) and a hierarchically ordered, planned sequence of interventions (Courtois, 1999).

The Therapeutic Relationship

The therapeutic relationship is the nexus of the treatment for CTSDs (Howell & Iskowitz, 2016; Kinsler, 2017; Kinsler, Courtois, & Frankel, 2009; Pearlman & Courtois, 2005). This is in keeping with the scientific finding that an alliance that is recognized and valued by both the patient and the therapist is a key component in the success of many types of treatment (Del Re, Flückiger, Horvath, Symonds, & Wampold, 2012; Fluckiger, Del Re, Wampold, & Horvath, 2018; Friedlander, Escudero, Welmers-van de Poll, & Heatherington, 2018; Niejenhuis et al., 2018; Norcross & Lambert, 2018), and may especially be the case in the treatment of those who have been subjected to complex interpersonal and developmental trauma (Kinsler, 2017; Kinsler et al., 2009; Schore, 2003; Siegel, 2009). The therapist's ability to maintain attunement and empathy with the patient and to repair ruptures in the therapeutic relationship also has been identified in research as a key predictor of therapeutic outcome across a range of therapeutic modalities (Eubanks, Muran, & Safran, 2018; Friedlander, Lee, Shaffer, & Cabrera, 2014).

Clinicians treating patients with CTSDs prioritize such attunement in order to model for the patient of how relationships can be genuinely trustworthy, safe, and mutual. Relational connection is provided, along with boundaries that preserve the physical and psychological safety and integrity of each participant. Boundaries are particularly important given that these patients' physical and psychological boundaries were repeatedly violated over the course of their victimization. In the aftermath (or in some cases, in a continuing context) of relationships that involve abuse, neglect, abandonment, betrayal, or exploitation, the relationship with the therapist is a crucial experience to begin to counteract the patient's experience of relational misuse, misattunement, loss, threat, and harm. Kinsler et al. (2009) noted that the therapeutic relationship is both a catalyst for reenactments of relational traumas and an opportunity for therapist and patient to become aware of, safely contain, understand, and transform the core beliefs and affects associated with having had to survive complex trauma. Change and healing occur as the therapist responds to the patient with respect, interest, and empathy by being attuned, respectful, culturally sensitive, and collaborative (see Chapters 4 and 8 for a more in-depth discussion of these issues).

It should be noted, however, that the relationship is not the "be-all, end-all" of the treatment and may create a stumbling block for those who are unable to respond to or incorporate empathy or attunement (or who experience it as unsafe due to their past experiences), some for extended periods of time over the course of treatment. For some individuals, it can trigger attachment anxiety and other uncomfortable emotions. In other words, attunement itself may be triggering, paradoxically making the therapy relationship unsafe and causing defensive reactions to be activated. For these reasons, some writers on complex trauma treatment are suggesting that therapists focus on "resourcing" the patient with skills to self-regulate (i.e., from the inside out, rather than from the outside in, or from "bottom up" rather than "top down"), with interventions designed to help the patient to learn to self-assess and self-regulate and to better manage in everyday life (Fisher, 2017). Relationships with others besides the therapist can be highly influential, and, therefore, attention to relationship building, providing information on how to distinguish safe and trustworthy individuals from those who are not, and personal discrimination and assertiveness is encouraged.

Trauma-Informed Care

The past decade in particular has witnessed the rapid growth of a survivor/consumer-led movement in the mental health, physical health/medical, social, educational, and legal fields based on a philosophy of policy and practice that has been described as trauma-informed care (TIC; Bassuk, Latta, Sember, Raja, & Richard, 2017; Levenson, 2017; Martin et al., 2017; Purtle, 2018; Sanders & Hall, 2018; Sullivan, Goodman, Virden, Strom, & Ramirez, 2018). The philosophy underlying TIC is based on the knowledge that the majority of clients in various service settings have had histories of childhood or other forms of complex trauma. It also shifts the focus from what is "wrong" with service recipients/patients to what has "happened" to them (*www.samhsa.gov/nctic/trauma-interventions*), and understanding that their survival skills were actually adaptations to adverse circumstances and that many of these became the symptoms they are presenting with in the service setting. TIC is based on acknowledging the experiences of trauma survivors and safely and respectfully supporting them and their recovery. It involves making providers aware of how insensitive actions (or inaction) can trigger traumatic stress reactions that exacerbate rather than ameliorate trauma-related symptoms. TIC therefore highlights the importance of therapist attunement, reliability, and consistency based on the therapist's knowledge of trauma and its consequences, their own self-awareness and ability to be self-regulated in their interactions, as well as respect for patients' perspectives and strengths. It calls on the therapist to take responsibility for providing services in a calm, professional but kind, down-to-earth, and responsive manner in spite of—or, better yet, in response to—the intensity and lability of traumatized patients' PTSD and CTSD memories and symptoms (i.e., the secondary traumatic stress that is inherent in CTSD treatment; Sprang, Ford, Kerig, & Bride, 2018).

TIC also emphasizes the importance of all members of the provider team (including nonpractitioner staff members and administrators) interacting in a respectful, accepting, and affirming manner with the patient (and collaterals/third parties; e.g., family members). Additionally, the physical environment in which services are delivered is considered highly important in TIC, in order to ensure that recipients/patients feel safe, comfortable, supported but not overwhelmed, and able to access resources (e.g., understandable directions to clinic sites; bathrooms that are clean and private; food, educational materials), all in a nonchaotic treatment environment that minimizes the presence of unintended triggers for posttraumatic stress reactions and the reactivation of survival coping (Bloom, 2013; Fallot & Harris, 2008).

At present, many treatment settings and organizations purport to be trauma informed, but not all practice in this way, despite what they intend and advertise (Branson, Baetz, Horwitz, & Hoagwood, 2017; Musicaro et al., 2019). TIC is in a relatively early stage of development; it can be expected to continue and grow as understanding of the number and needs of traumatized individuals in society increase, along with increased recognition of the need for professional training and programming that prioritize the delivery of services in ways that support trauma survivors' status and recovery (Courtois & Gold, 2009). TIC can be understood as a combination of humane, ethical, and effective approaches to services, with the additional proviso that treatment for complex trauma survivors must be provided in as comfortable, stable, and safe interpersonal and physical environment as possible.

Professional Training and Qualifications, and Ongoing Supervision and Consultation

Treatment for CTSDs is founded on the psychotherapist's professional training, suitable qualifications, emotional maturity, and psychological, interpersonal, and technical competence. Unfortunately, issues of interpersonal violence, traumatization, and dissociation continue to be omitted from most curricula in the mental health professions (Courtois & Gold, 2009), a situation that is changing, but only gradually. Training or supervision in the treatment of posttraumatic and dissociative conditions, especially as it concerns CTSDs, has been difficult to find (Courtois, 2001; Courtois & Gold, 2009), but it is becoming more available, especially now that competencies for treatment of trauma-related disorders have been established (American Psychological Association, 2015; Cook, Newman, & the New Haven Trauma Competency Work Group, 2014) and as textbooks focus on traumatic stress disorders and their assessment, treatment, and research (e.g., Briere & Scott, 2014; Ford, Grasso, Elhai, & Courtois, 2015). In addition to an appropriate knowledge and skills base, therapists must have enough emotional maturity to deal with affectively charged disclosures and relational dynamics associated with complex trauma histories and symptoms, as well as the often comorbid problems of substance abuse and addictions, mood disorders, personal risk taking, aggression, self-injury, suicidality, and severe mental illness. In addition, patients may have long histories of marginally effective or ineffective treatment or other services during which their experience of complex trauma and its impact on their lives and health in the form of CTSDs was not identified. Unfortunately, it is often the case that patients were blamed for their symptoms and misdiagnosed, without any assessment or consideration of a possible history of trauma on the part of a provider who is relatively blind to its ubiquity and does not ask about it during intake and psychosocial assessment.

Fortunately, providers are becoming more aware of the link between a history of complex trauma (especially from childhood) and subsequent mental health and medical problems. Nevertheless, they may lack the training to know how to assess and work effectively with these patients and their concerns. Therapists who have not had training and supervision to anticipate the challenges posed by therapeutic engagement with patients with either single-trauma or complex trauma histories and responses (including dissociation) may have great difficulty managing the transference and countertransference reactions that arise fairly routinely in this treatment, often as a result of vicarious trauma or secondary traumatic stress reactions (Pearlman & Caringi, 2009; Sprang et al., 2018). Unrecognized, unmodulated, and unmanaged countertransference can lead to otherwise avoidable therapeutic errors that can fundamentally compromise the therapeutic relationship and treatment outcomes (Kinsler et al., 2009). Without this preparation, therapists may become very frustrated and distressed in ways that may add to the patient's sense of stigma and reactivate or intensify patient distress rather than assist the patient therapeutically. In point of fact, many clients with unrecognized and untreated complex trauma histories have complained about having been reviled and revictimized by the very helpers they turned to for assistance, creating yet another layer of injury. TIC was developed specifically to educate providers about the needs of the traumatized and create a more accepting and healing (and less stigmatizing and antagonistic) atmosphere that is geared to their needs.

Best Practices for CTSD Assessment

Strategies and instruments for the assessment of traumatized individuals have developed significantly over the past several decades. A variety of specialized instruments is now available for the symptoms of both posttraumatic and dissociative conditions and disorders, and to document the trauma experience itself (Chapter 5). Nevertheless, no consensus measure is currently available specifically for the assessment of CTSDs, although Briere's Trauma Symptom Inventory–2 (TSI-2; Briere, 2011) covers many of the relevant dimensions and Brown (2009) described the use of a variety of standard instruments in devising a comprehensive assessment strategy for complex trauma responses. Therefore, in conducting assessment of patients with complex trauma histories, practitioners should adhere to several procedural guidelines, which is consistent with the approach espoused in trauma-informed care.

1. *Embed assessment of psychological trauma within a standard and broad-based psychosocial assessment for all patients.* From the point of screening or intake, the clinician should include open-ended questions about important relationships and personal goals, achievements (both those that were attempted without success and those that were realized), and memorable or formative experiences. From this personal history narrative, the therapist can begin to formulate hypotheses or note explicitly stated examples of the patient's experiences of psychological trauma and victimization, and subsequent alterations in biopsychosocial development that have evolved into posttraumatic and/or dissociative symptomatology. This type of open-ended and sensitively guided self-disclosure provides for the patient an experiential framework for how treatment can be genuinely respectful, collaborative, and empowering, beginning the development of a truly therapeutic relationship from the outset. With this foundation, the therapist can ask more specific questions about potentially traumatic experiences to which the patient has alluded, as well as check on other types of traumatic experiences and symptoms that the patient did not spontaneously disclose. Systematic inventories of potentially traumatic experiences such as the Traumatic Events Screening Instrument (Ford & Smith, 2008) and PTSD and CTSD symptoms such as the Trauma Symptoms Inventory–2 (Briere, 2011) can help to elicit information about traumatic circumstances and symptoms (see Chapter 5 for detailed information about instruments and methods of inquiry).

2. *Inquire about adverse and traumatic experiences, the patient's history, current life, or symptoms, but know that such an inquiry does not automatically result in disclosure, even when the history is positive for such events.* Many individuals with complex trauma histories are reluctant to disclose or are unable to recall sensitive information about themselves and their traumatic or related life experiences, especially early in the assessment or treatment process. The therapist must be nonjudgmentally aware when this is the case, and not misinterpret it as the patient's attempt to lie, manipulate, or mislead. Instead, it may be the case that patients do not know their history (due to dissociation, amnesia, repression, or other factors) or are so shamed, fearful, or confused that they have understandable difficulty discussing or even recalling it. Moreover, some patients may have been threatened with dire harm if they ever disclosed what

happened to them, and others may still be at risk, involved with, and/or under the influence or threat of the perpetrator or abusive others. Many patients from all backgrounds and life circumstances (including but not limited to complex trauma) first test the trustworthiness of the therapist before beginning to disclose any type of personally sensitive information. This "testing" may be either conscious and intentional (e.g., hypervigilance regarding the therapist's accessibility, reliability, and attunement during and between sessions) or unconscious (e.g., various forms of unintended challenging, confrontational or distancing behavior, or boundary overstepping). The therapist's willingness and ability to respond nonjudgmentally and empathically while upholding the conditions of the therapeutic contract and clear boundaries when faced with such "tests" can forestall premature flight or disengagement from treatment and, over time, give the patient the confidence to make more detailed disclosures.

3. *Approach the patient with respect and with the understanding that being asked about and/or disclosing a history of abuse can result in dysregulated emotions.* The therapist must convey an attitude of openness and sensitivity and ask questions from a position of genuine nonjudgmental interest in the patient, including support for the patient's absolute right to choose when and what to discuss or disclose. When patients are anxious or unwilling to share or examine their past and current traumas or traumatic stress reactions, this can test the therapist's patience and professional confidence (e.g., "Am I doing something wrong or insensitive that the patient won't open up or confide in me?"; "What will it take for this person to trust me?"). It is often the case however that being patient and accepting, and understanding a patient's reluctance to make sensitive (and/or potentially dangerous) disclosures, while supporting the patient's right to make personal choices about the timing and nature of such disclosures, can actually lead to more rapid and thorough disclosures. Patient can be assisted by recognizing that the therapist is sensitive to the difficulty of revisiting traumatic experiences or disclosing embarrassing, shameful, or troubling trauma-related symptoms.

4. *Recognize that disclosure and discussion of traumatic experiences or trauma-related symptom can result in the spontaneous emergence or intensification of PTSD, CTSD, or related symptoms (e.g., addictive urges, suicidality, hopelessness, shame, psychotic symptoms).* The therapist should be aware of this possibility and be prepared to respond in a way that helps the patient to reorient and restabilize in the moment and before leaving the session (Briere, 2004; Dorrepaal et al., 2012). The therapist must be knowledgeable about the possibility of acute symptomatic distress and responses and be able to calmly and sensitively reorient and restabilize the patient. In fact, this may provide an opportunity for the therapist to offer information about trauma and posttraumatic reactions and to teach self-management strategies in the moment.

By the same token, it is crucial that therapists not expect patients automatically to have intense or debilitating reactions to trauma-related assessment and disclosure. In most cases, patients with even the most severe complex trauma histories and CTSD symptoms are fully able to disclose and discuss many, and, in some cases, all of their traumatic experiences and trauma-related symptoms if the framework for assessment described earlier is provided. It is just as serious a mistake for a therapist to communicate personal anxiety and/ or a fear of the trauma story or a lack of confidence in the patient's ability to tolerate the discussion—which can create a self-fulfilling prophecy by triggering the patient to have the adverse reactions that the therapist fears—as it is to underestimate the stressfulness of disclosure of complex trauma experiences and CTSD symptoms. The best approach is a middle path of calm, sensitive, and collaborative inquiry that encourages disclosure but respects the patient's decision about when, what, and how to share, and that offers strategies for self-management of any difficulties in the aftermath of the disclosures.

5. *Specialized assessment might be introduced or repeated at different points in treatment, because new details and posttraumatic and dissociative symptoms may emerge as a consequence of the achievement of a modicum of safety and stabilization, after some precursor issues have been addressed, or the individual's traumatic stress disorder and associated symptoms may have been triggered in some way.* Although some symptoms are blatant and highly evident (i.e., flashbacks [Ford, 2018]), others are very subtle, such as dissociative fragmentation (see Chapters 5 and 6), hypervigilance-based avoidance (Kaczkurkin et al., 2017), and phobias. Dissociative episodes and flashbacks can be misdiagnosed as psychotic hallucinations or delusions if they are not recognized as reenactments (symbolic, as well as literal) of traumatic experiences (Brewin, 2015). Avoidance can be misdiagnosed as depression or malingering if it is not recognized as a hypervigilant or phobic attempt to protect against a perceived threat (which may include an intolerable memory of overwhelming distress as well as objective dangers) (Ford, 2017).

6. *Assessment begins in a general way and becomes more specialized according to the symptoms and needs of the individual.* The recommended strategy is to start with a general biopsychosocial assessment (in interview or written form, or both) and move toward trauma-focused screenings, instruments, and interviews, as indicated. Clinical signs of potential PTSD or CTSD (e.g., re-experiencing, numbing/dissociation, affect dysregulation, hypervigilance) symptoms should be carefully noted (i.e., when and how they emerge, their precipitants and their intensity, the patient's beliefs about and ability to control or manage them). This is followed by a more detailed specialized assessment. Because comorbid medical and psychological conditions and symptoms (e.g., problems with eating, sexuality, dysphoria, anxiety, addiction, physical illness, sleep, suicidality, self-harm) are common in patients with complex trauma histories, specialized instruments for these conditions are used as needed (see Chapter 5). In some cases, outside consultations or specialized corollary assessments (e.g., sleep monitoring, neuropsychological or neuroimag-

ing tests, medical tests) are necessary in order to rule in or rule out alternative (or co-occurring) causes of complex symptoms.

Best Practices for CTSD Treatment: 30 Principles

1. *Set treatment goals that flow from and are linked to the integrated assessment findings and to the patient's identified goals, preferences, and needs.* Several goals for the treatment of PTSD have been identified (Courtois, 1999; Schnyder & Cloitre, 2015; Schnyder et al., 2015). They include increased physical and psychological safety and stability; enhanced self-esteem and trust; reduced severity of PTSD symptoms; reestablishment of the normal stress response; deconditioning of anxiety/fear; processing of emotions and traumatic memories; recovery from comorbid problems; maintained or improved adaptive functioning and social and intimate relationships; reengagement in life; enhanced social support; and development of a relapse prevention plan.

CTSDs involve other developmental/attachment and self- and relationship difficulties that require additional treatment goals than those for more classic forms of PTSD (Courtois & Ford, 2009; Ford, 2017). These goals include but are not limited to: overcoming developmental blockages and fixations; acquiring skills for missed developmental milestones such as emotional identification/discrimination, experiencing, expression, and self-regulation; developing experiences of self-mastery that disrupt patterns of helplessness and hopelessness; developing strategies for maintaining personal safety (including discrimination of trustworthy from untrustworthy others and situations); developing personal assertion skills aimed at decreasing and ultimately ending revictimization; restoring or developing a capacity for secure, organized relational attachments ("earned secure" attachment); enhancing personality integration and recovery of dissociated knowledge and avoided emotions; restoring or acquiring personal authority over the remembering process through trauma and narrative processing; acknowledging and resolving issues of trauma-related beliefs and moral or spiritual injury; identifying and modifying trauma-based reenactments; and restoring or enhancing compromised physical health.

In order to achieve these goals, CTSD treatment must achieve several therapeutic objectives:

- Restoration of both bodily and mental functioning, including both sensorimotor integration and neurochemical and psychophysiological integrity.
- Enhancement of the capacity not just to identify and tolerate but to actively reflect on, understand, and modulate distressing emotions.
- Restoration or acquisition of organized and secure internal working models of attachment and the capacity to selectively engage with and trust others.

- Enhancement of skills for inhibiting risky, self-harming, or self-defeating behaviors, often used as means of self-regulation and self-integration.
- Enhancement of skills for inhibiting behaviors that elicit, collude with, passively tolerate or minimize, or intentionally or inadvertently escalate conflict, estrangement, exploitation, or physical or emotional aggression or microaggressions in relationships.
- Enhancement of skills for activating and consistently utilizing effective problem-solving, goal formulation and attainment, and life management tactics.
- Identification of dissociative processes and dissociative sequestering of emotions, thoughts, perceptions, and memories, up to and including the development of ego states and switching between them, while encouraging the reassociation of emotions and knowledge that have been dissociated, leading to greater personality integration.
- Identification and resolution of guilt and shame, including development of a sense of self as whole, integrated, worthy, and efficacious, while coming to understand the origins of beliefs about the self as defective, failing, incompetent, dependent, or irreversibly damaged.
- Prevention or enhancement of skills for safely managing and recovering from reenactments of past traumas and revictimization of self and others.
- Identification and enhancement of skills for overcoming the dynamics of betrayal-trauma, and for understanding and resolving ambivalent attachment to abusive and nonprotective caregivers.
- Restoration or acquisition of an existential sense of life as being worth living and a sense of spiritual connection and meaning.
- Support or restoration of the capacity for empathically taking the perspective of others who were harmed by, and finding prosocial ways to provide meaningful restitution for, actions of one's own that have caused or contributed to moral injury.

Goals may also be developed for highly individualized and idiosyncratic concerns raised by the patient. These include (a) stress-related problems with health, pain, or sleep; (b) specific sexual problems; (c) intimate partner relationships; (d) contact with family members or others who continue to be abusive or violent and how to safely maintain separation from or safe forms of contact with them; (e) difficulties with parenting and childrearing; (f) addictions and addictive behaviors; (g) conflict resolution in the family or at work; and (h) problems with learning or performance in school or at work. Individualized treatment goals may change according to the phase and focus of treatment and the emergence of crisis circumstances (e.g., separation and loss of significant others, death of the perpetrator or nonoffending others, suicide attempt, self-harm, additional abuse and domestic violence, community violence, addiction relapse).

The therapist should not be surprised that the achievement of a goal and/ or the resolution of an issue might lead to the emergence of other concerns that were previously dormant or not in evidence (e.g., sobriety might lead to the emergence of intrusive memories of abuse that the patient previously suppressed or did not find troubling; smoking cessation might lead to increased dissociation or problems with anger). Freedom from concerns about being subjected to unwanted contact with a perpetrator might lead to the emergence of patients' previously unacknowledged feelings and memories related to the perpetrator or the abuse. It is not advisable to predict any specific forms of symptom emergence, because this could lead to anticipatory anxiety and avoidance that are countertherapeutic; however, it is helpful to reassure patients in advance that unanticipated emotions, memories, and associated physical responses may emerge as current symptoms are addressed and worked through.

2. *Treatment should be based on the consensus-based metamodel most widely used in contemporary treatment of CTSDs, which involves three stages or phases of treatment organized to address specific issues sequentially and in a relatively hierarchical order* (Herman, 1992; Janet, 1889). Although the efficacy of this approach has been challenged as not yet having an evidence base and as unnecessarily delaying the processing of trauma due to an overly conservative focus on safety and stabilization before proceeding (De Jongh et al., 2016), the research of Brand and her colleagues on treatment phases and tasks for dissociative identity disorder suggests its efficacy for that subset of the complex trauma population (Brand et al., 2012, 2013). These findings support the viewpoint of the majority of clinicians treating CTSDs continues to be that sequencing is in the interest of "resourcing" and preparing the patient before explicitly processing trauma memories (Courtois & Ford, 2009, 2013; Schnyder et al., 2015). Moreover, there is no evidence that integrating interventions other than trauma memory processing or beginning treatment with attention to problems in daily life, has adverse effects in terms of dropouts, symptom exacerbation, or slower or poorer outcomes. Indeed, there is some evidence that the opposite is true: Psychotherapies that focus on emotion and interpersonal self-regulation in current life, along with psychoeducation and therapeutic exploration of the links between current symptoms and past traumatic experiences, have shown evidence of lower rates of premature termination (Bisson, Roberts, Andrew, Cooper, & Lewis, 2013) and comparable outcomes (Cloitre et al., 2010; Ford, Steinberg, Hawke, Levine, & Zhang, 2012; Ford, Steinberg, & Zhang, 2011; Markowitz et al., 2015) to therapies that emphasize beginning sustained intensive trauma memory processing as early as possible in treatment.

Contemporary guidance is emphasizing efforts to help clients to gain mastery experiences right from the start of treatment, starting with their physical responses, to counteract their sense of powerlessness and lack of skills (Blue Knot Foundation, 2019; Ogden, Minton, & Pain, 2006). Careful sequencing of therapeutic activities and tasks calls for initial emphasis on present-centered issues such as personal and environmental safety and the intentional development or strengthening of skills for emotion regulation and life management. Functionality may be reduced temporarily at critical junctures in therapy (e.g., at the outset, when disclosing trauma memories, or as the end of treatment approaches). The therapist must carefully monitor signs of such functional decline and, when it is identified, work with the patient to modulate the intensity of emotional reactions and build or enhance sources of support. Attention to the client's emotional capacity ("the window of tolerance") is also suggested throughout the course of treatment (Ogden et al., 2006).

Phase 1: Ensuring Safety and Preparing for Trauma Memory Processing

3. *Phase 1 lays the foundation for CTSD treatment.* It includes pretreatment issues, such as preliminary assessment, the development of motivation for treatment, informed consent, and education about what psychotherapy is about, how to participate most successfully, and ways to manage physical sensations and reactions. It begins with attention to the development of the treatment relationship in a way that fosters the possibility of a strong therapeutic alliance over time. Some patients already do so well in managing symptoms and maintaining or putting their lives back together that they either have no need to complete the other two phases of treatment or choose not to do so. Others never move beyond or complete this first phase, and instead use it as life maintenance and a source of needed support. Such person-centered and present-centered treatment approaches are increasingly endorsed by research studies (Hoge & Chard, 2018). At the very least, even for a patient who might precipitously leave treatment early on, the focus of this first phase gives them additional information and resources with which to approach their difficulties and improve their lives. This in and of itself can be therapeutic.

4. *Phase 1 focuses initially on personal and interpersonal safety, which may take considerable time to develop.* As noted earlier, complex trauma survivors often live in conditions of relational and life chaos and danger, lacking basic forms of safety in relation to others (e.g., ongoing or intermittent abuse, domestic or community violence) and themselves (e.g., self-harm, suicidality, addictions, risk taking). Therefore, a first order of treatment is to discuss safety and its importance and to establish conditions of safety to the fullest degree possible. Ongoing danger and vulnerability require the patient to continue to engage in defensive and protective strategies, without which they will be emotionally overwhelmed and even more vulnerable to further victimization. When the patient continues to be in an unsafe situation (ongoing domestic violence, incest, sexual harassment, political repression, migrancy, sex trafficking, etc.) or especially when they continue to engage in unsafe practices (ongoing and voluntary contact with abusers contrary to the plan, drug use and abuse, risk taking), therapist concern and countertransference (ranging from an urge to protect and rescue the patient to feelings of anger, disappointment, and disgust and an urge to detach from and abandon) are likely to be activated and

are times when the therapist most needs and benefits from outside support and perspective. The therapist must self-regulate and manage the countertransference in order to return the focus to safety and the patient's ultimate responsibility for their actions, assisting in the identification of blocks or challenges. Thus, when plans falter or fail, rather than castigating the patient, the therapist must understand such a relapse as a need for additional safety education, collaborative problem solving, and a revised safety plan based on what the patient believes to be feasible.

Even when patients' lives are objectively safe, they may have great difficulty in feeling safe engaging in the personal reflection, emotion expression, and disclosure that is inherent in psychotherapy. Helping patients to feel confident that the therapist nonjudgmentally understands how traumatic experiences and other adversities have made self-reflection and self-disclosure anxiety provoking or deeply distressing is therefore an essential aspect of creating a solid foundation of personal trust and safety in Phase 1.

5. *Treatment assists the patient in building emotion regulation capacities, identifying arousal states, and clarifying perceptions and thoughts.* Phase 1 focuses on enhancing the patient's ability to manage extreme arousal states by labeling emotions, learning strategies for their safe and modulated expression in order to prevent or manage the extremes of hyperarousal (e.g., panic, impulsive risk taking, rage, dissociation) or hypoarousal (e.g., emotional numbing, physical collapse, relational detachment, exhaustion, paralysis, hopelessness) associated with CTSDs. In this way, rather than remaining reactive or dissociated, the individual learns to self-modulate and manage states of arousal, through specific skills training interventions that may include skills that enhance self-soothing capacities (e.g., focused breathing) and self-awareness (e.g., mindfulness and somatic focusing). This also occurs when therapists sensitively respond and "stay present" when the patient remembers and/or discloses episodes of abuse and victimization, causing strong emotions to emerge in response. This support and coregulation of the evoked emotions provides *in vivo* modeling of this type of response and is utilized with the intention of helping the patient learn to self-regulate.

6. *Phase 1 also involves enhancing the patient's ability to approach and master rather than avoid internal bodily/affective states and external events that trigger posttraumatic reactions.* Avoidance that may have been lifesaving during the trauma and in its aftermath becomes problematic when it becomes automatic and becomes the individual's sole means of coping. Avoidance due to fear of facing what is painful becomes overgeneralized, creating heightened fear responses. This process is a hallmark of traumatic stress disorders; resolving avoidance has been identified as a benchmark for successful treatment (Foa & Jaycox, 1999). Reversing avoidance and developing ways of actively engaging with both positive and negative experiences, emotions, and memories requires growth in the form of a shift from automaticity and reactivity to one that is

conscious, self-reflective, and more self-regulating (Ford, 2018). A fundamental challenge beginning in Phase 1 and continuing in all treatment phases is to enhance awareness of both subtle and obvious forms of avoidance of anticipated danger or distress, and of the safety signals that may be used as focal points to modulate anxiety and lead to more effective active coping tactics. In this way, trauma processing begins in the first phase of treatment when, prior to intensive intentional reexperiencing or retelling of trauma memories, therapy assists the patient in recognizing, understanding, and choosing to not engage in habitual avoidance behaviors when feeling stressed or distressed (e.g., by spontaneous memories of the trauma and resultant re-experiencing reactions).

7. *Patient education is an integral component of Phase 1, optimally beginning immediately*. Education can demystify psychotherapy by explaining how it is a practical process in which therapist and patient together, as a team, figure out how the patient has had to deal with stressful experiences and circumstances, and how the patient can draw on their strengths to develop new ways of interacting and experiencing, all in the interest of self-mastery. Education about traumatic stress reactions as adaptive and self-protective responses under conditions that are overwhelming and constitute survival threats, and how and why these reactions can become chronic—but reversible—symptoms, further supports patients' confidence that therapy can provide a new approach for them to understand and overcome their reactions and symptoms. It is also geared to helping them identify their strengths and competencies and build on them to achieve new types of experiences and ways of coping. Psychoeducation thereby builds self-confidence and self-awareness, develops hope and motivation to change, and creates a practical framework for the subsequent teaching of specific skills for self-regulation, self-development, and trauma memory processing.

8. *Phase 1 of treatment introduces awareness about and supports the patient's sense of self and relational capacities*. Developmentally adverse interpersonal trauma fundamentally interferes with the acquisition of a sense of positive identity, personal control, and self-efficacy (see Chapters 1 and 2). Therefore, the therapist needs to assist the patient in developing and consolidating a personal and unique identity, and in recognizing ways that they are (or can be) personally and interpersonally capable. This process involves helping the patient to use personal attention to physical and emotional issues of which they had previously been unaware to stimulate self-exploration and self-knowledge, ultimately jump-starting or consolidating a more stable sense of self and improved self-esteem. The therapist can provide education about how early insecure or traumatic life experiences with caregivers shape the individual's "working model" of self and others and how this subsequently impacts their sense of self, and expectations for current and future relationships.

Building, restoring, or identifying possible new healthy relations with others and support networks is a crucial part of this phase. Mistrust of the motivation of others is a major interpersonal hallmark of many, if not most, complex trauma survivors. Thus, when it is expressed, whether directly or indirectly, it should be expected and not taken as a personal affront by the therapist. Educating the patient about insecure and disorganized attachment patterns and their origins and about betrayal-trauma and how mistrust of others and their motives is generated in these contexts, occurs simultaneously with the "real-time" exposure to and experience of a more attuned and responsive relationship with the therapist. This information provides both a contrast to the past and a corrective. Patients can also be educated in the identification of behaviors that differentiate individuals who are trustworthy from those who are not—and acquire the skills and the confidence necessary for personal assertion and self-protection.

9. *Although Phase 1 does not specifically center explicitly on trauma memory processing, the focus of this phase directly or indirectly relates to traumatic antecedents, their related developmental impacts, including encoding as implicit memory.* The major difference between this phase and the next is that in Phase 1, the impact of past traumatic experiences is addressed primarily by teaching the patient how posttraumatic stress and developmental problems are expectable and adaptive reactions to traumatic experiences and teaching about implicit memory and identifying somatic reactions and markers The patient's ongoing posttraumatic and additional symptoms, among other things, become the basis for determining whether formal trauma memory processing is required. If the patient continues to explicitly, intrusively reexperience trauma memories or to have other symptoms that indicate that intrusive reexperiencing is occurring (e.g., avoidance, dissociation, reenactments, hypervigilance, or emotion dysregulation in reaction to cues subtly, symbolically, or obviously related to traumatic events or the relational dynamics, threats, or harm experienced therein) and is willing to work more directly on trauma memories, then treatment proceeds to Phase 2. At times, this shift is explicitly initiated by the clinician, based on an evaluation of the patient's readiness. At other times, it proceeds rather seamlessly from cognitively based verbal recounting the identification and expression of associated feelings.

Patients can be expected to move back and forth between phases, especially in times of crisis, relapse, or overwhelm, and/or when they need to refresh skills, re-establish their sense of trust and confidence, or to apply, or reformulate, their safety plan and relationship involvements and commitments.

Phase 2: Processing of Traumatic Memories

10. *Phase 2 focuses on safe, self-reflective disclosure of traumatic memories and associated reactions in the form of a progressively elaborated and coherent autobiographical narrative and associated emotional responses.* Narrative reconstruction of memories must be timed and structured to support the patient's ability not only to tolerate trauma memories and emotions but also to develop a coherent life story that encompasses personal success and growth,

as well as psychological trauma and consequences, including decline. Patients are encouraged to feel the emotions associated with the traumatic experiences and relationships, in other words, to associate or reassociate rather than to dissociate or otherwise avoid their reactions. Thus, patients are assisted in feeling, rather than detaching from, the impact that past traumatic experiences had and continue to have, as they are helped to understand and to accept their trauma-related reactions. In CTSD treatment, the focal emotions are not limited to anxiety or fear as is often the case in PTSD treatment, in which other emotions may be considered secondary. Grief and mourning are often foci, as are shame, guilt, self-contempt and self-hatred, disgust, disappointment, and rage. Additionally, the patient may undertake specific actions to resolve relationships with abusers or others, for example, through disclosures and discussions, boundary development, separation or reconnection from a position of increased awareness, understanding, and interpersonal and self-regulatory skills. A variety of strategies and approaches to trauma memory processing have been developed to address these and various issues (described in Parts III and IV in this volume).

11. *Some treatment models specifically do not prescribe recall of traumatic memories in Phase 2 but focus instead on enhancing patients' capacities for self-regulation in their current lives without retelling traumatic memories in detailed or repetitive narratives* (see Chapters 13, 16, 17, 18). These therapies explicitly link the patient's processing of current stressful or emotionally evocative experiences to the resolution of the sense of distress and helplessness that can lead to avoidance of traumatic memories. They approach memory work with an emphasis on helping the patient to reconstruct and process memories and associated emotions as they prefer, to counter posttraumatic avoidance of feared or overwhelming memories by building self-regulation capacities for memory processing (Ford, 2018; Ford, Courtois, Steele, van der Hart, & Nijenhuis, 2005). This replaces the prescribing of memory recall as a required or even recommended component of treatment. Those self-regulation capacities can then be called upon by patient and therapist if and when traumatic memories are a source of concern, or if the patient wishes to tell their story in the therapy.

12. *Other treatment models specifically do not prescribe recall of traumatic memories in Phase 2 but focus instead on strengthening patients' abilities to examine reflectively the full range of past and recent memories.* Phase 2 may therefore involve an autobiographical "life narrative reconstruction" to assist patients in gaining a sense of mastery or authority over their memories, first in relation to the full range of life experiences, as a preparation for systematically revisiting and reconstructing traumatic memories in narrative form (see Chapters 12, 14, and 18). These approaches also include the continued strengthening of skills for emotional and interpersonal self-regulation prior to engaging the patient in formal narrative reconstruction of traumatic memo-

ries (see Chapters 16–18). The goal of narrative reconstruction is to restore both the patient's sense of authority over their own memories (Harvey, 1996) and the actual ability to recall traumatic memories using episodic/declarative memory operations (which may have been impaired by complex trauma; Ford, 2018). These processes often result in a much more integrated and coherent memory of the traumatic circumstances and an increased ability to tolerate them without automatic and uncontrolled reactivity or shutdown.

13. *An alternative approach to memory reconstruction is detailed narrative memory processing.* Methods include desensitization (i.e., graduated exposure; see Chapter 13), flooding (i.e., intensive or prolonged exposure; see Chapter 9), narrative reconstruction (i.e., personal storytelling; see Chapters 11, 14, and 17), cognitive restructuring (see Chapters 10 and 11), or experiential (i.e., selective focusing on key moments; see Chapters 13 and 15). Narrative memory processing therapies involve the patient recalling in written, imaginal, or verbal format, a specific traumatic memory as vividly as possible in first-person mode (i.e., as if it were happening in the present). Narrative memory processing therapy seeks to directly counter anxiety-based avoidance of traumatic recollection and to give the patient a sense of self-determination and confidence in recalling traumatic memories, in contrast to feeling that these memories are intolerable and uncontrollable when they spontaneously emerge in some way (Ford, 2018). Along with the intentional imaginal retelling of part or all of a traumatic memory, narrative memory processing can be combined with *in vivo* exposure interventions that help the patient to safely encounter cues and situations that elicit memories of past traumatic events in ways that do not cause them to reexperience them or decompensate. The goal is for the patient to intentionally anticipate and manage reactions using a variety of strategies they have learned rather than avoid trauma cues and reminders in daily life.

14. *No approach to memory reconstruction work has been definitively validated for patients with CTSDs.* Each of the psychotherapy models described in Part II of this volume has shown evidence of promising outcomes in patients with complex trauma histories and with some symptoms of CTSDs. However, as explained in Chapters 9–18, careful adaptation is needed for each individual patient in order to safely and effectively address CTSD symptoms. Therefore, trauma memory processing should be considered for use but be carefully adapted and titrated to meet the needs and capacities of the individual patient. The emotional and physical self-regulation and narrative reconstruction approaches warrant consideration in addition to (or as an alternative or preparation for) exposure-based traumatic memory work (Ford, 2018).

15. *Throughout Phase 2, it is essential to carefully monitor and assist the patient in maintaining an adequate level of functioning, consistent with past and current lifestyle and circumstances.* At no point should therapy be a substi-

tute for living life or be a direct precipitant of—or tacit collusion with—a view of the patient as without personal agency or permanently damaged. Empathizing with and showing respect for the resilience and adaptive intentions embodied in the patient's symptoms as a framework in Phase 2 is essential. Then the patient can begin to feel pride and a sense of self-confidence rather than shame and failure.

Phase 3: Reintegration—Fully Resuming Life

16. *Phase 3 is the culmination of the previous therapeutic work and can be an exciting time of growth as the patient feels increasingly able to have a meaningful life beyond simply surviving trauma.* In Phase 3, patients have gained assurance in their ability to handle the emotional reactivity that are triggered by reminders or memories of past trauma. They are able to draw on, and further bolster, this confidence by using the self-regulation skills they have learned (or fine-tuned) in the first phases of therapy. They also have gained a sense of resolution derived from facing, carefully reflecting on, and coming to terms with memories of past traumas and the survival adaptations that they necessitated. In Phase 3, these accomplishments are translated into daily living and into decisions and plans for the future that are based on goals and hopes that give the patient a sense of meaning and identity. The therapist's role in this phase is largely to serve as a resource and guide, while the patient charts a course and takes steps to live differently while pursuing key life goals. Serving as a "surrogate memory bank" for the patient also can be important, in order to provide occasional reminders when things patients have discovered and learned about themselves and can help a patient to approach a current life challenge or goal with awareness rather than in a state of distress or reactivity.

17. *However, Phase 3 may also be fraught with difficulty for patients who have never had the opportunity for such a life.* Phase 3 might be a time when patients specifically realize the dysfunction and pathology of the past (or present) and its associated losses as they attempt to move beyond its influence. This may result in intense grief and mourning for what never was (i.e., "I'm not the person I might have been"; "I had no childhood"; "I had no parenting"). Phase 3 continues the focus on developmental attainments that have been disrupted or remain unresolved, and on fine-tuning and gaining confidence in oneself and in self-regulatory, life, and relationship skills. Commonly encountered challenges include the continued development of trustworthy relationships and intimacy; sexual functioning; parenting; career and other life decisions; ongoing discussions or confrontations with abusive or neglectful others; determination of courses of action for ongoing self-protection; mourning and grieving of losses; and personal atonement and restitution if in the process of surviving trauma the patient has acted in ways that they regret or feel has caused others harm (i.e., moral injury). This is also the phase in which the patient may most productively consider taking legal (civil or criminal) or other action against

the perpetrator(s) or organization(s). In this phase, as in the others, the clinician continues to provide the secure base by being a respectful, empathically attuned, and affirming listener and guide, with the patient's goals and values in sharp focus. The therapist should scrupulously avoid influencing a patient in these decision points, instead providing relevant information where warranted, while encouraging autonomous decision making.

Treatment Considerations across All Phases of Therapy

18. *Dissociation, as a clinical issue and challenge.* As discussed in Chapter 6, dissociation was a highly likely response to a history of complex trauma, especially when it was repetitive over the course of childhood. Therapists treating this population will be faced with dissociative phenomena ranging from brief episodes of spacing out or inattention (dissociative process) to full-blown switches between different identity states each of which exercise some degree of executive control of the patient (dissociative identity disorder), or anywhere between the two (e.g., the "fragmented selves model" of Fisher [2017]—see also Chapter 24) or the "internal family system" model of Schwartz [Schwartz, Schwartz, & Galperin, 2009]. One of the major complications that arise in treatment is therapist unfamiliarity and inexperience with these phenomena, often due to a lack of attention to them in professional training and ongoing professional skepticism about them (critics often decry dissociation as fantasy). Training based on research findings and accurate information is urgently needed as a result.

Because dissociation is so ubiquitous in this population and because it is so implicated in the sequestration and disintegration of personal experience and associated personal fragmentation (once developed as an automatic coping mechanism in the face of chronic inescapable traumatic episodes and experiences, especially those that were sexual and physically intrusive), it is important for it to be assessed, identified, and then included in the treatment. To not do so is often to disregard an essential defensive operation and method of functioning that can highly compromise and have dire consequences in the patient's life. Also, it is worth noting that dissociation is the opposite of mindfulness and the ability to self-reflect and to mentalize (see Chapters 23 and 25 for discussion of these issues and why somatic and psychological mindfulness is essential to include in the treatment of complex trauma). Chapter 6 provides a comprehensive overview of assessing and treating complex dissociative conditions also referred to as complex developmental dissociative trauma and CSTDs.

19. *Treatment, like complex traumatic stress symptoms, is complex and multimodal.* As noted earlier, the range of symptoms and comorbidities involved may require a variety of treatment goals and different treatment approaches. Treatment should therefore incorporate a variety of theoretical perspectives and clinical modalities in an integrative rather than unimodal or

fragmented manner. Treatment is also individualized to the needs and capacities of the patient and is modified as needed (Cloitre, 2015; Courtois, 1999) and as suggested by periodic repeat assessments and goal evaluation New treatment approaches are emerging, many based on new findings in the neurosciences and some body-based and other approaches long considered complementary and alternative to talk therapy (see Chapters in Part IV).

20. *Therapists must be aware of and effectively manage patients' transference reactions and reenactments, and their own secondary traumatic stress reactions, vicarious traumatization, and countertransference.* The patient's transference in the context of CTSD treatment can be understood as being related to past experiences and adaptations enacted within or projected onto the therapeutic relationship ("traumatic transference"). The therapist's countertransference is understood as personal responses based on their personal history or character, apart from the traumatic transference but highly impacted by it. Countertransference may also be closely related to secondary traumatic stress or vicarious trauma responses colored by the emotional impact of the patient's trauma disclosures and traumatic stress reactions (see Chapter 8 for further discussion). The therapist must consciously model and utilize self-regulatory skills to manage their own secondary or vicarious trauma reactions and provide a secure emotional presence and reliable therapeutic boundaries for the patient (Kinsler et al., 2009; Sprang et al., 2018). Therapist self-care, intentional self-reflection (during and after treatment sessions), and professional support and development (including ongoing consultation or supervision and additional training) are crucial to being able to recognize and address transference, secondary/vicarious traumatic stress, and countertransference reactions and dynamics in a constructive, therapeutic manner.

21. *The patient's development of an outside support system must be encouraged within the realistic limits of the patient's relational capacities and resources, and with respect to the patient's peer group(s), gender identity, and cultural, racial–ethnic background, norms, and traditions.* The patient may start from the position that no one is to be trusted, because trusting others resulted in hurt or harm and caused betrayal-trauma. The therapist must, over time, counter these beliefs (while respecting their origin and reinforcing their basis in past reality and that some people are, in fact, exploitive and otherwise abusive), model and teach social skills when needed, and encourage outside engagement with trustworthy others in a range of settings. They also provide a model and reinforcement by being trustworthy and ethical in their therapeutic interactions and relationship with the patient. Other modalities such as group treatment, couple counseling, and family treatment might be helpful with regard to this issue. Additionally, tele-health and internet-based resources such as information and support forums might provide the patient with additional sources of information and support, but their quality varies markedly and patients should be so advised. It can be important for the therapist to ask

about them in the interest of staying informed about outside influences on the patient.

Duration of Treatment

22. *On average, CTSD treatment is longer-term than treatment for less complex clinical presentations.* For some patients, treatment may be quite delimited, but it rarely can be meaningful if completed in less than 10–20 sessions, unless its focus is on a specific problem or symptom. For others, treatment may last for decades, whether provided continuously or episodically. Even therapeutic modalities that are designed to be completed within 10–30 sessions may require more sessions or repetitions of "cycles," or episodes of the intervention. Determining the duration of treatment should be based on the patient's response to therapy rather than on a pre-determined basis. Of course, modularized interventions that have a preset duration can play a valuable role as part of a larger treatment (and case management) plan, but the overall treatment duration should be flexible and based on the attainment of key goals (e.g., safety, symptom management or resolution, secure and healthy relationships, personal autonomy and peace of mind).

23. *However, when multiple modalities are required (i.e., group and individual; substance abuse treatment in addition to psychotherapy; couple and/ or family work plus individual therapy; partial hospitalization in addition to or instead of individual therapy; inpatient treatment), more sessions per week are obviously needed.* Therapy should exceed the usual standard of frequency only when symptom and impairment severity/crisis stabilization warrant the additional costs to the patient, family, and payor(s), unless more intensive treatment is mandated by the therapeutic orientation (e.g., intensive forms of psychodynamic/analytic or cognitive-behavioral therapy conducted on a several-days-per-week basis; Foa et al., 2018; Sloan, Marx, Lee, & Resick, 2018) or pharmacologically assisted therapy conducted over a period of several consecutive hours) (Oehen, Traber, Widmer, & Schnyder, 2013). More frequent or prolonged sessions, especially if oriented toward memory processing (referred to by some as "memory work" and provided on an intensive basis such as over the course of several days or over a weekend), without a strong foundation of emotional regulation skills, most often destabilize patients and can cause them to decompensate; furthermore, they may cause an unhealthy dependence on the therapist and the therapy to develop. Strategies of this sort are therefore contraindicated in most cases. That said, massed or intensive treatments applied over a short period of time are currently being tested for the treatment of classic PTSD.

Treatment Frame

24. *Therapists must carefully set and maintain boundaries that are ultimately protective of the treatment efficacy and continuance.* As noted, a written document presented at the outset of treatment that spells out mutual rights

and responsibilities as the foundation of informed consent is recommended. Templates that therapists can individualize to their practice specifications are available from most professional organizations, and one tailored for use with this population is available (Courtois & Ford, 2013). It is advisable for treatment to begin with tighter boundaries and limitations that can be loosened over time and for the therapist to explain their importance since they may be very confusing to those whose boundaries were regularly violated or who were routinely engaged in dual relationships. While maintaining a consistent treatment frame, therapists must maintain a degree of flexibility, encourage collaborative problem solving, and take patient needs and preferences into consideration. The responsibility for the maintenance of therapeutic boundaries always rests with the therapist.

Continuity of Care

25. *Given the likelihood of patients having had neglectful and/or traumatic personal (and possibly treatment) histories of abandonment and betrayal, therapists and patients benefit from the availability of backup therapists or programs during times when the primary therapist is unavailable.* Backup resources provide some security against feelings of rejection and abandonment that often accompany separations. It must be recognized that separations often serve as reminders of past neglect or losses, so they may precipitate crises while a therapist is away. When treatment must end due to exigencies in the patient's or the therapist's life (e.g., geographic or career changes, illness), the end process may itself create a crisis of loss. It is a critical opportunity to support and sustain the patient's reactions as well as their gains in relational, emotional, and behavioral self-regulation. Not uncommonly, losses or changes in the patient's past were avoided or unaddressed, leaving them to deal with them without support. Endings thus present a critical opportunity to reverse the pattern and to offer support in the face of loss and separation. Incorporating strategies for the patient to preserve a sense of psychic connection to and continuity with the therapist (e.g., offering tangible and symbolic transitional objects that represent the therapist's continued interest and caring, despite the reduced or terminated physical availability) can be helpful. Integrating these transitional interventions with the patient's gradual and self-paced (if possible) engagement with a new therapist or treatment system/provider serves to extend therapy's benefits in terms of self-regulation, self-integration and efficacy, and trust in and ability to rely on caregiving resources.

Treatment Trajectories

26. *All patients do not heal the same way or to the same degree of completeness or health.* Therapists must be aware of differences in patients' capacities to engage in therapy and to resolve their symptoms and distress. There are as many degrees of self- and relational impairment as there are of healing

capacities and resources, resulting in different degrees and types of resolution and recovery. What might objectively be a partial success for one patient might meet another's full capacity (or that of the same patient at a different stage of treatment and recovery). For example, some patients never progress beyond life stabilization and/or sobriety, yet that constitutes a valuable attainment if it is meaningful for them, a genuine victory, and a profound change of life quality, even if no further change is undertaken. Different treatment trajectories have been identified (Kluft, 1994; Layne et al., 2008) and serve as reminders of patients' differing capacities and resolutions. It should also be expected that some patients have what Wang, Wilson, & Mason (1994) termed "cyclic decompensation," defined as a periodic exacerbation of their symptoms or a decline in their life status, which is best responded to with immediate acute intervention. Patients should also be cautioned about an ongoing susceptibility to unexpected triggering events or emotions and prepared with management strategies based on their skills development.

Service Settings

27. *Most treatment for patients with CTSDs take place in outpatient settings, whether a mental health center, a clinic, or a private practice.* At times, patients require specialized services and settings, including inpatient, partial hospital or day treatment, residential rehabilitation or supportive housing, or intensive outpatient programs (e.g., for substance abuse, eating disorders, sexual addiction, or compulsive and dangerous self-harm). These settings often provide, in addition to increased monitoring and stabilization resources, intensive individual and group skills-building programs; psychopharmacology services for medication evaluation and management; peer support programs (e.g., 12-step or other group recovery programs, day treatment, "clubhouses"); and case management and specialized consultants to address vocational, educational, residential, financial, criminal justice, and legal needs.

In some cases, inpatient care may be required due to the patient's acuity or inability to function. Unfortunately, it is often the case that hospitalization may cause the patient additional distress, such as when they are housed with actively manic and/or psychotic patients who are disruptive, intrusive or threatening, and even physically dangerous, or when a unit is understaffed and/or has staff members who are not trained and do not recognize posttraumatic distress and, as a consequence, misunderstand, stigmatize, and damage the patient. Outpatient therapists should be aware of the quality, or the lack thereof, of the inpatient or day hospital unit in which they hospitalize patients and seek to keep these hospitalizations as brief as possible. Optimally, they have attending privileges or other professional contacts with inpatient providers that allow for coordination of services and orientation.

Whatever treatment setting is the best fit or is clinically determined to be necessary, it is advisable for the outpatient therapist to communicate with and coordinate treatment with other involved treatment professionals for optimal continuity of care. Splitting between caregivers can complicate what may be an already complicated treatment, and it may also be a very habitual mode of functioning for patients with complex trauma, who may have observed this survival skill in their family and between their parents. Collaboration has the dual benefit of stopping the splitting process and introducing patients to another mode of interaction between themselves and authority figures. The decision to undertake intensive psychiatric, addiction recovery, and/or traumatic stress or dissociative disorder treatment should always be made collaboratively with the patient (i.e., as necessary and appropriate and in the absence of an acute life-threatening situation) and with spouse/partner, guardians, caregiver(s), or significant others, as available.

Psychopharmacology

28. *Several psychotropic medications (e.g., antidepressants, anxiolytics, adrenergic blockers, mood stabilizers, and antipsychotics) have shown promise in treating some PTSD symptoms* (American Psychological Association, 2017; International Society for Traumatic Stress Studies, 2019; U.S. Department of Veterans Affairs and Department of Defense, 2017). Patients with CTSDs may benefit from these medications, but they may also need more complex medication regimens (but not necessarily larger numbers or amounts of medications). It has often been the case that these patients have had their symptoms misdiagnosed and prescribed a wide variety of medications, frequently resulting in overmedication (a problem especially in women). Finding the right medication, combined medications, dosage, and titration may be a prolonged and complicated process that requires accurate diagnosis as well as careful, empathic therapeutic management. The risk of suicide and substance abuse (in addition to the patient's degree of adherence, trustworthiness, and motivation in relation to medication) requires specific consideration. Medication designed to reduce specific target symptoms' severity often is used in combination with psychotherapy in treatment of complex traumatic stress disorders (Krystal et al., 2017; Opler, Grennan, & Ford, 2009). Coordination and collaboration between the treating and prescribing therapists are highly advisable.

Recently, other drugs and substances (e.g., MDMA/ecstasy, medical marijuana, ketamine) have been investigated in terms of their effect on the symptoms of PTSD. It is expected that such studies will continue and that a role for these treatments will develop over time.

Facilitating Autonomy in Daily Life

29. *Throughout treatment, patients should be assisted in applying adaptive skills to daily life in order to enhance their autonomy and to lessen their dependence on the therapist.* Emotional reliance on the therapist as a source of support, affirmation, and guidance should not ever be viewed judgmentally, however, for this will iatrogenically replicate the self-stigma and self-doubt

that are tragic hallmarks of complex trauma experiences. Nor should it be technically interpreted as merely the regressive residue of an anxious or disorganized attachment style, although that may be a contributing factor due to a history of not having received reliable, responsive, and emotionally affirming and regulated caregiving in formative developmental periods. To a patient who was so deprived, the therapist's attention and caring may feel like "manna from heaven" and the therapist as a savior. Therapists must understand this felt sense of neediness/relief as a sign of the patient's resilient and adaptive ability to seek and value genuine relatedness. This is a strength that can be balanced with autonomous self-reliance when therapy provides a model for a mature caring relationship that the patient can generalize to other adult-to-adult relationships (and to being a caregiver in relationships as a parent or mentor to younger persons). When the therapist also models maintaining reasonable boundaries and limitations, this can simultaneously encourage the patient to both be self-confident and self-reliant, while also building supportive friendships and relationships with available others.

Ending Treatment and Posttreatment Contact

30. *At its best, ending treatment is part of the entire process and is related to the completion of stated goals; thus, it can be a cause for satisfaction and celebration. But, it often holds other meanings as well.* At whatever point treatment comes to an end, it poses special issues and often stirs up patients' feelings of abandonment, grief, fear/anxiety, betrayal, anger, and loss of security, as well as satisfaction. Whenever or however it occurs, the end of treatment is best completed as a mutual process with a clearly demarcated ending. It should be anticipated, prepared for, and should not come as a surprise to the patient. When a therapist must leave practice for some reason and unless it is an urgent situation and leave-taking, the patient should be informed of the situation and be given adequate time to process the change and plan for the future. In any event, *it is incumbent on the therapist not to abandon the patient.* This is especially the case with patients who have been relationally challenging to the therapist on an ongoing basis. In such cases, the therapist might act out a countertransference reaction of frustration or anger toward the patient by terminating treatment without warning or preparation (colloquially this is referred to as "dumping"). When a therapist makes a choice to discontinue a treatment, professional ethics require that they take care to respectfully communicate and discuss reasons to the patient and provide treatment referrals.

It is important to prepare for the possibility that the patient may self-terminate therapy. This can be done by putting an agreement in place that the patient will not abruptly discontinue treatment without a last session including a formal good-bye. The goal is to prevent a premature ending that might be based on miscommunication or misunderstanding. Such terminations may be the result of intensification or reactivation of the patient's CTSD symptoms due to events or circumstances in the patient's life over which the therapist has no influence. They may also occur when transference or countertransference reactions on the part of the patient and/or therapist are not recognized and addressed collaboratively and therapeutically. And, as noted by Kinsler (2017), they may be due to the patient's progress and readiness to end, often when "real life" becomes more meaningful and exceeds the need for therapy. He also noted that some patients leave in a "flight of independence" much like adolescents who leave home for the first time in a "flight of freedom" and urges therapists to understand (and even celebrate) this pattern. In most cases however it behooves the therapist to encourage an ending process, especially given that most abusive families and contexts rarely encourage notice or discussion of such changes and that separations are often abrupt and involve emotional and physical cut-offs. Additionally, terminating therapy without some sort of positive closure and accomplishment can leave the patient in a state of distress that could compromise safety or previous therapeutic gains. Even if limited to a single final session, having a mutually agreed-upon plan for a wrap-up session can be a way for the therapist to help the patient by validating their achievements and self-determination and by offering a farewell (and an invitation to return if issues and symptoms emerge in the future). Patients should be assured that such a return is not seen as a failure or "recidivism" but rather as a "check-in," "tune-up," or resumption of treatment to continue work on unfinished or newly emerged issues.

Finally, after therapy has been concluded, posttreatment contacts should be based on thoughtful prior discussion and agreement between the patient and therapist. Different therapists have their own unique perspectives on how to manage such contacts or communications or whether to have them at all. At the very least, outside relationships should be keep to a minimum and not develop into a friendship or something casual or ongoing. Dual relationships of any sort that might impede a return to and resumption of treatment should not be undertaken. In particular, the development of posttermination romantic and sexual relationships is forbidden as unethical by most professional mental health organizations As previously abused patients are especially susceptible to re-enactments and revictimization, they must be regarded as an especially vulnerable population in particular need of proper boundaries and ethics.

Conclusion

Psychotherapy for adults with CTSDs is widely practiced but still in the early phases of scientific and clinical validation. While awaiting the results of systematic clinical research, therapists can nevertheless benefit from the application of the practice principles and evolving treatment interventions developed specifically for CTSDs and dissociative disorders. Guidelines and models for the treatment of PTSD are applicable to patients with CTSDs, but they cannot be assumed to fully or even effectively sustain engagement in treatment or to ameliorate or resolve the complex self-regulation problems that originate when developmentally adverse interpersonal traumas have derailed or impaired adults' core biopsychosocial functioning. The extant clinical knowledge base suggests that safety-focused, strengths-based, physically as well as psychologically based, collaborative, self-regulation enhancing, self-integrating, avoidance-challenging, individualized approaches to treatment delivered by emotionally healthy and professionally responsible therapists, who have specialized training and professional resources to support this very demanding work, make an important difference in the lives of patients who have had substantial life adversity. Approaches and strategies continue to develop and evolve and therapists are therefore advised to continue their education on the treatment of this population.

References

American Psychological Association. (2002). Criteria for practice guideline development and evaluation [Evaluation Studies]. *American Psychologist, 57*(12), 1048–1051.

American Psychological Association. (2006). Evidence-based practice in psychology. *American Psychologist, 61*(4), 271–285.

American Psychological Association. (2015). Guidelines on trauma competencies for education and training. Retrieved from *www.apa.org/ed/resources/trauma-competencies-training.pdf*.

American Psychological Association. (2017). *Clinical practice guidelines for the treatment of PTSD in adults*. Washington, DC: American Psychological Association.

Bassuk, E. L., Latta, R. E., Sember, R., Raja, S., & Richard, M. (2017). Universal design for underserved populations: Person-centered, recovery-oriented and trauma-informed. *Journal of Health Care for the Poor and Underserved, 28*(3), 896–914.

Bisson, J. I., Roberts, N. P., Andrew, M., Cooper, R., & Lewis, C. (2013). Psychological therapies for chronic post-traumatic stress disorder (PTSD) in adults. *Cochrane Database Systematic Reviews, 12*, CD003388.

Bloom, S. L. (2013). The Sanctuary model. In J. D. Ford & C. A. Courtois (Eds.), *Treating complex traumatic stress disorders in children and adolescents: Scientific foundations and therapeutic models* (pp. 277–294). New York: Guilford Press.

Blue Knot Foundation. (2017). Practice guidelines for treatment of complex trauma and trauma informed care and service delivery. Retrieved from *www.blueknot.org.au/resources/publications/practice-guidelines*.

Blue Knot Foundation. (2019). Practice guidelines for clinical treatment of complex trauma. Retrieved from *www.blueknot.org.au/resources/publications/practice-guidelines*.

Brand, B. L., Myrick, A. C., Loewenstein, R. J., Classen, C. C., Lanius, R., McNary, S. W., . . . Putnam, F. W. (2012). A survey of practices and recommended treatment interventions among expert therapists treating patients with dissociative identity disorder and dissociative disorder not otherwise specified. *Psychological Trauma: Theory, Research, Practice, and Policy, 4*(5), 490–500.

Brand, B. L., McNary, S. W., Myrick, A. C., Loewenstein, R. J., Classen, C. C., Lanius, R. A., . . . Putnam, F. W. (2013). A longitudinal, naturalistic study of dissociative disorder patients treated by community clinicians. *Psychological Trauma: Theory, Research, Practice, and Policy, 5*(4), 301–308.

Branson, C. E., Baetz, C. L., Horwitz, S. M., & Hoagwood, K. E. (2017). Trauma-informed juvenile justice systems: A systematic review of definitions and core components. *Psychological Trauma, 9*(6), 635–646.

Brewin, C. R. (2015). Re-experiencing traumatic events in PTSD: New avenues in research on intrusive memories and flashbacks. *European Journal of Psychotraumatology, 6.*

Briere, J. N. (2004). *Psychological assessment of adult posttraumatic states: Phenomenology, diagnosis, and measurement* (2nd ed.). Washington, DC: American Psychological Association.

Briere, J. N. (2011). *Trauma Symptom Inventory–2 (TSI-2)*. Odessa, FL: Psychological Assessment Resources.

Briere, J. N., & Scott, C. (2014). *Principles of trauma therapy: A guide to symptoms, evaluation, and treatment* (2nd ed.). Thousand Oaks, CA: SAGE.

Brown, D. P. (2009). Assessment of attachment and abuse history, and adult attachment style. In C. A. Courtois & J. D. Ford (Eds.), *Treating complex traumatic stress disorders: An evidence-based guide* (pp. 124–144). New York: Guilford Press.

Cloitre, M. (2015). The "one size fits all" approach to trauma treatment: Should we be satisfied? *European Journal of Psychotraumatology, 6.*

Cloitre, M., Stovall-McClough, K. C., Nooner, K., Zorbas, P., Cherry, S., Jackson, C. L., . . . Petkova, E. (2010). Treatment for PTSD related to childhood abuse: A randomized controlled trial. *American Journal of Psychiatry, 167*(8), 915–924.

Cook, J. M., Newman, E., & the New Haven Trauma Competency Work Group. (2014). A consensus statement on trauma mental health: The New Haven Competency Conference process and major findings. *Psychological Trauma: Theory, Research, Practice and Policy, 6,* 300–307.

Cook, J. M., Rehman, O., Bufka, L., Dinnen, S., & Courtois, C. (2011). Responses of a sample of practicing psychologists to questions about clinical work with trauma and interest in specialized training. *Psychological Trauma, 3*(3), 253–257.

Courtois, C. A. (1999). *Recollections of sexual abuse: Treatment principles and guidelines.* New York: Norton.

Courtois, C. A. (2001). Traumatic stress studies: The need for curricula inclusion. *Journal of Trauma Practice, 1*(1), 33–58.

Courtois, C. A. (2004). Complex trauma, complex reactions: Assessment and treatment. *Psychotherapy: Theory, Research, Practice, Training, 41*(4), 412–425.

Courtois, C. A., & Brown, L. S. (2019). Guideline orthodoxy and resulting limitations of the *American Psychological Association Treatment Guideline for PTSD in Adults: Psychotherapy, 56*(3), 329–339.

Courtois, C. A., & Ford, J. D. (Eds.). (2009). *Treating complex traumatic stress disorders: An evidence-based guide.* New York: Guilford Press.

Courtois, C. A., & Ford, J. D. (2013). *Treating complex trauma: A sequenced relationship-based approach.* New York: Guilford Press.

Courtois, C. A., Ford, J. D., & Cloitre, M. (2009). Best practices in psychotherapy for adults. In C. A. Courtois & J. D. Ford (Eds.), *Treating complex traumatic stress disorders: An evidence-based guide* (pp. 82–103). New York: Guilford Press.

Courtois, C. A., & Gold, S. (2009). The need for inclusion of psychological trauma in the professional curriculum. *Psychological Trauma, 1*(1), 3–23.

De Jongh, A., Resick, P. A., Zoellner, L. A., van Minnen, A., Lee, C. W., Monson, C. M., . . . Bicanic, I. A. (2016). Critical analysis of the current treatment guidelines for complex PTSD in adults. *Depression and Anxiety, 33*(5), 359–369.

Del Re, A. C., Flückiger, C., Horvath, A. O., Symonds, D., & Wampold, B. E. (2012). Therapist effects in the therapeutic alliance–outcome relationship: A restricted-maximum likelihood meta-analysis. *Clinical Psychology Review, 32*(7), 642–649.

Dorrepaal, E., Thomaes, K., Smit, J. H., van Balkom, A. J., Veltman, D. J., Hoogendoorn, A. W., & Draijer, N. (2012). Stabilizing group treatment for complex posttraumatic stress disorder related to child abuse based on psychoeducation and cognitive behavioural therapy: A multisite randomized controlled trial. *Psychotherapy and Psychosomatics, 81*(4), 217–225.

Ducharme, E. L. (2017). Best practices in working with complex trauma and Dissociative Identity Disorder. *Practice Innovations, 2*(3), 150–161.

Eubanks, C. F., Muran, J. C., & Safran, J. D. (2018). Alliance rupture repair: A meta-analysis. *Psychotherapy, 55*(4), 508–519.

Fallot, R., & Harris, M. (2008). Trauma-informed services. In G. Reyes, J. D. Elhai, & J. Ford (Eds.), *The encyclopedia of psychological trauma* (pp. 660–662). Hoboken, NJ: Wiley.

Farber, B. A., Suzuki, J. Y., & Lynch, D. A. (2018). Positive regard and psychotherapy outcome: A meta-analytic review. *Psychotherapy, 55*(4), 411–423.

Fisher, J. (2017). *Healing the fragmented selves of trauma survivors: Overcoming internal self-alienation.* New York: Routledge.

Flückiger, C., Del Re, A. C., Wampold, B. E., & Horvath, A. O. (2018). The alliance in adult psychotherapy: A meta-analytic synthesis. *Psychotherapy, 55*(4), 316–340.

Foa, E., & Jaycox, L. (1999). Cognitive-behavioral treatment of posttraumatic stress disorder. In D. Spiegel (Eds.), *Psychotherapeutic frontiers: New principles and practices* (pp. 23–61). Washington, DC: American Psychiatric Press.

Foa, E. B., McLean, C. P., Zang, Y., Rosenfield, D., Yadin, E., Yarvis, J. S., . . . STRONG STAR Consortium. (2018). Effect of prolonged exposure therapy delivered over 2 weeks vs 8 weeks vs present-centered therapy on PTSD symptom severity in military personnel: A randomized clinical trial. *Journal of the American Medical Association, 319*(4), 354–364.

Forbes, D., Creamer, M., Bisson, J. I., Cohen, J. A., Crow, B. E., Foa, E. B., . . . Ursano, R. J. (2010). A guide to guidelines for the treatment of PTSD and related conditions. *Journal of Traumatic Stress, 23*(5), 537–552.

Ford, J. D. (2017). Complex trauma and complex PTSD. In J. Cook, S. Gold, & C. Dalenberg (Eds.), *Handbook of trauma psychology* (Vol. 1, pp. 322–349). Washington, DC: American Psychological Association.

Ford, J. D. (2018). Trauma memory processing in PTSD psychotherapy: A unifying framework. *Journal of Traumatic Stress, 31,* 933–942.

Ford, J. D., Courtois, C. A., Steele, K., van der Hart, O., & Nijenhuis, E. R. (2005). Treatment of complex posttraumatic self-dysregulation. *Journal of Traumatic Stress, 18*(5), 437–447.

Ford, J. D., Grasso, D. G., Elhai, J. D., & Courtois, C. A. (2015). *Posttraumatic stress disorder: Scientific and professional dimensions* (2nd ed.). New York: Academic Press.

Ford, J. D., & Smith, S. (2008). Complex posttraumatic stress disorder in trauma-exposed adults receiving public sector outpatient substance abuse disorder treatment. *Addiction Research and Theory, 16*(2), 193–203.

Ford, J. D., Steinberg, K. L., Hawke, J., Levine, J., & Zhang, W. (2012). Randomized trial comparison of emotion regulation and relational psychotherapies for PTSD with girls involved in delinquency. *Journal of Clinical Child and Adolescent Psychology, 41*(1), 27–37.

Ford, J. D., Steinberg, K. L., & Zhang, W. (2011). A randomized clinical trial comparing affect regulation and social problem-solving psychotherapies for mothers with victimization-related PTSD. *Behavior Therapy, 42*(4), 560–578.

Friedlander, M. L., Escudero, V., Welmers-van de Poll, M. J., & Heatherington, L. (2018). Meta-analysis of the alliance-outcome relation in couple and family therapy. *Psychotherapy, 55*(4), 356–371.

Friedlander, M. L., Lee, H. H., Shaffer, K. S., & Cabrera, P. (2014). Negotiating therapeutic alliances with a family at impasse. *Psychotherapy, 51*(1), 41–52.

Hamblen, J. L., Norman, S. B., Sonis, J., Phelps, A., Bisson, J., Delgado Nunes, V., Megnin-Viggars, O., . . . Schnurr, P. P. (2019). A guide to PTSD guidelines. *Psychotherapy, 56*(3), 359–373.

Harvey, M. (1996). An ecological view of psychological trauma and trauma recovery. *Journal of Traumatic Stress, 9*, 3–23.

Herman, J. L. (1992). *Trauma and recovery*. New York: Basic Books.

Hoge, C. W., & Chard, K. M. (2018). A window into the evolution of trauma-focused psychotherapies for posttraumatic stress disorder. *Journal of the American Medical Association, 319*(4), 343–345.

Howell, E. F., & Itzkowitz, S. (2016). *The dissociative mind in psychoanalysis: Understanding and working with trauma*. New York: Routledge Press, Taylor & Francis Group.

International Society for the Study of Trauma and Dissociation. (2011). Guidelines for treating dissociative identity disorder in adults. Retrieved from *www.isst-d.org/default.asp?contentID=49*.

International Society for Traumatic Stress Studies. (2012). The ISTSS expert consensus treatment guidelines for complex PTSD in adults. Retrieved from *http://www.istss.org*.

International Society for Traumatic Stress Studies. (2018a). ISTSS guidelines position paper on complex PTSD in adults. Retrieved from *www.istss.org/getattachment/treating-trauma/new-istss-prevention-and-treatment-guidelines/istss_cptsd-position-paper-(adults)_fnl.pdf.aspx*.

International Society for Traumatic Stress Studies. (2018b). ISTSS guidelines position paper on complex PTSD in children and adolescents. Retrieved from *www.istss.org/getattachment/treating-trauma/new-istss-prevention-and-treatment-guidelines/istss_cptsd-position-paper-(child_adol)_fnl.pdf.aspx*.

International Society for Traumatic Stress Studies. (2019). ISTSS treatment guidelines. Retrieved from *www.istss.org/treating-trauma/new-istss-prevention-and-treatment-guidelines.aspx*.

Janet, P. (1889). *L'automatisme psychologique*. Paris: Felix Alcan.

Jenness, J. L., & McLaughlin, K. A. (2015). Towards a person-centered approach to the developmental psychopathology of trauma. *Social Psychiatry and Psychiatric Epidemiology, 50*(8), 1219–1221.

Kaczkurkin, A. N., Zang, Y., Gay, N. G., Peterson, A. L., Yarvis, J. S., Borah, E. V., . . . Consortium, S. S. (2017). Cognitive emotion regulation strategies associated with the DSM-5 posttraumatic stress disorder criteria. *Journal of Traumatic Stress, 30*(4), 343–350.

Kinsler, P. J. (2017). *Complex psychological trauma: The centrality of relationship*. New York: Routledge, Taylor & Francis.

Kinsler, P. J., Courtois, C. A., & Frankel, A. S. (2009). Therapeutic alliance and risk management. In C. A. Courtois & J. D. Ford (Eds.), *Treating complex traumatic stress disorders: An evidence-based guide* (pp. 183–201). New York: Guilford Press.

Kluft, R. P. (1994). Treatment trajectories in multiple personality disorder. *Dissociation, 7*, 63–76.

Krystal, J. H., Davis, L. L., Neylan, T. C., Raskin, M. A., Schnurr, P. P., Stein, M. B., . . . Huang, G. D. (2017). It is time to address the crisis in the pharmacotherapy of posttraumatic stress disorder: A consensus statement of the PTSD Psychopharmacology Working Group [Letter]. *Biological Psychiatry, 82*(7), e51–e59.

Layne, C., Beck, C., Rimmasch, H., Southwick, J., Moreno, M., & Hobfoll, S. (2008). Promoting "resilient" posttraumatic adjustment in childhood and beyond. In D. Brom, R. Pat-Horenczyk, & J. D. Ford (Eds.), *Treating traumatized children: Risk, resilience, and recovery* (pp. 13–47). London: Routledge.

Levenson, J. (2017). Trauma-informed social work practice. *Social Work, 62*(2), 105–113.

Markowitz, J. C., Petkova, E., Neria, Y., Van Meter, P. E., Zhao, Y., Hembree, E., . . . Marshall, R. D. (2015). Is exposure necessary?: A randomized clinical trial of interpersonal psychotherapy for PTSD. *American Journal of Psychiatry, 172*(5), 430–440.

Martin, S. L., Ashley, O. S., White, L., Axelson, S., Clark, M., & Burrus, B. (2017). Incorporating trauma-informed care into school-based programs. *Journal of School Health, 87*(12), 958–967.

McEwen, B. S. (2017). Allostasis and the epigenetics of brain and body health over the life course: The brain on stress. *JAMA Psychiatry, 74*(6), 551–552.

McFetridge, J., Swan, A. H., Heke, S., Karatzias, T., Greenberg, N., Kitchiner, N., et al. (2017). *Guideline for the treatment and planning of services for complex post-traumatic stress disorder in adults*. Edinburgh: UK Psychological Trauma Society.

Musicaro, R. M., Spinazzola, J., Arvidson, J., Swaroop, S. R., Goldblatt Grace, L., Yarrow, A., . . . Ford, J. D. (2019). The complexity of adaptation to childhood polyvictimization in youth and young adults: Recommendations for multidisciplinary responders. *Trauma, Violence, and Abuse, 20,* 81–98.

Niejenhuis, J. B., Owen, J., Valentine, J. C., Winkeljohn Black, S., Halford, T. C., Parazak, S. E., . . . Hilsenroth, M. (2018). Therapeutic alliance, empathy, and genuineness in individual adult psychotherapy: A meta-analytic review. *Psychotherapy Research, 28*(4), 593–605.

Nijdam, M. J., van der Meer, C. A. I., van Zuiden, M., Dashtgard, P., Medema, D., Qing, Y., . . . Olff, M. (2018). Turning wounds into wisdom: Posttraumatic growth over the course of two types of trauma-focused psychotherapy in patients with PTSD. *Journal of Affective Disorders, 227,* 424–431.

Norcross, J. C., & Lambert, M. J. (2018). Psychotherapy relationships that work III. *Psychotherapy, 55*(4), 4–8.

Oehen, P., Traber, R., Widmer, V., & Schnyder, U. (2013). A randomized, controlled pilot study of MDMA (± 3,4-Methylenedioxymethamphetamine)-assisted psychotherapy for treatment of resistant, chronic post-traumatic stress disorder (PTSD). *Journal of Psychopharmacology, 27*(1), 40–52.

Ogden, P., Minton, K., & Pain, C. (2006). *Trauma and the body: A sensorimotor approach to psychotherapy*. New York: Norton.

Opler, L., Grennan, M., & Ford, J. D. (2009). Psychopharmacological treatment of complex traumatic stress disorders. In C. A. Courtois & J. D. Ford (Eds.), *Treating complex traumatic stress disorders: An evidence-based guide* (pp. 329–350). New York: Guilford Press.

Pearlman, L. A., & Caringi, J. (2009). Living and working self-reflectively to address vicarious trauma. In C. A. Courtois & J. D. Ford (Eds.), *Treating complex traumatic stress disorders: An evidence-based guide* (pp. 202–222). New York: Guilford Press.

Pearlman, L. A., & Courtois, C. A. (2005). Clinical applications of the attachment framework: Relational treatment of complex trauma. *Journal of Traumatic Stress, 18*(5), 449–459.

Phoenix Australia–Center for Posttraumatic Mental Health. (2013). Australian guidelines for the treatment of acute stress disorder and posttraumatic stress disorder. Retrieved from *www.phoenixaustralia.org/wp-content/uploads/2015/03/phoenix-asd-ptsd-guidelines.pdf.*

Porges, S. W. (2011). *The polyvagal theory: Neurophysiological foundations of emotions, attachment, communication, and self-regulation*. New York: Norton.

Purtle, J. (2018, August 5). Systematic review of evaluations of trauma-informed organizational interventions that include staff trainings. *Trauma, Violence, and Abuse.* [Epub ahead of print]

Sanders, M. R., & Hall, S. L. (2018). Trauma-informed care in the newborn intensive care unit: Promoting safety, security and connectedness. *Journal of Perinatology, 38*(1), 3–10.

Schnyder, U., & Cloitre, M. (Eds.). (2015). *Evidence based treatments for trauma-related psychological disorders*. Zurich, Switzerland: Springer.

Schnyder, U., Ehlers, A., Elbert, T., Foa, E. B., Gersons, B. P., Resick, P. A., . . . Cloitre, M. (2015). Psychotherapies for PTSD: What do they have in common? *European Journal of Psychotraumatology, 6.*

Schore, A. N. (2003). *Affect dysregulation and disorders of the self*. New York: Norton.

Schwartz, R. C., Schwartz, M. F., & Galperin, L. (2009). Internal family system therapy. In

C. A. Courtois & J. D. Ford (Eds.), *Treating complex traumatic stress disorders: An evidence-based guide* (pp. 353–370). New York: Guilford Press.

Siegel, D. J. (2009). *The developing mind: How relationships and the brain interact to shape who we are* (2nd ed.). New York: Guilford Press.

Simiola, V., Neilson, E. C., Thompson, R., & Cook, J. M. (2015). Preferences for trauma treatment: A systematic review of the empirical literature. *Psychological Trauma, 7*(6), 516–524.

Sloan, D. M., Marx, B. P., Lee, D. J., & Resick, P. A. (2018). A brief exposure-based treatment vs cognitive processing therapy for posttraumatic stress disorder: A randomized noninferiority clinical trial. *Journal of the American Medical Association Psychiatry, 75*(3), 233–239.

Sprang, G., Ford, J. D., Kerig, P. K., & Bride, B. (2019). Defining secondary traumatic stress and developing targeted assessments and interventions: Lessons learned from research and leading experts. *Traumatology, 25,* 72–81.

Stavropoulous, P., & Keselman, K. (2012). *"The last frontier:" Practice guidelines for treatment of complex trauma and trauma informed care and service delivery.* Melbourne, Australia: Adult Survivors of Abuse (now Blue Knot Foundation).

Sullivan, C. M., Goodman, L. A., Virden, T., Strom, J., & Ramirez, R. (2018). Evaluation of the effects of receiving trauma-informed practices on domestic violence shelter residents. *American Journal of Orthopsychiatry, 88*(5), 563–570.

U.S. Department of Veterans Affairs and Department of Defense. (2017). *VA/DOD clinical practice guideline for the management of posttraumatic stress disorder and acute stress disorder (Version 3.0)*. Washington, DC: Author.

Wang, S., Wilson, J. P., & Mason, J. W. (1996). Stages of decompensation in combat-related posttraumatic stress disorder: A new conceptual model. *Integrative Physiological and Behavioral Science, 31*(3), 237–253.

CHAPTER 4

Therapeutic Alliance and Risk Management

CHRISTINE A. COURTOIS

Complex traumas such as child abuse and attachment failure are relational events and experiences, occurring most often within families, not only between parents and other relatives and children, but also in other personal or fiduciary relationships. As a result, complex trauma has a profound effect on not only physiological/biological and psychological development but also the ability to form close and trusting relationships (Edwards, Holden, Felitti, & Anda, 2003). Moreover, complex trauma often is followed by revictimization in various relationships throughout the lifespan. However, although survivors of complex trauma have been *hurt in relationships,* paradoxically, *relationships can be a core component of healing from these injuries.* At times, special relationships, such as close friendships, mentorships, marriage/partnerships, and, in some cases, parenting of one's own children can be restorative, for example, when they provide the attachment security the individual needs to learn new ways of relating to and trusting others. For individuals for whom no place has been safe in their lives (Spinazzola, van der Kolk, & Ford, 2018), psychotherapy may also provide the needed "safe haven" within which to modify old relational patterns that were built on abuse, exploitation, betrayal, and disregard. Stated simply, whether it occurs within or outside of psychotherapy, healing from complex trauma (especially when this involves a fundamental compromise of primary attachment bonds) occurs in safe, dependable, responsive, kind, and bounded relationships. Therefore, it is essential that psychotherapy for survivors of complex trauma be carefully structured and sensitively provided to ensure that the therapeutic relationship is indeed genuinely safe for the client.

This chapter begins with a brief review of the impact of complex trauma and their outcomes and disorders (complex traumatic stress disorders [CTSDs]) on survivors' relationships and defines some major parameters of psychotherapy that help promote relational healing of traumatized persons. The client's relational history and the "lessons of abuse" are brought to the treatment relationship in ways that can create barriers to the development of a collaborative working alliance, despite a therapist's best efforts. They may also create tumultuous and challenging relationships that test client and therapist alike. Chu (1988) wrote of the treatment traps (including intense relational demands and ambivalence, extreme mistrust coupled with neediness and dependence, dysregulated emotions and behaviors, substance abuse and addictions in some, and ongoing risk taking or lack of ability to maintain personal safety) facing therapists in the course of their work with traumatized individuals, some of whom may still be in abusive or unsafe circumstances, or under the influence or alcohol or other drugs. In a later article, he characterized the treatment of previously abused adults as "the therapeutic roller coaster," because it can be highly intense and unstable, often in unpredictable, perplexing, and paradoxical ways. Chu advised therapists to be mindful of the many relational challenges that attend treatment with this population and the risks that they can pose for both therapists and their clients (Chu, 1992). This caution is especially relevant for trainees and novice therapists, although it applies to all, no matter how experienced. It is unfortunate that many seasoned therapists received little or no mention of trauma in their formal clinical training and practica and have had to "make do" or supplement their training, usually with attendance at continuing education courses. Courtois and Gold (2009) discussed how the lack of systemic training on the topic of trauma and the treatment of traumatized individuals and groups is less than ideal and may lead to "therapeutic misadventures." The second part of this chapter includes a review of some of these areas of risk, with a focus on their management within the treatment structure and process.

The Relational Histories of Individuals with CTSDs

The histories of individuals with CTSDs typically include a variety of repeated abusive and neglectful experiences, beginning in the family of origin, usually with parents or other primary caregivers, and spreading outward to the extended family and beyond, to others known to the child in some way, some within fiduciary relationships (i.e., teachers, coaches, clergy, therapists, bosses, and superior officers). This familial and relational context makes processing and resolving these experiences extremely difficult, since these are not typically benign contexts involving the occasional act of abuse. Rather, these frequently chronically abusive and/or neglectful environments *combine* various and cumulative combinations of emotional, physical, and sexual abuse; parental substance abuse; domestic violence; a parent or parents with mental illness or other impairment or limitation (including their own history of unresolved trauma and loss); and the loss of a parent through death, separation and divorce, outright abandonment, and criminal incarceration. A dose–

response relationship between the number of types of abuse suffered in childhood and later neurobiological, psychological and medical effects has been found (Edwards et al., 2003) modified by a variety of factors including resilience, duration, course of development, and so on. Recent research has also acknowledged the particularly virulent impact of emotional abuse (including forms such as ongoing antipathy, bullying, degradation, emotional smothering, and overdependence) and neglect that can involve the failure to provide for basic needs (housing, food, hygiene, clothing, schooling) in addition to indifference/nonresponse and nonprotection of the child (Hopper, Grossman, Spinazzola, & Zucker, 2019).

Multiple-category childhood victimization (also known as *polyvictimization*; Turner, Finkelhor, & Ormrod, 2010) has important consequences for how children view themselves and their worlds, influencing their identity, self-esteem, and relationships with and ability to be intimate with others. When abuse and neglect start early and continue over much of childhood and adolescence and especially when they are perpetrated by a parent/caregiver, when they intensify over time, and when there is no escape and no help from others (Spinazzola et al., 2018), how does the child understand and make sense of it? In general, persons who experience chronic abuse *come to believe, at a very deep level, that the world is unsafe, and that other people are not benign, safe, or trustworthy*. By virtue of their repeated experiences of abuse and neglect, they come to "know" *that they are somehow to blame and deserving of both the abuse and of not being responded to or protected*. They feel "in their bones" that they are bad and somehow highly defective, that it is fruitless to hope, that they will never be safe, and that they must not show or disclose their pain, as they will be stigmatized, ridiculed, and abandoned. They may look to others for help, but simultaneously they often expect to be beyond assistance and to be further abused and betrayed by the person(s) to whom they turn, including therapists and other professionals (unfortunately something they might have also experienced previously). Erik Erikson (1950) called this *basic mistrust* that can start very early in life and serve as a problematic foundation for future developmental tasks.

More recently, and building on Erikson's theory, findings from developmental psychology (formerly known as developmental psychopathology and now more appropriately termed *developmental traumatology*) have expanded understanding of the relational circumstances that usually precede frank physical, emotional, and/or sexual abuse in a family. Numerous researchers investigating the *quality* of early attachment experiences between primary caregivers (usually parents) and young children (before age 2) have found that seriously disrupted attachment and the lack of security it produces, without repair or intervention for the child, in and of itself, can be traumatic (labeled *attachment trauma* by Allen [2001], and Schore [2003a, 2003b]). Difficulties in early attachment patterns between infants and primary caregivers usually precede and interact with adverse childhood events and experiences over the course of childhood and adolescence.

In developing *attachment theory,* British psychiatrist John Bowlby (1969, 1980) pioneered the study of connection between caregiver and young child, and the significance of its quality to human development. He noted that children need a stable and reliable caregiver who is affectively attuned to them as valued and unique individuals, who teaches them social interaction skills and emotional identification and regulation through coregulating, and who offers soothing and protection from overstimulation and threat/danger. Bowlby (1969) introduced the concept of what he termed an *inner working model* (IWM) to describe cognitive and emotional representations of self and others that typically operate automatically and unconsciously after they are learned in the context of attachment experiences. These form the basis for adult relational style and interpersonal relationships and behavior. Four primary attachment styles/IWMs in childhood have been identified, each of which has a corresponding style in adulthood: (1) *secure;* (2) *insecure–ambivalent/resistant;* (3) *insecure–fearful/avoidant;* and (4) *insecure–disorganized/disoriented.* Accumulated evidence now strongly suggests that the majority of children who have been chronically abused and neglected develop one of the insecure and/or disorganized/disoriented attachment styles (Lyons-Ruth & Jacobovitz, 1999) that impacts their sense of self (both within and apart from relationships) and their view and ability to interact with others. Conscious and nonconscious beliefs, such as "No one is trustworthy," "It's a dog-eat-dog world," "Everyone is out to get their own," "To feel safe, I need to be in control," "I feel disconnected from other people," "Nobody gets to me," "I don't need anyone," "I am bad," and "I deserve to be treated badly by others," influence the quality of individuals' interactions and relationships.

When interactions are disappointing in some way, these beliefs get reinforced and can become a "closed loop" of erroneous reasoning that arises from the child's needs to protect themselves in the crucial relationship with the primary caregiver (see Chapter 2 for discussion of the "survival brain"). These styles, which research has determined are relatively stable over the life course, are subject to modification according to individual factors, such as the child's temperament, genetic profile, personal resilience, and perceptual style; contextual factors, such as culture and community; and idiosyncratic life events and experiences. Notably, these IWMs can be updated through new relational experiences with individuals (especially those with a secure attachment style) who convey personalized interest that is responsive and respectful. It is on this basis that the importance of the relationship in the treatment of clients with experiences of complex interpersonal trauma is founded.

Evidence-Based Psychotherapy Relationships

Research in psychotherapy effectiveness has largely focused on treatment provided according to manual-based protocols (Binder, 2004), designed in part to eliminate variations between therapists. In contrast, however, a long line of *therapeutic outcome research* (not trauma-focused) suggests that it is *pre-*

cisely these individual therapeutic relational differences, a unique part of each treatment relationship, that contribute to and predict outcome (Hubble, Duncan, & Miller, 1999) and that these have been almost totally dismissed in the available clinical practice guidelines. Client factors account for approximately 40% of therapeutic change; the therapeutic relationship, for 30%; expectancy effects, for 15%; and specific therapeutic techniques, for only 15% (Hubble et al., 1999; Norcross, 2011; Norcross & Lambert, 2019). Gelso and Silverberg (2016, p. 154) succinctly stated the case: "The relationship that exists between psychotherapist and client is almost universally viewed as a key factor in the success or failure of psychotherapy across all theoretical orientations."

Recently, the Society for the Advancement of Psychotherapy, Division 29, of the American Psychological Association published the third special issue of its journal *Psychotherapy* devoted to *evidence-based psychotherapy relationships* that were framed within the work of the Third Interdivisional (Divisions 17 and 29) American Psychological Association Task Force on Evidence-Based Relationships and Responsiveness. In the special issue, the devaluation of the therapy relationship in contemporary treatment guidelines and evidence-based practices is discussed and challenged. The findings reported for each of the various relational elements of psychotherapy are especially significant, because they were based on a review of the literature and a meta-analysis of the aggregate research studies on each element. Expert consensus by Task Force members regarding the findings of the meta-analyses deemed nine of the relationship elements as demonstrably effective (alliance in adult, child and adolescent, and couple and family therapy; collaboration; goal consensus; cohesion in group therapy; empathy; positive regard and affirmation; and collecting and delivering client feedback), seven as probably effective (congruence/genuineness, real relationship, emotional expression, cultivating positive expectations, promoting treatment credibility, managing countertransference, and repairing alliance rupture), and one as promising but with insufficient research to judge (self-disclosure and immediacy). The consensus conclusion was that decades of research evidence and clinical experience converge in supporting the substantial and consistent contributions of the psychotherapy relationship to outcome, independent of the type of treatment or the technique used.

By and large, these studies were with clinical populations with a variety of symptoms and mental health conditions and were not trauma-specific; nevertheless, they certainly apply to complex trauma treatment, although additional research on this specific type of treatment is needed. To date, one systematic review of evidence-based psychotherapy relationship variables in psychological treatment for adults who experienced trauma-related distress has been undertaken (Ellis, Simiola, Brown, Courtois, & Cook, 2018). Results of this review indicate that the alliance was predictive of or associated with a reduction in various symptoms. The authors called for additional research on the role of evidence-based psychotherapy relationships in the treatment of trauma survivors to help researchers, clinicians, and educators improve therapist training, as well as client engagement and retention in treatment.

Technique or Relationship or Both?

The consensus among therapists treating the severely traumatized is that *both technique and relationship* are important influences on outcome. Researchers are now studying this very issue as it pertains to the treatment of CTSDs. Cloitre, Stovall-McClough, Miranda, and Chemtob (2004) reported that "in the treatment of childhood abuse-related PTSD [posttraumatic stress disorder], the therapeutic alliance and the mediating influence of emotion regulation capacity appear to have significant roles in successful outcome" (p. 411). They also noted that two specific areas of technique are important in treating CTSDs: (1) teaching of stabilization/emotional regulation/self-soothing (what might also be labeled as *present-centered treatment*) and (2) processing of traumatic experiences. Each area requires specialized training, approaches, and interventions; therefore, therapists must be skilled and comfortable working in each.

Clients with complex trauma histories, especially those that occurred in the context of insecure attachment, often have emotional regulation deficits that may in turn cause reliance on a variety of problematic behaviors (i.e., addictions, compulsions, self-injury, chronic suicidality) in the interest of self-soothing that helps them with emotional and self-regulation. Thus, therapists need a repertoire of skills and methods to help clients approach rather than avoid emotion, and to learn to tolerate and modulate a variety of emotional states through more adaptive self-regulation and self-soothing strategies within the supportive context of the relationship. Therapists also must be able to tolerate their own reactions when working with these maladaptive coping strategies that often are based on self-harm and self-invalidation. A variety of available workbooks now provide specific information, guidance, and a series of exercises and worksheets on these various topics (Allen, 2005; Boon, Steele, & van der Hart, 2011; Cloitre, Cohen, & Koenen, 2006; Conterio & Lader, 1998; Copeland & Harris, 2000; Neff & Germer, 2017; Jobes, 2006; Linehan, 1993, 2017; Miller; 1994; Najavits, 2002; Porges & Dana, 2018; Schwartz, 2017; Vermilyea, 2000), and specialized workshops and training programs are now available (often under the topic heading of stabilization or emotional regulation skills), some of which include supervision and certification of practitioners in that particular method.

In addition to these important interventions geared toward client self-regulation, the consensus of many other clinicians and clinical researchers strongly supports the view that *the therapy relationship is itself a major vehicle of change* for this treatment population. In his recent book on the topic, Kinsler (2018) chose as his subtitle "the centrality of relationship." Optimally, the treatment relationship models a secure and responsive attachment style and provides containment of the client's anxiety, the opportunity for expression of other core emotions, a context within which to work out relational issues that arise in the therapeutic dyad and elsewhere, and a basic *valuing of or validation* of self and personhood that the client may never have had. Clients often express a variant of the following quote during the course of or at the end of their treatment: "You saw me and let me be me"; "You treated me like a person and not an 'it' or an irritant"; "You taught me by example"; "You both challenged and supported me"; "You showed me that you cared."

A healing therapy relationship handles relational distress, including mistrust, hypervigilance, and mistakes made by each member of the dyad, without defensiveness, retaliation, or detachment/abandonment on the part of the therapist. As such, it becomes a model for what can be. As attachment becomes more secure over the course of treatment, emotions become more accessible and less onerous, the client's sense of identity and self-regard increase, and relationship skills mature. As a result, the client has a new template (or IWM) termed *earned security* for self-understanding and relationships and new abilities to apply interpersonally.

The remainder of this chapter covers some aspects of what has been learned from available research studies in attempting to create this type of relationship with complex trauma clients, direct clinical experience, reading of expert literature, peer consultation, supervision, personal reflection, and professional training. Guidance is offered on how to approach the treatment relationship, as well as manage the risks inherent in it, because the relationship itself (since it so often is a reminder of relationships with parents and other caregivers and authority figures) tends to elicit strong feelings and reactions in the client and subsequently in the therapist. As noted earlier, without forethought, preparation, and specialized training, treatment mistakes—including major and serious misalliances and misadventures—can develop, an unfortunately common occurrence in the treatment of those with CTSDs including the dissociative disorders. My purpose in this chapter is to avoid or to offset some of these difficulties and mistakes by increasing awareness of their possibility and some the dynamics surrounding them.

A "Working Alliance"

Virtually all schools or orientations of psychotherapy discuss helpful qualities in the clinician–client relationship. It is the *quality of the therapeutic relationship that is of central concern*. The central features for most schools and writers include a sense that both clinician and client have shared goals, a common language (and, for that matter, a mutual recognition that there are trauma-based experiences for which there is no adequate language; see Dalenberg, 2000, p. 59), and a mutual respect for what they shared and learned together. The therapist must be open and responsive to the uniqueness of the client and work hard at understanding the client's issues, beliefs, and style. Among other things, this involves providing acceptance for any and all emotions. The therapist understands that acceptance and reflection are extremely significant in countering the invalidation and abuse of the past. In neurobiological terms, they help to stimulate new neuronal pathways that may literally change the client's brain and how it functions in relationship (see Chapter 2). Strategies such as these based on findings from neuroscience, the field of developmental psychopathology/traumatology, and attachment studies, have been labeled *interpersonal neurobiology* by Schore (2003a) and Siegel (2007). These are designed to assist the client in exploring and learning about self in the context of a relationship that is responsive and accepting. Moreover, the client can learn important self-regulation skills, such as emotional identification, discrimination, and modulation, healthy means of self-calming, and effective interpersonal response, negotiation, and action. In the treatment, the therapist strives to be "interpersonally transparent" (discussed more below) to counter the client's lack of information about relationship dynamics and to bolster the client's trust and security. Thus, the relationship becomes *catalyst, context,* and *container* for interpersonal experimentation and learning (Kinsler, Courtois, & Frankel, 2009).

Components of a Working Alliance with Complex Trauma Clients

Working alliances with trauma survivors are characterized primarily by the provision of basic interpersonal and environmental safety within the relationship (Herman, 1992). As a starting point, therapists must work from the principle of "Do no *more* harm" (Courtois, 1999, 2015), as they understand that their clients have been previously harmed (unfortunately and tragically, some in prior therapeutic and other types of professional relationships). They must seek to be responsive and emotionally accessible, yet with clear boundaries and limitations. Frankel's (2002) helpful list of central components of establishing safe treatment for this population is expanded upon here:

Trust and Testing

The clinician cannot and should not expect automatic trust on the part of the client, especially early on. Clients may present as totally untrusting and even contemptuous of the therapist's efforts to make a connection (a stance primarily related to the detached/avoidant IWM) or, alternatively and paradoxically, as totally trusting and dependent on the therapist (a premature and untested global trust expressed primarily by those with a preoccupied/anxious IWM). Those with a disorganized IWM veer between brittle trust and extreme mistrust, inconsistently and unpredictably moving toward attachment, then moving away from it, and they may be quite dissociative. Obviously, these inconsistent behaviors can be very confusing and are often associated with the diagnosis of borderline personality disorder, which is comparable in major ways to complex PTSD (Ford & Courtois, 2014). Whatever the presenting style, therapists start from the position that they must earn the client's trust (i.e., by having words match behaviors and vice versa; by expressing consistent interest in the individual's welfare; and by being reliable, steady, and reasonable in interactions). If and when trust develops, it does so *within the context of relational testing*. Trauma survivors, having been schooled in ways of betrayal and violation of personal boundaries (*betrayal trauma*; Freyd, 1996), know little about trust or trustworthiness, as the behaviors and signals indicative of trust have been crossed. Trust that arises in the therapy relationship is hard-earned and can be long in coming and, in some cases, remains limited. Few warning signs are more powerful to a trauma survivor than a clinician who asks or expects to be trusted or takes the client's trust for granted, and/or who takes mistrust personally rather than using it as a mechanism to understand the client's betrayal history and learned schema about self and others. Tests of trustworthiness are, at best, not failed rather than passed. Clients who claims to *"totally* trust you" early in therapy are likely to be placating the therapist as a dangerous potential betrayer, expressing extreme dependence without reasonable testing, trying to caretake the therapist into caring about them, or trying to get the therapist to endorse them as "special." In these scenarios, the client does not actually trust that the therapist will act in a manner that is caring and trustworthy. More specifically, these clients do not believe that the therapist will see them for themselves, and fear that anyone who does actually see them will see only their subjective "badness" and join them in their self-contempt before rejecting and abandoning them.

Blame and Behavior

Safety grows when therapists do not blame clients for their troubles, problems, lifestyles, "choices," failings, symptoms, and behaviors that appear to be (or actually are) manipulative. These behaviors usually developed as protective or adaptive strategies (survivor skills) and resulted from what clients learned and/or did not learn in formative relationships and in conditions of abuse and neglect in contexts that were generally entrapping and not easily escaped. Child victims and adult survivors of complex trauma (whether it occurred on a consistent or more ambient basis) are used to being blamed for all bad things in their lives, blame they have internalized. They perfectly illustrate the admonition that if blaming someone for their problems would help, then the client would have fully recovered years ago. An adequate response requires therapeutic steadiness and the ability to nonjudgmentally point out and reflect on problematic behaviors with the client, in other words, *to contain and analyze rather than react or criticize.* This can be an especially potent opportunity to problem-solve other means of coping with the client. Yet this process is not as easy as it might sound, since boundaries and limitations may be tested again and again. Therapists should be prepared to not only negotiate with clients but also hold to their standards and boundaries, as doing so replicates the limit setting of good parenting. Therapists are encouraged to consistently "reinforce the right thing" (Linehan, 1993).

Therapists should practice unconditional regard (Rogers, 1951) toward the client as a unique and worthy individual while being conditional about behavior. Clients who refuse to comply with basic guidelines and boundaries may need to be respectfully "invited" out of treatment until they change their behavior or increase their motivation or work ethic, at which point, they might be invited to reengage (Linehan, 1993). It is an unfortunate reality that some clients are not motivated to make changes, are totally depressed, hopeless, and in despair about having anything better, that they may be in relationships that inhibit, discourage, or punish change, or may not have "hit bottom" sufficiently to engage in change.

Shame and Symptoms

It is critically important that therapists not shame clients for their troubles, failings, symptoms, and behavioral repertoires (even in the case of "disinviting" them and stopping a treatment). The likelihood is high that they have already been shamed mightily by past traumatic and other relational experiences and are contemptuous of themselves and their needs. As a result, they bring their shame with them to treatment, where they may engage in reenactment behaviors. They require helpers who can be *sensitive to their shame* and to their shame-bound and shaming identity and behaviors, without adding to it while helping them to explore their negative self-worth and sense of being apart from/less than other humans. Moreover, to paraphrase Wurmser (1981) on shame and guilt: "Guilt brings things into therapy; shame keeps it out." Survivors may be very secretive due to their personal shame and quite dissociative in response to feeling this emotion. Therapists must be sensitive to clients with such dynamics, again understanding them as self-protective strategies in response to experiences of humiliation and being treated like an object of someone else's gratification or need, rather than as character flaws or solely as clients' intransigence or manipulation. It is likely that shame-bound dynamics will lessen as trust in the therapist develops, as shame issues are resolved, and self-understanding and self-compassion increase, a gradual process in most cases.

Consistency and Connection

The clinician must provide consistency in terms of personal style and behavior both within and outside the session, appointment times (start and finish), punctuality, and availability between sessions. Consistency applies to attachment, to the therapist's willingness to engage in a "close-enough" connection with the client that attends to the client's degree of comfort or discomfort, as some require more closeness or distance than others. Regardless, connection with, reliability of style and response, and support are essential elements of healing, especially from relational and interpersonal maltreatment. Real connection with others, including the therapist, often takes a long time and much testing to develop, but once it does, it may provide a model for other supportive relationships and generalize to them.

Humility

The clinician must have or must learn personal humility—the quality of not "being the authority on high" with all the answers or of not taking oneself too seriously. Schore (2003b) comments on *relational repair as a core strategy in the development of secure relationships*. The therapist must be interpersonally aware and acknowledge errors, blunders, and imperfections, ready and willing to engage in relational repair. This includes not being afraid to express their own emotions (in a manner that communicates a sense of responsibility to the client and their relationship, but not in any way to preempt or overshadow the client's emotions such as upset and anger), and working to repair damage to the therapeutic relationship when it occurs. Trauma survivors are not used to relationships with people who discuss and problem-solve issues in ways that are respectful, and who admit errors and foibles. This makes repair of therapeutic mistakes both difficult and incredibly helpful.

Competent clinicians maintain clear and firm boundaries and reveal only a modicum of information about their personal lives (and then only when there is a clear therapeutic rationale for such disclosure), but they judiciously use and disclose their feelings and reactions *within the treatment relationship* in order to be more transparent to the client, as a means of modeling communication and collaboration, and to break what was often a process of "gaslighting" the client's emotions by perpetrators skilled at deceit, deception, and denial. Dalenberg (2000),who studied individuals who had completed trauma treatment, commented on this relationship issue. Her study participants reported feeling that they would have benefited had their therapists been more transparent about their reactions and feelings "in the moment." Without this, these former clients reported they were left wondering and anxious about how their therapist *really* felt; this was especially the case with anger. They reported that when therapist anger was not openly acknowledged, it tended to get acted out, either passively or more directly, in ways that damaged rather than strengthened the relationship. This client feedback offers crucial information about one of the most difficult emotions for both trauma survivors and therapists. Therapists have a vital healing opportunity to model emotional acknowledgement and appropriate and bounded verbal expression, separating it from being expressed or acted out in hostile and destructive ways (i.e., aggressive outbursts and verbalizations, violent behavior, retribution, cutoffs). Importantly, *the parties can be angry with one another, acknowledge it rather than act it out, and still be in the relationship one with the other*. These relational experiences may be a first for the client and were not likely part of their repertoire from past interactions. As such, they can be profoundly influential in changing relational understandings and separating them from the past.

Demeanor

Safety grows when the clinician's demeanor is warm, kind, calm, gentle, interested, and empathically attuned and when they have physical prosody. Calm demeanor and empathic attunement contribute to a *holding environment* (Winnicott, 1965), within which respect is conveyed. It is in direct contrast to the ways abuse survivors are accustomed to being treated. Being treated with respect and attunement may initially be uncomfortable and may even be challenged or outright rejected by the client due to discomfort or shame. Therapists must understand this dynamic and not take such responses personally, and instead seek to provide a degree of closeness/distance that is most comfortable and workable for the client. When the therapist's attunement and empathy are accepted and internalized, they provide conditions for personal growth and change.

Awareness

Safety grows as the clinician is aware (mindful) of their own emotional states, life stresses, and countertransference and countertrauma reactions, and is willing to talk with clients about these "awarenesses," when it is appropriate to do so (Dalenberg, 2000; Pearlman & Courtois, 2005; Pearlman & Saakvitne, 1995; Schwartz, 2000). Therapist mindfulness is being promoted across all major treatment orientations, from psychoanalysis to cognitive-behavioral to somatosensory treatment, as a necessary component for client development (Fonagy, 1997; Linehan, 1993; Ogden, Pain, & Minton, 2006; Siegel, 2007; see also chapters in Parts II–IV of this volume). Psychophysiological synchrony and relational attunement communicate implicitly and contribute directly to the client's ability to self-explore, engage in identity development, and increase their overall well-being (Schore, 2003a, 2003b). Research findings offer support that such attunement on the part of a significant other can lead to development of new neural pathways in the brain that, in turn, can lead to changed behavior and a more secure attachment style. As noted earlier, as opposed to this in-session openness and transparency, therapists are encouraged to maintain discretion in disclosing much about their personal lives, so that the focus of the treatment does not shift to the therapist rather than remaining on the client. As these clients are highly interpersonally responsive to the needs of others and have learned to be caretakers or controllers early in life, therapists need to be aware of the potential for this dynamic to play out in the treatment dyad. It is a reenactment that is best noted and discussed when it takes place, with the client given new options for interactions (Courtois, 2010).

Professionalism

Safety is also founded on the therapist's professionalism. Most mental health professions recommend providing the client with a document or a contract that includes pertinent information regarding the therapist's (or organization's) practice, "the rules of the road," including, among others:

- Articulated practice policies involving boundaries and limitations, and methods of contact (something that has grown in importance with the advent of multiple electronic channels of communication and accessibility via social media).
- Defined and defensible billing practices.
- Maintenance of a confidential setting and clear information about when

confidentiality of session content might be breached (in the case of danger to self or others, legal mandates to report disclosures of past or present child abuse, reports of therapist sexual boundary violations, or judicial orders, all dependent on the jurisdiction).

- Open discussion and problem solving regarding boundary crossings and their effects.
- Maintenance of records that contain behaviorally based information and observations and that are respectful of the client.
- Maintenance of meetings within the established parameters and office setting, unless there is a well-planned and discussed reason for other arrangements.
- A planned ending of treatment, usually with a request that the client agree to return for a final session rather than precipitously ending without any discussion at the point of leave-taking. This is to identify or correct any misunderstandings and to provide a closing to the work.

In summary, *the essential therapeutic task is to provide relational conditions that encourage the safety of the attachment between client and therapist,* and safety in a more general sense. It is not unusual for clients with complex trauma histories to comment that they have never been treated this way or been seen as a unique individual nor had their safety or well-being emphasized, or their preferences taken into consideration. It is through provision of such conditions that the therapy work can lead to a change in the client's attachment style. The client can move to the *earned secure* attachment style within the therapy that can then extend to extratherapeutic relationships (Valory, 2007).

Importantly, *relational attunement increases client self-development and self-regulation, giving them new experiences in the world.* It includes the process of attending closely and reflecting on the relational meaning of therapeutic events and reactions. Perhaps the most important question for the therapist to ask repeatedly is "How will this (considered) statement/intervention increase the client's *reflection on self and on self-in-relationship?*" A safe relationship in which one may experientially explore is the goal of the treatment process rather than insight or correct interpretation on the part of the therapist (See Chapters 23–25 for discussion of these issues and approaches). Relational safety supports the client in learning new ways of seeing and understanding the self (including increased self-esteem and lessened shame; increased understanding of the dynamics and effects of the trauma) and new skills, especially ways of coping and relating. As the possibility of the safety and trustworthiness of others in the world and one's ability to respond and act rather than react is incorporated, there is less need for the client to dissociate and/or use other defensive operations to self-regulate or self-protect. The therapist is open to the client's feelings and experiences; thus, there is no longer a need to exclude them from awareness through dissociation or other means, in turn promoting an increase in personal coherence/personal narrative. There is less need for compartmentalization; rather than being overwhelmed by emotional reactions, the client begins to feel secure enough just to notice and experience emotions as they happen (labeled as *increased capacity for self-reflection, reflective aware-ness,* or *mindfulness* or *working experientially*) (see Fisher, 2017; Siegel, 2007). A clinical example serves to illustrate.

A client who began therapy was exceedingly sensitive to whether the thera-pist "cared." Any change in the established appointment times due to personal or professional obligations was personalized by the client and taken to signify that the therapist was indifferent to her. "You don't care. I'm just a marker in your book . . . another hour to fill . . . another paying customer. I'm always bad, wrong, the one no one gives a damn about!" The therapist had to work against feeling attacked or becoming defensive or reactive, instead respond-ing with comments such as the following: "It's hard to believe anyone cares if something that matters to you changes." Of particular importance were times when the treating therapist acknowledged his own mistakes in relationship management: "You're right. It was inconsiderate of me to wait too long to tell you I was going to be away. I apologize" or "I agree, I could have handled that better." This stance of nonretaliation toward the client's blame and attack was crucial. The client began to realize that she was important enough that the therapist took her position seriously and offered an apology. Making a mistake with her *mattered* to the therapist. Relational repairs of this sort often became major therapeutic change points for the client.

Another, more paradoxical change point came when the therapist expressed his irritation after the same client made a series of quasi-emergency phone calls with an escalating degree of desperation and helplessness in a short time period, straining the therapist's capacity and patience. After considering that the client had (he hoped) become strong enough to hear it, the therapist commented, "I understand that you are very upset, but this is the third time you've called in 2 hours and I can't be immediately available in such an ongo-ing way. Let's go back over your safety contract together and find some of the self-soothing or support-from-others strategies that you agreed to use when you get into these binds." By this time, the relationship was stable enough for the client to take this in, not as personal rejection or an indication that the therapist did not care but as an honest acknowledgment of the therapist's limitations and feelings, and an expectation that the client use agreed-upon self-management strategies. After acknowledging her initial hurt, she told the therapist in the subsequent session, "Sure I was taken aback, but it was good for me to realize you're human, too. Sometimes you run out of patience, some-times you get overwhelmed, just like I do. I can't rely only on you or expect you to always be available." These comments communicated a marked increase in the client's ability to obtain personal control over her initial emotional reac-tions, based in large measure on the long-term safety and holding environment of the relationship. She also became more open to seeking support in her other relationships. A further example follows.

As the therapy moved toward the end, the client was able to incorporate the relational lessons she learned in the laboratory of therapy into impor-tant life relationships. She became capable of mutual, collaborative, give-and-take relationships with her children. She became able to set limits on and avoid exploitive relationships with men. She came to accept that she no longer "deserved" to be exploited. She asserted herself gently but firmly in her romantic relationships. For the first time in many years, she lived an organized, nonchaotic life. There was an increase in her ability to relate to others in healthy ways in all types of relationships: intimate, parenting, friendship, and colleagueship. These changes were enormously satisfying for client and therapist alike.

In summary, *changing the entire self-in-the-world schema of how relationships and people work is the backbone and a goal of this therapy, a component of the trauma resolution.* The interpersonal nature of complex trauma and its usual occurrence over developmental epochs create extremely confusing messages about self and relationships (betrayal-trauma) and derail and compromise healthy development. As explained in other chapters of this text, explicit attention to the traumatic antecedents in the client's life is often necessary for the remission of posttraumatic symptoms. Such strategies are best undertaken in the context of a therapeutic alliance and after some trust has been established. The relationship facilitates the overall treatment and, in and of itself, is a therapeutic technique with strong empirical support.

Areas of Risk and Their Management

I turn next to a discussion of some of the most common relational "demands" made by these clients, whether explicitly or implicitly, that can challenge and flummox therapists, along with considerations of how to manage them ethically and with relational sensitivity.

1. *"Re-parent/rescue me."* Perhaps the most common mistake is trying to become the good parent the client never had, by rescuing and attempting to meet unmet dependency needs. Such a strategy, instead of emphasizing the client's responsibility for self and personal growth within and outside the therapy and the development of a support system apart from the therapist, can lead instead to increased dependence and demands and an entitled stance (e.g., needing more time, more sessions, special exceptions and treatment, multiple crisis contacts). In response and paradoxically, the therapist might try to do even more. Therapists who do not communicate their limitations or address when boundaries are tested, pushed, or crossed, can become trapped in a vicious cycle of trying to provide an impossible level of responsiveness and care. Inexperienced therapists and trainees may be most prone to make mistakes of this sort, but more experienced therapists can also overextend themselves, usually in response to compelling clients who might activate something in them that is normally dormant or managed. Examples of overresponse include sending postcards or letters and taking phone calls while on vacation; making nightly phone calls to assuage loneliness and to prove the therapist's caring; extended

and extra sessions or contacts (sometimes via electronic means such as e-mails or texts or on social media) on an ongoing basis with no clear therapeutic need or rationale; and continuous needs for crisis management, including emergency hospitalizations (often repeated admissions). Therapists learn the hard way that rescuing can boomerang as client demands and needs increase to the point that they seem insatiable and thus impossible to meet. Unfortunately, when therapists overindulge, overprovide, and seek to rescue, and find that nothing they do is enough and even more is demanded, at some point, they are likely to become angry, frustrated, and resentful. It is then not unusual for them to act out their feelings against the client in a way that is hostile, blaming, and shaming. In fact, unacknowledged or unaddressed anger and resentment can result in emotional detachment up to and including abrupt termination of treatment and client abandonment, a serious ethical breach, that can be profoundly damaging to trauma survivors who have previously been mistreated, neglected, and abandoned. To add insult to injury, therapists often blame the client for "causing" their reactions.

Instead, the therapeutic task is to give feedback when the demand is more than the therapist can provide and to problem-solve solutions with the client, who ultimately must be assisted in learning self-responsibility (as opposed to extreme self-sufficiency that may have led to relational "hunger and neediness" on one hand or overdependence/overreliance on the therapist, on the other) and to practice give-and-take with others. Therapists who maintain appropriate boundaries and limitations provide a model of self-care, while not diminishing the client's legitimate needs. Importantly, clients learn that therapy does not exist "outside of the bounds of other human relationships," that they may need to learn to develop an outside support system, find other ways to meet their needs, and that *their losses are not compensable by their therapist* and instead need to be faced and grieved (Calof, cited in Courtois, 1999).

2. *"Promise you won't ever leave or hurt me."* Clients who were seriously neglected in childhood understandably yearn for constancy and reassurance that they will not be abandoned or hurt by the therapist. They may test this out through hypervigilance, hypersensitivity, overreliance, and/or acting-out behavior. The therapist must be empathic about the seriousness of these issues and help clients understand how they developed. Concurrently, the therapist must address the issue openly, while not offering false reassurances and unreasonable promises (i.e., "I will never leave you"). Instead, the therapist can offer assurance of the intention to remain available as long as the relationship is working, the treatment is progressing, and other life circumstances do not interfere. All relationships are conditional: Therapists cannot guarantee what they are unable to control (e.g., their own health, the health and needs their families, the stability of their practice, change in life circumstance or life plans, and even death, or that they will never make a mistake).

3. *"You will neglect me, or you have abused me."* In a similar vein, it is inevitable that therapists will disappoint their clients by having other priorities

and life vicissitudes (e.g., at times, they may be late, distracted, tired, or over-worked; the pager may go off during a session; they may need to deal with an emergency or make a client wait; they may have a family emergency that may cause them to be unavailable for a period of time). Therapists have their own life issues that limit them and their availability. Therapeutic mistakes and limitations are "teachable moments" in which the lesson is "Yes, I am really tired today, and maybe I have not been as present as we both wish—but I can and do still care about you. This doesn't mean that I am going to abandon you." These moments teach the relational middle ground: Every letdown is *not* a prelude to neglect, abuse, or abandonment.

What has been identified as *traumatic transference* occurs when the survivor client, expecting that the therapist will be yet another abuser, is ever vigilant to that likelihood. This can be a very difficult projection for therapists to understand, because they entered their profession to be helpers, not abusers. They must work to counter resentment or otherwise not take this transference expectation personally, while helping clients to explore and understand its origin. They must also understand the relational paradox and insult of betrayal trauma and attachment insecurity (especially disorganized attachment) that is based on past abuse and the grooming or conditioning that preceded and occurred within it. Often, the relationship was the context and conduit within which the child victim was groomed and in which role relationships and responsibilities were perverted and misrepresented. It was often the case that *when the relationship became established and close, abuse occurred, rationalized as an important part of the relationship*. Thus, at the point when the therapeutic relationship deepens and trust begins to develop, the client may become most fearful and vigilant and detach in response, surprising the therapist who, in fact, may (correctly) feel more connected. When therapists do not behave in abusive, exploitive, or retaliatory ways, and when they help clients to understand their fears and reactions as legitimate and as projections of and attempts at mastery of past experiences, they provide a different model for relationships in which abuse/exploitation is not the inevitable outcome. Other people can be trusted because they are trustworthy.

4. *"How dare you have faults?"* Everyone wishes for a perfect father, mother, therapist, and so forth. The therapist's job is to help clients have more realistic expectations, while grieving the faults of those who were or are self-centered, abusive, or neglectful. As they let go of the wish for perfection, clients are freer to accept what therapists *do have* to give, namely, their genuine selves—imperfections, limitations, pettiness, and all. In taking this stance (i.e., "I can be helpful to you even if I am imperfect and will continue to care even when you are"), therapists also model that clients need not be perfect to be acceptable, challenging a belief held by many.

5. *"Your boundaries are killing me. Make me special/get involved in my life [including sexual involvement in some cases]."* Clients raised with abusive/exploitive caregivers in the context of insecure–disorganized attachment have

experienced a variety of boundary failures and violations. These may include overly stringent boundaries without any flexibility on the one hand, lack of boundaries on the other, or boundaries that are ever-changing and unpredictable. The fluidity of boundaries enables the development of dual relationships, something clients may be used to and try to establish with the therapist. Understandably, abused and neglected clients yearn for the "special-ness" they either never had with their primary caregivers or only had in the context of being abused and exploited (often referred to as "negative specialness"). Stable and predictable boundaries within the therapy work against the development of dual relationships and teach consistency, reliability, and integrity. Although the client might experience boundaries as rejection, the therapist must make clear that a sexual or other dual relationship would not be in the client's best interests, as it is unethical and will retraumatize: "Having a sexual relationship might feel special but would violate the terms of our relationship in many of the same ways your abuse did. This would involve retraumatization rather than healing." Therapists must heed their ethical mandates regarding dual relationships. Putnam's (1989) counsel is that it is preferable to end a treatment with a client than to become romantically and sexually engaged, no matter what the circumstance. Severe damage is the most common aftermath of personal and sexual involvement by therapists with their clients.

6. *"You solve this chaos/you make it all go away."* Some clients have the expectation that it is the therapist's responsibility to "fix it," optimally as soon as possible (or even yesterday!). Among other things, the therapist who takes on this expectation may inadvertently communicate that clients are weak and incapable of learning and changing, a reinforcement of the wrong thing and a stance that paradoxically can encourage oppositional and controlling behavior. Alternatively, clients' resilience and strength need to be supported and built upon: "I know you wish I could just fix it. I would like that, too, but no one can do that. You have a number of strengths and things going for you. Let's find ways to help you build on those use them to tackle your issues." "You are ultimately responsible for your own recovery."

7. *"You find my memories for me, or you tell me my memories."* Many clients have the hope or expectation that the therapist will "find" or "fill-in" their abuse memories for them (e.g., "My boyfriend/girlfriend was reading this checklist in a magazine and said I can't sleep and don't like sex because I was probably sexually abused. I want you to tell me if I was"). Without evidence, corroboration, or autobiographical memory, no one can say for sure whether a person was or was not abused. There is no specific symptom that *proves* abuse (sexual or otherwise) or that arises *only* from sexual abuse. The therapist must start *with the client's memories (if any are available), suspicions, and symptoms as they are presented* (Courtois, 1999). Since it is not unusual for clients to want to "export the authority for memories to the therapist" rather than have to struggle with uncertainty and the possibility of real abuse and neglect

in their backgrounds (Calof, in Courtois, 1999, p. 270), the therapist should not set themselves up as arbiter of the client's reality. Instead, they can work to resolve presenting problems and provide an interpersonal context in which the client can explore the possibility of abuse without suggestion or suppression. They can also work in somatic and experiential ways with clients, based on the neuroscientific findings regarding implicit encoding of memory and deep physical responses. The therapist's stance should be something along the lines of: "Without your explicit remembering and without evidence, I have no way of knowing whether you may have been abused. It is for you to explore and to make your own determinations about what might have happened to you. You have mentioned problems in your upbringing and your family that are worth exploring as to their personal meaning, and their possible influence on your sleep problems and sexual functioning. You've also described extreme body tension, especially when trying to sleep. Let's see if we can work on these."

8. *"Money: What am I worth to you?"* It is not unusual for severely abused clients to have been raised in poverty or a condition of financial instability (this should not be taken to mean that abuse and neglect do not occur in more well-to-do families, just that poverty is a risk factor for abuse). As a result, many survivors have not learned financial management skills, a deficit that keeps some in dire financial straits. At the opposite end of the spectrum, others are scrupulous about money management, having vowed as children to become independent and never have to rely on anyone for anything. Money can symbolize many things: For the self-sufficient and untrusting client who views every relationship as a give-and-take transaction, every session might start with payment, "cash on the barrelhead so I am not in your debt." The therapist is promptly paid for services, and either party is then free to walk away *without owing anything.* For others, the therapy fee is yet another way they must "pay for" or be encumbered in the present by their past. These clients are understandably resentful of the cost to them (financially and in other ways) and may directly or indirectly resist paying for services or may declare that they are merely paychecks for the therapist who takes payment in return for care and attention. Still others may use money as a yardstick by which to measure the therapist's caring: If the client is special enough, then the therapist will not charge, will extend credit over an unlimited period of time, or will lower the standard fee in accommodation. To resist these treatment traps, and in keeping with professional standards, the therapist should have consistent fee-setting and payment collection policies that do not allow clients to build large back balances. I recommend carefully examining the relational meaning when a client fails to pay, falls seriously behind, is allowed to build a large balance, and so forth. Often the latent meaning is a desire to be specially nurtured, a way to sabotage treatment, or a way to express anger or other emotions indirectly on the part of the client, or a way to avoid conflict regarding the payment of fees on the part of the therapist—issues that need to be made explicit and negotiated rather than avoided.

9. *"Emergencies: On call or on tap?"* In a population in which chaos and interpersonal revictimization might be the norm, at least early in treatment, it is important to set clear standards regarding personal safety and how emergencies are defined and handled. It is optimal to have these detailed in the written treatment document mentioned earlier or in the client's safety plan. Additionally, it is highly advisable to conduct a risk and safety assessment at the start of therapy. For those clients in clear danger to themselves or others, periodic assessments are a necessity, as is the need to develop a plan of action (i.e., safety planning) that the client agrees to put into place in an ongoing manner (and is not time-limited or with an expiration date), but especially in the event of an emergency. The client may be taught a wide variety of self-soothing and emotion regulation techniques to implement in the initial stabilization portion of treatment. These form the foundation of self-management, and the therapist serves as a backup resource on an as-needed basis, when a situation of risk or danger escalates or in an emergency.

When clients do reach out for contact in dire circumstances, and in accordance with the agreements spelled out in the safety plan, the therapist must respond positively and in ways that reinforce that the client honored the plan *before* taking action. Nevertheless, for clients used to instability and living in danger, change might be difficult and even threatening. There may be a number of lapses and relapses before the client can achieve some modicum of safety. When safety remains seriously compromised, it may be due to present-day danger and threats, a trauma reenactment of some sort, or in the dissociative client, the emergence of a self-state that is controlling, self-destructive, or in conflict with other self-states that the therapist should seek to explore and understand with the client (and/or explore in consultation). This may require directly delving into the trauma "out of the normal order" to process it and to desensitize the client to its insidious effects.

Additional Risk Management Tools

The following tools are widely recommended as aids in the management of risk in the general client population but especially in the interpersonally traumatized.

Record Keeping

Treatment notes concerning the content of each session are generally required by professional ethics codes and can be important in managing risk. Many notes follow a format that resembles the following: (1) session content/topics/disclosures; (2) interventions; (3) client comments and behaviors; (4) changes in focal symptoms and risks (including suicidality and self-harm); and (5) plans for continued treatment or closure, and extrasession assignments and tasks. This format is especially helpful in addressing two areas of compromised function in many adult survivors: the ability to engage in self-reflection ("observing ego functions") and discontinuous memory caused by dissociation or other defensive operations. Both functions are addressed when notes are reviewed in the context of a treatment session covering topics that have been discussed previously. In this way, factual note taking and reminders reinforce memory retention. The "client comments and behaviors" section, which is primarily a record of things said/done by the client, can clarify the meaning of material discussed, reinforcing an observing ego. Furthermore, this section can contain documentation of "boundary pushes" and how these are handled (e.g., a client may ask to be touched or held after a session in which an exposure treatment for flashbacks was done) and safety risks, and how the therapist responded to them, or the plan for doing so. The therapist makes a verbatim record of what the client said and the therapist's response. Such documentation can be especially valuable in the event of a licensing board of ethics complaint or a lawsuit and shows that the therapist is aware of boundary and safety issues and has plans in place to address them that are consistent with the standard of care.

When Content Speaks Indirectly about Process

Process observations and comments—made by the therapist about what is transpiring in the therapeutic interaction—are typical in psychotherapy. As part of the process, it can be helpful for the therapist to periodically check in with the client about how the therapy is going and how the client is feeling, and to request feedback about what is working and what is not. A therapist may be surprised by the client's responses, for example, learning that something they said or did had a negative impact on the client, with intensity varying from mild to very strong. Feedback of this sort can assist the therapist in making "course corrections," thereby reinforcing the client's collaboration and personal empowerment. Such a strategy is in keeping with the therapy movement that involves ongoing elicitation of client feedback and shifts in strategy to better meet the client's needs, a strategy that has support as an evidence-based relational element.

Discussions of the Future

Therapists should expect or initiate discussions about the future in general and as it relates to the therapy relationship. In addition to avoiding impossible commitments and promises, these conversations open discussion about issues such as "How will I know I'm done with treatment?"; "Will you tell me that it's time to stop?"; "Will I be having flashbacks like this forever?"; and so forth. Again, clients should be encouraged to discuss such issues.

The Therapeutic Impasse

Treatment impasses can develop for many reasons. When it becomes apparent that a stalemate has occurred, it is useful for the therapist to note it and to try to discuss what events or feelings might have contributed to it. If enough goodwill exists (depending on the seriousness and intensity of the impasse), it may be helpful to seek consultation, optimally with another clinician experienced in the treatment of CTSDs and the negotiation of impasses. As an alternative to a consultant, some dyads may decide to begin recording sessions—either by audio- or videotaping—so that perceptions of the process may be measured against the "reality" offered by the recording. The clinician's best approach to impasse consultation and discussion involves openness to understanding and appreciating all factors that may be at work, and willingness to avoid blame or shame and to work toward a resolution that moves treatment forward or toward a decision to wrap it up and to make referrals as needed.

Ending the Relationship on a Positive Note

Powerful connections develop in relationship-based therapy. The end of treatment may activate or recapitulate feelings associated with past abandonment or other losses and may lead to bereavement. Thus, termination needs to be handled carefully, because inattentive management can undo some of the gains of "earned security." Generally, termination should be discussed as the client naturally begins to reconnect with the outside community. The client may begin to cancel appointments, change appointment times, reduce frequency of sessions, and ask for telephone check-ins as opposed to in-person sessions, and so forth. As therapy winds down, enough time should be given for discussion of the impact and the feelings that leave-taking elicits. The relational lesson is "I and our work will always be with you as you move on." For some clients, discussing leave-taking as a normal part of healthy relationships can prompt strong feelings of elation and also of sadness and loss. The use of a metaphor (e.g., when a child leaves home for the first time for camp, college, or the military, a family's job is to prepare and successfully "launch" the child into a wider world) can put perspective on the ending.

It is standard practice for therapists to ask clients to attend one last session even if they have unilaterally decided to end treatment. This is especially important in order to identify or clear up any misunderstandings that may have led to the urge to abruptly end in a "flight into health," a "flight into independence," or a "flight into avoidance" among other motivations. It is helpful for them to learn to say good-bye or farewell rather than to just avoid or have a cutoff as the ending of the treatment (as may have been typical behavior in their family of origin). Yet, at times, the client cannot leave this way, and manufactures a reason to storm out and slam the door or creates an abrupt emotional cutoff. Therapists may need to cope with being left in an incomplete or less than optimal way, just as parents cope when their adolescent distances in terms of achieving independence. Leaving home—and a safe haven—is difficult. As with other issues in relational treatment, it is best if the issue is discussed, mutually decided, and undertaken with preparation, but that is not always the way it happens. The question of termination, of course, raises the question of what the outline may be for a posttherapy relationship, if any.

Posttherapy Contacts

Therapists have different values and policies regarding posttherapy contact. Some accept phone calls, e-mails, and visits, possibly even a meeting for coffee or lunch while others do not agree to any form of contact. Whatever the therapist's stance, it should be based on a careful assessment of what is in the former client's best interests, whether it will be manageable, and whether it will interfere with the ending of treatment and the client's newly developed independence. An extratherapeutic relationship may make a return to therapy for additional treatment difficult, if not impossible, so the situation calls for caution and informed consent.

Although some professional ethics codes allow the establishment of romantic or sexual relationship with past clients several years posttherapy (American Psychological Association, 2002), others are adamant in strictly forbidding such a relationship. Due to the power dynamics involved in the relationship, the development of a romantic/sexual relationship is fraught with high potential to damage. For this reason, such a relationship with complex trauma clients is inadvisable under any circumstance and patently unethical in some instances.

The Outcome

When therapy for CTSDs works, changes can be dramatic and very satisfying for both parties. A client can move from a life centered on reliving past trauma and anticipating continued or additional trauma to relative stability, coherence, safety, warmth, and human connection. This review and discussion of the relational interactions and "teachings" that occur in treating clients with complex trauma histories has presented an approach to the structure and delivery of therapy based on relational healing, along with the parameters for managing the risks inherent in this deeply interconnected treatment. A dual focus on engaging with the client in a manner that builds and maintains a genuine working alliance, while also monitoring and addressing personal empowerment and development, and limiting risks to safety within or outside the therapy session, is the *sine qua non* for a relational healing approach within every evidence-based approach to treatment of CTSDs.

Acknowledgment

I acknowledge the contributions of Philip J. Kinsler and A. Steven Frankel to the prior edition of this chapter (Kinsler, Courtois, & Frankel, 2009).

References

Allen, J. G. (2001). *Traumatic relationships and serious mental disorders*. Chichester, UK: Wiley.

Allen, J. G. (2005). *Coping with trauma: Hope through understanding* (2nd ed.). Washington, DC: American Psychiatric Press.

American Psychological Association. (2002). *Ethical principles of psychologists and code of conduct.* Washington, DC: Author.

Binder, J. L. (2004). *Key competencies in brief dynamic psychotherapy: Clinical practice beyond the manual.* New York: Guilford Press.

Boon, S., Steele, K., & van der Hart, O. (2011). *Coping with trauma-related dissociation: Skills training for patients and therapists.* New York: Norton.

Bowlby, J. (1969). *Attachment and loss: Vol. 1. Attachment.* New York: Basic Books.

Bowlby, J. (1980). *Attachment and loss: Vol. 3. Loss.* New York: Basic Books.

Chu, J. (1988). Ten traps for therapists in the treatment of trauma survivors. *Dissociation, 1*(4), 24–32.

Chu, J. (1992). The therapeutic roller coaster: Dilemmas in the treatment of childhood abuse survivors. *Journal of Psychotherapy: Practice and Research, 1,* 351–370.

Cloitre, M., Cohen, L. R., & Koenen, K. C. (2006). *Treating survivors of childhood abuse: Psychotherapy for the interrupted life.* New York: Guilford Press.

Cloitre, M., Stovall-McClough, C., Miranda, K., & Chemtob, C. M. (2004). Therapeutic alliance, negative mood regulation, and treatment outcome in child abuse-related posttraumatic stress disorder. *Journal of Consulting and Clinical Psychology, 72*(3), 411–416.

Conterio, K., & Lader, W. (1998). *Bodily self-harm: The breakthrough healing program for self-injurers.* New York: Hyperion.

Copeland, M. E., & Harris, M. (2000). *Healing the trauma of abuse: A women's workbook.* Oakland, CA: New Harbinger.

Courtois, C. A. (1999). *Recollections of sexual abuse: Treatment principles and guidelines.* New York: Norton.

Courtois, C. A. (2010). *Healing the incest wound: Adult survivors in therapy* (2nd ed.). New York: Norton.

Courtois, C. A. (2015). First, do no *more* harm. In D. Walker, C. A. Courtois, & J. Aten, (Eds.), *Spirituality oriented psychotherapy for trauma* (pp. 55–76). Washington, DC: American Psychological Association Press.

Courtois, C. A., & Gold, S. N. (2009). The need for inclusion of psychological trauma in the professional curriculum: A call to action. *Psychological Trauma: Theory, Research, Practice, and Policy, 1*(1), 3–23.

Dalenberg, C. (2000). *Countertransference and the treatment of trauma.* Washington, DC: American Psychological Association. *www.healthquality.va.gov/guidelines/mh/ptsd/vadodptsdcpgfinal082917.pdf.*

Edwards, V., Holden, G., Felitti, V., & Anda, R. (2003). Relationship between multiple forms of childhood maltreatment and adult mental health in community respondents. *American Journal of Psychiatry, 160*(8), 1453–1460.

Ellis, A. E., Simiola, V., Brown, L., Courtois, C., & Cook, J. M. (2018). The role of evidence-based therapy relationships on treatment outcome in adults with trauma: A systematic review. *Journal of Trauma and Dissociation, 19*(2), 185–213.

Erikson, E. H. (1950). *Childhood and society.* New York: Norton.

Fisher, J. (2017). *Healing the fragmented selves of trauma survivors: Overcoming internal self-alienation.* New York: Routledge.

Fonagy, P. (1997). Attachment and theory of mind: Overlapping constructs? *Association for Child Psychology and Psychiatry Occasional Papers, 14,* 31–40.

Ford, J. D., & Courtois, C. A. (2014). Complex PTSD, affect dysregulation, and borderline personality disorder. *Borderline Personality Disorder and Emotion Dysregulation, 1,* 9.

Frankel, A. S. (2002). *What I have learned.* Presidential Plenary Lecture, 19th Annual Fall Conference of the International Society for the Study of Dissociation, Baltimore, MD.

Freyd, J. J. (1996). *Betrayal trauma: The logic of forgetting childhood abuse.* Cambridge, MA: Harvard University Press.

Gelso, C. J., & Silberberg, A. (2016). Strengthening the real relationship: What is a psychotherapist to do? *Practice Innovations, 1*(3), 154–163.

Herman, J. L. (1992). *Trauma and recovery*. New York: Basic Books.

Hopper, E., Grossman, F., Spinazzola, J., & Zucker, M. (2019). *Treatment of adult survivors of childhood emotional abuse and neglect: Reaching across the abyss*. New York: Guilford Press.

Hubble, M., Duncan, B., & Miller, S. (1999). *The heart and soul of change: What works in psychotherapy*. Washington, DC: American Psychological Association.

Jobes, D. A. (2006). *Managing suicidal risk: A collaborative approach*. New York: Guilford Press.

Kinsler, P. J. (2018). *Complex psychological trauma: The centrality of relationship*. New York: Routledge/Taylor & Francis Group.

Kinsler, P. J., Courtois, C. A., & Frankel, A. S. (2009). Therapeutic alliance and risk management. In C. A. Courtois & J. D. Ford (Eds.), *Treating complex traumatic stress disorders: An evidence-based guide* (pp. 183–201). New York: Guilford Press.

Linehan, M. M. (1993). *Cognitive-behavioral treatment of borderline personality disorder*. New York: Guilford Press.

Linehan, M. M. (2017). *Cognitive-behavioral treatment of borderline personality disorder* (2nd ed.). New York: Guilford Press.

Lyons-Ruth, K., & Jacobovitz, D. (1999). Attachment disorganization unresolved loss, relational violence, and lapses in behavioral and attentional strategies. In J. Cassidy & P. R. Shaver (Eds.), *Handbook of attachment: Theory, research, and clinical applications* (pp. 520–554). New York: Guilford Press.

Miller, D. (1994). *Women who hurt themselves*. New York: Basic Books.

Najavits, L. (2002). *A women's addiction workbook*. Oakland, CA: New Harbinger.

Neff, K., & Germer, C. (2017). *Mindful self-compassion workbook for self-compassion practitioners*. New York: Guilford Press.

Norcross, J. C. (Ed.). (2011). *Psychotherapy relationships that work* (2nd ed.). New York: Oxford University Press.

Norcross, J. C., & Lambert, M. (2019). *Psychotherapy relationships that work* (3rd ed.). New York: Oxford University Press.

Ogden, P., Pain, C., & Minton, K. (2006). *Trauma and the body*. New York: Norton.

Pearlman, L. A., & Courtois, C. A. (2005). Clinical applications of the attachment framework: Relational treatment of complex trauma. *Journal of Traumatic Stress, 18*(5), 449–459.

Pearlman, L. A., & Saakvitne, K. W. (1995). *Trauma and the therapist: Countertransference and vicarious traumatization in psychotherapy with incest survivors*. New York: Norton.

Porges, S., & Dana, D. (Eds.). (2018). *Clinical applications of the polyvagal theory*. New York: Norton.

Putnam, F. W. (1989). *Diagnosis and treatment of multiple personality disorder*. New York: Guilford Press.

Rogers, C. R. (1951). *Client-centered therapy: Its current practice, implications and theory*. London: Constable.

Schore, A. N. (2003a). *Affect dysregulation and disorders of the self*. New York: Norton.

Schore, A. N. (2003b). *Affect dysregulation and the repair of the self*. New York: Norton.

Schwartz, A. (2017). *The complex PTSD workbook: A mind body aproach to regaining emotional control and becoming whole*. Berkeley, CA: Althea Press.

Schwartz, H. L. (2000). *Dialogues with forgotten voices: Relational perspective on child abuse trauma and treatment of dissociative disorders*. New York: Basic Books.

Schwarz, R. (2002). *Tools for transforming trauma*. New York: Routledge.

Siegel, D. (2007). *The mindful brain: Reflection and attunement in the cultivation of well-being*. New York: Norton.

Spinazzola, J., van der Kolk, B., & Ford, J. D. (2018). When nowhere is safe: Trauma history antecedents of posttraumatic stress disorder and developmental trauma disorder in childhood. *Journal of Traumatic Stress, 31*(5), 631–642.

Turner, H. A., Finkelhor, D., & Ormrod, R. (2010). Poly-victimization in a national sample of children and youth. *American Journal of Preventive Medicine, 38*(3), 323–330.

Valory, M. (2007). Earning a secure attachment style: A narrative of personality change in adulthood. In R. Josselson, A. Lieblich, & D. P. McAdams (Eds.), *The meaning of others* (pp. 93–116). Washington, DC: American Psychological Association.

Vermilyea, E. (2000). *Growing beyond survival: A self-help toolkit for managing traumatic stress.* Baltimore: Sidran Press.

Winnicott, D. W. (1965). *The maturational process and the facilitating environment: Studies in the theory of emotional development.* New York: International Universities Press.

Wurmser, L. (1981). *The mask of shame.* Baltimore: Johns Hopkins University Press.

CHAPTER 5

Evidence-Based Psychological Assessment of the Sequelae of Complex Trauma

JOSEPH SPINAZZOLA
JOHN BRIERE

Research conducted in the 1990s and the first decade of the 21st century revealed an incremental relationship between the amount of trauma experienced and the breadth and severity of associated psychological difficulties and risk outcomes, reported in the psychiatric, traumatic stress, victimology, and public health literatures. It yielded several prominent constructs addressing the accumulating effects of trauma exposure, including *cumulative trauma* (Briere, Kaltman, & Green, 2008; Cloitre et al., 2009; Follette, Polusny, Bechtle, & Naugle, 1996), *polyvictimization* (Finkelhor, Ormrod, & Turner, 2007; Musicaro et al., 2019), and *adverse childhood experiences (ACEs)* (Anda et al., 2006).

Research conducted over the past decade has illuminated more nuanced relationships between trauma exposure and outcomes, lending credence to the formulation of *complex trauma* as a dual construct defined by the interconnection of cumulative exposure to interpersonal victimization and evolving (mal) adaptation (Spinazzola et al., 2005, 2013). For example, cumulative interpersonal trauma exposure during childhood was found to contribute more significantly to adult symptom complexity than cumulative exposure during adulthood (Cloitre et al., 2009). Operationalizing complex trauma as exposure to traumatic experiences that are chronic, early childhood in onset, and interpersonal in nature, Wamser-Nanney and Vandenberg (2013) demonstrated an association between complex trauma exposure and higher levels of behavior problems and psychiatric symptoms than observed in response to other trauma exposure ecologies, including impersonal trauma; acute interpersonal trauma;

125

or chronic interpersonal trauma with later childhood or adolescent onset. Similarly, the intersection of early developmental timing with accumulation or recurrence of interpersonal trauma has been found to be a strongly predictive of more severe psychopathology (Dierkhising, Ford, Branson, Grasso, & Lee, 2019).

Recent research has shown that exposure to particular types of interpersonal trauma in childhood further contributes to the complexity of associated outcomes. Childhood psychological maltreatment (i.e., emotional abuse/neglect) and sexual abuse have been linked to greater frequency and severity of psychopathology and risk outcomes than other forms of childhood maltreatment (Kisiel et al., 2014; Spinazzola et al., 2014). Specific multi-type constellations of trauma (e.g., combined psychological and physical abuse; impaired primary caregiving combined with family and community violence) have also been associated with more complex and severe clinical presentations (Hodgdon et al., 2018b; Spinazzola, van der Kolk, & Ford, 2018). Applied neuroscientific research has shown that specific forms of childhood maltreatment and neglect result in survival-driven changes to brain structures and physiology that over time are associated with distinct patterns of developmentally evolving psychopathology, maladaptive coping and risk trajectories (Teicher & Sampson, 2016).

These converging bodies of research lend support to what may be referred to as a *complexity theory* of trauma exposure and adaptation. The central tenet of complexity theory is that certain types or characteristics of traumatic experiences exhibit a weighted, synergistic, or otherwise disproportionate effect on subsequent symptomatology and risk trajectories. This raises the possibility that certain forms of trauma exposure might lead to distinct and replicable symptom presentations and impairments, i.e., to one or more complex trauma diagnoses (Courtois, 2008).

A Complex Trauma Diagnosis?

Beginning in the early 1990s, recognition of the complexities of adaptation to psychological trauma led select traumatic stress scholars to propose alternate diagnostic constructs to posttraumatic stress disorder (PTSD). Foremost among these, complex posttraumatic stress disorder (Herman, 1992) was initially postulated to consist of six empirically supported, concurrently experienced symptom clusters: affect dysregulation and distress reduction behaviors, dissociation, somatization, and negative attributions regarding self-image, relationships and systems of meaning (Pelcovitz et al., 1997). During the DSM-IV Field Trials, this construct was briefly renamed disorders of extreme stress not otherwise specified (DESNOS) to distinguish it from classic PTSD. Although DESNOS was ultimately not included as a formal diagnosis, facets of this construct were acknowledged under Associated Features of PTSD in DSM-IV (American Psychiatric Association, 2000).

The current configuration of complex PTSD has gained substantial traction in the international research community and has been included as a formal diagnostic entity in the 11th revision to the World Health Organization's *International Classification of Diseases* (ICD-11; World Health Organization, 2018) (Cloitre, Gavert, Brewin, Bryant, & Maercker, 2013). PTSD itself has evolved in DSM-5 to incorporate several facets of symptom complexity originally introduced by the DESNOS construct, including negative attributions about self, others and the world; reckless or destructive behaviors; and dissociative reactions (American Psychiatric Association, 2013).

Most recently, the need for a developmentally anchored complex trauma diagnosis has been asserted (D'Andrea, Ford, Stolbach, Spinazzola, & van der Kolk, 2012). The perceived distinctness and utility of such a developmental trauma disorder (DTD) has been bolstered by an international clinician survey (Ford et al., 2013). Diagnostic field trial results provide strong preliminary validation for this construct (Ford, Spinazzola, van der Kolk, & Grasso, 2018; Spinazzola et al., 2018; van der Kolk, Ford, & Spinazzola, 2019).

Despite the attraction of models such as complex PTSD and DTD, the manifold effects of complex trauma ultimately are not easily encapsulated within the parameters of any single diagnostic framework. Symptom complexity may vary as a function of the nature, number, and timing of the specific traumas a given individual has experienced, as well as the presence of relevant biological, psychological, contextual and epigenetic risk factors. Evidence-based assessment of this diverse clinical population should embrace its inherent complexity and eschew reliance upon fixed definitions of complex trauma exposure or rigid compositions of complex trauma symptoms. In recognition of the limitations of subscribing to a unitary complex trauma diagnosis, this chapter offers a deconstructed, phenomenologically based guide to assessment of psychological responses that may be associated with exposure to complex traumatic stressors.

Factors Further Complicating Complex Trauma Outcomes

More severe and complex posttraumatic outcomes frequently are associated with preexisting nervous system hyperreactivity (Perry & Pollard, 1998); comorbid anxiety, depressive, personality or substance disorders (Acierno, Resnick, Kilpatrick, Saunders, & Best, 1999); an avoidant response style (Briere, 2019); and impaired attachment relationships (Spinazzola et al., 2005). Trauma symptomatology also may be intensified by environmental variables, such as poverty (Golin et al., 2016), incarceration (Kubiak, 2005), social marginalization and oppression (Carter, 2007) and trauma-related stigmatization (e.g., Sorsoli, Kia-Keating, & Grossman, 2008), and may vary according to culture-specific idioms of distress (Marsella, Friedman, Gerrity, & Scurfield, 1996). Structural violence and oppression in such forms as racism, sexism, homo- and transphobia, and xenophobia constitutes a serious type of trauma exposure in its own right (Holmes, Facemire, & Da Fonseca, 2016), and public health research has demonstrated greater prevalence of trauma exposure and severity of associated symptomatology in a number of minority racial, ethnic and sexual orientation populations (Roberts, Austin, Corliss, Vandermorris, & Koenen, 2010; Nobles et al., 2016). Finally, ancestral trauma exposure is believed to contribute to greater disease prevalence and health disparities across generations of afflicted communities (Sotero, 2006), and should be considered for its potential compounding effect on the complexity of symptom expression in response to present-day trauma exposures as well as from the epigenetic repercussions and ongoing societal expressions of historical trauma.

Complex Posttraumatic Outcomes

Because complex trauma outcomes vary widely, psychological assessment in this area must potentially address a wide range of symptoms. These can be viewed in terms of a number of intrinsically overlapping, phenomenological categories (Briere & Spinazzola, 2005; Kliethermes, Schacht, & Drewry, 2014). For the sake of illustration, the complex array of potential trauma-related symptoms and impairments identified in empirical and clinical studies include the following:

- Classic and complex PTSD symptoms and disorders
- Mood disturbance, such as anxiety (including panic and phobias), depression, and anger
- Emotional and affect dysregulation
- Somatization, somatic dysregulation and sensory integration difficulties
- Cognitive and identity disturbance, such as low self-esteem, self-blame, hopelessness, expectations of rejection, and preoccupation with danger
- Interpersonal difficulties including maladaptive attachment patterns
- Executive functioning difficulties, including impaired perspective taking, impulse control, working memory, problem solving, decision making, and goal setting
- Dissociation
- Distress reduction activities or maladaptive coping behaviors, such as compulsive sexual behavior, disordered eating, aggression, substance abuse, self-mutilation, and suicidality

Given the broad range of potential posttraumatic outcomes, it is unlikely that the psychological assessment of traumatized individuals can be adequately captured through the administration of a test for PTSD. Instead, once it has been determined that trauma exposure is part of the clinical picture, the number of possible assessment targets proliferate. The remainder of this chapter concerns the technical aspects of this expanded assessment process.

The Role of Assessment in Trauma Intervention: Assessment-Based Treatment

Other than in forensic contexts, the primary function of psychological assessment is to inform treatment. This may be especially true for complex posttraumatic presentations. Without structured assessment, the clinician may inadvertently miss important intervention targets, leading to inadequate or incomplete treatment. Accurate specification of initial treatment targets is especially critical for *components-based* approaches to complex trauma treatment (e.g., Briere & Scott, 2014; Hopper, Grossman, Spinazzola, & Zucker, 2018). Such approaches suggest that complex trauma intervention be customized, matching treatment elements to clients' specific clinical presentations. In this context, a battery of psychometrically valid psychological tests is necessarily the first step in the development of a treatment plan.

When repeated over time, psychological testing also can signal the need to change or augment the focus of treatment. For example, ongoing assessment may suggest a shift in approach when posttraumatic stress symptoms begin to respond to treatment but other symptoms (e.g., eating disturbances) continue relatively unabated or even increase (Courtois, 2008). Repeated administration of measures also can increase accountability and quality control and add to the clinical knowledge base regarding the effectiveness of various trauma-related psychotherapies. Ongoing assessment should be an essential element of complex trauma intervention with adults and integrated into the fabric of psychotherapy as an alliance and empowerment-building partnership between clinician and client.

Psychometric Issues

As is true of psychological tests in general, those used to evaluate the effects of complex trauma exposure must have adequate reliability and validity, and should be standardized on demographically representative samples of the general population (American Educational Research Association, 2014). Such tests also should have good sensitivity and specificity if they are offered as diagnostic instruments. For example, a measure intended to identify PTSD should be able to predict with reasonable accuracy both true cases of PTSD (sensitivity) and those cases in which PTSD is not present (specificity). Nevertheless, numerous trauma-specific instruments have been developed, primarily in the context of research, and continue to be used despite not meeting current standards for clinical psychological tests. Although many of these tests are intriguing and internally consistent, their actual clinical applicability is often unknown.

Equally problematic, some trauma impact measures have not been normed on the general population. Without normative data, clinicians are unable to compare a given score on a measure with "healthy" individuals' scores on that measure; thus, they cannot determine the extent to which said score represents dysfunction or disorder. The clinician is advised to avoid, whenever possible, nonstandardized measures in the assessment of trauma effects. In the case of solely diagnostic screening instruments, the absence of normative data is generally not a problem, because the only issue is whether a given set of symptoms is—or is not—present.

For these reasons, the majority of the measures recommended in this chapter are *evidence-based*: normed on the general population, or in the case of diagnostic measures, shown to possess adequate sensitivity and specificity in well-controlled research. Nevertheless, even those measures that have been standardized and normed in the United States or with other Western countries vary widely in the extent to which they have been linguistically translated or evaluated for construct equivalence across cultures. Accordingly, clinicians working with diverse clinical populations should invariably interpret psychometric tests with caution. Therapists should integrate clinical expertise, supervision, and available collateral information in their careful consideration of the extent to which results gleamed from diagnostic interviews or self-report measures accurately reflect client psychopathology versus culturally normative behavior, the manifestation of systemic adversity, or conflation with other contextual factors.

Approaches to Assessing Complex Trauma in Adult Clients

Because complex posttraumatic outcomes vary widely, the initial approach to assessment is critically important. In a sense, the clinician must make an educated guess as to the likely relevant areas of distress or dysfunction for a given client, even though he or she has yet to determine them psychometrically. In most cases, this determination is made during the initial interview, when presenting complaints and trauma history are elicited and the client's overall clinical presentation is considered. This process may be assisted by the early use of broad-spectrum screening instruments that assess numerous areas of symptomatology simultaneously. These include broadband measures that tap phenomena such as anxiety, depression, or psychosis, as well as instruments that evaluate a range of posttraumatic outcomes.

Adult Self-Report Measures

Psychological tests of complex trauma effects in adults can be divided into two groups: instruments that tap a wide range of generic (i.e., non-trauma-specific) psychological symptoms, and tests that directly assess various forms of posttraumatic disturbance.

Broadband Measures to Screen for Psychopathology

A variety of psychological tests are available for the assessment of non-trauma-specific symptoms in adult complex trauma survivors. Several evaluate syndromes relevant to a wide range of psychiatric diagnoses, most notably the *Millon Clinical Multiaxial Inventory–IV* (MCMI-IV; Millon, Grossman, & Millon, 2015), the *Minnesota Multiphasic Personality Inventory-2* (MMPI-2; Butcher et al., 2001) and the *Personality Assessment Inventory* (PAI; Morey, 2007). Each of these instruments yields detailed information on self-capacity difficulties frequently associated with complex posttraumatic outcomes and include PTSD scales of moderate sensitivity and specificity (Carlson, 1997). These instruments also include validity scales developed to detect under- or overreporting of symptoms. While helpful, multiple studies have found that elevated validity indices observed in adults with histories of chronic interpersonal trauma are more often reflective of genuine difficulties than malingering (Klotz Flitter, Elhai, & Gold, 2003). Finally, the *Symptom Checklist 90* (SCL-90-R), along with its short version, the *Brief Symptom Inventory* (BSI), offers a more parsimonious option for assessment of multiple clinical dimensions relevant to complex trauma, including Somatization, Interpersonal Sensitivity, and Hostility (Derogatis & Savitz, 2000).

Posttraumatic Sequelae Measures

Psychological tests of posttraumatic disturbance, in turn, can be organized into three categories: (1) PTSD measures; (2) trauma-focused measures specifically designed to assess domains of complex posttraumatic stress; and (3) non-trauma-focused instruments that measure other symptoms and difficulties that may be relevant to one or more of the conceptually overlapping phenomenological categories of complex trauma sequelae listed above.

PTSD Measures

To date, self-report measures of DSM-5 PTSD have yet to be standardized and normed on general population samples. This limits the definitiveness with which posttraumatic stress symptoms reported by clinical populations can be distinguished from normative stress reactions. Nevertheless, two PTSD self-report measures updated for DSM-5 demonstrate strong psychometric properties including good predictive validity as screening tools for provisional diagnosis of DSM-5 PTSD.

PTSD Checklist for DSM-5

The PTSD Checklist for DSM-5 (PCL-5; Weathers et al., 2013b) is a 20-item measure designed to assess the DSM-5 symptoms of PTSD. Psychometric research to date on trauma-exposed active military, veteran and civilian samples indicate that the PCL-5 possesses strong internal consistency, test-retest reliability, convergent, discriminant, factorial and predictive validity, and sensitivity to treatment change over time (Blevins, Weathers, Davis, Witte, & Domino, 2015; Bovin et al., 2016; Wortmann et al., 2016).

Posttraumatic Diagnostic Scale for DSM-5

The Posttraumatic Diagnostic Scale for DSM-5 (PDS-5; Foa et al., 2016a) is a 49-item measure designed to assess PTSD symptom severity in response to a single event. Items cover all DSM-5 Criteria for PTSD, including trauma exposure type, symptoms clusters, duration, and impact on functioning. PDS-5 exhibits good initial evidence of reliability (internal consistency, test–retest) and validity (convergent, discriminant, and predictive).

The Dissociative Subtype of PTSD Scale

The Dissociative Subtype of PTSD Scale (DSPS) is a 15-item instrument. Its three scales (Derealization/Depersonalization, Loss of Awareness, and Psychogenic Amnesia) were designed to measure the dissociative subtype of DSM-5 PTSD. It can be administered as either a self-report measure or a semi-structured interview. This measure has yet to be normed or standardized, but has positive preliminary factor validation with a military veteran sample (Wolf et al., 2017).

Other PTSD Symptom Scales in Widespread Use

The *Detailed Assessment of Posttraumatic Stress* (DAPS; Briere, 2001) is the only standardized and normed self-report measure of PTSD; however, it has yet to be updated for DSM-5. Many other empirically validated but unstandardized self-report measures of PTSD exist but are not recommended for continued use until at minimum they are updated for DSM-5 and retested.

Complex Posttraumatic Stress and Adaptation Measures

A small number of self-report instruments have been specifically developed to measure complex posttraumatic reactions. Three measures in particular possess robust psychometric properties. Two of these measures (TSI-2 and IASC) were standardized and normed to distinguish clinical impairment across various dimensions of complex posttraumatic psychopathology. A third (ITQ), while not yet standardized, has been extensively validated internationally on large clinical samples and normed on multiple large nationally representative population samples for use as the primary diagnostic measure for ICD-11 PTSD and complex PTSD.

Trauma Symptom Inventory-2

The Trauma Symptom Inventory–2 (TSI-2; Briere, 2011) taps overall level of acute and chronic posttraumatic symptomatology without reference to a specific traumatic event. Because DSM-5 allows for traumatic stress disorders arising from multiple events (American Psychiatric Association, 2013), measures of potentially more complex etiologies, such as the TSI-2, may be increasingly relevant to modern assessment scenarios. The TSI-2 consists of 12 clinical scales (Anxious Arousal, Depression, Anger, Intrusive Experiences, Defensive Avoidance, Dissociation, Sexual Disturbance, Impaired Self-Reference, Tension Reduction Behavior, Insecure Attachment, Somatic Preoccupations, and Suicidality), and four summary factors (Self-Disturbance, Posttraumatic Stress, Externalization, and Somatization) that capture many dimensions of complex trauma maladaptation.

The Inventory of Altered Self-Capacities

The Inventory of Altered Self-Capacities (IASC; Briere, 2000b), a 63-item standardized instrument, comprises scales spanning at least four areas of complex trauma sequelae. Its scales assess various facets of interpersonal difficulties, identity disturbance, affect dysregulation, and maladaptive coping/tension reduction. Elevated scores on the IASC have been shown to predict adult attachment style, childhood trauma history, interpersonal problems, suicidality, and substance abuse history in various samples (e.g., Allen, 2011; Bigras, Godbout, Hébert, Runtz, & Daspe, 2015; Briere & Rickards, 2007).

The International Trauma Questionnaire

The International Trauma Questionnaire (ITQ; Cloitre, Roberts, Bisson, & Brewin, 2017) is an 18-item self-report measure of ICD-11 PTSD and complex PTSD. With emphasis on maximizing its clinical utility, the ITQ was intentionally developed as a brief and simply worded self-report instrument validated to function as an easily administered and scored diagnostic tool for PTSD and complex PTSD across diverse international practice settings and cultures. Items cover the three clusters of ICD-11 PTSD symptoms (re-experiencing, avoidance of reminders, and persistent sense of threat) in addition to three clusters of "disturbances in self-organization" (affective dysregulation, negative self-concept, and disturbances in relationships). In adherence to ICD-11 scoring criteria, diagnoses of PTSD and complex PTSD are mutually exclusive and all six symptom clusters must be present for a diagnosis of complex PTSD to be assigned. In contrast to DSM-5 PTSD, no restrictions are set on the type(s) or magnitude of traumatic experience(s) with which symptoms are associated. Research has supported the psychometric properties of the ITQ (Karatzias et al., 2016, 2017), including its ability to distinguish both complex PTSD and PTSD from borderline personality disorder (Cloitre, Garvert, Weiss, Carlson, & Bryant, 2014).

Non-Trauma-Specific Measures Relevant to Complex Posttraumatic States

Complex posttraumatic outcomes often include problems that span a wide range of psychological and behavioral functioning, including affect dysregulation and mood disturbance; somatization; cognitive, identity, and relational disturbance; executive dysfunction; dissociation; and maladaptive coping or distress reduction activities. Thorough and accurate assessment of complex trauma effects typically requires inclusion of multiple evidence-based measures, client-tailored selection of which is informed by collateral information, records review, and initial clinical presentation.

Mood Disturbance Measures

There is a greater abundance of standardized, normed, and validated measures for mood disturbance than for any other category of symptoms and difficulties relevant to the effects of complex trauma. Given the pervasiveness of these issues for adult complex trauma clients, clinicians should select at least one evidence-based self-report measure of depression, anxiety, and problems with anger to include in their assessment arsenal. The following rank among the principal tests in these categories: the *Beck Anxiety Inventory* (BAI; Beck & Steer, 1993), the *Beck Depression Inventory–II* (BDI-II; Beck, Steer, & Brown, 1996), the *State–Trait Anger Expression Inventory–2* (STAXI-2; Spielberger, 1999); and the *State–Trait Anxiety Inventory* (STAI; Spielberger, Gorsuch, Lushene, Vagg, & Jacobs, 1983).

Emotion and Affect Dysregulation Measures

Clinical research has revealed affect dysregulation to be a predominant effect of complex trauma exposure for children (Spinazzola et al., 2005, 2018) and adults (van der Kolk et al., 2005). Expert consensus surveys and best practice guidelines have identified increasing client capacity for emotion regulation as a primary element of complex trauma treatment (Cloitre et al., 2011). A number of self-report measures of emotional, affective, and related forms of dysregulation exist, including the *Difficulties in Emotion Regulation Scale* (DERS; Gratz & Roemer, 2004), the *Negative Mood Regulation Scale* (NMR; Catanzaro & Mearns, 1990), and the *Abbreviated Dysregulation Inventory* (ADI; Mezzich, Tarter, Giancola, & Kirisci, 2001). Despite reasonable overall psychometric properties, these measures were developed primarily for research purposes and have not been normed or standardized with representative population samples. To gauge whether client endorsement of difficulties with emotion regulation reflects actual clinical impairment, it is recommended that clinicians utilize specific scales of the IASC or the ITQ that have been developed and validated for this purpose.

Somatization Measures

Clinicians seeking efficient, evidence-based assessment of somatic problems and complaints have primarily had to distill relevant information from specific scales of broad-based instruments (e.g., MCMI-III; MMPI-2; PAI; SCL-90-R). An underutilized option is the *Patient Health Questionaire-15* (PHQ-15; Kroenke, Spitzer, & Williams, 2002), a validated self-report measure of somatic symptom severity with clinical cutoffs derived from large-scale administration in diverse medical practice settings. A second viable option, the TSI-2 (discussed earlier) includes both a clinical scale and a summary factor addressing somatic concerns (Briere, 2011).

Cognitive, Self-Image, and Relational Disturbance Measures

Complex trauma exposures often are followed by chronic cognitive symptoms and impair sense of self and attributions about relationships. Fortunately, a number of reliable, well-validated, standardized, and normed measures are available that tap cognitive distortions and negative self- and relational schemas.

The *Tennessee Self-Concept Scale, Second Edition* (TSCS-2; Fitts & Warren, 1996) is a widely used multidimensional measure of self-concept in general clinical practice and research. Although it is not routinely included in trauma assessment batteries, clinical experience indicates that it is sensitive to the effects of childhood trauma on subsequent psychological functioning.

The *Cognitive Distortions Scale* (CDS; Briere, 2000a) is a 40-item instrument that measures five types of cognitive distortion: Self-Criticism, Helplessness, Hopelessness, Self-Blame, and Preoccupation with Danger. CDS scales predict past exposure to interpersonal violence, as well as suicidality, depression, and posttraumatic stress.

The *Trauma and Attachment Belief Scale* (TABS; Pearlman, 2003) is an 84-item measure of disrupted cognitive schemas across five areas rated for both "self" and "other": Safety, Trust, Esteem, Intimacy, and Control. The TABS may be helpful in understanding important assumptions that clients carry in their relationships, including their therapeutic relationships.

In addition, several broader tests have scales that tap aspects of impaired self-capacities, including the Borderline Features scale of the PAI, the Impaired Self-Reference scale of the TSI-2, the negative self-concept symptom cluster of the ITQ, various personality scales of the MCMI-IV and the Rorschach, and the Demoralization factor of the SIDES-R (see below).

Executive Functioning Measures

Self-report measures addressing domains of executive functioning in adults exist, and at least one such measure has been empirically validated and standardized with a U.S. normative sample (Behavior Rating Inventory of Executive Function—Adult Version; Roth, Isquith, & Gioia, 2005). While the child version of this measure has been more widely used in research (e.g., Hodgdon et al., 2018a), there remains a dearth of empirical studies in peer-review journals utilizing this or other standardized executive function measures with adult populations. Alternatively, when feasible clinicians should consider partnering when with a neuropsychologist to administer a validated, broad-based neuropsychological screening instrument or domain-specific tests tailored to their client's presenting executive function issues.

Dissociation Measures

Dissociation refers to a defensive alteration in consciousness or awareness, frequently invoked to reduce the distress associated with psychologically traumatic events. Despite the potential importance of dissociation in complex posttraumatic stress, there are few standardized or validated measures of this construct available to clinicians.

The *Multiscale Dissociation Inventory* (MDI; Briere, 2002) is the only standardized and normed measure of dissociative responses. Based on the empirically supported premise that dissociation is a multidimensional phenomenon (Bernstein & Putnam, 1986; Briere, Weathers, & Runtz, 2005), the MDI consists of 30-items comprising six scales (Disengagement, Depersonalization, Derealization, Memory Disturbance, Emotional Constriction, and Identity Dissociation) that form an overall "dissociation profile." The MDI has demonstrated acceptable psychometric properties in various samples (e.g., Parlar, Frewen, Oremus, Lanius, & McKinnon, 2016; Resick, Suvak, Johnides, Mitchell, & Iverson, 2012).

The *Dissociative Experiences Scale* (DES; Bernstein & Putnam, 1986) is an unstandardized but historically widely used, free-access, 28-item, single-scale instrument measuring overall frequency of dissociative symptoms. Several studies have offered widely variable factor structures and study sample-specific norms for the DES. A meta-analysis of validation studies on the DES revealed mixed psychometric properties and associated limitations regarding usage and interpretation of this measure (van IJzendoorn & Schuengel, 1996). For example, in contrast to the proposed score of 30 to discriminate presence of a dissociative disorder, research comparing clinical versus nonclinical samples has indicated need for a much more conservative cutoff of 45–55 to minimize false positives. Moreover, research suggests that the DES should be administered across multiple timepoints and raters (client, therapist) to obtain an accurate measurement of dissociative symptomatology. Among other concerns, this calls into question the suitability of the DES as a dependent measure of treatment outcome. Ultimately, the DES may have greatest utility as a brief, no-cost tool that provides an initial impression of the presence and general extent of dissociative symptomatology.

The *Multidimensional Inventory of Dissociation* (MID; Dell, 2006) provides an intriguing alternative to the DES. The MID comprising 278 items, is an exhaustive inventory of dissociative symptoms and processes. It employs a hybrid administration methodology: clinician-guided self-report supplemented by clinical interview and exploration of positively endorsed items. The MID instrument comes with an extensive interpretation manual, and training and technical assistance on measure administration and interpretation is available. While not normed or standardized, the MID has been empirically validated and has demonstrated good overall psychometric properties.

Maladaptive Coping and Distress Reduction Measures

As noted earlier in this chapter, many individuals with complex traumatic stress disorders (perhaps especially those with emotional regulation problems) engage in externalization, maladaptive coping or other distress reduction behaviors when confronted with trauma-related memories, emotions and physiological reactivity (Briere, 2019). In addition to the Tension Reduction Behavior (TRB) subscale of the TSI-2, and the Tension Reduction Activities (TRA) subscale of the IASC, various measures can be used to assess specific dysfunctional behaviors common to complex posttraumatic distress. These include the Dysfunctional Sexual Behavior (DSB) subscale of the TSI-2, the Substance Abuse and Suicidality subscales of the DAPS, and various scales of the MCMI-IV MMPI-2, and PAI. In addition, a number of freestanding, evidence-based measures are available. These include the *Eating Disorder Inventory–3* (EDI-3; Garner, 2004), the *Adult Substance Abuse Subtle Screening Inventory-4* (SASSI-4; Lazowski & Geary, 2019) and the *Adult Suicidal Ideation Questionnaire* (ASIQ; Reynolds, 1991).

Clinician-Administered Measures

Clinician-administered measures pertinent to complex trauma outcomes in adults primarily take the form of structured and semistructured interviews. However, one classic projective test with indices of relevance to traumatic sequelae is also considered in this section.

Broadband Diagnostic Interviews

Several clinician interviews have been validated for measurement of DSM and ICD diagnoses pertinent to assessment of the full range of complex trauma reactions.

The Structured Clinical Interview for DSM-5 Disorders

The Structured Clinical Interview for DSM-5 Disorders (SCID-5; First, Williams, Karg, & Spitzer, 2016) is the most comprehensive measure of psychiatric diagnoses. Its clinical use version includes full diagnostic modules for a wide range of disorders, with screening items for additional diagnoses of relevance to complex trauma adaptation, including eating disorders, intermittent explosive disorder, somatic symptom disorder, and hoarding disorder. The SCID-5 includes detailed handbooks guiding administration and scoring; optional live training is also available. While SCID-5 content and scoring has been updated for DSM-5, the preponderance of psychometric research was conducted on earlier versions measuring DSM-IV-based diagnoses. One newer study of SCID-5 (Shankman et al., 2017) found that an adapted version enabling dimensional scoring of symptom severity demonstrated superior reliability and validity compared to the standard diagnostic scoring.

The World Health Organization World Mental Health Composite International Diagnostic Interview

The World Health Organization World Mental Health Composite International Diagnostic Interview (WHO WMH-CIDI; Kessler et al., 2004) is the most cited diagnostic interview in worldwide clinical research. It includes a two-page screener of its most common diagnostic modules. However, in contrast to the SCID, the extensive training required to gain access to the WMH-CIDI is likely to be prohibitive to many practicing clinicians. While an updated version aligned to DSM-5 and ICD-11 is reported to be in development, no further training is available for earlier versions of this instrument.

The Mini International Neuropsychiatric Interview

The Mini International Neuropsychiatric Interview (M.I.N.I.; Sheehan et al., 1998) enables rapid evaluation of 17 prevalent DSM diagnoses, with screening questions for additional diagnoses and more detailed modules for specific disorders. Content and scoring of its latest version (MINI 7.0.2) have been updated for DSM-5, but as with the SCID and CIDI, research to date on psychometric properties is based on previous versions.

None of these broadband diagnostic interviews include assessment of dissociative disorders or new DSM-5 diagnoses relevant to complex trauma adaptation (i.e., disruptive mood dysregulation disorder; disinhibited social engagement disorder). Given their diagnostic foci, these clinical interviews also do not measure prominent, dimensional elements of maladaptation associated with complex trauma exposure such as emotion dysregulation, negative self-image, executive dysfunction, and relationship problems. Cautions regarding limitations to the cross-cultural validity and construct equivalence of these and other diagnostic instruments with non-Western, developing, and postconflict countries have been raised (Rosenman, 2012) and in some instances empirically substantiated (deJong, Komproe, Spinazzola, van der Kolk, & van Ommeren, 2005).

Trauma-Specific Clinician Interviews

The Clinician-Administered PTSD Scale

The Clinician-Administered PTSD Scale (CAPS-5; Weathers et al., 2013a) is a widely used structured diagnostic interview that generates both dichotomous and continuous scores for current and lifetime PTSD. Previous versions of the CAPS have been extensively validated. The CAPS-5 has been updated to enable diagnosis of PTSD based on DSM-5. In contrast to earlier versions, the 30-item CAPS-5 no longer measures supplemental symptoms associated with complex trauma reactions.

The Posttraumatic Stress Disorder Symptom Scale Interview for DSM-5

The Posttraumatic Stress Disorder Symptom Scale Interview for DSM-5 (PSSI-5; Foa et al., 2016b), a 24-item, semistructured interview of PTSD diagnosis and symptom severity, has been updated for DSM-5. Preliminary psychometric research has indicated good to excellent validity and reliability of the PSSI-5 (Foa et al., 2016b).

The Structured Interview for Disorders of Extreme Stress

The Structured Interview for Disorders of Extreme Stress (SIDES; van der Kolk, Roth, Pelcovitz, Sunday, & Spinazzola, 2005) was the first instrument developed to measure complex trauma-specific (i.e., DESNOS or early complex PTSD) reactions in adults. The SIDES is not slated to be updated to align it with the ICD-11 diagnosis of complex PTSD, and use of the SIDES has diminished over the past decade, attributable in part to unresolved scale-design flaws, proliferation of inconsistent scoring rules, and lack of agreement among experts about scale and item composition. Consequently, the original 37-item version of the SIDES is not recommended for further use. A well-designed set of studies undertaken to improve the psychometric properties of the SIDES (Scoboria, Ford, Lin, & Frisman, 2008) resulted in delineation of the SIDES-R, a 20-item measure comprises five scales: Somatic Dysregulation, Anger Dysregulation, Risk/Self-Harm, and Altered Sexuality, and Demoralization. Given its status as one of few measures capturing multiple domains of complex trauma adaptation, including some dimensions not covered by other evidence-based measures, the SIDES-R merits consideration as a research tool for studies in which its factors are of interest, or as a secondary dimensional measure of complex trauma adaptation with select clients.

Interview Measures of Dissociative Symptoms and Disorders

Clinician-administered measures of dissociation possess relevance and appeal as a component of more extensive evaluation of complex trauma reactions given the prominence of dissociative phenomena in adults with histories of complex trauma, the inherent limitations in client awareness and self-report of dissociative symptoms, and the exclusion of dissociative disorders from broadband diagnostic instruments.

The Structured Clinical Interview for DSM-IV Dissociative Disorders

The Structured Clinical Interview for DSM-IV Dissociative Disorders (SCID-D; Steinberg, 1994) is the best validated measure of dissociative symptoms and disorders. The SCID-D focuses on measurement of five manifestations of clinical dissociation: amnesia, depersonalization, derealization, identity confusion, and identity alteration. The SCID-D has been widely used in clinical research and has been translated and validated for use in numerous countries. An interviewer's guide is available, and an updated edition of the SCID-D enabling diagnosis of dissociative disorders based on DSM-5 and ICD-11 criteria is reported to be in development.

The Dissociative Disorders Interview Schedule

The Dissociative Disorders Interview Schedule (DDIS DSM-5; Ross et al., 1989) is a 132-item structured interview that has been updated to enable diagnosis of all DSM-5 dissociative disorders. The DDIS measures several additional diagnoses and conditions associated with dissociative disorders including borderline personality disorder, somatic symptom disorder, positive symptoms of schizophrenia, substance abuse, childhood abuse, developmental manifestations of dissociation, and extrasensory experiences. The psychometric properties of the DDIS have yet to be tested for DSM-5; earlier versions demonstrated good sensitivity and specificity in diagnosis of dissociative identity disorder.

Other Clinician-Administered Measures of Relevance to Complex Trauma

Adult Attachment Interview

The Adult Attachment Interview (AAI; George, Kaplan, & Main, 1985) is a well-validated, semistructured interview addressing internal representations of attachment in adults informed by core childhood relationships. The AAI assigns adults to one four primary attachment statuses: (1) Autonomous, (2) Dismissing, (3) Preoccupied, and (4) Unresolved/Disorganized. Whereas the fourth category has most directly been associated with traumatic loss or abuse, the second and third categories may be pertinent to adults with histories of severe emotional abuse or emotional neglect in childhood, or other subtle forms of early or pervasive psychological maltreatment (e.g., excessive parental demands; gaslighting). Initially developed as a research tool, scholars have illustrated the usefulness of the AAI in the context of adult psychotherapy, including trauma-focused treatment (Steele & Steele, 2008). Nevertheless, use this instrument in routine clinical practice has been heavily limited by the infrequency, cost, and time-intensive nature of the required training regimen for AAI administration, scoring, and interpretation.

Rorschach

The Rorschach differs from the other instruments described in this chapter in that it is a projective test rather than a self-report or interview measure. This test can yield meaningful information about various constructs relevant to complex posttraumatic symptoms, such as psychological defenses, ego strength, reality testing, self-capacities, aggression, and bodily concerns (Exner, 2003), as well as posttraumatic stress and dissociation (Luxenberg & Levin, 2004). Contemporary efforts to enhance empirical validation of the Rorscach have resulted in the development of a revised and generally well-received system for administration, scoring and interpretation (Meyer, Viglione, Mihura, Erard, & Erdberg, 2011). When interpreted by those without specific training in assessment of clients with complex posttraumatic clinical presentations, however, some trauma-related outcomes may be misrepresented as impaired reality testing or personality disorder on the Rorschach (Luxenberg & Levin, 2004). As with the AAI, the requisite training and investment of time and resources to establish proficiency in use of the Rorschach may be impractical for most practicing clinicians.

Recommendations

Several recommendations can be made for the assessment of the complex effects of trauma in adults. First, in most cases, at least two broadband screening instruments should be administered: at least one for either general psychological symptomatology or psychiatric diagnoses, and at least one for complex trauma-specific disturbance. In addition, those trained in projective testing or attachment theory should consider using the Rorschach or the AAI when indicated and when time permits. If, based on these tests and/or the general clinical interview, PTSD is suspected, a structured clinical interview should be administered if feasible. Otherwise a self-report instrument with good predictive validity for PTSD diagnosis or clinical symptom severity may be used. When additional facets of complex trauma adaptation are suspected, the evaluator should administer whatever psychometrically valid tests or interviews seem most relevant, including those tapping dissociation, self-image, or disturbed self-capacities. When emotion dysregulation, mood disturbance, somatization, maladaptive coping, or distress reduction activities are particular concerns, administration of instruments containing particular scales that address these specific areas of difficulty may be helpful.

Conclusion

Complex posttraumatic responses reflect the wide variety of potential adverse experiences in the world and the many biological, social, cultural, and psychological variables that moderate the impact of these experiences. As a result, these outcomes are quite variable and cover many domains, and the notion of a one-size-fits-all diagnosis often is untenable. Instead, the clinician should consider the entire range of posttraumatic responses potentially attributable to a given client's history and risk factors. In many cases, this may require the administration of a wide range of psychological tests, both generic and more trauma-specific, followed by, or concurrent with, other tests relevant to the individual's specific clinical presentation.

Thorough assessment of complex posttraumatic responses informs diagnosis and guides treatment. Evaluation approaches that examine the full range of trauma-related outcomes may highlight treatment targets that might otherwise be overlooked, identifying trauma symptoms within more generic syndromes and generic symptoms within a stress disorder. Assessment of complex traumatic stress sequelae also may identify phenomena that interfere with effective treatment. For example, information that a client in trauma-focused therapy has a significant drug abuse history or emotional regulation difficulties may lead the clinician to use an empirically supported intervention that more directly addresses substance abuse issues or increases affect regulation capacities, either prior to, in conjunction with, or in lieu of a more classical memory processing-focused approach to posttraumatic stress symptoms.

The mental health field has become increasingly aware of complex trauma as a meaningful construct and focus of clinical attention. This realization has catalyzed tremendous innovation in the development of evidence-based treatment approaches for trauma-exposed adults presenting with complex psychological difficulties. Innovation in the development, validation, and standardization of evidence-based assessment measures of complex trauma reactions is of equal importance. Such tools are essential to inform selection, combination, and sequencing of treatment models; to monitor symptom change over the course of treatment; and to guide empirically driven intervention adjustments in effort to optimize treatment effectiveness.

Note

The DAPS, TSI-2, CDS, and IASC, described in this chapter, were written by John Briere, who receives royalties from Psychological Assessment Resources.

References

Acierno, R., Resnick, H. S., Kilpatrick, D. G., Saunders, B. E., & Best, C. L. (1999). Risk factors for rape, physical assault, and posttraumatic stress disorder in women: Examination of differential multivariate relationships. *Journal of Anxiety Disorders, 13*, 541–563.

Allen, B. (2011). Childhood psychological abuse and adult aggression: The mediating role of self-capacities. *Journal of Interpersonal Violence, 26*, 2093–2110.

American Educational Research Association, American Psychological Association, National Council on Measurement in Education, & Joint Committee on Standards for Educational and Psychological Testing (U.S.). (2014). *Standards for educational and psychological testing*. Washington, DC: Author.

American Psychiatric Association. (2000). *Diagnostic and statistical manual of mental disorders* (4th ed., text rev.). Washington, DC: Author.

American Psychiatric Association. (2013). *Diagnostic and statistical manual of mental disorders* (5th ed.). Arlington, VA: Author.

Anda, R., Felitti, V., Bremner, J. D., Walker, J. D., Whitfield, C., Perry, B. D., . . . , Giles, W. H. (2006). The enduring effects of abuse and related adverse experiences in childhood: A convergence of evidence from neurobiology and epidemiology. *European Archives of Psychiatry and Clinical Neuroscience, 256*, 174–186.

Banyard, V. L., Williams, L. M., & Siegel, J. A. (2001). The long-term mental health consequences of childhood sexual abuse: An exploratory study of the impact of multiple traumas in a sample of women. *Journal of Traumatic Stress, 14*, 697–715.

Beck, A. T., & Steer, R. A. (1993). *Beck Anxiety Inventory manual*. San Antonio, TX: Psychological Corporation.

Beck, A. T., Steer, R. A., & Brown, G. K. (1996). *Manual for the Beck Depression Inventory–II*. San Antonio, TX: Psychological Corporation.

Bernstein, E. M., & Putnam, F. W. (1986). Development, reliability, and validity of a dissociation scale. *Journal of Nervous and Mental Disease, 174*, 727–734.

Bigras, N., Godbout, N., Hébert, M., Runtz, M., & Daspe, M. È. (2015). Identity and relatedness as mediators between child emotional abuse and adult couple adjustment in women. *Child Abuse and Neglect, 50*, 85–93.

Blevins, C. A., Weathers, F. W., Davis, M. T., Witte, T. K., & Domino, J. L. (2015). The Posttraumatic Stress Disorder Checklist for DSM-5 (PCL-5): Development and initial psychometric evaluation. *Journal of Traumatic Stress, 28*, 489–498.

Bovin, M. J., Marx, B. P., Weathers, F. W., Gallagher, M. W., Rodriguez, P., Schnurr, P. P., & Keane, T. M. (2016). Psychometric properties of the PTSD Checklist for Diagnostic and Statistical Manual of Mental Disorders-Fifth Edition (PCL-5) in veterans. *Psychological Assessment, 28*(11), 1379–1391.

Briere, J. (2000a). *Cognitive Distortions Scale (CDS)*. Odessa, FL: Psychological Assessment Resources.

Briere, J. (2000b). *Inventory of Altered Self-Capacities (IASC)*. Odessa, FL: Psychological Assessment Resources.

Briere, J. (2001). *Detailed Assessment of Posttraumatic Stress (DAPS)*. Odessa, FL: Psychological Assessment Resources.

Briere, J. (2002). *Multiscale Dissociation Inventory*. Odessa, FL: Psychological Assessment Resources.

Briere, J. (2011). *Trauma Symptom Inventory-2 (TSI-2)*. Odessa, FL: Psychological Assessment Resources.

Briere, J. (2019). *Treating risky and compulsive behavior in trauma survivors*. New York: Guilford Press.

Briere, J., Kaltman, S., & Green, B. L. (2008). Accumulated childhood trauma and symptom complexity. *Journal of Traumatic Stress, 21*(2), 223–226.

Briere, J., & Rickards, S. (2007). Self-awareness, affect regulation, and relatedness: Differential sequelae of childhood versus adult victimization experiences. *Journal of Nervous and Mental Disease, 195,* 497–503.

Briere, J., & Scott, C. (2014). *Principles of trauma therapy: A guide to symptoms, evaluation, and treatment* (2nd ed.). Thousand Oaks, CA: SAGE.

Briere, J., & Spinazzola, J. (2005). Phenomenology and psychological assessment of complex posttraumatic states. *Journal of Traumatic Stress, 18*(5), 401–412.

Briere, J., Weathers, F. W., & Runtz, M. (2005). Is dissociation a multidimensional construct?: Data from the Multiscale Dissociation Inventory. *Journal of Traumatic Stress, 18,* 221–231.

Butcher, J. N., Graham, J. R., Ben-Porath, Y. S., Tellegen, A., Dahlstrom, W. G., & Kaemmer, B. (2001). *Minnesota Multiphasic Personality Inventory (MMPI-2): Manual for administration and scoring.* Minneapolis: University of Minnesota Press.

Carlson, E. B. (1997). *Trauma assessments: A clinician's guide.* New York: Guilford Press.

Carter, R. T. (2007). Racism and psychological and emotional injury: Recognizing and assessing race-based traumatic stress. *Counseling Psychologist, 35,* 257–266.

Catanzaro, S. J., & Mearns, J. (1990). Measuring generalized expectancies for negative mood regulation: Initial scale development and implications. *Journal of Personality Assessment, 54,* 546–563.

Cloitre, M., Courtois, C. A., Charuvastra, A., Carapezza, R., Stolbach, B. C., & Green, B. L. (2011). Treatment of complex PTSD: Results of the ISTSS expert clinician survey on best practices. *Journal of Traumatic Stress, 24*(6), 615–627.

Cloitre, M., Garvert, D. W., Brewin, C. R., Bryant, R. A., & Maercker, A. (2013). Evidence for proposed ICD-11 PTSD and complex PTSD: A latent profile analysis. *European Journal of Psychotraumatology, 4,* 20706.

Cloitre, M., Garvert, D. W., Weiss, B., Carlson, E. B., & Bryant, R. A. (2014). Distinguishing PTSD, complex PTSD, and borderline personality disorder: A latent class analysis. *European Journal of Psychotraumatology, 5,* 25097.

Cloitre, M., Roberts, N. P., Bisson, J. I., & Brewin, C. R. (2017). *The International Trauma Questionnaire (ITQ).* Unpublished measure.

Cloitre, M., Stolbach, B. C., Herman, J. L., van der Kolk, B., Pynoos, R., Wang, J., & Petkova, E. A. (2009). Developmental approach to complex PTSD: Childhood and adult cumulative trauma as predictors of symptom complexity. *Journal of Traumatic Stress, 22,* 399–408.

Courtois, C. A. (2008). Complex trauma, complex reactions: Assessment and treatment. *Psychological Trauma: Theory, Research, Practice, and Policy, 1*(1), 86–100.

D'Andrea, W., Ford, J., Stolbach, B., Spinazzola, J., & van der Kolk, B. (2012). Understanding interpersonal trauma in children: Why we need a developmentally appropriate trauma diagnosis. *American Journal of Orthopsychiatry, 82*(2), 187–200.

de Jong, J. T., Komproe, I. H., Spinazzola, J., van der Kolk, B. A., & Van Ommeren, M. H. (2005). DESNOS in three post-conflict settings: Assessing cross-cultural construct equivalence. *Journal of Traumatic Stress, 18,* 13–21.

Dell, P. F. (2006). The Multidimensional Inventory of Dissociation (MID): A comprehensive measure of pathological dissociation. *Journal of Trauma and Dissocation, 72*(2), 77–106.

Derogatis, L., & Savitz, K. (2000). The SCL-90-R and the Brief Symptom Inventory (BSI) in primary care. In M. Maruish (Ed.), *Handbook of psychological assessment in primary care settings* (pp. 297–334). Mahwah, NJ: Erlbaum.

Dierkhising, C. B., Ford, J. D., Branson, C., Grasso, D. J., & Lee, R. (2019). Developmental timing of polyvictimization: Continuity, change, and association with adverse outcomes in adolescence. *Child Abuse and Neglect, 87,* 40–50.

Exner, J. E. (2003). *The Rorschach: A comprehensive system* (2nd ed.). New York: Wiley.

Finkelhor, D., Ormrod, R. K., & Turner, H. A. (2007). Polyvictimization and trauma in a national longitudinal cohort. *Developmental Psychopathology, 19,* 149–166.

First, M., Williams, J., Karg, R., & Spitzer, R. (2016). *Structured Clinical Interview for DSM-5 Disorders, Clinician Version (SCID-5-CV)*. Arlington, VA: American Psychiatric Association.

Fitts, W. H., & Warren, W. L. (1996). *Tennessee Self-Concept Scale, second edition*. Torrance, CA: Western Psychological Services.

Foa, E. B., McLean, C. P., Zang, Y., Zhong, J., Powers, M. B., Kauffman, B. Y., . . . Knowles, K. (2016a). Psychometric properties of the Posttraumatic Diagnostic Scale for DSM-5 (PDS-5). *Psychological Assessment, 28*(10), 1166–1171.

Foa, E. B., McLean, C. P., Zang, Y., Zhong, J., Rauch, S., Porter, K., . . . Kauffman, B. Y. (2016b). Psychometric properties of the Posttraumatic Stress Disorder Symptom Scale Interview for DSM-5 (PSSI-5). *Psychological Assessment, 28*(10), 1159–1165.

Follette, V. M., Polusny, M. A., Bechtle, A. E., & Naugle, A. E. (1996). Cumulative trauma: The impact of child sexual abuse, adult sexual assault, and spouse abuse. *Journal of Traumatic Stress, 9*, 25–35.

Ford, J., Grasso, D., Green, C., Levine, J., Spinazzola, J., & van der Kolk, B. (2013). Clinical significance of a proposed developmental trauma diagnosis: Results of an international survey of clinicians. *Journal of Clinical Psychiatry, 74*(8), 841–849.

Ford, J. D., Spinazzola, J., van der Kolk, B., & Grasso, D. J. (2018). Toward an empirically based developmental trauma disorder diagnosis for children: Factor structure, item characteristics, reliability, and validity of the Developmental Trauma Disorder Semi-Structured Interview (DTD-SI). *Journal of Clinical Psychiatry, 79*(5), ii.

Garner, D. M. (2004). *Eating Disorder Inventory–3 professional manual*. Odessa, FL: Psychological Assessment Resources.

George, C., Kaplan, N., & Main, M. (1985). *The Adult Attachment Interview*. Unpublished manuscript, University of California at Berkeley, Berkeley, CA.

Golin, C. E., Haley, D. F., Wang, J., Hughes, J. P., Kuo, I., Justman, J., . . . Hodder, S. (2016). Posttraumatic stress disorder symptoms and mental health over time among low-income women at increased risk of HIV in the U.S. *Journal of Health Care for the Poor and Underserved, 27*(2), 891–910.

Gratz, K. L., & Roemer, L. (2004). Multidimensional assessment of emotion regulation and dysregulation: Development, factor structure, and initial validation of the Difficulties in Emotion Regulation Scale. *Journal of Psychopathology and Behavioral Assessment, 26*, 41–54.

Herman, J. L. (1992). Complex PTSD: A syndrome in survivors of prolonged and repeated trauma. *Journal of Traumatic Stress, 5*, 377–391.

Hodgdon, H., Liebman, R., Martin, L., Suvak, M., Beserra, K., Rosenblum, W., & Spinazzola, J. (2018a). The effects of trauma type and executive dysfunction on symptom expression of polyvictimized youth in residential care. *Journal of Traumatic Stress 31*, 255–264.

Hodgdon, H., Spinazzola, J., Briggs, E., Liang, L., Steinberg, A., & Layne, C. (2018b). Maltreatment type, exposure characteristics, and mental health outcomes among clinic referred trauma-exposed youth. *Child Abuse and Neglect, 82*, 12–22.

Holmes, S. C., Facemire, V. C., & DaFonseca, A. M. (2016). Expanding criterion A for posttraumatic stress disorder: Considering the deleterious impact of oppression. *Traumatology, 22*(4), 314–321.

Hopper, E. K., Grossman, F. K., Spinazzola, J., & Zucker, M. (2018). *Treating adult survivors of emotional abuse and neglect: Component-based psychotherapy*. New York: Guilford Press.

Karatzias, T., Cloitre, M., Maercker, A., Kazlauskas, E., Shevlin, M., Hyland, P., . . . Brewin, C. R. (2017). PTSD and complex PTSD: ICD-11 updates on concept and measurement in the UK, USA, Germany and Lithuania. *European Journal of Traumatology, 8*(Suppl. 7), 1418103.

Karatzias, T., Shevlin, M., Fyvie, C., Hyland, P., Efthymiadou, E., Wilson, D., . . . Cloitre, M. (2016). An initial psychometric assessment of an ICD-11 based measure of PTSD and complex PTSD (ICD-TQ): Evidence of construct validity. *Journal of Anxiety Disorders,* *44,* 73–79.

Kessler, R., Abelson, J., Demler, O., Escobar, J., Gibbon, M., Guyer, M., . . . Zheng, H. (2004). Clinical calibration of DSM-IV diagnoses in the World Mental Health (WMH) version of the World Health Organization (WHO) Composite International Diagnostic Interview (WMH-CIDI). *International Journal of Methods in Psychiatric Research,* *13*(2), 122–139.

Kisiel, C., Fehrenbach, T., Liang, L., Stolbach. B., Griffin. G., McClelland, G., . . . Spinazzola, J. (2014). Examining child sexual abuse in relation to complex patterns of trauma exposure within the National Child Traumatic Stress Network. *Psychological Trauma: Theory, Research, Practice and Policy, 6*(Suppl. 1), S29–S39.

Kliethermes, M., Schacht, M., & Drewry, K. (2014). Complex trauma. *Child and Adolescent Psychiatric Clinics of North America, 23,* 339–361.

Klotz Flitter, J. M., Elhai, J. D., & Gold, S. N. (2003). MMPI-2 F scale elevations in adult victims of child sexual abuse. *Journal of Traumatic Stress, 16*(3), 269–274.

Kroenke, K., Spitzer, R. L., & Williams, J. B. (2002). The PHQ-15: Validity of a new measure for evaluating the severity of somatic symptoms. *Psychosomatic Medicine, 64*(2), 258–266.

Kubiak, S. P. (2005). Trauma and cumulative adversity in women of a disadvantaged social location. *American Journal of Orthopsychiatry, 75,* 451–465.

Lazowski, L. E., & Geary, B. B. (2019). Validation of the Adult Substance Abuse Subtle Screening Inventory-4 (SASSI-4). *European Journal of Psychological Assessment, 35*(1), 86–97.

Luxenberg, T., & Levin, P. (2004). The role of the Rorschach in the assessment and treatment of trauma. In J. P. Wilson & T. M. Keane (Eds.), *Assessing psychological trauma and PTSD* (2nd ed., pp. 190–225). New York: Guilford Press.

Marsella, A. J., Friedman, M. J., Gerrity, E. T., & Scurfield, R. M. (Eds.). (1996). *Ethnocultural aspects of posttraumatic stress disorder: Issues, research, and clinical applications.* Washington, DC: American Psychological Association.

Meyer, G. J., Viglione, D. J., Mihura, J. L., Erard, R. E., & Erdberg, P. (2011). *Rorschach Performance Assessment System: Administration, coding, interpretation, and technical manual.* Toledo, OH: Rorschach Performance Assessment System.

Mezzich, A. C., Tarter, R. E., Giancola, P. R., & Kirisci, L. (2001). The Dysregulation Inventory: A new scale to assess the risk for substance use disorder. *Journal of Child and Adolescent Substance Abuse, 10,* 35–43.

Millon, T., Grossman, S., & Millon, C. (2015). *Millon Clinical Multiaxial Inventory–IV: Manual.* Bloomington, MN: NCS Pearson.

Morey, L. C. (2007). *Personality Assessment Inventory professional manual* (2nd ed.). Odessa, FL: Psychological Assessment Resources.

Musicaro, R., Spinazzola, J., Arvidson, J., Swaroop, S., Goldblatt Grace, L., Yarrow, A., . . . Ford, J. (2019). The complexity of adaptation to childhood polyvictimization in youth and young adults: Recommendations for multidisciplinary responders. *Trauma, Violence and Abuse, 20*(1), 81–98.

Nobles, C. J., Valentine, S. E., Borba, C. P. C., Gerber, M. W., Shtasel, D. L., & Marques, L. (2016). Black-white disparities in the association between posttraumatic stress disorder and chronic illness. *Journal of Psychosomatic Research, 85,* 19–25.

Parlar, M., Frewen, P. A., Oremus, C., Lanius, R. A., & McKinnon, M. C. (2016). Dissociative symptoms are associated with reduced neuropsychological performance in patients with recurrent depression and a history of trauma exposure. *European Journal of Psychotraumatology, 7,* 29061.

Pearlman, L. A. (2003). *Trauma and Attachment Belief Scale.* Los Angeles: Western Psychological Services.

Pelcovitz, D., van der Kolk, B. A., Roth, S., Mandel, F., Kaplan, S., & Resick, P. (1997).

Development of a criteria set and a structured interview for disorders of extreme stress (SIDES). *Journal of Traumatic Stress, 10,* 3–16.

Perry, B. D., & Pollard, R. (1998). Homeostasis, stress, trauma, and adaptation: A neurodevelopmental view of childhood trauma. *Child and Adolescent Psychiatric Clinics of North America, 7,* 33–51.

Ray, W. J., & Faith, M. (1995). Dissociative experiences in a college age population: Follow-up with 1190 subjects. *Personality and Individual Differences, 18*(2), 223–230.

Resick, P. A., Suvak, M. K., Johnides, B. D., Mitchell, K. S., & Iverson, K. M. (2012). The impact of dissociation on PTSD treatment with cognitive processing therapy. *Depression and Anxiety, 29*(8), 718–730.

Reynolds, W. M. (1991). Psychometric characteristics of the Adult Suicidal Ideation Questionnaire in college students. *Journal of Personality Assessment, 56,* 289–307.

Roberts, A. L., Austin, B., Corliss, H. L., Vandermorris, A. K., & Koenen, K. C. (2010). Pervasive trauma exposure among US sexual orientation minority adults and risk of posttraumatic stress disorder. *American Journal of Public Health, 100*(12), 2433–2441.

Rosenman, S. (2012). Cause for caution: Culture, sensitivity and the World Mental Health Survey Initiative. *Australasian Psychiatry, 20*(1), 14–19.

Ross, C. A., Heber, S., Norton, G. R., Anderson, G., Anderson, D., & Barchet, P. (1989). The Dissociative Disorders Interview Schedule: A structured interview. *Dissociation, 2*(3), 169–189.

Roth, R. M., Isquith, P. K., & Gioia, G. A. (2005). *Behavior Rating Inventory of Executive Function–Adult Version (BRIEF-A).* Odessa, FL: Psychological Assessment Resources.

Scoboria, A., Ford, J., Lin, H. J., & Frisman, L. (2008). Exploratory and confirmatory factor analyses of the Structured Interview for Disorders of Extreme Stress. *Assessment, 15*(4), 404–425.

Sheehan, D., Lecrubier, Y., Harnett-Sheehan, K., Amorim, P., Janavs, J., Weiller, E., . . . Dunbar, G. (1998). The Mini International Neuropsychiatric Interview (M.I.N.I.): The development and validation of a structured diagnostic psychiatric interview. *Journal of Clinical Psychiatry, 59*(Suppl. 20), 22–33.

Sorsoli, L., Kia-Keating, M., & Grossman, F. K. (2008). "I keep that hush hush: Male survivors of sexual abuse and the challenges of disclosure. *Journal of Counseling Psychology, 55*(3), 333–345.

Sotero, M. M. (2006). Conceptual model of historical trauma: Implications for public health practice and research. *Journal of Health Disparities Research and Practice, 1*(1) 93–108.

Spielberger, C. D. (1999). *STAXI-2 State–Trait Anger Expression Inventory–2: Professional manual.* Lutz, FL: Psychological Assessment Resources.

Spielberger, C. D., Gorsuch, R. L., Lushene, R., Vagg, P. R., & Jacobs, G. A. (1983). *Manual for the State–Trait Anxiety Inventory.* Palo Alto, CA: Consulting Psychologists Press.

Spinazzola, J., Ford, J., Zucker, M., van der Kolk, B., Silva, S., Smith, S., & Blaustein, M. (2005). National survey of complex trauma exposure, outcome and intervention for children and adolescents. *Psychiatric Annals, 35*(5), 433–439.

Spinazzola, J., Habib, M., Knoverek, A., Arvidson, J., Nisenbaum, J., Wentworth, R., & Pond, A. (2013, Winter). The heart of the matter: Complex trauma in child welfare. *CW360°: Trauma-Informed Child Welfare Pratice,* pp. 8–9, 37.

Spinazzola, J., Hodgdon, H., Liang, L., Ford, J., Layne, C., Pynoos, R., . . . Kisiel, C. (2014). Unseen wounds: The contribution of psychological maltreatment to child and adolescent mental health and risk outcomes in a national sample. *Psychological Trauma: Theory, Research, Practice and Policy, 6*(Suppl. 1), S18–S28.

Spinazzola, J., van der Kolk, B., & Ford, J. (2018). When nowhere is safe: Interpersonal trauma and attachment adversity as antecedents of posttraumatic stress disorder and developmental trauma disorder. *Journal of Traumatic Stress, 31*(5), 631–642.

Steele, H., & Steele, M. (Eds). (2008). *Clinical applications of the Adult Attachment Interview.* New York: Guilford Press.

Steinberg, M. (1994). *Structured Clinical Interview for DSM-IV Dissociative Disorders—Revised (SCID-D-R).* Washington, DC: American Psychiatric Press.

van der Kolk, B., Ford, J., & Spinazzola, J. (2019). Comorbidity of developmental trauma disorder and posttraumatic stress disorder: Findings from the DTD field trial. *European Journal of Psychotraumatology, 10*(1), 1562841.

van der Kolk, B. A., Roth, S. H., Pelcovitz, D., Sunday, S., & Spinazzola, J. (2005). Disorders of extreme stress. *Journal of Traumatic Stress, 18,* 389–399.

van IJzendoorn, M. H., & Schuengel, C. (1996). The measurement of dissociation in normal and clinical populations: Meta-analytic validation of the Dissociative Experiences Scale (DES). *Clinical Psychology Review, 16*(5), 365–382.

Wamser-Nanney, R., & Vandenberg, B. R. (2013). Empirical support for the definition of a complex trauma event in children and adolescents. *Journal of Traumatic Stress, 26*(6), 671–678.

Weathers, F. W., Blake, D. D., Schnurr, P. P., Kaloupek, D. G., Marx, B. P., & Keane, T. M. (2013a). The Clinician-Administered PTSD Scale for DSM-5 (CAPS-5). Retrieved from the National Center for PTSD from *www.ptsd.va.gov.*

Weathers, F. W., Litz, B. T., Keane, T. M., Palmieri, P. A., Marx, B. P., & Schnurr, P. P. (2013b). The PTSD Checklist for DSM-5 (PCL-5). Retrieved from the National Center for PTSD at *www.ptsd.va.gov.*

Wolf, E. J., Mitchell, K. S., Sadeh, N., Hein, C., Fuhrman, I., Pietrzak, R. H., & Miller, M. W. (2017). The Dissociative Subtype of PTSD Scale (DSPS): Initial evaluation in a national sample of trauma-exposed veterans. *Assessment, 24*(4), 503–516.

World Health Organization. (2018). *International classification of diseases* (11th ed.). Geneva, Switzerland: Author.

Wortmann, J. H., Jordan, A. H., Weathers, F. W., Resick, P. A., Dondanville, K. A., Hall-Clark, B., . . . Litz, B. T. (2016). Psychometric analysis of the PTSD Checklist-5 (PCL-5) among treatment-seeking military service members. *Psychological Assessment, 28*(11), 1392–1403.

CHAPTER 6

Assessing and Treating Complex Dissociative Disorders

KATHY STEELE
ONNO VAN DER HART

We focus in this chapter on the two dissociative disorders that manifest in distinctive dissociative symptoms and include a division or compartmentalization of sense of self and identity. These complex disorders are considered to be extreme reactions to developmental trauma and require a specific treatment approach. They include dissociative identity disorder (DID) and other specified dissociative disorder—type 1 (OSDD-1; American Psychiatric Association, 2013). OSDD includes a diverse range of four dissociative problems, but OSDD-1 is considered to be very much like DID, with less distinct symptoms. Because so many phenomena are now considered to be dissociative, we briefly explore the several definitions of dissociation, as they have different treatment implications, as well as offer a brief overview of assessment and treatment of OSDD-1 and DID.

Definitions of Dissociation in the Literature

More and more symptoms have been brought under the umbrella of dissociation since its original and more limited description over a century ago, a compartmentalization of the personality, including sense of self and identity (Janet, 1907). *Dissociation* has been defined as (1) a "normal" experience involving attentional phenomena such as absorption, detachment, and imaginative involvement; (2) physiological hypoarousal, with resulting disconnection from present experience; (3) a broad array of symptoms of depersonalization and derealization; and (4) a "pathological" type involving trauma-related division of personality and identity.

Alterations in Attention and Awareness of the Present

This definition, which sometimes has been referred to as "normal" dissociation, includes various manifestations of alterations in conscious awareness and attention, such as absorption (overfocus on thoughts or activities, such that one is not aware of surroundings); detachment (thinking of nothing and being unaware of surroundings); spaciness resulting in forgetfulness and inattention; excessive daydreaming; and other types of imaginative involvement (Dalenberg & Paulson, 2009; Holmes et al., 2005). These phenomena are considered "normal" because all humans experience them in everyday life, especially when tired, ill, preoccupied, stressed, or so focused on one thing (e.g., reading an interesting book or thinking about an upsetting interaction with someone) that we do not notice or register others. They are found in both normal and clinical populations and are therefore not specific to dissociative and other trauma-related disorders, though they are typically present in these disorders. While changes in conscious awareness are generally present in OSDD-1 and DID, they are not sufficient in themselves to cause or entirely explain the broad range of mental and somatic symptoms of dissociation that are common in these two disorders.

Treatment of Alterations in Awareness

When alterations in conscious awareness are in the "normal" range, they require no treatment other than a return to a focus on the present, and good self-care that remedies stress, fatigue, illness, or a tendency toward distraction and absorption. The treatment of serious and chronic problems that interfere with daily functioning, such as chronic absorption, detachment, and maladaptive daydreaming (Somer, 2002; Somer & Herscu, 2017), primarily includes mindfulness training and development of reflective functioning. These skills are highly recommended for trauma survivors but are not sufficient in themselves to treat OSDD-1 and DID (Steele, Dorahy, Van der Hart, & Nijenhuis, 2009).

Physiological Shutdown

Dissociation is also described in some of the literature as a physiological shutdown or extreme hypoarousal due to excessive parasympathetic activation (Porges, 2003, 2011; Schore, 2003, 2012). This is an innate defense reaction against life threat that results in rapid loss of energy and movement ("flag") and ultimately in total collapse or death feint ("faint") (Nijenhuis, 2015; Porges, 2003, 2011; Schauer & Elbert, 2010; Steele, Boon, & van der Hart, 2017; Van der Hart, Nijenhuis, & Steele, 2006). Porges has called this the *dorsal vagal response* (2003, 2011). Physiological shutdown involves a severe disconnect from present awareness and is often trauma-related, which is why some call it *dissociation*. The problem with this definition is that dissociation also may involve extreme hyperarousal, as well as dysregulated alternation between hyper- and hypoarousal commonly found in OSDD-1 and DID. It also does not include other mental and physical symptoms that have been described as dissociative in much of the literature (Steele, Van der Hart, & Nijenhuis, 2009; Steele et al., 2017).

Treatment of Dorsal Vagal Reactions

Treatment of the dorsal vagal response involves activation of the ventral vagal parasympathetic system, which regulates the nervous system. This might include use of the therapist's voice (calm and slightly singsong and repetitive) and other sounds that activate the ventral vagal system, breathing exercises, somatic resourcing, concrete orientation to the present (e.g., "Can you touch the fabric of the sofa to remind you that you are here and now and safe?"), present-centered postural change or movement, and activation of curiosity and relationally collaborative efforts (e.g., "Let's together find a way to help you feel more grounded") (Dana, 2018; Ogden & Fisher, 2016).

Depersonalization and Derealization

Severe and persistent symptoms of depersonalization and derealization include out-of-body experiences, somatic and perceptual distortions, feeling as if in a dream or on a stage, and slowed time sense before, during, or in the immediate aftermath of traumatic experiences (Bryant & Harvey, 2000). These symptoms are hallmarks of depersonalization disorder (American Psychiatric Association, 2013). They are common acute peritraumatic experiences (Bryant & Harvey, 2000), and are included in criteria for acute stress disorder and in OSDD— type 3 (American Psychiatric Association, 2013). Depersonalization is also a major criterion for the relatively new dissociative subtype of PTSD that is now included in the fifth edition of the *Diagnostic and Statistical Manual of Mental Disorders* (DSM-5; American Psychiatric Association, 2013; also see Lanius, Brand, Vermetten, Frewen, & Spiegel, 2012).

More transient symptoms of depersonalization are ubiquitous, found in many mental disorders (Aderibigbe, Bloch, & Walker, 2001; American Psychiatric Association, 2013), and also in the general population as occasional phenomena during periods of stress, illness, or fatigue (Catrell & Catrell, 1974).

Treatment of Depersonalization

Treatment of depersonalization disorder is challenging and to date there is no evidence-based treatment. The treatment of the dissociative subtype of post-traumatic stress disorder (PTSD) involves the need for the client to learn emotion recognition and tolerance, and reflective functioning, along with mindfulness and grounding skills, what are generally considered to be stabilization skills. Generally, a combination of dynamic psychotherapy, cognitive-behavioral therapy (CBT), skills training, and medication can be helpful, both for persistent depersonalization symptoms (Simeon & Abugel, 2006) and for the dissociative subtype of PTSD.

The Original Definition of Dissociation: Division of the Personality

Dissociation was originally described by Pierre Janet under the rubric of *hysteria*, the old term for what is now considered to be a wide range of trauma-related disorders, including not only OSDD-1 and DID but also the somatoform dissociative disorders described in the *International Classification of Diseases, Tenth Revision* (ICD-10; World Health Organization [WHO], 1992). Janet noted that hysteria was an integrative failure "characterized by the retraction of the field of personal consciousness and a tendency to the dissociation and emancipation of the systems of ideas and functions that constitute personality" (1907, p. 332). Thus, the original definition notes that changes in conscious awareness are a necessary component of dissociation, but a division of personality is also necessary, a phenomenon not acknowledged in more recent definitions of dissociation. Alterations in conscious awareness only involve attentional and perhaps perceptual components of experience; the original term *dissociation* encompasses the whole of personality, which can include attention, cognition, emotion, somatic experiences, perception, prediction, and systems of meaning and identity (Nijenhuis & Van der Hart, 2011; Steele et al., 2009, 2017).

Because of the treatment differences we outlined earlier among the many phenomena that are called dissociation in the clinical literature, we make the case for distinguishing what we call *structural dissociation (of the personality)*, as originally described by Janet. Structural dissociation involves an inner organization or structure of divided subsystems within an individual's whole personality system that lack adequate cohesion and coherence, what we identify as *dissociative parts of the personality* (Boon, Steele, & Van der Hart, 2011; Nijenhuis, 2015; Steele et al., 2017; Van der Hart et al., 2006). This term emphasizes that dissociation is at the level of personality, not a simple isolation of affect or attentional loss, for example. Many other labels exist for these subsystems, such as alters, alternate personalities or identities, dissociative states, disaggregate self-states, self-states, ego states, self-aspects, and part-selves. Regardless of what they are called, these subsystems have their own sense of self and first-person perspective in dissociative disorders, have unusually closed (but still semipermeable) boundaries between each other, and can, in principle, interact with each other and other people, unlike the normal subsystems in individuals who do not have a dissociative disorder.

While some clinicians and researchers question whether "parts" language is potentially suggestive for clients, the majority of dissociative individuals report that this language fits their experience and helps them feel more understood. There is consensus among experts in the dissociative disorders field that dissociative subsystems are not separate things or beings within the same person, nor should they be treated as such. Neither are they mere role playing; rather, they are manifestations of significant and chronic breaches in the integrity of a single personality—including sense of self—across time and contexts. Thus, a systemic approach that considers dissociative parts as interrelated subsystems of the individual should be the fundamental foundation for all therapeutic interventions in OSDD-1 and DID.

Because treatment differs among the various phenomena included under the rubric of dissociation, for clarity, we propose that alterations in conscious awareness without accompanying division of personality be called by those names (e.g., absorption, detachment, imaginative involvement); that physiological hypoarousal be distinguished from dissociative symptoms per se and from dissociative disorders; that more attention be paid to somatoform dissociative symptoms that are emphasized in the ICD-10 (WHO, 1992); and that symptoms of depersonalization and derealization be distinguished from the disturbances of identity in OSDD-1 and DID.

The Roots of Structural Dissociation

Normal integration of self and personality is an ongoing developmental endeavor (Putnam, 1997) that requires continual updating and adaptation across the individual's life (Damasio, 1999; Janet, 1929; Schore, 2003). Dissociative divisions in OSDD-1 and DID prevent the individual from engaging in the normal updating that lends itself to personality adaptation and a single autobiographical sense of self across time, situations, and experiences. Instead each dissociative part is organized by fixed and rather limited ways of thinking, feeling, perceiving, and behaving, impervious to normal changes and updating. The individual is unable to integrate these discrepant parts into his or her personality and into a single encompassing sense of self without further skills building. Thus, an important treatment point is that OSDD-1 and DID are not merely dissociative defenses, but rather are deficits in the integration of the self that require a period of ego strengthening in therapy.

DID and OSDD-1 likely have both psychological and biological underpinnings. The psychological value of dissociation is to avoid awareness and ownership of what is perceived to be intolerable. Biologically, structural dissociation seems to occur along evolutionary lines of (1) defending against danger and life threat, and (2) functioning in daily life via distinct neural networks that organize and regulate attention, perception, emotion, physiology and, behavior (Liotti, 2006, 2009, 2017; Nijenhuis, 2015; Panksepp, 1998; Porges, 2003, 2011; Steele et al., 2017; Van der Hart et al., 2006). These innate neural pathways are called *motivational* or *action systems,* because they motivate us to act in particular ways. They are mediated by primary affects, directing us toward experiences that increase chances of survival and away from danger and threat. For example, most of the action systems of daily life direct us toward prosocial activities: attachment, collaboration, competition, caregiving, play, and sexuality (Lichenberg & Kindler, 1994; Liotti, 2017; Panksepp, 1998; Steele et al., 2017). Defensive systems against threat include flight, fight, freeze, and faint (death feigning or collapse). Action systems of daily life and those of defense involve very different physiological states.

Several authors have proposed that these two opposing systems are the underpinnings of disorganized attachment and dissociative disorders such as OSDD-1 and DID (Liotti, 2006, 2009, 2017; Nijenhuis, 2015; Steele et al., 2017; Van der Hart et al., 2006). The traumatized child has an insoluble dilemma of meeting two competing biological needs to attach to and defend against the same caregiver, what Main and Hesse (1990) have called "fright without solution." This results in a collapse of attachment strategies and in subsequent discordant alternation between attachment and defense strategies with their very different physiological, attentional, emotional, perceptual, and cognitive components. This early fragmentation leaves the child vulnerable to further dissociation across the lifespan (Ogawa, Sroufe, Weinfield, Carlson, & Egeland, 1997). The development of different dissociative parts can be understood, at least in part, by these chronic involuntary and inharmonious alternations between discrepant action systems (Liotti, 2006, 2009, 2017; Steele et al., 2017; Van der Hart et al., 2006).

In OSDD-1 and DID, dissociative parts of the individual may be said to develop in relative isolation from each other, dependent on their functional organization via either daily life or threat action systems, and via avoidance of overwhelming emotion, sensations, meanings, and memories. The individual tries to go on with everyday life in dissociative parts that are primarily organized by daily life systems, typically highly avoidant of the trauma. When the individual is directed by dissociative parts primarily fixed in threat defense, he or she is often reliving and reenacting the trauma, unable to realize it is over, and unable to participate in daily life effectively. These two types of parts can become increasingly separate, organized by conflicting motivations, emotions, and needs.

Before effective treatment can commence, thorough assessment of dissociative disorders should be undertaken. Below we summarize the major indications of OSDD-1 and DID.

Assessment of Dissociative Disorders

A major clinical challenge to adequate assessment is the lack of training available to clinicians, resulting in problems of both over- and underdiagnosis (Steele et al., 2017). Underdiagnosis is the major problem, as most clinicians do not even consider the possibility of dissociative disorders. Overdiagnosis can occur when clinicians mistake phenomena such as borderline dynamics, normal ego states, or metaphorical "inner child" states for dissociative parts. It also can occur when an individual presents with malingering or a factitious disorder (Draijer & Boon, 1999; Thomas, 2001).

The dissociative symptoms in OSDD-1 and DID are qualitatively different than in other disorders or problems, which can help in accurate diagnosis (Boon & Draijer, 1993; Korzekwa, Dell, & Pain, 2009; Rodewald, Dell, Wilhelm-Gößling, & Gast, 2011).

Amnesia

Dissociative amnesia is a disorder in its own right when other symptoms of dissociation are not present (dissociative amnesia; American Psychiatric Association, 2013). It is required for the diagnosis of DID but is commonly found in most trauma-related disorders, and is therefore not a unique marker of DID and OSDD-1. However, many individuals with DID experience not only amnesia for past trauma—a relatively common phenomenon in traumatized populations—but also amnesia for the present, indicating that dissociative parts are acting outside of awareness in daily life. When an individual is reporting significant recall difficulties in either the past or present, clinicians need to distinguish between dissociative amnesia and failures of encoding involving absorption and detachment, as treatment will differ (Allen, Console, & Lewis, 1999; Steele et al., 2009, 2017).

Present-day amnesia can be accompanied by reports of engaging in significant activities the individual does not remember doing ("I know that big report was turned in to my boss, but I have no recollection of doing it"); of finding strange things among one's belongings ("I find cigarette butts in the house, but I don't smoke and don't know how they got there"; "I unpacked my groceries and found several boxes of cookies—I don't even like cookies!"); or finding writings or drawings ("Sometimes I find scary drawings like a little kid would make, with a big 'HELP' written in red"; "I found threatening notes in my bedroom written to me, calling me bad names and telling me I deserve to die"). Individuals may be unable to recall their therapy sessions or remember significant events such as graduations, weddings, birth of a child, or a funeral of a significant other. Some individuals report pervasive amnesia for the past ("I don't remember anything before age 16"; "I can remember being at school, but nothing about living at home"; "I remember a lot about my father, but don't seem to have any memories of my mother"; "I just draw a big blank between the ages of 8 and 12").

Schneiderian Symptoms

In addition to amnesia, many clients with OSDD-1 or DID show puzzling outward manifestations of dissociative parts that function in an internally constructed world, working "behind the scenes" to influence the individual. This phenomenon has been termed *passive influence* (Kluft,1987) or *partial intrusions* (Dell, 2009), and can be identified through questions about so-called

"Schneiderian symptoms" of schizophrenia (Dell, 2009; Foote & Park, 2008; Kluft, 1987; Steele et al., 2017; Steinberg & Siegel, 2008). These 11 symptoms, originally meant to identify schizophrenia, are more often found in individuals with OSDD-1 and DID. They include (1) hearing voices commenting; (2) hearing voices arguing; (3) visual and perceptual hallucinations; (4) feeling as though one's body is controlled by an outside force; (5) the sense that one's emotions, (6) thoughts, or (7) impulses are controlled by outside forces; (8) the sense that an outside force is adding to, or (9) censoring or withdrawing one's thoughts; (10) thought broadcasting (e.g., believing that one's thoughts are broadcast through the radio or TV); and (11) delusions. Thought broadcasting is rare in DID, but the other symptoms are quite common. Visual hallucinations are typically related to flashbacks or other intrusions of trauma. Likewise, delusions are generally found to be trauma-related. For example, many dissociative individuals are terrified that their abuser will hurt them in the present, even though the person may live very far away or even be dead. Delusions and visual hallucinations typically resolve when the trauma can be integrated.

Hearing Voices

Many dissociative individuals—like many others with trauma-related disorders—hear auditory hallucinations that are the "voices" of other parts of themselves arguing and commenting internally, a symptom that sometimes leads to a misdiagnosis of psychosis. Dissociative voices can typically be distinguished from psychotic auditory hallucinations (Dorahy et al., 2009; Foote & Park, 2008; Steele et al., 2017) in the following ways: (1) they usually begin in childhood, long before the onset of psychosis is typical; (2) they include voices of children and adults; (3) they include the voices of people from the client's past; (4) they are heard regularly or constantly instead of intermittently; (5) they comment about the person or have conversations about him or her that are "overheard" by the client; (6) they are generally not accompanied by social and occupational decline or evidence of thought disorder; (7) they have their own sense of self, even if very limited in some cases; and, most importantly (8) they can engage in dialogue with the therapist and the individual, unlike psychotic voices. Reality testing is generally intact in those with dissociative disorders, and there is no evidence of thought disorder commonly associated with psychosis (Foote & Park, 2008).

Other Intrusions and Losses

Many individuals with OSDD-1 and DID experience puzzling and sometimes jarring symptoms of losses of and intrusions into experience, both mental and somatic (Dell, 2006, 2009; Nijenhuis, 2015; Van der Hart et al., 2006). These are related to the partial intrusions of various dissociative parts into conscious awareness. These symptoms are rarely found in other disorders and are more common than complete shifts from one part to another. Losses might include somatic changes not due to medical conditions, such as temporary paralysis, contracture, physical numbness (anesthesia) and inability to feel pain (analgesia), deafness, blindness, pseudoepileptic seizures, or abrupt (but temporary) loss of a skill such as driving or cooking (see somatic dissociative disorders in ICD-10; WHO, 1992). Mental losses include the sudden loss of emotion ("My sadness just disappeared!") or thoughts ("That thought was taken away"), or censoring ("Something inside won't let me talk about my mother").

Somatoform intrusions might involve intense and unexplained pain or other sensations that begin and end suddenly without medical explanation (often eventually traced back to sensations felt during a traumatic memory), tics and other movements (again, typically related to trauma). *Mental intrusions* include sudden emotions or thoughts that are unrelated to the current moment and which the client disavows ("That is not my anger"; "There is a thought in my head that you are going to hurt me, but it doesn't come from me: I trust you and know you wouldn't hurt me").

Other Problems with a Dissociative Underpinning

On the surface, structural dissociation may also appear to mimic other problems and disorders. For example, many severely traumatized clients use self-harm as a common strategy to cope with self-dysregulation and distress. However, in individuals with OSDD-1 or DID, self-injury may also be the result of conflicts among dissociative parts. For example, an individual can experience one part cutting or otherwise harming another part as punishment for telling about abuse and not maintaining the protection of silence, or to quiet distressed "child" parts that are experienced as crying internally.

To the untrained observer, structural dissociation can sometimes appear indistinguishable from other problems, such as bipolar disorder, borderline personality disorder, and a host of other problems. It may underlie chronic depression or anxiety, sleep and eating problems, sexual problems, and addictions, among others. On the other hand, comorbid disorders are common in individuals with developmental trauma, including those with OSDD-1 and DID. Clinicians must determine whether the disorder is stand-alone, or whether it is a symptom of underlying dissociation, as treatment will differ. For example, shifts in mood may be labeled as rapid-cycling bipolar disorder, but in OSDD and DID, rapid mood changes may be related to shifts among dissociative parts, and treatment will differ.

Differentiation between Ego States, Borderline Modes, and Dissociative Parts

Ego States

Work in ego-state therapy (EST; Watkins & Watkins, 1997), schema therapy (Young, Klosko, & Weishaar, 2003), and recent studies in neurobiology (Putnam, 2016) indicate that consciousness and self are never completely unitary. We all have multiple self-states or ego states that comprise our "self." *Ego states* are defined as "an organized system of behavior and experience whose elements are bound together by some common principle and which is separated from other such states by a boundary that is more or less permeable" (Watkins & Watkins, 1977, p. 25). It is likely that dissociative parts are extreme variants of ego states (Kluft, 1987; Steele et al., 2017; Watkins & Watkins, 1997). However, normal ego states differ from dissociative parts in their lack of autonomy and elaboration, personal experience and memory, and unique self-representation and first-person perspective (Kluft, 1987). Most people recognize normal ego states as belonging to themselves and do not experience amnesia, hallucinations, Schneiderian symptoms, or other dissociative mental and somatic intrusions and losses (Moskowitz & Van der Hart, 2019).

Borderline Modes

Young and colleagues (2003) refer to different modes in individuals with borderline personality disorder (BPD). *Modes* are comparable to normal ego states and are defined as particular states of mind that cluster schemas and coping styles into a temporary "way of being" to which an individual can shift suddenly (Young et al., 2003). The individual may recognize the mode as belonging to self, but as somewhat independent and dichotomous, for example, "That was the bad Susie that got drunk; good Susie knows better." Susie remembers drinking (she does not have amnesia) and when questioned is able to recognize that she herself was drinking. Like ego states, modes are not accompanied by Schneiderian symptoms.

Many individuals with BPD have a wide array of dissociative symptoms beyond alterations in awareness, but still do not necessarily meet criteria for a dissociative disorder (Korzekwa et al., 2009). Thus, distinguishing BPD from OSDD-1 and DID can be challenging in some cases. However, in most instances, the unique characteristics and severity and chronicity of the dissociative symptoms clarifies the diagnosis of OSDD-1 or DID. A substantial minority (approximately 24%) of individuals with BPD do have co-occurring DID, and about the same number (approximately 24%) meet criteria for OSDD-1 (Korzekwa et al., 2009), so significant comorbidity may be present in about half of individuals with BPD.

Resources for Assessment of OSDD-1 and DID

Resources for assessment of dissociative disorders include Brand and Loewenstein (2010); Dell (2006); Dell and O'Neil (2009); Kluft (1987); Loewenstein (1991); Ross (1989, 1997); Spinazzola and Briere, Chapter 5, this volume; Steele et al. (2017); Steinberg, (1995, 2004); Steinberg and Siegel (2008); and Van der Hart et al. (2006).

There are several instruments that aid in diagnosis, including the *Struc-*

tured *Clinical Interview for Dissociative Disorders* (SCID-D [not currently updated to DSM-5]; Steinberg, 1995, 2004); the *Multidimensional Inventory for Dissociation* (MID; Dell, 2006); and the *Dissociative Disorders Interview Scale* (DDIS [now updated to DSM-5]; Ross, 1989). Several instruments are not diagnostic, but they do screen individuals who warrant further clinical assessment for OSDD-1 and DID. The *Multiscale Dissociation Inventory* (MDI, Briere, 2002) includes a subscale on Identity Dissociation. Should an individual score generally high on the MDI and specifically on the Identity Dissociation scale, further assessment is warranted. The *Dissociative Experiences Scale–II* (DES-II; Carlson & Putnam, 1996) examines experiences of amnesia, absorption, and depersonalization. A taxon for pathological dissociation (DES-T, Waller, Putnam, & Carlson, 1996) includes eight items of the DES-II that are more accurate markers for pathological dissociation, distinguishing it from absorption. A high score on the DES-T warrants further assessment. Finally, the *Somatoform Dissociation Questionnaire* (SDQ-20; Nijenhuis, Spinhoven, Van Dyck, Van der Hart, & Vanderlinden, 1996) can help identify individuals who have somatic dissociation commonly found in OSDD-1 and DID, phenomena that are less likely to be identified and assessed as part of a dissociative profile.

A Brief Overview of Treatment

There is growing evidence that individuals with OSDD-1 and DID benefit from having their structural dissociation directly assessed and addressed. Clinical research shows that managing dissociation leads to decreased levels of dissociation, PTSD symptoms, general distress, drug use, physical pain, and depression, along with an increased sense of self-control and self-knowledge over the course of treatment (Brand et al., 2013, 2019; Jepsen, Langeland, Sexton, & Heir, 2014). Individuals in these studies reported increased ability to socialize, work, study, or do volunteer work, and reported feeling better overall. They engaged in less self-injurious behavior and had fewer hospitalizations than before treatment and demonstrated increased global assessment of functioning (GAF) scores, and improved adaptive capacities over time (Brand et al., 2013, 2019). On the other hand, highly dissociative individuals who do not receive treatment for dissociation do not tend to improve or may not be able to maintain temporary treatment gains (Jepsen et al., 2014). They are prone to ongoing social and occupational difficulties, depression and anxiety, self-harm, suicidality, poor response to treatment, and frequent medical and psychiatric interventions, including hospitalizations.

The treatment guidelines for DID (International Society for the Study of Trauma and Dissociation [ISSTD], 2011) are helpful in directing approaches to OSDD-1 and DID, as is the expert consensus survey for complex PTSD (Cloitre et al., 2011) and the Australian Practice Guidelines for Treatment of Complex Trauma (Kezelman & Stavropoulos, 2012). The latter two can serve as a foundation for treatment to which specialized approaches for structural dissociation are added. Trauma-informed and present-centered experiential or psychodynamic psychotherapy are mainstays of the treatment of dissociative disorders, with the addition of specialized techniques and approaches that directly address the undue separation of dissociative parts, the resolution of traumatic memories, and the facilitation of integration of self and personality.

The standard of care for treating dissociative disorders, as with complex PTSD, is a phase-oriented approach (Brand et al., 2013; Boon et al., 2011; Chu, 2011; Howell, 2011; ISSTD, 2011; Steele et al., 2005, 2017; Van der Hart et al., 2006) that involves the following components:

- Phase 1: Safety, stabilization, symptom reduction, skills building, and development of a collaborative alliance.
- Phase 2: Processing and integration of traumatic memories.
- Phase 3: Further personality (re)integration and (re)habilitation, along with the establishment of a life that is less compromised by dissociation, traumatic memories, and other symptoms.

These treatment phases are not linear, often periodically requiring a return to an earlier phase to relearn skills, or the occasional short excursion into the next phase (Courtois, 2004, 2010; Courtois & Ford, 2012; Steele et al., 2005, 2017; Van der Hart et al., 2006). It is a treatment that explicitly acknowledges stages of change (Prochaska & Norcross, 2018) that involve different rates of motivation and learning and considers the likelihood of relapse as an opportunity for further problem solving.

Each phase of treatment should have a specific focus on eroding the need for ongoing structural dissociation. To this end, in addition to helping individuals learn more effective regulation and reflecting strategies, clinicians can target trauma-related phobic avoidance of (1) inner experience (e.g., thoughts, emotions, sensations, conflicts); (2) attachment and attachment loss (rejection and abandonment); (3) dissociative parts; (4) traumatic memories; and (5) adaptive change and risk-taking (Steele et al., 2005, 2017; Van der Hart et al., 2006).

Phase 1: Stabilization

Treatment begins with an initial phase of stabilization, safety, ego strengthening, education, and skills building to improve the individual's adaptive functioning and capacity to engage effectively in therapy. A collaborative therapeutic approach is typically effective, with a clear therapeutic frame and boundaries, including careful limits on number of sessions per week and contact outside of sessions via email, text, or phone calls. Excessive caretaking of individuals with dissociation should be avoided, as dependency issues are frequent and intense. Clinicians should be mindful not to activate further the client's already stressed attachment system with either too much closeness or too much distance (Brown & Elliott, 2016; Cortina & Liotti, 2014; Steele, 2018; Steele et al., 2017).

Individuals with dissociation need to learn how to decrease conflicts among dissociative parts and support regulation of specific parts that may not always be directly accessible to them as a whole. Education and skills-based training in identifying and effectively managing dissociation are helpful (Boon et al., 2011; Brand et al., 2013, 2019; Brand & Loewenstein, 2010; ISSTD, 2011; Steele et al., 2017). A number of authors have discussed how to specifically help individuals with dissociation with these skills and take stepwise approaches to decrease conflict among dissociative parts (Boon et al., 2011; Chu, 2011; Fisher, 2017; Gelinas, 2003; Gonzalez & Mosquera, 2012; Howell, 2011; Kluft, 2000; Knipe, 2018; Ogden & Fisher, 2016; Phillips & Frederick, 1995; Steele et al., 2017; Twombly, 2005; Van der Hart et al., 2006).

We cannot emphasize enough that clinicians should not treat dissociative parts as separate individuals, nor should they ignore them in the hope that they will just "go away." The goal in treating dissociative disorders is always to support integration of the personality and to eliminate the reasons and need for ongoing dissociation. Self-compassion, sharing of experience, collaboration, and negotiation among all dissociative parts of the individual are key to successful integration (e.g., Boon et al., 2011; Kluft, 2000; Steele et al., 2017; Van der Hart et al., 2006). When possible, treatment should be directed to the individual as whole. While this is not always feasible due to the client's low integrative capacity and high dissociative tendencies, it is a good foundation from which to start and to which one returns as often and as long as possible. Clinicians can invite "all parts of the mind" to be present in therapy, with the adult part of the individual remaining present when possible. The therapist does not seek to establish an individual relationship with each part; rather, he or she serves as an integrative "bridge" between various parts to improve the coherence of the entire system of the individual.

When a shift from one part to another or a partial intrusion occurs in session, the process should be noted and explored: What just happened? Why now? What dynamics are at play? Is there a conflict that is being avoided or expressed? What in the therapeutic relationship might be relevant? For instance, is there a shift to a young part that is expressing dependency yearnings that the adult cannot tolerate? In this way, the individual is supported in identifying and resolving reasons for dissociation in real time, and therapy can stay on track and not be diverted by the different agendas and conflicts among various dissociative parts.

When it is not feasible to make systemic interventions at the level of the whole personality because of the individual's extreme phobic avoidance, the therapist may intervene directly with two or more dissociative parts (Steele et al., 2017; Van der Hart et al., 2006). For example, several parts may be encouraged to collaborate in accomplishing a task in which other parts are not yet able to participate (e.g., emotion regulation, maintaining safety). Or one part can be encouraged to care for or alleviate the suffering of other parts. There are times when the therapist may elect to work with a single part. Often, due to phobic avoidance of disruptive parts, the individual is unable or unwilling to directly address them. In such cases, the therapist may choose to work directly with a single part to build integrative connections with the individual as a whole. As soon as feasible, the therapist supports more direct connection between the parts, thereby reducing phobic avoidance and raising the integrative capacity of the individual.

In stepwise fashion, dissociative parts can be supported to become consciously aware of each other to diminish avoidance reactions, orient to the present, and foster understanding and empathy for their various roles; next to facilitate cooperation in daily life functioning; and only then to share traumatic experiences. This work must be carefully paced, as premature attempts to focus on dissociative parts in therapy, before the client is ready, can result in increased dissociation, decompensation, or flight from therapy. Once the individual is more accepting of parts, has adequate capacities to regulate, and inner conflicts among parts are decreased, Phase 2 treatment can begin. However, with highly dissociative individuals, this work usually needs significant titration, as discussed below.

Phase 2: Integrating Traumatic Memories

Exposure to traumatic memories with simultaneous prevention of maladaptive reactions is considered a fundamental intervention in trauma-related disorders. Although exposure proponents in the field of PTSD have noted that therapists are often more hesitant than is warranted to employ exposure techniques for fear of overwhelming the client (Cahill, Foa, Hembree, Marshall, & Nacash, 2006), therapists in the dissociative disorders field have learned that premature and prolonged trauma memory processing in dissociative clients lacking the capacity to safely experience and modulate arousal can have serious iatrogenic results. Due to the severe integrative deficits found in highly dissociative clients, early and direct confrontation with traumatic memories can be acutely destabilizing, sometimes leading to decompensation and posttraumatic decline. In this regard, treatment of OSDD-1 and particularly DID (as well as many cases of complex PTSD) differs significantly from a more immediate approach to processing traumatic memories suggested for the treatment of PTSD.

When Phase 2 interventions are initiated in OSDD-1 and DID, several caveats apply. First, clinicians need to understand that not all dissociative parts may have access to a given traumatic memory. Second, exposure does not automatically occur across all dissociative parts. Third, exposure that seems tolerable to one dissociative part may not be to another. Fourth, when arousal is too high, a dissociative individual will respond with further separation between and shifting among parts in an attempt to regulate.

Special approaches to the treatment of traumatic memories, including titration techniques, can be found in a variety of sources (Howell, 2011; Frederick & Phillips, 1995; Kluft, 1996, 2013; Knipe, 2018; Gonzalez & Mosquera, 2012; Steele et al., 2017; Twombly, 2005; Van der Hart et al., 1993, 2006, 2017).

Phase 3: Further Integration of the Personality and Rehabilitation

Phase 3 involves a greater focus on integration of the personality, grieving, and continued attention to improving quality of life. The oscillation of the individual between the joy of a new "self," new competencies and enjoyment, and the grieving of loss leads to further integration. Individuals with dissociation experience incremental gains in the ability to experience themselves as whole individuals across the phases of treatment. This integrative process mostly occurs in a gradual fashion, but it is often brought to fruition in Phase 3, as the reasons for ongoing dissociation are eliminated. It is not unusual for additional traumatic memories and dissociative parts to emerge in Phase 3 in response to a growing capacity to integrate. During such times, excursion back to Phase 1 and Phase 2 work will need to occur. Some integration of parts occurs spontaneously, while other parts seem to "fade" or simply cease separate activity. In some cases, integration may not be possible or may be resisted by an individual who is invested in remaining dissociative. These individuals may need ongoing support to remain stable.

Conclusion

The complex dissociative disorders of OSDD-1 and DID can be diagnosed with accuracy and be distinguished from other disorders. There is growing empirical evidence supporting clinical observations that treatment focused on dissociation is effective in reducing not only dissociative symptoms but also other distressing problems. Yet many myths, misconceptions, and prejudices about OSDD-1 and DID remain. Clinical training often does not include sufficient attention to dissociation and dissociative disorders; thus, clinicians have little or no knowledge about how to effectively assess or treat these conditions. Another difficulty is confusion about the symptoms and definition(s) of dissociation; more clarity among the diverse symptoms and their different treatments would be helpful. Obviously, a proper therapeutic focus on dissociative process and experiences should not promote a further sense of separateness. Individuals with OSDD-1 and DID can benefit from stable, rational, and well-boundaried treatment that addresses the many complexities of chronic developmental trauma, with an emphasis on integration of dissociative parts of the personality.

References

Aderibigbe, Y. A., Bloch, R. M., & Walker, W. R. (2001). Prevalence of depersonalization and derealization in a rural population. *Social Psychiatry and Psychiatric Epidemiology, 36,* 63–69.

Allen, J. G., Console, D. A., & Lewis, L. (1999). Dissociative detachment and memory impairment: Reversible amnesia or encoding failure? *Comprehensive Psychiatry, 40,* 160–171.

American Psychiatric Association. (2013). *Diagnostic and statistical manual of mental disorders* (5th ed.). Arlington, VA: Author.

Boon, S., & Draijer, N. (1993). *Multiple personality disorder in the Netherlands*. Lisse, the Netherlands: Swets & Zeitlinger.

Boon, S., Steele, K., & Van der Hart, O. (2011). *Coping with trauma-related dissociation: Skills training for clients and therapists*. New York: Norton.

Brand, B., & Loewenstein, R. (2010, October). Dissociative disorders: An overview of assessment, phenomenology, and treatment. *Psychiatric Times*, pp. 62–69.

Brand, B. L., McNary, S. W., Myrick, A. C., Loewenstein, R. J., Classen, C. C., Lanius, R. A., . . . Putnam, F. W. (2013). A longitudinal, naturalistic study of dissociative identity disorder patients treated by community clinicians. *Psychological Trauma: Theory, Research, Practice, and Policy, 5*, 301–308.

Brand, B., Schielke, H. J., Putnam, K., Putnam, F., Loewenstein, R. J., Myrick, A., . . . Lanius, R. (2019). An online educational program for individuals with dissociative disorders and their clinicians: One year and two-year follow-up. *Journal of Traumatic Stress, 32*(1), 156–166.

Briere, J. (2002). *Multiscale Dissociation Inventory*. Odessa, FL: Psychological Assessment Resources.

Brown, D. P., & Elliott, D. S. (2016). *Attachment disturbances in adults: Treatment for comprehensive repair*. New York: Norton.

Bryant, R. A., & Harvey, A. G. (2000). *Acute stress disorder: A handbook of theory, assessment, and treatment*. Washington, DC: American Psychological Association.

Cahill, S. P., Foa, E. B., Hembree, E. A., Marshall, R. D., & Nacash, N. (2006). Dissemination of exposure therapy in the treatment of posttraumatic stress disorder. *Journal of Traumatic Stress, 19*, 597–610.

Carlson, E. B., & Putnam, F. W. (1993). An update on the Dissociative Experiences Scale. *Dissociation, 6*(1), 16–27.

Catrell, J. P., & Catrell, J. S. (1974). Depersonalization: Psychological and social perspectives. In S. Arieti (Ed.), *American handbook of psychiatry* (2nd ed., pp. 766–799). New York: Basic Books.

Chu, J. A. (2011). *Rebuilding shattered lives* (2nd ed.). New York: Wiley.

Cloitre, M., Courtois, C. A., Charuvastra, A., Carapezza, R., Stolbach, B. C., & Green, B. L. (2011). Treatment of complex PTSD: Results of the ISTSS expert clinician survey on best practices. *Journal of Traumatic Stress, 24*, 615–627.

Cortina, M., & Liotti, G. (2014). An evolutionary outlook on motivation: Implications for the clinical dialogue. *Psychoanalytic Inquiry, 34*, 864–899.

Courtois, C. A. (2004). Complex trauma, complex reactions: Assessment and treatment. *Psychotherapy: Theory, Research, Practice, and Training, 41*, 412–425.

Courtois, C. A. (2010). *Healing the incest wound: Adult survivors in therapy* (2nd ed.). New York: Norton.

Courtois, C. A., & Ford, J. (2012). *Treatment of complex trauma: A sequenced, relationship based approach*. New York: Guilford Press.

Dalenberg, C. J., & Paulson, K. (2009). The case for the study of "normal" dissociative processes. In P. F. Dell & J. A. O'Neil (Eds.), *Dissociation and the dissociative disorders: DSM-V and beyond* (pp. 145–154). New York: Routledge.

Damasio, A. (1999). *The feeling of what happens: Body and emotion in the making of consciousness*. Boston: Houghton Mifflin Harcourt.

Dana, D. (2018). *The polyvagal theory in therapy: Engaging the rhythms of regulation*. New York: Norton.

Dell, P. F. (2006). The Multidimensional Inventory of Dissociation (MID): A comprehensive measure of pathological dissociation. *Journal of Trauma and Dissociation, 7*, 77–106.

Dell, P. F. (2009). The long struggle to diagnose multiple personality disorder (MPD): Partial MPD. In P. F. Dell & J. A O'Neil (Eds.), *Dissociation and the dissociative disorders: DSM-V and beyond* (pp. 383–402). New York: Routledge.

Dell, P. F., & O'Neil, J. A. (Eds.). *Dissociation and the dissociative disorders: DSM-V and beyond*. New York: Routledge.

Dorahy, M. J., Shannon, C., Seagar, L., Corr, M., Stewart, K., Hanna, D., . . . Middleton, W. (2009). Differentiating auditory hallucinations in DID from schizophrenics with and without a trauma history. *Journal of Nervous and Mental Disease, 197,* 892–898.

Fisher, J. (2017). *Healing the fragmented selves of trauma survivors: Overcoming internal self-alienation*. New York: Routledge.

Foote, B., & Park, J. (2008). Dissociative identity disorder and schizophrenia: Differential diagnosis and theoretical issues. *Current Psychiatry Reports, 10,* 217–222.

Gelinas, D. J. (2003). Integrating EMDR into phase-oriented treatment for trauma. *Journal of Trauma and Dissociation, 4*(3), 91–135.

Gonzalez, A., & Mosquera, D. (2012). *EMDR and dissociation: The progressive approach*. Charleston, SC: Amazon Imprint.

Holmes, E. A., Brown, R. J., Mansell, W., Fearon, R. P., Hunter, E. C., Frasquilho, F., & Oakley, D. A. (2005). Are there two qualitatively distinct forms of dissociation?: A review and some clinical implications. *Clinical Psychology Review, 25,* 1–23.

Howell, E. F. (2011). *Understanding and treating dissociative identity disorder: A relational approach*. New York: Routledge.

International Society for the Study of Trauma and Dissociation. (2011). Guidelines for treating dissociative identity disorder in adults. *Journal of Trauma and Dissociation, 6,* 69–149.

Janet, P. (1907). *Major symptoms of hysteria*. New York: Macmillan.

Janet, P. (1929). *L'évolution de la personnalité*. Paris: A. Chahine.

Jepsen, E. K. K., Langeland, W., Sexton, H., & Heir, T. (2014). Inpatient treatment for early sexually abused adults: A naturalistic 12-month follow-up study. *Psychological Trauma: Theory, Research, Practice, Policy, 6*(2), 142–151.

Kezelman, C., & Stavropoulos, P. (2012). *The last frontier: Practice guidelines for treatment of complex trauma and trauma-informed care and service delivery*. Kirribilli, NSW: Adults Surviving Child Abuse.

Kluft, R. P. (1987). First-rank symptoms of schizophrenia as a diagnostic clue to multiple personality disorder. *American Journal of Psychiatry, 144,* 293–298.

Kluft, R. P. (1996). Treating the traumatic memories of patients with dissociative identity disorder. *American Journal of Psychiatry, 153,* 103–110.

Kluft, R. P. (2000). The psychoanalytic psychotherapy of dissociative identity disorder in the context of trauma therapy. *Psychoanalytic Inquiry, 20,* 259–286.

Kluft, R. P. (2013). *Shelter from the storm*. North Charleston, SC: CreateSpace.

Knipe, J. (2018). *EMDR Toolbox: Theory and treatment of complex PTSD and dissociation* (2nd ed.). New York: Springer.

Korzekwa, M. I., Dell, P. F., & Pain, C. (2009). Dissociation and borderline personality disorder: An update of clinicians. *Current Psychiatry Reports, 11,* 82–88.

Lanius, R. A., Brand, B., Vermetten, E., Frewen, P. A., & Spiegel, D. (2012). The dissociative subtype of posttraumatic stress disorder: Rationale, clinical and neurobiological evidence, and implications. *Depression and Anxiety, 29,* 701–708.

Lichtenberg, J. D., & Kindler, A. R. (1994). A motivational systems approach to the clinical experience. *Journal of the American Psychoanalytic Association, 42,* 405–420.

Liotti, G. (2006). A model of dissociation based on attachment theory and research. *Journal of Trauma and Dissociation, 7*(4), 55–74.

Liotti, G. (2009). Attachment and dissociation. In P. F. Dell & J. A. O'Neil (Eds.), *Dissociation and the dissociative disorders: DSM-V and beyond* (pp. 53–65). New York: Routledge.

Liotti, G. (2017). Conflicts between motivational systems related to attachment trauma: Key to understanding the intra-family relationship between abused children and their abusers. *Journal of Trauma and Dissociation, 18,* 304–318.

Loewenstein, R. J. (1991). An office mental status examination for complex chronic dissociative symptoms and multiple personality disorder. *Psychiatric Clinics of North America, 14, 567–604.*

Main, M., & Hesse, E. (1990). Parents' unresolved traumatic experiences are related to infant disorganized/disoriented attachment status: Is frightened and/or frightening behavior the linking mechanism? In M. T. Greenberg, D. Cicchetti, & E. M. Cummings (Eds.), *Attachment in the preschool years* (pp. 161–182). Chicago: University of Chicago Press.

Moskowitz, A., & Van der Hart, O. (2019). Historical and contemporary conceptions of trauma-related dissociation: A neo-Janetian critique of models of divided personality. *European Journal of Trauma and Dissociation.* [Epub ahead of print].

Nijenhuis, E. R. S. (2015). *The trinity of trauma: Ignorance, fragility, and control* (Vol. 1). Göttingen, Germany: Vendenhoeck & Ruprecht.

Nijenhuis, E. R. S., Spinhoven, P., Van Dyck, R., Van der Hart, O., & Vanderlinden, J. (1996). The development and psychometric characteristics of the Somatoform Dissociation Questionnaire (SDQ-20). *Journal of Nervous and Mental Disease, 184,* 688–694.

Nijenhuis, E. R. S., & Van der Hart, O. (2011). Defining dissociation in trauma. *Journal of Trauma and Dissociation, 12,* 469–473.

Ogawa, J. R., Sroufe, L. A., Weinfield, N. S., Carlson, E. A., & Egeland, B. (1997). Development and the fragmented self: Longitudinal study of dissociative symptomatology in a nonclinical sample. *Development and Psychopathology, 9,* 855–879.

Ogden, P., & Fisher, J. (2016). *Sensorimotor psychotherapy: Interventions for trauma and attachment.* New York: Norton.

Panksepp, J. (1998). *Affective neuroscience.* New York: Oxford University Press.

Phillips, M., & Frederick, C. (1995). *Healing the divided self.* New York: Norton.

Porges, S. W. (2003). The polyvagal theory: Phylogenetic contributions to social behavior. *Physiology and Behavior, 79,* 503–513.

Porges, S. W. (2011). *The polyvagal theory: Neurophysiological foundations of emotions, attachment, communication, and self-regulation.* New York: Norton.

Prochaska, J. O., & Norcross, J. C. (2018). *Systems of psychotherapy: A transtheoretical analysis* (9th ed.). London: Oxford University Press.

Putnam, F. W. (1997). *Dissociation in children and adolescents: A developmental perspective.* New York: Guilford Press.

Putnam, F. W. (2016). *The way we are: How states of mind influence our identities, personality and potential for change.* New York: International Psychoanalytic Books.

Rodewald, F., Dell, P. F., Wilhelm-Gößling, C., & Gast, U. (2011). Are major dissociative disorders characterized by a qualitatively different kind of dissociation? *Journal of Trauma and Dissociation, 12,* 9–24.

Ross, C. A. (1989). *Multiple personality disorder: Diagnosis, clinical features, and treatment.* New York: Wiley.

Ross, C. A. (1997). *Dissociative identity disorder: Diagnosis, clinical features, and treatment of multiple personality.* New York: Wiley.

Schauer, M., & Elbert, T. (2010). Dissociation following traumatic stress: Etiology and treatment. *Zeitschrift für Psychologie, 218,* 109–127.

Schore, A. N. (2003). *Affect regulation and the repair of the self.* New York: Norton.

Schore, A. N. (2012). *The science of the art of psychotherapy.* New York: Norton.

Simeon, D., & Abugel, J. (2006). *Feeling unreal: Depersonalization disorder and the loss of the self.* London: Oxford University Press.

Somer, E. (2002). Maladaptive daydreaming: A qualitative inquiry. *Journal of Contemporary Psychotherapy, 32,* 197–212.

Somer, E., & Herscu, O. (2017). Childhood trauma, social anxiety, absorption and fantasy dependence: Two potential mediated pathways to maladaptive daydreaming. *Journal of Addictive Behaviors, Therapy and Rehabilitation, 6*(4), 1–5.

Steele, K. (2018). Dependency in the psychotherapy of chronically traumatized individuals: Using motivational systems to guide effective treatment. *Cognitivismo Clinico, 15,* 221–226.

Steele, K., Boon, S., & Van der Hart, O. (2017). *Treating trauma-related dissociation: A practical, integrative approach.* New York: Norton.

Steele, K., Dorahy, M., Van der Hart, O., & Nijenhuis, E. R. S. (2009). Dissociation versus alterations in consciousness: Related but different concepts. In P. F. Dell & J. A. O'Neil (Eds.), *Dissociation and the dissociative disorders: DSM-V and beyond* (pp. 155–170). New York: Routledge.

Steele, K., Van der Hart, O., & Nijenhuis, E. R. S. (2005). Phase-oriented treatment of structural dissociation in complex traumatization: Overcoming trauma-related phobias. *Journal of Trauma and Dissociation, 6*(3), 11–53.

Steinberg, M. (1995). *Handbook for assessment of dissociation: A clinical guide.* Washington, DC: American Psychiatric Press.

Steinberg, M. (2004). *Interviewer's Guide to the Structured Clinical Interview for DSM-IV Dissociative Disorders—Revised (SCID-D-R)* (2nd ed.). Washington, DC: American Psychiatric Press.

Steinberg, M., & Siegel, H. D. (2008). Advances in assessment: The differential diagnosis of dissociative identity disorder and schizophrenia. In A. Moskowitz, I. Schäfer, & M. J. Dorahy (Eds.), *Psychosis, trauma and dissociation: Emerging perspectives on severe psychopathology* (pp. 177–189). New York: Wiley-Blackwell.

Thomas, A. (2001). Factitious and malingered dissociative identity disorder: Clinical features observed in 18 cases. *Journal of Trauma and Dissociation, 2,* 59–77.

Twombly, J. H. (2005). EMDR for clients with dissociative identity disorder, DDNOS, and ego states. In R. Shapiro (Ed.), *EMDR solutions: Pathways to healing* (pp. 86–120). New York: Norton.

Van der Hart, O., Nijenhuis, E. R. S., & Steele, K. (2006). *The haunted self: Structural dissociation and the treatment of chronic traumatization.* New York: Norton.

Van der Hart, O., Steele, K., Boon, S., & Brown, P. (1993). The treatment of traumatic memories: Synthesis, realization and integration. *Dissociation, 6,* 162–180.

Van der Hart, O., Steele, K., & Nijenhuis, E. R. S. (2017). The treatment of traumatic memories in patients with complex dissociative disorders. *European Journal of Trauma and Dissociation, 1*(1), 25–35.

Waller, N. G., Putnam, F. W., & Carlson, E. B. (1996). Types of dissociation and dissociative types: A taxonomic analysis of dissociative experiences. *Psychological Methods, 1,* 300–321.

Watkins, J. G., & Watkins, H. H. (1997). *Ego states: Theory and therapy.* New York: Norton.

World Health Organization. (1992). *International statistical classification of diseases and related health problems, 10th Revision* (ICD-10). Geneva, Switzerland: Author.

Young, J., Klosko, J. S., & Weishaar, M. E. (2003). *Schema therapy: A practitioner's guide.* New York: Guilford Press.

CHAPTER 7

Cultural Humility and Spiritual Awareness

LAURA S. BROWN

Complex trauma occurs within the psychosocial framework of external cultural realities, and the internal, intrapsychic representations of those realities. It also occurs within existential and spiritual meaning-making systems. A child who is being repeatedly abused and neglected, an adult trapped in painful and apparently inescapable intimate partner violence or held captive and tortured, is not a generic human being experiencing these traumata. Each survivor is always a person who is unique, and perhaps uniquely targeted for traumatic experiences, because of the various and multiple strands of their[1] intersectional identities. They then experience the distress of the trauma, and develop their attempts to cope with that distress, in the psychosocial and spiritual/existential realities of a particular time, place, and location in the social, emotional, spiritual, and political worlds in which their trauma is happening. Finally, the psychotherapist working with the complex trauma survivor is also a product of this same process of identity development and as such will symbolize meanings to trauma survivors that may assist, or undermine, the development of a therapeutic alliance and the conduct of psychotherapy itself.

Responding effectively to these realities in clinical work requires the development of cultural humility and self-awareness by all psychotherapists working with complex trauma survivors, a construct commonly referred to by the term *cultural competence*. In this chapter, I use *cultural humility* as a preferred term to indicate that moving toward culturally competent practice is a process, not a goal or a box that can be checked off. This process of developing awareness of cultural and spiritual dynamics in therapy has often seemed daunting, largely because of how this aspect of clinical work has been historically defined. The notion that one should learn rules for treating "diverse populations," to use

---

[1] "They" and "their" have been used in the chapter to represent nongendered pronouns.

the language common in training settings in the last 30 or so years, has led many therapists to distance themselves from work with individuals whom they perceive as sufficiently different from them in some way that might preclude practicing well. This stance is not unique to therapists working with complex trauma; such distancing from issues of difference, often accompanied by feelings of guilt, shame, and inadequacy, parallels how trauma itself has been marginalized in the larger psychotherapy fields until very recently. *A goal of this chapter is both to disrupt the common narrative of how therapists develop cultural humility and spiritual awareness in their work, and to engage those working with survivors of complex trauma in the project of joining this process.*

This chapter focuses on an overarching stance about cultural humility and spiritual awareness that can, and should, be woven into the fabric of any and all specific treatment models for working with complex trauma. Every client has intersectional identities that include a meaning-making system, and those intersectional identities and meaning-making systems can be crucial components of success, or otherwise, in treatment. The theoretical frameworks presented here focus on creating heightened awareness of personal, inevitable biases and distortions, and on developing overarching epistemologies of difference rather than algorithms for working with so-called "diverse populations." Another goal of this chapter is to offer models of how intersectional identities affect both the experience of complex trauma and also the later development of both distress and dysfunction (aka pathology), as well as resilience, hopefulness, and posttraumatic growth.

Why should a clinician working with complex trauma survivors be centrally concerned with developing cultural humility and awareness of spiritual and existential issues? Why not simply take the stance of referring the survivor who is a member of group X to the specialist in that group, and maintain competence and ethical practice by means of limiting the populations with whom one works? Or why not see all clients as simply human and take a stance of "color-blindness"? The first reason is that, more than any other form of psychic distress, the very nature of complex trauma is inherently concerned with culture, context, politics, spiritual and meaning-making systems, and identity. All complex psychological trauma is interpersonal in nature, and each person comes to the experience of trauma, whether as perpetrator or target, as a human with intersectional identities and social realities that, if denied or avoided in therapy, can silence the survivor just as surely as denying or avoiding the trauma itself. Complex trauma is a trauma of intimacy, of shared physical and social realities, and frequently of cultures and meaning-making systems that are shared by both victims and perpetrators. In consequence, the violations of body, mind, and spirit at the core of complex traumatic stress disorders are each flavored and shaped by those psychosocial, contextual, political, spiritual, and cultural milieus in which that trauma occurs. Herman (1992) directly recognized and addressed these social and political realities when she first proposed the construct of complex trauma, but others have not always followed her lead, because the bulk of subsequent clinical and research discussions of complex trauma have shifted to the specifics of symptom pictures and treatment strategies. Ironically, within a subject matter that gives voice to previously unspoken realities, culture, identity, spirituality, and social context have largely been the invisible components of conceptualizations of working with complex trauma survivors. "If you pretend not to see my color or the ways in which I pray, then you do not see me, you cannot help me heal, and for sure you do not see how I see you," says my Native American client to me, her Euro-American therapist.

The second reason to undertake this process is that, for readers who do not live in large metropolitan areas, replete with specialists in working with every possible population, the option of making a referral to such a specialist is not an option. Furthermore, as I explore later in this chapter, this strategy is itself a means of emotional distancing from difference, disguised as maintaining the boundaries of competence, a methodology that is likely to have continuing problematic results for the psyche of the clinician. Finally, this "refer-out" strategy reflects an epistemology of difference that, although revolutionary and valuable when it emerged in the 1970s, is no longer a tenable stance for understanding human difference, or a foundation for culturally competent practice. It "ghettoizes" the experiences of those who differ from the dominant cultural norm. Ultimately, developing cultural humility and spiritual awareness is but one brick in the foundation of general competencies and areas of self-reflection that clinicians working with survivors of complex trauma should bring to their work. As I discuss later in this chapter, all of us have every single marker of identity present in ourselves. To routinely decline to work with people who do not appear to share our identity markers reduces our capacities to examine those markers thoughtfully and critically in ourselves, as well as in clients who appear to resemble us. Because cultural humility and spiritual awareness are not skills that we develop for those who differ from us; they are ways of being as therapists that apply equally with everyone we treat.

A Few Words about Language

Mental health coursework and textbooks on working with difference have commonly used the term *minority group* to refer to those populations defined as "other" than that of the author. This terminology is not used in this contribution, because it is both numerically inaccurate in many instances and it carries a metamessage experienced by many "minorities" as pejorative. Instead, the terms *target* and *dominant/agent* groups are used. *Target groups* are defined as those groups in a given cultural and political setting that have been historically, and/or currently are the targets of systemic discrimination, oppression, violence, and/or prejudice. *Dominant/agent groups* are defined as those groups in a particular cultural and political setting that represent the norm and are assigned power within that setting's hierarchy and institutions. Not all members of dominant/agent groups will experience benefit from their group membership; not all members of target groups will experience disadvantage. Most individuals' identities contain some mixture of dominant/agent and target experiences. These group memberships, although they may be defined as being due to biological variables such as sex assigned at birth or phenotype, are socially constructed and thus have social meanings that differ from context to context. These strands of identity are then given meaning and value by the specific cultural, social, political, and spiritual/existential realities in which a person exists. In consequence, these meanings may change as the narrative themes of those settings transform or a person moves from one milieu to another. Trauma survivors comprise one large, diverse target group, marginalized by a dominant/agent culture that wishes to obscure the realities of human capacities for cruelty.

Defining *Cultural Humility*: Standpoints and Worldviews

Beginning in the 1960s, emergent literatures in the various mental health disciplines noted that the science and scholarship of those fields were distorted through the lenses of dominant/agent cultures, with almost everything written about human beings reflecting, in reality, only the limited experiences of human beings who were assigned male at birth, of entirely one ancestry (i.e., European), and middle or upper class—members of the cultural-dominant groups in the culture, in other words. In contrast, the decades of the 1970s and 1980s were marked by an explosion of scholarship on the psychological experiences and needs of target groups, with volumes dedicated to cisgender women, people of color, sexual minorities, older adults, people with disabilities, and other, similar specific target groups.

The Etic Epistemological Approach to Understanding Culture and Identity

This sort of scholarship that focuses on within-group similarities, as well as differences between target and dominant/agent groups, is referred to as an *etic* epistemology. Etic strategies for knowledge are those emphasizing allegedly objective collections of information about a group based on categories of analysis developed by scholars who position themselves intellectually outside of the group. In the instance of this "Handbook of psychotherapy with Bajorans" period of scholarship, the etic knowledge offered about members of target groups referred to how they did or did not fit into the dominant/agent culture's diagnostic categories, and how they did or did not respond to conventional, dominant/agent cultural approaches to psychotherapy. (Bajorans are an ethnic group from the television series *Star Trek: Deep Space Nine*. Like many of Earth's target groups, they have a history of colonization, oppression, and resistance, making them an excellent fictive placeholder for actual target groups. Their colonizers and oppressors, the Cardassians, serve as the fictive placeholder for dominant/agent groups.)

Cultural competence within this etic epistemology of difference discouraged humility. Instead, clinicians were urged to acquire large amounts of information about specific groups, developing sets of clinical rules and algorithms for working with clients who were group members. Etic epistemologies, and the scholarship arising from them, tended to downplay within-group differences, emphasize the homogeneity of groups, and highlight the differences between target and dominant groups. Implicit assumptions in this scholarship were that the specific group membership is always a core and foreground component of an individual's identity, and target group memberships are relatively fixed, rather than fluid, categories of experience. Thus, a competent practitioner in this model would have specific limits to his or her competence, for instance, being able to work well with Bajorans but not with Klingons.

Etic models of cultural competence were important and necessary correctives to the state of the mental health disciplines in an era when all behavioral norms were defined unquestioningly through those of the dominant/agent group. They were a valuable and irreplaceable initial step in moving these disciplines and their practitioners toward the capacity to work with people from the full range of human experience, punctuating as they did the varieties of human experience and the diversity of expressions of psychological distress and behavioral dysfunction.

But these etic models were also problematic in some ways. Problems included the tendency to enhance the clinician's sense of self as expert via the acquisition of specific knowledge, and as a credible source of authority about cultural variables present in a client's problems. Humility was never a value of these models, nor was awareness of a client's existential, spiritual, and meaning-making systems. The clinician, having read "the Handbook," presumed to know something about a Bajoran client, and in fact, perhaps more than would Bajoran clients themselves. Also problematic were unquestioned assumptions about the value of dominant/agent cultural diagnostic categories and practices. Etic models simply demonstrated, for the most part, how dominant/agent categories of analysis of distress often applied poorly to members of some target groups, rather than raising fundamental questions about the inherent value of diagnoses or therapeutic strategies that might have had implications for work with all clients. A conceptual ghetto was created in which a "diverse populations" literature flourished but had little impact on the dominant culture of the mental health disciplines. One acquired a certain set of information to become competent to treat Bajorans only if one were interested in working with Bajorans; *cultural competence* itself became defined as a type of special focus in the work of a clinician, with subcategories of "Bajoran specialist" and Klingon specialist" creating ever-narrower islands of supposed expertise.

Etic models also have had another unfortunate set of unintended consequences. By creating a standard for competence based on the acquisition of specific knowledge, many clinicians who did not wish to memorize the list of rules for a particular group defined themselves as not competent to work with members of most target groups. In the attempt to practice ethically, these clinicians withdrew from working with members of target groups, feeling uncomfortable and in some instances ashamed of not knowing the correct information. As I discuss later in this chapter, actual and emotional withdrawal, and feelings of shame about difference in members of dominant/agent groups, frequently fuel nonconscious biases that themselves render the development of cultural humility and spiritual awareness more daunting.

Paradigm Shift: Emic Epistemological Approaches to Understanding Culture and Identity

For these reasons, and because of changes in how the study of difference has been approached since the late 20th century, *emic* epistemologies of difference and human diversity have emerged in the mental health disciplines as a new paradigm for culturally competent practice. These models support cultural humility and a vision of competence as being a continuous progression of growing awareness on the part of the clinician. Emic models do not assume an invariant human behavioral norm, nor do they impose standardized categories for understanding and analyzing human experiences. They do not; they place authority in the hands of the external expert no matter how much that person has memorized about the norms and traditions of a particular target group. Rather, these models are more qualitative and phenomenological in nature, assuming the presence of within-group differences that are meaningful to people in those groups, even if they are not easily apparent to outside observers. These models invite the development of categories of analysis of experience from within a group, disclaiming the existence of the objective or universal. Emic models create an epistemic framework in which members of target groups are themselves the experts on the realities and meanings of their experiences, and in which the experience of intersectional identity is normative and assumed.

Additionally, within the mental health disciplines, these models have emphasized the importance of clinicians' understanding and examining the meaning of their own identities and biases, as well as the implications of those variables for the accurate observation of the distress of others, and the design and implementation of healing strategies. The clinician is adjured to take a stance of humility and openness rather than one of "competence-through-knowing-data." Thus, emic models are not simply about understanding data about Bajorans; they are also about understanding humanness, and about apprehending for all parties the intersubjective meanings of being a human psychotherapist working with a Bajoran client. In emic models, both parties are observers and participants, with both parties co-constructing the meanings of experiences.

Emic models assume not a stance of expertise on the part of the clinician, but a stance of curiosity, humility, and ignorance, as the foundations for culturally competent practice. Culturally competent therapists are humble. They know and embrace the reality that they are indeed ignorant, lacking in sufficient knowledge of the person of the client; they embrace the ambiguity of psychotherapeutic situation and create space in which to experience compassionately, and without judgment, how they may fail to understand their client, because the client is both apparently different and apparently similar. They explore the transcendent and meaning-making aspects of both the trauma itself and the process of recovery and healing rather than assuming that these realms of experience should be exiled from psychotherapy. Ironically, such a stance of high tolerance for ambiguity is generally considered necessary for the effective practice of psychotherapy and the development of therapeutic relationships. Embracing ambiguity about cultural phenomena implies that clinicians cannot assume they know what it means that the client is assigned female at birth, has darker-toned skin, is a practicing Roman Catholic, and has parents who were born in Cape Verde. Instead, the ambiguous potentials arising from those observable facts become the core of cultural humility that increases competence for being that person's therapist. The same stance of humility requires the clinician to embrace the same ambiguity with a complex trauma survivor who is Euro-American, sports straight blonde hair, professes no religion, and comes from the sixth generation of her family to inhabit a small, Midwestern U.S. town. This curiosity and openness to not-knowing are equally core to working with that second person.

However, the effects of guilt and shame that frequently distort dynamics in relationships between target and dominant/agent groups members seem to disconnect otherwise emotionally capable psychotherapists from their willingness to be uncertain and tentative with clients who represent the cultural other, whatever that might be. Because of the problematic narrative of etic competence, psychotherapists frequently experience themselves as more different, more deficient, and less competent to consider engaging with clients who visibly differ from them. In work with survivors of complex trauma, in which the psychotherapist's own emotional responses will be captured, read, and interpreted by clients whose interpersonal realities have been dangerous and confusing, the presence of such distortions, and the performance anxieties placed upon themselves by therapists to emit evidence of etic knowledge can lead to serious, difficult-to-repair ruptures in the therapeutic alliance. Consequently, a step toward the development of capacity for cultural humility and spiritual awareness in psychotherapists is the direct confrontation and acceptance of the realities of personal bias.

Bias: Yours, Mine, All of Ours

As people of goodwill, psychotherapists tend to see themselves as nonjudgmental and lacking in malignant bias. They are, in many instances, trained to become aware of their judgments and to let them go, and cautioned to maintain neutral, objective stances in relationship to clients. This narrative of the unbiased, nonjudgmental therapist is both unrealistic in general and deadly to the development of a culturally competent stance of practice, because it presumes a way of being that is difficult, if not possible, for most human beings to achieve. Ironically, although there is a place in the world of psychotherapy for negative countertransferences that emerge from therapists' relationships to their parents, there has been little to no room for the parallel challenges arising from the biases inherent in our intersectional identities and experiences.

Evolutionary biology and psychology indicate that humans are coded to notice difference. Our limbic systems, also implicated in the trauma response, light up and become active when data become available that another human differs in some way. Their limbic systems are what Data, the android character from the *Star Trek* series, referred to as the "subroutine for emotions," the component of human brains that runs in parallel with the cognitions of the prefrontal cortex, and that, as any trauma therapist knows only too well, usually overpower that thinking brain, firing more quickly and with more impact. The neural networks built by early trauma, and those generated by bias, are more potent, as they are often operating on an implicit basis than the more explicit cognitive overlay grown later in life. The notion that a therapist can be unbiased about human difference presumes the absence of limbic system input, as well as of any personal life history that has ascribed meaning to difference, either positive or otherwise. No psychotherapist matches these criteria, nor should any psychotherapist aspire to do so.

By the time that the first Bajoran survivor of complex trauma enters their office, the average psychotherapist will have had multiple experiences of classically conditioned associations with the visual, auditory, kinesthetic, and other sensory cues presented by that individual. The psychotherapist will have bias simply by virtue of being alive. In the second decade of the 21st century, we are all also inundated with information from numerous uncurated and not peer-reviewed sources; social media abound with inaccurate information, some of which affects our belief systems about people in ways that are difficult to change even when the truth of a matter is finally made available. Acknowledging this reality of our human tendency toward bias and suggestibility is akin to acknowledging any sort of affect or countertransferential response evoked by clients. As noted by Pope and Tabachnick (1993), it is normal for psychotherapists to experience disgust, hate, fear, or sexual feelings in response to their clients. Dalenberg (2000), and Pearlman and Saakvitne (1995), have similarly noted that work with survivors of complex trauma is particularly likely to elicit in psychotherapists these kinds of painful and confusing emotional responses.

Yet when the client is identified as a member of a target group, and the therapist's identity is largely that of dominant/agent group status, therapists seem to forget all of what they know about the normative nature of problematic countertransference in trauma treatment and instead confuse themselves with guilt and shame about this particular set of affects and biases that arise from cultural and identity difference rather than one's family of origin. Such shame and guilt are components of a larger phenomenon known as *aversive* or *modern* bias (Gaertner & Dovidio, 1986, 2005), an understanding of which is another core aspect of developing the humility necessary for moving toward cultural competence.

Aversive Bias

Aversive bias refers to nonconscious biases held by individuals who consciously eschew overt expressions of bias. It appears to have emerged during the latter half of the 20th century, as the holding of overt bias became socially stigmatized and unacceptable among groups of people that often included members of mental health professions (although, sadly, overt expressions of bias have become a cultural norm in the United States and many other countries globally). For many such people of goodwill a split developed between their expressed, conscious beliefs that were not biased and that emphasized values of fairness and honoring difference, and their well-conditioned, nonconscious, now ego-dystonic biases that had become consciously aversive to them. Social psychological research suggested that around 85% of Euro-American individuals hold aversive (also known as *implicit*) bias toward persons of color, even when their consciously held attitudes and behaviors are devoid of overt bias.

The presence of aversive or implicit bias has observable impacts on people's interactions with others; thus, rather than being simply a private affair, it is an intersubjective phenomenon with specific effects on the interpersonal field. Given the sensitivity of complex trauma survivors to a therapist's own unexplored or denied feelings, it stands to reason that aversive bias can play a large part in undermining the therapeutic relationship, thus reducing treatment effectiveness.

Aversive bias is supported by denial and undoing, and leads to shame, discomfort, and distancing by dominant/agent group members from target group members. Members of target groups, who, like trauma survivors, are often highly attuned to cues about bias emanating from members of dominant/agent groups, report experiencing their interactions with such dominant/agent group persons as crazy making and fraught with inauthenticity. Similarly, the psychotherapy client encountering a therapist who claims to have no angry feelings, while emitting cues of angry affect, is likely to feel discounted and be made crazy. Therapists who are unaware of their aversive or implicit biases thus may emit interpersonal cues that undermine their conscious intentions to do well. Given the heightened importance of the therapeutic alliance for clients who have anxious, avoidant, disorganized, or ambivalent attachment styles, which is true for many survivors of complex trauma (Norcross & Lambert, 2005), the presence of such nonconscious and disowned bias in psychotherapists, along with the distancing, detachment, and even hostility it often produces, may be particularly toxic to the alliance in psychotherapy with this population.

The humility that leads to culturally competent practice does not rest solely in knowing, in theory, about personal aversive bias, however. It requires a willingness to acknowledge its presence in oneself compassionately, without shaming oneself or inducing guilt, as a step toward greater congruence and authenticity. As noted earlier, humans are biologically wired to respond to difference, and psychosocially conditioned to associate difference with negative ascriptions that are inescapable in the familial and cultural contexts in which each psychotherapist has been raised. Because all humans have bias, acknowledging that reality as a simple given that must be observed, described, and eventually transformed enhances therapists' capacities to work across difference.

Shame about bias, however, undermines effectiveness. Nathanson (1992) has argued that humans have four predictable responses to shame: withdrawing or distancing from the source of the shame, attacking the self for being shameful, attacking the source of the shame, or denial. Each of these inter- and intrapersonal strategies is counter to psychotherapeutic effectiveness; ironically, the strategy of withdrawal (e.g., "I'm not trained to work with Bajorans") has been one accepted mode of behaving in a competent manner in etic models of cultural competence. Compassionate acceptance of the reality of psychotherapist bias allows for approach and relationship between dominant/ agent and target group members, an interpersonal style more consistent with the development of a therapeutic alliance with the survivor of complex trauma. If I am able to compassionately accept the reality of my biases and make them conscious, so that I can make the choice to not enact them, I enact them less and distance less from clients who evoke these biases. I need not employ distancing strategies, because I am experiencing less shame and greater humility about my own humanity. Then I am more willing to learn about the individual with curiosity helping me to be able to withstand being confronted by a client without responding defensively. Cultural humility creates therapeutic competence.

Understanding Privilege

When psychotherapists embrace the reality of their personal bias without shame, they are free to take the next step of moving toward cultural competence, the acknowledgment of cultural privilege and disadvantage. *Privilege* has become a somewhat radioactive term in some academic and political settings. Nonetheless, it is a real sociocultural phenomenon with very real health and mental health consequences. Psychotherapists thus need to get past the cultural radioactivity that has been associated with this construct, as it has important utility for those of us pursuing a path toward cultural competence.

Privilege should be a simple, neutral, observable phenomenon, as neither privilege nor disadvantage is earned or deserved. Like the acquisition of bias, these experiences accrue to the individual because of the circumstances and realities of life, few of which, until adulthood, occur in response to personal desires or actions. Not all who have privilege have access to its benefits; not all of the benefits are easy to identify as such, particularly when a person has intersectional identities in which the nonprivileged components of identity become more powerful than do the privileged one. Privilege is more easily noticed in when it is absent for some and present for others. Trauma survivors, whatever their other intersectional identities, have lost the privilege of being able to ignore traumatic events in their emotional and social environments; being able to deny or minimize ubiquitous trauma is a function of the privilege of not yet having experienced one's own trauma.

What is *privilege*? McIntosh (1998) described it as an "invisible backpack" of safety and positive experiences that is carried by each member of a dominant/agent group. It cannot usually be taken off, and it is rarely noticed by the person who carries it unless it is identified, and until the cultural context changes and privilege becomes redistributed. Rather, for most dominant/agent group individuals, privilege is simply how life is, the description of "normal." Much of the so-called "populist" politics emerging in the second decade of the 21st century is an expression of anger about cultural changes that have changed privilege, accompanied by demands to return to an earlier state of affairs. There is shame associated with this redistribution, in large part because in many dominant/agent cultures, the absence of privilege is explained as deriving from some real or imagined deficiencies in the target group, thus justifying the denial of privilege, and implying that privilege might be earned through correction of those alleged deficiencies, when such is never the case. An excellent example of this is the case of Dr. Henry Louis Gates, Harvard professor, being arrested in his own home because a neighbor saw him struggling with his lock and assumed that he was a burglar. He is African American. The privilege to simply struggle with one's own lock without having the police called, and of not being arrested in one's own home when no laws were broken, was not available to Dr. Gates despite his PhD, his Harvard professorship, his reputation, and his many honors; his racial phenotype, which creates disadvantage in the United States, was more powerful in influencing others' perceptions of him than anything he had earned through his own talent and hard work.

Privilege and its opposite, disadvantage, have known effects on mental health and functioning, expressed in the form of risk and resiliency factors (e.g., childhood poverty as a risk factor, good health as a resiliency factor) in the pathways to psychological and somatic distress and dysfunction. Health and mental health disparities are evidence of privilege and disadvantage in access to care, healthy food, safe water and air, and the presence or absence of endemic violence, some of it perpetrated in spasms of long-simmering rage, self-directed hatred, and violence within the target group communities, and some of it perpetrated by law enforcement on members of those target communities.

Some examples of dominant group privilege include the following:

- While driving your car, you are unlikely to be stopped by the police so long as you obey traffic laws. If stopped, you are unlikely to be killed by that police officer.
- If your daughter or son argues with a teacher or is returning home from

a party at night, she or he will not be taken into custody by policy and sent to juvenile hall.

- You can walk into any store wearing anything you want, pretty well assured that you will not be followed or harassed by store security.
- You can check out of a rental house and not have the police called on you. You can receive a loan to purchase a home if you meet the basic financial requirements.
- Your culture's holidays are always days off from work or school. You will not have to observe a fast day while at work surrounded by people eating lunch.
- You can be imperfect, and few people will generalize from your imperfections to those of everyone in your group. You need not represent your group to the world.
- If your day, week, or year is going badly, you need not ask whether there are overtones of bias, or whether you are being paranoid; thus, no excess emotional energy needs to be spent parsing the meanings of a situation, and when you do not like what is happening, it is rare that you will be accused of overreacting or being paranoid.
- Something traumatic can be publicized on the news or social media and your day will not be affected by floods of posttraumatic emotions.

Most individuals have some mixture of privilege and disadvantage due to the mingling of dominant/agent and target group status in their intersectional identities. Invidious comparisons between experiences of disadvantage (e.g., is racism worse than homophobia?) frequently have the effect of creating divisions between target groups, while obscuring the psychological reality that for every person who experiences privilege or its absence, there are psychosocial effects. Privilege creates ease, safety, and a sense of clarity (whether false or real) about what happens in the world, thus fostering resilience and giving access to resources that speed the healing process.

Acknowledging privilege, like acknowledging one's aversive bias, is a process that often initially induces shame and guilt. Like aversive bias, privilege should be an occasion for neither; being born with pale skin or a penis in a culture that values these characteristics and gives privilege to those who have them is an accident of fate and genetics. Just as therapists working with the survivors of complex trauma convey that the terrible things done to clients were not their fault, so, too, a cultural humility teaches therapists that whatever privilege they have accrued by accident of birth is not their fault.

Shame or guilt over privilege, similar to shame about aversive bias, can undermine both effective assessment and psychotherapy. Most centrally, empathic relating may be undermined when the powerful and sometimes insidious effects of the absence of privilege on well-being and psychological robustness are denied or downplayed, leading to overpathologizing of a survivor's behaviors by the therapist, who operates from unexamined assumptions of privilege and the resources that privilege makes available. A therapist who denies privilege can also become numb to how the absence of privilege shapes life's realities. To call oneself color-blind is an excellent example of privilege at work; only if the shade of my skin has not systemically disadvantaged me can I act as if this variable matters little.

The issue of privilege appears in the realm of spirituality and meaning-making practice as well. Some faiths teach that they alone are true and right, and condone persecution of those who believe otherwise. Some practitioners of particular spiritual paths define their ways as more enlightened, imposing other cultural values ("We preach peace"; "We are egalitarian"; "We keep kosher more strictly"; and so on, *ad infinitum*) onto the structure of spiritual practice. Those whose meaning-making systems do not include a divinity similarly may judge or be judged. Because such beliefs are often implicit biases that occur in the realm of the precognitive that is the unspoken foundation for meaning, and because meaning-making systems can be so central to healing from complex trauma, therapists need to be willing to do in-depth exploration of the ways in which bias may have hidden in their own spiritual and meaning-making systems.

Representation: Transference, Plus

Paradoxically, when bias and privilege are persistently observed and re-cognized, the *sine qua non* of psychotherapy—to know, value, and be of assistance to the unique individual who is the client—becomes a possibility. Moreover, therapists who are able to unflinchingly observe their bias and privilege also are better equipped to comprehend the limits of the aspiration to be truly client-centered that are created by the complex phenomenon of *representation*. The 19th-century African American suffrage activist Anna Julia Cooper said, "When and where I enter, then and there the whole race enters with me" (quoted in Giddings, 1996, p. 14). Cooper's statement is true for each therapist and for each client. When and where therapy occurs, into the room enter personal and cultural histories, privileges, and biases. Therapists represent things to their clients, who represent things in return. These phenomena are more than simply transference or countertransference, because the things represented (i.e., ethnicity, gender, social class, and others, to be discussed later in this chapter) are currently active in the social environment rather than existing largely in past experiences that are symbolically or unconsciously evoked or transferred into the therapeutic environment. The dynamics of representation, even when symbolic, are not merely nonconscious representations of personal history; they are the interpersonal, social, spiritual, and political realities in which therapy takes place.

The humility leading to culturally competent practice, with trauma survivors or with others, requires a heightened awareness of what is represented by both parties. This is especially the case when one or the other represents a component of personal or historical trauma to the other. For cultural competence to be infused into the work, therapists must consider how both visible and invisible aspects of identities may carry meanings to which clients are not insensitive. Therapists may attempt to deny social realities by telling themselves (and sometimes their clients) that they are inattentive to clients' phenotype, sex, gender, size, or accent; such statements, reflecting experiences of privilege or the problematic pedagogy of etic models, are experienced as invalidating to clients from target groups, who rarely are not perceived, and treated in the world in ways informed by their intersectional identities.

Privilege, ironically, confers a lack of awareness, because an aspect of privilege is that one member is not expected to represent the entire group. The divorcing heterosexual person, for example, is not seen as evidence of the failure of that sexual orientation but simply as someone having a bad relationship experience, nor is the Euro-American child who performs poorly in math seen as evidence that math capacities are lacking for persons with that ancestry and phenotype. For those psychotherapists whose primary intersectional identities derive from dominant/agent groups, and who are most likely to be affected by the nonconscious assumptions of privilege, heightened attention to how and what one represents is essential for the humility leading to culturally competent practice. This interrogation of personal identities may also deepen empathy as dominant/agent group therapists begin dimly to apprehend what it means to live as a visible, audible, or palpable symbol of something—good, bad, or indifferent. A basic assumption of cultural humility is never to assume that we have the trust of our clients. This dovetails with what is known about working with complex trauma. Trauma is itself destructive to trust; survivors of interpersonal trauma may take years to believe that their therapists will not become one of their perpetrators. When therapists overtly represent difference in a way that, consciously or not, conveys a message of threat because of what the therapist appears to represent, or if the client evokes a parallel reaction in the therapist, the willingness to bring these dynamics of difference and representation into shared awareness not only increases cultural competence but also takes steps toward the deepening of empathy and attunement.

When therapists represent current or historical trauma to clients and are aware of it, however, they increase the possibility of earning trust when they tell truths about accepting their role as representatives of their culture. Acknowledging and validating the presence of dynamics arising from such representations in the therapy office can communicate to clients a willingness to tell truths that are uncomfortable for therapists, not simply to invite clients to experience the therapists' own discomfort. Power becomes more balanced when therapists eschew the anonymity of privilege, and bring to the foreground their own identities, as their target group clients must do often in their daily lives.

Thus, simply saying, "I'm wondering what it means for our work together that I'm apparently able-bodied and you're a person with a visible disability," communicates a psychotherapist's cultural humility in several ways. First, the therapist is being honest about privilege, and about the power dynamics engendered by that privilege. Second, the therapist is taking responsibility for opening the discussion, which is usually more uncomfortable (because it is potentially a source of guilt and/or shame) for a member of a dominant/agent group, withdrawing from neither the topic, the discomfort, nor the client's realities. Finally, the therapist is acknowledging the awareness that they are representing their dominant/agent group in this dyad. These, and similar interventions, are not a formula for "how to be culturally competent." Such embrace of difficult dialogues of difference is, however, one of many ways in which cultural humility can enhance practice with complex trauma survivors, who may feel a modicum more safe knowing that they are not alone in their awareness of disparities of privilege, and that they do not carry the sole responsibility for making that visible and integrated into the therapy.

Diversity Is about Everyone: The ADDRESSING Model

Finally, this practice stands on a foundation of belief that each human being represents the range of aspects of intersectional identity, and that moving toward cultural competence requires therapists to be aware of the dynamics of their own identities and social locations, not only those of clients. Human diversity is not about "special populations," but about the nature of being human. Challenging oppressive norms is something we do not only altruistically, on behalf of traumatized survivors, but also from enlightened self-interest, with the assumption that each person is in some manner harmed by current social structures of hierarchies of value. This further moves the definitions of cultural competence away from the *etic* "Handbook of psychotherapy with Bajorans" model to one that positions dominant/agent group members of goodwill as allies to members of targets group, in part by disrupting the narrative of "normal" and "other," with a discourse of multiple and intersectional identities across social locations that are present in everyone. Using epistemologies of difference that invite psychotherapists to consider how to think about and analyze experiences of identity supports cultural competence, because the therapist need not acquire discrete data bits about Bajorans; rather, the therapist learns how to think about what it might mean to be this particular Bajoran whose intersectional identities also include being assigned male at birth, being cisgender, growing up in an internment camp, being a refugee, being a parent, and having experienced childhood complex trauma.

A variety of epistemologies of difference have been proposed tor cultural competence in psychotherapy; the one I discuss here is Hays's ADDRESSING model (2001, 2007, 2016). This acronym stands for a nonexhaustive yet useful list of varieties of intersectional identity:

- A: Age-related factors, including chronological age and age cohort.
- DD: Disability–ability, and illness, born with and acquired, visible and invisible.

- R: Religion, spirituality, and systems of meaning making.
- E: Ethnic origins, ancestry, race/phenotype, and culture.
- S: Social class, current and former.
- S: Sexual orientation—lesbian, gay, bisexual, transgender, heterosexual, pansexual, asexual, questioning.
- I: Indigenous heritage/colonization, history/colonizer history.
- N: National origin/immigration status/refugee/offspring of immigrants.
- G: Gender—sex assigned at birth, gender identity, and orientation.

This model makes explicit that all humans have multiple and intersectional identities. Although one aspect may become central phenomenologically or assume the foreground interpersonally, each individual is the unique intersection of some combination of these social locations. Identity emerges in the dialectical struggle between individual experiences including attachment style and experiences of trauma and temperament, and between group/collective and individual experiences and norms. Not all of these variables have the same effect in any two persons; they are additive, multiplicative, or variable, depending on the situation. The intersections may vary within the lifetime of a given person as well.

Trauma: Another Intersectional Identity

Trauma is another component of identity; this is as true for some therapists (Pope & Feldman-Summers, 1992) as for their clients. Many clients with complex trauma histories are children of trauma survivors, living with legacies of intergenerational transmission of trauma experiences (Danieli, 1998). Still others identify with cultures that have historically been so affected by systemic trauma, such as Native American or First Nations, African American, Jewish, Khmer, Native Hawaiian or Alaskan, or Armenian, that historical and systemic trauma has been woven into other aspects of identity by the centrality of historical trauma to that component of identity (Comas-Díaz & Jacobsen, 2001; Pole, Gone, & Kulkarni, 2008).

Perpetration is another facet of many people's identities, a variable that fuels some of the shame that leads to denial of bias. The descendants of slaveholders, of soldiers who shot women and children in this country's genocidal wars against its indigenous people, of those who imprisoned or tortured others in the countries from which they came, are among the survivors of complex trauma. The police officers who shot an innocent man because they scared themselves with the color of his skin, the border guard required to separate parents from their crying children, these and other people whose work and lives invite them to do harm, also can be complex trauma survivors. They or their ancestors suffered what Shay (1995) calls the "moral injury" of being trauma perpetrators, a wound that has been shown to equal other forms of trauma. Both therapists and clients can be the inheritors of moral injury that was often traumatic to the family cultures that it created. For some individuals of mixed heritage, the inner conflict between having descended from both target and oppressor is yet another component of identity flavoring the experiences of complex trauma.

Each component of identity in the ADDRESSING model can be linked to the experience of trauma in some manner; this may be due to direct targeting, as is the case for hate crimes or gender-based violations, or it may have occurred more indirectly (e.g., with poverty being a risk factor for exposure to violence). A complete discussion of this topic far exceeds the parameters of this chapter; readers are referred to Brown (2008) for a book-length discussion and review of pertinent literature on specific relationships between ADDRESSING variables and trauma exposure. Individuals may also, accurately or not, attribute their experiences of victimization to some component of their identities, and struggle with their hatred of an inescapable fact about themselves that they believe has rendered them vulnerable.

For example, the survivor of complex trauma who hates herself for having been a vulnerable child, unable to protect herself against abuse or soothe herself in the face of neglect, may have developed an intolerance of anything youthful or child-like in herself. In the extreme, this may lead to structural dissociation, in which inner "children" are punished by other ego states for being young, thus representing the supposed cause of the experience of victimization. In a similar vein, a man who is sexually assaulted as a child because of his supposed effeminacy may develop a hypermasculine style as an adult, expressing hatred of effeminate men or of women.

Because perpetrators of complex trauma are so frequently those with whom a survivor was or is emotionally intimate, many of the survivor's intersectional identities may overlap with those of the perpetrator, creating understandable confusion and difficulties when defenses of splitting are engaged, as is so frequently the case in the aftermath of overwhelming abuse or neglect. "I hate the white person in me," cries the mixed-race survivor of incest at the hands of her Euro-American father. Struggles with identity and meaning making, which are commonplace among survivors of complex trauma, may be intensified by the ways in which identification with or loyalty to a group has become contaminated by shared membership with the ones who did harm. Cultural competence can be enhanced by a psychotherapist's ability to embrace, and to invite clients to embrace, these painful contradictions and experiences of betrayal (along with related feelings of ambivalence, i.e., love and hate; affection and contempt), and to see identity development as fluid rather than fixed and reflecting many different intersectional variables.

Trauma and Identity Development

Maria Root, an identity theorist who has used the experiences of people of mixed phenotype and ancestry (aka *racially mixed*) to develop her models

(Root, 1998, 2000, 2004), has argued that several factors need to be present to develop an ecologically valid identity theory for persons of recent mixed heritage. First, this model needs to account for within-group bias and oppression, the sort of expression of internalized oppression or horizontal hostility that can occur when target group membership is present. Second, such a model must see as positive the experience of identities that are socially defined as being in conflict with one another. Root's model, a useful paradigm for humility in understanding the identity experiences of trauma survivors, construes these sorts of apparently conflicting mixes of identities as being potentially mentally healthy in contrast to prior models, which were pathologizing. Her model next notes the importance of changes in social and political contexts, and social reference groups that are available to persons and affect their own understanding of their particular intersectional identities. Finally, the model must acknowledge the interaction of experiences in people's social ecology, including family environment, history, and biological heritage. Root portrays her model graphically as a series of nested, interactive, overlapping boxes in which these various factors are in constant interplay, and in which identity is in a continuous process of development rather than moving toward a fixed and apparently stable state (see *www.drmariaroot.com*).

Cultural humility in trauma practice is enhanced by this or similar models of identity formation, because it allows the clinician to conceptualize their own and their clients' identities as a continuously transforming matrix of multiple social locations that does not require a fixed and stable state to be functional. Many survivors of trauma exist in a liminal identity state, one in which transition is a constant. What is less obvious but equally important for the culturally competent trauma psychotherapist to take into account is the degree to which liminal identities emerge as a function of a posttraumatic healing process, in which identity as a trauma survivor becomes integrated in a positive fashion into other aspects of identity.

Culturally competent practice takes clients' and psychotherapists' varying and intersectional identities into account in making sense of what occurs in the interpersonal field of the therapy process: the poverty-class Euro-American cisgender woman client who has risen into middle management, and the upper-middle-class Euro-American cisgender woman therapist who struggles to make a middle-class income in an independent practice, may need to interrogate one another regarding the centrality of social class to their respective identities to discover how their relationship has been plagued by disconnects. In this example, the hidden aspect of intersectional identities that is social class may have had important effects on sense of self for both women in ways that are obscured by current apparent similarities. Because, as Root notes, one way to consciously embrace one's intersectional identity is to refuse to accept a solo identity assigned by others. Thus, cultural competence in psychotherapy is enhanced by thoughtful consideration of all potential aspects of identity. The humility inherent in not assuming the strands of intersectionality or the ways in which they entwine in any other person allows the therapy process to embrace each person's strategy for weaving those aspects into a coherent whole.

Therapy in the Real World

Finally, each aspect of identity and each way that those variables have become embedded in the experiences of trauma and recovery are affected by the social and political realities of the world. Cultural competence requires therapists to remain attuned to the ways that external events, which may seem distal to the therapy process, are proximal in their capacities to evoke affect, intensify bias, or change the meaning of the relationships between people in that process.

This does not mean therapists have to be constantly scanning the news or social media for evidence of some emerging danger; in fact, with the emergence of social media, the presence of danger for members of target groups and their allies has finally become as visible to dominant/agent culture as it has always been to people who are systemically at risk. Rather, it means a consideration that shifts in the therapy, steps back and to the side, and intensifications of painful affects and feelings of hopelessness or despair may not only represent an intrapsychic process but also reflect encounters with meaningful external realities. Watching children of color wrenched from their parents at the U.S. border in the spring of 2018 spoke powerfully and painfully to many trauma survivors. Root's (1992) concept of "insidious trauma" is a useful construct for considering how this might be the case. She describes how exposure to what Essed (1991) refers to as "everyday" bias operates as a continuous stream of small traumatizations that may appear to have no immediate effect, but that can have a cumulative effect when the latest act of bias goes viral on Facebook. Exacerbation of symptoms may not require news of a hate crime against members of one's own group; it can occur in response to the latest exposure to everyday bias, discrimination, or invisibility, which is itself a form of psychic violence. This heightened awareness of the retraumatizing capacities of the present moment lead therapists to actively explore how triggering life events are not simply Criterion B reminders of a trauma, but representations of threat to some aspect of identity, including a component of intersectionality that might have remained in the background of the therapy process.

Conclusion

The cultural humility that can lead to greater levels of cultural competence as a psychotherapist is a process with no clear conclusion. As one grows in this domain, one grows in self-awareness of one's ignorance and how one might stretch intellectual, experiential, spiritual, and emotional edges to better develop empathy. Deepening cultural competence leads the therapist, paradoxically, to make more errors of commission at first, in place of the errors of omission and avoidance that are more common when the "refer to the Bajoran specialist" strategy is engaged. The deepening of intimacy and relationship, whether in psychotherapy or elsewhere in life, allows sufficient contact that errors can be made. Aversive biases express themselves behaviorally, countertransferences evoked by representation are acted out, and willingness to acknowledge error and listen to distress is called upon repeatedly. Cultural competence requires that therapists seek ongoing consultation and training, as well as continuing acquisition of specific knowledge. A therapist never *achieves* cultural competence but is always moving toward the repeated yet compassionate self-examination of bias, privilege, and self-representation. The parallel processes and skills inherent in working with complex trauma serve psychotherapists well on the journey to cultural competence; deepening cultural humility, in turn, sharpens the skills of the psychotherapist entering the world of complex trauma.

References

Brown, L. S. (2008). *Cultural competence in trauma therapy: Beyond the flashback.* Washington, DC: American Psychological Association.

Comas-Díaz, L., & Jacobsen, F. (2001). Ethnocultural allodynia. *Journal of Psychotherapy Practice and Research, 10,* 246–252.

Dalenberg, C. I. (2000). *Countertransference and the treatment of trauma.* Washington, DC: American Psychological Association.

Danieli, Y. (Ed.). (1998). *International handbook of multigenerational legacies of trauma.* New York: Plenum Press.

Essed, P. (1991). *Everyday racism: Reports from women of two cultures.* New York: Hunter House.

Gaertner, S., & Dovidio, J. (1986). The aversive form of racism. In J. Dovidio & S. Gaertner (Eds.), *Prejudice, discrimination and racism* (pp. 61–89). Orlando, FL: Academic Press.

Gaertner, S., & Dovidio, J. (2005). Understanding and addressing contemporary racism: From aversive racism to the common in-group identity model. *Journal of Social Issues, 61,* 615–639.

Giddings, P. (1996). *When and where I enter: The impact of race and sex on black women's lives.* New York: Amistad.

Hays, P. A. (2001). *Addressing cultural complexities in practice: A framework for clinicians and counselors.* Washington, DC: American Psychological Association.

Hays, P. A. (2007). *Addressing cultural complexities in practice: Assessment, diagnosis, and therapy* (2nd ed.). Washington, DC: American Psychological Association.

Hays, P. A. (2016). *Addressing cultural complexities in practice: Assessment, diagnosis, and therapy* (3rd ed.). Washington, DC: American Psychological Association.

Herman, J. L. (1992). *Trauma and recovery.* New York: Basic Books.

McIntosh, P. (1998). White privilege: Unpacking the invisible knapsack. In M. McGoldrick (Ed.), *Re-visioning family therapy: Race, culture, and gender in clinical practice* (pp. 147–152). New York: Guilford Press.

Nathanson, D. (1992). *Shame and pride: Affect, sex, and the birth of the self.* New York: Norton.

Norcross, J. C., & Lambert, M. J. (2005). The therapy relationship. In J. C. Norcross, L. E. Beutler, & R. F. Levant (Eds.), *Evidence-based practice in mental health: Debate and dialogue on the fundamental questions* (pp. 208–217). Washington, DC: American Psychological Association.

Pearlman, L. A., & Saakvitne, K. W. (1995). *Trauma and the therapist: Countertransference and vicarious traumatization in psychotherapy with incest survivors.* New York: Norton.

Pole, N., Gone, J., & Kulkarni, M. (2008). Posttraumatic stress disorder among ethnoracial minorities in the United States. *Clinical Psychology: Science and Practice, 15,* 35–61.

Pope, K. S., & Feldman-Summers, S. (1992). National survey of psychologists' sexual and physical abuse history and their evaluation of training and competence in these areas. *Professional Psychology: Research and Practice, 23,* 353–361.

Pope, K. S., & Tabachnick, B. G. (1993). Therapists' anger, hate, fear, and sexual feelings. *Professional Psychology: Research and Practice, 23,* 142–152.

Root, M. P. P. (1992). Reconstructing the impact of trauma on personality. In L. S. Brown & M. Ballou (Eds.), *Personality and psychopathology: Feminist reappraisals* (pp. 229–265). New York: Guilford Press.

Root, M. P. P. (1998). Preliminary findings from the biracial sibling project. *Cultural Diversity and Mental Health, 4,* 237–247.

Root, M. P. P. (2000). Rethinking racial identity development: An ecological framework. In P. Spickard & J. Burroughs (Eds.), *We are a people: Narrative and multiplicity in constructing na ethnic identity* (pp. 205–220). Philadelphia: Temple University Press.

Root, M. P. P. (2004). From exotic to a dime a dozen. *Women and Therapy, 27,* 19–32.

Shay, J. (1995). *Achilles in Vietnam: Combat trauma and the undoing of character.* New York: Simon & Schuster.

CHAPTER 8

New Perspectives on Vicarious
Traumatization and Complex Trauma

LAURIE ANNE PEARLMAN
JAMES CARINGI
ASHLEY R. TRAUTMAN

Trauma clinicians face many challenges in working with clients with complex trauma adaptations, as these symptoms and styles of relating are often woven into the fabric of survivors' internal and interpersonal lives. While remaining attuned to their complex trauma clients' needs, therapists must maintain self-awareness through attention to their own emotional responses and the effects of the work on themselves in order to provide ethical, effective treatment.

The empathic engagement necessary for truly therapeutic relationships with these clients, as well as with other traumatized populations, has trans-formative personal repercussions for the therapist, a process that has been labeled *vicarious traumatization* (VT; McCann & Pearlman, 1990a; Pearlman & Saakvitne, 1995). While this work can also present many rewards to thera-pists, our primary focus here is on the deleterious effects of trauma work on therapists. Trauma therapists must develop ways to work sustainably over the course of treatment relationships that may be long term and, in some cases, span their entire careers. We refer the reader to the many Internet resources that have been developed since the first publication of this chapter (*https://vtt. ovc.ojp.gov*; *https://vtt.ovc.ojp.gov/compendium*; *www.counseling.org/docs/ trauma-disaster/fact-sheet-9---vicarious-trauma.pdf*).

In this chapter, we describe VT from our vantage point as clinicians who have worked extensively with complex trauma survivors describe it, briefly discuss both a possible mechanism for and particular factors that contribute to VT, suggest ways clinicians and institutions can address it, and suggest research and policy directions. Our goal is to support therapists and others who work with survivors with complex trauma in protecting and maintaining themselves so they and their clients can thrive as a result of their therapeutic work.

Definition

VT is defined as the negative transformation in the clinician that results from empathic engagement with trauma survivors and their trauma stories and ways of relating, combined with a commitment or responsibility to help them (McCann & Pearlman, 1990a; Pearlman & Saakvitne, 1995). Its hallmark is disrupted spirituality, just as with direct psychological trauma, in which the signature loss is of meaning and hope. The VT construct emerged primarily from observations of the effects on therapists of working with trauma survivor clients who had experienced multiple forms of childhood abuse and neglect (McCann & Pearlman, 1990b). Although the VT literature does not explicitly differentiate between those who work with persons with histories of complex or repetitive ("Type II") and time-limited or one-time ("Type I") traumatic events and experiences (Terr, 1989), the theoretical literature on VT largely refers to, and the research literature has primarily studied, clinicians who work with complex trauma. However, helpers working with survivors with all forms of trauma may experience VT. The VT experience parallels that of direct trauma, with similar, if less intense, characteristic responses; however, if left unaddressed, it can escalate in severity until it meets criteria for a psychiatric diagnosis such as posttraumatic stress disorder (PTSD)/secondary traumatic stress variant, anxiety, mood, and substance abuse disorders. The alterations in meaning, relationships, and overall life satisfaction can resemble those of complex trauma survivor clients, although they are usually less severe than those resulting from direct traumatic experiences.

Although psychoanalytic theory has long been interested in the self of the therapist as a technical factor in the success of a treatment, the focus on the clinician's well-being is a newer area of study. We draw here from some of the relevant therapist well-being literature, focusing specifically on VT, its risk factors, mechanism(s) of development, and antidotes as they apply to sustaining clinicians working with people with complex trauma.

Constructivist self development theory (CSDT; McCann & Pearlman, 1990b; Pearlman & Saakvitne, 1995), the theoretical foundation for the VT construct, suggests that each clinician's unique VT responses arise from an interaction between the clinician and the client, including the specifics of both parties' histories and current life situations, attachment and relational styles, capacity for affect regulation, and posttraumatic reactions and adaptations (McCann & Pearlman, 1990a). The unique value of the VT construct is this theoretical base, which allows for making connections among observations (signs, symptoms, adaptations) and suggests etiology and possibilities for addressing and transforming VT. CSDT frames symptoms as adaptations rather than pathologizing normal responses to abnormal events. But rather than focusing on symptoms, it identifies areas of the self that are affected by both direct and indirect trauma, providing a basis for understanding myriad individual responses (e.g., social withdrawal, dissociation, substance misuse) that can arise from negative effects on one area of self-functioning (e.g., affect tolerance). Thus, the theoretical base of the VT construct allows for a depth and complexity of comprehension and avenues for intervention. The theory base supports clinicians and their organizations in understanding, anticipating, and preventing VT and in addressing it, so that it is less likely to interfere with or curtail work-related effectiveness and satisfaction.

Researchers have identified in trauma therapists symptoms of posttraumatic stress, such as avoidance, intrusive thoughts, flashbacks, hyperarousal, numbing, and cognitive disruptions; relational changes, such as aggression, reenactments, difficulty with boundary management, personal withdrawal, and alienation; as well as more general psychological stress and distress (Arvay & Uhlemann, 1996; Bober, Regehr, & Zhou, 2006; Lee, Gottfried, & Bride, 2018; Ortlepp & Friedman, 2002; Schauben & Frazier, 1995). Accounts from clinicians who treat complex trauma also include reports of therapist dissociation and depersonalization during sessions, intimacy and sexual difficulties, increased use of alcohol or other substances to self-soothe or self-medicate, somatization, social isolation, loss of meaning and hope, increased mistrust of others and their intentions and motives, hypervigilance, and even paranoia (Benatar, 2000; Sui & Padmanabhanunni, 2016).

Wilson and Thomas (2004) reported results of the Clinicians' Trauma Reaction Survey, a study conducted with 345 therapists (Thomas, 1998). Using the conceptual frameworks of empathic strain (Wilson & Lindy, 1994), vicarious traumatization (McCann & Pearlman, 1990a; Pearlman & Saakvitne, 1995), and compassion fatigue (Figley, 1995), this study documented five primary aspects of clinicians' reactions to trauma work: (1) unmodulated affect in response to clients' trauma narratives; (2) somatic complaints; (3) PTSD symptoms; (4) impact on personal frames of reference such as beliefs, values, worldview, and sense of self; and (5) symptoms of acute traumatic stress disorder, depression, and anxiety (Wilson & Thomas, 2004, p. 154). These categories closely parallel the adaptations of complex trauma survivors.

VT can be differentiated from the related constructs of countertransference, burnout, compassion fatigue, and countertrauma. VT refers to the negative changes that can take place across time in clinicians who treat trauma, as an interaction among client, therapist, and work setting factors, in a particular social–cultural context. *Countertransference* (Freud, 1912) refers to the analyst's (or therapist's) responses to a single client, based on the therapist's personal issues, whether client trauma is involved or not (see Pearlman & Saakvitne, 1995, for a discussion of this distinction). *Burnout* (Freudenberger, 1974) focuses on the gap between what the clinician is expected to do (or what the client needs; Williamson, 2018) and what he or she is able to provide. It also refers to the therapist's increasing alienation from the work and a sense of increased hopelessness, helplessness, and despair. In contrast to burnout, *compassion fatigue* (formerly known as *secondary traumatic stress disorder*; Figley, 1995) focuses on the parallel trauma symptoms that clinicians may develop in working with traumatized clients, often due to overinvolvement that paradoxically results in exhaustion and withdrawal/detachment. *Countertrauma* "focuses on the dynamic between patient and therapist" (Gartner, 2017, p. 8), much like VT.

It is not yet known whether VT is inevitable in trauma treatment. Research findings, as well as anecdotal evidence from experienced clinicians, suggest that most experience some negative transformation of their personal frame of reference (spirituality, worldview, and identity), relationships, ability to regulate emotional states, judgment or decision-making abilities, or bodily experiences. It is important to emphasize that *neither clients nor clinicians are responsible for the development of VT*. Rather, it is an occupational hazard, a cost of doing the work that arises as therapists confront and deal with the toxicity of trauma (Munroe et al., 1995). Clinicians and their organizational work settings must respond through recognizing and legitimizing rather than stigmatizing its occurrence, and managing it rather than ignoring it.

Finally, VT is neither an endpoint, nor is it best understood by its symptoms. Because VT is a process, there are many points at which clinicians and those who support them can intervene to mitigate the negative effects. The symptoms are signals that change is needed to sustain the clinician in the work over time.

Contributing Factors

Contributing factors are predisposing or risk factors that increase the therapist's likelihood of developing VT. The first category of contributing factors includes aspects of the work (*situation variables*), such as exposure to clients' sometimes horrific histories and challenging attachment styles and relational dynamics, and the nature of the work, such as the interaction between the dynamics and the details of the clients' stories on the one hand, and the confidentiality demands of the work on the other.

Additional significant situational contributing factors come from the organizational, social, and cultural context of the treatment. These include work-setting variables, such as demands of the workplace for productivity that might exceed the therapist's personal resources and emotional capacity; the focus on paperwork and other administrative tasks that overwhelm clinicians and invite them to dehumanize clients; lack of support for self-care, such as no health insurance and inadequate time off; lack of structures (e.g., trauma-focused peer and expert clinical consultation) to maintain the confidentiality of the work and to sustain the worker; a work culture that undermines the work by using sarcasm or humor that can dehumanize clients, as well as workers; lack of training and consultation related to both clinical issues and

VT; an organizational culture that demands a tough demeanor; and the isola-tion of private practice. In addition, we work in a broader social context that includes racism, sexism, poverty, injustice, and politics and media, which often are elements of complex trauma clients' traumatic experiences and can open old wounds and impede healing.

The other major category of contributing factors, aspects of the clini-cian (*person variables*), includes both personal dimensions, such as therapist personal trauma history and the degree of its resolution, coping and attach-ment style, current life stressors, emotional maturity, judgment (especially as it relates to maintaining boundaries), support system and relationship satisfac-tion; parallels in the therapist's life that promote identification; and profes-sional dimensions such as trauma-specific training and therapeutic skill.

A Hypothesized Mechanism Underlying VT

The presence of risk or contributing factors alone does not create VT. There must also be an activating mechanism. We hypothesize a certain type of empathic engagement as the process that catalyzes contributing factors into VT. Batson, Fultz, and Schoenrade (1987) presented a model that can be applied to under-standing this mechanism in therapists. When clinicians open themselves to oth-ers' pain, they may experience personal distress or empathy, or both. *Personal distress* arises when one imagines *personally experiencing* the traumatic event, a process that can result in negative feelings. These uncomfortable feelings may lead therapists to distance themselves from clients or, alternatively, to become overinvolved, both stances reducing therapists' ability to be helpful and giving rise to more problematic client behaviors. On the other hand, *empathy* arises from the therapist imagining *what the client experienced,* resulting in compas-sion for clients and prosocial behavior. The research by Batson et al. can be applied to suggest that we may be more compassionate and effective therapists, and we may have greater endurance and work-related satisfaction, if we can modulate our engagement with our clients and remain in a place of empathy rather than identification. Moosman (2002) studied empathy in trauma thera-pists as a possible element in the development of VT. While empathy alone did not contribute to VT, Moosman found that therapists who were "highly emotionally *reactive*" due to identification were more likely to experience VT, lending support to our hypothesis.

Individual Approaches to
Coping with and Transforming VT

Most of the work on addressing VT has focused on general approaches rather than on interventions targeted to clinicians' specific contributing factors and manifestations of VT. In our opinion, VT interventions should focus on specific contributing factors and responses/symptoms. General approaches may be essential to strengthening the therapist's foundation for resilience related to VT, but will not address, for example, intrusive imagery, social withdrawal, or spiritual depletion. Clinicians (perhaps with the assistance of their consultants, supervisors, or therapists) must identify the particular factors that are increasing their VT and the specific ways trauma work is affecting them, then seek remedies for those specific issues. For example, trauma-specific interventions such as eye movement desensitization and reprocessing therapy (EMDR) and cognitive-behavioral therapy (CBT) are likely to be useful to therapists who are experiencing PTSD symptoms. Those experiencing increased cynicism may need to engage in spiritual renewal activities or may be helped by CBT.

Here we describe five individual realms that may help the clinician develop a strong foundation: social support, professional consultation, spiritual renewal, committed self-care, and working sustainably. Clinicians also must continuously monitor and respond to their specific personal needs.

Social Support

One of the effects of VT is for the clinician to withdraw from relationships and to isolate (possibly due to depression, the need to regulate affect by distancing from closeness, or interpersonal depletion). Therapists may also withdraw from clients. Since working in isolation can reduce the therapist's ability to consult colleagues for clinical and emotional support, it is important for trauma clinicians to cultivate personal and professional support as an antidote to the demands of their work (Catherall, 1995; Munroe et al., 1995; Rosenbloom, Pratt, & Pearlman, 1995). Research demonstrates that social support is associated with higher rates of *posttraumatic growth*, positive change experienced as a result of the struggle with a major life crisis or a traumatic event (Calhoun & Tedeschi, 2006) among clinicians (Mâirean, 2016; Manning-Jones, De Terte, & Stephens, 2016). Social support can be a source of both emotional and instrumental assistance. It provides inoculation against the corrosive effects of trauma work by defining and creating meaningful and supportive communities that serve to broaden identity beyond that of "trauma clinician," and that promote personal well-being through interpersonal connection and support.

Professional Consultation

Because of the intensity and intricacy of transference–countertransference dynamics in psychotherapies with complex trauma clients, working without clinical consultation, at any level of clinician experience, can pose great hazards for both clients and therapists. Consultation allows clinicians to acknowledge and reflect on their reactions to complex trauma clients' often intense feelings and sometimes extreme behaviors and relational demands and interactions (Pearlman & Courtois, 2005; Pearlman & Saakvitne, 1995). In our experience, examining personal responses in a supportive, confidential, trauma-informed, professional consulting relationship can be a powerful source of support in identifying and managing VT. Consultation provides a forum for processing personal distress, as well as for developing strategies for mitigating VT. Professional consultation relationships can also protect against inappropriate therapist disclosure of clinical material to the therapist's friends or family members, which often happens in a bid for support. We discuss organizations' responsibilities related to clinical consultation below.

Spiritual Renewal and Vicarious Transformation

We believe that the most important process in ameliorating VT responses, especially despair and hopelessness, is the development of a *spiritual life,* a practice or set of practices that makes room for reflection, putting the work into a larger context, and finding or creating meaning. Given the posited central role of spirituality, or meaning systems, to trauma, it is essential to attend to the development of whatever is self-nourishing. There are many paths to spirituality. For some, it involves engaging in traditional practices such as prayer and organized religion. For others, it means creating or finding community; being useful to others; enjoying nature; or seeking awe, joy, beauty, and wonder. We encourage clinicians to find or to create their own meaningful spiritual practices to counter the dispiriting challenges that can accompany work with complex trauma.

One of the best antidotes to VT is to be transformed in positive ways by the work, a process that we term *vicarious transformation* (Pearlman & Caringi, 2009). Others have used related, but distinct, concepts such as vicarious posttraumatic growth (the positive consequences of working with trauma survivors; Arnold, Calhoun, Tedeschi, & Cann, 2005), vicarious resilience (therapists' ability to learn about resilience from clients and apply it to their own lives; Hernández, Gangsei, & Engstrom, 2007), and counterresilience (psychological and spiritual growth in the analyst, arising from engaging deeply with traumatized clients; Gartner, 2017).

Opening oneself to the darker aspects of human experience can contribute to personal and professional perspective and growth. Developing a frame of reference that includes some way of making sense of the human capacity for cruelty and evil allows the clinician to approach the work with more comprehension. Understanding why such horrors occur is not the same as accepting their inevitability or forgiving harmdoers. Trauma clinicians may be moved to social activism, another strategy that might help to transform VT (Pearlman & Saakvitne, 1995).

Committed Self-Care

We encourage trauma clinicians to understand self-care not as an indulgence or afterthought but rather as essential to their physical and mental health, and to their ability to engage constructively with their clients (Norcross &

Guy, 2007; van Dernoot Lipsky & Burk, 2009; Wicks, 2008). We have termed this orientation *committed self-care*. This means *intentionally and frequently* creating opportunities for respite and replenishment (i.e., engaging in activities that offer distraction or personal growth; exercising, having fun, resting, relaxing, and connecting with one's body; and developing and maintaining intimate interpersonal relationships). It also means, wherever possible, disengaging from activities and relationships that are depleting and replacing them with those that are sustaining. *Such self-care is an ethical imperative for all therapists, but it is especially important for those working with trauma survivors.* While self-care alone will not ameliorate VT (Bober & Regehr, 2006), it provides an essential foundation as well as a counterbalance.

Working Sustainably

Perspective

In this section, we address ways of thinking about the work that may prove valuable to the management of VT. *The development of a theoretical basis* that guides the use of countertransference responses is invaluable, because accumulated unprocessed countertransference responses (especially those outside of conscious awareness) can contribute to VT. A theoretical framework is the map that gives therapy direction and provides guideposts to the therapist. Theory offers possible reasons for complex trauma clients' ways of interacting and coping, and a rational basis for responding to them constructively. For example, the therapist may become frustrated with a client who repeatedly engages in self-harming behavior. Rather than continuing to explain to the client why such behavior is problematic, therapists who understand trauma reenactments can engage clients in delving deeper into their histories, and invite them to explore and connect childhood experiences with current behaviors.

Staying connected to personal experience, being aware of personal emotions while sitting with clients, helps to maximize empathic attunement. At the same time, clinicians need to *remain aware of the present moment and the treatment frame* (the fact that they are the responsible party in a therapy relationship; that they have a fiduciary duty to the client; that the relationship is bounded by time constraints, ethical rules and laws, professional roles, etc.). It is easy to be caught up in the intensity of complex trauma clients' needs and feelings, and to lose perspective. It is the clinician's job to think before responding, to put clients' immediate needs into a larger therapeutic context, and to respond in a way that conveys respect, collaboration, empowerment, and sound professional judgment.

Accepting the inevitably of VT can, perhaps paradoxically, be helpful, as can *accepting personal and professional limitations*. Realizing that psychotherapy, although a powerful process, cannot accomplish miracles, that it can neither undo the past nor protect clients from all future harm, and that it will not go on forever, keeps the therapist connected to the realities of human relationships. This in turn can lessen wishful thinking, a strategy that Norcross and Guy (2007) identify as ineffective in their discussion of empirically proven self-care strategies for psychotherapists. Wishing things were different impedes accepting what is. Acceptance frees the clinician to change what can be changed, reinforcing agency and countering the helplessness of direct and indirect trauma.

Many clinicians recognize the value of *focusing on process rather than on outcomes*. For many trauma survivors with complex trauma adaptations, healing is a long, slow process. Many understandably want treatment to be as brief as possible for psychological and financial reasons, and, as a result, might overload themselves emotionally in an attempt to be "done with it." They might also feel pressure from family members or others who want them to "get back to normal" as soon as possible. A focus on doing what needs to and can be done rather than on the client's ability to live differently immediately will likely result in less frustration for both therapist and client (family members might need to be involved and educated about the strategy in order to be supportive). Similarly, *focusing on the positive, reinforcing desired behaviors and outcomes rather than highlighting shortcomings and disappointments,* can also enhance the therapeutic relationship and provide encouragement and support for both parties. As much as possible, therapists must work with their clients to maintain or to increase their functioning in daily life settings (Kinsler, 2017; Norcross & Guy, 2007).

Practice

How can clinicians apply a sustainable perspective to their work? In addition to promoting restorative relationships with complex trauma survivors, managing boundaries appropriately helps to limit VT. *Appropriate boundary management* means many things; it includes remembering the therapist's role and mandate, treating the client with respect, leaving work at the office (Kinsler, 2017; Kinsler, Courtois, & Frankel, 2009; Norcross & Guy, 2007), and participating authentically, while keeping the goals of the treatment and the client's needs in focus. Boundaries are particularly salient with clients who have been subjected to violations, exploitations, and dual relationships. These clients often enter treatment without a well-formed ability to negotiate or manage boundaries in relationships, and often expect harm or abuse rather than care and protection. For example, after 2 years of therapy, a survivor of childhood sexual abuse by multiple perpetrators told her therapist she felt that everyone who had ever been kind to her had wanted something from her. When the therapist asked, "Has that happened in here?", the client replied, "Not yet." Therapists must not be "thrown" by such a remark, which might result in distancing, self-protective anger or outrage, or efforts to save or rescue the client (in order to differentiate oneself from harmful and exploitive others). Rather, the therapist's nondefensive understanding can go a long way toward increasing trust. When therapists anticipate such responses on the part of traumatized clients, they are less likely to personalize them and react with defensiveness, retaliation, or excessive caregiving.

Some therapeutic relationships have more built-in boundaries than others. At one end of the spectrum are those that are highly structured (i.e., the 50-minute therapy session, payment for professional services, and client privacy statutes) and at the other are those with less structure and fewer boundaries (i.e., a clergy or therapist visit to homebound clients in their homes or care facilities, field work with war-affected refugee children, residential care, foreign language translation for psychotherapies). Yet, even more boundaried relationships are often unsupervised, confidential, and take place behind closed doors. Professional boundaries support the specialized nature of the therapist's professional responsibilities and invite self-awareness and regulation on the part of the therapist. Therapists who are having difficulties or crises in their personal lives must be especially mindful not to use their clients to take care of or support them in what is often a familiar role reversal for childhood trauma survivors. We strongly recommend that therapists at all levels of experience increase their personal and professional support and lessen or modify their caseloads when in the throes of life difficulties.

To attune to and adequately understand clients, clinicians must *listen with respect and an open mind and heart.* This implies entering the client's world, imagining his or her experience both during the traumatic events of the past and while the client is recounting and perhaps reliving them in the present relationship. It means feeling the pain of the victim, and the fear and confusion of the survivor. Such an intense process can induce VT when clients' experiences are horrific, including, for example, torture, violence, sadism, or, prolonged abuse or neglect. It is not only possible but essential both to *engage with clients empathically and to maintain and respect boundaries.* That means that clinicians let clients know through words and actions that they care deeply about them, the harm they experienced, and their struggle to recover. And it means collaborating with the client to modify the frame (including clinician availability, fees, consultation arrangements, means of communication, third-party involvement, frequency of sessions, treatment goals, etc.) as needed, so both parties can live with it throughout the duration of the therapy relationship. Empathy allows the development of healing connections. Boundaries help to ensure that the relationship is therapeutic and not exploitive, that clients' needs come first, and that therapists will not promise things they cannot sustain over the long haul. For example, agreeing that a client may call when in crisis may make sense at certain points during a therapy. But if therapists encourage clients to call freely and engage in therapy during extended phone calls over a period of months, they will likely suffer from resentment and burnout, and clients may find it more difficult to develop essential self-regulation skills and outside sources of support, including mutually supportive friendships.

Writing a progress note at the end of each session according to professional record-keeping guidelines documents the healing process. It can also assist the therapist in decompressing and gaining perspective on the session and the overall process of therapy. Personal journal writing allows clinicians to explore their responses to the challenges they face and connects them to their personal experience.

Clinicians may also find it useful to *do something very different between therapy sessions,* especially when they are heavily scheduled. Activities that encourage the clinician's physical engagement may provide an antidote to bodily tension or may counter the sedentary nature of the therapeutic process. Examples include meditating, deep breathing, stretching, office yoga, taking a walk, exercising, listening to a favorite piece of music, and having lunch alone or with colleagues. Some clinicians find it useful to engage in brief creative activities, such as making a quick sketch or drawing, or debriefing with a colleague after particularly challenging sessions. One therapist we know debriefs between sessions with jokes and comedy material she pulls up from different sites on her computer.

Some trauma clinicians suggest that the therapist *attend to and use his or her bodily responses and experiences* and associated emotional states while working with traumatized clients as a way to identify and then address physical and psychological effects of empathic attunement and resonance (e.g., Fisher & Ogden, 2009; Rothschild, 2006; Schore, 2003). Awareness of and adjustments to bodily states that help clinicians to remain grounded and emotionally contained may protect them from the effects of VT. *Using countertransference responses to promote the client's growth* is a powerful antidote to the lack of control that clinicians (as well as clients) often feel in the trauma recovery process. The therapist's feelings about the client's experience provide important information. Using that information to move the therapy forward counters the powerlessness that clinicians often feel as they bear witness to reports of atrocities and their painful aftermath. The therapist's personal reactions can contribute to understanding clients and to feeling more empathy and compassion for them (Pearlman & Saakvitne, 1995). Sorting out those feelings might require (and certainly may be enhanced by) professional consultation.

Organizational Approaches and Policy Implications

Organizational approaches to addressing VT have policy implications. It is often only through enlightened policy that organizations prioritize clinicians' experience, recognizing that effective, ethical treatment depends on clinicians who can sustain themselves in the work.

Professional training programs have a responsibility to ensure that trainees have basic knowledge and skills competency to practice psychotherapy ethically and responsibly. Unfortunately, even now, many graduate programs do not include training specific to trauma treatment (Courtois & Gold, 2009), a travesty given that the majority of mental health clients have a history of trauma. Professionals and consumer-survivors have developed trauma-informed care to address this issue. Division 56 (Trauma Psychology) of the American Psychological Association has published a set of trauma competencies for therapists, administrators, and organizations at different levels of expertise to use (Cook, Newman, & the New Haven Trauma Competency Group, 2014). An integral part of these efforts is recognition of the impact of the work on the therapist.

Training that addresses the impact of trauma work and VT is essential, not optional. Trainings for this purpose exist in experiential, workbook, and online formats (e.g., Pearlman & McKay, 2008; Pryce, Shackelford, & Pryce, 2007; Saakvitne, Gamble, Pearlman, & Lev, 2000; Saakvitne, Pearlman, & the Staff of the Traumatic Stress Institute, 1996), yet state and agency policies frequently neither address these issues nor make such training available (Caringi, 2007; Caringi et al., 2015; Pryce et al., 2007), although this seems to be changing.

Organizations can institutionalize trainings to address VT by implementing curricula with components designed to increase the ability of clinicians to identify, recognize, and respond to it (Naturale & Pulido, 2012; NSW Rape Crisis Centre, 2009; Saakvitne et al., 2000). Such training should be implemented on an ongoing basis, starting with orientation for new clinicians and as an advanced offering for seasoned clinicians. Organizations with policies that include education about the risks and effects of VT as part of the agency's core practice curriculum may help clinicians prepare for work-related stress (Bell, Kulkarni, & Dalton, 2003).

Clinicians providing trauma services do not operate in a vacuum. Across work settings, clinicians (and their clients) are affected by policies regarding the services they render. Research is beginning to show the impact that agency, state, and federal policies and procedures and insurance limitations and challenges can have on VT levels (Bell et al., 2003; Bloom & Farragher, 2011; Hormann & Vivian, 2005). In some settings, it is common for the least experienced professional or paraprofessional clinicians to provide care to the most traumatized and challenged individuals. This is not to say that grassroots clinicians or paraprofessionals are ineffective, or that they do not provide valuable and therapeutic services; rather, it is often the case that undertrained and/or newly degreed clinicians are "thrown into the deep end of the pool," with little or no attention to whether they can "swim," often without adequate training, consultation, or supervision. Such a scenario is a recipe for therapeutic disaster for both client and therapist, as well as for VT and early burnout. It may also result in serious misjudgments and missteps, including boundary crossings and violations with clients. Therefore, it is essential to take policy and training into account when examining the causes, prevention, and treatment of VT.

The ABC (awareness, balance, and connection) model of preventing and mitigating VT for individuals (Saakvitne et al., 1996) offers a way to frame how agency, state, and federal policy may be formulated and implemented to support clinicians in treating complex trauma. Recent research offers preliminary evidence that *awareness* at the policy level may help to prevent VT (Caringi, 2007; Caringi et al., 2015). Policy offers an avenue for clinicians in agencies to know that their leaders acknowledge and understand the difficult nature of trauma treatment and the potential impact of VT.

Policy at the agency level can impact how clinicians are able to achieve *balance* in their work and personal lives. Two of the most basic and important ways that organizations can help to balance the challenges of working with complex trauma clients relate to caseload size and composition, and clinical consultation/organizational support.

Agency policy often dictates a hierarchical top-down management style, with little communication up or down; too much work due to short staffing; too much paperwork; and little or no clinical supervision or consultation. In social service agencies, these realities often result from insurance and managed care restrictions in which services can be driven by time-limiting, cost-cutting strategies. Top-down leadership style, in which managers question and sometimes invalidate clinicians' practice knowledge and attempts at balance and self-care, or create policies that ignore clinicians' daily work realities, can be particularly disruptive. For example, policies that inhibit clinicians' abilities to take breaks, work flexible schedules, and access vacation time impact the balance needed to work in a service setting. Policies that allow flexible work schedules and mandate that staff use compensatory and annual leave in a timely manner provide opportunities to rest and to process and integrate the effects of the work.

Connection both inside and outside the workplace is necessary. Peer support teams within agencies can offer a first line of defense in dealing with VT (Caringi, 2007; Caringi et al., 2015) and multidisciplinary teams such as those found in inpatient settings can offer different perspectives and approaches to working with clients. Peer support teams require administrative support or a mandate in the form of policy. Two states, Massachusetts and New York, are currently piloting a "teaming" method of casework in an attempt to break the isolation and stress that often exist in difficult, trauma-involved child welfare cases.

In addition to peer support, regular clinical consultation or supervision can help to create resilience related to VT (e.g., Gil & Weinberg, 2015). Effective supervision that is relational recognizes the clinician's distress as a result of the work and normalizes these reactions may help reduce the levels of VT (Knight, 2005). In addition, organizations that foster strong alliances between supervisors and clinicians, and promote relationships that are less authoritarian and more mutual may reduce VT (Peled-Avram, 2017). Such policies and practices have great potential and require research on their effectiveness.

Organizations that acknowledge the pervasiveness of VT and respond accordingly may prevent stigmatizing the emotional impact of working with those who have experienced trauma. Such acknowledgment can help sustain clinicians over time and encourage them to engage in individual VT-relevant practices. Policies and practices designed to respond to the needs of clinicians exposed to clients' trauma are one component of a comprehensive trauma-informed systems approach.

Conclusion

Supporting the recovery of survivors with complex trauma requires great skill, compassion, and awareness. Our detailed examination of the manifestations, contributing factors, and mechanism related to VT may assist in increasing clinicians' and agencies' awareness of VT, and their ability to address it. This in turn may increase the likelihood of providing effective and ethical treatment for this population, and sustaining clinicians in this challenging work.

References

Arnold, D., Calhoun, L. G., Tedeschi, R., & Cann, A. (2005). Vicarious posttraumatic growth in psychotherapy. *Journal of Humanistic Psychology, 45*(2), 239–263.

Arvay, M. J., & Uhlemann, M. R. (1996). Counsellor stress in the field of trauma: A preliminary study. *Canadian Journal of Counselling, 30,* 193–210.

Batson, C. D., Fultz, J., & Schoenrade, P. A. (1987). Distress and empathy. *Journal of Personality, 55,* 19–39.

Bell, H., Kulkarni, S., & Dalton, L. (2003). Organizational prevention of vicarious trauma. *Families in Society, 84,* 463–473.

Benatar, M. (2000). A qualitative study of the effect of a history of childhood sexual abuse on therapists who treat survivors of sexual abuse. *Journal of Trauma and Dissociation, 1,* 9–28.

Bloom, S. L., & Farragher, B. (2011). *Destroying sanctuary: The crisis in human service delivery systems.* New York: Oxford University Press.

Bober, T., & Regehr, C. (2006). Strategies for reducing secondary or vicarious trauma: Do they work? *Brief Treatment and Crisis Intervention, 6*(1), 1–9.

Bober, T., Regehr, C., & Zhou, Y. R. (2006). Development of the Coping Strategies Inventory for trauma counsellors. *Journal of Loss and Trauma, 11*(1), 71–83.

Calhoun, L. G. , & Tedeschi, R. G. (Eds.). (2006). *The handbook of posttraumatic growth: Rsearch and practice.* Mahwah, NJ: Erlbaum.

Caringi, J. (2007). *Secondary traumatic stress in New York State child welfare clinicians.* Doctoral dissertation, State University of New York, Albany, NY.

Caringi, J., Stanick, C., Trautman, A., Crosby, L., Devlin, M., & Adams, S. (2015). Secondary traumatic stress in public school teachers: Contributing and mitigating factors. *Advances in School Mental Health Promotion, 8*(4), 244–256.

Catherall, D. R. (1995). Coping with secondary traumatic stress: The importance of the therapist's peer group. In B. H. Stamm (Ed.), *Secondary traumatic stress: Self-care for clinicians, educators and researchers* (pp. 80–92). Lutherville, MD: Sidran Press.

Cook, J. M., Newman, E., & New Haven Trauma Competency Group. (2014). A consensus statement on trauma mental health: The New Haven Competency Conference process and major findings. *Psychological Trauma: Theory, Research, Practice, and Policy, 6*(4), 300–307.

Courtois, C. A., & Gold, S. N. (2009). The need for inclusion of psychological trauma in the professional curriculum: A call to action. *Psychological Trauma: Theory, Research, Practice, and Policy, 1*(1), 3–23.

Figley, C. R. (Ed.). (1995). *Compassion fatigue: Coping with secondary traumatic stress disorder in those who treat the traumatized.* New York: Brunner/Mazel.

Fisher, J., & Ogden, P. (2009). Sensorimotor psychotherapy. In C. A. Courtois & J. D. Ford (Eds.), *Treating complex traumatic stress disorders: An evidence-based guide* (pp. 312–328). New York: Guilford Press.

Freud, S. (1912). The future prospects of psychoanalytic therapy. In J. Strachey (Ed. & Trans.), *The standard edition of the complete psychological works of Sigmund Freud* (Vol. 7, pp. 3–122). New York: Norton.

Freudenberger, H. R. (1974). Staff burnout. *Journal of Social Issues, 30*(1), 159–165.

Gartner, R. B. (Ed.). (2017). *Trauma and countertrauma, resilience and counterresilience: Insights from psychoanalysts and trauma experts.* Oxford, UK: Routledge.

Gil, S., & Weinberg, M. (2015). Secondary trauma among social workers treating trauma clients: The role of coping strategies and internal resources. *International Social Work, 58*(4), 551–561.

Hernández, P., Gangsei, D., & Engstrom, D. (2007). Vicarious resilience: A new concept in work with those who survive trauma. *Family Process, 46*(2), 229–241.

Hormann, S., & Vivian, P. (2005). Toward an understanding of traumatized organizations and how to intervene in them. *Traumatology, 11*(3), 159–169.

Kinsler, P. J. (2017). *Complex psychological trauma: The centrality of relationship.* New York: Routledge.

Kinsler, P. J., Courtois, C. A., & Frankel, A. S. (2009). Therapeutic alliance and risk management. In C. A. Courtois & J. D. Ford (Eds.), *Treating complex traumatic stress disorders* (pp. 183–201). New York: Guilford Press.

Knight, C. (2005). Working with survivors of childhood trauma: Implications for clinical supervision. *Clinical Supervisor, 23*(2), 81–105.

Lee, J., Gottfried, R., & Bride, B. (2018). Exposure to client trauma, secondary traumatic stress, and the health of clinical social workers: A mediation analysis. *Clinical Social Work Journal, 46,* 228–235.

Mâirean, C. (2016). Secondary traumatic stress and posttraumatic growth: Social support as a moderator. *Social Science Journal, 53*(1), 14–21.

Manning-Jones, S., De Terte, I., & Stephens, C. (2016). Secondary traumatic stress, vicarious posttraumatic growth, and coping among health professionals: A comparison study. *New Zealand Journal of Psychology, 45*(1), 20–29.

McCann, I. L., & Pearlman, L. A. (1990a). Vicarious traumatization: A framework for understanding the psychological effects of working with victims. *Journal of Traumatic Stress, 3*(1), 131–149.

McCann, I. L., & Pearlman, L. A. (1990b). *Psychological trauma and the adult survivor: Theory, therapy, and transformation.* New York: Brunner/Mazel.

Moosman, J. (2002). *Vicarious traumatization.* Doctoral dissertation, George Mason University, Fairfax, VA.

Munroe, J. F., Shay, J., Fisher, L., Makary, C., Rapperport, K., & Zimering, R. (1995). Preventing compassion fatigue: A team treatment model. In C. R. Figley (Ed.), *Compassion fatigue: Coping with secondary traumatic stress disorder in those who treat the traumatized* (pp. 209–231). New York: Brunner/Mazel.

Naturale, A., & Pulido, M. L. (2012). Helping the helpers: Ameliorating secondary traumatic stress in disaster workers. In J. Framingham & M. L. Teasley (Eds.), *Behavioral health reponses to disasters* (pp. 189–208). Boca Raton, FL: Taylor & Francis Group.

Norcross, J. C., & Guy, J. D. (2007). *Leaving it at the office: A guide to psychotherapist self-care.* New York: Guilford Press.

NSW Rape Crisis Centre. (2009). *The NSW Rape Crisis Centre vicarious trauma management program.* Drummoyne, Australia: Author.

Ortlepp, K., & Friedman, M. (2002). Prevalence and correlates of secondary traumatic stress in workplace lay counselors. *Journal of Traumatic Stress, 15,* 213–222.

Pearlman, L. A., & Caringi, J. (2009). Living and working self-reflectively to address vicarious trauma. In C. A. Courtois & J. D. Ford (Eds.), *Complex traumatic stress disorders: An evidence-based guide* (pp. 202–224). New York: Guilford Press.

Pearlman, L. A., & Courtois, C. A. (2005). Clinical applications of the attachment framework: Relational treatment of complex trauma. *Journal of Traumatic Stress, 18*, 449–460.

Pearlman, L. A., & McKay, L. (2008). *Understanding and coping with vicarious trauma: Online training module.* Pasadena, CA: Headington Institute.

Pearlman, L. A., & Saakvitne, K. W. (1995). *Trauma and the therapist: Countertransference and vicarious traumatization in psychotherapy with incest survivors.* New York: Norton.

Peled-Avram, M. (2017). The role of relational-oriented supervision and personal and work-related factors in the development of vicarious traumatization. *Clinical Social Work Journal, 45*(1), 22–32.

Pryce, J. G., Shackelford, K. K., & Pryce, D. H. (2007). *Secondary traumatic stress and the child welfare professional.* Chicago: Lyceum Books.

Rosenbloom, D. J., Pratt, A. C., & Pearlman, L. A. (1995). Clinicians' responses to trauma work: Understanding and intervening in an organization. In B. H. Stamm (Ed.), *Secondary traumatic stress: Self-care issues for clinicians, researchers, and educators* (pp. 65–79). Lutherville, MD: Sidran Press.

Rothschild, B. (2006). *Help for the helper: The psychophysiology of compassion fatigue and vicarious trauma.* New York: Norton.

Saakvitne, K. W., Gamble, S., Pearlman, L., & Lev, B. (2000). *Risking connection: A training curriculum for working with survivors of childhood abuse.* Lutherville, MD: Sidran Press.

Saakvitne, K. W., Pearlman, L. A., & Staff of the Traumatic Stress Institute. (1996). *Transforming the pain: A workbook on vicarious traumatization.* New York: Norton.

Schauben, L. J., & Frazier, P. A. (1995). Vicarious trauma: The effects on female counselors of working with sexual violence survivors. *Psychology of Women Quarterly, 19*, 49–64.

Schore, A. N. (2003). *Affect regulation and the repair of the self.* New York: Norton.

Sui, X., & Padmanabhanunni, A. (2016). Vicarious trauma: The psychological impact of working with survivors of trauma for South African psychologists. *Journal of Psychology in Africa, 26*(2), 127–133.

Terr, L. C. (1989). Treating psychic trauma in children: A preliminary discussion. *Journal of Traumatic Stress, 2*(1), 3–20.

Thomas, R. (1998). *An investigation of empathic stress reactions among mental health professionals working with PTSD.* Unpublished doctoral dissertation, Union Institute, Cincinnati, OH.

van Dernoot Lipsky, L., & Burk, C. (2009). *Trauma stewardship: An everyday guide to caring for self while caring for others.* San Francisco: Berrett-Koehler.

Wicks, R. J. J. (2008). *The resilient clinician.* New York: Oxford University Press.

Williamson, R. (2018, June 22). *Vicarious traumatization, stress, and psychological resilience: Addressing the psychological hazards of work with refugees, immigrants and displaced populations.* Webinar, American Psychological Association Trauma Division.

Wilson, J. P., & Lindy, J. D. (1994). Empathic strain and countertransference. In J. P. Wilson & J. D. Lindy (Eds.), *Countertransference in the treatment of PTSD* (pp. 5–30). New York: Guilford Press.

Wilson, J. P., & Thomas, R. B. (2004). *Empathy in the treatment of trauma and PTSD.* New York: Brunner/Routledge.

PART II

EVIDENCE-SUPPORTED INDIVIDUAL TREATMENT MODALITIES AND MODELS

CHAPTER 9

Prolonged Exposure Therapy

ELIZABETH A. HEMBREE
EDNA B. FOA

Prolonged exposure (PE) is a cognitive-behavioral therapy that was developed 30 years ago with the aim of reducing posttraumatic stress disorder (PTSD) by helping individuals to emotionally process traumatic experiences. Over the years, numerous studies have been conducted in many centers to evaluate the efficacy and effectiveness of this treatment. These studies revealed that PE was effective in reducing not only PTSD but also depression, general anxiety, and other trauma-related symptoms. In this section of the chapter, we first introduce the treatment by briefly describing the PE components and how they are implemented in a course of therapy. We then describe the theory underlying PE and the rationale for treatment, and finally present a brief summary of empirical support.

Overview of PE

PE comprises the following key procedures:

- Psychoeducation via discussion of PTSD symptoms and common reactions to trauma, what factors maintain trauma-related symptoms over time, and how PE addresses these factors and thereby reduces PTSD and related symptoms.
- Repeated *in vivo* exposure to situations, places, people, or activities that are realistically safe or low risk but that the client is avoiding because of

excessive fear or other trauma-related emotions, including shame, grief, guilt, and anger, or because of PTSD-related beliefs.
- Repeated imaginal exposure (revisiting trauma memories in imagination) followed by processing the experience with the therapist and discussing the thoughts and feelings that arose during the revisiting.

The overall aim of *in vivo* and imaginal exposure is to enhance emotional processing of traumatic experiences by helping PTSD sufferers to face trauma memories and reminders, and to process the emotions and thoughts that ensue. In doing so, clients develop a realistic perspective that differentiates trauma memories and reminders from the traumatic events themselves. The client learns that talking and thinking about the trauma are not the same as being in the trauma, that they can safely experience memories and reminders, and tolerate the distress that initially results from confrontations, and that the distress decreases over time.

As described in the PE therapist guide (Foa, Hembree, Rothbaum, 2007; Foa, Hembree, Rothbaum, & Rauch, 2019), treatment is typically implemented in eight to 15, 90-minute sessions. By the time a client enters Session 1 of PE, he or she will have had a thorough evaluation that includes assessment of lifetime trauma history, PTSD, other psychiatric disorders, social/family and relationship functioning, and role functioning. Thus, a client who receives PE has either a diagnosis of PTSD or subthreshold PTSD with significant symptoms that are causing distress and interference.

In Session 1, the therapist begins forming a therapeutic relationship with the client, presents the logistics of the treatment, and provides the overall rationale for PE. We introduce the idea that trauma symptoms and distress are maintained over the long term by two primary factors: (1) avoidance of trauma-related memories, thoughts, and feelings, and avoidance of situations and activities that are similar to or are reminders of the trauma and therefore are perceived as dangerous; and (2) the presence of PTSD-related beliefs or views that the world is extremely dangerous, and the self is extremely incompetent, weak, or unable to cope. The avoidance strategies prevent the client from processing the trauma experiences and from modifying these unhelpful and often inaccurate cognitions. Imaginal and *in vivo* exposure are described as procedures for addressing and reducing these maintaining factors by approaching rather than avoiding trauma memories, feelings, and thoughts (imaginal exposure) and the safe or low-risk situations, places, people, and activities that the person is avoiding in order to not stir up trauma-related thoughts, fear, or other negative emotions (*in vivo* exposure). The remainder of the session is devoted to gathering trauma-relevant information that aids in treatment planning and tailoring the treatment to the individual. A form of breathing retraining is taught to clients and practiced at the end of Session 1. This slow, calm breathing is not paired with exposure procedures, but is described as a skill that may be practiced and used to manage general anxiety. All sessions are audio-recorded and listened to as part of homework between sessions. All subsequent sessions begin with a review of the week's homework, with much positive feedback and reinforcement for the client's efforts, and discussion of what he or she has learned.

Psychoeducation continues in Session 2 with a discussion of common trauma-related symptoms and problems, with the aims of providing information, eliciting and discussing the client's own symptoms and reactions to his or her traumatic experiences, validating and normalizing his or her reactions in the context of PTSD, and instilling hope by communicating to the client that a good deal of these distressing symptoms and problems is directly related to PTSD, and much of this may improve through treatment. Session 2 continues as the therapist revisits the rationale for *in vivo* exposure, reminding the client that avoidance helps in the short run by reducing distress and anxiety, but in the long run, maintains trauma-related emotions and beliefs. The therapist explains that repeated *in vivo* exposure to safe/ low-risk situations has several benefits: blocking the reinforcing effects of avoidance; helping the client to experience the reality of what actually happened in these situations, thus differentiating the actual traumatic events from trauma reminders; habituation (reduction of anxiety) and disconfirmation of the belief that anxiety will last forever; and bringing about an enhanced sense of competence. They together construct a list of avoided situations and activities the client will approach throughout the treatment, arranging them in an ascending hierarchy based on the client's predicted discomfort level in each situation. In each session thereafter, the therapist helps the client choose which exposure exercises to practice, working up the hierarchy as therapy progresses. The client generally does the *in vivo* exercises as homework between sessions, but if an exercise is particularly challenging, the therapist may do it with the client in session.

Imaginal exposure is introduced in Session 3. The therapist provides the rationale for imaginal exposure, emphasizing why repeatedly revisiting and recounting traumatic memories in imagination aids healing. Imaginal exposure helps the client to organize and make sense of the trauma memory; learn that memories are not dangerous (differentiating the trauma from the memories of the trauma); reduce intensity of distress and increase tolerance of negative emotions; learn that engaging in trauma memories does not result in loss of control; and increase his or her sense of competence. The standard procedure for imaginal exposure is designed to promote emotional engagement by asking the client to close his or her eyes, vividly imagine or visualize the trauma memory while describing it in the present tense, including details of what happened, as well as what he or she was thinking, feeling, and sensing during the experience. Imaginal exposure is then conducted for 35–40 minutes and is followed by "processing," which is a discussion of the emotions and thoughts that emerged for the client while revisiting the traumatic memory. Imaginal exposure is conducted in each of the remaining treatment sessions and is always followed by processing, then the assignment of homework.

The intermediate sessions of PE (Session 4 through the next-to-final session) are similar to Session 3, consisting of homework review, followed by imaginal exposure, processing of thoughts and feelings, and assigning homework. As treatment progresses, the client is encouraged to describe the trauma memory in greater detail during the imaginal revisiting and to focus on the currently most distressing parts of the trauma memory, or "hot spots."

The final session of PE includes homework review, a brief imaginal exposure, processing with emphasis on how the imaginal exposure experience and the client's perspective on the trauma(s) have changed over the course of therapy, and a detailed review of what the client has learned and experienced that brought about changes in symptoms and functioning. The latter part of the session is devoted to discussing the continued application of all that the client has learned in treatment (e.g., that facing rather than avoiding trauma memories and reminders has facilitated recovery), relapse prevention, and treatment termination.

Emotional Processing Theory

A thorough presentation of emotional processing theory, the conceptual backbone of PE, is beyond the scope of this chapter. Interested readers are directed to the references cited in this section for more information. Foa and Kozak (1985, 1986) first proposed emotional processing theory to explain the mechanisms involved in anxiety disorders and in exposure therapy for these disorders. Foa and colleagues subsequently elaborated on the original theory of emotional processing in applying it to the development, maintenance, and recovery from PTSD (Foa, Steketee, & Rothbaum, 1989; Foa & Riggs, 1993; Foa & Jaycox, 1999; Foa & Cahill, 2001; Foa, Huppert, & Cahill, 2006; Rauch & Foa, 2006). In this conceptualization, the trauma memory is viewed as a cognitive structure that includes representations of the stimuli that were present during the trauma, the person's responses during the trauma, and the meaning of the stimuli and responses. This includes not only fear and anxiety responses but also responses such as guilt, shame, helplessness, and anger. Because of the large number of stimuli in the trauma memory that are perceived as dangerous or threatening, individuals with PTSD tend to perceive the world as extremely dangerous. In addition, aspects of how one behaved during the trauma, current PTSD symptoms, and negative interpretation of symptoms are associated with meanings that include perception of oneself as weak, guilty, and incompetent, and prevents recovery from the traumatic event. These negative cognitions that underlie PTSD (e.g., "The world is entirely dangerous"; "I am completely incompetent") further promote the maintenance of PTSD symptoms, which in turn reinforce the faulty cognitions (Foa & Cahill, 2001). As briefly explained in the chapter opening, the exposure work in PE is designed to provide experiences that disconfirm these unhelpful and inaccurate expectations of harm and beliefs about inadequacy, and reduce the associated fear, anxiety, guilt, self-blame, shame, and anger.

Empirical Support for PE

PE has been studied for over 30 years and has received extensive empirical evidence for treating PTSD. PE has demonstrated efficacy in studies with a wide range of trauma populations, including adult and adolescent female sexual and physical assault survivors, survivors of childhood sexual and physical abuse, combat veterans and active duty military service members, and mixed-gender samples exposed to a variety of traumatic experiences, such as motor vehicle accidents, torture, and criminal victimization (McLean, Asaani, & Foa, 2015; Powers, Halpern, Ferenschak, Gillihan, & Foa, 2010). Many studies have compared PE's outcome with other cognitive-behavioral treatments, medications, and active non-trauma-focused treatments such as supportive counseling and relaxation training. In comparative trials, PE has generally shown similar efficacy to other cognitive-behavioral trauma-focused interventions for the reduction of PTSD and related symptoms.

Some researchers have investigated the usefulness of adding other techniques such as cognitive restructuring, anxiety management/relaxation, and stress inoculation training (SIT) to PE. The vast majority of these studies has failed to demonstrate that PE combined with other trauma-focused interventions produces outcome better than PE alone. For example, Foa et al. (2005) compared PE alone and PE combined with cognitive restructuring (CR) in 179 women with chronic PTSD resulting from rape, nonsexual assault, and/ or childhood sexual abuse. Results demonstrated comparable efficacy for both PE and PE/CR, as each resulted in greatly reduced symptoms of PTSD, anxiety, and depression at posttreatment and at a 1-year follow-up.

To our knowledge, there are no published studies of PE implemented specifically with a population diagnosed with complex PTSD, which is not surprising given that complex PTSD was introduced as a diagnosis by the World Health Organization's diagnostic system, the *International Classification of Diseases and Related Health Problems* (ICD-11) in 2018, and this version is not yet in effect. There are published analyses of data from randomized trials comparing the treatment outcomes of PE and other trauma-focused treatments on symptoms of PTSD among clients with and without childhood abuse histories and/or severe comorbidities. Resick, Nishith, Weaver, Astin, and Feuer (2002) compared PE with cognitive processing therapy (CPT) in women with rape-related PTSD. In comparison to the wait list, both PE and CPT yielded significant improvement in PTSD symptoms and depression, with gains maintained through long-term follow-up of 5–10 years (Resick, Williams, Suvak, Monson, & Gradus, 2012). The effect size of these treatments did not differ for women with or without childhood abuse histories, and there was no difference in dropouts between these subgroups (Resick, Nishith, & Griffin, 2003; Resick, Suvak, & Wells, 2014). Similarly, Foa et al. (2005) found no difference in reduction of PTSD and depression when comparing the outcomes of women with PTSD resulting from adult rape, adult nonsexual assault, and childhood sexual abuse.

Van Minnen, Harned, Zoellner, and Mills (2012) examined evidence addressing use of PE in clients with problems consistent with complex PTSD that were comorbid with PTSD, including dissociation, borderline personality disorder, psychosis, suicidal behavior and nonsuicidal self-injury, substance use disorders, and major depression. They concluded from their review of empirical studies that PE can be safely and effectively used for clients with these conditions, often with a decrease in the comorbid problem as well as the PTSD symptoms. We therefore turn next to a discussion of several key features of PE that may account for its safety and effectiveness in treating symptoms described as more common in complex traumatic stress disorders than in "classic" PTSD.

Key Clinical Features of PE Relevant to Complex Traumatic Stress Disorders

Facilitating and Sustaining Client Engagement in PE

Important in any psychotherapeutic treatment, sustained engagement is a particularly high priority in trauma-focused therapy, because avoidance is a prominent feature of PTSD, and one that maintains the disorder and may lead to treatment dropout. Engaging clients begins in the first contact and is nurtured throughout PE in multiple ways. Assessment and therapy procedures are conducted in a respectful, compassionate, and nonjudgmental manner. When indicated by client ambivalence or low confidence, we preface PE with several sessions aimed at exploring the client's desires and doubts about engaging in treatment for PTSD and enhancing motivation and hopefulness. The foundational rationale for PE is built over the first three to four sessions and with effort to ensure that the client really understands it. We expect that intellectual comprehension of the rationale may precede emotional acceptance. The logic of using *in vivo* and imaginal exposure to overcome avoidance is explained in straightforward language, tailored to the client's presentation, and made relevant and meaningful by sprinkling the discussion with examples from the symptoms and history that the client has shared. We expect clients to struggle with avoidance and often predict this will happen; when it does, the therapist meets it with understanding, validation, and support, as well as an individualized response. This may involve returning to the rationale by reminding the client that while avoidance makes perfect sense and is part of PTSD, in the long run, it keeps a person stuck. Or the therapist may modify the way that the imaginal exposure is conducted or suggest that the client change an *in vivo* exposure by doing it at a different time of day or accompanied by a friend, but with gentle encouragement to stay the course. Therapists conducting PE provide ample positive reinforcement and cheerleading for the client's efforts, may also schedule phone calls between sessions when needed to touch base or discuss how an exposure went, and continually highlight evidence of improvement, courage, increased tolerance of emotion, and learning.

The Role of the Client–Therapist Therapeutic Alliance in PE

Building a strong therapeutic alliance is another fundamental cornerstone of PE. It makes sense that Cloitre, Koenen, Cohen and Han (2002) found therapeutic alliance to be a predictor of reduction in PTSD via imaginal exposure. Facing trauma memories and reminders is often very difficult, and being accompanied through the process by a trusted and reliable therapist is as important as having a thorough understanding of *why* it is helpful to face these reminders. Forging a strong therapeutic relationship goes hand in hand with engaging and sustaining the client in treatment, and in PE it is supported in a number of ways. The therapist acknowledges the client's courage in coming in for treatment and sharing the traumatic experiences he or she has had. We gather information about and clearly communicate our understanding of the client's symptoms and incorporate these symptoms into the rationale for treatment and the discussion of common reactions to trauma. PE therapists are sensitive to clients' statements that reflect avoidance and safety behaviors. *Safety behaviors* are subtle avoidance behaviors in which the person approaches a situation or activity while engaging in a behavior (thought or action) that minimizes or prevents anxiety or discomfort, such as shopping at a time of day the store is very empty, or always sitting with one's back to a wall or near the exit. Individuals with chronic PTSD are often unaccustomed to thinking of their behavior in terms of avoidance, especially when the behavior has long been present and just feels like a preference. Asking about these examples of subtle avoidance communicates to the client that the therapist is actively listening and thinking about what is being shared.

In nurturing the therapeutic alliance, PE therapists validate the client's experience and emotion in an empathic and nonjudgmental manner, maintaining awareness that the client may be disclosing his or her trauma experience for the first time, or with a more detailed narrative than ever before. Finally, PE is conducted in a truly collaborative manner that fosters trust and conveys the therapist's respect for the client. It is important that the PE therapist openly acknowledges that while he or she may serve as an experienced and knowledgeable guide, clients are the expert on themselves. We share decision making with the client and incorporate his or her judgment about the targets and pace of the therapy in deciding things such as what *in vivo* exposure exercises will be done or whether to move on to the next hot spot in imaginal exposure. The correct response to a client asking, "Do I have to do that?" in response to the therapist's suggestion that an exposure should be done that day is "No. Of course not. You are in control of this decision and what you do or don't do . . . but why are you here? How is it that the PTSD is controlling your life or dictating what you do and when you do it? And does it make sense that doing this [exposure] is part of taking that control back?"

Addressing Complex Traumatic Stress Symptoms in PE

PE therapists often encounter a wide range of clients with trauma-related symptoms that are sometimes categorized as part of complex traumatic stress disorders. These include difficulties with regulating intense emotions, dissociation, and interpersonal difficulties and isolation. The emotional processing work of PE provides many opportunities to practice engaging in and tolerating strong emotions. Grounded in the rationale and drawing on the alliance with the therapist, the client is asked to engage in imaginal exposure experiences that may arouse anxiety, sadness, grief, shame, anger, and/or guilt. This requires tolerating emotion, remaining in the exposure situation without avoiding or escaping, accessing memories of past experiences yet paying attention and being rooted in the present in order to learn and to foster the development of perspective. PE therapists aim to conduct exposure in a way that promotes the client being in an effective range of emotional engagement: high enough that the trauma-related memories, thoughts, and feelings are accessible and available for emotional processing, yet not so high that the client is overwhelmed and/or unable to retain the capacity to process information. To accomplish this, the therapist may modify the standard way that imaginal exposure is conducted in order to increase emotional connection for those who are *underengaged* or decrease emotional connection for those who are *overengaged*.

The latter group of clients may include those who struggle with dissociation. In these cases, education about staying grounded in the present is provided—we sometimes refer to this as keeping "one foot in the memory and the other firmly grounded in the present"—and skills for staying grounded are taught. These include modification of procedures such as keeping one's eyes open while revisiting the memory, narrating it in the past tense, reducing visualization, making it more conversational with the therapist, or writing rather than verbalizing the trauma narrative. The therapist may suggest to the client that he or she breathe in the slow, calming way taught in Session 1 of PE to reduce arousal and promote grounding. Other standard tools include using sensory inputs to stay grounded: holding or manipulating objects, using ice water or cold washcloths on the skin, standing up, walking around while talking. For those clients who are underengaged, we may use sensory inputs to increase access to the memory, while following the standard procedure for imaginal exposure closely, as it is designed to promote emotional engagement, and asking clients to focus on and describe bodily sensations or other sensory information that is part of the trauma memory.

Finally, relational/interpersonal difficulties are addressed through both the therapeutic relationship and by doing and processing *in vivo* exposure exercises. This type of exposure is typically considered a procedure for approaching and becoming more comfortable with situations that are feared excessively. In PE, *in vivo* exposure is also used for behavioral activation: getting active, exercising, changing routines, going out. These activities are not necessarily feared excessively, but they often occur infrequently when one is isolated and alone.

Therapists often include activities on the hierarchy that will create opportunity for connecting with others, even briefly, and social interactions, both casual and more meaningful. These may include situations such as attending meetings or religious services, calling a friend or family member, taking an exercise class, inviting someone for a meal, making eye contact with other people, getting in the longest line at the supermarket and greeting/speaking to the cashier and starting a conversation with someone next in line, going to the mall and walking into every store, finding a clerk, and making eye contact while asking where to find something. If clients are extremely avoidant of social contact, therapists may help them ease into it by role-playing conversations or by walking out in public with them and modeling greeting, asking simple questions, or smiling and looking at people. Breaking avoidant routines and engaging with other people, even casually, often creates worthwhile learning opportunities and can help PTSD sufferers to feel more empowered and confident.

Implementing Exposure Skills in the Service of Recovery

Over many years of implementing PE with trauma survivors, we have learned that exposure is a powerful learning tool and an elegant way to modify cognition. Overcoming avoidance and approaching memories or situations that are realistically safe or low risk, even if frightening or unpleasant, creates opportunity to learn *what really happens,* and that *I can handle this.* Doing so modifies the PTSD-related beliefs that the *world is dangerous* and that *I am incompetent* and enhances confidence and self-esteem. As described in the rationale for PE, it also provides repeated opportunities to differentiate trauma reminders from the traumas themselves, so that people become less afraid of having memories and feelings triggered.

Clinical Case Example Illustrating PE with a Survivor of Repeated Childhood Sexual Abuse

Identifying information and other details in this case have been altered in the interest of confidentiality. Kelly sought treatment at age 34. At intake, she disclosed for the first time that she had been sexually abused between ages 5 and 13, and raped by an acquaintance at age 20. Several different men, some who were family members, perpetrated the sexual abuse. She identified the worst of these experiences as repeated abuse by her grandfather, who sexually assaulted her several times per week between ages of 7 and 10. Kelly was unemployed at the time of intake, living with a man in a discordant relationship but unable to support herself living alone. She was isolated and reported having no real friends. Kelly met criteria for severe PTSD with extensive avoidance; major depressive disorder, recurrent; binge-eating disorder; panic disorder, and obsessive–compulsive disorder. In addition, she reported a clinically significant level of dissociative symptoms. She strongly endorsed negative beliefs, including "If people knew what happened they would look down on me"; "I have to be on guard all the time"; "People can't be trusted"; "I will never be able to feel normal emotions again"; "I feel isolated and set apart from others"; "If people knew what happened, they would be disgusted"; and "I should be over this by now." The primary emotions that Kelly reported feeling were shame, disgust (self-directed), and sadness.

Kelly received 10 sessions of PE. In Session 2, the therapist worked with her to create the *in vivo* hierarchy. The items on Kelly's hierarchy were of several different types:

1. Safe situations that she was avoiding because they were reminders of her abuse (e.g., walking into dark rooms in her apartment, sleeping with the lights and TV off in her bedroom, consensual sexual activity).
2. Situations that she avoided or felt uncomfortable with because she viewed the world and other people as dangerous (e.g., someone walking behind her on the street, riding on a bus, taking a subway, being in crowds).
3. Situations involving being around people and social interactions (e.g., being with a group of people in a class or at church, talking to new people, hanging out with her new friend, having a conversation with a family member).

Kelly attended sessions regularly, engaged in her *in vivo* exposure homework, and listened to recordings of the therapy sessions. She expressed understanding of the rationale for treatment, was cautiously willing to do the exposure, and fearful of the emotions it would trigger.

Imaginal exposure began in Session 3, and Kelly revisited one of her most distressing memories of rape by her grandfather at age 8. Although crying hard and reporting extremely high levels of distress as she described this painful experience, Kelly was able to stay with it and repeated the narrative of this experience twice during that session. In the processing that followed, she described how sad and scared and alone she felt during that time of her life. The following excerpt is part of the discussion she and the therapist had about listening to the recording of her imaginal exposure for homework in the coming week:

THERAPIST: What worries you about knowing that you're going to listen to this tape?

KELLY: I guess I feel like when I start feeling certain emotions, I don't know what to do with them. I don't know how to feel. I don't know if I'm supposed to be feeling this way. . . . I just don't want to feel sad. I just don't want to remember. And the more I remember, the more pain comes. I also don't want to do it because I don't want those pains to come back at me and go back to feeling like I was a child.

Kelly's therapist responded by validating her desire to avoid the painful feelings stirred up by the revisiting, praising her courage in allowing herself to connect with them the way she did in this session, and reminding her that while painful, this would help her heal the emotional wounds left by these traumatic experiences.

Kelly was able to listen to the session recordings regularly and practice her *in vivo* exposures. Her self-reported PTSD and depression symptoms, which were assessed every other session, began to come down by Session 4. In the beginning of Session 5, Kelly discussed her response to the trauma memories and images that regularly intruded during the previous week:

THERAPIST: The pictures and thoughts about your grandfather abusing you that came to your mind. Did you try to push them away?

KELLY: No.

THERAPIST: OK. And how was that?

KELLY: At first it was hard . . . but I was thinking like, it's a part of me. It's a part of something that happened to me. I have to live with it. I've been trying to tell myself there's no sense in trying to avoid it. I'm learning to deal with it and get past it. Normally I would just avoid thinking about it and that would just delay it. But now, for me right now it's just normal. Something I should be feeling and going through . . .

THERAPIST: Wow. That is great.

KELLY: . . . instead of trying to avoid it. It's like trying to walk through something, instead of going around it, just walking through it. It's easier. That's how I feel. That's how I felt this week. Might as well just live with it.

Session 6 was notable in that Kelly realized during her imaginal exposure that she had said "no" to her grandfather. In the processing afterward, the discussion focused in part on this realization:

KELLY: I just didn't know . . . that I said "no" (*voice low and tearful*).

THERAPIST: You felt like this is bad; I'm not supposed to be doing this. . . . But he's standing there telling you to do it or you'll get in trouble. . . . How do little kids respond?

KELLY: They do what they're supposed to do.

THERAPIST: Yeah. What the adult's telling them to do.

KELLY: (*crying*)

THERAPIST: Is this the first time you remember saying "no"? How does that feel, knowing that you said "no"?

KELLY: It makes me feel better. But I haven't said no to someone again since I was 8, since I was that young. At the same time, it lets me know that I didn't want it. I didn't want it to happen. It lets me know that I didn't want it to happen and I knew that it was wrong (*crying*). I don't know why. It just it just let me know I didn't want it to happen. Because for a long time I've wondered why didn't I stop it. Why didn't I say "no"? And actually, I never remembered saying "no." All the years I just never thought I said "no."

THERAPIST: Does it feel good to remember that?

KELLY: Yeah. And I'm starting to think it really wasn't my fault. . . . I really didn't have any control over it.

THERAPIST: Yeah. What made you start thinking like that?

KELLY: When you told me to stop thinking or judging myself as if I were an adult then . . . my thinking is like an adult when I think about what happened to me at 8 and I am thinking that I should have been able to control it . . . but I was 8 and I wasn't able to control it.

THERAPIST: Right. Right.

KELLY: I wasn't able to control it. Most children at 8 . . . aren't thinking like they're 34. I *wasn't* 34.

THERAPIST: You're right.

KELLY: And it took me a long time to know that because I was still thinking how my mind is now, like I should have been able to control it. Like I could have stopped it. But I couldn't have. What was I gonna do?

THERAPIST: It sounds like you're starting to forgive yourself and let go of some of that blame . . .

In Session 8, the thoughts and emotions that Kelly shared in the processing after imaginal exposure reflected significant shifts in her perspective, as she described how the revisiting feels differently to her now, and how it feels to be less distressed:

KELLY: I was there then, but I'm not there now. And I felt like it can't affect me now the same way that it did then. I don't have to cry or be upset. I feel like I just go through it and learn from it. Crying for me means that it affected me, and I don't have to allow it to affect me anymore the way it did. That's how I felt last week, and I guess that's why I didn't get upset today.

THERAPIST: You've learned so much. And processed so much. Does that feel really powerful to say, "That was *then* and this is how I feel *now?*"

KELLY: I didn't think I'd ever see it. (*crying*)

THERAPIST: I'm really proud of you.

KELLY: I thought all of my life I'd have this cloud over me. And that it would just stay here even though I get better sometimes. But I feel like the cloud is slowly moving away. So, it doesn't feel like it's always raining on me. I'm crying now because I'm happy. I feel like I never thought that I'd get to this point. I never thought that. And now I'm here. I was just sitting on the bed this morning. Even though I was rushing, I sat down and said, "I feel like I'm a whole new person." And I'm starting to see the changes in my life. Outside, I don't get so upset. I don't fly off the handle with people so often. I don't have to put them in their place. All the time I used to feel like people made judgments about me. I felt I had to go out of my way to put them in their place. And I don't feel like I have to do that. I'm not a talker—only with close people I know. And now I actually hold conversations with people. Like I was in a conversation with this girl on the bus, and I don't even know her. I almost feel like I'm normal now. Like for a long time I didn't feel like I was normal. And now I feel like I'm normal. So that's the only way I can explain it. I feel like I'm normal. And I was thinking last week, with my life the way it is, I was looking in the mirror and thinking, "I don't have any money, I'm broke as I can be. And I'm actually really happy." I haven't felt like that in a long time. At first, I started to get upset about money. And then I said, "*I'm not doing that.* I'll look for a job and fix my resume to the best of my ability. And what happens will happen. I can't get upset over what I have no control over."

Later in this session, Kelly comments on how hard it was for her to admit to being abused by four different perpetrators, and how her sense of shame has lessened:

"I kept thinking that maybe I'll just tell them about my grandfather. Because maybe people will understand it more. They can't understand it if I let them know that it happened with three other people. And when I came here for my first visit, with that intake counselor, she was the first person I had ever admitted that to . . . that I was molested. Because I felt ashamed about being molested. Ashamed as an adult, *but I was a child.* And something came over me, just tell her about all of it. Just tell her that I was molested by four different men. She was the first person I ever admitted it to. I felt so much shame for that. Now I don't feel shame, *because it happened.* It *happened.* As much as people think that it's not happening, *incest happens!*"

In the final session, the therapist and Kelly review the changes she has made in her therapy and how she is seeing the future. The therapist has asked Kelly to rate her current levels of discomfort for the situations on her *in vivo* exposure hierarchy, and all have gone down markedly, even for some *in vivo* exposures that she had not yet attempted:

KELLY: I'm not going to say that it [referring to her childhood abuse] doesn't bother me, but *it doesn't hurt anymore.* I have the mechanisms to deal with it now, and I didn't have that before. Like I'm able to deal with it if

I have a memory. Before I wasn't able to do that. The only thing I can say is that I'm equipped. I know what to do.

THERAPIST: Do you think that's just for the memories or is that for other things, too?

KELLY: Everything. For me it's been everything.

THERAPIST: So, like the other things you haven't worked on, for example, like moving ahead with different sexual behaviors with your boyfriend. Are you going to think, "Oh, I'll just forget about it, we didn't get to it" or are you going to still be working on it?

KELLY: I'm going to still keep moving on, because it's all a process. I don't think my healing is going to stop when the therapy stops. It's still going to be there. My healing doesn't end in 10 weeks. I don't know when it's going to stop. I'm still healing. I went through years and years of abuse. It doesn't stop in a few months. I keep healing. I'll be healing for years and years. But I don't have to let what happened weigh me down anymore. Like it doesn't control me. I control *it*. So, I guess the things I haven't done off the list, I'm not afraid to try. That's the only thing I can say, I'm not afraid to try.

Posttreatment evaluation indicated that Kelly's PTSD and depression symptoms decreased markedly over the course of PE. By both independent evaluator and her own self-report, she lost the diagnosis of PTSD. Follow-up evaluations at 1- and 2-years posttreatment revealed excellent maintenance of gains, with only a few mild symptoms present.

Commentary on the Use of PE with Complex Traumatic Stress Disorder

Working through Client Reactions and Emotions

In using PE with clients with long-term PTSD and much comorbidity, we *expect* the client to struggle with intense emotions and to experience urges to avoid engaging in exposures both in and between sessions. Working through this begins with the essential foundation of a compelling rationale and a strong therapeutic alliance and continues as we collaborate with the client in planning and implementing exposures. We aim to conduct imaginal exposure in an effective manner, helping the client learn to access and express emotion while managing or regulating that emotion so that he or she feels safe. As described, this sometimes requires modifications to standard procedures, monitoring of response to treatment, practicing skills for tolerating and managing intense emotions, pacing the therapy to match the client's rate of learning, and offering ample encouragement and reinforcement.

Although exposure therapy was originally conceptualized as a treatment for excessive anxiety, treating PTSD sufferers has taught us that PE facilitates the emotional processing of much more than fear and anxiety (Foa et al., 2019). In addition, PTSD treatment studies examining changes in anger, shame, guilt, and other negative emotions have reported PE outcomes that include significant reductions in these emotions (Harned, Korslund, Foa, & Linehan, 2012; Harned, Korslund, & Linehan, 2014; Langkaas et al., 2017). How does PE facilitate the emotional processing of emotions other than fear? Imaginal exposure guides the client to engage emotionally with the traumatic memory while visualizing and verbalizing these events, and to allow and tolerate the emotions that arise during this process. As illustrated by Kelly remembering in her third session of imaginal revisiting that she said "no" to her perpetrator, this sometimes enables the person to observe and integrate important information that has been ignored, discarded, or forgotten over time, due to the avoidance behaviors that are part of PTSD. Repeatedly listening to the audio recordings of the imaginal exposure sessions furthers this processing.

Tolerating unpleasant feelings allows information to be processed and integrated, often involving the incorporation of corrective information. For example, shame was the primary emotion Kelly felt in relation to her history of sexual abuse. Shame is often prominent in individuals with PTSD related to childhood sexual abuse, rape, or in those with trauma-related beliefs involving self-blame, being "dirty," or that "Something about *me* made it happen" and "I didn't do anything to stop it." Clients like Kelly with intense feelings of shame often struggle with disclosing their traumatic experiences. Describing these memories in the therapist's presence may amplify the shame, leading the client to avoid imaginal exposure or certain parts of the narrative, or avoid eye contact, hide his or her face behind hands or clothing, or turn the body away from the therapist. When shame blocks engagement and processing, we discuss this with the client, identifying and labeling the feelings of shame, and providing education. We explain that shame is maintained by keeping traumatic experiences buried like a secret that must be kept in the dark, which prevents the associated thoughts and feelings from being examined. We encourage the person to share these memories with the therapist, thereby creating the opportunity to see these events from a different and more realistic perspective. We encourage facing or looking at the therapist while revisiting and processing the memories, inviting the person to see the therapist's response. It can be powerfully healing to see a compassionate and nonjudgmental response rather than the blaming or disgusted response that Kelly anticipated. The corrective information in repeated interactions like this often reduces shame and self-blame. Indeed, as can be seen in the transcript excerpts, Kelly's shame did abate, along with her self-blame and thoughts of people being disgusted by her "if they knew."

Kelly's treatment illustrates the implementation of PE with a case that at the outset might have seemed too complicated for a 10-session course of cognitive-behavioral trauma treatment given her history of repeated interpersonal trauma, chronic and severe PTSD with extensive avoidance, multiple psychiatric disorders, dearth of supportive relationships, and serious psychosocial stressors. It also illustrates the capacity of people to benefit from good, focused, short-term therapy.

Helping the Client to Manage Dissociative Reactions

It can be difficult with some clients for the therapist to distinguish dissociative reactions from periods of intense emotional engagement, with or without signs of overt distress. One quick check on this is to ask clients brief and simple questions about what they are feeling or thinking (during the revisiting) just to have an opportunity to observe their response. The therapist may also assess for dissociation by asking him- or herself whether the client's emotional experience in the revisiting, as best the therapist can discern this from observation, is likely to promote a distinction between "thinking about" the traumatic event and actually "reencountering" it. Is this exposure proceeding in a fashion that will help the client learn that he or she can safely engage with the memory and remain grounded in the present? If not, the therapist will begin modifying the revisiting in a way that decreases emotional engagement and grounds the client in the present, as discussed earlier in the chapter.

Enhancing the Client's Awareness and Acceptance of Bodily States

Clients who are able to strongly engage emotionally with the trauma memory and are vulnerable to dissociative symptoms may experience intense physical sensations during imaginal exposure that are essentially somatic reexperiencing symptoms or "body memories." When this happens, we label these as body memories and explain to the client that they are memories of sensations (e.g., tactile, taste, smell, sight, or pain) that were part of the trauma experience, and encourage the client to think of them as the same as an intrusive image or flashback, but in the body. The client is encouraged to be aware of and tolerate the sensation, knowing that it will subside. We have observed that with repeated revisiting of the memories associated with the somatic reexperiencing, the sensation does subside. These body memories are often frightening to clients, as they can involve acute pain in some part of the body, nausea, vomiting, tasting blood or other substances, sensations of ropes on the skin where they had been tied, or smelling odors. One of our clients experienced many body memories like this and learned to accept them just as she accepted the images and emotions that arose during her imaginal exposure. When body memories were strong, she would remind herself that these were just memory, and she was safe.

Facilitating Involvement in Supportive Relationships

As we mentioned earlier in the chapter, social contact and interaction is very often included on the *in vivo* exposure hierarchy and can create wonderful opportunities to learn that there are safe and pleasant people in the world. The benefits of this type of social exposure was illustrated in Kelly's case when she described the changes in her interactions with people and how this made her feel: "I was in a conversation with this girl on the bus, and I don't even know her. I almost feel like I'm normal now." *In vivo* exposures that involve greeting or talking with people in safe settings decreases isolation and creates opportunities to have experiences that help to modify the PTSD-related beliefs such as "I am bad," "unlikeable," "disgusting," or "unable to relate to others."

Identifying and Managing Safety Risks

A general guideline in PE is that if initial assessment determines PTSD to be a primary problem and no life-threatening or higher priority problems are identified, our goal is to maintain the focus on PTSD, with periodic reassessment of other problem areas as needed. If problems that pose an imminent risk (e.g., of suicide, serious self-injury, harm to others) are present upon initial evaluation, therapists are advised to prioritize treatment for these very high-risk behaviors before proceeding with PE. However, comorbidity of other psychiatric disorders with PTSD is quite high, and clients with severe PTSD are often dealing with multiple psychosocial stressors. Crises during treatment are common. Impulse control problems (e.g., alcohol binges, substance abuse, risky behaviors) also may be present.

However, if a crisis arises during PE without imminent risk, our goal is to remind the client that adhering to treatment, and thereby decreasing PTSD and associated symptoms, is the best help we can give. If appropriate, we may link the crisis to PTSD, and predict that these situations will improve as PTSD improves. We clearly state support for the client's desire to recover from PTSD and applaud healthy coping. Thus, the overall aim is to provide emotional support through the crisis, yet keep PTSD as the major focus of treatment. We agree with van Minnen et al. (2012) that in cases with severe comorbidity (e.g., substance or alcohol dependence, recent or current high-risk suicidal or self-injurious behavior), PTSD may be treated with PE, while integrated or concurrent treatment to monitor and address the comorbid problems is provided.

Final Comment

The therapist interested in using PE should first acquire training in this model of treatment. It is also important that the therapist be thoroughly grounded in the foundation of the theory and rationale for prolonged exposure, as this is what guides therapists' decision making and response to client reactions to treatment. To encourage a client like Kelly to visualize and describe a painful memory of being raped as a child, and to support her while she connects with and expresses the anguish and shame she felt (and may feel to some degree in the session), requires the therapist's trust as well as his or her skill: trust in the process, in the client's capacity to heal, and in him- or herself to support this healing while tolerating and managing personal feelings and reactions.

References

Cloitre, M., Koenen, K. C., Cohen, L. R., & Han, H. (2002). Skills training in affective and interpersonal regulation followed by exposure: A phase-based treatment for PTSD related to childhood abuse. *Journal of Consulting and Clinical Psychology, 70,* 1067–1074.

Foa, E. B., & Cahill, S. P. (2001). Psychological therapies: Emotional processing. In N. J. Smelser & P. B. Bates (Eds.), *International encyclopedia of the social and behavioral sciences* (pp. 12363–12369). Oxford, UK: Elsevier.

Foa, E. B., Hembree, E. A., Cahill, S. P., Rauch, S. A., Riggs, D. S., Feeny, N. C., & Yadin, E. (2005). Randomized trial of prolonged exposure for PTSD with and without cognitive restructuring: Outcome at academic and community clinics. *Journal of Consulting and Clinical Psychology, 73,* 953–964.

Foa, E. B., Hembree, E. A., & Rothbaum, B. O. (2007). *Prolonged exposure therapy for PTSD: Emotional processing of traumatic experiences.* New York: Oxford University Press. (Translations in Hebrew, Spanish, Japanese, Chinese, Polish, Korean, Swedish)

Foa, E. B., Hembree, E. A., Rothbaum, B. O., & Rauch, S. A. M. (2019). *Prolonged exposure therapy for PTSD: Emotional processing of traumatic experiences* (2nd ed.). New York: Oxford University Press.

Foa, E. B., Huppert, J. D., & Cahill, S. P. (2006). Emotional processing theory: An update. In B. O. Rothbaum (Ed.), *The nature and treatment of pathological anxiety* (pp. 3–24). New York: Guilford Press.

Foa, E. B., & Jaycox, L. H. (1999). Cognitive-behavioral theory and treatment of post-traumatic stress disorder. In D. Spiegel (Ed.), *Efficacy and cost-effectiveness of psychotherapy* (pp. 23–61). Washington, DC: American Psychiatric Press.

Foa, E. B., & Kozak, M. J. (1985). Treatment of anxiety disorders: Implications for psychopathology. In A. H. Tuma & J. D. Maser (Eds.), *Anxiety and the anxiety disorders* (pp. 421–452). Hillsdale, NJ: Erlbaum.

Foa, E. B., & Kozak, M. J. (1986). Emotional processing of fear: Exposure to corrective information. *Psychological Bulletin, 99,* 20–35.

Foa, E. B., & Riggs, D. S. (1993). Post-traumatic stress disorder in rape victims. In J. Oldham, M. B. Riba, & A. Tasman (Eds.), *American Psychiatric Press review of psychiatry* (Vol. 12, pp. 285–309). Washington, DC: American Psychiatric Press.

Foa, E. B., Steketee, G. S., & Rothbaum, B. O. (1989). Behavioral/cognitive conceptualizations of post-traumatic stress disorder. *Behavior Therapy, 20,* 155–176.

Harned, M. S., Korslund, K. E., Foa, E. B., & Linehan, M. M. (2012). Treating PTSD in suicidal and self-injuring women with borderline personality disorder: Development and preliminary evaluation of a dialectical behavior therapy prolonged exposure protocol. *Behaviour Research and Therapy, 50*(6), 381–386.

Harned, M. S., Korslund, K. E., & Linehan, M. M. (2014). A pilot randomized controlled trial of dialectical behavior therapy with and without the dialectical behavior therapy prolonged exposure protocol for suicidal and self-injuring women with borderline personality disorder and PTSD. *Behaviour Research and Therapy, 55,* 7–17.

Langkaas, T. F., Hoffart, A., Oktedalen, T., Ulvenes, P. G., Hembree, E. A., & Smucker, M. (2017). Exposure and non-fear emotions: A randomized controlled study of exposure-based and rescripting-based imagery in PTSD treatment. *Behaviour Research and Therapy, 97,* 33–42.

McLean, C., Asaani, A., & Foa, E. B. (2015). Prolonged exposure therapy. In U. Schnyder & M. Cloitre (Eds.), *Evidence based treatments for trauma-related psychological dis-*

orders: A practical guide for clinicians (pp. 143–159). Cham, Switzerland: Springer International.

Powers, M. B., Halpern, J. M., Ferenschak, M. P., Gillihan, S. J., & Foa, E. B. (2010). A meta-analytic review of prolonged exposure for posttraumatic stress disorder. *Clinical Psychology Review, 30,* 635–641.

Rauch, S., & Foa, E. (2006). Emotional processing theory (EPT) and exposure therapy for PTSD. *Journal of Contemporary Psychotherapy, 36*(2), 61–65.

Resick, P. A., Nishith, P., & Griffin, M. G. (2003). How well does cognitive behavioral therapy treat symptoms of complex PTSD?: An examination of child sexual abuse survivors within a clinical trial. *CNS Spectrums, 8,* 340–355.

Resick, P. A., Nishith, P., Weaver, T. L., Astin, M. C., & Feuer, C. A. (2002). A comparison of cognitive-processing therapy with prolonged exposure and a waiting condition for the treatment of chronic posttraumatic stress disorder in female rape victims. *Journal of Consulting and Clinical Psychology, 70,* 867–879.

Resick, P. A., Suvak, M. K., & Wells, S. Y. (2014).The impact of childhood abuse among women with assault-related PTSD receiving short-term CBT. *Journal of Traumatic Stress, 27,* 558–567.

Resick, P. A., Williams, L. F., Suvak, M. K., Monson, C. M., & Gradus, J. L. (2012). Long-term outcomes of cognitive-behavioral treatments for posttraumatic stress disorder among female rape survivors. *Journal of Consulting and Clinical Psychology, 80,* 201–210.

van Minnen, A., Harned, M. S., Zoellner, L., & Mills, K. (2012). Examining potential contraindications for prolonged exposure therapy for PTSD. *European Journal of Psychotraumatology, 3,* 18805.

CHAPTER 10

Cognitive Therapy

ANKE EHLERS
HANNAH MURRAY

Cognitive therapy for posttraumatic stress disorder (CT-PTSD) aims to help an individual update the idiosyncratic, often highly personal distressing meanings that they have taken from traumatic experiences, so that these meanings become less threatening to their sense of self and their perception of the world. This central aim remains essential to treatment even when aspects of complexity are apparent, whether that may be experiences of multiple traumatic events over a lifetime, the presence of comorbid social or psychological difficulties, or complicating features such as dissociative episodes. In this chapter, we first outline Ehlers and Clark's (2000) cognitive model for PTSD, the core treatment procedures, and the evidence base for CT-PTSD. We then describe how the treatment interventions can be applied when working with various issues of complexity. In a case study, we describe how CT-PTSD was used to treat a multiply traumatized woman with a complex presentation of PTSD.

Cognitive Therapy for PTSD

Traumatic events are extremely negative events that everyone would find highly threatening and distressing. Yet what people find *most* distressing about a traumatic event, and what it means to them, varies greatly from person to person, and influences the probability of developing PTSD. The personal meanings of trauma and their relationship with features of trauma memories are central to Ehlers and Clark's (2000) cognitive model of PTSD, which suggests that PTSD develops when traumatic experiences are processed in a way that produces a sense of serious current threat, driven by two key processes (Figure 10.1).

The first source of current threat is *negative appraisals* (personal mean-

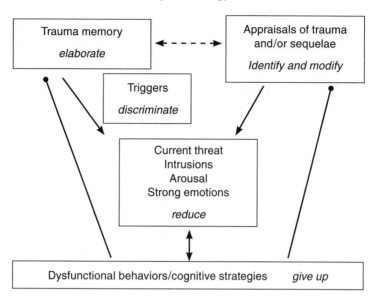

FIGURE 10.1. Treatment goals (in italics) in cognitive therapy for PTSD (Ehlers & Clark, 2000). Pointed arrows stand for "leads to." Round-arrows stand for "prevents a change in." Dashed arrows stand for "influences." From Ehlers (2013). Copyright © 2013 by Wiley. Reprinted by permission.

ings) of the trauma and/or its sequelae (e.g., reactions of other people, initial PTSD symptoms, physical consequences of the trauma). The perceived threat can be external or internal, and the negative emotions depend on the type of appraisal: Perceived *external* threat can result from appraisals about impending danger (e.g., "I cannot trust anyone"), leading to excessive fear, or appraisals about the unfairness of the trauma or its aftermath (e.g., "I will never be able to accept that the perpetrator got away with it"), leading to persistent anger. Perceived *internal* threat often relates to negative appraisals of one's behavior, emotions, or reactions during the trauma, or to the perpetrator's or other people's humiliating or derogatory statements, and may lead to guilt (e.g., "It was my fault"), or shame (e.g., "I am a bad person"). A common negative appraisal of consequences of the trauma in PTSD is perceived permanent change of the self or one's life (e.g., "I have permanently changed for the worse"), which can lead to sadness and hopelessness. For multiply traumatized individuals, personal meanings tend to become more generalized (e.g., "I do not matter"; "I deserve bad things happening to me"; "I am worthless"), leading to an enduring sense of degradation, defeat, or low self-worth. The appraisals can become more embedded in a person's internal belief systems over time. For example, if an early life trauma has led a person to feel that he or she is damaged in some way, or unlucky in life, experiencing further trauma is likely to further confirm this belief.

The second source of perceived current threat according to Ehlers and Clark (2000) is characteristics of the individual's memory of the trauma. The worst moments of the trauma are poorly elaborated in memory, that is, inadequately integrated into their context (both within the event, and within the context of previous and subsequent experiences/information). The effect of this is that a person with PTSD remembers the trauma in a disjointed way. When he or she recalls the worst moments, it may be difficult to access other information that could correct impressions he or she had or his or her predictions at the time: In other words, the memory for these moments has not been updated with what the person knows now. The effect of this is that the threat experienced during these moments is reexperienced as if it were happening right now rather than being a memory from the past. This "nowness" of the memories can be so severe that a person may experience a dissociative flashback and lose awareness of his or her present surroundings. The reexperiencing can include reexperiencing of bodily sensations and emotions from the trauma in the absence of a recollection of the event itself. The disjointedness of memories may also be affected by repeated exposure to traumatic experiences, with poorer integration into autobiographical memory with each subsequent trauma exposure, explaining in part why repeated exposure to traumatic events makes PTSD more likely to develop, and why dissociation is common.

Ehlers and Clark (2000) also noted that intrusive trauma memories are easily triggered in PTSD by sensory cues that overlap perceptually with those occurring during trauma (e.g., a similar sound, color, smell, shape, movement, or bodily sensations). They suggest that if people during trauma mainly process perceptual features of the experience (data-driven processing), this will lead to strong perceptual priming, such that stimuli similar to those in the trauma are more easily identified in the environment. Through learned associations, the stimuli also become associated with strong affective responses, which can generalize to similar stimuli. Both priming and generalized associative learning lead to a poor discrimination of the stimuli in the current environment from those in the trauma. This means that perceptually similar stimuli are easily spotted and can trigger reexperiencing symptoms.

The third factor that maintains a sense of current threat in Ehlers and Clark's model is cognitive strategies and behaviors that people with PTSD use in response to the perceived current threat. These correspond to the problematic appraisals in meaningful ways and include effortful suppression of memories, avoidance of reminders, rumination, excessive precautions to prevent future trauma ("safety behaviors") and alcohol or drug use. These behaviors and cognitive strategies maintain PTSD by preventing change in the appraisals or trauma memory, and/or by increasing symptoms, and thus keep the sense of current threat going. For some individuals, especially those with long-standing PTSD, these behaviors may become highly disabling, and may be the reason an individual comes into therapy.

Figure 10.1 illustrates the three factors (appraisals, memory characteristics, cognitive/behavioral strategies) that maintain a sense of current threat and PTSD symptoms according to Ehlers and Clark's (2000) model. CT-PTSD uses the theoretical framework of this model and targets these three factors. The model suggests three treatment goals:

1. To modify threatening appraisals (personal meanings) of the trauma and its sequelae.
2. To reduce reexperiencing by elaboration of the trauma memories and discrimination of triggers.
3. To reduce cognitive strategies and behaviors that maintain a sense of current threat.

Core treatment procedures (described in greater detail below) in CT-PTSD include the following[1]:

- *Individualized case formulation.* The therapist and client collaboratively develop an individualized version of Ehlers and Clark's (2000) model of PTSD, which serves as the framework for therapy. Treatment procedures are tailored to the formulation.
- *Reclaiming/rebuilding one's life assignments* is designed from the first session onwards to address the client's perceived permanent change after trauma and involves reclaiming or rebuilding activities and social contacts.
- *Changing problematic appraisals* of the traumas and their sequelae through guided discovery and behavioral experiments.
- *Updating trauma memories* is a three-step procedure that includes (1) accessing memories of the worst moments during the traumatic events and their currently threatening meanings, (2) identifying information that updates these meanings (information from either the course of events during the trauma, or from cognitive restructuring and testing of predictions), and (3) linking the new meanings to the worst moments in the memory.
- *Discrimination training with triggers of reexperiencing* involves systematically spotting idiosyncratic triggers (often subtle sensory cues) and learning to discriminate between "now" (cues in a new safe context) and "then" (cue in the traumatic event).
- *A site visit* completes the memory updating and trigger discrimination.
- *Dropping unhelpful behaviours and cognitive processes* commonly includes discussing their advantages and disadvantages and *behavioral experiments* in which the patient experiments with reducing unhelpful strategies such as rumination, hypervigilance for threat, thought suppression, and excessive precautions (safety behaviors).
- *A blueprint* summarizes what the client has learned in treatment and includes plans for any setbacks.

---

[1] Video extracts of the procedures and therapy materials can be accessed at *https://oxcadatresources.com*.

Empirical Support

The factors proposed to maintain PTSD in Ehlers and Clark's (2000) model of PTSD have been supported in prospective and experimental studies (e.g., Beierl, Böllinghaus, Clark, Glucksman & Ehlers, 2019; Ehlers, Mayou, & Bryant, 1998; Ehlers, Maercker, & Boos, 2000; Ehlers, Ehring, & Kleim, 2012; Ehring, Ehlers, & Glucksman, 2008; Kleim, Ehlers, & Glucksman, 2007; Kleim, Ehring, & Ehlers, 2012). The efficacy of CT-PTSD has been evaluated in several randomized controlled trials in adults (Ehlers et al., 2003, 2014, 2019b; Ehlers, Clark, Hackmann, McManus, & Fennell, 2005) and children (Meiser-Stedman et al., 2017; Smith et al., 2007). In these research trials, CT-PTSD was found to be highly acceptable to clients, as indicated by very low dropout rates (3% on average) and high client satisfaction scores. It led to clinically significant improvements in PTSD symptoms (intent-to-treat pre–post treatment effect sizes around 2.5), disability, depression, anxiety, and quality of life. Over 70% of these studies' participants fully recovered from PTSD. Outreach open trials treating consecutive samples of survivors of the Omagh and London bombings replicated these results (Brewin et al., 2010; Gillespie, Duffy, Hackmann, & Clark, 2002). The percentage of clients whose symptoms worsened with treatment was close to zero, and smaller than in clients waiting for treatment (Ehlers et al., 2014). This suggests that CT-PTSD is a safe and efficacious treatment.

Three further studies (Duffy et al., 2007; Ehlers et al., 2013, 2019a) implemented CT-PTSD in routine clinical services. The samples treated in these studies included a very wide range of clients, including those with complicating factors such as serious social problems, living currently in danger, very severe depression, borderline personality disorder, or multiple traumatic events and losses. Therapists included trainees, as well as experienced therapists. Outcomes remained very good, with large intent-to-treat effect sizes of 1.25 and higher for PTSD symptoms. Around 60% of the clients who started therapy remitted from PTSD. Dropout rates were somewhat higher than in the randomized controlled trials of CT-PTSD (around 15%), but rates were still below the average for trials of trauma-focused cognitive-behavioral therapy of 23% (Bisson, Roberts, Andrew, Cooper, & Lewis, 2013). Very few clients experienced a mild degree of symptom worsening (1.2% in Ehlers et al., 2013). Thus, the evidence suggests that CT-PTSD is an effective treatment for individuals with a broad range of presentations, including many of the complex symptoms experienced by people with prolonged trauma histories.

CT-PTSD has also been successfully used in an intensive format in which therapy is delivered daily over the course of 5–7 working days (Ehlers et al., 2014; Murray, El-Leithy, & Billings, 2017), and in a briefer self-study assisted[2] format (Ehlers et al., 2019b).

---

[2]The self-study modules will be made available at *https://oxcadatresources.com.*

Treatment Procedures

Format of Treatment

CT-PTSD is usually delivered in up to 12 weekly treatment sessions for clients who currently reexperience a small number of traumas, and up to 20 weekly sessions for clients with multiple traumas and complex presentations. Sessions that involve work on trauma memories should be 90 minutes long to allow the client time to refocus on the present before leaving the session. Weekly measures of PTSD symptoms, depression, and cognitions are helpful in monitoring the effects of interventions and spotting problems that remain.

Therapeutic Style and the Therapeutic Relationship

In common with other forms of cognitive therapy, CT-PTSD uses guided discovery as the primary therapeutic style. As the main focus of the intervention is the cognitions that stem from the traumas and induce a sense of current threat, strategies such as Socratic questioning aim to gently guide the client to explore and examine a wider range of evidence by asking questions that help him or her consider the problem from different perspectives, with the aim to generate a less threatening alternative interpretation. CT encourages a perspective of curiosity rather than trying to undermine or prove the client's perspective to be wrong.

A nonthreatening, collaborative style of working is essential to working with trauma survivors, particularly those with complex presentations. Establishing a good therapeutic relationship based on mutual trust, respect, and warmth is fundamental, especially with individuals who have had experiences of interpersonal trauma and may believe they can no longer trust people. Setting up an open and collaborative alliance is also important to empower clients to have control over the therapeutic relationship, to question the therapist and the interventions if they are uncertain or uncomfortable. For those with interpersonal difficulties, this enables swifter resolution of issues that could lead to an impasse in the therapeutic relationship or to treatment dropout.

Generating an alternative interpretation (insight) is usually not sufficient to generate a large emotional shift. Crucial steps in therapy are therefore to test the client's appraisals in behavioral experiments, which create experiential new evidence against the client's threatening interpretations, and to link the new meanings to the relevant moments during the trauma in memory with the updating memories procedure (i.e., by simultaneously holding the moment and the new meanings in mind to facilitate an emotional shift). This is also important to address "head–heart lag," which can be a problem when beliefs have been long-held and may shift intellectually but not emotionally.

Case Formulation, Psychoeducation, and Treatment Planning

At the start of treatment, therapist and client discuss the client's symptoms and treatment goals, and explore cognitions to develop an individualized case formulation.

The therapist normalizes the PTSD symptoms by explaining that they are common reactions to extremely stressful, overwhelming events, and that many of the symptoms are a sign that the memories of the traumas are not fully processed yet.

The therapist asks the client to give a brief account of the traumas and starts exploring the personal meanings ("What was the worst thing about the trauma?"; "What were the worst moments, and what did they mean to you?"). The emotions that the client experiences are further indicators of the type of problematic meanings that need to the addressed in treatment, and the *Posttraumatic Cognitions Inventory* (Foa, Ehlers, Clark, Tolin, & Orsillo, 1999) can help with identifying cognitive themes, some of which the client may not mention in the early sessions.

In the case of clients with histories of multiple traumatic events, it is important to determine which events are linked to the current PTSD. The therapist aims to discover which events the client is reexperiencing, since these will be the primary focus of the intervention. The therapist also may assist the client in developing a timeline of the client's life, or trauma history, to facilitate the identification of focal traumas.

The therapist asks the client what strategies he or she has used so far to cope with his or her distressing memories. Suppression of memories, avoidance, and numbing of emotions (including substance use) are common, as well as rumination. The therapist then uses a *thought suppression experiment* (asking the client to try hard not to think about an image such as a green rabbit sitting on the therapist's shoulder) to demonstrate experientially that suppressing mental images has paradoxical effects.

The model in Figure 10.1 is rarely presented to clients, due to its complexity. Rather, the therapist summarizes with clients an individualized case conceptualization and treatment plan that relates to the three main processes inherent to the model:

1. Many of their symptoms are caused by the nature of trauma memories. Addressing these during treatment will reduce the intrusions and make the traumas feel more like memories from the past.
2. Understandably, the traumas have affected clients' views of themselves and the world, leading them to feel more under threat and more negative about themselves. These views will be considered in therapy, to understand whether they are being colored by the trauma memories.
3. Some strategies that clients have used so far to control the symptoms and threat are understandable, but may be inadvertently counterpro-

ductive (as clients have experienced in the thought suppression experiment). Clients will experiment with replacing these strategies with alternatives that may be more helpful.

As the CT-PTSD case formulation is tailored to each individual, it can be applied to a wide variety of presentations, traumas, and cultural backgrounds, and can incorporate comorbid conditions and the effects of multiple traumas. For example, comorbid depression may be related to some of the client's appraisals of the trauma and other life experiences (e.g., "I am worthless") and cognitive strategies (e.g., rumination). Comorbid panic disorder may have developed from interpretations of the reexperiencing symptoms (e.g., reexperiencing difficulty breathing leading to the thought "I will suffocate"). And comorbid obsessive–compulsive disorder (OCD) may be linked to appraisals such as "I am contaminated" and linked to behaviors such as excessive washing. Cultural beliefs may influence an individual's personal meanings of trauma and his or her attempts to come to terms with trauma memories in helpful and unhelpful ways. Treatment is tailored to the individual's beliefs, including cultural beliefs.

CT-PTSD allows for flexibility in the order in which the core treatment procedures are delivered, depending on the individual formulation and client preference. The memory updating procedure often has a fast and profound effect on symptoms and is generally attempted early on, if possible. For patients with severe dissociative symptoms, training in stimulus discrimination is conducted first, and narrative writing is preferred over imaginal reliving. In addition, for certain cognitive patterns, the memory work is prepared through discussion of the client's appraisals and cognitive processing at the time of the trauma. For example, when a client profoundly believes him- or herself to be at fault for a trauma, and the resultant guilt and/or shame prevents the client from being able to describe it fully to the therapist, therapy would start with addressing these appraisals. If a client experienced mental defeat (the perceived loss of all autonomy) during an interpersonal trauma, therapy would start with discussing the traumatic situation from a wider perspective to raise the client's awareness that the perpetrators intended to control and manipulate his or her feelings and thoughts at the time, but that they are not exerting control now.

For clients displaying complex features of PTSD, other problems may need to be an initial priority. Particularly, if reexperiencing symptoms and coping strategies are currently placing a client at risk, for example, through severe dissociative episodes, excessive use of substances, self-harm, or risky sexual behavior, these behaviors require immediate attention. In addition, a comorbid condition, such as severe depression with acute suicidal intent or acute psychosis, is a clinical priority that would interfere with the successful or safe delivery of CT-PTSD and would require prior treatment. In some cases, it may also be necessary to prioritize other problems or events for a few sessions during treatment if they become the client's primary problem.

Reclaiming/Rebuilding Your Life

An early intervention in CT-PTSD is to encourage clients to reintroduce activities and relationships that were important to them before the trauma but have been relinquished, in order to address the common appraisal that their lives have been permanently changed since the trauma. This involves a discussion of previous interests and activities, and a gradual reintroduction to them via homework assignments. For the individual who has a long history of trauma and cannot readily identify previously valued activities, who was very young when the trauma occurred, or who has lost much of his or her former life since the trauma (e.g., loss of a significant other or home, life-changing injuries), the focus is on "(re)building your life." The therapist and client identify together what activities and interests would fit with the client's goals for the future, and plan small achievable steps toward them.

Stimulus Discrimination

Although they may appear to come "out of the blue," many reexperiencing symptoms of PTSD are triggered by subtle sensory reminders of the trauma, such as visual patterns or colors, sounds, smells, tastes, or bodily sensations. One sensory similarity between the trauma and the current situation may be sufficient to trigger reexperiencing. This makes the triggers hard to spot. Helping a client to become more aware of his or her triggers using systematic observation in the session, and as homework, helps the client to feel more control over the intrusions, and learn to break the link between the trigger and the trauma memory.

This involves several steps. First, the client learns to distinguish between "then" and "now" (i.e., to focus on how the present triggers and their context ("now") differ from the trauma ("then"). Second, the therapist and client practice focusing on the differences, while intentionally introducing triggers during a therapy session (e.g., the sound of shouting or brakes squealing on Internet audio libraries, red fluids that look like blood, pictures of people who look like the perpetrator). The "then" versus "now" discrimination can be facilitated by carrying out actions that were not possible during the trauma (e.g., moving around if the client was trapped in the trauma, touching objects or looking at photos that remind the client of his or her present life). Finally, clients apply the "then" versus "now" discrimination between sessions as triggers arise.

Updating Trauma Memories

In CT-PTSD, the meaning of the trauma to an individual is central to understanding the maintenance of PTSD. These meanings are often associated with so-called "hot spots" (Foa & Rothbaum, 1998), the moments in the trauma memory that are most distressing and have the strongest sense of "nowness." These moments may be accessed through imaginal reliving (Foa & Rothbaum, 1998) or narrative writing (Resick & Schnicke, 1993). Imaginal reliv-ing involves the client visualizing the traumatic event (usually with his or her eyes closed) and describing to the therapist, moment by moment, what is hap-pening, including sensory details, thoughts, and feelings. Narrative writing involves preparing a written account of the trauma, usually with the therapist, with a similar level of detail. Imaginal reliving is generally more immersive than narrative writing and can lead to quicker access to the difficult thoughts and feelings associated with a particular hot spot in trauma memory. For some individuals, this can be overwhelming, and narrative writing is recommended in preference to imaginal reliving for those who dissociate easily or experience strong physical reactions when accessing the trauma memory (e.g., vomiting or feeling faint). Narrative writing is also preferable when a trauma memory is very long, or when the client is very confused about what happened or has long gaps in memory (e.g., due to loss of consciousness or drugs).

In CT-PTSD, the aim of memory work is not to relive the trauma repeat-edly until habituation occurs, but to identify hot spots and their meanings, and information that will help understand and update them. This usually takes only one or two sessions. Once a hot spot has been identified, the personal meanings are carefully explored. The therapist and client then begin to identify infor-mation that does not fit with the problematic meanings, which can "update" the hot spot. In some cases, this will be simple, factual updates the client may already be aware of, but may not yet have fully integrated into the trauma memory. For example, if the client believes he or she was going to die and leave his or her children behind, it may be helpful to update the hot spot with the knowledge that he or she survived, and to look at a recent family photo to help consolidate this information. In other cases, it may take research and psychoeducation to identify updating information, for example, interviewing experts to understand why an event occurred. Some appraisals require more thorough cognitive techniques to generate meaningful updates. For example, if someone believes that he or she is to blame for a trauma, techniques such as Socratic questioning, systematic discussion of evidence, behavioral experi-ments, pie charts, discussing hindsight bias, or a survey may be required to access an alternative explanation. Imagery may also be helpful in generating a new perspective, for example, imagining what would have happened if the client had fought back when being threatened with a knife.

Once updating information that the client finds compelling has been iden-tified, it is actively incorporated into the trauma memory, by holding the rel-evant hot spot and its original meanings in mind (through imaginal reliving or reading the corresponding part of the narrative) simultaneously with the updat-ing information. This may be done verbally (e.g., "I know now that . . . "), through imagery (e.g., visualizing how one's wounds have healed; visualizing the perpetrator in prison; visualizing a deceased in a peaceful place; looking at a recent family photo), using movements or actions that are incompatible with the original meaning of this moment (e.g., jumping up and down for hotspots that involved predictions about dying or being paralyzed), or incompatible sensations (e.g., touching a healed arm; eating or drinking something with a taste different from blood). It is important to look for an emotional shift during the updating to see whether the updating information has been adequately processed. Clients report feeling surprised or relieved when the updating is successful, and reexperiencing decreases and sleep improves in the following days (Woodward et al., 2017). For clients with severe dissociation, it can take a few attempts to find the best way to make the updating information "sink in" when recalling their hot spots.

Addressing Unhelpful Behaviors and Dissociation

Usually, the first step in addressing cognitive strategies and behaviors that maintain PTSD is to discuss their problematic consequences. This is generally done using guided discovery, listing the advantages and disadvantages of the behavior, and behavioral experiments to demonstrate their effects. For a nonrisky behavior, this may include increasing the behavior. For example, the effects of selective attention to danger cues can be demonstrated by asking the client to attend to possible signs of danger unrelated to trauma, such as watching traffic on a busy road. This demonstrates experientially that hypervigilance can lead to anxiety based on a heightened appraisal of risk. Behavioral experiments in dropping the behavior and observing the consequences can then be attempted.

Many cognitive strategies and behaviors that maintain PTSD, such as thought suppression and hypervigilance to danger, do not place clients directly at risk. However, strategies such as excessive use of drugs and/or alcohol, self-harm, risky sexual behavior, and severe dissociation can be dangerous. The therapist and client work together to understand the role the behavior is playing in maintaining PTSD and how it is contributing to other psychological, social, relationship, health, and financial problems. A plan is then developed to reduce the behavior, anticipating potential obstacles and how they can be overcome. Behavioral experiments allow the testing of beliefs associated with coping strategies (e.g., "I won't be able to sleep without alcohol"). In some cases, associated beliefs require additional cognitive work, for example, when someone believes that he or she deserves to be harmed by others, and deliberately places him- or herself in risky situations. For individuals who have a long history of trauma and may struggle to assess how risky a situation is, work on recognizing and assessing danger may be required.

Dissociation can also be formulated as a coping strategy, albeit an unintentional one. The therapist and client explore how and why dissociation occurs, and learn to recognize triggers to dissociation. Clients are taught to use stimulus discrimination (discussed earlier) to deal with triggers. In cases in which the client is experiencing strong loss of awareness, he or she is encouraged to experiment with strategies that make the difference between the trauma and the current situation more salient. Such strategies are often referred to as *grounding strategies* or reminders of the "here and now." Therapist and client discuss and practice these in the session to find the most effective strategy. The best strategies are generally easily accessible, with powerful cues to the present moment, such as strong tastes, smells, or sensations, or visual or auditory cues that were not present at the time of the trauma. Once the client's attention has been refocused on the here and now, therapist and client try to identify what triggered the dissociation, and use stimulus discrimination.

Further Imagery Work

If reexperiencing symptoms persist after successful updating of the client's hot spots and discrimination of triggers, imagery transformation techniques can be useful. The client transforms the trauma image into a new image that signifies the trauma is over. Transformed images can provide compelling evidence that the intrusions are a product of the client's mind rather than perceptions of current reality. Image transformation is also particularly helpful with intrusions that represent images of things that did not actually happen during the trauma (e.g., images of the future that represented the client's worst fears, such as images of his or her children growing up sad and alone).

Revisiting the Scene of the Trauma

A visit to the site of the trauma completes the work on trauma memories and appraisals. Visiting the site can help correct remaining problematic appraisals, as the site provides many retrieval cues and helps access further information to update the appraisals. The site visit also helps complete the stimulus discrimination work. Clients realize that the site "now" is very different from the way it was "then," which helps place the trauma in the past. Using Google Street View to visit the site virtually can be an effective alternative when it is unsafe or impractical to visit the site in person. In other cases, it can be a useful preparation for visiting a site, when the client is reluctant or anxious. In all cases, giving a clear rationale for the visit, addressing beliefs about returning to the site of the trauma, and planning for any potential difficulties is helpful preparation for the returning to the scene of the trauma (for further details, see Murray, Merritt, & Grey, 2015).

Clinical Case Example

Case Description

Carmen (whose name and details are disguised), a 35-year-old Colombian woman referred for treatment of PTSD, had a long history of traumatic experiences, beginning when she was a child. Her father would shout and insult Carmen if she displeased him, which was often, and beat her with his belt or a stick if she was disobedient. He would require her to stand absolutely still while she was being punished, and he would beat Carmen harder if she moved.

At the age of 16, Carmen married and moved out of the house, with the primary motivation of escaping her father. However, the man she married was also violent. Carmen described him as a local "bad man," involved with criminal gangs in the neighborhood. He was twice Carmen's age and was unfaithful to her throughout their marriage, as well as being sexually and physically violent toward her. Carmen explained that as a woman in Colombia, she was expected to stay at home and raise their children, but she had ambitions to work and study, having done well at school despite the violence at home.

Carmen was isolated, with little support, but she did manage to stay in touch with her sister, who had moved to the United Kingdom and was working as a nurse. With her help, Carmen left her husband and traveled to London with her three children. Carmen was also training to be a nurse, although at the time of treatment, she had taken a break from her studies.

At assessment, Carmen met criteria for PTSD and had reexperiencing symptoms relating to five episodes of violence at the hands of her ex-husband. She was also suffering from depression, and fulfilled most, but not all, criteria for a diagnosis of borderline personality disorder. Her sister had persuaded her to come for treatment when she had found Carmen self-harming by cutting her inner thighs, a long-standing behavior. She denied suicidal intent, citing her children as a protective factor, but described an occasion in which she had wandered alone at night to a bridge over the river, in an apparently dissociated state, and a member of the public had alerted the police, who took her home.

Treatment

Carmen received 18 sessions of treatment. The early sessions focused on engagement, risk management, and developing a shared understanding of Carmen's problems. Carmen expressed reluctance to come to the sessions and often gave brief answers or said "I don't know" when asked certain questions, particularly relating to her trauma history. The therapist focused on normalizing her symptoms and giving information about PTSD. She also agreed to write a letter to the housing association that accommodated Carmen and her sister, as they were hoping to move to a bigger flat now that her children were older.

Carmen had a flashback during Session 2, triggered by the sound of a male voice shouting nearby. The therapist took this opportunity to begin the process of helping Carmen to identify her triggers and to learn stimulus discrimination. They also experimented with different reminders of the here and now. Carmen began to carry a stress ball in her purse that she could squeeze if she began to dissociate, and also taught her sister how to recognize whether she was dissociating and help her. Carmen's self-harm tended to occur when she was dissociating in response to a trauma trigger. The use of stimulus discrimination as an alternative proved effective in reducing the self-harm.

After three sessions working on these techniques, Carmen and her therapist began to construct a timeline of her traumatic experiences. She was able to identify which of the events she reexperienced in nightmares, flashbacks, and intrusive memories, and which events were important in terms of belief formation. For example, she reported that the belief "I deserve to be punished" (which she believed 100%) started when her father would beat her for minor misdemeanors, but it grew stronger during her marriage.

The most distressing trauma memory for Carmen was the first time she was raped by her husband, which was on her wedding night. Carmen understood that she was expected to have sex with her husband that night, but she asked him to stop because she was experiencing pain, which he refused to do. As their marriage continued, Carmen was raped many times, and learned to dissociate when it was happening, something she had also done when her father was punishing her. Understanding dissociation as a strategy that had helped her in dangerous situations, but was no longer needed, was an important step in making sense of Carmen's trauma symptoms, which had previously made her believe she was going mad.

Due to her dissociation, Carmen and her therapist worked on the trauma memories using written narratives. The first trauma memory revealed many important cognitive themes, including a sense of shame, degradation, and contamination linked to Carmen's belief that she deserved such treatment. They worked on these beliefs using a range of techniques, including a review of the evidence and a survey. The survey was sent to a range of respondents via Survey Monkey for anonymous responses. Carmen and her therapist devised several questions to address Carmen's beliefs (e.g., "Does a woman have a right to refuse sex, even once she is married?"). The new evidence was then used to update the trauma memory ("I know now that he is wrong and I do not deserve to be treated this way"). Her belief that she deserved bad treatment dropped to 20%, although she still described head–heart lag. To consolidate the verbal updates, Carmen wrote a letter to her younger self, and read it to her in imagery, telling her that she was a good person, who did not deserve bad treatment.

Work on the other reexperienced memories progressed quickly, as many of the same emotions and appraisals were present, and could be updated rapidly. Carmen and her therapist wrote the updates into the trauma narratives and, in later sessions when her dissociation was better controlled, Carmen was able to read the narratives and the updates aloud, taking in the new updated meanings while holding her hot spots in mind.

As her reexperiencing symptoms reduced, Carmen was able to increase her range of activities, and she and her therapist reviewed the "reclaiming your life" plan she had made at the start of treatment. She determined with nursing college personnel when she would restart her course and began to study at home. Carmen had previously avoided situations in which she would be alone with men, and she and her therapist planned some behavioral experiments in which Carmen could safely experience and discriminate triggers, such as ordering an online shopping item and conversing with the deliveryman. She had also avoided events with the Colombian community in London, for fear that someone might know her husband, but through a risk calculation with her therapist, Carmen concluded that this was highly unlikely, and experimented with visiting a Colombian café with her sister.

Toward the end of treatment (Session 15), Carmen and her therapist used Google Street View to find the house where she had lived with her husband in Colombia. To her surprise, she could zoom in on the exact house on their old street. With encouragement from her therapist, Carmen noticed several differences in how the house and the street had looked when she lived there. The front garden was tidier and the front door had been painted (leading Carmen to conclude that her husband had moved away), signage on the street had changed, and some graffiti had been painted over.

Carmen and her therapist prepared a blueprint summarizing her work in treatment, and identifying a plan for any possible setbacks in the future. Carmen was adamant that she would never again enter a romantic relationship, but in the final few sessions of treatment had agreed to go on a date with a friend of her sister. She felt anxiety about the possibility of violence, and a lack of confidence in recognizing whether he could be trusted. Given that Carmen had limited experience in nonabusive relationships, her therapist helped her to make a list of acceptable and unacceptable behaviors to watch out for. They agreed on a plan for what to do if he behaved in an unacceptable manner, including to check with her sister if she was unsure.

Session Transcript

This session transcript is taken from Session 9, after Carmen and her therapist had completed a detailed narrative of the first rape she experienced.

THERAPIST: You've done such a brilliant job with this. I'm really impressed.

CARMEN: I didn't think I would be able to say it all.

THERAPIST: You've said lots, and we've got it written down now. How does it feel to see it?

CARMEN: It's a bit much, you know, but I'm glad I did it.

THERAPIST: Are you feeling OK? Are you fully in the here and now?

CARMEN: Yes, I'm here, I've got my ball! (*showing the therapist her stress ball*)

THERAPIST: That's great. Are you OK to talk a bit more about what we've written down?

CARMEN: Yes.

THERAPIST: OK, good. Tell me if you want a little break or if you need anything. Squeeze the ball if you feel like you are losing touch, yes?

CARMEN: I am. I will.

THERAPIST: So, I know the whole story is really horrible, but sometimes there are certain moments which are stronger than others, that feel really bad. Are there any moments like that here?

CARMEN: When he is on me and I can't move. And he pressing here (*indicating her throat*).

THERAPIST: On your neck?

CARMEN: Yes, I can't breathe, too scary. I dream about it, and I wake up like this (*gasping*).

THERAPIST: That must be very scary.

CARMEN: Very scary and, I don't know . . .

THERAPIST: It gives you another feeling, too?

CARMEN: Him on me, it's so nasty, makes me (*shuddering and scratching her arms*) . . .

THERAPIST: It feels nasty? What kind of nasty? Like it makes you feel dirty?

CARMEN: Nasty, dirty, bad.

THERAPIST: You are scratching your arms a bit. I don't want you to hurt yourself. Can you squeeze the ball instead?

CARMEN: Yes.

THERAPIST: Well done. So, with this moment, when he was on you and pressing on your neck, what were you thinking? What was in your mind?

CARMEN: That maybe he will kill me. He is very heavy, and I can't breathe.

THERAPIST: So you were thinking he might kill you? It might sound a strange question, but what would have been the worst thing about that?

CARMEN: Well for me it would be bad, I am so young. But also it is disgrace for my family.

THERAPIST: Can you explain a bit more about that to me?

CARMEN: I don't know. People would talk about it in the town, it would be a big thing. And he is an important man, people know him. He would say it was my fault maybe.

THERAPIST: Your fault that he killed you?

CARMEN: Yes, he is clever. He would make it like it was my fault.

THERAPIST: OK, so at that moment you were thinking "I can't breathe; he might kill me, and I would be causing a disgrace to my family, people will think it is my fault."

CARMEN: Yes, all that.

THERAPIST: And you were feeling frightened, and also nasty, dirty? Tell me more about that.

CARMEN: It's like I am covered in him, he is sweaty, disgusting. And I am wrong somehow . . .

THERAPIST: So he is sweaty and disgusting, and it is also making you feel disgusting?

CARMEN: I think it is the sex thing. You know, in my country, young girl has sex, she is dirty.

THERAPIST: Even when you are married?

CARMEN: Well, not so much, but this wasn't normal, didn't seem like normal husband–wife sex. It was wrong somehow, so it seemed like I was making it wrong.

THERAPIST: OK, let me check if I understand: He is disgusting, but also you are feeling like you are doing something wrong because this isn't normal sex?

CARMEN: Yes, and my dad always said I was a slut, you know, even though I didn't do nothing, so maybe that was in my mind.

THERAPIST: I think you've noticed something really important there. It makes sense that some of those thoughts were influenced by everything you had already been through, like some of the things your dad used to say and do.

CARMEN: Yes, he got in my mind too much. In some ways my dad and my husband were the same. Both want to scare me, be the big man.

THERAPIST: Yes, that's interesting, isn't it? And it makes sense that some of the things they said to you got in your head. One thing I want us to do together is try and understand whether what they said is true.

CARMEN: I know it isn't true, most of it. I didn't know then, but I know now. And sometimes it is hard to believe it. If I feel down, it's like they are still here, still telling me things.

THERAPIST: That makes a lot of sense. Do you remember how we talked about, with PTSD, that things from the past can feel like they are happening now? You might know it isn't true now, but when the memories come, or you feel down, it feels true again.

CARMEN: Yes, exactly that.

THERAPIST: OK, so let's think about how you were thinking that night, on your wedding night, when he was pressing on top of you. And we can start thinking about whether those things are true, and whether we know anything now which is different.

Commentary on the Case Example

Building an Alliance

A major priority, especially when working with someone with interpersonal difficulties, is to build a strong therapeutic alliance. Carmen had been persuaded to attend treatment by her sister, and initially expressed reservations about the process. The therapist was concerned that she might drop out of treatment, so she focused primarily on creating a shared understanding of Carmen's difficulties and creating hope that they could be overcome. Having a better understanding of what was causing and maintaining her problems helped Carmen to believe that they were treatable. Engagement was also increased by teaching Carmen usable skills during the early sessions, such as stimulus discrimination, giving her more control over her symptoms and helping her to see that therapy could be helpful. This took priority in early sessions over beginning the trauma narrative. It was important that Carmen have control over the pace of therapy, and not feel pushed or coerced at any point.

Working with Risk

Another priority was to establish Carmen's safety. This involved developing an accurate profile of the nature and frequency of Carmen's self-harm and any risky behavior when she dissociated. In Carmen's case, the self-harm occurred when she was dissociating, and was an effective means of "grounding" her. Carmen found the behavior distressing, and was willing to learn alternative methods of returning her attention to the here and now. Given Carmen's history of abuse by others, the therapist hypothesized that there was also an element of self-punishment to her self-harm. Carmen found it hard to identify what thoughts triggered the urge to self-harm, but she did link it to intrusive memories of sexual assaults by her husband. These memories, and their related meanings, were prioritized in treatment.

Carmen was suffering from dissociative episodes, both in the form of flashbacks and "blanks," in which she was unaware of her surroundings for periods of time. In such cases, it is important to assess whether a client is at risk when dissociated, for example, if he or she is driving or entering risky situations. In Carmen's case, this had occurred on only one occasion, when she had wandered onto a bridge after a row with a neighbor. Again, identification of triggers and practicing stimulus discrimination were effective in reducing this risk in Carmen's case. However, the dissociative episodes and self-harm were monitored throughout treatment, especially while working on the trauma memories, and narrative writing was used as an alternative to imaginal reliving to minimize the risk of triggering a dissociative flashback.

Carmen's risk from others was also assessed. She did not judge either her father or ex-husband to currently pose a risk, as they continued to live in Colombia, and there had been no recent contact or threats made. In cases where individuals are still at risk, for example from ex-partners, establishing safety should be a priority before treatment continues. This usually involves developing a safety plan, and contacting the police and relevant safeguarding organizations.

Comorbid Social and Psychological Problems

Like most people with PTSD, Carmen met criteria for at least one comorbid psychological disorder. In her case, depression had developed as a consequence of her traumatic experiences and of having PTSD. The main maintenance factors in Carmen's depression were negative, self-critical thinking and a reduction in positive activities. The symptoms of depression, which did not interfere with her PTSD treatment and were regarded as a secondary problem, began to improve as her PTSD symptoms lifted. In other cases, comorbid conditions would require treatment in their own right if deemed to be the primary problem for a client, if related closely to the client's treatment goals, or if they interfered with PTSD treatment or remained problematic even after PTSD has been successfully addressed.

Social problems are also common for individuals with PTSD and, likewise, may take priority over PTSD treatment if they having a significantly negative impact. In Carmen's case, her main problem was with housing, which, although not an urgent issue, was causing her distress. Her therapist helped her problem-solve the issue and helped her access the Citizen's Advice Bureau, and wrote a letter in support of her housing application. They then agreed to prioritize work on PTSD for the remainder of the sessions.

Working Cross-Culturally

Cultural beliefs may influence an individual's personal meanings of trauma and their attempts to come to terms with trauma memories in helpful and unhelpful ways. As CT-PTSD uses an individual case formulation, treatment is tailored to the individual's beliefs, including cultural beliefs. Carmen often spoke about gender roles in Colombian culture and on the normalization of violence within relationships. The therapist took a stance of empathic curiosity, encouraging Carmen to reflect on how her cultural background had impacted on her beliefs. Updates to memories must feel relevant to clients in order to be effective, so the therapist also took care to work collaboratively with Carmen to identify updates and to make sure that they felt personally meaningful.

English was Carmen's second language, and she spoke it well, without the need for interpreter. The therapist took care to avoid jargon and to check understanding, using Carmen's words where possible. CT-PTSD can be conducted via an interpreter, if needed, although awareness of the additional interpersonal dynamics requires consideration (Tribe & Raval, 2014), and some practical adaptations, such as longer sessions, may be needed. Additional issues should also be considered when working with refugees and asylum seekers; for further details, see Grey and Young (2008).

Working with Multiple Trauma Memories

Working with clients who have experienced multiple traumatic experiences raises several issues, including a decision about which memories to prioritize. It can be helpful to make a timeline of the client's life, or the period in which he or she experienced traumas, to start putting the events in the context of a narrative, to identify the most troublesome experiences, and to understand when different beliefs developed. Working on the most problematic event, in terms of distress and frequency of reexperiencing symptoms (using an intrusions diary can help identify this, if needed), has the biggest impact on PTSD symptoms. However, not all clients are willing to tackle the worst trauma first and, if there are concerns about risk, dissociation, or dropout, it can be preferable to work on a less distressing memory first that has straightforward updates, such as "I did not die." This can often have the effect of demonstrating the updating procedure and, hopefully, its effectiveness, thereby building confidence to repeat it with other traumas.

Carmen had identified five traumatic events that she reexperienced, all from adulthood. Although her childhood experiences were traumatic, she did not reexperience them. They were, however, very important in formulating her PTSD, as they laid the foundation for the development of relevant beliefs such as "I attract bad people" and "I deserve to be punished," and influenced how she experienced the adult traumas. As such, her childhood experiences were discussed in therapy but were not the subject of detailed narrative writing and updating. Had she been experiencing intrusive memories, nightmares, or flashbacks to her childhood, these techniques could have been applied. However, it should be noted that CT-PTSD has been developed and tested primarily for traumatic events in adolescence and adulthood, and is only recently being subjected to rigorous testing with clients who primarily experienced early childhood trauma.

Working with Long-Standing Beliefs

Many clients who have experienced multiple traumatic experiences, especially early life trauma, present with long-standing beliefs that are strongly held. These beliefs require targeting in treatment, in order to develop meaningful alternatives. Carmen had believed since childhood that there was something defective about her that attracted bad people, and meant that she deserved punishment. She often experienced "head–heart lag," for example, knowing that her experiences were not her fault but not truly believing it. Carmen and her therapist addressed these beliefs with a range of techniques. As well as cognitive discussion techniques, such as drawing up a list of evidence for and against her beliefs, they also arranged a survey to hear opinions from a range of other people. To help Carmen connect with this new information at an emotional level, the therapist used experiential techniques, such as writing a compassionate letter and reading it to her younger self in imagery.

One of Carmen's beliefs was that she could no longer trust her judgment and would be vulnerable to further abuse in the future. Because Carmen had very limited experience of nonabusive relationships, she found it difficult to clearly judge what behavior within a relationship was acceptable, and what was a warning sign of future violence. To address this, Carmen and her therapist took a more skills-based approach to develop a "warning sign" system to help Carmen recognize, and deal with, risky situations.

Virtual Site Visits

Returning to the scene of the trauma is a recommended procedure in CT-PTSD. However, in some cases, there are practical or safety considerations that make it impossible, for example, when the trauma happened in another country. In these cases, a virtual site visit can be used. Online tools such as Google Street View and Google Earth can be used to locate the scene of the trauma. This allows many of the same activities as a real site visit, such as noticing the differences between the trauma memory and the site as it currently appears. For Carmen, seeing how her old street had changed made the memories of domestic abuse feel more remote. She also believed that she would see her ex-husband when she looked up her old address (a sign of the "nowness" of her memories) and felt relieved that he no longer seemed to live at their old house.

Conclusion

CT-PTSD is an effective treatment for individuals with PTSD, including those with more complex presentations. The formulation-based treatment allows for flexibility in how and when different interventions are applied according to clinical need and client choice. The focus on individual meanings of the trauma and its consequences means that treatment is highly individualized to each client. The therapist aims to see the trauma through the eyes of the client, and help the client to develop less threatening appraisals of what has occurred, which can then be linked back into the trauma memory. As such, CT-PTSD is a collaborative and flexible approach to addressing complex traumatic stress disorders.

Acknowledgment

The development and evaluation of CT-PTSD was funded by the Wellcome Trust (069777, 200796).

References

Bisson, J. I., Roberts, N. P., Andrew, M., Cooper, R., & Lewis, C. (2013). Psychological therapies for chronic post-traumatic stress disorder (PTSD) in adults. *Cochrane Database of Systematic Reviews, 12,* CD003388.

Beierl, E. T., Böllinghaus, I., Clark, D. M., Glucksman, E., & Ehlers, A. (2019, September 11). Cognitive paths from trauma to posttraumatic stress disorder: A prospective study of Ehlers and Clark's model in survivors of assaults or road traffic collisions. *Psychological Medicine, 11,* 1–10.

Brewin, C. R., Fuchkan, N., Huntley, Z., Robertson, M., Thompson, M., Scragg, P., . . . Ehlers, A. (2010). Outreach and screening following the 2005 London bombings: Usage and outcomes. *Psychological Medicine, 40,* 2049–2057.

Duffy, M., Gillespie, K., & Clark, D. M. (2007). Post-traumatic stress disorder in the context of terrorism and other civil conflict in Northern Ireland: Randomised controlled trial. *British Medical Journal, 334,* 1147.

Ehlers, A. (2013). Trauma-focused cognitive behavior therapy for posttraumatic stress disorder and acute stress disorder. In G. Simos & S. G. Hofmann (Eds.), *Textbook of CBT for anxiety disorders* (pp. 161–189). New York: Wiley.

Ehlers, A., & Clark, D. M. (2000). A cognitive model of posttraumatic stress disorder. *Behaviour Research and Therapy, 38,* 319–345.

Ehlers, A., Clark, D. M., Hackmann, A., McManus, F., & Fennell, M. (2005). Cognitive therapy for post-traumatic stress disorder: Development and evaluation. *Behaviour Research and Therapy, 43,* 413–431.

Ehlers, A., Clark, D. M., Hackmann, A., McManus, F., Fennell, M., Herbert, C., & Mayou, R. (2003). A randomized controlled trial of cognitive therapy, a self-help booklet, and repeated assessments as early interventions for posttraumatic stress disorder. *Archives of General Psychiatry, 60,* 1024–1032.

Ehlers, A., Ehring, T., & Kleim, B. (2012). Information processing in posttraumatic stress disorder. In J. G. Beck & D. M. Sloan (Eds.), *The Oxford handbook of traumatic disorders* (pp. 191–218). New York: Oxford University Press.

Ehlers, A., Grey, N., Stott, R., Warnock-Parkes, W., Wild, J., . . . Clark, D. M. (2019a). *Effectiveness of cognitive therapy in routine clinical care: Second phase implementation.* Manuscript in preparation.

Ehlers, A., Grey, N., Wild, J., Stott, R., Liness, S., Deale, A., . . . Clark, D. M. (2013). Implementation of cognitive therapy in routine clinical care: Effectiveness and moderators of outcome in a consecutive sample. *Behaviour Research and Therapy, 51,* 742–752.

Ehlers, A., Hackmann, A., Grey, N., Wild, J., Liness, S., . . . Clark, D. M. (2014). A randomized controlled trial of 7-day intensive and standard weekly cognitive therapy for PTSD and emotion-focused supportive therapy. *American Journal of Psychiatry. 171,* 294–304.

Ehlers, A., Maercker, A., & Boos, A. (2000). PTSD following political imprisonment: The role of mental defeat, alienation, and permanent change. *Journal of Abnormal Psychology, 109,* 45–55.

Ehlers, A., Mayou, R. A., & Bryant, B. (1998). Psychological predictors of chronic PTSD after motor vehicle accidents. *Journal of Abnormal Psychology, 107,* 508–519.

Ehlers, A., Wild, J., Stott, R., Warnock-Parkes, E., Grey, N., & Clark, D. M. (2019b). *Efficient use of therapist time in the treatment of posttraumatic stress disorder: A randomized clinical trial of brief self-study assisted and standard weekly cognitive therapy for PTSD.* Manuscript submitted for publication.

Ehring, T., Ehlers, A., & Glucksman, E. (2008). Do cognitive models help in predicting the severity of posttraumatic stress disorder, phobia and depression after motor vehicle accidents?: A prospective longitudinal study. *Journal of Consulting and Clinical Psychology, 76,* 219–230.

Foa, E. B., Ehlers, A., Clark, D. M., Tolin, D., & Orsillo, S. (1999). The Post-Traumatic Cognitions Inventory (PTCI): Development and validation. *Psychological Assessment, 11,* 303–314.

Foa, E. B., & Rothbaum, B. O. (1998). *Treating the trauma of rape: Cognitive-behavioral therapy for PTSD.* New York: Guilford Press.

Gillespie, K., Duffy, M., Hackmann, A., & Clark, D. M. (2002). Community based cognitive therapy in the treatment of post-traumatic stress disorder following the Omagh bomb. *Behaviour Research and Therapy, 40,* 345–357.

Grey, N., & Young, K. (2008). Cognitive behaviour therapy with refugees and asylum seekers experiencing traumatic stress symptoms. *Behavioural and Cognitive Psychotherapy, 36,* 3–19.

Kleim, B., Ehlers, A., & Glucksman, E. (2007). Early predictors of chronic post-traumatic stress disorder in assault survivors. *Psychological Medicine, 37,* 1457–1468.

Kleim, B., Ehring, T, & Ehlers, A. (2012). Perceptual processing advantages for trauma-related visual cues in posttraumatic stress disorder. *Psychological Medicine, 42,* 173–181.

Meiser-Stedman, R., Smith, P., McKinnon, A., Dixon, C., Trickey, D., Ehlers, A., . . . Dalgleish, T. (2017). Cognitive therapy as an early intervention for PTSD in children and adolescents: A randomized controlled trial addressing preliminary efficacy and mechanisms of action. *Journal of Child Psychology and Psychiatry, 58*(5), 623–633.

Murray, H., El-Leithy, S., & Billings, J. (2017). Intensive cognitive therapy for post-traumatic stress disorder in routine clinical practice: A matched comparison audit. *British Journal of Clinical Psychology, 56,* 476–478.

Murray, H., Merritt, C., & Grey, N. (2015). Returning to the scene of the trauma in PTSD treatment—why, how and when? *Cognitive Behaviour Therapist, 8,* e28.

Resick, P. A., & Schnicke, M. K. (1993). *Cognitive processing therapy for rape victims.* Newbury Park, CA: SAGE.

Smith, P., Yule, W., Perrin, S., Tranah, T., Dalgleish, T., & Clark, D. M. (2007). Cognitive behavioral therapy for PTSD in children and adolescents: A preliminary randomized controlled trial. *Journal of the American Academy of Child and Adolescent Psychiatry, 46,* 1051–1061.

Tribe, R., & Raval, H. (Eds.). (2014). *Working with interpreters in mental health.* London, UK: Routledge.

Woodward, E., Hackmann, A., Wild, J., Grey, N., Clark, D. M., & Ehlers, A. (2017). Effects of psychotherapies for posttraumatic stress disorder on sleep disturbances: Results from a randomized clinical trial. *Behaviour Research and Therapy, 97,* 75–85.

CHAPTER 11

Cognitive Processing Therapy

KATHLEEN M. CHARD
ELLEN T. HEALY
COLLEEN E. MARTIN

Cognitive processing therapy (CPT), a manualized, evidence-based treatment, was initially developed by Resick and Schnicke (1993) to treat posttraumatic stress disorder (PTSD) in individuals with sexual trauma histories. This treatment is grounded in cognitive theory, which posits that certain maladaptive posttraumatic cognitions develop at the time of the trauma and can serve to maintain PTSD symptoms over time (Resick, Monson, & Chard, 2017). These cognitions can be reinforced with evidence from prior events or with information obtained from future events. Beliefs may exist about the individual's role in the cause of the trauma, potentially leading the individual to internalize blame for the event, whereas others may place inappropriate blame on others involved in the event. The beliefs the individual has about the trauma may be distorted and unrealistic based on his or her interpretation of the event, which then serves to maintain emotions such as guilt and shame. CPT also incorporates components of information processing theory, which posits that when individuals take in information that is discrepant from their existing schemas (i.e., traumatic events), the information can either be assimilated into the existing schemas, or existing beliefs are changed to reflect the discrepant information (Hollon & Garber, 1988). When assimilation occurs, the way the individual views the event may be altered in order to fit the trauma into his or her existing belief system (e.g., "I must have done something to cause it"). When change of existing schemas or beliefs is based on the trauma, the individual may then change his or her thinking about the self, others, and the world in extreme or exaggerated ways (e.g., "No one can be trusted"). Strategies employed during CPT, such as identification of maladaptive thoughts (which in CPT are called "stuck points") and the use of Socratic dialogue, allow for the development of more balanced and realistic beliefs.

In addition to a focus on cognitions, CPT addresses the wide range of emotions that can stem from a traumatic event. The CPT model differentiates "natural" and "manufactured" emotions that individuals with PTSD may experience following a trauma. Natural emotions are those that are universal and flow directly from the event (e.g., fear elicited by the fight–flight–freeze response), whereas manufactured emotions are based on the maladaptive thoughts about the event (e.g., guilt based on the individual's belief that it was his or her fault). When the cognitions underlying manufactured emotions are modified to reflect more accurate beliefs about the trauma, the manufactured emotions are likely to subside.

For individuals with trauma histories, certain core beliefs (e.g., "I am unlovable"; "I am unworthy") develop and/or become reinforced at the time of the trauma, and this is particularly true for those with more complex PTSD presentations. Negative beliefs about the self, others, and the world may be repeatedly reinforced if the individual has been exposed to multiple traumatic events from childhood through adulthood. CPT allows for a specific focus on how individuals see themselves, other people, and the world, as well as a focus on where these beliefs originated to determine whether the thoughts came from an unbiased and dependable source.

Evolution of CPT

In its inception, CPT was conducted in groups for female survivors of sexual trauma. Several randomized controlled trials were then conducted to determine its efficacy in treating PTSD in a variety of formats, with a variety of trauma samples. A version of CPT created by Kathleen Chard specifically for individuals with childhood sexual assault trauma (CPT-SA) includes a combined group and individual format. For this population, the treatment included additional topics of family rules, developmental capabilities of children, assertive communication, ways of giving and taking power, and social support (Chard, 2005).

Given the early evidence-base in treating PTSD stemming from various types of traumatic events (e.g., sexual assault, interpersonal violence, combat), Resick and colleagues (2008) wanted to better understand the mechanisms of change in CPT, so they conducted a trial that dismantled the components of CPT. This study highlighted that CPT with a written trauma account did not result is better outcomes than CPT without the trauma account. Given evidence that both modes of CPT are effective, CPT is now offered with ("CPT + A") or without the use of a written trauma account ("CPT") (Resick et al., 2017). CPT can be delivered in individual, group, and combined group and individual formats. Additionally, based on a study by Galovski, Blain, Mott, Elwood, and Houle (2012), there is now an appreciation that patients benefit from CPT that has variable length based on their treatment needs. The protocol has also been disseminated nationally and internationally, and most notably, throughout the U.S. Veterans Healthcare Administration both in person and via telehealth. It has also been translated into 12 different languages to provide treatment across cultures.

Evidence for CPT

There is a substantial evidence base to support CPT for PTSD in a wide variety of samples. CPT and/or CPT + A have been compared in randomized controlled trials (RCTs) to diverse comparison conditions, including prolonged exposure (PE), present-centered therapy, dialogical exposure therapy, treatment as usual, and wait-list conditions (e.g., Resick, Nishith, Weaver, Astin, & Feuer, 2002; Suris, Link-Malcolm, Chard, Ahn, & North, 2013; Butollo, Karl, Konig, & Rosner, 2015; Resick et al., 2015). Several meta-analytic studies have also revealed high effect sizes for CPT + A (e.g., Haagen, Smid, Knipscheer, & Kleber, 2015; Watts et al., 2013). The first RCT conducted compared CPT + A versus PE versus a minimal attention wait-list condition in a sample of women in the community with histories of rape (85% had additional interpersonal traumas; 41% had childhood sexual abuse histories; Resick et al., 2002). In this study, there were few differences between the two active treatments; however, individuals in the CPT + A condition had significantly more reductions in guilt, health-related concerns, hopelessness, and suicidal ideation. Resick, Suvak, Johnides, Mitchell, and Iverson (2012a) conducted a long-term follow-up study with the participants used in this first RCT and found that there were no differences between CPT + A and PE on PTSD and depression symptoms 5–10 years following treatment.

CPT-SA was compared to a wait-list condition in a sample of individuals with histories of childhood sexual abuse (Chard, 2005). There were significant differences between CPT-SA and the wait-list condition on PTSD symptoms, depression, and dissociation. Specifically, for those in the CPT-SA condition, only 7% met criteria for a PTSD diagnosis at posttreatment, 3% met criteria for a diagnosis at 3-month follow-up, and 6% met criteria at 12-month follow-up. In the first controlled study with a veteran sample, Monson and colleagues (2006) compared CPT + A to treatment as usual and found that 40% of the sample had remitted from PTSD after 12 sessions of CPT + A. The findings from this study highlighted CPT's applicability to samples with different types of index traumas. In order to expand its applicability to real-world settings, Forbes and colleagues (2012) conducted an RCT examining CPT for military-related PTSD delivered by therapists in Australian veteran's community clinics. Compared to a treatment-as-usual condition, CPT+A was associated with significant reductions in PTSD symptoms, anxiety, depression, and improvement in social relationships and dyadic relationships at posttreatment.

Studies of secondary treatment outcomes relevant to complex PTSD have been based on data from these studies. Specifically, analyses have examined the role of childhood physical and sexual abuse, as well as borderline personality disorder characteristics, on CPT outcomes. The effects of childhood abuse on treatment outcomes in the CPT + A versus PE versus minimal attention RCT (Resick et al., 2002) were examined, and no significant differences existed in dissociation, dysfunctional sexual behavior, impaired self-reference, or tension reduction behavior in those with and without childhood sexual abuse. In Resick et al.'s (2008) dismantling study, participants with low pretreatment levels of dissociation responded best to CPT, while those high in dissociation at pretreatment responded best to CPT + A (Resick et al., 2012a). Additionally, there were no differences in PTSD symptom severity at posttreatment for those with or without histories of childhood sexual or physical abuse. Interestingly, participants with more frequent childhood abuse fared better in CPT, as compared to CPT + A or wait-list (Resick et al., 2008; Resick, Suvak, & Wells, 2014). In a separate study, female veterans with military sexual trauma histories did not significantly differ on any pretreatment variables or on any PTSD outcomes regardless of whether they did or did not have histories of childhood sexual abuse (Walter, Buckley, Simpson, & Chard, 2014).

Finally, two studies have examined borderline personality characteristics in association with treatment outcomes in CPT. Individuals with high levels of borderline personality disorder characteristics, who also had more severe PTSD and depression symptoms, had greater gains in CPT than did individuals with low levels of borderline personality disorder characteristics (Clarke, Rizvi, & Resick, 2008). In a residential PTSD treatment setting, no significant differences in PTSD treatment gains existed between those with and without personality disorders; however, there were significant pretreatment differences in depression symptoms. Individuals with personality disorders experienced greater improvement in depressive symptoms over the course of CPT (Walter, Bolte, Owens, & Chard, 2012). In other studies, clients with complex PTSD presentations also have shown no differences from those without complex PTSD in dropout rates from CPT (e.g., Holder, Holliday, Pai, & Suris, 2017).

Clinical Application of CPT to Complex PTSD

Client Engagement in CPT

CPT actively encourages significant client engagement in therapeutic process. Although CPT has specific exercises for each session, the content for these exercises and ultimate outcomes are decided by the client. The therapist is a facilitator and guide through each worksheet. To set the stage, in the first session of CPT, the therapist discusses the role of avoidance in treatment with the client in the context of avoidance symptoms maintaining PTSD symptomatology. This transparent discussion focuses on anticipating avoidance (e.g., homework noncompliance, missing sessions) and how therapist and client can work to solve any individualized avoidance-related issues that are interfering with treatment. Because avoidance of internal and external experiences is typically heightened in individuals with PTSD, perhaps even more so in those with complex PTSD, therapist and client discuss the costs of avoidance the client has experienced as a result of avoiding the trauma(s). By normalizing these topics and addressing them at the outset of treatment, clients have an opportunity to discuss their level of engagement in the treatment and gain a better understanding of the rationale behind the treatment. The structure of CPT lends itself well to populations that present with instability and dysregulation. The client is informed of the expectations and structure of the therapy from the very beginning of treatment, which can provide stability during times of dysregulation.

Throughout CPT, the therapist is encouraged to explicitly discuss thoughts and emotions related to completing certain assignments. For example, the therapist assigns an "Impact Statement" in Session 1 for the client to complete on why the client believes the trauma occurred and how it has affected his or her beliefs in five areas: safety, trust, power and control, esteem, and intimacy. When this is assigned, the client is invited to explore any thoughts that arise about completing the assignment and/or engaging in treatment on an ABC Worksheet. This sheet guides the client in identifying antecedents ("A"), associated beliefs/thoughts ("B"), and consequences/feelings ("C") related to trauma, as well as events that occur on a daily basis. During this process, the client identifies his or her beliefs about completing the assignment and emotions connected to these beliefs. The client also evaluates whether these beliefs are (1) realistic and (2) whether there is anything else he or she can say to him- or herself in the future.

Individuals with complex PTSD often naturally, or with the assistance of the therapist, focus more heavily on beliefs that arise from their experiences with, and their expressions of, emotions. These emotions-focused beliefs are also addressed throughout treatment (e.g., "If I feel scared, I must cut myself"). For individuals with complex PTSD, there are likely several core beliefs about themselves and expressing emotions that have been severely influenced by trauma(s) throughout their lives. Based on the cognitive theoretical framework of CPT, if beliefs can be modified to become more realistic, the emotional responses associated with them will be more manageable. If stuck points about experiencing and showing emotions are addressed early in treatment, it is more likely that the individual who experiences significant affect dysregulation may see greater benefit from therapy as a result of using these skills from the outset of treatment.

The Therapeutic Relationship in CPT

In CPT, the relationship between client and therapist provides the important context for the client to learn cognitive strategies and to challenge stuck points. For clients with complex PTSD, often histories of interpersonal trauma can impact trust and willingness to fully engage in a therapeutic relationship. Thus, in CPT, the focus is on reevaluating beliefs about opening up to others and establishing relationships, and specifically a focus on five themes that may impact relationships (safety, trust, power and control, esteem, and intimacy). For example, if there are specific stuck points about trust in interpersonal relationships, the therapist can use the therapeutic relationship as evidence to help clients challenge their thoughts.

The therapeutic relationship also allows for testing of stuck points related to showing emotion; often the therapist may be the first person the individual has told about the trauma(s). Through this experiential approach of emotion, rather than avoidance, clients can learn strategies to appropriately regulate their emotions by identifying and describing them with the therapist. Additionally, the therapeutic alliance allows clients to have a space to challenge their long-standing beliefs about the trauma and themselves in a secure setting. For those with complex PTSD symptoms, beliefs about trusting others may be more long-standing due to the potentially repeated and interpersonal nature of traumas that lead to complex PTSD symptoms. Some therapists have expressed a concern that clients require additional supportive sessions prior to starting trauma-focused therapy, but that concern has not been borne out in the data on CPT, because clients with complex PTSD do not drop out of CPT more than clients without complex PTSD, and it is the working alliance in early CPT sessions that is most predictive of ultimate treatment outcome (Brady, Warnock-Parkes, Barker, & Ehlers, 2015; Forbes et al., 2012).

Targeting Complex PTSD Symptoms in CPT

The symptoms of complex PTSD align with the primary targets of CPT. The primary goal of CPT is to address maladaptive cognitions about the trauma, as well as about the self, others, and the world, to create more balanced belief systems. Research has shown that negative trauma-related cognitions about the self are central features of complex PTSD (Karatzias et al., 2018). Those with childhood trauma and histories of multiple interpersonal traumas have negative belief systems that likely influence other complex PTSD symptoms such as affect dysregulation, relational difficulties, and dissociation. Therefore, the CPT model fits well for this population, as these cognitions are addressed beginning in the first sessions of the treatment.

CPT also directly targets difficulties with affect dysregulation, which is another primary symptom of complex PTSD. By teaching clients to explicitly identify and label their automatic thoughts and subsequent emotions, they are learning to engage their frontal lobe and decrease activity in the amygdala (e.g., Hariri, Mattay, Tessitore, Fera, & Weinberger, 2003). Clients with complex PTSD may never have learned how to identify emotions or learned that their emotions were valid, and CPT provides them with a corrective experience to engage in emotion identification. Dissociation, also a symptom of complex PTSD, is addressed during CPT through the modification of stuck points and decreasing avoidance of the trauma and trauma reminders. In a sample of women with PTSD who were enrolled in CPT, there were significant reductions in dissociative symptoms from pre- to posttreatment that were maintained at

6-month follow-up (Resick, Williams, Suvak, Monson, & Gradus, 2012b). In another study examining differences in men and women with PTSD enrolled in CPT, dissociative symptoms were measured as a secondary outcome and significantly decreased across treatment overall; however, women initially evidenced more rapid decreases than men in dissociative symptoms (Galovski, Blain, Chappuis, & Fletcher, 2013). CPT has also been shown to decrease symptoms of dissociation in a sample of individuals with eating disorders, which is a population that shares overlapping symptoms with complex PTSD (e.g., Mitchell, Wells, Mendes, & Resick, 2012).

In the beginning sessions of CPT, the therapist provides the client with psychoeducation about how the goals of CPT are to help facilitate the natural recovery process from PTSD through modification of maladaptive cognitions and through emotional processing of the traumatic event. The therapist explains that traumatic events can shatter preexisting beliefs the client had about him- or herself if the client had generally positive experiences in childhood. For others, who grew up with more negative experiences, the traumatic event reinforces preexisting beliefs about their worth and self-concept. In this portion of the psychoeducation, the therapist can tailor this discussion specifically to the experiences of those with complex PTSD presentations regarding the beliefs that have been created and solidified through repeated trauma exposure. Discussion of the role of emotions in trauma in CPT is framed by description of the fight–flight–freeze response, as well as distinguishing between natural and manufactured emotions. For example, those with complex PTSD who have difficulties regulating affect may in fact experience the fight–flight–freeze response during periods of dysregulation. They may feel that they are constantly under threat; thus, their fear network becomes activated, making it difficult to regulate emotions. The therapist explains this process and why it may be difficult to regulate emotions when the amygdala is activated. Additionally, dissociative symptoms can occur in the context of this fear response. CPT teaches clients how to engage the frontal lobe during these processes, to increase affect regulation and decrease dissociative symptoms.

In the second half of treatment, individuals are asked to engage in behavioral activities to promote increased use of the new alternative beliefs they have created to rebuild their self-concept. The practice assignment following Session 10 asks clients to do one nice thing for themselves daily and to practice giving and receiving compliments without judgment. These activities are pertinent to those with complex PTSD, reinforcing newly formed alternative beliefs about the self. By practicing new beliefs through the behavioral assignments, clients may come to repair the distorted views previously held about their worth and overall self-concept.

CPT and Trauma Processing

Trauma processing in CPT involves helping clients identify what they have been telling themselves about the trauma, then using Socratic dialogue to help them evaluate their thinking. By exploring the context of the trauma, learning to recognize hindsight bias, and differentiating between what was unforeseeable from what was intended, clients can begin to see their trauma in a more accurate light. As this happens, the disruptive manufactured emotions are reduced, and there is greater opportunity to feel natural emotions and grieve losses.

In CPT + A, in addition to trauma processing through Socratic dialogue and cognitive worksheets, clients are given the practice assignment of writing a trauma account. This assignment entails writing out a detailed description of the traumatic event (i.e., thoughts, feelings, sensations) from the time they realized they were in danger until the danger was over. This account is written in the past tense to highlight the point that the event is a memory, and that the trauma is not happening now. Clients are prepared for this assignment by completing ABC Worksheets on any thoughts that arise in writing about their trauma (e.g., "I will be retraumatized" or "If I write this, I will completely lose control"). Therapist and client work collaboratively together to determine whether these thoughts about completing the account are realistic, and they generate alternative thoughts that are more realistic for the client to use.

After the client has written the trauma account, the client reads the account aloud to the therapist. The processing of this account is focused on the natural emotions experienced by the client while writing it and reading it in session. The trauma account gives the client a chance to organize the memory and determine whether he or she is leaving any important details out, and to experience any emotions that he or she has not let him- or herself feel since the trauma occurred. Once the client has read the account and identified his or her emotional reaction to it, the therapist uses Socratic dialogue to focus on stuck points. Of particular relevance to those with complex PTSD is resolving stuck points involving negative, trauma-related cognitions about the self and their potential role in the event(s).

Clinical Case Study Example

The following CPT session transcript excerpts with "Jessica," a composite client, are presented as a clinical case example of treating complex PTSD with CPT, highlighting common issues and concerns across a range of CPT sessions. Jessica, a 37-year-old African American, divorced female, has a history of repeated childhood sexual abuse perpetrated by her stepfather when she was ages 5–11. Additionally, she was raped when she was 18 years old, while she was drinking at a party. She married at age 25; her husband was physically abusive throughout their marriage, and she divorced him after 5 years. She has two children from her marriage, who are now ages 8 and 10. She endorses suicidal thoughts and has a history of multiple suicide attempts by ingesting pills, though no attempt resulted in medical intervention. She has a long history of polysubstance use, and she continues to use alcohol almost every day.

CPT Session 1: Selecting an Index Trauma and Addressing Avoidance

Session 1 of CPT involves introducing the treatment rationale and describing PTSD symptoms and etiology. Additionally, with someone who has a history of multiple traumas, determining the index trauma is an important task during this session. The traumatic experience that bothers the client the most is selected for the index trauma, then this trauma serves as the starting focus for treatment. The therapist explains the rationale for selecting an index trauma while also validating that selecting one trauma does not mean that the other experiences are not addressed in treatment. Selecting an index trauma can be particularly challenging for those who have experienced prolonged, repeated traumas and/or many types of traumas, but it remains important to select an incident of trauma rather than selecting a prolonged period of abuse on which to focus to identify the point at which the client may have become stuck in recovery and to reduce potential avoidance. Strategies for helping the client to determine the index trauma include asking about the focus of current reexperiencing symptoms, looking at a timeline of when PTSD symptoms worsened, and inquiring about what events the client avoids thinking about the most.

Introducing the role of avoidance in PTSD is an important part of CPT Session 1. The discussion should help the client identify ways in which she tends to avoid and to identify ways that avoidance may interfere with treatment, so that therapist and client can prevent this from happening.

THERAPIST: Which trauma do you think bothers you the most?

JESSICA: It's hard to say. It all bothers me.

THERAPIST: I'm sure. I know it's hard, and remember, by choosing to focus on one experience, it doesn't mean the other experiences do not matter. This gives us a focus, a place to start. Is there one experience that you avoid thinking about the most or that you do not want to talk about?

JESSICA: I guess I'd say what my stepfather did to me.

THERAPIST: OK, and that happened several times? Is there a particular incident that bothers you the most?

JESSICA: I don't even remember a lot of the times given how many times it happened. But I do remember a time when I was about 9, and I decided I would stop him, so I fought back, but he was stronger than me and overpowered me. I'd say that really bothers me.

THERAPIST: OK, let's start there. We are going to look at what you are saying to yourself about that event specifically first. Together we will ask questions to examine what the facts were in that situation and whether your conclusions about them are accurate. Then we'll take a broader view from there to look at the impact that event and other experiences have had on your thoughts about yourself and others.

JESSICA: That makes sense.

THERAPIST: Good. As with anytime a person learns a new skill, the more time you put into it, the more you will get out of it. So it will be important to practice the skills you are learning here. However, we know that avoidance is a key part of PTSD and that your desire to avoid thinking about the trauma and avoid feeling emotions that come up is expected. There are many ways people avoid feelings or thinking about their trauma. What are the ways that you avoid?

JESSICA: I'm quite good at avoiding things. I tend to look for things to numb out my feelings. I guess that's why I drink so much. But I hate to be alone, so I avoid that too—sometimes even staying in relationships or friendships that aren't good for me.

THERAPIST: Are there ways in which you can anticipate that your avoidance might interfere with treatment?

JESSICA: Well, yeah. In the past, when I didn't want to deal, I'd just check out—and I missed therapy sessions and stopped answering my phone. When it was really bad, I'd think about killing myself. I guess that's the ultimate level of avoidance.

THERAPIST: These are all things we should look out for and catch when you start avoiding, so we can keep you in therapy, as treatment won't work if you are not here.

JESSICA: I know.

THERAPIST: We want to make sure you are not avoiding your thoughts and feelings, and as you mentioned, alcohol is one of the ways you have coped with your symptoms and avoided emotions. Can you refrain from using alcohol before and right after our sessions, as well as before, during, and after your practice assignments?

JESSICA: I will try.

THERAPIST: Let's check in each session and monitor how your alcohol use is going and whether suicidal thoughts are arising.

CPT Session 3: Addressing Concerns about Escalation of Symptoms

It is not uncommon for clients with a history of emotion regulation concerns to become alarmed if they experience distress in the context of trauma-focused treatment. Often, the avoidance of emotions has been so strong that any feelings that start to arise in the context of treatment may be catastrophized, with clients describing stuck points such as "I can't handle it" or "If I feel my feelings, I will fall apart." Addressing these beliefs as they arise is important to prevent these beliefs from interfering with therapy engagement.

JESSICA: This was a really hard week. I don't think I can do this treatment anymore.

THERAPIST: Why is that?

JESSICA: This is just too much. I am afraid I will fall apart. It feels like I am starting to.

THERAPIST: What would falling apart look like?

JESSICA: I don't know, giving up, not caring anymore.

THERAPIST: Are you having any thoughts of hurting yourself?

JESSICA: Well, I think about dying all time. It might be easier that way. But then I remind myself about my kids, and I really don't want to hurt them. So I wouldn't do it. I'm not there right now. I have been in the past, but I'm not right now. I'm afraid I will open Pandora's box and I won't be able to handle it and I'll become suicidal.

THERAPIST: I think I hear a stuck point there. Can we take a look at this on an ABC sheet and see if we can find some thoughts we can work on? This thought sounds a bit like an "if . . . then. . . . Can you finish the sentence "If I keep doing CPT, then . . . "?

JESSICA: OK, so in column A, goes "Continuing CPT"; in column B goes, "If I keep doing CPT, then I will fall apart."

THERAPIST: Great, that sounds like a stuck point we should add to the log! And in column C, how does that thought make you feel?

JESSICA: Scared.

THERAPIST: OK, scared. Does thinking about your traumas in treatment make you as scared as you were at the time of the trauma?

JESSICA: Well, no. It's different—it's not happening now.

THERAPIST: Right, that's probably an important reminder: It's not happening now, it's a memory. And even then, did you fall apart?

JESSICA: I felt like it at times, even to the point of considering suicide. But I've learned a lot. I have more support now than I did then.

THERAPIST: Yes, you do. And what can you if you feel like you are falling apart?

JESSICA: I can remind myself that I haven't fallen apart yet, even if I sometimes felt like I was. I am strong. I can reach out to a friend. And like you said, I can remind myself that it is not happening now.

CPT Session 4: Socratic Dialogue Targeting Assimilated Stuck Points

Cognitive change is facilitated using Socratic dialogue, in which the therapist poses questions to help clients explore their thinking. Early on in therapy, the first type of stuck points to target are those that are *assimilated*, which means those that reflect clients' interpretations of how and why the trauma happened. When working on assimilated stuck points with clients who have had many traumas, Socratic dialogue should be focused on a particular incident. There are a range of questions that can help clients examine what they have been saying to themselves, which includes clarifying questions, challenging assumptions, evaluating evidence, and challenging the underlying beliefs. The goal of Socratic dialogue is to help clients reexamine what they have been telling themselves about the trauma and come to more realistic conclusions. Successfully challenged assimilated stuck points often result in a reduction in manufactured feelings such as guilt. As clients are more able to accept the reality of the event, which includes acknowledging what was outside of their control, they may experience an increase of natural feelings, such as sadness. Sadness or grief is considered part of the natural recovery process from trauma, and this shift in emotion from guilt to sadness can be a productive step toward recovery.

JESSICA: I just keep coming back to the thought should have done more to stop him over all those years. I should have put an end to it.

THERAPIST: It sounds like that thought comes up a lot, and you mentioned that it's a thought that comes up when you think about the index trauma specifically, right? Let's focus on that day.

JESSICA: Yes, that's right, I do think I should have fought harder to stop my stepdad that day.

THERAPIST: So, what exactly did you do?

JESSICA: First I said, "I don't want to do this. Can you stop?" And I used my right hand to push at his chest. He grabbed my wrist, his whole hand wrapped around it, and he pushed me back and pinned my wrist to the bed. Then he grabbed my other wrist before I could do anything.

THERAPIST: So he was a lot stronger than you?

JESSICA: Well, yeah, I was only 9. And I was a petite kid. He was so much bigger and stronger than me. My wrists hurt so much and my arm was twisted. I knew if I fought harder, he would hurt me more. He told me that if I knew what was good for me, I'd quit it.

THERAPIST: And then what?

JESSICA: So, I gave up. I didn't fight anymore, I just wanted it over so he'd leave. But I should never have given up.

THERAPIST: What other choice did you have?

JESSICA: I guess I didn't have another choice. I tried. But there was nothing I could do. (*Starts to cry.*)

THERAPIST: So realistically, could you, as a 9-year-old, have changed the outcome by fighting back?

JESSICA: I wish I could have, but no, I can see now that I had no chance.

CPT Session 6: New Trauma Disclosed

When clients have experienced many traumatic events, sometimes they avoid disclosing a traumatic experience that is shameful or particularly upsetting, or sharing specific details of traumas that they have discussed. It is important for the therapist to explore this possibility, especially when PTSD symptoms have not come down despite changes in thinking. When new traumas are disclosed midway through CPT, the therapist should help the client find his or her stuck points related to this new event and begin challenging those stuck points as well.

THERAPIST: You mentioned that you are starting to think about the abuse from your stepfather differently and not blaming yourself as much, but your PTSD symptoms are still high. Do you think we've been missing anything in what we are focusing on? Are there any other traumas that you haven't told me about?

JESSICA: I do have to tell you something. Oh, this is hard . . .

THERAPIST: It's OK, what is it?

JESSICA: You know that guy I told you I have been dating on and off?

THERAPIST: Yeah.

JESSICA: This is embarrassing, and I haven't told anyone this. He asks me to do things sexually that involve me inflicting pain on myself, like burning myself with hot wax, and more . . . oh God. I can't believe I am telling you this.

THERAPIST: Does he force you do this?

JESSICA: Well, yes and no. I do it to myself. But it is at his insistence. Sometimes he is there in the room, sometimes it happens over video chat. I have said I want to stop doing this, but he begs me. He threatens to leave me. He says I'll never find someone to love me like he does. He says pretty awful things.

THERAPIST: Where do things stand now? Are you still seeing him?

JESSICA: I just broke up with him, I know he's not good for me. I feel terrible, but it's all my own doing. I'm so disgusting.

THERAPIST: Thank you for telling me this. I can see this is hard for you to talk about.

JESSICA: Yeah, it's been my "dirty secret" for a long time. My friends have no idea how bad it is.

THERAPIST: OK, sounds like we should look at this experience here in therapy. We're about halfway through CPT, and you've started to make some good progress on your traumas with your stepfather. Does it feel that way to you?

JESSICA: Yeah, I am beginning to see that it wasn't my fault. I still wish I fought back harder, but I am working on that.

THERAPIST: Yes, you are. Given what you just told me, I think we should look for what stuck points you might have related to what has been happening with your ex-boyfriend. Then we can prioritize what stuck points to work on next. Does that sound like a plan?

JESSICA: OK, but this feels different, because it's all my own doing. I am disgusting.

THERAPIST: Sounds like some stuck points—"It's all my own doing"; "I am disgusting." Let's add those to the stuck point log.

JESSICA: He makes me feel so undeserving. So unlovable.

THERAPIST: OK, what might be the stuck point there?

JESSICA: I am undeserving of love. No one will ever treat me well. I am damaged goods.

THERAPIST: Yes. Let's write those down. It sounds like there is a lot of shame. What are some of your thoughts that lead to shame?

JESSICA: Well, I don't know why I do it. It's all my fault.

THERAPIST: OK, let's look at what you are saying is your fault here and go through a worksheet on that stuck point.

Session 12: Final Impact Statement

At the end of a course of CPT, clients are asked to write a final impact statement to describe how they view the trauma now. This is an opportunity to reflect on the cognitive and behavioral changes that have occurred in the context of treatment. The hope is for clients to demonstrate both changes in how they view their traumas and broader changes in how they view their worth, their ability to trust themselves and others, their willingness to engage in relationships, and their sense of safety and control. For those with complex PTSD, CPT teaches cognitive skills to challenge the core beliefs about themselves that may have led to despondence and disconnection.

THERAPIST: Did you write your final impact statement?

JESSICA: Yes, I have it here.

THERAPIST: OK, excellent. First, we'll have you read your newly written impact statement. Then I am going to read yours from the beginning of treatment back to you. Can you read the impact statement you wrote this week?

JESSICA: Sure.

"I am coming to realize that my stepfather's actions were his alone and he was responsible for what he did. It's his fault. I wish I could have stopped it, but I was only 9. I tried to fight back, but I couldn't. I am still sad for that little girl who had no one looking out for her. I have a better understanding now that 'no' means no and that people who don't respect that are in the wrong. I can say 'no.' Sometimes that will mean I lose people, but I am growing to realize it might be better to be alone than with someone who hurts me. That's tough though. I still really struggle with what it means to be alone. I am doing better at being present, I used to disconnect anytime I was reminded of my trauma or upset emotionally. I am also working on my self-esteem. I know intellectually that I have value, that everyone does, I'm going to keep working on that as it can be hard to remember sometimes. I also am realizing that it's OK to be sad. Sad things have happened to me. I hope I don't always feel this way, but it's something I can handle now."

THERAPIST: Wow! Nice work. I'm hearing a lot of change in what you are saying to yourself. OK, now I am going to read your initial impact statement.

"My traumas happened because I let them. My stepfather knew how to manipulate everyone, but in the end, I didn't stop him, so it is my fault that it went on for so long. I am so ashamed of what he did to me. I am forever tarnished. My mother should have known what was going on. She should have protected me. I think she feared being alone too much to see what was right under her eyes. My stepfather's actions ruined me and set me up for a life of trauma. . . . I can't trust anyone, everyone is out for themselves. Men can't be trusted, I have been hurt by so many. And yet, being alone is terrifying. I need to be in control at all times or I will get hurt. I don't think I'll ever get better. Sometimes I wonder if it is even worth trying."

JESSICA: Wow. I can't believe I said that. Well, I mean, I know I did, but that almost feels like someone else now.

THERAPIST: What differences did you hear?

JESSICA: There were a lot of differences. I blame myself much less than I used to and I now feel like I have tools I can use when I start to think painful thoughts. I need to keep catching when my thinking floats back to all the "I should haves . . . " but I have the sheets to use for that.

THERAPIST: Yes! Exactly, we want you to keep using the sheets for past events and new things that come up.

JESSICA: Yes, and I am realizing I can handle much more than I thought I could. It's OK to be sad sometimes, I don't want to be sad all the time, but it doesn't need to be dangerous or scary. I have cut down on my alcohol and really haven't been using it. I am also trying to reach out to friends more and get out for social events and that really feels nice.

Commentary on the Case Example

As a case example, Jessica demonstrates how CPT can benefit someone with a complicated trauma history and comorbid concerns, such as alcohol use, self-harming behaviors, and a history of suicidality. Despite concerns early on about her ability to tolerate the treatment and the new disclosure partway through treatment, Jessica stayed with the treatment and endorsed substantial change in 12 sessions of CPT. She still has some areas to continue working on, including self-esteem, acceptance of emotions, and being comfortable being with herself, but she now has learned the skills to challenge her thinking and has an increased sense of agency that she can handle her distress. Given these new skills, we find that clients no longer need the therapy sessions to continue to use the techniques, and in fact, many CPT clients continue to show improvement in their scores even after therapy ends. Typically, we ask clients to return for a check-in session 1 month after CPT ends, and this gives us an opportunity to reinforce the skills that they have learned and identify areas for continued focus and improvement.

In complex PTSD, there can be safety risks or behaviors that interfere with therapy, such as ongoing suicidality, substance use, or self-harm. In CPT, these behaviors are monitored, and the connection between these behaviors and PTSD-related avoidance is highlighted. There is an active, collaborative, problem-solving approach to help keep clients on track with their treatment goals. The cognitive skills teach clients to analyze what they are telling themselves and to check how true this is. Jessica voiced a common worry about "falling apart" and by using the ABC worksheet, the therapist helped her examine how realistic that was.

Conclusion

Throughout CPT, therapists look at all thoughts objectively, using tools to examine evidence and root out assumptions in a structured and stepwise cognitive approach that can be containing and reassuring. By facing the trauma and coming to see what happened through a more accurate lens, clients' misinterpretations and assumptions are clarified, which then leaves room to feel the natural emotions (e.g., sadness) and promotes acceptance of the reality of the event. As this happens, clients are more able to stay grounded in the present, rather than avoiding or dissociating, as they learn that they can tolerate their memories. CPT's cognitive skills not only help clients make sense of their trauma experiences but also help them identify and challenge their thinking that contributes to difficulties in emotional dysregulation and interpersonal disruption often seen in complex PTSD.

References

Brady, F., Warnock-Parkes, E., Barker, C., & Ehlers, A. (2015). Early in-session predictors of response to trauma-focused cognitive therapy for posttraumatic stress disorder. *Behaviour Research and Therapy, 74,* 40–47.

Butollo, W., Karl, R., Konig, J., & Rosner, R. (2015). A randomized controlled clinical trial of dialogical exposure therapy vs. cognitive processing therapy for adult outpatients suffering from PTSD after type I trauma in adulthood. *Psychotherapy and Psychosomatics, 85,* 16–26.

Chard, K. M. (2005). An evaluation of cognitive processing therapy for the treatment of posttraumatic stress disorder related to childhood sexual abuse. *Journal of Consulting and Clinical Psychology, 75,* 965–971.

Clarke, S. B., Rizvi, S. L., & Resick, P. A. (2008). Borderline personality characteristics and treatment outcome in cognitive-behavioral treatments for PTSD in female rape victims. *Behavior Therapy, 39,* 72–78.

Forbes, D., Lloyd, D., Nixon, R. D., Elliott, P., Varker, T., Perry, D., . . . Creamer, M. (2012). A multisite randomized controlled effectiveness trial of cognitive processing therapy for military-related posttraumatic stress disorder. *Journal of Anxiety Disorders, 26,* 442–452.

Galovski, T. E., Blain, L. M., Chappuis, C., & Fletcher, T. (2013). Sex differences in recovery from PTSD in male and female interpersonal assault survivors. *Behaviour Research and Therapy, 51,* 247–255.

Galovski, T. E., Blain, L. M., Mott, J. M., Elwood, L., & Houle, T. (2012). Manualized therapy for PTSD: Flexing the structure of cognitive processing therapy. *Journal of Consulting and Clinical Psychology, 80,* 968–981.

Haagen, J. F. G., Smid, G. E., Knipscheer, J. W., & Kleber, R. J. (2015). The efficacy of recommended treatment for veterans with PTSD: A metaregression analysis. *Clinical Psychology Review, 40,* 184–194.

Hariri, A. R., Mattay, V. S., Tessitore, A., Fera, F., & Weinberger, D. R. (2003). Neocortical modulation of the amygdala response to fearful stimuli. *Biological Psychiatry, 53,* 494–501.

Holder, N., Holliday, R., Pai, A., & Suris, A. (2017). Role of borderline personality disorder in the treatment of military sexual trauma-related posttraumatic stress disorder with cognitive processing therapy. *Behavioral Medicine, 43,* 184–190.

Hollon, S. D., & Garver, J. (1988). Cognitive therapy. In L. Y. Abramson (Ed.), *Social cognition and clinical psychology: A synthesis* (pp. 204–253). New York: Guilford Press.

Karatzias, T., Shevlin, M., Hyland, P., Brewin, B. R., Cloitre, M., Bradley, A., . . . Roberts, N. P. (2018). The role of negative cognitions, emotion regulation strategies, and attachment style in complex post-traumatic stress disorder: Implications for new and existing therapies. *British Journal of Clinical Psychology, 57,* 177–185.

Mitchell, K. S., Wells, S. Y., Mendes, A., & Resick, P. A. (2012). Treatment improves symptoms shared by PTSD and disordered eating. *Journal of Traumatic Stress, 25,* 535–542.

Monson, C. M., Schnurr, P. P., Resick, P. A., Friedman, M. J., Young-Xu, Y., & Stevens, S. P. (2006). Cognitive processing therapy for veterans with military-related posttraumatic stress disorder. *Journal of Consulting and Clinical Psychology, 74,* 898–907.

Resick, P. A., Galovski, T. E., Uhlmansiek, M. O., Scher, C. D., Clum, G. A., & Young-Xu, Y. (2008). A randomized clinical trial to dismantle components of cognitive processing therapy for posttraumatic stress disorder in female victims of interpersonal violence. *Journal of Consulting and Clinical Psychology, 76,* 243–258.

Resick, P. A., Monson, C. M., & Chard, K. M. (2017). *Cognitive processing therapy for PTSD: A comprehensive manual.* New York: Guilford Press.

Resick, P. A., Nishith, P., Weaver, T. L., Astin, M. C., & Feuer, C. A. (2002). A comparison of cognitive-processing therapy with prolonged exposure and a waiting condition for the treatment of chronic posttraumatic stress disorder in female rape victims. *Journal of Consulting and Clinical Psychology, 70,* 867–879.

Resick, P. A., & Schnicke, M. K. (1993). *Cognitive processing therapy for rape victims: A treatment manual.* Newbury Park, CA: SAGE.

Resick, P. A., Suvak, M. K., Johnides, B. D., Mitchell, K. S., & Iverson, K. M. (2012a). The impact of dissociation on PTSD treatment with cognitive processing therapy. *Depression and Anxiety, 29,* 718–730.

Resick, P. A., Suvak, M. K., & Wells, S. Y. (2014). The impact of childhood abuse among women with assault-related PTSD receiving short-term cognitive-behavioral therapy. *Journal of Traumatic Stress, 27,* 558–567.

Resick, P. A., Wachen, J. S., Mintz, J., Young-McCaughan, S., Roache, J. D., Borah, A. M., . . . Peterson, A. L. (2015). A randomized clinical trial of group cognitive processing therapy compared with group present-centered therapy for PTSD among active duty military personnel. *Journal of Consulting and Clinical Psychology, 83,* 1058–1068.

Resick, P. A., Williams, L. F., Suvak, M. K., Monson, C. M., & Gradus, J. L. (2012b). Long-term outcomes of cognitive-behavioral treatments for posttraumatic stress disorder among female rape survivors. *Journal of Consulting and Clinical Psychology, 80,* 201–210.

Suris, A., Link-Malcolm, J., Chard, K., Ahn, C., & North, C. (2013). A randomized clinical trial of cognitive processing therapy for veterans with PTSD related to military sexual trauma. *Journal of Traumatic Stress, 26,* 28–37.

Walter, K. H., Bolte, T. A., Owens, G. P., & Chard, K. M. (2012). The impact of personality disorders on treatment outcomes for veterans in a posttraumatic stress disorder residential treatment program. *Cognitive Therapy and Research, 36,* 576–584.

Walter, K. H., Buckley, A., Simpson, J. M., & Chard, K. M. (2014). Residential PTSD treatment for female veterans with military sexual trauma: Does a history of childhood sexual abuse influence outcome? *Journal of Interpersonal Violence, 29,* 971–986.

Watts, B. V., Schnurr, P. P., Mayo, L., Young-Xu, Y., Weeks, W. B., & Friedman, M. J. (2013). Meta-analysis of the efficacy of treatments for posttraumatic stress disorder. *Journal of Clinical Psychiatry, 74,* 541–550.

CHAPTER 12

Brief Eclectic Psychotherapy

BERTHOLD GERSONS
MIRJAM J. NIJDAM
GEERT E. SMID
ULRICH SCHNYDER

Brief eclectic psychotherapy for posttraumatic stress disorder (BEPP), an evidence-based treatment that focuses on working through difficult emotions and grief originating from traumatic events, aims not only to reduce symptoms but also to enable trauma survivors to learn from devastating experiences (Gersons & Schnyder, 2013). As we describe in this chapter, BEPP has unique characteristics that distinguish it from other evidence-based treatments and are highly relevant in the treatment of complex posttraumatic stress disorders (CTSDs).

In 1980 in Amsterdam, police officers dealing with the traumatic sequelae of shooting incidents sought help. One of us, Berthold Gersons, discovered that many of these police officers were suffering from posttraumatic stress disorder (PTSD; Gersons, 1989). In 1980, PTSD also was first formally recognized as a psychiatric disorder. Initially, BEPP was specifically designed for the treatment of police officers with PTSD. Gersons started with short psychodynamic therapy (Luborsky, 1984), which resulted in a decrease of the police officers' symptoms of avoidance. The officers were keen to gain insight into themselves, often learning how both their childhood experiences and the traumatic events they experienced in police duties had influenced their views of the world. However, their PTSD intrusive reliving symptoms did not diminish. As a result, Gersons modified BEPP, using techniques from crisis intervention, cognitive therapy, grief therapy, and psychodynamic psychotherapy.

In BEPP, the therapist first pays attention to fear and other overwhelming emotions, followed by a focus on meaning and learning from traumatic events. The therapy consists of 16 sessions, and its five essential elements are psychoeducation, imaginal exposure to the traumatic event, writing letters and working with memorabilia (objects that are linked to the traumatic event), meaning making and integration, and a farewell ritual (see Figure 12.1).

BEPP was further developed in the 1980s and 1990s, simultaneous with the development of other trauma-focused psychotherapies such as trauma-focused cognitive behavioral therapy (TF-CBT) and eye movement desensitization and reprocessing (EMDR) therapy. The first randomized controlled trials (RCTs), which demonstrated the efficacy of BEPP, EMDR, and TF-CBT, all emerged in the 1990s and 2000s (Foa, Rothbaum, Riggs, & Murdock, 1991; Gersons, Carlier, Lamberts, & van der Kolk, 2000; Vaughan et al., 1994). Although the treatment has several aspects in common with other trauma-focused treatments (Schnyder et al., 2015), the clinical rationale for BEPP differs from the rationale of other PTSD treatments. In BEPP, the imaginal exposure phase is not primarily focused on habituation to and extinction of the fear responses related to the traumatic event. Instead, the focus is on experiencing and accepting the overwhelming emotional reactions such as anxiety, sadness, anger, guilt, shame, helplessness, and so on.

The fundamental idea is that someone develops PTSD when the strong emotional responses originating from traumatic events are suppressed and postponed. Traumatic events can cause insecurity in a person about him- or herself, and this leads to anxiety and negative mood states (Horowitz, 1976). Lack of understanding or care from family, friends, and others for the individual can result in suppression and delay of the emotional processing needed to rebuild a sense of security. Emotional responses that are logically connected to a traumatic event can subsequently evolve into disordered states with an increasing level of chronicity over time. According to Horowitz, the ability to tolerate these extreme emotions is the key to healthy processing of trauma, and this is also the central hypothesis of how exposure works in BEPP. The development of PTSD often can be traced back to one core event, after which the PTSD symptoms started. Imaginal exposure is focused on reliving this traumatic event from hot spot to hot spot during several sessions, until all relevant emotions have sufficiently been felt and expressed (Nijdam, Baas, Olff, & Gersons, 2013). In the exposure, this primarily concerns the helplessness, sorrow, and grief connected to the trauma. Secondarily, fear reactions also diminish. In parallel, the person writes one or more angry letters (which are never actually sent) to the person or organization he or she holds responsible for the trauma.

Another important element in the clinical rationale for BEPP is the assumption that traumatic events frequently go together with substantial losses, which bring forth a lasting change in the person. Often the person wants to go back to the "old self," but in BEPP, the message is that these changes make the person "sadder and wiser," and that one can search and find a new equilibrium with the changed perspective on the world. This is addressed in the meaning making and integration phase of BEPP and encompasses a broader perspective

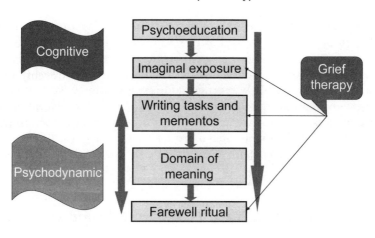

FIGURE 12.1. Essential elements of BEPP. Copyright © 1996 B. P. R. Gersons.

than just the core traumatic event. Often, other traumatic events and their consequences for the person and their identity are discussed as well. Life lessons and coping patterns brought about by a disrupted childhood are addressed and connected to the core traumatic event. It is often hard for the person to fully leave behind the traumatic events and their sequelae. The farewell ritual at the end of the treatment is a symbolic way to mark this milestone, and consists of a farewell part and a celebration part. During the ritual, the person parts with the trauma and often a long period of disturbed life. This enables the person to turn his or her perspective from the past to the here and now, and the future. The person also celebrates the resumption of "normal" life again and being reunited with important others.

After the first RCT that showed the efficacy of BEPP as compared to a wait list in police officers with PTSD (Gersons et al., 2000), several RCTs followed. BEPP proved to be efficacious in patients in a psychiatric outpatient clinic as compared to wait list (Lindauer et al., 2005). Schnyder, Müller, Maercker, and Wittman (2011) performed a replication study in patients in a psychiatric outpatient clinic in Switzerland who had sustained various types of traumatic events and suffered from a range of comorbidities, and similarly found good results for BEPP as compared to a minimal attention control condition. These studies showed that BEPP could be applied well to patient populations other than police officers. A study comparing BEPP and EMDR showed both treatments to be equally effective on a range of clinical and neuropsychological outcomes, and they also showed similar increases in posttraumatic growth (Nijdam, Gersons, Reitsma, de Jongh & Olff, 2012; Nijdam, Martens, Reitsma, Gersons, & Olff, 2018a; Nijdam et al., 2018b). In these trials in the Netherlands and Switzerland, patients with complex trauma were prevalent.

Outcomes in the RCTs with BEPP have been limited to structured interviews and questionnaires to assess PTSD and comorbid disorders, and have not yet included instruments to investigate complex stress disorders and how these conditions, symptoms, and aftereffects respond to treatment. From our clinical experience, however, it is apparent that many patients enroll in BEPP treatment because of the (consequences of) complex symptoms of PTSD and/ or traumatic bereavement. We further address this in the next section of this chapter in which we describe the symptoms of CTSDs we commonly see in our clinical practices, and how these are addressed in BEPP. The case example we present in the third section provides a further illustration of the BEPP approach with complex PTSD symptoms. We conclude with key points of the treatment and its clinical tactics.

BEPP and Key Clinical Features Relevant to CTSDs

In complex PTSD, three additional symptom domains, above and beyond those of PTSD, are present: difficulties in emotion regulation, negative self-concept, and difficulties in sustaining relationships (Maercker et al., 2013). In DSM-5 (American Psychiatric Association, 2013), the dissociative subtype of PTSD includes symptoms of depersonalization and derealization (Lanius, Brand, Vermetten, Frewen, & Spiegel, 2012). We use these definitions to describe how the key symptoms of CTSDs are targeted in BEPP, and how the model is helpful in promoting engagement and building the therapeutic relationship. Furthermore, we describe how trauma processing is viewed in the therapy model and psychosocial skills building.

The theoretical model of BEPP takes into account that many, if not most, patients who seek treatment for trauma-related disorders do not suffer from the repercussions of a single traumatic event but rather from multiple traumatization (Gersons, 1989; Gersons, Meewisse, & Nijdam, 2015). The primary targets of BEPP are the symptoms of PTSD, such as reexperiencing the traumatic event(s) and avoiding trauma-related stimuli. With regard to the additional symptoms frequently observed in complex PTSD, the patient's negative self-concept and difficulties in sustaining trusting and fulfilling relationships are addressed during the second half of treatment, particularly when working in the domain of meaning and integration (i.e., when the patient moves his or her attention away from the trauma and starts to focus more on current exigencies in the here and now in private, social, and occupational aspects of life).

Engagement in BEPP starts in the first treatment session. To engage the patient as much as possible in psychoeducation is of crucial importance. The patient needs to be recognized as a victim of what happened. Moreover, psychopathological symptoms, as well as severe sequelae regarding daily life functioning and relating to others, should be acknowledged. However, at the same time, the patient should also be recognized as a "strong" person who is motivated for treatment. Psychoeducation aims at helping the patient to understand the relationship between his or her symptoms and the traumatic experiences. It is also valuable to explain how these symptoms and events have heavily influenced difficulties in relationships with others and often in daily functioning. The psychoeducation should be well understood by the patient and partner or important other trusted person present at the first encounter (Gersons, Meewisse, Nijdam, & Olff, 2011). This is provided in a way that uses the patient's language to make sure he or she understand how complex trauma can lead to complex PTSD, and how the different therapeutic elements can help the patient overcome his or her symptoms, stop being haunted by the past, and reengage in private, social, and occupational life as the treatment progresses. Halfway through the treatment, the partner is invited again to attend and is asked to report to both patient and therapist any progress made from his or her viewpoint. Moreover, the patient is engaged in homework assignments, particularly by being asked to bring memorabilia to work with during therapy sessions and encouraging him or her to write an ongoing letter in order to process aggressive emotions.

The therapeutic relationship helps to improve positive expectations about the outcome of the BEPP treatment (Kazlauskas et al., 2017). While transference phenomena are not explicitly addressed, unless there is an immediate and urgent clinical need to do so (e.g., when the patient falls in love with the therapist or expects the therapist to behave abusively, and tries to act out on his or her feelings), the therapist sees to it that mutual trust develops in the therapeutic relationship, so that the patient feels safe and encouraged to confront the difficult issues at stake. This is also facilitated by the fact that the BEPP protocol comprises a total of 16 sessions, which is longer than most evidence-based treatments for PTSD.

Psychosocial skills are not explicitly taught in BEPP. In the domain of the meaning making phase, the focus is very much on understanding how one's view of oneself and of important others has been changed by the traumatic past, and how this has led to a world with less trust in other people in general. When patients realize this and learn from this insight, they become encouraged to "practice" new relationships with others, often in work situations. Learning psychosocial skills in BEPP therefore occurs in a more implicit way, as a result of being encouraged to gain new learning experiences based on one's personal goals. The BEPP protocol is designed to help patients not only recover from their symptoms but also ultimately to take charge of their lives, to enjoy their relationships with significant others, and to resume work, thus reconnecting to the world.

In BEPP, the perspective on how trauma processing works is different, for instance, than classical CBT approaches or EMDR. In the BEPP model, it is not necessary to do imaginal exposure to the traumatic memory in a "prolonged" way, for example, as in prolonged exposure (PE) therapy (Foa, Hembree, & Rothbaum, 2007) or to repeatedly go back to the most stressful images of the event and alternate these with a distracting task, as in EMDR (Shapiro, 2001). After relaxation, one closes one's eyes and goes back to the day or days of the traumatic experiences. This very slow process mainly focuses on the catharsis of emotions such as sadness and sorrow. Especially when this goes slowly and is spread over four to six sessions, it is not unusual for new memories to come up. The person revisits in a detailed manner the moments during which, for example, his or her life was in danger and reflects on how he or she felt then and now, in the reflection with the therapist after the imaginal exposure. The use of memorabilia, which the patient is encouraged to bring to the therapy session, also helps to bring back the experiences in a vivid way. The task to write angry letters to those whom one holds responsible for the traumatic events or the sequelae of the traumatic events, and to those who did not help or who sheltered an abuser at their expense helps the patient to remember the details of what exactly happened and the order in which the events took place. When the memory is more complete and more detailed, the person can reflect on the reality of it in a different way, and this is one of the important goals before moving on to meaning making in the second phase of the treatment.

Clinical Case Example

A young female police officer, Mrs. S, came in for diagnosis and treatment with BEPP. Her trauma story and her symptom profile were consistent with a diagnosis of complex PTSD. She was successfully treated in 16 sessions.

The Key Traumatic Event

Mrs. S is a regular police officer. Her daily work is to patrol the streets mostly with colleagues and to attend to all kinds of emergencies. She has been working with the police for about 5 years. In these years she has frequently been exposed to potentially traumatic events, such as finding dead bodies of people who killed themselves or died in traffic incidents or criminal shootings. Being beaten by drunk people and being threatened was a regular experience for her. However, she did not develop PTSD until the key traumatic experience we describe later on. Of course, these experiences had always been very unpleasant or even shocking, but she saw it as her professional duty to find solutions in those situations, deescalating tensions between people involved and calming down the public. She stated that the misbehavior of some colleagues at her police station often worried her more than the work-related stressors in the streets. That was unacceptable for her, but she did not feel capable to change this herself.

The key traumatic event happened at the end of a weekend day. A colleague of hers got an assignment to track down a car whose driver refused to stop when ordered by other police. She and her colleague got into their police car and started to drive around in the area. She tried to receive more precise information from the police alarm room. When they spotted the car they were looking for, they signaled the driver to stop. However, the driver did not react. Then they signaled the driver to stop, using the blue light and even the siren. This still did not result in getting the car to halt. The two police officers got increasingly nervous and felt uneasy. Why did that driver not react? Mrs. S had no clue.

The drive ended in a neighborhood of old housing, where the driver finally parked his car. The police officers stopped also behind the car. The driver stepped out of the car, as did two ladies, one of whom later proved to be his daughter and the other, a niece. The man was very agitated and was lambasting the officers. Mrs. S's colleague asked the man to behave, but when this did not help to calm him down, he grabbed the man to arrest him. The intention was to transport the man to the police station, where he could be interrogated. Instead, the man freed himself and a tremendous fight broke out in which Mrs. S and the two ladies were heavily involved. Because of the siren, many bystanders showed up from the area, and one of them mingled in the fight. Her colleague was wounded. She saw how exhausted he was and she also saw blood on the ground. Meanwhile, she had asked for backup on her transceiver. She was heavily beaten and became increasingly afraid that she and her colleague would not survive before the backup arrived. At a certain point, she was so frightened that she decided to pull her gun and shoot in the air. She was aware that the man and the ladies were unarmed, and she was unsure whether it was acceptable to use the gun. When she shot into the air, everyone withdrew; the driver, his daughters and the audience. People started to shout: "She has drawn her gun!" After this had happened, colleagues of hers arrived and took control of the situation. The driver and the ladies were arrested and brought to the police station. Mrs. S was extremely shaken and, together with her colleague, returned to the station. Following this event, she developed PTSD.

Mrs. S was descended from a migrant family. She grew up in the Netherlands. Her childhood until the age of 7 was rather normal. But when she failed to accomplish at school, a cascade of traumatic experiences started. At the end of the school year, her grades were too low for her to be promoted to the next year. To prevent her father from seeing the low grades, she had torn out a page from her school report. When her father discovered one page was missing, he exploded in rage. He started to hit her with a leather belt and even acted as if he wanted to cut her throat to kill her. She was banished to the attic for 2 months. She was not allowed to leave the attic; she also secretly received some food from her mother. The beatings continued. It nearly became a daily ritual, often initiated by moments when she made mistakes while being forced to read religious verses aloud. Her brothers were also hit by her father, for instance, when they came home from school when other boys had snatched the cheese from their sandwiches. The boys were blamed for not sufficiently defending themselves. The beating stopped when she was around 14 years old. Then a cousin raped her and started to abuse her sexually. In the beginning, her brothers gave this nephew a beating, but this did not end the abuse. Also, her mother did nothing to prevent the abuse. During a trip to the country from which her father and mother had migrated, she was forced to sign a document. It turned out that by doing that she was married to her cousin. Back in the Netherlands, she ran away from home. Later on, she started her education to become a police officer. She also divorced her cousin/husband and brought him to court, where he was sentenced. At age 22, she married again but divorced some years later.

Obviously, Mrs. S had suffered a variety of diverse repetitive traumas in childhood, as well as later on. Her PTSD symptoms included recurrent and intrusive distressing recollections from the key traumatic event and also nightmares combined with sleeping problems. At her work, she panicked often, as if a traumatic event was about to happen again. Also she got frightened when seeing dark-skinned people, because they reminded her of the skin color of the perpetrator and his daughters. She also generalized a negative stigma of being "asocial," although she was a person of color herself. She often panicked when she had to drive out to an incident. She then felt her heart rate increasing and she started sweating. Still she did not want to stop working, because of she was afraid to lose her job. At best, she tried to avoid being ordered to go out on the street again. Regarding the key traumatic incident, she lost memory of a certain period when the beatings were most intense. That seemed to be a dissociative moment. Her recall of the event started again the moment she felt pain in her limbs and head from the beating and the ladies' nails pushed into her flesh. Coming home from work she felt exhausted and depressed. She increasingly avoided visiting friends. She felt as if she had lost her cheerful self, becoming increasingly irritable. Her sister told her how unfriendly and aggressive she had become. She had difficulty concentrating and forgot normal things. She was hypervigilant, always sitting with her back to the door, and was often startled in stressful work situations. She felt badly about her aggressiveness and was always afraid to disappoint friends and family. She also had a tendency to drink too much alcohol.

BEPP Treatment

The psychotherapy Mrs. S had undergone before starting BEPP had not been successful. She had been in treatment two times with different psychologists. These therapies involved talking about events in her current life and about her childhood experiences, and had not resulted in a decrease in symptoms and in improvement of her psychological condition.

She was very happy with her first session of BEPP devoted to psychoeducation. She appreciated learning how her symptoms originated from the key traumatic event and how this event still programmed her here-and-now reactions. She also understood very well how the different elements of the BEPP treatment could be helpful to resolve her PTSD. This motivated her very much to start the next sessions of imaginal exposure. "I am looking forward to starting with the exposure," she told the therapist. At the first exposure session after the relaxation exercise, she revisited *in vivo* how she was assigned to stop the car and how the driver refused to stop. In BEPP, the patient needs to progress very slowly with eyes closed to become aware of feeling the increasing tension and strong related emotions. As more and more details of the event came to the surface, her tension increased enormously. When her story reached the moment she pulled her gun, the therapist stopped the exposure. Mrs. S was very sad and overwhelmed, especially because she realized how frightened she had been of dying. Also, the dilemma of shooting in the air when others were not armed was still bothering her. She also felt very much abandoned by her colleague and by the police organization in general.

At the following exposure session, Mrs. S still felt very sad. The therapist explained to her that this was understandable after reexperiencing the traumatic event in this controlled way and realizing how terrible it had been and how much it disrupted her life afterward. That helped her to accept her intense sadness. This second exposure started with the shooting and the strange experience of "silence" directly afterward. People then started shouting, "She has drawn her gun!" while her incoming colleagues were cuffing the driver and his daughters, and calming the public. She remembered that she cried later when sitting in the courtyard of the police station with her colleague smoking a cigarette together. She felt very disappointed by her colleague whom she believed, as a "man," should have saved her and not the other way around. Two more exposure sessions were needed to process other emotions, including anger.

The expressions of anger, grief, and intense feelings of helplessness were very much facilitated by the letter writing task. Letter writing is used to feel anger as much as possible and to put it into words. The letters are not meant to be sent. Mrs. S wrote to the police how she was handled by the public and by the organization as "a small lady to be spit on and beaten." The most important letter was to her father and mother about the aggressive childhood incidents of beatings by her father and his act of threatening to kill her, as well as the rape and abuse by her cousin, and the absence of any comfort or protection from her mother. She often cried, but she became more relaxed after each session. It was not necessary to use the imaginal exposure procedure here for the discharge of the strong emotions. Also, nonverbal signs, such as a decreased body tension and the clothes she wore in the next sessions, showed that she was more relaxed and self-confident.

Then began the important second part of BEPP, which is called the *domain of meaning*. She realized how difficult it had become for her to trust others due to the events she suffered during childhood. She started to understand how she avoided any vulnerability toward others and how she therefore had to suppress emotions. Instead, she wanted to be a strong policewoman. But now she felt disappointed by the police organization. The police, she realized, was to be a "substitute safe and comforting family" for her. Now it turned out it was not. Instead, dishonesty, danger, and denial were key elements in the substitute family. She recognized how she always tried to start anew, as if she could leave the bad things of her life behind and start again. She now increasingly accepted how she had been harmed during her childhood. When grieving this, more and more she started to appreciate life. Importantly, she realized how she had always been afraid of being abandoned by people close to her, such as her friends and family. As a result, she never dared to refuse a request for help from others. She felt she was now a happy person again, as she had been prior to the traumatic event. She also felt much wiser. Before, she suffered so much that other people did not like her, because she was so aggressive. Now that she felt relaxed and joyful, others liked her better. She understood her own behavior and hidden fears very well. For the farewell ritual, she decided to burn the audio disk of the police emergency, together with a female friend. On the disk was a tape of the whole traumatic event, from the assignment to find the car until Mrs. S shot in the air. She felt very much relieved when the disk was burned.

After finishing BEPP treatment, Mrs. S no longer met criteria for PTSD. At follow-up half a year later, her symptoms had not reappeared. She was grateful for the treatment. She continued working at the police station and informed her colleagues about her positive experience in the treatment.

The BEPP Model's Clinical Tactics

BEPP has several specific tactics for the treatment of patients with complex PTSD.

Working through Dysregulation Regarding Distrust, Detachment, Anger, Grief, and Shame

The BEPP components employed during the first phase of BEPP, specifically, psychoeducation, exposure, writing assignments, and use of mementos, are helpful in addressing different aspects of emotional dysregulation.

Distrust

A trusting relationship is initiated during psychoeducation, the first BEPP session. Importantly, a partner, family member, or friend is invited to this session. By providing clear information about both the treatment and complex traumatic stress symptoms, and by involving the patient's support network, trust is encouraged. The therapist mentions distrust as a common PTSD symptom and invites the client and the close other to reflect on this: Do they recognize it? What is helpful in such instances? During exposure, the therapist is supportive and repeats psychoeducation as needed, thereby continuing to build trust. If breeches in trust between therapist and patient occur during therapy, the close other may be reinvited to aid the client in reflecting on the situation and thereby facilitate working through distrust.

Detachment

Detachment often results from intense emotions that the client feels unable to tolerate, including anger, grief, and shame. Detachment may also result from depressive and dissociative avoidance. Working through detachment starts during the exposure sessions, when the therapist encourages emotional engagement. Essential in this process is that the therapist does not go too fast but instead adjusts the pace of the interventions in the exposure adequately to the patient's ability and capacities. Exposure helps the patient to fully realize what happened and often helps to reorganize the personal trauma story in the patient's mind so that it becomes more chronological and complete. This facilitates engagement. Other BEPP components, such as writing tasks and the use of mementos, also contribute to engagement and integration and are thus helpful in reducing detachment. During the meaning making and integration phase of BEPP, a reorientation relative to personal goals and values may enhance behavioral and cognitive activation and thus counteract depressive avoidance.

Anger

Working through anger is the primary aim of the writing tasks. Writing an angry letter may be especially helpful for patients struggling with a sense of injustice, who have difficulties in dealing with feelings of anger, and aggressive thoughts and impulses. A letter can be written to a perpetrator, negligent bystanders, or the government or another agency that is held responsible for the trauma or its sequelae. In the letter, uncensored anger, including insults and diatribes, may be expressed. Sometimes, burning the angry letter is integrated into the farewell ritual.

> A 35-year-old refugee from Bosnia was preoccupied with thoughts of revenge toward the perpetrator who had killed his best friend during the armed conflict in his home country. He wrote and read aloud his thoughts of revenge in graphic detail. During the meaning making and integration phase, he realized that not taking revenge was not the same as being disloyal to his friend. He was able to burn the letter during the farewell ritual.

Grief

Grief about the loss of real or desired resources—for example, in situations where the patient has been confronted with unwanted childlessness, job loss, breakup of a romantic relationship, loss of functional capacity due to medical or accidental causes, or loss of social status following migration—is addressed in BEPP by increasing awareness and encouraging emotional processing. As illustrated in the previous case, grief may concern having missed (parts of) childhood. Mrs. S realized that her childhood had been damaging, and she grieved the childhood ideal that was lost. Processing grief can help the client realize his or her emotional needs and thus fosters self-compassion and self-forgiveness (Young, Klosko, & Weishaar, 2003). Increased understanding of one's own emotional needs may also enhance a client's relational capacities and thereby diminish the risk of damaging relationships and revictimization.

Since the sudden and unexpected death of loved ones due to violent or otherwise traumatic circumstances involves separation distress in addition to traumatic distress, additional interventions may be useful to promote working through grief. A variant of the BEPP protocol that incorporates these interventions is named *brief eclectic psychotherapy for traumatic grief* (BEP-TG; Smid et al., 2015). If the loss of a loved one comprises the central traumatic event, psychoeducation includes information about grief reactions. Grief-focused exposure may include stimulus exposure, such as visiting the grave or looking at pictures of the deceased loved one, if avoidance of grief-related stimuli appears to play a role in blocking emotional processing. Conversely, if excessive grieving behavior is present, whereby the deceased person is symbolically kept alive in order to avoid confronting and accepting the reality of the loss, diminishing such behavior may be necessary to catalyze emotional processing of the loss.

In grief following bereavement, finding meaning encompasses the bereaved individual's evaluation of the loss of the loved person and its implications for the future, a cognitive, emotional, and spiritual process aimed at strengthening the individual's ability to live with the loss within his or her personal and cultural context. Writing assignments are useful tools to enable patients to evaluate meanings and to help bereaved individuals to confront painful aspects of the loss at their own pace. An ongoing farewell letter is a letter to the deceased in which the patient writes what he or she has always wanted to say, what he or she misses most, expressing longing for the deceased. In clients who have difficulties allowing feelings of sadness, it may promote emotional processing and finding meaning.

> Mrs. C, a 59-year-old married mother of two children, engaged in treatment a few months after the sudden death of a colleague. Her symptoms were consistent with a diagnosis of persistent complex bereavement disorder and PTSD. The colleague's death had reactivated memories and emotional pain associated with the loss of her younger sister 20 years earlier. The sister, with whom she had a very close relationship, had been murdered by an unknown perpetrator, who had never been found. After the sister's death, a very difficult period had followed during which there had been a lack of effective police actions, leaving Mrs. C frustrated and feeling unsafe and unable to work for over a year. There had been no mental health support at that time. This time, a BEP-TG treatment was begun. After explaining the treatment to both Mrs. C and her husband, grief-focused exposure was started. Both general and imaginary exposure took place. Mrs. C related loving memories of her sister, about how she had been informed by telephone about the death of her sister. She had not seen the sister's body, but she had been informed that it was heavily damaged. She had formed vivid images about her sister's last moments. These images were discussed in detail. Mrs. C felt very anxious during the exposure, but she also felt relieved to share her thoughts with someone. Since the children had been young at the time of her sister's death, Mrs. C and

her husband had avoided talking about the sister's death most of the time. Mrs. C wrote letters to her sister and became very sad. She experienced it as a breakthrough. She still felt guilty that she had not been able to protect her sister better. The meaning making and integration phase was focused on the changes in her life that were the result of the murder of her sister. Mrs. C realized that she did not need to feel responsible for things beyond her control. Her feeling of guilt about her sister decreased. She performed a ritual during dinner with her husband, in which she lighted a candle in honor of her sister and shared some of the feelings that had troubled her, and experienced support from her husband.

Shame

Shame arises in dependent or involuntary relationships in which dominance and subordination are established; the family of shame emotions includes humiliation, self-loathing, and feelings of defilement, disgrace, or dishonor (Herman, 2011). Following sexual assault and torture, shame may be accompanied by disgust and somatic distress. Following war-related atrocities, shame, survivor guilt, remorse, and meaninglessness are elements of *moral injury* (Shay, 2014).

Exposure is used to work through shame, with the therapist actively exploring sensitive areas of the client's story, in addition to providing psychoeducation, normalization of responses and feelings, and building trust (Herman, 2011). Disclosure in the context of the therapeutic relationship is a mastery experience that leads to greater self-knowledge, greater self-compassion, and reduced feelings of detachment (Herman, 2011). The therapist draws attention to the patient's shame reactions as they occur. Self-depreciative words can indicate feelings of shame, along with confusion of thought, hesitation, soft speech, silences, stammering, or rapid speech, as well as hiding behaviors, such as covering all or parts of one's face, gaze aversion, hanging one's head, or hunching shoulders. The therapist then invites the patient to make eye contact to enable empathic connection. Thus, the therapist encourages self-compassion (i.e., being kind and supportive to oneself and viewing suffering as part of the shared human experience; Dahm et al., 2015).

Helping the Client to Recover from Dissociative Episodes/Flashbacks

Dissociative episodes during exposure may be prevented by adjusting the speed of exposure to the client (i.e., slowing down). Therapist and the patient may agree on a sign (i.e., raising a finger) if exposure is experienced as being too fast or too difficult. Recovery from flashbacks and dissociative episodes is supported by making eye contact, providing reassurance and psychoeducation, and involving supportive others if needed and possible.

A 30-year-old woman from Sierra Leone was raped at age 18 by rebels after she saw them murder both her parents. She often showed dissociative absorption in traumatic memories during initial contacts: Each time the therapist referred to her traumatic past, she became silent, started staring, and did not respond for several minutes. Extensive psychoeducation and gradual exposure, starting with the grief about the death of her parents, enabled her to share the full story while staying in contact with her therapist.

Enhancing the Client's Awareness and Acceptance of Bodily and Emotion States

BEPP emphasizes learning from traumatic experiences (Gersons & Schnyder, 2013), which requires both awareness and acceptance. Therefore, the majority of BEPP sessions are devoted to the domain of meaning, and a ritual is planned toward the end of the therapy.

Aimed at promoting awareness and acceptance in the treatment of CTSDs, symbolic interactions with important others are included in BEPP (e.g., through writing assignments or the farewell ritual). Such symbolic interactions may also include imaginal conversations (Smid et al., 2015) in the variant BEP-TG. These allow the client to reconstruct cultural intersubjective realities (Smid & Boelen, in press) by symbolic means. Use of imaginal conversation to reconstruct a cultural intersubjective reality is illustrated below.

> M, a 36-year-old refugee from Iraq who lived in the Netherlands, felt very guilty following the violent death of his brother. Because the death happened after M's flight, M had not been able to bury his brother. The fate of his parents was unknown. An imaginary conversation was performed, in which M asked his brother for forgiveness and answered on behalf of his brother. His brother forgave him and hoped that M would find his parents, so that he could take care of them. For M, this conversation felt like saying good-bye.

Bodily States

In BEPP, each exposure session may start with a progressive muscle relaxation exercise (Jacobson, 1977). The client learns to reduce muscular tension by consciously tensing muscle groups, usually starting with the hands. If clients are especially tense and nervous at the first time, the therapist may start with "contralateral relaxation" of the fists. The client only needs to squeeze one fist while keeping the other fist relaxed. This reinforces a feeling of control that may specifically benefit clients with a tendency to dissociate.

Somatic sensations can evoke traumatic memories, and traumatic memories can involve somatic sensations. For example, a client who recalls being hit on the head may experience feelings of dizziness and head pain. Somatic sensations following trauma can result from several mechanisms: a "somatic flashback," imaginative reconstruction and reliving of the event, and anxiety (Hinton, Howes, & Kirmayer, 2008). If a client's distress includes somatic sensations, exploring sensation schemes during the domain of meaning phase of BEPP may be helpful to evaluate cultural and emotional meanings (Hinton et al., 2008). A sensation may become part of a script indicating what typically causes the sensation, what occurs when one has the sensation, and what consequences follow. The therapist may aid in modifying this script through gentle Socratic questioning. Some emotions may be expressed physically during exposure sessions as well. Grief is sometimes be put into words such as "pain in my heart," and the client may mimic certain facial or bodily expressions connected to a traumatic event. The therapist pays attention to these expressions in the reflection after the imaginal exposure.

Emotion States

CTSDs result from prolonged or repeated exposure to potentially traumatic events or exposure to events that have profound implications beyond a threat to one's own physical integrity. Emotion states that result may include guilt, shame, anger, alienation, and a state of intense fear/terror. Different social meaning systems that are implicated may be strongly culturally influenced. Awareness and acceptance of these emotion states is facilitated by interventions that support finding meaning in a culturally sensitive way (Smid & Boelen, in press).

In the case of traumatic grief, the therapist may guide an imaginal conversation with the person who died, in which the patient talks to the deceased person and also answers. This technique may mitigate feelings of guilt and may foster disclosure of things that still need to be expressed to the lost person ("unfinished business").

> A 52-year-old man, who had fled Afghanistan following an attack that killed his father, felt extremely guilty because he had asked his father to come along with him before the attack took place. Because of his flight, he was unable to take care of his younger brothers and sisters, and to fulfill other family duties. The therapist asked him to look upon himself through the loving eyes of his father. This was the first time he understood what self-compassion meant.

The role of the therapist in the imaginal conversation applied in BEP-TG is to encourage the bereaved individual to articulate meaningful questions, thoughts, and feelings toward the lost person, and to validate emotions that may arise during the conversation. Imaginal conversations represent experiential techniques that foster the transition from knowing intellectually that certain cognitions rooted in traumatic experiences are unhelpful to understanding them emotionally.

Imaginal conversations with a person who acted as a moral authority in the client's life may be used to deal with moral injury (Litz et al., 2009). In dealing with the effects of childhood adversities, imaginal conversations with the dysfunctional caretaker may play a role (Kellogg, 2012). The expression of anger is encouraged during the therapy session.

Rituals provide powerful and affirming experiences for bereaved individuals in mediating the transition of the individual from one social status to another, affirming the importance of the deceased person, channeling emotions, and offering vehicles for continuity and social cohesion of the social community (e.g., Romanoff & Terenzio, 1998). The loss of loved ones under traumatic circumstances often coincides with an impossibility to perform culturally appropriate rituals. The farewell ritual symbolizes a revised attachment bond with the deceased: The memory of the deceased may still be cherished, but the deceased is no longer symbolically kept alive (van der Hart & Boelen, 2003). Rituals can be a bridge to the patient's culture or spirituality. They may symbolize both continuity and transition and serve both reconciliation and affirmation (Doka, 2012).

The client designs a farewell ritual that he or she finds appropriate. Examples of farewell rituals include visiting a special place; creating a symbol of remembrance; performing a culturally appropriate ritual; renouncing things related to the traumatic circumstances of the death; burning the angry letter. The therapist is not present at the ritual, as it also constitutes the end of the treatment.

Facilitating the Client's Proactive Involvement in Supportive Relationships

The client is encouraged to involve supportive others, especially in the beginning and at the end of the therapy. A partner or friend is invited to the psychoeducation session. The farewell ritual implies a reunion with loved ones; therefore, the patient is encouraged to share the farewell ritual with a partner or a close friend.

Finding meaning includes a focus on important others, as well as values, priorities, goals, and activities. The therapist explores what kind of activities a patient undertakes and to what extent these activities are satisfactory. What has changed since the traumatic event? The therapist challenges the patient to look ahead and encourages him or her to think of important social, recreational, and, if relevant, work-related goals in the near future.

Identifying and Managing Safety Risks

Immediate suicidal risk is a contraindication for starting BEPP. However, long-standing safety risks, such as chronic suicidal ideation, self-harm, and addictions, may be addressed in an individual treatment plan promoting the reduction of safety risks. The involvement of a partner or friend in the therapy may support tailoring of the treatment plan to safety risks. It is important that both the client and the supportive person learn about the potential of trauma-focused treatment to bring about a temporary increase in distress. It is helpful for the therapist, client, and the supportive person to anticipate increases in distress, as well as risk behaviors, and to agree about how then to proceed (e.g., reschedule a joint consultation).

Conclusion

BEPP was originally developed to treat police officers with PTSD, but over the years, several studies have shown its efficacy for a wider range of trauma types and backgrounds. Many of the patients who enroll in treatment show symptoms of CTSDs, such as affect dysregulation, negative self-image, dissociative symptoms, and problems in sustaining relationships. BEPP encourages the formation and maintenance of a strong therapeutic relationship through psychoeducation and learning that one can handle the confrontation with traumatic material in the imaginal exposure. An essential part of BEPP is to work through core traumatic experiences in detail in the imaginal exposure, focusing on feelings of helplessness and grief. Other traumatic experiences and messages inherent in the person's background and childhood are addressed in the meaning-making phase in connection to the view of oneself, others, the world and the future. Writing letters is helpful in expressing unresolved emotions of anger, aggression, and grief, and often serves as a starting point for sessions in the meaning making and integration phase. Acknowledging the reality of the traumatic events and the strong accompanying emotions stimulates the person to learn from them, and to find a new equilibrium in relationships with others, and the view of him- or herself. BEPP is therefore a unique and useful model for the treatment of CTSDs, as well as related syndromes such as traumatic grief and complicated bereavement.

References

American Psychiatric Association. (2013). *Diagnostic and statistical manual of mental disorders* (5th ed.). Arlington, VA: Author.

Dahm, K. A., Meyer, E. C., Neff, K. D., Kimbrel, N. A., Gulliver, S. B., & Morissette, S. B. (2015). Mindfulness, self-compassion, posttraumatic stress disorder symptoms, and functional disability in U.S. Iraq and Afghanistan war veterans. *Journal of Traumatic Stress, 28,* 460–464.

Doka, K. J. (2012). Therapeutic ritual. In R. A. Neimeyer (Ed.), *Techniques of grief therapy: Creative practices for counseling the bereaved* (pp. 341–343). New York: Routledge.

Foa, E. B., Hembree, E. A., & Rothbaum, B. O. (2007). *Prolonged exposure therapy for PTSD: Emotional processing of traumatic experiences* (Therapist guide). Oxford, UK: Oxford University Press.

Foa, E. B., Rothbaum, B. O., Riggs, D. S., & Murdock, T. B. (1991). Treatment of posttraumatic stress disorder in rape victims: A comparison between cognitive behavioral procedures and counseling. *Journal of Consulting and Clinical Psychology, 59,* 715–723.

Gersons, B. P. R. (1989). Patterns of PTSD among police officers following shooting incidents: A two-dimensional model and treatment implications. *Journal of Traumatic Stress 2,* 247–257.

Gersons, B. P. R., Carlier, I. V. E., Lamberts, R. D., & van der Kolk, B. A. (2000). Random-ized clinical trial of brief eclectic psychotherapy for police officers with posttraumatic stress disorder. *Journal of Traumatic Stress, 13*, 333–347.

Gersons, B. P. R., Meewisse, M. L., & Nijdam, M. J. (2011). Brief eclectic psychotherapy for PTSD. In U. Schnyder & M. Cloitre (Eds.), *Evidence-based treatments for trauma-related psychological disorders: A practical guide for clinicians* (pp. 255–276). Cham, Switzerland: Springer International.

Gersons, B. P. R., Meewisse, M. L., Nijdam, M. J., & Olff, M. (2011). Protocol: Brief eclectic psychotherapy for PTSD (BEPP) (3rd English version). Amsterdam, the Netherlands: Academic Medical Centre at the University of Amsterdam.

Gersons, B. P. R., & Schnyder, U. (2013, December 20). Learning from traumatic experi-ences with brief eclectic psychotherapy for PTSD. *European Journal of Psychotrau-matology, 4.*

Herman, J. L. (2011). Shattered shame states and their repair. In J. Yellin & K. White (Eds.), *Shattered states: Disorganized attachment and its repair* (pp. 157–170). London: Kar-nac.

Hinton, D. E., Howes, D., & Kirmayer, L. J. (2008). Toward a medical anthropology of sensations: Definitions and research agenda. *Transcultural Psychiatry, 45*, 142–162.

Horowitz, M. J. (1976). *Stress response syndromes.* Northvale, NJ: Jason Aronson.

Jacobson, E. (1977). The origins and development of progressive relaxation. *Journal of Behavior Therapy and Experimental Psychiatry, 8*, 119–123.

Kazlauskas, E., Jovarauskaite, L., Mazulyte, E., Skruibis, P., Dovydaitiene, M., Eimontas, J., & Zelviene, P. (2017). "It will get even better": Preliminary findings from a trauma-focused psychotherapy effectiveness study reveal false positive patients' long-term out-come expectations after the treatment. *Nordic Journal of Psychiatry, 71*(4), 277–281.

Kellogg, S. (2012). On speaking one's mind: Using chair-work dialogues in schema therapy. In M. V. Vreeswijk, J. Broersen, & M. Nadort (Eds.), *The Wiley-Blackwell handbook of schema therapy: Theory, research, and practice* (pp. 197–207). Chichester, UK: Wiley.

Lanius, R. A., Brand, B., Vermetten, E., Frewen, P. A., & Spiegel, D. (2012). The dissocia-tive subtype of posttraumatic stress disorder: Rationale, clinical and neurobiological evidence, and implications. *Depression and Anxiety, 29*(8), 701–708.

Lindauer, R. J. L., Gersons, B. P. R., van Meijel, E. P. M., Blom, K., Carlier, I. V. E., Vri-jlandt, I., & Olff, M. (2005), Effects of brief eclectic psychotherapy in patients with posttraumatic stress disorder: Randomized clinical trial. *Journal of Traumatic Stress, 18*, 205 –212.

Litz, B. T., Stein, N., Delaney, E., Lebowitz, L., Nash, W. P., Silva, C., & Maguen, S. (2009). Moral injury and moral repair in war veterans: A preliminary model and intervention strategy. *Clinical Psychology Review, 29*, 695–706.

Luborsky, L. (1984). *Principles of psychoanalytic psychotherapy: A manual for supportive-expressive treatment.* New York: Basic Books.

Maercker, A., Brewin, C. R., Bryant, R. A., Cloitre, M., van Ommeren, M., Jones, L. M., . . . Reed, G. M. (2013). Diagnosis and classification of disorders specifically associated with stress: Proposals for ICD-11. *World Psychiatry, 12*, 198–206.

Nijdam, M. J., Baas, M. A., Olff, M., & Gersons, B. P. (2013). Hotspots in trauma memo-ries and their relationship to successful trauma-focused psychotherapy: A pilot study. *Journal of Traumatic Stress, 26*(1), 38–44.

Nijdam, M. J., Gersons, B. P. R., Reitsma, J. B., de Jongh, A., & Olff, M. (2012). Brief eclec-tic psychotherapy versus eye movement desensitisation and reprocessing therapy in the treatment of posttraumatic stress disorder: Randomised controlled trial. *British Journal of Psychiatry, 200*(3), 224–231.

Nijdam, M. J., Martens, I. J., Reitsma, J. B., Gersons, B. P., & Olff, M. (2018a). Neurocogni-tive functioning over the course of trauma-focused psychotherapy for PTSD: Changes in verbal memory and executive functioning. *British Journal of Clinical Psychology, 57*, 1–17.

Nijdam, M. J., van der Meer, C. A. I., van Zuiden, M., Dashtgard, P., Medema, D., Qing, Y., . . . Olff, M. (2018b). Turning wounds into wisdom: Posttraumatic growth over the course of two types of trauma-focused psychotherapy in patients with PTSD. *Journal of Affective Disorders, 227,* 424–431.

Romanoff, B. D., & Terenzio, M. (1998). Rituals and the grieving process. *Death Studies, 22,* 697–711.

Schnyder, U., Ehlers, A., Elbert, T., Foa, E., Gersons, B., Resick, P., . . . Cloitre, M. (2015, August 14). Psychotherapies for PTSD: What do they have in common? *European Journal of Psychotraumatology, 6.*

Schnyder, U., Müller, J., Maercker, A., & Wittmann, L. (2011). Brief eclectic psychotherapy for PTSD: A randomized controlled trial. *Journal of Clinical Psychiatry, 72,* 564–566.

Shapiro, F. (2001). *Eye movement desensitization and processing: Basic principles, protocols, and procedures* (2nd ed.). New York: Guilford Press.

Shay, J. (2014). Moral injury. *Psychoanalytic Psychology, 31,* 182–191.

Smid, G. E., & Boelen, P. A. (in press). Culturally sensitive approaches to finding meaning in traumatic bereavement. In R. A. Neimeyer (Ed.), *New techniques of grief therapy: Bereavement and beyond.* New York: Routledge.

Smid, G. E., Kleber, R. J., de la Rie, S. M., Bos, J. B. A., Gersons, B. P. R., & Boelen, P. A. (2015). Brief eclectic psychotherapy for traumatic grief (BEP-TG): Toward integrated treatment of symptoms related to traumatic loss. *European Journal of Psychotraumatology, 6*(1), 27324.

van der Hart, O., & Boelen, P. A. (2003). Therapeutische afscheidsrituelen in de behandeling van problematische rouw: Een integratie [Therapeutic farewell rituals in the treatment of problematic grief: An integration]. In O. van der Hart (Ed.), *Afscheidsrituelen: Achterblijven en verder gaan* (pp. 221–235). Lisse: Swets en Zeitlinger.

Vaughan, K., Armstrong, M. S., Gold, R., O'Connor, N., Jenneke, W., & Tarrier, N. (1994). A trial of eye movement desensitization compared to image habituation training and applied muscle relaxation in post-traumatic stress disorder. *Journal of Behavior Therapy and Experimental Psychiatry, 25,* 283–291.

Young, J. E., Klosko, J. S., & Weishaar, M. E. (2003). *Schema therapy: A practitioner's guide.* New York: Guilford Press.

CHAPTER 13

Eye Movement Desensitization and Reprocessing Therapy

DEBORAH L. KORN
FRANCINE SHAPIRO

Eye movement desensitization and reprocessing (EMDR) therapy is an integrative, phase-oriented psychotherapy that highlights the role of the brain's information processing system in the development and treatment of a wide range of mental health issues. It is guided by the adaptive information processing (AIP) model, which proposes that psychopathology is due to a failure to adequately process traumatic or other adverse life experiences to a point of "adaptive resolution" (Shapiro, 2018). In nontraumatic circumstances, disturbing events are spontaneously resolved when links are established with neural networks containing relevant and helpful information (e.g., "I am a responsible person"; "I am not alone"). However, in overwhelming traumatic situations with high levels of psychophysiological arousal and concomitant emotional dysregulation, information processing becomes blocked, preventing the forging of connections between memories of these experiences (encoded in a static, state-specific network) and more adaptive information held in other memory networks. The traumatic experience, with all of its components—feelings, sensations, impulses, cognitions, images, and other sensory elements—remains "frozen" in the nervous system. Inadequately processed memories are later reactivated by internal or external triggers (environmental or interpersonal stressors, feelings, or sensory experiences related to a traumatic episode), leading to classic posttraumtic stress disorder (PTSD) symptoms and other problematic psychological and physiologic reactions. Through an EMDR lens, "triggered" symptoms reflect the activation of one or more traumatic memories within the nervous system (Shapiro, 2018).

According to the AIP model, if earlier memories, characterized by negative feelings (e.g., shame and fear), impulses or behaviors (e.g., freezing), and maladaptive beliefs developed during the trauma or afterwards (e.g., "I'm powerless"), remain unprocessed and stored in the nervous system in a disturbing, state-specific form, individuals may find themselves responding emotionally, behaviorally, cognitively, and/or somatically to current situations as if they were still living in the past, in danger and without choices. They remain quite limited in their ability to respond adaptively to challenging situations in the present, because they are still influenced by the schemas and response sets associated with earlier traumatic experiences. In the AIP model, the brain's information processing system is compared to other body-based systems (e.g., the immune system) and is viewed as physiologically geared toward the achievement of optimal health. In EMDR treatment, the therapist helps mobilize the client's own inherent healing mechanism, with the goal of fully processing traumatic memories until they no longer cause symptoms and can be recalled without distress.

During EMDR therapy, an individual is asked to focus on a traumatic memory while engaged in bilateral stimulation (typically, repetitive lateral eye movements). This creates a condition of dual attention—a simultaneous focus on an external stimulus and an internal memory—that facilitates the processing of the memory. Although eye movements are the most commonly used form of bilateral stimulation and the type most supported by research (Lee & Cuijpers, 2013), other forms, such as auditory or tactile bilateral stimulation, can be used. EMDR therapy employs a comprehensive three-pronged approach that targets (1) relevant unprocessed or "stuck" memories linked to the client's current symptoms, (2) current triggers and symptoms associated with psychological distress, and (3) goals for adaptive future functioning and performance. Within a comprehensive EMDR therapy treatment plan, each of these dimensions of an individual's experience is identified and targeted for processing. The goal is to reduce the level of distress associated with a memory and its triggers and to shift the client's self-appraisal from negative to positive. As traumatic or adverse experiences and triggers are processed to a point of completion, current symptoms, maladaptive defenses, and dysfunctional interpersonal patterns begin to shift and are ultimately transformed, ideally to the point of elimination.

The symptoms of complex traumatic stress disorders (CTSDs) can be understood in terms of what happened (e.g., different forms of abuse and exploitation), what did not happen (e.g., response, rescue, attachment repair, protection), and the individual's unique adaptation to adverse life circumstances, including negative self-appraisals developed during or subsequent to the traumatic experience. Ubiquitous, "small-t" adverse life events (e.g., microaggressions, rejection, humiliation, failure, loss, neglect, deprivation), often quite common in the histories of individuals with CTSDs, are regularly addressed in EMDR therapy and are not considered secondary to or less relevant than the "big-T" traumas defined in DSM-5 PTSD criteria (American Psychiatric Association, 2013).

The Evolution of a Psychotherapy: From EMD to EMDR to EMDR Therapy

When Shapiro first reported on her novel methodology in a randomized controlled trial (RCT), it was referred to as EMD, or eye movement desensitization, and viewed simply as a desensitization technique for lowering the distress associated with posttraumatic memories (Shapiro, 1989). Since then, EMD has evolved into a comprehensive and multifaceted psychotherapy. In 1991, in recognition of the profound cognitive shifts and insights reported during treatment, Shapiro changed the name to EMDR (eye movement desensitization and reprocessing), and subsequently developed the AIP theory to explain the changes being observed. Today, this approach, recognized as much more than a narrowly focused technique, is referred to as EMDR therapy (Shapiro, 2018).

Over the last several decades, influenced by advances in the understanding of complex trauma, interpersonal neurobiology, affective neuroscience, and attachment theory, EMDR therapy has become much more expansive and integrative. In addition to the continued attention to trauma processing, there is now a greater emphasis on addressing clients' developmental deficits and patterns of dysregulation, as well as the maladaptive strategies learned to cope with or defend against emotional pain. Complex interpersonal trauma is treated within a relational context (Rosoff, 2019), with the therapist actively accompanying the client through trauma processing, co-regulating, providing support, reassurance and validation, working with fears, shame, and defenses, delighting in transformational moments, and explicitly helping the client to feel and to be seen, heard, and deeply understood. Both verbal (e.g., recognition, validation) and nonverbal (e.g., eye contact, facial expression, gestures, prosody) attunement are critical in creating a secure base from which the client can explore previously unbearable experiences.

An array of specialized EMDR protocols and interventions has been developed to address the challenges of working with the multiplicity of issues (as detailed in the chapters of this text) associated with complex trauma. These interventions, along with moment-to-moment attunement, titration, and the maintenance of secure attachment, enable EMDR clinicians to efficiently move clients into actual trauma processing, while keeping them within what Siegel (1999) has termed their "window of tolerance"—a zone of arousal within which they can receive, process, and integrate information effectively without becoming hyper- or hypoaroused. Also, as additional EMDR protocols have been developed to treat an increasingly wide range of comorbid mental health issues (e.g., psychotic disorders, chronic pain, addictions), the treatment of CTSDs with EMDR therapy, has become significantly more comprehensive (see Shapiro, 2018).

Empirical Evidence for EMDR Therapy

Considerable controversy surrounded EMDR during its early years due largely to its unique eye movement procedure. However, its efficacy in the amelioration and eradication of symptoms of PTSD is now well established in the research and clinical literature. The findings of early RCTs indicated that up to 90% of survivors of a single trauma no longer had a PTSD diagnosis after only three 90-minute sessions, and with no homework (Rothbaum, 1997; Wilson, Becker, & Tinker, 1997). More recent studies have reported numbers as high as 95% for loss of PTSD diagnosis (Capezzani et al., 2013). Over time, the efficacy of EMDR has been validated by more than 30 RCTs. Moreover, 13 RCTs, compared EMDR therapy to either general cognitive-behavioral therapy (CBT) or trauma-focused cognitive-behavioral therapy (TF-CBT). Five of the studies found equivalent effectiveness for EMDR and CBT in reducing PTSD symptoms. However, two of the studies found that TF-CBT was significantly more effective than EMDR therapy, while six found EMDR therapy to be more effective (de Jongh, Benedikt, Hofmann, Farrell, & Lee, 2019a). Four additional papers found that EMDR therapy achieved the desired treatment effects in fewer sessions (de Jongh et al., 2019a). Also, dropout rates for EMDR therapy are low. A meta-analysis, by Swift and Greenberg (2014) reported a dropout rate of 17% for EMDR therapy, compared to rates of 23–28% for full CBT, prolonged exposure (PE), and cognitive processing therapy (CPT), although the differences did not reach statistical significance.

Though EMDR therapy is similar to TF-CBT in its focus on lowering or eliminating subjective distress and changing maladaptive beliefs, it is not simply a variant of CBT. According to the World Health Organization (2013, p. 1), "Unlike CBT with a trauma focus, EMDR does not involve a) detailed descriptions of the event, b) direct challenging of beliefs, c) extended exposure, or d) homework." In EMDR therapy, all processing of traumatic material is done within session, with the therapist present to co-regulate and intervene as needed. Exposure to traumatic material is imaginal, brief, and intermittent. Unlike in most forms of exposure therapy, clients are not required to repeatedly tell, write, or listen to their trauma narrative within or outside of session and are simply asked to self-monitor and record observations between sessions. These factors, along with EMDR's efficacy, likely play a role in keeping dropout rates low.

Thus far, more than 36 RCTs have substantiated the positive effects of the eye movement component. One meta-analysis (Lee & Cuijpers, 2013) of 26 trials with 849 participants confirmed that eye movements significantly reduce negative emotions and imagery vividness. Other studies provide evidence that eye movements facilitate episodic memory retrieval, increase the recognition of true information, lower emotional arousal, and increase relaxation, cognitive flexibility, and neurophysiological changes (for a review, see Shapiro, 2018). Shapiro (2018) proposed that the theories of underlying mechanisms of action with the most empirical support suggest that eye movements (1) elicit an orienting response that activates the parasympathetic nervous system, (2) interfere with working memory, and (3) stimulate the same neurological processes that occur in rapid eye movement (REM) sleep. All are consistent with the AIP model. Landin-Romero, Moreno-Alcazar, Pagani, and Amann (2018) provide a systematic review of proposed mechanisms of action.

EMDR is thought to reprocess the trauma with short and intermittent exposures resulting in memory reconsolidation, in which the memory is changed and then re-stored in its altered form (Suzuki et al., 2004). This is in contrast to the prolonged exposures of CBT, which result in extinction, creating a new memory while leaving the original one intact.

There is growing evidence that EMDR therapy is a first-line treatment not just for PTSD, but also for individuals with a history of childhood interpersonal trauma, or other forms of prolonged or repeated trauma, who report the kinds of symptoms associated with complex PTSD (CPTSD; Chen et al., 2018). In their systematic review and meta-analysis of psychological interventions for the symptoms of CPTSD, as defined in the most recent WHO International Classification of Diseases (ICD-11), Kartatzias et al. (2019) reported that EMDR was effective in treating negative self-concept, disturbances in relationships, and affect dysregulation, as well as PTSD symptoms. EMDR therapy has also been found to be effective with individuals with CPTSD who display significant dissociation (for review, see de Jongh et al., 2019b).

Not surprisingly, evidence suggests that complex or repetitive trauma requires more sessions to achieve positive outcomes. For example, in an eight-session RCT, van der Kolk et al. (2007) found that 100% of the adult-onset trauma participants in the EMDR treatment group lost their PTSD diagnosis by the end of treatment as compared to only 75% of the child-onset participants, who were most likely to have CTSDs. At 6-month follow-up, 89% of the childhood-onset group had lost their PTSD diagnosis, but only 33% were considered asymptomatic, compared to 75% of those with adult-onset trauma exposure. These findings suggest the need for a lengthier course of treatment for individuals with CTSD.

EMDR therapy for CTSDs is a phase-oriented approach that emphasizes the importance of client preparation prior to trauma-focused processing. There has been significant discussion about how to determine readiness and whether or not certain clients need a prolonged stabilization period. Client safety and maintenance of functioning are always priorities in EMDR therapy, yet there remains an emphasis on getting to trauma processing as quickly as possible to alleviate distress.

Some EMDR studies indicate that a prolonged phase of stabilization is not always necessary. For example, although 37 patients (42%) in the van der Kolk et al. (2007) study met the criteria for CPTSD or disorders of extreme stress not otherwise specified (DESNOS), or reported index traumas of childhood sexual or physical abuse, only one participant in the EMDR therapy condition required additional stabilization interventions beyond the standard safe/calm place exercise in the preparation phase (both discussed below). In a second study (van den Berg et al., 2015), examining the efficacy of trauma-focused treatment for patients with a psychotic disorder and comorbid PTSD, 60% of those in the EMDR condition were found to have lost their PTSD diagnosis after eight treatment sessions. Of these, 67% reported a history of sexual abuse with 36.4% indicating childhood sexual abuse before the age of 12. There was no stabilization phase in this study and the safe/calm place exercise was removed from the standard EMDR therapy protocol. More recently, Bongaerts, Minnen, and de Jongh (2017) published a report with seven participants diagnosed with CPTSD and other conditions indicating the feasibility and effectiveness of intensive EMDR therapy without a stabilization phase.

As concluded by Bongaerts et al. (2017) and other recently published studies (for review, see de Jongh et al., 2019b), there is mounting evidence that intensive EMDR therapy formats can be safely and effectively used with complex trauma populations yielding high effect sizes and retention rates. That said, rigorous RCTs with participants specifically diagnosed with CPTSD are needed to determine the most efficacious treatment regimens.

Based on this firm foundation of research findings, EMDR therapy has been designated an effective trauma treatment, receiving strong recommendations in the guidelines of numerous internationally recognized organizations, including the World Health Organization (2013), International Society for Traumatic Stress Studies (ISTSS Guidelines Committee, 2019), Clinical Resource Efficiency Support Team of the Northern Ireland Department of Health, Social Services and Public Safety (CREST, 2003), Australian Centre for Posttraumatic Mental Health (2013), the U.S. Department of Veterans Affairs and Department of Defense (2017), and a conditional recommendation in one other (American Psychological Association; Courtois et al., 2017). As such, EMDR is among the most strongly endorsed treatments for PTSD.

Key Clinical Features:
The Eight Phases of EMDR Therapy

From the outset of treatment, EMDR therapists provide traumatized clients with psychoeducation about the AIP model and the relationship between "stuck" or dysfunctionally stored memories and ongoing symptoms. Treatment explores an individual's exposure to acts of commission (e.g., harm, abuse, loss) as well as omission (e.g., abandonment, neglect, invalidation, nonprotection). The targets addressed in EMDR therapy include not only actual traumatic memories but also current triggers and symptoms. Acts of omission resulting in attachment-related developmental interruptions or injuries are also targeted. EMDR therapy for CTSDs, like that for PTSD, consists of eight phases: (1) history taking and treatment planning, (2) preparation, (3) assessment, (4) desensitization, (5) installation, (6) body scan, (7) closure, and (8) reevaluation.

History Taking and Treatment Planning

During this initial phase of treatment, the therapist gathers background bio-psychosocial information about the client, using relevant inventories and clinical questioning. The therapist develops a case conceptualization and treatment plan to address the client's vulnerability to emotional dysregulation and dissociation, as well as skills deficits, stabilization needs, and attachment status. Relevant past experiences, current triggers and symptoms, and future coping and performance goals are identified for later processing. An AIP-driven approach to history taking often involves the use of "floatback" and/or "affect scan" techniques to identify targets for processing. Using these techniques, the therapist asks the client to access the feelings, sensations and, sometimes, beliefs associated with a recent symptom episode, and then invites the client to follow them back to an earlier time, when the client experienced something similar.

In considering readiness for trauma processing, the therapist assesses whether the individual has a reasonable repertoire of adaptive coping skills and, in turn, the capacity to access affect without negative consequences. Clients need to be able to maintain dual attention—in this case, attending to memories and distressing internal experiences while remaining oriented to the present environment—and manage any defensive or dissociative impulses. There is also a need for sufficient security within the therapeutic relationship.

The therapist tracks the client's capacity to remain present-focused and responsive. If the client becomes increasingly anxious or defensive (e.g., spontaneously shutting down or stating, "I don't want to talk about that"), the therapist helps with regulation and orienting (e.g., "Come back to me. You're safe now and in my office. Feel your feet on the ground"). If the client continues to struggle, the therapist might opt to begin with the preparation phase instead, in which the therapist directs efforts at strengthening the therapeutic relationship and building self- and dyadic regulation capacities. Clients diagnosed with severe behavioral dysregulation (e.g., addictions, parasuicidal or suicidal behaviors, aggression toward others, eating disorders) and/or dissociative disorders often need to begin with the preparation phase.

Preparation

Psychoeducation about the AIP model and the procedural steps of EMDR therapy are provided, along with relevant coping or resourcing strategies as needed; clients are given an opportunity to learn and practice a variety of strategies to help them stay regulated. Using an established protocol, all clients are introduced to the concept of the safe/calm place (Shapiro, 2018) and invited to "imagine a place that is soothing and comfortable, where nothing bad has ever happened." In order to strengthen and "install" this resource, sets of bilateral stimulation are used as the client focuses on the safe/calm place image and the feelings, sensations, and words associated with it. This safe/calm place can then be cued if and when the client is triggered or to help with closure at the end of a processing session.

Therapists may also guide their clients through a resource development and installation (RDI) protocol (Korn & Leeds, 2002; Leeds, 2009) that focuses on identifying and accessing (via positive memories of experiences and people) the personal qualities (e.g., courage, confidence, connection) needed to directly address traumatic experiences in treatment and to cope more effectively with symptoms and real life stressors. The therapist asks questions to identify memories or images associated with these qualities in at least three different areas: (1) personal mastery experiences (e.g., winning a race); (2) helpful others and role models (e.g., a beloved relative or best friend); and (3) symbolic resource images (e.g., a firmly rooted tree). Once the memory or image is identified, the client is asked to notice the positive feelings, sensations, and words associated with the resource as sets of bilateral stimulation are commenced. Typically, the client feels more "resourced" with every set and, eventually, is encouraged to visualize a connection with this resource when dealing with a difficult situation. Behavioral goals are set for using relevant resources to manage the fears associated with confronting traumatic memories and for addressing particular life stressors. EMDR therapists also teach clients numerous other techniques designed to help with self-management (see Shapiro, 2018).

Based on the stabilization needs of their clients, therapists can integrate material from other well-established models during the preparation phase, including personal safety, stabilization, or skills-focused interventions from models such as Dialectical Behavior Therapy (DBT; Linehan, 2015), Seeking Safety (Najavits, 2002), skills training in affective and interpersonal regulation (STAIR; Cloitre, Cohen, & Koenen, 2006) or Trauma Affect Regulation: Guide for Education and Therapy (TARGET; Ford, 2015). They might choose to introduce skills, strategies, or imaginal resources that the client can use for grounding, distancing, titrating, modulating, containing, soothing, or orienting (Korn, 2009). Finally, they may introduce ego-state interventions, primarily during this phase, to decrease destabilizing and defensive behaviors, resolve internal conflicts, increase commitment to treatment, and help prepare for trauma-focused work (Forgash & Copeley, 2008; Gonzalez & Mosquera, 2012; Knipe, 2015; van der Hart, Groenendijk, Gonzalez, Mosquera, & Solomon, 2013). In this context, an "ego state" is a state of mind or a part of the personality that is typically stable over time, accessible, and associated with a particular role, emotion, memory, kind of behavior, or cognitive function.

The length of the preparation phase varies. There are no required interventions in the preparation phase other than the "safe/calm place" exercise and no set number of sessions required prior to the start of trauma processing. Some survivors of complex trauma (i.e., those with a secure attachment style, who generally have stable resources) meet readiness criteria at intake or after only a few sessions. Memory processing is started as quickly as possible, but there are some clients who require a more extended preparation phase—several weeks to many months—due to their limited self-capacities, skills deficits, and unstable life circumstances. The therapist may return to the preparation phase at various times during the course of treatment if it becomes apparent that the client needs new skills or strengthened self-capacities.

Assessment

This brief phase is used to select and activate a relevant memory for processing. The therapist asks the client to focus on one particular target, a memory associated with a specific traumatic experience (e.g., physical attack at age 8 by one's father), symptom (e.g., nightmare, feeling of shame or self-hatred, flashback image), or trigger (e.g., criticism from boss). The target is activated by the therapist through a series of questions designed to access the image, negative cognition (e.g., "I'm not good enough"), feelings, and somatic sensations associated with it. A desired positive cognition (e.g., "I'm good enough") is also identified as a goal, and baseline readings on the Subjective Units of Disturbance (SUD) scale (Wolpe, 1982) and Validity of the (Positive) Cognition (VOC) scale (Shapiro, 1989) are obtained. The SUD scale (0–10, 0 = *no disturbance*, 10 = *maximum disturbance*) is used to rate the intensity of the distress the client feels when focusing on the target. The VOC scale (1–7, 1 = *not true at all*, 7 = *totally true*) is used to rate how "true" the positive cognition feels while accessing the traumatic memory. Starting in this phase, both scales are used at various points over the course of a session to track progress.

Desensitization

The actual trauma processing begins when the therapist asks the client to focus on the components of the target memory (image, negative cognition, feelings, and sensations), while simultaneously focusing on some form of bilateral stimulation (tracking fingers or a light moving back and forth for visual stimulation, listening to binaural tones, and/or receiving alternating taps on each hand). The client is instructed: "Just notice and let whatever happens happen." At the end of a set of bilateral stimulation (typically lasting about 30 seconds, though sometimes much longer), the therapist asks, "What do you get now?" The range of possible responses is large. Clients may express various emotions, report on the experiencing of various sensations or impulses, or describe images or unfolding scenes. They also may offer additional details about the target experience and/or share new memories, thoughts, or insights. Clients may spontaneously address a "child self" or perpetrator, or imagine completing an action (e.g., fighting back or speaking up) that had not been possible at the time of the trauma. Other thematically related "feeder" memories of earlier events may also emerge. This new material generally becomes the focus of the next processing set. Processing of the target continues until no new material emerges and the client indicates that the SUD level when focusing on the original memory is no higher than 1 (preferably 0).

Even after considerable work in the preparation phase, it is rather common for clients to encounter phobias, "blocking beliefs," dissociation, or various other defensive responses, upon beginning trauma processing. Therapists track responses on a moment-to-moment basis, coregulating and working to keep clients within their window of tolerance. Therapists might slow the speed of the bilateral stimulation, decrease the number of back and forth passes (auditory, tactile, or visual), or offer reassurance by reminding their clients that they are safe, that it is "old stuff" that they are processing, and that they are not alone anymore. When hypoarousal is evident, the client is directed to notice certain sensations, micromovements, or signs of emotion to increase arousal. For hyperarousal, the client is encouraged to reconnect with the therapist, get grounded, take a deep breath, or use some modulation-focused resource imagery. The therapist may opt to use EMD (Shapiro, 2018) with clients who are having difficulties tolerating the work at hand. With EMD, as opposed to EMDR, the therapist applies much shorter sets of bilateral stimulation and returns to the target after each set to take a SUD level. The client can choose to focus on just one small aspect of the memory (e.g., image, feeling, sensation) and associations to material beyond the target memory are deliberately limited by the therapist.

When processing gets stuck (e.g., ruminative perseveration on a distressing aspect of a memory, or failure to spontaneously progress in an adaptive direction), the therapist probes to determine what fears, blocking beliefs, or defenses are inhibiting or interfering (e.g., "What are you afraid might happen if you let yourself feel sad?" or "What message from childhood is holding you back right now?") Typically, clients get stuck because they are unable to access more adaptive memory networks, information, or thoughts (e.g., "Children are not responsible for abuse" or "Sadness is a healthy, appropriate emotion to feel when you lose someone that you love"), and/or have compromised affect regulation (e.g., "If I let myself feel, I'll go crazy or die").

Clients tend to get stuck at regular intervals on three different "informational plateaus" associated with themes of (1) responsibility and defectiveness, (2) safety and vulnerability, and (3) power and control (Shapiro, 2018). The therapist anticipates and responds to emerging fears and blocks with "cognitive interweaves" (Korn & Laliotis, 2015; Shapiro, 2018), providing missing information and adult perspectives or asking questions that invite a client to consider certain conclusions, insights, emotional responses, and imagined actions and scenes. For example, for clients who are burdened with self-hatred for failing to fight back during an assault, therapists might provide psychoeducation about the normal "freeze" response or ask their clients to consider what would likely have happened if they had actually tried to fight back. Therapists might ask, "What would you say if this was your daughter telling you the same story? Would you think that it was her fault that she was raped?" Or therapists may encourage clients to imagine what they might say or do to the abuser if they could safely take revenge, with no concern for consequences. When appropriate, clients are encouraged to verbalize pain or anger out loud, directing it toward a perpetrator or bystander. If the client reports a body sensation that seems to represent an inhibited action, movements such as running in place, pushing, or pounding with fists may be encouraged during processing sets (Levine, 1997; Shapiro, 1995, 2018). When the necessary adaptive information or responses are accessed, the therapist responds affirmatively and encourages the client to "just notice," continuing with bilateral stimulation.

Installation

When a target memory appears to have been fully desensitized (i.e., SUD = 0), work proceeds to the "installation" of the desired positive cognition. The client is asked whether the positive cognition (e.g., "I am fine as I am") identified earlier still fits or whether another fits better (e.g., "I'm good") The strongest positive cognition, along with the original incident, is held in mind and a VOC rating (1–7) is taken. Sets of bilateral stimulation are administered until the client reports that the positive cognition feels optimally true and integrated (VOC = 7). The therapist attempts to identify blocking beliefs, fears, and other material (e.g., "I don't want you to think that I'm bragging") that need to get processed in order for the positive cognition to be fully integrated. Once identified, the client is asked to focus on the block, and processing with bilateral stimulation continues until the VOC = 7; interweaves may be used if processing remains blocked.

Body Scan

In this phase, the client is asked to hold the original target in mind, along with the positive cognition, while physically "scanning" for any remaining feelings or signs of distress or discomfort in the body. If any remain, the client is asked to focus on the sensations while processing with bilateral stimulation continues, until no residual disturbance is reported. The body scan phase thus serves as a final check on whether the target memory is fully processed. It is designed to identify additional aspects of the target memory or related memories that still need to be addressed.

Closure

In this next-to-last phase, the therapist shifts away from trauma-related material, with an emphasis on returning the client to a grounded, present-focused state. If the processing is incomplete, the client is encouraged to put the material into an imagined container, then to engage in a self-soothing exercise, such as the safe/calm place. Client and therapist typically debrief, and the client is asked about the most important thing learned during the session. Out-of-session goals and self-care strategies for the week are also discussed. The client is encouraged to maintain a log or journal, noting observations related to presenting issues and current work. This phase serves to deepen the trust and security of the therapeutic relationship as client and therapist reflect on working together. When processing is incomplete (SUD level above 0 and VOC less than 7) at the end of a session (not an uncommon occurrence), attention returns to the incomplete target in the next session.

Reevaluation

Each session begins with a client report of changes experienced since the last processing session; the target from that session is then re-evaluated to determine whether further processing is needed. Additional material (e.g., new memories, details, realizations or insights, previously dissociated affect) may have emerged, especially in clients with significant dissociation. It is not unusual for additional elements of a given traumatic experience (or related experiences) to emerge as dissociative barriers weaken. Newly emergent material either becomes the focus of the current session or gets added to the treatment plan for later processing. The reevaluation phase provides an important checkpoint, ensuring that relevant new targets are identified as they emerge and that older targets are fully resolved before proceeding. As additional material emerges over the course of treatment, the treatment plan evolves.

The Three-Pronged Protocol: Past, Present, and Future

As the client completes the processing of each target, the treatment plan is reassessed and modified to determine which memory, current trigger, or future goal should be addressed next. Ultimately, the clinical goal is to identify, reprocess, and resolve all relevant targets (past memories and present triggers) related to current symptomatology and to assist the client, through an imagined "future template" rehearsal procedure, to effectively deal with day-to-day challenges and personal initiatives. Using the "future template protocol," therapists encourage their clients to first imagine a future scene, and then run a movie in their mind's eye, with a beginning, middle, and end, that involves coping effectively with a challenging situation. If difficulties are encountered, the client problem-solves, role-plays, or receives coaching from the therapist. Bilateral stimulation is then used to neutralize any anxiety and eliminate blocks to successful rehearsal. Once the client has achieved mastery with the imagined future template movie, bilateral stimulation is added to fully "install" or integrate this positive goal state.

Complex Decision Making: Selecting Targets, Sequencing Interventions, and Adapting the Standard Protocol for Treating CTSDs

With classic PTSD, treatment planning and decision making are often quite straightforward. For individuals with CTSDs, these processes tend to be more complicated, as the therapist is faced with multiple decisions. The priorities for treatment, targets chosen for processing, and the client's capacity to do the work need to be continually reevaluated. With classic PTSD, targets from the past are usually addressed first, but with CTSD, the therapist considers the client's affect tolerance, dissociative vulnerabilities, current life stability, and readiness to address painful material in setting up targets and sequencing.

Although EMDR is a phase-based therapy, treatment is not linear. At times, therapy begins with or diverts to a future-change goal, using a future template, to help the client prepare for, and ultimately achieve, that goal (e.g., preparing for a long-avoided doctor's appointment, a difficult conversation with a partner, or a visit to an Alcoholics Anonymous meeting). In focusing on future targets first, the goal is to help clarify goals, access hope and motivation, and stabilize daily functioning. At other times, present-day triggers and symptoms may be addressed first in an effort to decrease fears, blocking beliefs, and dysregulating emotions that might hinder the client's capacity to address critical past traumas. Successful work with current triggers and symptoms helps clients develop a sense of confidence in their capacity to tolerate present-day affect and arousal, and a chance to experience the support and commitment of their therapist prior to addressing more painful and possibly overwhelming memories. This "corrective emotional experience" can be explicitly highlighted, then integrated into a client's present-day positive memory network (e.g., "Notice what it was like to do this work with me today"), with a "set" of bilateral stimulation.

In working with past traumatic experiences, therapist and client collaboratively decide on the sequencing of targets, utilizing any of a number of approaches to identify and organize relevant targets. They may decide to start with the earliest known exposure to a particular kind of trauma or experience (e.g., abandonment, shaming, abuse, invalidation), the worst instance of that kind of trauma or experience, or some other, related experience. They may opt to sequence targets using a more developmental approach, addressing the earliest to the most recent traumas and adverse events in chronological order. However, with chronically traumatized clients, starting with the earliest or worst traumatic memories may be particularly challenging due to an overabundance of traumatic memories, dissociation, limited affect tolerance, and extensive phobias of inner experience (van der Hart, Nijenhuis, & Steele, 2006). It is often preferable to use a symptom-focused approach in which the therapist identifies the most disruptive present-day symptoms—feelings, sensations, beliefs, and reactions to triggers—and uses the floatback or affect scan technique to search for the memories most directly related to these symptoms. This approach may lead to memories that were not previously conscious and ones that are highly activated or charged. Clients are always given a choice as to whether they are, indeed, ready to address such highly charged memories or whether they would prefer to address a memory with a lower SUD level.

If memories involve developmental trauma—neglect, deprivation, loss of or separation from a caregiver, unmet needs—the therapist may decide to use a "positive resourcing" protocol (i.e., RDI) to strengthen the positive memory network (e.g., filling in some of the client's significant deficits with imagined or actual experiences of positive caregiving or personal resilience) prior to accessing emotionally charged memories. And, in the actual processing, the therapist may actively use interweaves to facilitate developmental repair (e.g., "Imagine that you could offer that little girl exactly what she needed. What would you want to say to her or do for her?") When dealing with comorbid issues such as addictions, eating disorders, obsessive–compulsive disorder (OCD), phobias, or self-injury, the therapist may decide to use additional specialized EMDR protocols (as discussed in Shapiro, 2018).

It is important to note that it is not necessary to target every traumatic memory, since spontaneous generalization of changed perspectives operates across memory networks; if one memory is processed to resolution, it is often the case that thematically related experiences are also resolved. In addition, treatment plans are continually reevaluated and revised, and clients regularly revisit territory previously addressed but with an increased sense of integration and new levels of understanding.

Clinical Case Example

Molly, a 29-year-old single, white female, employed full-time, was referred for outpatient treatment after a 1-week stay in an inpatient psychiatric facility. Upon discharge, she still had debilitating symptoms of depression and PTSD with passive suicidal ideation, urges to stab her hand, and significant dissociation. She reported a history of sexual, physical, and emotional abuse and neglect by multiple perpetrators, beginning at an early age. She and her two brothers were raised by an emotionally and physically abusive, alcoholic mother and a passive, absent father, who would leave home for extended periods of time. At age 6, she was sexually abused on several occasions by a sadistic male neighbor who, she later learned, had also abused other children in the neighborhood. He physically forced her to kill a baby rabbit with a knife after telling her that he would kill her if she did not comply. Her mother, when intoxicated, would come after her with knives and hairbrushes, telling her that she was the worst daughter imaginable, that she should have never been born, and that she did not deserve to live.

Molly saw herself as "damaged goods" and believed that she was "dirty, disgusting, and shameful." She maintained a sense of extreme mistrust and anticipated revictimization in every relationship, from both men and women. She was disgusted with herself for having been hospitalized and reported that she had come out worse than she was when admitted. She was also terrified of losing her self-control and somehow harming others, though she had no previous history of doing so. She described a profound sense of loneliness and despair, repeatedly saying, "I'm not sure why I'm alive." Despite her horrific history and internal struggles, Molly was successful in many areas of her life (e.g., work), had several close friends, and was generally viewed by others as kind and considerate.

In her first session, Molly explained that she had requested EMDR therapy upon discharge because she had a sense that her despair was somehow connected to her childhood. However, she was clear that she could not attend to her traumatic past until she felt safe in her therapist's office and able to manage her emotions and symptoms more effectively at home and at work. Honoring Molly's position, the therapist chose to reverse Phase I (history taking and treatment planning) and Phase II (preparation) and delayed all exploration of her past until Molly felt more regulated and secure. Despite this, Molly quickly became dysregulated (pressured speech and heightened anxiety, alternating with dissociative fogginess and fragmentation of her narrative) as she described her recent experience in the hospital. This provided an opportunity for the therapist to introduce a number of different self-regulation strategies. Molly learned and practiced diaphragmatic breathing and some grounding, orienting, and distancing strategies, and was able to develop a secure imaginal container to hold intrusive material. She was reassured that the work would be paced according to her expressed need, thus reinforcing her assertiveness and sense of control. The therapist validated Molly's disappointment in her recent hospital stay and explicitly stated that she would work hard to earn Molly's trust; she encouraged her ongoing feedback about how she (the therapist) was doing.

Over the first four sessions, the therapist provided an overview of EMDR and AIP theory, and education about complex trauma and its impact. Molly was introduced to bilateral stimulation and resources were "installed" using the safe/calm place and RDI protocols. As Molly felt safer in the therapeutic relationship and better able to regulate her emotions, the therapist shifted the focus to exploring Molly's upbringing and trauma history. Multiple targets were identified for processing (past events, current symptoms, and distress triggers), as were goals for psychological and social functioning. The first target, a negative, invalidating interpersonal experience from her hospitalization (with a relatively low SUD level) was processed in Sessions 5 and 6. In Sessions 7 and 8, the remaining fears related to focusing on childhood traumas were targeted, and Molly emerged with a sense of confidence and the positive cognition "I can handle this" (VOC = 7).

In the next session, recounted in the following transcript, Molly presented in a state of heightened arousal with pronounced suicidal ideation. With Molly's permission, the therapist guided her in a floatback exercise to explore touchstone memories of events related to her distress, and Molly quickly acknowledged and articulated the previously unavailable memory of killing a baby rabbit. This memory had not emerged during history taking, even though sexual abuse by her neighbor had been discussed.

Session 9

MOLLY: Every time I see or hear a young child crying, I start to feel depressed and start thinking about suicide. I just hate myself and want to die. I made a sincere commitment to you about safety. I'm not going to act on this, but it feels pretty unbearable at times.

THERAPIST: Molly, when was the last time you were triggered in this way?

MOLLY: Just yesterday, I was at the supermarket and I saw a mother yelling at her little girl. The girl was crying and refusing to leave the store, because she wanted a small toy. I just stood there, frozen, watching her cry, feeling worse and worse about myself.

THERAPIST: That sounds like it was really difficult. Would it be OK if we float back from that experience to see what it connects to? I'll be right here with you, guiding the process.

MOLLY: OK. I think that it makes sense to float back even though I'm scared.

THERAPIST: I don't want you to feel this way anymore, either. I know that you are going to feel so much better once we sort this out and address what's underneath these symptoms. Does this make sense to you?

MOLLY: Yes. I have felt a bit better with each session. I'm scared but willing to try.

[Starting with the image, negative cognition, emotions, and sensations associated with the experience at the supermarket, Molly floated back to earlier, related traumatic experiences. She first went to a memory of her mother screaming at her when she was 12 years old, holding a knife and telling her that she wished that she had never been born. At one point, Molly froze and said that she was starting to feel foggy and dizzy, so the therapist asked her to ground herself by looking at her (the therapist), stomping her feet, and feeling the texture of her chair's upholstery. When she was solidly back in the present moment, the therapist asked her if she could float back further.]

MOLLY: (*with tears in her eyes*) I am remembering a time that Jim, our neighbor, forced me to kill a baby animal. I was about 6 years old. I felt like the worst person in the whole world and wanted to die. How could I have done that! I loved animals! I've spent a lifetime trying not to think about that experience. Maybe it's time to talk about it and work on it.

THERAPIST: OK. You are really courageous, Molly, and I applaud your willingness to work on this awful memory with me. Before we begin our processing work, I'd like you to imagine your circle of support and the image of you successfully doing volunteer work. Can you get to these resources?

MOLLY: Yes. I can see everyone in my circle of support and can connect with the part of me that feels good about my volunteer work at the food pantry.

THERAPIST: Good. So, when you think about the memory with Jim, what picture represents the worst part of that experience?

MOLLY: (*in a tremulous, child-like voice*) He is standing over me and making me hold a knife to the bunny rabbit. I can hear that evil man's voice and feel his breath on my neck.

THERAPIST: It's a memory. It's old stuff. Keep it on the screen. You want to be an observer . . . a witness. What's the negative belief you're having about yourself as you think of this memory right now?

MOLLY: I'm bad. I don't deserve to live.

THERAPIST: And, as you bring up that picture, what would you prefer to believe about yourself?

MOLLY: I'd rather believe that I am good and deserve to live.

THERAPIST: How true does that feel to you now, on a scale of 1 to 7, where 1 feels completely false and 7 feels completely true?

MOLLY: 2.

THERAPIST: And what do you feel now as you think about this memory?

MOLLY: Scared. Ashamed. Disgusted with myself.

THERAPIST: Stay with me as you connect with these feelings. They are part of the old experience. And on a scale of 0 to 10, where 0 is no disturbance and 10 is the highest disturbance you can imagine, how disturbing does this memory feel to you now?

MOLLY: 10.

THERAPIST: Where do you feel this distress in your body? And, are there any impulses or urges that accompany this distress?

MOLLY: I feel it in my stomach and in my hands. I also feel the urge to scream and to stab myself.

THERAPIST: OK. Remember that you have your stop signal and that you are totally in control of this process. Bring up this memory of being forced to kill this rabbit. Focus on the words "I'm bad. I don't deserve to live." Be aware of the feelings and sensations in your body. And follow my fingers. [*SEM*; "set of eye movements"] Take a break and a breath. What do you notice? (These words are repeated after each *SEM*, but are not included in this transcript hereafter.)

MOLLY: I hate myself so much. I just don't know how I could have done something like that. I want to vomit. I didn't fight back. I didn't run.

THERAPIST: It's old stuff, Molly. Keep it on the screen. Remember, you were just a little girl and he was a big, strong, mean man who had threatened your life more than a few times. Stay with that. [*SEM*]

MOLLY: Yes. He said that he would kill me if I didn't do what he told me to do. I was terrified of him. (*Starts to cry, freezes, and covers her face with her hands.*)

THERAPIST: (*in a very gentle voice*) Tears are welcome here. Just let them come. I'm right here with you. No judgment from me, just care and concern. Stay with me and with what's coming up for you. [*SEM*]

MOLLY: I just don't know how to forgive myself. I'm so ashamed. After he made me do that, I wanted to die. I fantasized about taking that knife and plunging it into my hand and my heart.

THERAPIST: Molly, how old were you? Six years old, right? (*Uses her hand to show how tall a 6-year-old might be.*) You were just a little girl. If your friend Laura's little girl told you this same story, would you think that she was disgusting? Weak for not fighting back or running away? Responsible for what happened? (*Molly signals "No" with her head after each question.*) Go with that. [*SEM*]

MOLLY: (*looking collapsed*) But my mother always said that I was bad and that everything was my fault.

THERAPIST: Let's put your mother's voice to the side, OK? (*Molly nods, "OK."*) [*SEM*]

MOLLY: But it was my fault that this all happened, because I went to this man's house after he offered to give me a new toy.

THERAPIST: You didn't know what he was planning, did you? You did what any 6-year-old kid would have done, right? (*Molly signals with a shrug that she is unsure.*) How many other innocent children were tricked by this man and later abused by him?

MOLLY: (*with tears and a flash of recognition*) A lot, I think. We were actually all really good kids. No one deserved to be tortured and abused. We were all completely innocent and powerless. I didn't want to kill that rabbit! Even though there were parts of me that wanted to die right in that moment, I ultimately wanted to live. I *had* to go along with him.

THERAPIST: Yes! I am so glad that you chose to live! Notice what you're feeling and what's happening in your body now—sensations and urges.

MOLLY: I feel anger and an urge to run.

THERAPIST: Yes! Of course. I know that you would have run right out the front door of your neighbor's house if you had had the chance to safely get away. Stay with that. [*SEM*]

MOLLY: I like what you said. I imagined my adult self taking that little girl by the hand. As we ran out that front door, I looked back and screamed, "You are an evil man and a killer. I hate you and hope you rot in hell!" Now, I see myself sitting by a campfire in the mountains, holding her, rocking her, and wiping away her tears.

THERAPIST: And perhaps there's something that you want to say to her. [*SEM*]

MOLLY: I told her that she didn't do anything wrong, and that she couldn't have known what that man was going to do. I said that I was so sorry that this happened to her. I told her that I loved her and that I would never leave her. I now know why I was initially drawn to that man. He was kind to me and paid attention to me. I got nothing but crumbs and cruelty at home. I was vulnerable to his invitation.

THERAPIST: Yes. Stay with that and stay with her. Notice what's changing inside, what you're feeling and sensing. [*SEM*]

MOLLY: I feel so much less pressure in my body, like a weight has been lifted, and I don't feel as foggy. I feel less frozen. I feel like she is resting in my arms and I can maybe start to relax a little bit. It's over and she's safe. Maybe I can even begin to forgive myself for being there when that baby rabbit was killed. He was the killer, not me. (*Tears start rolling down her face. This time she does not cover her face; instead, she makes eye contact and gently smiles.*)

At the end of the session, when the therapist returned to check the SUD level of the original incident, Molly reported that her level was at a 2 (out of 10). When asked what was keeping it at a 2, she said that she knew that she still needed to process her anger, but that it was no longer self-directed. When asked what the most important thing she learned about herself was, Molly stated that she felt like maybe she wasn't so bad after all. She felt like she had accomplished a lot and expressed a sense of hope about the plans for continued processing. Over the next two sessions, processing continued until an SUD level of 0 and a VOC of 7 were reported.

Commentary on the Case Example

As Molly searched for memories related to her present-day triggered state, it was critical that her therapist urged her to scan back farther, beyond age 12, when her mother had chased her with a knife, to the previously dissociated memory at age 6 of being forced by an abusive, sadistic neighbor to kill a baby rabbit. In targeting this horrific experience over the course of three sessions, it became clear that this memory held the key to Molly's suicidal and parasuicidal ideation and impulses. It had been a pivotal experience in her life, constituting a "moral injury" (Litz, Lebowitz, Gray, & Nash, 2016) that had turned her against herself and destroyed her self-respect. In her mind, she had become a perpetrator and had started to experience herself as the "bad person" her mother had endlessly declared "should never have been born." She understood all that happened in her life as confirmation that she was "bad and therefore doomed and deserving of further misfortune." Molly's negative cognition, "I'm bad," and its correlate, "I don't deserve to live," along with her feelings of shame, fear, and self-disgust, suggested that her misattribution of responsibility needed to be a primary focus during processing.

As Molly processed this memory, the therapist used various interweaves to help her remain within her window of tolerance, to relinquish her self-blame, and to begin to regard this experience from a new, adult perspective. She helped Molly access information that was critical to a more adaptive and accurate assessment of responsibility, using Socratic questioning and noting that Molly was quite young at the time, that her perpetrator had repeatedly sexually abused her and threatened her life, that he was much bigger and stronger, and that he had lured many other innocent children to his house. As Molly recognized that she had, indeed, been powerless at the time, and that she had submitted only in response to his threats, she spontaneously moved from shame and self-hatred to grief and a sense of compassion for her younger self.

The therapist continually asked Molly to notice what she was feeling in her body, keeping the work in the experiential and somatosensory realm. The therapist's suggestion that Molly would have undoubtedly run, if she could have, gave her permission to imagine an escape and to direct her anger toward her perpetrator; she imaginally moved from immobilization and submission to mobilization and triumphant assertion. The therapist facilitated developmental repair by encouraging Molly to communicate directly with her "child self," offering the nurturance and understanding that she had failed to receive from her parents. Throughout the session, the therapist offered cheerleading, validation, permission, and explicit recognition to counter Molly's aloneness and to support her emerging sense of clarity and truth.

Whereas some clients are able to process their trauma targets with little therapist involvement and few interweaves, most clients with complex trauma require significant assistance. Due to Molly's severe shame and self-hatred, the therapist began the interweaves right after the very first set of eye movements. The therapist did not wait for Molly to get stuck and dysregulated, anticipating that it would be difficult to get her back on track. Though the primary focus in Session 9 was the "informational plateau" of responsibility and defectiveness, Molly also made progress in shifting her beliefs related to powerlessness and safety. In imagining her escape, speaking up to the perpetrator, and offering compassion and safety to her child self, she was able to feel more empowered and capable of separating her traumatic past from her much safer present-day life. In her next session, Molly recognized that the urge to stab herself in the hand and heart was related to her long-standing guilt. Unable to fight her abuser at the time, she redirected the rage, hatred, and violent impulses at herself. She recognized that she had spent a lifetime punishing herself as a result of being unable to "adaptively resolve" her anger toward this man. In Session 10, she conclusively decided to hold the perpetrator rather than herself responsible.

In Session 11, the third and final session focused on this memory, Molly imagined pushing away the perpetrator's hand and stabbing him with the knife. At first she was frightened by this, but then she realized that imagining these actions was necessary if she wanted to free herself from her suicidal and parasuicidal ideation and impulses. These thoughts and impulses did not reappear at any point later in Molly's treatment. She reported being much less disturbed when in a situation involving crying children. Eventually, she completed a future template, imagining herself successfully coping with and responding to a distressed child. In later sessions, Molly processed additional memories of abuse by her mother and the neighbor, as well as her father's disinterest and nonprotection. She experienced a profound reduction in the symptoms that had brought her into treatment. Upon termination, Molly reported that she felt like a worthwhile and lovable person who had a lot to offer others. Her self-compassion and capacity to trust herself and others had grown immensely. At six-month follow-up, Molly shared that she had started a new romantic relationship. She reported no signs of depression or PTSD and stated that the quality of her life had only continued to improve.

Conclusion

Endorsed by numerous domestic and international organizations as a first-tier, empirically validated intervention for PTSD, EMDR therapy is also widely used in treating an extensive range of complex trauma-related disorders and problems. It is an eight-phase, integrative psychotherapy, guided by the AIP theory, which proposes that inadequately processed memories of adverse and traumatic life experiences lead to the psychological and stress-induced physical problems seen in PTSD and CTSDs. EMDR therapy addresses the link between current symptoms—emotional, somatic, behavioral, and cognitive—and exposure to both "big-T" and "small-t" traumas, including sexual, physical, and emotional abuse, atrocities related to ethno- and geopolitical violence, attachment disruptions, neglect, unmet psychological needs, and even everyday failures, humiliations, and losses. EMDR therapy is effective, safe, efficient, and comprehensive in treating survivors of complex trauma, not only decreasing their symptoms, but also supporting their postraumatic growth.

References

American Psychiatric Association. (2013). *Diagnostic and statistical manual of mental disorders* (5th ed.). Arlington, VA: Author.

Australian Centre for Posttraumatic Mental Health. (2013). *Australian guidelines for the treatment of acute stress disorder and posttraumatic stress disorder*. Melbourne, Australia: Author.

Bongaerts, H., Minnen, A. V., & de Jongh, A. (2017). Intensive EMDR to treat patients with complex posttraumatic stress disorder: A case series. *Journal of EMDR Practice and Research, 11*(2), 84–95.

Capezzani, L., Ostacoli, L., Cavallo, M., Carletto, S., Fernandez, I., Solomon, R., Pagani, M., & Cantelmi, T. (2013). EMDR and CBT for cancer patients: Comparative study of effects on PTSD, anxiety, and depression. *Journal of EMDR Practice and Research, 7*(3), 134–143.

Chen, R., Gillespie, A., Zhao, Y., Xi, Y., Ren, Y., & McLean, L. (2018). The efficacy of eye movement desensitization and reprocessing in children and adults who have experienced complex childhood trauma: A systematic review of randomized controlled trials. *Frontiers in Psychology, 9*, 534.

Cloitre, M., Cohen, L., & Koenen, K. C. (2006). *Treating survivors of childhood abuse: Psychotherapy for the interrupted life*. New York: Guilford Press.

Courtois, C. A., Sonis, J., Brown, L. S., Cook, J., Fairbank, J. A., Friedman, M., . . . Schulz,

P. (2017). *Clinical practice guideline for the treatment of posttraumatic stress disorder (PTSD) in adults.* Washington, DC: American Psychological Association.

CREST. (2003). *The management of post traumatic stress disorder in adults.* Belfast: Clinical Resource Efficiency Support Team of the Northern Ireland Department of Health, Social Services and Public Safety.

de Jongh, A., Amann, B. L., Hofmann, A., Farrell, D., & Lee, C.W. (2019a). The status of EMDR therapy in the treatment of posttraumatic stress disorder 30 years after its introduction. *Journal of EMDR Practice and Research, 13*(4), 261–269.

de Jongh, A., Bicanic, I., Matthijssen, S., Amann, B. L., Hofmann, A., Farrell, D., Lee, C. W., & Maxfield, L. (2019b). The current status of EMDR therapy involving the treatment of Complex PTSD. *Journal of EMDR Practice and Research, 13*(4), 284–294.

Department of Veterans Affairs & Department of Defense. (2017). *VA/DOD clinical practice guideline for the management of posttraumatic stress disorder and acute stress disorder.* Washington, DC: Veterans Health Administration, Department of Veterans Affairs and Health Affairs, Department of Defense.

Ford, J. D. (2015). An affective cognitive neuroscience-based approach to PTSD psychotherapy: The target model. *Journal of Cognitive Psychotherapy, 29*(1), 69–91.

Forgash, C., & Copeley, M. (2008). *Healing the heart of trauma and dissociation with EMDR and ego state therapy.* New York: Springer.

Gonzalez, A., & Mosquera, D. (2012). *EMDR and dissociation: The progressive approach* (rev. 1st ed.). CreateSpace, independent publishing platform.

ISTSS Guidelines Committee. (2019). Posttraumatic stress disorder prevention and treatment guidelines: Methodology and recommendations. Retrieved from *www.istss.org/treating-trauma/new-istss-prevention-and-treatment-guidelines.aspx.*

Karatzias, T., Murphy, P., Cloitre, M., Bisson, J., Roberts, N., Shevlin, M., . . . Hutton, P. (2019). Psychological interventions for ICD-11 complex PTSD symptoms: Systematic review and meta-analysis. *Psychological Medicine, 49*(11), 1–15.

Knipe, J. (2015). *EMDR toolbox: Theory and treatment of complex PTSD and dissociation.* New York: Springer.

Korn, D. L. (2009). EMDR and the treatment of complex PTSD: A review. *Journal of EMDR Practice and Research, 3*(4), 264–278.

Korn, D. L., & Laliotis, D. A. (2015). Clinical interweave categories. In B. J. Hensley (Ed.), *An EMDR primer: From practicum to practice* (2nd ed., pp. 264–276). New York: Springer.

Korn, D. L., & Leeds, A. M. (2002). Preliminary evidence of efficacy for EMDR resource development and installation in the stabilization phase of treatment of complex posttraumatic stress disorder. *Journal of Clinical Psychology, 58*(12), 1465–1487.

Landin-Romero, R., Moreno-Alcazar, A., Pagani, M., & Amann, B. L. (2018). How does eye movement desensitization and reprocessing therapy work?: A systematic review on suggested mechanisms of action. *Frontiers in Psychology, 9*, 1395.

Lee, C. W., & Cuijpers, P. (2013). A meta-analysis of the contribution of eye movements in processing emotional memories. *Journal of Behavior Therapy and Experimental Psychiatry, 44*(2), 231–239.

Leeds, A. M. (2009). Resources in EMDR and other trauma focused psychotherapy: A review. *Journal of EMDR Practice and Research, 3*(3), 152–160.

Levine, P. A. (1997). *Waking the tiger: Healing trauma.* Berkeley, CA: North Atlantic Books.

Linehan, M. (2015). *DBT skills training manual* (2nd ed.). New York: Guilford Press.

Litz, B. T., Lebowitz, L., Gray, M. J., & Nash, W. P. (2016). *Adaptive disclosure: A new treatment for military trauma, loss, and moral injury.* New York: Guilford Press.

Najavits, L. M. (2002). *Seeking Safety: A treatment manual for PTSD and substance abuse.* New York: Guilford Press.

Rosoff, A. (2019). How we do what we do: The therapist, EMDR, and the treatment of complex trauma. *Journal of EMDR Practice and Research, 13*(1), 60–73.

Rothbaum, B. O. (1997). A controlled study of eye movement desensitization and reprocessing in the treatment of posttraumatic stress disordered sexual assault victims. *Bulletin of the Menninger Clinic, 61*(3), 317–334.

Shapiro, F. (1989). Eye movement desensitization: A new treatment for post-traumatic stress disorder. *Journal of Behavior Therapy and Experimental Psychiatry, 20*(3), 211–217.

Shapiro, F. (1991). Eye movement desensitization and reprocessing procedure: From EMD to EMDR—a new treatment model for anxiety and related traumata. *Behavior Therapist, 14*, 133–135.

Shapiro, F. (1995). *Eye movement desensitization and reprocessing: Basic principles, protocols, and procedures.* New York: Guilford Press.

Shapiro, F. (2018). *Eye movement desensitization and reprocessing (EMDR) therapy: Basic principles, protocols, and procedures* (3rd ed.). New York: Guilford Press.

Siegel, D. J. (1999). *The developing mind: Toward a neurobiology of interpersonal experience.* New York: Guilford Press.

Suzuki, A., Josselyn, S. A., Frankland, P. W., Masushige, S., Silva, A. J., & Kida, S. (2004). Memory reconsolidation and extinction have distinct temporal and biochemical signatures. *Journal of Neuroscience, 24*(20), 4787–4795.

Swift, J. K., & Greenberg, R. P. (2014). A treatment by disorder meta-analysis of drop-out from psychotherapy. *Journal of Psychotherapy Integration, 24*(3), 193–207.

van den Berg, D. P. G., de Bont, P. A. J. M., van der Vleugel, B. M., De Roos, C., de Jongh A., Van Minnen, A., & van der Gaag, M. (2015). Prolonged exposure versus eye movement desensitization and reprocessing versus waiting list for posttraumatic stress disorder in patients with a psychotic disorder: A randomized clinical trial. *Journal of the American Medical Association, Psychiatry, 72*(3), 259–267.

van der Hart, O., Groenendijk, M., Gonzalez, A., Mosquera, D., & Solomon, R. (2013). Dissociation of the personality and EMDR therapy in complex trauma-related disorders: Applications in the stabilization phase. *Journal of EMDR Practice and Research, 7*(2), 81–94.

van der Hart, O., Nijenhuis, E. R. S., & Steele, K. (2006). *The haunted self: Structural dissociation and the treatment of chronic traumatization.* New York: Norton.

van der Kolk, B. A., Spinazzola, J., Blaustein, M. E., Hopper, J. W., Hopper, E. K., Korn, D. L., & Simpson, W. (2007). A randomized clinical trial of eye movement desensitization and reprocessing (EMDR), fluoxetine, and pill placebo in the treatment of posttraumatic stress disorder: Treatment effects and long-term maintenance. *Journal of Clinical Psychiatry, 68*(1), 37–46.

Wilson, S., Becker, L. A., & Tinker, R. H. (1997). Fifteen-month follow-up of eye movement desensitization and reprocessing (EMDR) treatment of post-traumatic stress disorder and psychological trauma. *Journal of Consulting and Clinical Psychology, 65*(6), 1047–1056.

Wolpe, J. (1982). *The practice of behavior therapy.* Boston: Allyn & Bacon.

World Health Organization. (2013). *Guidelines for the management of conditions that are specifically related to stress.* Geneva, Switzerland: Author.

World Health Organization. (2018). *The ICD-11 for mortality and morbidity statistics.* Geneva, Switzerland: Author. Retrieved from *https://icd.who.int/browse11/lm/en#/ http%3a%2f%2fid.who.int%2ficd%2fentity%2f585833559.*

CHAPTER 14

Narrative Exposure Therapy

MAGGIE SCHAUER
KATY ROBJANT
THOMAS ELBERT
FRANK NEUNER

Narrative exposure therapy (NET) is a treatment for adult and child survivors who continue to suffer from past experiences of traumatic stressors. It is specifically designed for individuals who have been exposed to complex and multiple traumata, after having survived severe and repeated physical and social threats to life and integrity. NET enables individuals to establish a coherent autobiographical narrative of their most significant experiences. The narration contextualizes life events that were highly arousing, so that internal reminders, threat-related cues, lose their dominance over the person's experience of emotions, physiological responses, cognitive patterns, and relationships to self and others in the present. Consequently, NET has been frequently used to treat individuals who suffer from deliberate, repeated, and prolonged interpersonal trauma (Schauer, Neuner, & Elbert, 2011).

In order to be universally applicable for the treatment of traumatic stress disorders in diverse populations affected by continuous domestic, community, or organized violence, NET was designed to meet the following requirements (Schauer, Neuner, & Elbert, 2005; Elbert, Schauer, & Neuner, 2015):

1. The therapy is applicable to various traumatized groups. Exclusions are not made on the basis of demographics such as age (when capable of episodic memory), gender, or education. Traumatized people are not excluded due to ethnicity or social group. It is possible to sensitively adapt the procedure to different environments and cultural settings.

2. NET has been evaluated in ecologically valid, real-world settings. The intervention shows cumulative beneficial effects, evident after only a few sessions. This is especially important in attending to resource-poor communities in low-income countries or crisis regions, and relevant in providing trauma treatment for children and adults living in informal urban poverty areas, asylum centers, refugee settlements, or difficult-to-access areas around the globe.

3. The simplicity and robustness of NET and its potential for dissemination is such that integration into large-scale service provision within a cascade model of public mental health care is possible (Schauer & Schauer, 2010).

4. *Complex trauma* inevitably involves the abuse of human rights. In NET, acknowledgment of this fact is fundamental, since it allows both survivor and therapist to compare the atrocities that have occurred against objective, agreed-upon principles of how human beings should behave toward each other. Sharing information about the cruelties of war, torture, and abuse may be used to counter stigma associated with survivors (Schneider et al., 2018) and raise awareness of human rights violations in the younger generation (Winkler, 2017). For victims, regaining access to their biographies and communicating their history to others can empower them to stand up for their rights as victims of violence and overcome feelings of anger, hopelessness, and powerlessness.

Rationale for NET

Individuals with complex trauma histories typically had to cope with several forms of interpersonal traumatic stressors—*stones,* as we refer to them—including sexual abuse, neglect, exploitation, relational betrayal, rejection, physical violence, and so forth, often from the earliest days of childhood onward, but sometimes under adult conditions of detention and torture. The expectation that other humans (especially caregivers) are trustworthy, nurturing, and protective may have been severely violated. Such environments often frustrate basic needs for human belonging, control and autonomy, personal appreciation, and physical care. This leads to negative beliefs about the self and others, and to corresponding behavioral patterns and survival-based schemas of "struggle without protection," as well as unhealthy coping strategies, such as addictions and self-injurious or suicidal behavior. "Many survivors of relational and other forms of early life trauma are deeply troubled, and often struggle with feelings of anger, grief, alienation, distrust, confusion, low self-esteem, loneliness, shame and self-loathing. . . . They often have diffuse identity issues and feel like outsiders, different from other people . . . They often feel a sense of personal contamination and that no one understands or can help them" (Courtois & Ford, 2009, p. 4). As a result of this distress and acquired survival-oriented patterns of interacting with others, professionals may feel challenged by complex trauma survivors' dependence, aggression, self-destructiveness, and distrust. Therapists may feel frustrated, confused, angry, and exhausted by patterns of behaviors and relations that are perceived to be akin to personality disorders. However, the corollary of having developed strategies for survival is that complex trauma survivors often also show a remarkable capacity for resilience and empathy toward others. These individuals' sensitivity and compassionate advocacy for weaker, less powerful individuals and animals often go unacknowledged as achievements—*flowers*, so to speak, in their autobiographies. Prior to, during, or after times of trauma, each life story contains sources of strength, joy, mastery, happiness, and love. Consequences of the negative, stressful and traumatic times are buffered by individual resilience factors and beneficial experiences such as corrective relationships, events with positive valence, achievements, experiences of social recognition and pride, and so forth, that form resources (Schauer, Neuner, & Elbert, 2005, 2011).

The rationale for NET begins with this fundamental understanding of harm due to cumulative "building blocks" (Schauer & Robjant, 2018) caused by increasing experiences of "threats to human life." These include events and adverse experiences that risk physical health, survival of self and kin, and social status. Events that damage each of these domains have predictable impacts on regulatory systems (neural, immune, epigenetic) and in turn on mental health (see, e.g., Elbert & Schauer, 2014). Memories of trauma share common emotions and cognitions such as fear, horror, or helplessness and thoughts about the imminence of death, powerlessness, and extreme loneliness. Therefore, an associative network of these "hot" memories with mutually excitatory connections is formed (i.e., memories of the fear experienced during one event may also call into play memories of other arousing events). Connections become particularly strong the higher the arousal, and with it, the autonomic responding (e.g., Schauer et al., 2011, Elbert & Schauer, 2014). Remembering threats can activate this memory network and may trigger a flight–fight response, with its high sympathetic arousal, a fright response with tonic immobility, and excessive dual autonomic tone, and a flag–faint dissociative *shutdown* with parasympathetic dominance (Schauer & Elbert, 2010).

The representation of the first single event of its type is stored in connection to the particular context, the *when* and *where* it happened ("cold" memory). If the event is recalled, place and time are also remembered well. Additional stressful experiences then interconnect with the existing memory of previous traumatic experiences inasmuch as they share a similar context— sometimes to the degree that they share the emotions (fear, shame, etc.) and cognitions ("I will die, I cannot do anything . . . "). At the same time, the connection to the context, to the "cold" memory is lost, as it is not possible to relate the rising fear to different times and places. In contrast, the sensory, cognitive, emotional, and physiological representations ("hot" memory) connect with increasingly mutual excitatory power. With more experiences, more and more hot elements become associated with each other. The fear/trauma network loses its connections to *time and place*. Therefore, fear, horror, and helplessness generalize, giving rise to feelings of impending threat even months and years after the events. NET is thought to reverse this process by recon-necting hot and cold memories, while segregating the memory traces of the different events. Since trauma memory is decontextualized, there is need for a biographical timeline approach that focuses on the arousing and important situations and their evolving schemas within life periods during development: the *lifeline* (Schauer et al., 2011).

Trauma survivors experience both threats and strengthening and soothing human (and animal) contacts in a uniquely personal sequence of specific events at different stages of their development. Trauma-focused therapies often try to identify an "index trauma" to target with exposure techniques (Schnyder et al., 2015), together with the instruction to hide or dissociate other trauma material. However, after multiple severe trauma experiences, it is not advisable to aim to identify or single out a *worst event* to be reprocessed (Priebe et al., 2018). Earlier experiences determine the perception, response to, and process-ing of the subsequent events. Consequently, NET suggests going through all of the significant life events in chronological order: Long-term healing in psy-chotherapy is achieved through attention to the entire life biography. Working through the life history with empathic therapeutic support is a robust variant of effective trauma therapy and allows the emergence of personal identity. Spe-cific, highly arousing events are uncovered within the lifetime periods and are revisited, recounted, processed, and contextualized.

Evidence for NET

It has been demonstrated that adult and child survivors with multiple trau-matizing life events benefit from NET (Schauer et al., 2011; Jacob, Wilker, & Isele, 2017, Nosè et al., 2017). Individuals from diverse backgrounds, with lives torn apart by stressful events such as childhood abuse and neglect, loss of caregivers, adoption, forced recruitment into armed groups or gangs, migration, political violence and torture, life-threatening illnesses, severe disas-ters, and so forth, show significantly reduced clinical symptomatology, and enhanced quality of life and level of occupational and social functioning. NET has been used to successfully treat survivors of organized violence and severe torture experiences, producing large effect sizes (Hensel-Dittmann et al., 2011; Neuner et al., 2010) as well as other complex trauma survivors (e.g., Pabst et al., 2014; Domen, Ejiri, & Mori, 2012; Mauritz et al., 2016; Steuwe et al., 2016). Stenmark, Catani, Neuner, Elbert, and Holen (2013) demonstrated that with NET, asylum seekers can be successfully treated for posttraumatic stress disorder (PTSD) and depression in a general psychiatric health care sys-tem. The most pronounced improvements are observed at (long-term) follow-up. This suggests that NET delivered in a relatively short time period elicits a significant enough change in self-perception and self-regulation to trigger a longer term healing process that leads to a sustained improvement in psy-chopathological symptoms, physical health, functioning, and quality of life. NET has been effectively and safely applied in situations that remain volatile and insecure, such as conditions of continuous trauma (i.e., ongoing domestic violence; Orang et al., 2018) or objective life threat in war and conflict, reducing symptoms while enabling the individual to bear witness to the atrocities endured. Reviews identified NET as an evidence-based treatment for different groups of survivors of violence (e.g., Nosè et al., 2017; Thompson, Vidgen, & Roberts, 2018).

Manuals have appeared in print in Dutch, English, Farsi, French, Italian, Japanese, Korean, and Slovakian; Arab, Spanish, and German translations are in preparation. NET is available in special adaptations for child soldiers and ex-combatants (forensic offender rehabilitation [FORNET]; Elbert, Hermenau, Hecker, Weierstall, & Schauer, 2012; Robjant et al., 2019) or street children (Crombach & Elbert, 2015) with previous family violence, and a child-friendly version for other children and adolescents (KIDNET; Schauer et al., 2011; Schauer, Neuner, & Elbert, 2017). NET also has been suggested as a promising approach in inhibiting the transgenerational transmission of trauma (Ullmann et a., 2017). The effect of NET has been demonstrated in improvements in clinical and social symptoms and in validating these results in neurophysiological and molecular biomarkers. Using neuroimaging, Adenauer et al. (2011) observed that NET enhances cortical top-down regulation, which is associated with the ability to inhibit the fear response. NET also was shown to improve health parameters (e.g., frequencies of cough, diarrhea, and fever), even under harsh living conditions (Neuner et al., 2008). In the immune system, T cells are critical for maintaining balance, regulating the immune response, and preventing autoimmune diseases. Morath et al. (2014a) demonstrated a treatment-related increase in the previously reduced proportion of regulatory T cells in the NET group at 1-year follow-up. NET is able to reverse the pathological levels of damaged DNA in individuals with PTSD back to a normal level (Morath et al., 2014b). These findings have obvious implications for physical health, including autoimmune diseases. Key strengths of NET are its low dropout rate, even for complex cases (e.g., 91% individuals suffering from borderline personality disorder completed NET in a German study; Steuwe et al., 2016) and due to its robust nature, the potential for dissemination, including to counselors in low-income countries, war zones, and crisis regions (Schauer & Schauer, 2010; Neuner et al., 2008, Jacob, Neuner, Mädl, Schaal, & Elbert, 2014; Koebach, Schaal, Hecker, & Elbert, 2017).

The Sequence of the Therapeutic Intervention in NET

NET proceeds in three essential steps (see Figure 14.1). Since survivors of complex trauma fear a loss of control or abandonment, and expect an unpredictable response, the therapeutic alliance in NET commences at the diagnostic interview with the therapist who will conduct the treatment. To allow a sense of mastery, the initial interview (Step 1) is highly structured and predictable, including event checklists matching the experiences of the client (e.g., torture or sexual abuse events). Childhood experiences are specifically targeted (e.g., the Maltreatment and Abuse Chronology of Exposure [MACE]), as well as dissociative phenomena following traumatic stress (using the Shutdown Dissociation Scale [Shut-D], which is able to discriminate the *dissociative subtype*; Schalinski, Schauer, & Elbert, 2015). A brief psychoeducation and a step-by-step explanation of the therapeutic procedure is then used to normalize, legitimize, and explain complex trauma reactions, as well as fears, resistances, and worries about the treatment protocol and exposure work ahead.

In the following 90-minute session, a *lifeline* is laid out (Step 2), symbolizing the person's life from birth to the present. The therapist helps classify specific life events within lifetime periods along this time axis (spatiotemporal integration into the individual development context). The creation of a biographical overview of highly arousing and significant moments (Schauer et al., 2011; Schauer & Ruf-Leuschner, 2014) is a reparative experience for traumatized children and adults with fragmented episodic memory. This spatiotemporal allocation and header-like naming of the most important personal events (general and specific events) in the successive lifetime periods is a meaningful component of NET, carried out from an allocentric (an observer's) position (Schauer et al., 2011).

In step 3 of NET, the autobiographically explicit, episodic memory is formed and completed by narration. The therapist invites the survivor to tell his or her life story now from an egocentric position within several double sessions, from the time of birth and early childhood until the present (see Schauer et al., 2011). Where there are long periods that do not contain highly arousing events, the narration is summarized, providing an overview of situations that the person has experienced, so that the course of life becomes evident. The therapist takes the role of a witness to the testimony of the narrator. This genuine interest and active listening promotes and encourages narration.

The therapist has an empathic and accepting attitude, while also clearly condemning violations of the client's human rights (cf. Neuner, Elbert, & Schauer, 2018). The life narrative contextualizes the network of cognitive, affective, and sensory memories of a person's traumatic and other highly arousing memories by filling in the details of fragmentary memories and developing a coherent autobiographical story. Each slowed-down narrative, with a focus on specific life events from the biography, attentive to all levels of experiencing and remembering, makes it possible to connect essential elements of the trauma and the meaning of this for the person's whole life. At subsequent sessions, the narration is read back to the client, who completes missing details or makes corrections, demonstrating to the narrator that the therapist has truly heard every detail and recorded it, and emphasizing the collaborative nature of the approach.

Key elements of the therapist's behavior include compassionate understanding, active listening, therapeutic alliance, and unequivocal positive regard and encouragement. The therapist asks the survivor to describe emotions, thoughts, sensory information, and physiological and bodily responses in detail

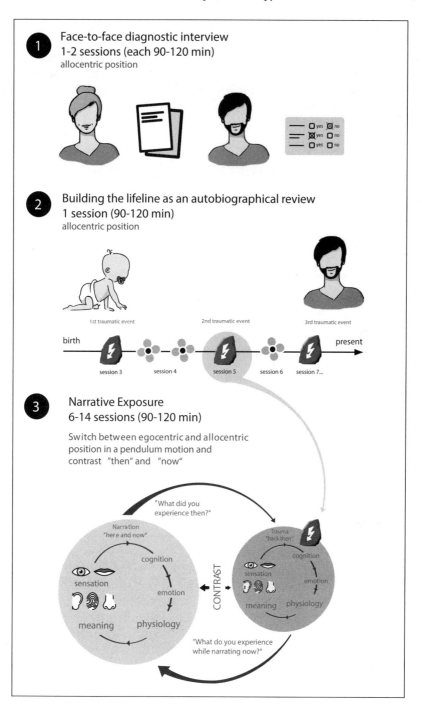

FIGURE 14.1. NET step by step: Structured, gradual approach to the trauma material.

(see Figure 14.1) and invites a "slow-motion" reliving without losing connection to the present. Staying present is achieved by utilizing permanent reminders that the emotions and physical responses sparked by memories are linked to episodic facts (e.g., time and place) and filled with meaning. When treatment ends, a documented autobiography created by the therapist (or in well-educated clients, with the help of the therapist) is presented to the survivor.

How Does NET Facilitate and Sustain Client Engagement in Treatment?

Engagement of complex traumatized individuals in NET requires recognition and comprehensive acknowledgment of key barriers inherent in trauma-related disorders.

Autobiographical Memory Disturbance

NET enables the client to approach and recover memories of the past in a structured, stepwise manner following this sequence: First, the individual's experiences of life events are explored (a simple acknowledgment of these events on a checklist that does not require details: yes/no it did/did not ("What?") happen to me, date ("When?"), place ("Where?"). Afterward, symptoms of suffering are identified using a structured interview, followed by an informed consent (according the cognitive development, age, and education of the client), a brief psychoeducation, and an explanation about the therapeutic procedure (90–120 minutes).

Second, in the next session, a biographic overview along a timeline is constructed with the *lifeline* exercise (90 minutes). At this stage, the specific (highly arousing) events are differentiated from general events and contextualized within a lifetime period. This helps the client identify which specific events are most distressing. Marking the lifetime period enables the client to order events more easily. During the lifeline stage, the therapist guides the client away from submerging into "hot" memory material and helps him or her stay on the "cold" memory side. The final (longest) part is *narrative exposure*, which is the narration of the whole life in chronological order, from birth to the present, highlighting with imaginal exposure the "hot" memory content. Important and arousing moments of positive and negative valence (e.g., traumata, loss/grief, meaningful moments, specific events with important attachment figures, personal achievements, and one's own aggressive acts) are now processed fully and in depth. Chronological processing of each event in context and within life periods enables further memory recall and "lightbulb moments" of linkage: Emotional episodes are coded in memory as networks of mutually activating information units. When processing the network, activity in one unit is transmitted to adjacent units, and depending on the strength of activation, the entire structure may be engaged. An extremely decelerated and emotion- and body-focused narration of a remembered biographical scene (the hot spot of a specific event) leads to priming and finally the appearance of the older, underlying trauma material.

Belief That the Trauma Is the Actual Reality in the Present

This belief is a result of the distorted memory representations (threat structure without context memory) that are being repaired through NET, so that a memory feels like a memory, as a past event in the context of life. The therapist enables the client to establish a sense of "past" by working through the *lifeline* in which a "bird's-eye view" of the client's life is obtained, and fragmented and chaotic memories are organized and situated in context. While processing in the *narrative exposure* stage, the therapist regularly invites the narrator to change focus between the past time and the here and now, as well as facilitating a *pendulum motion* between the egocentric and the allocentric view (see Figure 14.1). The narrator is constantly helped and grounded, and safety is reinforced. The therapist is asking primarily closed questions, while being clearly directive, making suggestions about emotions, cognitions, physical experiences, and meaning content that the client may have experienced at the time, so that the "stones" are relived in the present, as differentiated from the client's experience of them in the past.

Fear of Being Reminded of and Reliving Painful States, and Fear of Loss of Control over One's Mental State

Initially, the therapist assists the client in reducing this fear through psychoeducation about the rationale for therapy and reinforcement of the therapist's confidence in the ability of the client to complete the therapy and to withstand the emotions. During exposure to the "stones," active involvement of the therapist in an "exposure conversation" style (Robjant, Roberts, & Katona, 2017)—unique among trauma exposure therapies—allows the client to experience the therapist as constantly present in the narration. Listening to the life account and understanding its meaning reaches far beyond mere confrontation of worst events and instead honors the individual's way of living, surviving, and reacting. With the help of a supportive, nonjudgmental, accepting, and empathic therapist, the trauma material is approached step by step and in a foreseeable, directive, and structured manner. At each stage of the process, the client is aware of how far they have come, and what must still be done before reaching the present day on the lifeline.

The Inner Conflict between the desire to Communicate and the Perceived Incommunicability of Trauma

Responding to the strong, innate human motivation to communicate and to feel, the therapist understands the inability to voluntarily access trauma material and takes care of this by offering explanation for the suffering and inviting the client to listen to an empathic version of his or her life story. Overcoming gaps in cold memory is supported by working through the biographic contexts, exploring carefully the perceptions/sensations, cognitions, emotions, bodily reactions, and meaning contents (see Figure 14.1). The therapist signals patience in supporting efforts of the survivor to talk about what has happened. A firm belief in the survivor's ability to remember his or her own biographic events, and a persistent willingness to listen and stay in close contact throughout the process is vital. Where clients become "stuck" for words, the therapist redirects the survivor's attention to the here and now, and gently helps him or her focus on sources for cues: bodily reactions, emotions, and so forth. The therapist can help the narration by asking questions or suggesting a word or a description for the client's experience at that time (past) or in the moment (present), for the narrator to acknowledge or refute. The pendulum motion inherent in NET of exploring the highly arousing past moments and contrasting them in the same moment in time with the current experience in the present, thereby constructing an allocentric perspective, helps the client to restructure and understand the traumatic memory and its sequelae. The testimony focus in NET recognizes suffering not only as a medical/psychological condition and the consequence of abuse but also as a human rights violation and injustice. Traumas are occurring within a specific context of meaning, and this is specifically recognized and acknowledged.

Unsettled Identity: "Who Am I?"

People with broken lifelines need a comprehensive approach of narrative restructuring of not only their trauma memories but also their entire biography, especially their highly arousing negative and positive events: "I am what I remember about myself, my life and the meaning of it." A stable sense of identity requires an autobiography, sometimes including even the history of the family or tribe. NET offers corrective relationship experiences while reliving and linking past interpersonal situations and their ensuing schemas. From the lifeline onward, the client is aware that the therapist is interested in the whole life, and understands the context of traumas. Offering therapeutic suggestions when survivors cannot find words helps the client to feel connected to the therapist and to understand that the therapist is willing and able to understand the whole story. The testimony focus acknowledges that trauma has involved human rights abuse and injustice.

Self-Injurious/Deliberate Self-Harm and Dissociation

Implicit reliving of trauma cues causes anxiety and inner tension. In contrast, self-harm (especially pain caused by tissue damage) initiates a parasympathetic relief response with dissociation. In NET, imaginal exposure is combined with active anti-dissociative maneuvers. This is why the therapist must be active while the survivor recounts the trauma story, stimulating sensory perception and applied muscle tensing in the here and now to prevent dissociative shutdown. Active management of dissociative states is achieved by continuously contrasting the past trauma and the current reality and counteracting shutdown dissociation (Schauer & Elbert, 2010) during NET exposure sessions. When there is a risk of an intrusion (top-down processing only) and fusion of the trauma with the present reality or of dissociation (Schalinski et al., 2015; Schauer et al., 2011), the therapist increases the contrast between the here and now and the past. Sensory contrasting the past event to the present is crucial for overcoming dissociation (e.g., context: war scene vs. treatment room). They direct the attention of the survivor into the present (orienting/grounding) and afterward return to the trauma scene, with the help of spatiotemporal differentiation, sensory distinctions, and active motoric countermaneuvers as antidissociative strategies (Schauer & Elbert, 2010). In this way, the narrator is continually reoriented in the present when reliving the past: In NET attention should oscillate like a *pendulum* between then and now. This allows *ex-posure* (Latin for "exit a position") in a dual awareness.

Other measures are used during narrative exposure to counteract fainting, loss of muscle tension, and bodily weakness. The survivor is engaged in active body movement, managing vasovagal (pre-)syncope by leg crossing, muscle arm tensing, physical counterpressure maneuvers (e.g., squeezing a ball) and stabilizing blood pressure (e.g., cycling, staircase or a lying position). These techniques must be used *during* the imaginal exposure sessions, *while* the survivor is narrating the hot memory traumatic events, together with the help of the therapist (not as a homework exercise between sessions).

Comorbid Feelings of Shame and Guilt

Guilt-prone individuals, with their strong desire to understand what has happened in order to control the future, try to prepare for upcoming (social) threats and make sure of group inclusion by showing remorse and the will to take reparative action. A coherent and detailed narrative can significantly help to reduce cognitive distortions that lead to guilt. A complementary exercise often performed in trauma therapies is the allocation of a more objective percentage of one's own wrongdoing or failure set against the proportion of that of others and the circumstances involved in the incident. Reasons for one's own behavior at the time become apparent when experiences are thoroughly worked through in slow motion, by sorting out the sequence of events, knowledge, and decisions, and by fostering self-acceptance and enabling understanding of one's own decisions and actions in the context, including the emotional and physiological states. For example, one can understand that decisions that turned out to be wrong were made in exceptional moments under the highest stress, with no time and limited knowledge. Survivor guilt can be understood as a fear of being rejected by the social group when having survived while others have not. The therapist's welcoming reception is therefore key, and sharing the narrative can help.

Shame is a painful emotional reaction signaling social devaluation, status loss, and degradation. The validating eye of the other is needed to balance the humiliation caused by complex trauma experiences. The close "exposure conversation" style of the NET therapist is supportive, empathic, and involved, and therefore the client feels accepted. Social appreciation in therapeutic contact, as well as narration and sensitive processing of hurtful moments of rejection, also are key. Redirecting shame to the perpetrator to balance the social dominance situation and learning to publicly show self-confidence alongside social support can counter the suffering of social pain and allow the individual to regain dignity. The survivor is likely to be discussing the most shameful moments for the first time, and to be met with empathy and care rather than rejection is a hugely reparative experience that can also inspire confidence in engaging in social relationships again.

Difficulties with Relationships

When a client has been in abusive relationships, attention is paid to the positive and negative feelings associated with relationships, as well as moments of disappointment, when the client failed to get the much longed for love and care for which he or she hoped. When clients have been multiply exploited but do not recognize this (e.g., when the trauma occurred at a very young age), gradual narration through the "stones" can lead to realizing for the first time that the relationship was abusive. Great care is then needed in responding to the loss and grief of this idealized relationship if the client comes to a more realistic understanding. The process of NET can produce meaningful attachment repair, as the client can experience true empathy, compassion, and care from a person who listens and responds with emotion. This may lead the client subsequently to seek more healthy relationships in the future.

Fear of Overwhelming the Therapist with Dissociation/Flashbacks

During recall of past trauma, the therapist is reliably there ("shoulder to shoulder") every second with the client, an empathic monitor of the experience, who contrasts past and present feelings and thoughts and slows down the reexperiencing to ensure mastery. There is never a moment when the client is left alone. The therapist assists the client in achieving a sense of control, supports staying in a window of emotional tolerance throughout the work (no overengagement or underengagement). NET prepares therapists to handle *freeze, flight,* and *fight* stages, as well as to countermaneuver *fright, flag,* or *faint* stages (Schauer & Elbert, 2010). This creates predictability and gives the client a feeling of strength, calmness and competence in dealing with the various previously uncontrollable stages of the defense cascade. By referring to the proper context, focusing on the work to be done (i.e., enabling emotional processing), and sticking to the role of a witness of the testimony, the therapist is able to avoid excessive or inappropriate psychological identification (overidentifying) or getting caught in a conspiracy of silence. Therapists with their own trauma histories are advised to ensure that their own trauma work is complete before providing care for others. In contexts in which traumata are highly likely to have been experienced by therapists, NET trainings are set up in such a way that trainees process their own traumatic events.

Concerns of Both Therapists and Survivors about Causing Harm, Prompting Rejection, or Worsening Symptoms

Therapists are advised to manage their own overwhelming emotional feelings with appropriate self-care, professional boundaries, and use of clinical supervision. In addition, the very act of writing out the narration after the client has left the session helps the therapist to maintain a boundary with the client, to realize that these experiences were part of the client's life and not the therapist's, so that both are able to contextualize the events appropriately. Finally, the human rights focus in NET, acknowledging shattered beliefs, bitterness, and anger that both client and therapist may feel about the violations that have occurred (directed clearly toward the perpetrators), as well as "encouragement" for the therapist to act as advocate when appropriate and not remain "neutral" enables the therapist to resolve difficult feelings associated with having witnessed the client's extreme distress in response to horrific experiences.

Fear of Being Abandoned by the Attachment Figure/Inability to Let Go of the Therapist

The pain of having been abandoned and violated in the past by attachment figures is tied back to the context in which it originally occurred. For the new relationship with the listener (the therapist), the narrator (client) can experience the undivided and unconditional attention and warmth of the therapist as the narration unfolds, step by step. This is highly structured along the chronological flow of the person's biography, and is therefore predictable, boundaried, and contained. The testimony approach provides respect and dignity, and it satisfies the need for acknowledgment. When nearing the end of the narration in the present, closing rituals finalize the process with a natural ending: two persons who respect each other and let go. NET is time limited. This is an advantage in contrast to long-lasting therapies forming intense bonds that may foster dependencies.

Clinical Case Example

This case was referred to a specialist trauma service after the client described dissociative experiences, self-harm, and suicidality to her family doctor during a routine medical appointment. During the assessment session, the therapist administered the Life Events Checklist and suspected the client had been a victim of trafficking. The client acknowledged experiencing different types of multiple traumatic events, including severe abuse and adversities beginning in early childhood, and exposure later to life-threatening events such as severe hunger, risk of suffocation while being transported in a container, and the loss of a child. The therapist used the Posttraumatic Stress Diagnostic Scale to ascertain a diagnosis of PTSD. The Shut-D (Schalinski et al., 2015) revealed extensive dissociative experiences. The client was failing to eat regularly and was self-harming by cutting her abdomen and thighs. The client had no social contact and spent most of her time alone in her flat, leaving the house as rarely as possible.

During psychoeducation, the therapist explained the nature of the treatment, and the client was extremely ambivalent, believing herself unable to "put the pieces together and remember what happened," as well as fearing that she would become overwhelmed by emotion if she purposefully thought and talked about her experiences and "lose the last will to live that I have." The therapist explained that together they would take this journey to explore her life history, and that this time, the client would have with her someone who cared, every step of the way, through every detail. The client agreed to try the treatment on the following condition: If she wanted to stop the treatment, she would not be contacted by the therapist ever again. This request not only displayed her initial ambivalence toward the treatment but also her distrust of the therapist, with strong feelings of both needing and rejecting close contact.

During the lifeline session, events frequently had to be reordered to obtain as accurate a history as possible. Later, the client recalled further events, and three events were reordered as her autobiographical memory was restored. By the end of the lifeline session, the skeletal details of the client's life were as follows. Born in Cambodia, her early life included multiple events of severe physical and emotional abuse by her mother, and sexual abuse by her father. She was severely punished for mild misdemeanors and accidents, and lived in fear of both parents. She attended school but did not like talking to other children, afraid that they would not like her because she was poorly cared for and often bruised.

Following the lifeline session, the therapist immediately started the narration, beginning with the earliest arousing events. Excerpts from the narrations are detailed here, with the contrasting "here-and-now" information obtained by therapist shown in brackets. For the purposes of description, parts of the narration are shown at different points during the exposition. In an actual session, the therapist must start at the beginning with the general details of the life at the time of the trauma, before establishing the exact details before the trauma occurred, then slowing down and exploring each moment of the trauma in slow motion, attending to all the elements of the hot memory and connecting to the cold memory.

Narration Excerpt 1 from Exposition Session 1:
My Father Abusing Me

[After describing sensory details—pictures, sounds, smells . . .]

"I could tell from his face that he was angry and I was terrified (I still feel ter-rified now as we talk about it). I was screaming out for help (I just wanted someone to help me, I still do), my heart was beating (it's beating now and I feel panicky) and I tried to get off the bed but he pushed me back hard against it (I can feel where his hands were on my chest, even as I talk about it now, so heavy and strong). He put his hand over my mouth (yes, it was like this—[the client shows the therapist the position of the man's hand over her mouth]—and his face came right up to my face (I can still see the look in his eyes, but no—I can't see him now—I see you). He smelled of alcohol (here in this room I smell the orange oil [orange oil was used to counter dissociation in this session]). I thought, 'It will be worse because he has had beer.' I felt terrified and disgusted (now I just feel like crying. My heart is so heavy and I feel such pity for myself. I am angry now too. In my chest and arms I can feel it. He was my father! I was a child! He should have been protecting me, not using me for sex. Ugh, he was disgusting.) My heart was racing and I felt sick (no, I don't feel sick now, just angry). My arms were gripped against the side of the bed (like this, how I'm holding the chair now, except then it was the side of the bed). I was holding tightly. He said I would do as he wanted, as I was his little girl. I started crying because I was so scared, and I just didn't want it to happen again tonight. . . . "

Later her father died unexpectedly in an accident, and she was sold to a brothel by her mother when she was 9 years old. She was raped on the first night of entering the brothel and was introduced to a woman who ran the busi-ness, who regularly physically abused her as a way of controlling her.

Narration Excerpt 2 from Exposition Session 4:
Meeting the Brothel Owner

In this excerpt, the beginning of the event is explored. The therapist has already identified the lifetime period in which the event occurred, and initially gathers as much cold memory (context) information as possible before beginning to process the "stone."

"I met her on the third day after I had been left in the brothel. It was in the evening and there were some more people arriving. I couldn't see them, as I was in another room. I had been so scared and in so much pain from the rape the day before and I hadn't eaten anything. I didn't understand the words she used all of the time. I thought she was from a different country.

She looked different. She was glamorous, had beautiful clothes and jewelry, and wore lots of makeup. She smelled nice, and was so kind to me that first day. She told me that she was sorry that my mother had left me and I started to cry (I feel sad now, even though I hate my mother now; back then I was just longing for her to come back and take me from that place). I felt like I had knots and rocks in my stomach (I feel it a bit now, too). I felt so sad and wanted to see my mother again so much, even though I knew she would beat me if I ran away (now I feel so angry toward her. I hate her now as we talk about it. I could kill her if I saw her now. I feel it in my fists and in my chest). I was so scared of everyone that I had seen since I went into this place (I don't feel that fear now, well a tiny bit, my heart is a bit fast). There were no other children there, I just wanted to go home (I feel the sadness of that now, the longing is still there. I still feel like I never found my way back home. I wonder if I will ever have a home that is safe). The woman patted the seat next to her, which had a beautiful golden-colored cushion on it. Lots of things in this room looked like they cost a lot of money. I sat down and I felt a bit better as she was smiling at me, and no one had paid any attention to me for ages. She told me I mustn't cry, as it wasn't pretty. She grabbed my chin and turned it from side to side as she was looking at me. Then she put one hand under each breast, although I didn't have any yet, and then moved her hands down to my waist. I had no idea what she was doing and was confused (now I know exactly what she was doing. She was seeing how far into puberty I was. She was disgusting. She was pleased because there was demand for children who showed no signs of development, she knew I would make her a lot of money [the client stands up]. I feel so angry I could kill that witch. [The therapist at this point reinforces the anger the client feels now toward the woman who forced her to have sex with men, and that this was a violation of her rights.] Back then, I felt a bit uncomfortable but she was smiling at me. I didn't understand her, but I didn't want her to go away, and she was still smiling. I think I giggled, even though I was scared (now I just feel angry). I didn't want her to get bored of me and leave me alone (I feel so sad now as I talk about that [the client starts crying]—I was so young, so vulnerable, how could they do that to me? I feel so much pity for myself now as I think about how alone I was). She said she was going to make me very pretty and she told me I would make her happy if I made money for her and that one day I would be rich and I could do whatever I wanted."

The client placed on the lifeline multiple "stones" of being raped in the brothel over a 10-year period. At the time of the lifeline session, the client was unable to identify specific events within this life period of living within the brothel, so this was done later, once the early childhood memories of abuse had been processed, since the client frequently confused memories of the two different rape event contexts.

Narration Excerpt 3 from Exposition Session 6:
Refusing to Have Sex with a Client

"He laughed at me and asked me who I thought I was wearing this beautiful underwear if I wasn't a prostitute? (I feel shame now. I know that I shouldn't, but it is there. Those laughing eyes. I can see them now. He looked at me as if I was completely worthless. Now I can feel it, that heavy shame.) [The client is looking at the ground, her body hunched over in shame—the therapist asks if the client was positioned like this back then, and the client recalls that she was half-sitting, half-lying on the bed at the time, but she was avoiding his eyes. The therapist encourages the client to look at her. The client replies that she can see the therapist's eyes now and not the rapist's eyes. The client, when asked, says that the therapist's eyes look different, there is no hatred, only kindness. The therapist praises the client's courage, summarizes the last few moments, and asks what happens next, and the client continues.] I thought he was very angry and unpredictable, and I was sure that I was going to be in a lot of trouble for saying I didn't want to have sex with him. I was terrified, my heart racing (yes, I can feel it racing now, it's the same feeling, I'm scared). I looked to the door and it was shut. I thought, I know there are guards nearby, there is nothing I can do. I felt hopeless and desperate but so afraid (I feel hopeless now, and desperate, too. I feel this knot in my chest, but that's not how I felt in my body then; then there was nothing). He came toward me and hit the side of my face very hard (I can't feel anything now on my face). He put his hands around my neck and he squeezed very hard. I could hardly breathe (I feel a bit breathless now) and I thought I was going to die (now I feel I could have died, but I didn't). He didn't release my neck (my neck hurts now as we talk about it) but he took off his belt and his trousers fell down. I shut my eyes. [The client shuts her eyes in the present and the therapist encourages her to open them.] I felt very warm (I feel warm now, and weak) and suddenly I noticed I could hardly hear him anymore. [The therapist asks if client can hear her now, if she can see her clearly. The client says she can, but cannot hear well. The therapist reinforces that they are together, that the client should focus on the therapist, and notices the client start to slump in her chair and asks the client to cross her legs and to begin physical activation, clenching her hands around a two soft balls and releasing. Then the therapist asks what happens next.] I couldn't feel my body anymore properly (I can feel it a bit now, but it's a bit numb.) [The therapist and client continue physical activation.] I felt confused (I feel a bit confused, but now, I know I am here with you. I know what we are doing). Then he released my neck and I coughed [the client gasps] (yes, that is what I did then, I could breathe again a bit more, I can breathe again a bit more now), then I said 'please' and started to cry and beg. He laughed, turned me around and the rape started again. He pinned me down, leaned his sweating torso heavy on my back so that his hot breath was in my ear and then forced his big penis into my vagina. What a terrible pain. I thought, I will crack open. [They continue the narration until the point where the rapist leaves the room.]"

Ten years later, the client was sold on to another group of traffickers, working as a prostitute but living with six other women. She was under the constant surveillance of a guard initially, but over time was "trusted" by her traffickers and gained some independence, including being allowed to prepare her own meals and leave the flat. It was during this phase of her life that she started cutting her abdomen and thighs, usually in response to intrusive memories of the abuse by her parents and as a child in the brothel. During the *lifeline* session in therapy, she had placed a *flower* for this event and labeled it "my comforting friend." She described feeling numb after self-harm. During this period, a customer paying for sex with the client complained to her traffickers about her self-harm, and she was severely beaten as a punishment. She began restricting her eating after she realized that this could also lead to similar feelings of numbness. She gave birth to a child, who was taken from her by the traffickers. She does not know what happened to the child.

Narration Excerpt 4 from Exposition Session 10: Losing My Baby

This excerpt is midway through the exposition of the "stone."

"I sat back down on the bed and I screamed and wept (I am so sad, I am so lost, where is my baby now? What did they do to her?) [The client is weeping and sobbing.] I thought, 'How could they take her from me?' Nothing can describe the despair (I cannot describe it even now, ever since that moment there is a hole in my soul. I feel it now, too. Emptiness, nothingness, I feel it across my chest and down my arms. [She moves to adopt a position as if cradling a baby and continues to cry.] My heart was so heavy with agony and longing. (It is still like this, this never changes, this will never go away.) My arms felt empty where they had torn her from my arms. I couldn't think anything except 'I've lost her, I've lost her, I cannot live without her. I am nothing again.' I realized she had helped me so much, given me a reason to keep going (I think this still, she was my world. She made me think I wasn't worthless, I was at least loving to her dear soul). And now this terrible hell of emptiness. I just wanted to die (no, I don't feel this now, now I want to find her). I felt my insides sort of harden (yes, I feel this now, my stomach tightness, my body is stiff, I start to freeze over) and I threw the mirror on the floor and it shattered. I picked up the glass and slashed my thighs and the blood was beautiful and slowly I could feel myself losing any feelings (yes, I can feel it now, the tension going). [The therapist restarts physical activation with the client.] I prayed and prayed that I would die (now I feel it. Death would be so easy, but now I want her back. I can try to find her. Even if it takes my life. Oh, but there is no hope [the client begins sobbing again]. . . . "

The therapist is in close emotional contact, showing the client empathy, continuously summarizing and trying to phrase with the client's own words what she understands, as well as helping to label feelings. The therapist continues narrating through the "stone" of the abduction of the child, including when the client lost consciousness during the event, until the point at which the client had regained consciousness, tended her wounds somewhat and eaten something given to her by the traffickers. After a final period of captivity, she managed to escape while working and traveled to the United Kingdom via an agent. In the final session, therapist and client reviewed the client's lifeline, since there had been many changes over the course of the therapy. The therapist reread a summary of the entire narration from the therapy. The therapist discussed the client's wish to join a survivors' group and to search for her daughter, and appropriate referrals were made by the therapist for these purposes.

Key Points of the Intervention

Slowing down the narrative flow in moments of high physiological excitement ensures improved awareness of internal processing to avoid overwhelming and confusing feelings. In this way, the therapist ensures that the narration creates a safe space. The process consists of stages: (1) Exploring *perceptions*: ("What did you perceive?"; "What sensory impressions were there: seeing, hearing, smelling, tasting, touching?"); (2) question about the *thoughts* ("When you heard/saw/felt/tasted/smelled this, what did you think at that moment? What did you think it was? What happened in your mind and body then?"); (3) this raises the question of *emotional and physical experience* ("How did you feel then? Which emotion—fear, disgust, joy, shame, anger, contempt—came up when you saw this and thought this?"; "How did your body feel? Can you describe this bodily feeling? What quality is it—hot, cold, heavy . . . ? What is it? Where exactly do you feel it in your body now?"); (4) finally the *meaning* of this moment is explored, which anchors the experience ("When you perceived this and thought it and had this bodily feeling, what did it mean to you at that moment? What changed? What did you understand?") and the *behavior* at the time as a consequence of all of this evaluating ("So what did you actually do? How did you react when you felt/thought/understood? Which behavior did you show, maybe in contrast to your thoughts and feelings?")

While the survivor is talking, the therapist actively helps to clearly separate the trauma level "then" from the narrative level in the "here and now" ("Can you feel that it smells, looks, sounds, etc., quite different here? Can you experience that X is not in this room? Be invited to look to around and really check out the difference. Maybe you move your body in a way you couldn't do then because you were restrained. Feel free to say now, what you were afraid to express at the time of trauma.").

All of this reality checking needs to happen literally in the very same second of the intense remembering in order to introduce and increase a contrast between then and now and to let the survivor's brain and psychological self experience the proof that "the past" is not here. States of distrust, detachment, anger, grief, shame, and other painful and impulsive moments are understood in the context of their past appearance in the personal biography. Sensory perceptions, cognitions, emotions, bodily reactions, and actual behavioral responses, as well as meanings of the trauma scenes, are connected back to the past where they belong, and where they originated. In this way, clients' dysregulations become comprehensible, legitimized, and fade.

Humans use an internalized view of the other as a self-control measure in the struggle for social recognition and rank, fueled by intense, often painful, emotions. These unrecognized internal forces of suffering (in particular "shame" and "guilt") are explicitly illuminated during the telling of the life story in the narrative exposure. Moreover, NET processes not only the traumatic events ("stones") but also the highly arousing positive experiences ("flowers"), which are important and meaningful resources to revisit and regain. The mental representation of "me" as self-reflected awareness is supported throughout this process. The dependence on the thoughts, feelings, and actions of the other people in the survivor's life story as experienced, recalled, anticipated, or imagined is explored, as well as interpretation of actions and reaction to this introspection related to the social environment. The individual is mirrored in the eyes of the empathic and validating listener, the therapist, allowing corrective relationship experiences that weave together broken lifelines of complex trauma survivors.

References

Adenauer, H., Catani, C., Gola, H., Keil, J., Ruf, M., Schauer, M., & Neuner, F. (2011). Narrative exposure therapy for PTSD increases top-down processing of aversive stimuli—evidence from a randomized controlled treatment trial. *BMC Neuroscience, 12*(1), 127.

Courtois, C. A., & Ford, J. D. (Eds.). (2009). *Treating complex traumatic stress disorders: An evidence-based guide.* New York: Guilford Press.

Crombach, A., & Elbert, T. (2015). Controlling offensive behavior using narrative exposure therapy: A randomized controlled trial of former street children. *Clinical Psychological Science, 3*(2), 270–282.

Domen, I., Ejiri, M., & Mori, S. (2012). Narrative exposure therapy for the treatment of complex PTSD: An examination of the effect and adaptation. *Japanese Journal of Psychotherapy, 13*(1), 67–74.

Elbert, T., Hermenau, K., Hecker, T., Weierstall, R., & Schauer, M. (2012). FORNET: Behandlung von traumatisierten und nicht-traumatisierten Gewalttätern mittels Narrativer Expositions therapie [Treatment of traumatized and non-traumatized offenders by means of narrative exposure therapy]. In J. Endrass, A. Rossegger, F. Urbaniok, & B. Borchard (Eds.), *Interventionen bei Gewalt- und Sexualstraftätern: Risk-Management, Methoden und Konzepte der forensischen Therapie* [Interventions for violent and sexual offenders: Risk-management, methods and concepts of forensic therapy] (pp. 255–276). Berlin: Medizinisch Wissenschaftliche Verlagsgesellschaft.

Elbert, T., & Schauer, M. (2014). Epigenetic, neural and cognitive memories of traumatic stress and violence. In S. Cooper & K. Ratele (Eds.), *Psychology serving humanity: Proceedings of the 30th International Congress of Psychology: Vol. 2. Western psychology* (pp. 215–227). East Sussex, UK: Psychology Press.

Elbert, T., Schauer, M., & Neuner, F. (2015). Narrative exposure therapy (NET): Reorganizing memories of traumatic stress, fear and violence. In U. Schnyder & M. Cloitre (Eds.), *Evidence based treatments for trauma-related psychological disorders: A practical guide for clinicians* (pp. 229–254). Cham, Switzerland: Springer International.

Hensel-Dittmann, D., Schauer, M., Ruf, M., Catani, C., Odenwald, M., Elbert, T., & Neuner, F. (2011). The treatment of traumatized victims of war and torture: A randomized controlled comparison of narrative exposure therapy and stress inoculation training. *Psychotherapy and Psychosomatics, 80,* 345–352.

Jacob, N., Neuner, F., Mädl, A., Schaal, S., & Elbert, T. (2014). Dissemination of psychotherapy for trauma-spectrum disorders in resource-poor countries: A randomized controlled trial in Rwanda. *Psychotherapy and Psychosomatics, 83,* 354–363.

Jacob, N., Wilker, S., & Isele, T. (2017). Die Narrative Expositionstherapie (NET) zur Behandlung von Traumafolgestörungen: Evidenz, Dissemination und neueste Entwicklungen weltweit [Treating trauma spectrum disorders with narrative exposure therapy (NET): Evidence, dissemination and latest developments worldwide]. *Swiss Archives of Neurology, Psychiatry and Psychotherapie, 168*(4), 99–106.

Köebach, A., Schaal, S., Hecker, T., & Elbert, T. (2017). Psychotherapeutic intervention in the demobilization process: Addressing combat-related mental injuries with narrative exposure in a first and second dissemination stage. *Clinical Psychology and Psychotherapy, 24*(4), 807–825.

Mauritz, M. W., van Gaal, B. G. I., Jongedijk, R. A., Schoonhoven, L., Nijhuis-van der Sanden, M. W. G., & Goossens, P. J. J. (2016, September 21). Narrative exposure therapy for posttraumatic stress disorder associated with repeated interpersonal trauma in patients with severe mental illness: A mixed methods design. *European Journal of Psychotraumatology.* [Epub ahead of print]

Morath, J., Gola, H., Sommershof, A., Hamuni, G., Kolassa, S., Catani, C., . . . Kolassa, I. T. (2014a). The effect of trauma-focused therapy on the altered T cell distribution in individuals with PTSD: Evidence from a randomized controlled trial. *Journal of Psychiatric Research, 54,* 1–10.

Morath, J., Moreno-Villanueva, M., Hamuni, G., Kolassa, S., Ruf-Leuschner, M., Schauer, M., . . . Kolassa, I. T. (2014b). Effects of p-sychotherapy on DNA strand break accumulation originating from traumatic stress. *Psychotherapy and Psychosomatics, 83*(5), 289–297.

Neuner, F., Elbert, T., & Schauer, M. (2018). Narrative exposure therapy (NET) as a treatment for traumatized refugees and post-conflict populations. In N. Morina & A. Nickerson (Eds.), *Mental health of refugee and conflict-affected populations* (pp. 183–199). Cham, Switzerland: Springer International.

Neuner, F., Kurreck, S., Ruf, M., Odenwald, M., Elbert, T., & Schauer, M. (2010). Can asylum-seekers with posttraumatic stress disorder be successfully treated?: A randomized controlled pilot study. *Cognitive Behavior Therapy, 39,* 81–91.

Neuner, F., Onyut, P. L., Ertl, V., Odenwald, M., Schauer, E., & Elbert, T. (2008). Treatment of posttraumatic stress disorder by trained lay counselors in an African refugee settlement: A randomized controlled trial. *Journal of Consulting and Clinical Psychology, 76,* 686–694.

Nosè, M., Ballette, F., Bighelli, I., Turrini, G., Purgato, M., Tol, W., . . . Barbui, C. (2017). Psychosocial interventions for post-traumatic stress disorder in refugees and asylum seekers resettled in high-income countries: Systematic review and meta-analysis. *PLOS ONE, 12*(2), e0171030.

Orang, T., Ayoughi, S., Moran, J. K., Ghaffari, H., Mostafavi, S., Rasoulian, M., & Elbert, T. (2018). The efficacy of narrative exposure therapy (NET) in a sample of Iranian women exposed to ongoing intimate partner violence (IPV)—A randomized controlled trial. *Clinical Psychology and Psychotherapy, 25,* 827–841.

Pabst, A., Schauer, M., Bernhardt, K., Ruf, M., Goder, R., Elbert, T., . . . Seeck-Hirschner, M. (2014). Evaluation of narrative exposure therapy (NET) for borderline personality disorder with comorbid posttraumatic stress disorder. *Clinical Neuropsychiatry, 11*(4), 108–117.

Priebe, K., Kleindienst, N., Schropp, A., Dyer, A., Krüger-Gottschalk, A., Schmahl, C., . . . Bohus, M. (2018). Defining the index trauma in post-traumatic stress disorder patients with multiple trauma exposure: Impact on severity scores and treatment effects of using worst single incident versus multiple traumatic events. *European Journal of Psychotraumatology, 9*(1), 1486124.

Robjant, K., Köbach, A., Schmitt, S., Chibashimba, A., Carleial, S., & Elbert, T. (2019). The treatment of posttraumatic stress symptoms and aggression in female former child soldiers using adapted Narrative Exposure Therapy—a RCT in Eastern Democratic Republic of Congo. *Behaviour Research and Therapy, 123,* 103482.

Robjant, K., Roberts, J., & Katona, C. (2017). Treating posttraumatic stress disorder in female victims of trafficking using narrative exposure therapy: A retrospective audit. *Frontiers in Psychiatry, 8,* 63.

Schalinski, I., Schauer, M., & Elbert, T. (2015). The Shutdown Dissociation Scale (Shut-D). *European Journal of Psychotraumatology, 6.*

Schauer, M., & Elbert, T. (2010). Dissociation following traumatic stress: Etiology and treatment. *Journal of Psychology, 218*(2), 109–127.

Schauer, M., Neuner, F., & Elbert, T. (2005). *Narrative exposure therapy: A short-term intervention for traumatic stress disorders after war, terror, or torture.* Ashland, OH: Hogrefe & Huber.

Schauer, M., Neuner, F., & Elbert, T. (2012). *Narrative exposure therapy (NET): A short-term intervention for traumatic stress disorders* (2nd ed.). Göttingen, Germany: Hogrefe & Huber.

Schauer, M., Neuner, F., & Elbert, T. (2017). Narrative exposure therapy for children and adolescents (KIDNET). In M. Landolt, M. Cloitre, & U. Schnyder (Eds.), *Evidence-based treatments for trauma related disorders in children and adolescents* (pp. 227–250). Cham, Switzerland: Springer International.

Schauer, M., & Robjant, K. (2018). Commentary on Scheidell et al.: En-counting adversities; the "building blocks" of psychopathology. *Addiction, 113*(1), 57–58.

Schauer, M., & Ruf-Leuschner, M. (2014). Die Lifeline in der Narrativen Expositionstherapie (NET) [The "lifeline' in narrative exposure therapy (NET)]. *Psychotherapeut, 59,* 226–238.

Schauer, M., & Schauer, E. (2010). Trauma-focused public mental-health interventions: A paradigm shift in humanitarian assistance and aid work. In E. Martz (Ed.), *Trauma rehabilitation after war and conflict* (pp. 361–430). New York: Springer.

Schneider, A., Conrad, D., Pfeiffer, A., Elbert, T., Kolassa, I. T., & Wilker, S. (2018). Stigmatization is associated with increased PTSD risk and symptom severity after traumatic stress and diminished likelihood of spontaneous remission—A study with East-African conflict survivors. *Frontiers in Psychiatry, 9,* 423.

Schnyder, U., Ehlers, A., Elbert, T., Foa, E., Gersons, B., Resick, P., . . . Cloitre, M. (2015). Psychotherapies for PTSD: What do they have in common? *European Journal of Psychotraumatology, 6.*

Stenmark, H., Catani, C., Neuner, F., Elbert, T., & Holen, A. (2013). Treating PTSD in refugees and asylum seekers within the general health care system: A randomized controlled multicenter study. *Behaviour Research and Therapy, 51,* 641–647.

Steuwe, C., Rullkötter, N., Ertl, V., Berg, M., Neuner, F., Beblo, T., & Driessen, M. (2016). Effectiveness and feasibility of narrative exposure therapy (NET) in patients with borderline personality disorder and posttraumatic stress disorder—a pilot study. *BMC Psychiatry, 16*(1), 254.

Thompson, C. T., Vidgen, A., & Roberts, N. P. (2018). Psychological interventions for post-traumatic stress disorder in refugees and asylum seekers: A systematic review and meta-analysis. *Clinical Psychology Review, 63,* 66–79.

Ullmann, E., Licinio, N., Bornstein, S. R., Lanzman, R. S., Kirschbaum, C., Sierau, S., . . . Ziegenhain, U. (2017). Counteracting posttraumatic LHPA activation in refugee mothers and their infants. *Molecular Psychiatry, 23,* 2–5.

Winkler, N. (2017). *Feasibility and effectiveness of school-based interventions promoting trauma rehabilitation and reconciliation after the war in Uganda.* Dissertation, University of Konstanz, Konstanz, Germany.

CHAPTER 15

Emotion-Focused Therapy

SANDRA C. PAIVIO
LYNNE E. ANGUS

In this chapter, we specify the sources of disturbance that are consequences of complex trauma that become the focus of emotion-focused therapy for trauma (EFTT). This is followed by a description of the basic theory and fundamental assumptions underlying EFTT, its development specifically for complex trauma, and research evidence supporting efficacy and proposed mechanisms of change. We then describe the treatment model's phases and the therapeutic tasks it provides to help clients overcome processing difficulties. Finally, we present an excerpt from an EFTT session with a client (composite), dealing with sexual abuse at the hands of a neighbor when she was age 5, in order to illustrate the essential features of EFTT.

Complex Trauma

Complex trauma in childhood is here defined as repeated exposure to violence and betrayals of trust at the hands of loved ones and caregivers, often attachment figures. This is distinguished from *single-incident trauma*, which typically is associated with a diagnosis of posttraumatic stress disorder (PTSD; American Psychiatric Association, 2013), in that it results in a more complex array of disturbances. Whereas exposure to trauma at any age can result in disruptions in narrative and emotion processes, complex trauma in childhood is particularly devastating, because emotional competencies and enduring perceptions of self and intimate others are developed in the context of early attachment relationships.

Sources of Disturbance That Are the Focus of EFTT

Complex trauma is thought to involve three primary, interrelated sources of disturbance, each of which is associated with negative, long-term psychological effects. First, repeated exposure to the terror and helplessness of trauma is associated with psychological disorders, including symptoms of PTSD, anxiety, and depression. Second, negative and insecure attachment experiences in infancy and childhood can result in enduring perceptions of the self as worthless, incompetent, or negligible, and perceptions of intimate others as unavailable, hurtful, or dangerous. These enduring maladaptive perceptions of self and others may be out of context in adult life and may in turn result in difficulties with intimacy, parenting, and transgenerational transmission of trauma in adulthood. Third, children growing up in abusive environments typically receive limited support for expressing and coping with the intense negative feelings generated by abuse; thus, they learn to rely on emotional avoidance as a coping strategy, often cycling between feeling overwhelmed and shutting down engagement with painful emotions. Chronic avoidance of core feelings can result in limited awareness of emotional experience (*alexithymia*) and thus limited reflective awareness of the emotional impact of life events and personal memories resulting in self-narrative incoherence (Angus et al., 2017). Importantly, prolonged avoidance of trauma feelings and memories can also interfere with recovery and processing of trauma experiences (Foa, Huppert, & Cahill, 2006) and has been associated with a host of other mental health problems, including anxiety, substance abuse, eating disorders, and self-harm behaviors often used in an ultimately maladaptive effort at self soothing (Hayes, Strosahl, & Wilson, 1999).

Features of EFTT

EFTT is a short-term, trauma-focused approach that primarily targets negative attachment experiences (Bowlby, 1969/1997; Sroufe, 2005; van der Kolk, 2003) and avoidance of trauma feelings and memories that underlie and perpetuate symptoms (Paivio & Pascual-Leone, 2010). Grounded in the general model of emotion-focused therapy (EFT; Greenberg, 2011; Greenberg & Paivio, 1997), EFTT is informed by theory and research in the areas of emotion (Izard, 2002), narrative process (Angus & Greenberg, 2011) and affective neuroscience (e.g., LeDoux, 1996). According to EFT theory, emotion structures or schemes are multimodal personal meaning systems that, when activated in therapy, are rich source of information about thoughts, feelings, needs, bodily sensations, behavioral tendencies, and personal memories. The term *scheme* is used to emphasize emotion as embodying action plans rather than simply static mental representations. Specific, discrete adaptive emotions (e.g., anger at violation, sadness at deprivation and loss), contextualized within trauma narratives, are key sources of information that can help guide adaptive functioning. We describe later in detail the process of emotional transformation, wherein adaptive emotional responses are accessed to change meanings related to maladaptive emotional reactions (e.g., fear, shame) and trauma narratives.

EFTT includes features that are *common factors* across effective approaches described in this book. These include ensuring client safety, both in and out of therapy sessions; attention to emotion regulation (since it is usually dysregulated); construction of new meaning concerning view of self, others, and traumatic memories; and a phased approach, beginning with establishing client relational safety, then reexperiencing and working through and integrating trauma feelings and memories (exposure and emotional processing), followed by the enhancement of client agency, self-compassion, and self-narrative reconstruction that results in a more coherent, emotionally differentiated view of self and others (Paivio & Angus, 2017).

EFTT also is characterized by several *distinctive features*. First, empathic *responding* is the primary intervention for emotion regulation and resolution. A safe, empathically responsive, and collaborative relationship is the basis of therapy and all procedures, providing the security necessary for exploring confusing, painful, and frightening feelings and memories. Explicit empathic responding is more than empathic attunement to clients' feelings and needs, which characterizes all good therapy. Expressed empathy is a sophisticated response that conveys warmth, concern, and acceptance, as well as understanding of client's inner worlds—both expressed and implied feelings, and the cognitive/meaning framework of those feelings—that results in heightened reflective awareness on the client's part. Empathic responding plays a central role in enhancing emotion regulation and resolution. From a developmental perspective (Gross, 1999), *emotion regulation* is defined in terms of the capacity to (1) experience the full range of emotion (so that information associated with each is available), (2) modulate frequency and intensity (again, so that information is available), and (3) engage in appropriate expression of emotions, so that associated interpersonal needs can be met. Empathic responses can enhance each of these emotion regulation capacities by (1) helping clients to accurately label and symbolize (i.e., give language to its meaning), thus facilitating more differentiated narrative contextualization and integration of emotional experience; (2) soothing or heightening intensity/arousal of emotional experience in the process enhancing modulation and the capacity for exploration of that experience; and (3) helping clients to appropriately communicate feelings and meanings and thus facilitate experiential storytelling (i.e., telling their personal narratives) and enhanced relational bonds.

A second distinguishing feature of EFTT is that client "experiencing" is the primary source of new meaning and narrative–emotion integration. The construct of experiencing has some similarities to that of mindfulness, in the sense that both require a quiet and introspective stance, as well as nonjudgmental observation and acceptance of the flow of thoughts, feelings, and bodily sensations. However, the process of experiencing in therapy is a dyadic, interpersonal process that is exclusively intended to construct new meaning, whereby internal experience is a source of wisdom rather than emotion regulation. The construct of experiencing, derived from the phenomenological tradition (Gendlin, 1996), also bears some resemblance to the developmental concept of mentalization (Bowlby 1969/1997; Fonagy, Gergely, Jurist, & Target, 2002). The basic assumption underlying both constructs is that understanding of self and others is dependent on reflective functioning, that is, awareness of subjective internal processes (i.e., emotions, thoughts, feelings, desires). Moreover, a secure relational bond is viewed as facilitating client security that is necessary for exploring and symbolizing emerging internal states in therapy sessions (Paivio & Angus, 2017) and in life. The construct of "client experiencing" refers to the moment-by-moment *process* of in-session exploration leading to increased capacity for self-reflection.

The *Experiencing Scale* (EXP; Klein, Mathieu-Coughlan, & Kiesler, 1986) operationalizes this construct, with lower levels referring to dialogue that is externally and behaviorally focused, moderate levels that are affective and entail disclosure of specific personal memories, and higher levels involving exploration of and insight into intrapersonal and interpersonal patterns and the articulation of a new view of self and sense of heightened self-narrative coherence. Research using the EXP supports the contribution of clients' experiencing to outcome across insight-oriented therapeutic approaches, including EFTT (Pascual-Leone & Yeryomenko, 2017). Helping clients to explore their internal experience requires optimal arousal that is high enough to activate emotion structures or schemes and low enough to explore the associated meanings without overtaxing the client. This is consistent with the "window of tolerance" or emotional arousal necessary for optimal emotion regulation in processing trauma memories described by Ogden and Fisher (2015).

A third distinctive feature of EFTT is the primary focus on resolving or healing attachment injuries. Clients are not only distressed by current self and interpersonal problems (which also are discussed in therapy) but they also continue to be haunted by negative feelings, including betrayal and unmet needs concerning specific individuals from the past—perpetrators and attachment figures. These unresolved issues are the origins of current difficulties, whereby old feelings and unmet needs ("unfinished business") get activated in current situations and relationships.

Finally, EFTT is based on an empirically verified model of "unfinished business" resolution using an empty-chair dialogue intervention (Greenberg & Foerster, 1996). In this procedure, clients are asked to imagine perpetrators in an empty chair and to express previously constricted thoughts and feelings directly to this imagined other. Analyses identified the following four process steps that discriminate clients who resolve issues from those who do not: (1) a perceived globally powerful and negative other ("bad object" in object-relations terms), (2) expression of previously constricted adaptive emotion (e.g., anger at violation, betrayal, and sadness at loss), (3) a sense of entitlement to unmet needs (e.g., for protection, love), and (4) more adaptive perceptions of self as competent and worthwhile, more assertive interpersonal interactions, and a more differentiated perspective of the other as more human and life-size. In the case of clients dealing with childhood abuse, this procedure would occur in the context of clients accessing and disclosing painful traumatic memories of abuse, and/or the procedure could activate traumatic memories for further exploration.

Research Support for EFTT

EFTT is based on more than 30 years of process and outcome research (see Paivio & Pascual-Leone, 2010) beginning with a clinical trial (Paivio & Greenberg; 1995) evaluating therapy ($N = 34$) for "unfinished business" with a general clinical sample. Therapy (12 sessions) was based on the empirically verified model of steps in the process of resolving unfinished business with a significant other, as described earlier (Greenberg & Foerster, 1996). Clinical observation yielded several distinct processes for the subgroup of clients in the sample who were dealing with issues of child abuse trauma. These processes included activation of fear, avoidance, and shame in response to imagining perpetrators in the empty chair, and more time required to resolve these intrapersonal issues before clients could engage in imaginal confrontation (IC) and resolve issues with perpetrators. A revised model of EFT specifically for complex trauma was based on analyses of videotaped sessions with this subgroup. Revisions included conceptualizing the process specifically in terms of trauma—the empty chair intervention was reframed as imaginal confrontation of perpetrators; change was thought to involve both exposure and interpersonal processes; emotional processing of trauma memories was thought to be a mechanism of change; and a greater emphasis was placed on self-development in the middle phase of therapy, that is, on reducing the fear/avoidance, shame, and self-blame activated in the process of confronting trauma material.

A clinical trial ($N = 37$) evaluating 16 sessions of EFTT with IC (Paivio & Nieuwenhuis, 2001) resulted in large effect sizes in multiple domains of disturbance (symptom distress; self-esteem; global interpersonal problems; specific target complaints; resolution of issues with specifically identified perpetrators of abuse and neglect, who were the focus of therapy). These effects were maintained at 6-month follow-up. Subsequent process–outcome studies supported proposed mechanisms of change: Emotional engagement with traumatic autobiographical memory narratives during IC independently contributed to outcome beyond contributions made by the therapeutic alliance (Paivio, Hall, Holowaty, Jellis, & Tran, 2001). However, 20% of clients in the Paivio and Nieuwenhuis (2001) study declined participation in the evocative IC intervention. This was the impetus for developing a less stressful empathic exploration (EE) procedure to address unresolved complex trauma. EE is based on the identical model of resolution and steps in the process as IC, except that clients imagine perpetrators in their "mind's eye" and express evoked thoughts and feelings exclusively in an empathic, co-constructive interaction with the therapist.

A randomized controlled trial (RCT) (Paivio, Jarry, Chagigiorgis, Hall, & Ralston; 2010) comparing 16 sessions of EFTT with IC (*n* = 24) and EFTT with EE (*n* = 20) yielded comparably large effect sizes in multiple domains (see Paivio & Nieuwenhuis, 2001) in both treatment conditions, and effects were maintained at 1-year follow-up. Process–outcome studies yielded comparable processes (e.g., Ralston, 2008) during the IC and EE procedures (e.g., alliance quality, quality of engagement, depth of experiencing, levels of distress). However, there were lower levels of arousal during EE compared to IC and a lower dropout rate in EFTT with EE compared to EFTT with IC (5% vs. 21%). These findings support the intended function of EE as a comparable and less stressful procedure. Other studies have supported the contributions of depth of experiencing, adaptive anger expression, and therapist expressed empathy to outcome in EFTT with IC and EE (see Paivio & Pascual-Leone, 2010).

In terms of client variables, analyses of the previous samples (Paivio & Nieuwenhuis, 2001; Paivio et al., 2010) resulted in no differential effects for abuse severity or type, or gender, thus indicating broad applicability of EFTT. Severity of personality pathology was the only client variable associated with more limited treatment gains; this is consistent with expectations for short-term therapeutic approaches. The caveat in interpreting these research findings is client suitability for short-term therapy. Clients were excluded from EFTT clinical trials based on severity of disturbances that preclude short-term therapy and that frequently can occur in this client group (e.g., severe emotion dysregulation, substance abuse, suicidality, comorbid diagnoses). However, the standard EFTT short-term protocol can to be modified and phases may be extended to meet the needs of clients with more severe disturbance. For example, Phase 1, which focuses on establishing safety, can be prolonged for very fragile clients with severe affect dysregulation problems, and Phase 2, which focuses on self-development and emotional processing of trauma material, can be prolonged with clients who are severely avoidant. It is likely that the more limited gains achieved by clients with more severe personality pathology in EFTT clinical trials (Paivio & Nieuwenhuis, 2001; Paivio et al., 2010) is a function of their need for a longer course of therapy. EFTT also can assimilate strategies from other approaches (e.g., Seeking Safety for addictions: Najavits, 2002; dialectical behavior therapy: Linehan, 1993) as needed and appropriate to address problems with severe emotion dysregulation, suicidality, substance abuse, and self-harm behaviors.

Numerous process–outcome studies have examined narrative–emotion processes in EFTT (Paivio & Angus, 2017). There is now abundant evidence supporting impoverished narrative processes in unresolved trauma related to attachment style, especially the disorganized/dissociative style, including memory gaps, incoherence, negative content, limited use of emotion words, and limited insight or meaning (for review, see O'Kearney & Perrot, 2006). More recently, Angus and colleagues (2017) have empirically validated a narrative–

emotion process model and coding system that identifies three broad types of narrative–emotion processes. These are defined in terms of multidimensional indicators or markers of content and quality of client storytelling and emotional engagement in therapy sessions, including EFTT (Paivio & Angus, 2017). "Problem" storytelling typically occurs in the early phase of therapy and indicates unresolved trauma, such that clients are stuck in the "same old story," with a maladaptive, negative view of self and others. Additionally, narrative quality may be abstract, intellectual, and lacking in emotion or indicate overwhelming emotion without narrative context (e.g., dissociation), and evidence low levels of client experiencing. "Transition" storytelling typically occurs in the middle phase of therapy for successful clients as they begin to access adaptive resources that can be integrated into and begin to shift the "same old story." Client storytelling becomes more personal and experientially focused, evidencing higher levels of client experiencing. For example, it is when EFTT clients hold perpetrators accountable in the context of IC and EE interventions, and challenge their maladaptive emotions and beliefs, that more adaptive and assertive feelings, needs, beliefs, and behaviors emerge in therapy sessions. Next, narrative–emotion process "change" markers indicate the resolution and, in some instances, reconsolidation of maladaptive interpersonal patterns embedded in trauma memory narratives (Angus et al., 2017). For example, unexpected outcome and discovery storytelling occurs when clients access new insights into long-standing concerns and are willing to take assertive action to have core needs met. These insights are the basis for the articulation of a more agentic and differentiated experience of self and view of others (positive self-narrative identity change). The identification of narrative–emotion problem, transition, and change markers makes explicit what EFTT therapists implicitly notice and respond to in client storytelling to further enhance client experiential engagement and meaning making. These are an additional tool to guide responsive, moment-by-moment facilitation of productive client processes (Paivio & Angus, 2017).

The EFTT Treatment Model

EFTT consists of specific therapeutic tasks and associated narrative–emotion processing difficulties and interventions designed to address these difficulties. These are the primary foci of different phases of therapy. Clients reiteratively cycle through these tasks and processes over the course of therapy. Maintaining a safe therapeutic relationship and promoting client experiencing are basic tasks that are part of all phases, tasks, and interventions. These facilitate engagement in the process of therapy—a collaborative process of disclosing, exploring, and understanding the meaning of deeply personal, experientially alive self-narratives. EFTT uses a variety of interventions for working directly with emotion, accessing trauma feelings and narratives, in the context of a safe, collaborative, and empathically responsive therapeutic relationship.

Phases and Tasks

The overarching therapeutic task in EFTT is to resolve issues with significant others from the past who had a profoundly negative impact on development (perpetrators and attachment figures). *Resolution* is defined in terms of the following dimensions: (1) reduced symptom distress and negative feelings such as anger, sadness, fear, shame, alienation, concerning these others; (2) increased self-esteem, a more empowered, agentic view of self, and interpersonal boundary definition; (3) letting go of expectations that the other will change or make amends and looking toward one's own resources to meet existential or interpersonal needs; (4) a more differentiated perspective of significant others, appropriately holding perpetrators responsible for harm (rather than the self), and possibly forgiveness and recognition that other people can be safe and responsive rather than abusive and exploitive. We described steps in the resolution process earlier in the section on the model of unfinished business resolution.

Early Phase

The focus of the first phase of therapy (typically four sessions) is to establish a strong therapeutic alliance. Attention to the relationship is essential to all phases, tasks, and procedures throughout therapy, but it is the exclusive focus of the early phase and sets the course for the remainder of therapy. The alliance functions as both a direct and indirect mechanism of change. Safety and trust (1) are new relational experiences that help counteract negative attachment experiences and (2) provide a safe context that facilitates engagement in evocative reexperiencing and reprocessing procedures in which the client feels heard and supported.

Beginning in Session 1, empathic responding and validation of client perceptions and experience facilitate narrative disclosure of both current and past experiences. This begins the process of helping clients to approach the profound emotional pain of abuse and neglect which, in later sessions, can be allowed, tolerated, and explored for meaning. In one study of EFTT processes ($N = 45$), Mlotek (2013) found that the quality of therapist expressed empathy during Session 1 predicted client engagement in reexperiencing procedures (IC/EE) over the course of therapy and treatment outcome at the end of therapy.

During early sessions, the therapist provides clear expectations for therapy and specifically asks about and addresses client hopes and fears concerning therapy processes and change. The therapist also provides information about trauma and trauma recovery, including the importance of traumatic memory reexperiencing/emotional engagement and reduced emotional avoidance, a rationale for interventions, as well as immediacy and process observations, and transparency regarding client processing difficulties. Treatment goals are collaboratively formulated in the context of responding to client struggles, emotional pain, and desires for change. All these features help to reduce anxiety and promote safety and client sense of control and engagement in the process of therapy.

Over the course of the first few sessions, the therapist also is implicitly assessing both the content and quality of clients' narratives (e.g., presence of emotion words, coherence, ability to self-reflect, availability of adaptive internal resources), their capacity for emotion regulation, for attending to and exploring internal experience, and responsiveness to therapist interventions aimed at deepening experiencing and reflective meaning making. A clear understanding of client problems is collaboratively developed in plain language tailored to the individual client. This case formulation involves identifying the following components: (1) the core maladaptive emotion scheme (the "same old story"), emerging in the context of clients' storytelling, which comprises the core maladaptive emotion (e.g., rejecting anger, fear/shame, alienation, lonely abandonment) and sense of self and others that need to be changed, as well as core unmet needs and the effects of these on self and relationships; (2) the dominant emotional processing difficulties—poor awareness, regulation (hyper- and hypoarousal, avoidance/overcontrol, dysregulation), reflection/meaning making; and limited access to specific adaptive emotions (e.g., anger, sadness) that can be used to facilitate emotional transformation; (3) markers for narrative–emotion subtypes—problem storytelling (e.g., absent or overwhelming emotion, abstract or superficial), transition storytelling (e.g., experiential, self-reflective) and change storytelling (e.g., discoveries or insight and new behaviors); and (4) markers for therapeutic tasks (e.g., lack of clarity about internal experience, self-criticism/blame, avoidance and self-interruption, unresolved issues or unfinished business with particular perpetrators). Together these elements have clear implications for the process of therapy, and they are shared with the client, again, as a means of clarifying expectations, reducing anxiety, enhancing clients' sense of control, and engagement in the process.

The primary IC/EE procedures used in EFTT typically are introduced during Session 4 once a safe therapeutic relationship has been established. Again, provision of a clear rationale tailored to the individual client's story and treatment needs, and intervention options (e.g., to use chair work or not) help to promote engagement and contribute to client sense of control. The decision about whether to initially implement IC or the less evocative EE is based on knowledge of the individual client. There are several reasons why we recommend using IC, unless it is clearly contraindicated. First, imagining a perpetrator sitting across from the client in the room is highly evocative and quickly activates core trauma-related memories and emotional reactions, including blocks to resolution such as fear/avoidance and shame that become the focus of Phase 2 of therapy. Second, use of the chairs provides helpful structure in terms of clearly distinguishing between perceptions of the imagined other and reactions of the self for both client and therapist. Finally, the empty chair/IC procedure has been more extensively researched in terms of the process steps related to resolution and good outcome (e.g., Greenberg & Foerster, 1996; Paivio & Greenberg, 1995; Greenberg, 2011; Paivio et al., 2001). Contraindications for using IC in Session 4 (and therefore using EE as an alternative) include client problems with severe emotion dysregulation when focusing on a cruel and malevolent other and, of course, when the client refuses to participate or has extreme difficulties participating in IC. It is possible to briefly introduce IC later in the session, for example, at markers of assertive expression of adaptive feelings or needs, when the client is more resolved or regulated, and with a less frightening or toxic perpetrator. Importantly, EE is not simply trauma exploration in the overall relationship context of therapy; it is based on the IC process model and intervention principles (described earlier). Therapists need to be trained and competent in implementing this model.

Middle Phase

The focus of the middle phase of EFTT is to resolve self-related difficulties and internal conflicts observed in the early phase of therapy and activated in the initial IC/EE. These difficulties act as blocks to interpersonal resolution. Thus, the primary task of the middle phase is to promote self-development by reducing fear/avoidance, shame, and self-blame; enhancing emotion regulation and narrative–emotion integration; increasing self-esteem, self-empowerment, and the capacity to tolerate and explore the meaning of emotional pain; and to access self-soothing resources.

A variety of interventions are used in conjunction with IC/EE to resolve these difficulties. These include experiential focusing (Gendlin, 1996) to help clients symbolize the meaning of unclear or confusing internal experience; two-chair dialogues between parts of self to heighten awareness of the negative impact of self-criticism, -catastrophizing, or -interruption; access to healthy protest and self-soothing to challenge these maladaptive processes; memory work to explore distal situations in which the core maladaptive sense of self was formed; or recent situations in which that self-narrative was activated, with the goal of activating alternative adaptive resources (feelings, needs, beliefs) to construct a more adaptive self-narrative. The change mechanism here is emotional transformation. Steps in the process of resolving difficulties using these procedures have been clearly articulated (e.g., Paivio & Pascual-Leone, 2010).

A fundamental process that is essential to all tasks and procedures in EFTT is to promote and deepen client experiencing. It is widely accepted that the capacity to attend to and explore internal experience is essential to reexperiencing and emotional processing of trauma memories (e.g., chapters in the present text). Interventions that deepen experiencing help clients transition from an externally oriented, superficial, or intellectual stance (e.g., problem storytelling) to accessing and disclosing experientially alive episodic memories that are concrete, specific, personal, affective, and sensorial (transition storytelling)—these are the basis for deeply reflective self-exploration, new meaning making, and self-narrative change. This reexperiencing of traumatic events goes beyond simple disclosure that takes place in the early sessions and involves helping clients to (1) allow, tolerate, and explore the meaning of intensely painful emotional experience, and (2) to re-story that experience in light of a new positive, agentic view of self that includes clearly holdings perpetrators (rather than self) responsible for harm.

Typically, interventions used in EFTT involve implicit rather than explicit skills training. For example, emotion awareness is enhanced through advanced empathic responding and promoting experiencing. Research (Paivio et al., 2010) indicates that 80% of clients in EFTT met criteria for alexithymia before therapy, and this dropped to 20% at the end of therapy. In another study, Mundorf and Paivio (2011) found that depth of experiencing in written trauma narratives increased from pre- to posttreatment. In terms of IC of significant others who might still be in the client's current life, this is not intended as behavioral rehearsal but rather is designed to promote awareness of thoughts, feelings, wants, and needs. Such awareness can inform interpersonal interaction such as assertiveness and boundary definition. Two-chair dialogues between parts of the self are intended to increase experiential awareness, in the moment, of the negative effects of maladaptive processes, such as self-criticism or self-interruption of authentic feelings and needs. Such awareness can activate alternative adaptive processes. Two-chair dialogues also can be used to access self-compassion and self-soothing capacities in response to experiencing emotional pain, in the moment. This "hot process" is distinct from self-compassion skills training, which is used to regulate intense negative emotion when appropriate (e.g., at the end of a session) but is thought to be less transformative. One example of explicit skills training in EFTT involves teaching experiential focusing (Gendlin, 1996) as a structured procedure to promote understanding of internal experience, which clients can practice at home. Clients also can be assigned awareness homework ("Over the week, pay attention to your thoughts and feelings during troublesome situations; don't try to change anything, just notice"). Mindfulness and distress tolerance skills also may be taught as needed and appropriate.

Late Phase

The focus of the late phase of EFTT is to resolve issues with perpetrators and attachment figures who have been the focus of therapy, to integrate therapy experiences, and to form a bridge between the present and future. Once clients are feeling stronger, they are better able to confront and stand up to imagined perpetrators and uninhibitedly express feelings and entitlement to unmet needs. Experience and expression of adaptive anger and sadness/grief are considered catalysts for change because, once fully activated, the adaptive information associated with these emotions is available for integration into maladaptive emotion schemes (the "same old story") and construction of new meaning and view of self (e.g., discovery storytelling). Again, this is an integrative process of emotional transformation and self-narrative change. An important step in this resolution process involves promoting clients' sense of entitlement to unmet needs associated with adaptive emotions such as anger at violation and sadness/grief over losses. For example, clients may acknowledge wanting and needing their parents undivided attention or a childhood that was carefree and innocent, but it is not until they feel fully deserving of this that profound self-narrative change begins to occur.

The final two or three sessions of EFTT include a final IC/EE and explicitly processing observed changes (e.g., emotional processes, perceptions of self and other) compared to the initial dialogue during the early phase of therapy. Termination involves mutual feedback and meaning co-construction, which includes noticing and exploring client change stories, that is, reports of new behavior or insight. Just as in problem or transition storytelling, therapists help clients to engage and explore the importance and personal meaning of new experiences of agency and empowerment and consolidate self-narrative change.

The next section illustrates key processes in EFTT with a composite client who sought therapy for issues related to sexual abuse by a neighbor (ages 6–12), and past and current issues with her mother. She also struggled as a parent and, like many clients with histories of childhood abuse, was motivated to break the cycle of abuse and make a better life for her children.

Clinical Case Example

Bonnie, a 45-year-old single mother with two young children, suffered from low self-worth and confidence, perceived herself as "damaged" and "disposable," and had difficulties establishing interpersonal boundaries with her demanding, alcoholic mother, whom she perceived as self-centered, controlling, and neglectful. During Session 1, Bonnie disclosed details of childhood abuse by a male neighbor—playing hide and seek, which led to repeated physical and sexual abuse, including penetration, and being afraid to tell anyone—with an external storytelling quality devoid of emotional arousal. Therapist empathic responses and process observations ("It must be so hard to get in touch with the reality of those experiences, very painful") were not effective in evoking emotional experiencing, and Bonnie described herself as "not very emotional, more a matter-of-fact type person" (low-level experiencing). The therapist validated that this was another effect of her childhood—protection from pain that had the unintended effect of depriving her life of emotional color, to which she agreed. This set the stage for a focus on helping Bonnie get in touch with her feelings.

Early sessions primarily focused on past and present issues concerning Bonnie's mother. When asked about memories of herself as a child, Bonnie recalled feeling ignored and neglected by her, and wishing she had a different mother. Bonnie also stated that she had always wanted to be "the apple of her [mother's] eye." The therapist's validation and empathy ("Of course, wanting to feel loved, special") evoked tears, indicating the client's capacity for emotional experiencing; however, when the therapist empathically responded,

"I see how important this is to you," she quickly collapsed into resignation: "What is the point of wishing for what I never had?" The therapist validated her experience—"It's true you can't change the past, you missed out on a lot, you got gypped. I'm sure you've never had a chance to fully grieve those losses, and this is how healing occurs"—which collaboratively set the stage for future therapeutic work. Thus, goals for therapy included helping Bonnie acknowledge and grieve losses, access self-compassion and anger at abuse and neglect that, in turn, led to increased self-empowerment and the ability to better assert interpersonal boundaries. Over the next few sessions, with explicit guidance, Bonnie was better able to access her feelings. The following excerpt illustrates memory evocation, reexperiencing and reprocessing sexual abuse (experiential storytelling), accessing adaptive anger and sadness, therapist attunement to the shifting nature of these adaptive emotions, and fluid use of the IC procedure to activate feelings and promote entitlement to unmet needs and self-empowerment.

At the beginning of Session 6, Bonnie was highly distressed as she reported having had a nightmare the preceding week about her own little girl being abused, and being unable to protect her. The therapist suggested focusing in depth on her own sexual abuse and provided a rationale: "You never had a chance to process this, it still lives inside you, comes back to haunt you, that little girl in your dream is you." He suggested reexperiencing a specific incident of abuse, ensured that Bonnie was willing to do this (collaboration on the task), provided reassurance that they would go at her pace, and evoked a specific episodic memory.

THERAPIST: When you think of your experiences of sexual abuse, what comes to mind—the backyard or the house?

BONNIE: The house, that's where it mostly happened.

THERAPIST: OK, tell me a specific episode, bring the scene alive for me, you are in the house, whereabouts? What does it look like? Is it night or day? And he is there, doing what . . . ? [Invites experiential trauma storytelling.]

BONNIE: We are in the basement. I remember it always smelled musty. Sunlight is coming through the window. I wanted to go outside, but he is wanting to play hide and seek again . . . then he starts touching me. I don't stop him, I go along with it. (*tears*)

THERAPIST: I know it's hard, you are doing fine. [Provides empathic affirmation of vulnerability, support and encouragement.] So you are in the basement, 6 years old, and here is this grown man, your neighbor Roger, coming on to you sexually, touching you in sexual ways. What else do you remember? [Continues to evoke concrete, specific, personal, episodic memories; promotes experiential storytelling.]

BONNIE: I can smell his jacket hanging on the wall, his old baseball jacket, ghakk.

THERAPIST: Stay with "ghakk," like disgust? [Directs attention to emergent feelings, adaptive protest, thus promoting transition storytelling to change maladaptive self-narrative, and helps Bonnie accurately label her feelings.]

BONNIE: Yes, disgust. It makes me sick just thinking about it. But I didn't say no or stop him or say anything to my mother, like I was a willing participant (*voice breaking, tears*).

THERAPIST: OK, stay with what you felt at the time. He is touching you and you don't stop him, you go along with it . . . [Highlights and promotes exploration of maladaptive self-blame, the same old story, in the context of experiential trauma storytelling.]

BONNIE: At first, I liked the attention, but after a while, I didn't like it, I wanted him to stop. I dreaded going over there, begged my mother not to send me over there again, but she never listened. Probably she just wanted me out of the house so she could be with her boyfriend.

THERAPIST: So he gave you the attention you needed and craved, but you didn't want the sexual part? [Focuses on emergent adaptive unmet needs and healthy protest, transition storytelling, to help counteract self-blame and promote self-narrative change.]

BONNIE: (*under her breath, softly*) Yes.

THERAPIST: Dreaded it in fact. [Focuses again on adaptive emotion to help promote self-narrative change.]

BONNIE: (*under her breath, softly*) Yes.

THERAPIST: Begged for help but no one listened, completely powerless child. [Evocative empathy intended to heighten arousal and activate emotional experience.]

BONNIE: (*silence*)

THERAPIST: What are you feeling? [Empathic attunement to a shift in Bonnie's internal experience and invites Bonnie to explore and symbolize emerging emotions, promotes transition storytelling.]

BONNIE: Angry.

THERAPIST: Angry, say more, at him?

BONNIE: Yes, very angry at him.

THERAPIST: Yes, you should be very angry at him. [Provides validation and support for emergent experience of primary adaptive anger.] Can you imagine him over there (points to empty chair)? What would you like to say, now, from your adult perspective? [Initiates IC to heighten arousal and promotes assertive expression of adaptive anger.]

BONNIE: You used and abused me. You had no right.

THERAPIST: No right! Say more.

BONNIE: You were old enough to know better. I wish I had told on you. You should have gone to jail. (*tears, looks away from empty chair, at therapist*) Someone should have protected me.

THERAPIST: Yes, just a little girl, you needed protection. Who? Who should have protected you? [Empathic attunement to and follows the shift in Bonnie's experience of anger at perpetrator.]

BONNIE: My mother should have.

THERAPIST: Ah mother, yes, of course. Say "I needed protection, I was just a child." Can you imagine her over there, tell her? [Promotes assertive expression and entitlement to unmet need.]

BONNIE: Yes, I needed you to look out for me. You should have known something was wrong, you should have listened to me . . . (*more tears*)

THERAPIST: Something touches you, what's going on? [Empathic attunement to a shift in Bonnie's experience and promotes expression of that emerging new experience.]

BONNIE: I just feel so sad for that little girl.

THERAPIST: OK, yes, so sad for that little girl. Say more. (*Pulls empty chair closer, strokes seat of chair*). Can you imagine her here, little Bonnie, how does she feel—afraid, alone? [Empathic responding and guidance promote self-compassion and self-soothing in response to Bonnie's experience of emotional pain, intended to help to transform self-blame and promote self-narrative change.]

BONNIE: Dirty!

THERAPIST: Ah dirty, like there's something wrong with her.

BONNIE: Always!

THERAPIST: So unfair that this innocent little girl, you, Bonnie, feels like there's something wrong with her. What do you think she needs to hear? (*Strokes seat of chair.*)

BONNIE: (*tears*) I'm so sorry all that stuff happened to you. It wasn't your fault. I wish I could give you back all that lost innocence.

THERAPIST: Feel so bad for her, what do you want to do—comfort her or . . . ?

BONNIE: Very much, comfort her, take care of her (*tears*).

THERAPIST: Can you imagine how good that would feel, how much she needed that, still needs that? (*touches heart*) [Helps Bonnie experience, in the moment, the positive impact of self-soothing, which is a critical aspect of emotional transformation and consolidating self-narrative change.]

BONNIE: Yes, it feels good. . . . (*silence*)

THERAPIST: What is happening? [Attunement to a shift in Bonnie's experience and encourages expression of emerging new experience.]

BONNIE: I just feel angry.

THERAPIST: Angry, at who? Him?

BONNIE: Yes, at him. (*The therapist moves the chair further away.*) You thought you could get away with it, you did get away with it, hurting a little girl. I hope you rot in hell!

THERAPIST: So he deserves to be punished, it was not right, a crime.

BONNIE: No, it absolutely was not right. There's no excuse, you ruined so much of my life . . .

THERAPIST: Tell him the effects on you. [Promotes symbolization of meaning and deepening of experiencing, reflective storytelling.]

BONNIE: All my life I felt like something was wrong with me . . . keeping that dirty secret, hiding all the time, so busy focused on pleasing everyone else, never knowing what I thought or felt, even protecting you for god's sake! It's you who should be ashamed, not me. I was a child, you were the adult, you knew better, you knew it was wrong. (*Turns to the therapist.*) Why do I always think I have to please everyone else? I am not going to hide, protect him anymore.

THERAPIST: That sounds very important to you, say more. [Promotes exploration of Bonnie's desire for change in context of discovery storytelling.]

Bonnie decides she wants to tell her mother about the sexual abuse, and she and the therapist agree to focus on this in future sessions. In a later session, she imagines her mother's defensive and dismissive response: "Well, I hope you do not intend to blame me for that!" The therapist helps Bonnie work through activated feelings of resignation, express sadness at her mother's lack of care, then anger at her invalidation and neglect, and to assert Bonnie's entitlement to adult protection as a child and to hold her mother accountable. She is then in a better position to confront her mother in real life. When and if she decides to do this, therapy will support her in that process as well. Similarly, later sessions focus on helping Bonnie to express her needs and set realistic boundaries in the relationship with her mother. This is the basis for the emergence of a more assertive, resilient, and agentic view of self and positive self-identity narrative change.

Conclusion

Disrupted narrative and affective processes, some due to dissociation, are at the core of the constellation of disturbances stemming from complex childhood trauma. EFTT is an effective short-term, trauma-focused therapy that addresses this constellation of disturbances in both men and women with histories of different types of childhood abuse and neglect. Therapy is based on a solid theoretical foundation and more than 30 years of process and outcome research. Therapy employs a variety of powerful and systematically articulated strategies for working directly with emotion and narrative–emotional processing difficulties specific to complex trauma. The treatment protocol is specified in published treatment manuals (Paivio & Pascual-Leone, 2010; Paivio & Angus, 2017) and may be tailored to meet individual client needs, for example, by extending phases and tasks or assimilating aspects of other approaches, as appropriate. Overall, there is a need for effective treatment options for vulnerable clients with histories of complex child abuse trauma, and EFTT makes a distinct contribution to this treatment literature.

References

American Psychiatric Association. (2013). *Diagnostic and statistical manual of mental disorders* (5th ed.). Arlington, VA: Author.

Angus, L., Boritz, T., Bryntwick, E., Carpenter, N., Macaulay, C., & Khattra, J. (2017). The Narrative-Emotion Process Coding System 2.0: A multi-methodological approach to identifying and assessing narrative-emotion process markers in psychotherapy. *Psychotherapy Research, 27*(3), 253–269.

Angus, L., & Greenberg, L. (2011). *Working with narrative in emotion-focused therapy: Changing stories, healing lives.* Washington, DC: American Psychological Association Press.

Bowlby, J. (1997). *Attachment and loss.* London: Pimlico. (Original work published 1969)

Foa, E. B., Huppert, J. D., & Cahill, S. P. (2006). Emotional processing theory: An update. In B. O. Rothbaum (Ed.), *Pathological anxiety: Emotional processing in etiology and treatment* (pp. 3–24). New York: Guilford Press.

Fonagy, P., Gergely, G., Jurist, E., & Target, M. (2002). *Affect regulation, mentalization and the development of the self.* New York: Other Press.

Gendlin, E. T. (1996). *Focusing-oriented psychotherapy: A manual of the experiential method.* New York: Guilford Press.

Greenberg, L. S. (2011). *Emotion-focused therapy.* Washington, DC: American Psychological Association.

Greenberg, L. S., & Foerster, F. S. (1996). Task analysis exemplified: The process of resolving unfinished business. *Journal of Consulting and Clinical Psychology, 64,* 439–446.

Greenberg, L. S., & Paivio, S. C. (1997). *Working with emotions in psychotherapy.* New York: Guilford Press.

Gross, J. J. (1999). Emotion regulation: Past, present, future. *Cognition and Emotion, 13,* 551–573.

Hayes, S. C., Strosahl, K. D., & Wilson, K. G. (1999). *Acceptance and commitment therapy.* New York: Guilford Press.

Izard, C. E. (2002). Translating emotion theory and research into preventive interventions. *Psychological Bulletin, 128,* 796–824.

Klein, M. H., Mathieu-Coughlan, P., & Kiesler, D. J. (1986). The experiencing scales. In L. S. Greenberg & W. M. Pinsof (Eds.), *The psychotherapeutic process: A research handbook* (pp. 21–71). New York: Guilford Press.

LeDoux, J. (1996). *The emotional brain: The mysterious underpinnings of emotional life.* New York: Simon & Schuster.

Linehan, M. M. (1993). *Cognitive behavioral treatment of borderline personality disorder.* New York: Guilford Press.

Mlotek, A. (2013). *Contributions of therapist empathy to client engagement and outcome in emotion-focused therapy for complex trauma.* Unpublished masters thesis, University of Windsor, Windsor, ON, Canada.

Mundorf, E. S., & Paivio, S. C. (2011). Narrative quality and disturbance pre- and post-emotion-focused therapy for child abuse trauma. *Journal of Traumatic Stress, 24*(6), 643–650.

Najavits, L. M. (2002). *Seeking Safety: A treatment manual for PTSD and substance abuse.* New York: Guilford Press.

Ogden, P., & Fisher, J. (2015). *Sensorimotor psychotherapy.* New York: Norton.

O'Kearney, R., & Perrot, K. (2006). Trauma narratives in posttraumatic stress disorder: A review. *Journal of Traumatic Stress, 19*(1), 81–93.

Paivio, S. C., & Angus, L. E. (2017). *Narrative processes in emotion-focused therapy for trauma.* Washington, DC: American Psychological Association.

Paivio, S. C., & Greenberg, L. S. (1995). Resolving "unfinished business": Efficacy of experiential therapy using empty-chair dialogue. *Journal of Consulting and Clinical Psychology, 63,* 419–425.

Paivio, S. C., Hall, I., Holowaty, K. A. M., Jellis, J., & Tran, N. (2001). Imaginal confrontation for resolving child abuse issues. *Psychotherapy Research, 11,* 433–453.

Paivio, S. C., Jarry, J. L., Chagigiorgis, H., Hall, I., & Ralston, M. (2010). Efficacy of two versions of emotion-focused therapy for resolving child abuse trauma. *Psychotherapy Research, 20*(3), 353–366.

Paivio, S. C., & Nieuwenhuis, J. A. (2001). Efficacy of emotion focused therapy for adult survivors of child abuse: A preliminary study. *Journal of Traumatic Stress, 14*(1), 115–133.

Paivio, S. C., & Pascual-Leone, A. (2010). *Emotion-focused therapy for complex trauma: An integrative approach.* Washington, DC: American Psychological Association.

Pascual-Leone, A., & Yeryomenko, N. (2017). The experiencing scale as a predictor of treatment outcomes: A meta-analysis of psychotherapy process. *Psychotherapy Research, 27*(6), 653–665.

Ralston, M. B. (2008). *Imaginal confrontation versus evocative empathy in emotion focused trauma therapy.* Unpublished doctoral dissertation. University of Windsor, Windsor, ON, Canada.

Sroufe, L. A. (2005). Attachment and development: A prospective, longitudinal study from birth to adulthood. *Attachment and Human Development, 7*(4), 349–367.

van der Kolk, B. A. (2003). Posttraumatic stress disorder and the nature of trauma. In M. Solomon & D. Siegel (Eds.), *Healing trauma: Attachment, mind, body, and brain* (pp. 168–195). New York: Norton.

CHAPTER 16

Interpersonal Psychotherapy

ARI LOWELL

ANDREA LOPEZ-YIANILOS

JOHN C. MARKOWITZ

Guidelines for the treatment of posttraumatic stress disorder (PTSD) endorse exposure therapies as the intervention of choice (American Psychological Association, 2017; Cusack et al., 2016; Department of Veteran Affairs & Department of Defense, 2017; Institute of Medicine, 2014). Exposure therapies operate via repeated imaginal and *in vivo* "exposure" to feared stimuli, including recounting of the traumatic experience and reengagement in avoided activities that evoke anxiety (Foa, 2011). While these treatments yield considerable improvement for most patients who complete treatment (Cusack et al., 2016), exposure therapy for PTSD has limitations: the dropout rate is high, often exceeding 20% (Imel, Laska, Jakupcak, & Simpson, 2013); some patients refuse treatment; and other patients, including military veterans and others with complex PTSD symptoms, show lower response rates compared to other populations (Gerger, Munder, & Barth, 2014; Steenkamp, Litz, Hoge, & Marmar, 2015).

For these reasons, Bleiberg and Markowitz (2005) adapted interpersonal psychotherapy (IPT) for PTSD as a 14-week, manualized psychotherapy. In contrast to most other PTSD interventions, IPT does not encourage exposure to traumatic memories or require homework targeting avoidance of stimuli that evoke traumatic reminders. Rather, IPT addresses some of the devastating interpersonal effects of trauma exposure: affective detachment, social withdrawal, loss of self-efficacy, mistrust of the environment, and loss of trust in people. The primary hypothesis was that just as social support powerfully protects individuals exposed to trauma from developing PTSD (Guay, Billette, & Marchand, 2006; Ozer, Best, Lipsey, & Weiss, 2003; Pietrzak et al., 2010), bolstering patients' ability to identify and trust their feelings and use these feelings as a basis for communicating effectively with others might improve social functioning, galvanize sources of support, provide a sense of environmental mastery, and reverse the devastating effects of trauma. The focus of IPT is not on the traumatic event itself, but on its aftereffects, specifically on shuttered emotions and damaged social relationships. The hope is that individuals who eschew or do not respond to exposure therapy might find this focus more tolerable and efficacious.

Origin and Structure of IPT

IPT originally was developed to treat major depressive disorder in experimental arms of a 1974 medication treatment study, during an era when combining medication and psychotherapy was a novel idea (Markowitz & Weissman, 2012). Following multiple successful randomized controlled trials (RCTs), IPT for depression has been recognized as equipotent and in some instances superior to other leading forms of psychotherapy for depression, including cognitive-behavioral therapy (CBT; Cuijpers et al., 2011). IPT has since been adapted for use with depressed adolescents (Mufson, Dorta, Moreau, & Weissman, 2004); postpartum (O'Hara, Stuart, Gorman, & Wenzel, 2000) and geriatric patients (Reynolds et al., 1999); and people with other diagnoses, such as eating disorders (Murphy, Straebler, Basden, Cooper, & Fairburn, 2012) and substance use disorders (Carroll, Rounsaville, & Gawin, 1991). It is offered in other formats such as group therapy (Wilfley, MacKenzie, Welch, Ayres, & Weissman, 2000). Regardless of adaptation, the core principles of IPT remain the same:

- Psychopathology, be it depression or another disorder, is a treatable medical illness and not the patient's fault.
- Whatever the "cause" of a disorder, it occurs in an interpersonal context and involves social disruption; many disorders have interpersonal triggers and consequences.
- Improving social functioning and social support relieves symptoms.

Structure of IPT

IPT is a time-limited treatment delivered in three stages. The goals of the first stage, typically completed in one to three sessions, include assessment and diagnosis; exploring the patient's interpersonal context, including the context within which the current problem developed; and setting the framework for treatment. The therapist gathers an *interpersonal inventory,* cataloguing how the patient has interacted with others across the lifespan. Questions the therapist asks include the following: Who are the important people in the patient's life? What does the patient do when feeling sad, upset, or angry? In whom does the patient confide, if anyone? This history lends a sense of the patient's interpersonal functioning, intimacy, and current interpersonal disputes, while identifying potential sources of social support. In addition to conducting the interpersonal inventory, the therapist assigns the patient the *sick role,* explaining that the patient has a treatable illness that is not his or her fault, and emphasizes that the disorder and the interpersonal environment are responsible for the symptoms, not the patient, and under these circumstances no one is expected to be at his or her best (Parsons, 1951). The therapist sets a time limit and emphasizes that treatment will focus on feelings and interpersonal relationships.

In the last part of the first stage of treatment, the therapist presents a formulation (Markowitz & Swartz, 2007). An IPT formulation defines a focus for the treatment. The focus derives from the history and depends on what is most likely to be fruitful and helpful to the patient, usually either an event central to the development of the disorder or a current situation that is maintaining or worsening the problem. The primary focal areas are *grief (complicated bereavement),* an unresolved reaction to the death of a significant other; *role dispute,* a struggle with a significant other; or *role transition,* a major life change, such as a move, shift in job or position, or beginning or ending a relationship. If none of these categories fit, a fourth focus, *interpersonal deficits,* is used, usually focusing on loneliness and social isolation, and bolstering interpersonal skills. The therapist presents the formulation as a summary linking the patient's primary diagnosis and difficulties to an interpersonal context, and suggests using the focal area to explore interpersonal relationships and functioning in the patient's present symptomatic crisis. The therapist does not assign homework but does encourage the patient to "live dangerously," that is, to take emotional, interpersonal risks beyond the patient's initial comfort zone, which can be discussed in treatment.

In the second stage, comprising most of the treatment, the IPT therapist opens sessions by asking, "How have things been since we last met?" This question elicits either a feeling or an event, and the therapist's first task is to help the patient link the two. The therapist does this by asking questions about what has happened; what the patient felt, said, or did; what the response was; and, at each stage, how the patient was feeling and whether he or she thinks these feelings make sense. The therapist's goal is to help the patient identify, understand, and name feelings, and to recognize these feelings as valid, important, and interpersonally useful. Finally, the therapist asks the patient whether he or she is satisfied with the results of what he or she did or said. If not, the therapist asks, "What are your options?" and helps the patient explore alternatives. They typically practice options using role play. The time limit of treatment pressures patients to make changes and try the options practiced in treatment. The therapist applauds the patient for efforts toward "speaking up" in the service of feelings, needs, and wants. If the patient's efforts succeed, the therapist offers congratulations. If not, the therapist praises the effort, provides support, and helps the patient explore what went wrong and how the situation might be improved now or in the future. What other options exist?

In the last stage of treatment, the therapist works with the patient to consolidate gains, increase a sense of competence, and process the emotional termination of treatment. Treatment ending is acknowledged as bittersweet, because it is sad to end a relationship and also hopefully brings a sense of accomplishment. If the patient remains symptomatic, the therapist works with the him or her to identify next steps and plan for the future. An option for some patients who have completed IPT may be maintenance IPT, which has demonstrated efficacy over a longer term (Miller, Frank, & Levenson, 2012; Weissman, Markowitz, & Klerman, 2018).

IPT for PTSD: Theoretical Underpinnings and Differences from IPT for Depression

Theoretical foundations of IPT in its original form include the diathesis–stress model, medical model, and attachment theory (Lipsitz & Markowitz, 2013, 2016). The diathesis–stress model infers multiple causes for psychopathology, both biological and environmental. IPT focuses on the stress side of this model by identifying psychosocial factors, life events, or interpersonal problems that precipitate and maintain psychopathology (Lipsitz & Markowitz, 2013). Through the lens of the medical model, IPT creates for the patient a new characterization focused on externalizing the patient's problem and defining it as a medical illness, not a characterological attribute of the patient.

Bowlby (1973, 1998) proposed a human instinctual drive to form attachments that enhance infants' survival by evoking protective and nurturing behaviors by adults. In secure attachments, toddlers begin to explore their environment by venturing away from their supportive and encouraging caregiver (Bowlby, 1973, 1998). Positive reinforcement from the caregiver gives the child confidence to develop independently, while also relying on supportive relationships, and delivers the perspective that the environment is reasonably safe and populated with potential social supports. However, conflicts or mistreatment (or neglect) in this early developmental stage may lead to an insecure attachment style, yielding an outlook that environments and people in them are unsafe. This is associated with adult vulnerability, such as fearful avoidance (Markowitz, Milrod, Bleiberg, & Marshall, 2009). With regard to PTSD, securely attached individuals may have the confidence to explore their environment and risk "exposing" themselves to trauma reminders, while trusting social supports to help them process and manage fearful reactions. Conversely, insecurely attached individuals are further compromised by trauma, having fewer social supports to turn to and lacking confidence in relying on them, often leading to isolation and exacerbation of PTSD symptoms (Markowitz et al., 2009). IPT for PTSD is thus informed by attachment theory, in that treatment specifically focuses on a person's ability to trust the self and connect effectively with others.

In practice, IPT for PTSD is very similar to IPT for depression, and treatment sometimes covers both disorders given the high rate of comorbidity between the two (Rytwinski, Scur, Feeny, & Youngstrom, 2013). IPT for PTSD includes several key adaptations, however. In the opening phase, the therapist describes PTSD as a debilitating but treatable disorder that is not the patient's fault. As the trauma is usually identified as a change event, the formulation of *role transition* is often selected. A patient with PTSD may have been fine before a traumatic event occurred but afterward find life very different. For example, after experiencing a horrific car accident, a parent may suddenly stop volunteering to transport children to events, withdraw from social activities, and become irritable and depressed with others rather than friendly and outgoing. The treating therapist identifies this as a life role that has changed, and treatment might focus on understanding and reversing the interpersonal consequences of the trauma, so that the patient may transition (back) to a healthier way of being. As part of diagnosis and formulation, the therapist explains that PTSD induces interpersonal problems that compound the patient's situation, and that addressing these problems fuels recovery. The therapist also notes that although the traumatic event is important, the treatment focuses not on recalling the event but on addressing its intrapersonal/interpersonal consequences, including numbed emotions, isolation, and mistrust and hypervigilance.

Precisely because of the affective numbing of PTSD, IPT for PTSD places great emphasis on affective expression and the recognition that emotions, although powerful, are not dangerous. In contrast to patients with depression, who generally can identify and express some feelings, patients with PTSD are frequently detached, "numb" to feeling, and lack the ability to identify emotions or else fear them. Whether these deficits were present before the traumatic event is clinically interesting but largely immaterial to the treatment; regardless, PTSD exacerbates these problems, eroding a patient's ability to distinguish between threatening individuals and trustworthy social support. Like patients with depression, patients with PTSD are encouraged to take emotional risks. For those with PTSD, therapists typically frame this in the context of feeling anxious and frightened, whereas for patients with depression or comorbid depression, they may emphasize despondency and hopelessness. Anxiety and anger are validated as normal, adaptive emotions rather than "bad" or dangerous: Anger tells you something important about conflict in a relationship. Maladaptive coping mechanisms (e.g., numbing or avoidance) that may have helped a patient survive a traumatic ordeal are acknowledged as sensible in the face of danger but less helpful in the context of the patient's here-and-now interpersonal life (Markowitz, 2016).

Evidence and Efficacy of IPT for PTSD

Research studies have increasingly established the efficacy of IPT for PTSD. Following the initial pilot study (Bleiberg & Markowitz, 2005), the National Institute of Mental Health (NIMH) funded a randomized controlled study comparing 110 unmedicated patients with chronic PTSD in three treatment groups (Markowitz et al., 2015a, 2015b): prolonged exposure (PE; Foa, Hembree, & Rothbaum, 2007), the "gold standard" treatment for PTSD; relaxation therapy; and IPT for PTSD. Results were clear: IPT performed as well as PE, and, in fact, better for those with comorbid major depression (Markowitz et al., 2015b) or a history of sexual assault (Markowitz, Neria, Lovell, Van Meter, & Petkova, 2017). Although this study did not specifically assess complex PTSD, the comorbid PTSD + depression subgroup and chronic sexual assault subgroup were reporting, respectively, symptoms and trauma histories consistent with complex PTSD. Other research has demonstrated the efficacy of IPT for PTSD in group format (Campanini et al., 2010; Krupnick et al., 2008). While additional research is needed, the primary emerging message is that, contrary to common wisdom, exposure is not a necessary component of recovery from PTSD, and that IPT is a safe and effective alternative that some patients and therapists may find preferable and more palatable (Markowitz et al., 2016). Growing recognition of the potential of IPT for PTSD and the need for alternatives to exposure therapy has led to increased funding for additional research. Treatment guidelines have also begun to include IPT for PTSD as an evidence-based treatment, including the most recent iteration of the Department of Veterans Affairs and Department of Defense (VA/DoD; 2017) guidelines for PTSD.

IPT's Key Clinical Features Relevant to Complex Trauma

Complex trauma has been described as repetitive or prolonged stressors that involve harm or abandonment by caregivers at developmentally vulnerable times (Ford & Courtois, 2014). In contrast, *simple(r) trauma* (typically referred to as "trauma") usually entails a single, distinguishable event that is threatening or harmful to the life, physical safety, or integrity of the individual or another individual (van der Kolk, 2005). Many argue that DSM-5 PTSD captures the effects of simple(r) trauma but ignores the more complicated and chronic interpersonal trauma described by complex trauma (Briere & Spinazzola, 2005; Courtois & Ford, 2009; van der Kolk, 2005). Although IPT for PTSD was not specifically developed to treat complex trauma, empirical research has shown its efficacy in treating highly comorbid chronic PTSD (Markowitz et al., 2015a, 2015b), a diagnosis that shares many sequelae of complex trauma. IPT for PTSD targets several features of "complex traumatic stress": affect dysregulation, impaired self-development, somatic distress, and poor attachment patterns.

Targets of IPT When Treating Complex Trauma

Individuals who experience complex trauma, especially in critical developmental periods, often have insecure attachment styles and difficulty in regulating affect (Cloitre, Stovall-McClough, Zorbas, & Charuvastra, 2008; Courtois & Ford, 2009; van der Kolk et al., 1996). With its focus on affect and building social skills (Klerman, Weissman, Rounsaville, & Chevron, 1984; Weissman, Klerman, Prusoff, Sholmskas, & Padian, 1981), IPT for PTSD addresses patients' maladaptive attachment patterns, frequently the consequence of complex trauma. Focusing the patient on his or her emotions and affective response to interactions with others provides an emotional understanding of how to interpret and react to others, improving interpersonal relationships. Markowitz and colleagues (2009) proposed that *reflective functioning* (Bateman & Fonagy, 2004), or the ability to understand and distinguish one's own and others' emotional states, might mediate change in IPT for patients with chronic PTSD.

In contrast to "simple" PTSD, complex PTSD usually reflects not a singular traumatic event but a pervasive pattern that persists throughout a critical developmental period, making the typical target formulation of *role transition* harder to establish. As such, the therapist may instead suggest that the patient's entire traumatic childhood or other complex trauma environment disrupted expected psychosocial developmental, creating a trajectory that includes the unfortunate consequences of PTSD (simple or complex), such as avoidance, emotional numbness, and lack of trust. These consequences may be framed as formerly adaptive, having aided the patient's survival and enabled the patient to endure extremely difficult circumstances; however, the patient may then be reminded that he or she no longer faces these circumstances and no longer needs these strategies, which have the unfortunate consequence of maintaining symptoms of PTSD and social isolation. For complex or chronic PTSD, this then becomes the new *role transition*: a shift from a protective mode that emerged out of survival necessity to a new, healthier and more adaptive present.

In treating complex PTSD, the therapist explains emotions as the patient's guide to social interactions, highlighting the importance of understanding emotions such as anger as responses to encounters and the utility of expressing emotions productively to achieve a desired interpersonal result. Emotional understanding provides the patient with additional information to make better informed decisions about the self and relationships. The therapist encourages the patient to use these emotions as a guide to take appropriate emotional risks in relationships, which might feel dangerous. In taking appropriate, role-play-rehearsed social risks, the patient learns that the emotions (1) are valid, (2) can be expressed in healthy ways, and (3) provide feedback about the relationship or situation. Patients with PTSD initiate IPT sessions with interpersonal material, which the therapist guides by pursuing affect and using role plays to disentangle and work through successes, and safely meet and overcome the challenges in "living dangerously." As the patient begins to change his or her social interactions, he or she learns that relationships can involve trust, nurturance, and a sense of security.

Individuals with complex traumatic stress symptoms often have a poor sense of self and mistrust their own emotions and intuitions, which may lead them into unhealthy relationships that do not fulfill their needs. The IPT focus on affect and social functioning bolsters patients' sense of self by encouraging them to trust their feelings and use them to confirm their ability to effectively navigate their interpersonal world. The therapist works at providing positive praise for the patient's affective expression and emotional risk taking both in and out of sessions.

The IPT for PTSD framework gives the therapist tools to acknowledge and address symptoms related to complex trauma, such as somatic distress. Just as in the initial phase of treatment the therapist presents psychoeducation to the patient regarding trauma, PTSD, and the links among traumatic events, symptoms, and interpersonal problems, patients who experience somatic distress (e.g., gastric distress occurring just before a triggering situation) can similarly connect trauma to physical symptoms. Such symptoms presumptively stem from suppressed emotion; hence, they are as expectable as dissociation or panic attacks might be in another patient with PTSD and usually link to a currently stressful, isolative, or conflictual interpersonal context. IPT grants the patient a medically based explanation for his or her current hardships and the tools to improve interpersonal relationships, with the goal of alleviating symptoms.

Patient Engagement and the Therapeutic Relationship

IPT for PTSD, a time-limited (14-session), affect-based therapy, is structured to allow patients to actively participate in their treatment and recovery. The "here-and-now" focus of IPT engages the patient. Although the therapeutic relationship is central to IPT, as it is to any psychotherapy (Frank, 1971), IPT therapists do not focus on or interpret the therapeutic relationship itself. Rather, they facilitate a strong alliance while focusing treatment outside the office, on relationships in the patient's daily life. Still, as the therapeutic alliance deepens, the patient experiences a different type of relationship, one that is supportive, responsive, respectful, honest, and that encourages emotional expression. The therapeutic relationship, therefore, becomes part of a corrective emotional experience (Alexander & French, 1946), one to which the patient may subsequently refer when initiating and maintaining interpersonal relationships. When upset or uncomfortable, patients are encouraged to bring up their concerns to the therapist to allow a productive discussion, which exercises the patient's identification of emotions and social skills, as well as self-assertion and empowerment.

IPT for PTSD is emotionally intense in a different way than exposure treatment. The emotional intensity may make patients anxious or fearful of the process of feeling, as individuals with PTSD, especially with complex trauma histories, may have been emotionally numb for years. The therapist encourages these patients to identify and verbalize their emotions. Some patients have described "getting worse" due to feeling their emotions. The therapist serves as an emotional anchor, modeling for the patient that intense emotions are tolerable, valid, and useful in navigating relationships and the world.

Trauma Memory Processing

Unlike exposure-based treatments, IPT for PTSD does not require trauma memory processing. Not having to confront trauma memories and cues is part of what makes IPT for PTSD appealing to many patients. Nonetheless, in anecdotal experience, patients progressing through IPT for PTSD may begin to reference or discuss the trauma and their emotions related to it (Bleiberg & Markowitz, 2005; Markowitz, 2016). As a consequence of treatment, patients begin to understand that feelings may be powerful but are not dangerous, and by extension, recounting traumatic details may be uncomfortable or anxiety provoking but ultimately will not cause harm. The experience of recounting traumatic memories to potential social supports and receiving a positive response may become part of the recovery process for some patients with PTSD, while others benefit simply from realizing that if they want to, they *can* share these experiences. While traumatic retellings in session are not encouraged, an IPT therapist may react to such an occurrence by processing feelings about the event and the retelling itself, as well as highlighting that both patient and therapist have survived the conversation, and in fact usually feel closer and more connected afterward.

Clinical Case Example

Background

Janine, a 31-year-old African American woman, lived with her boyfriend of 3 years. Janine did not present seeking treatment; rather, she expressed interest in entering a research study, as she believed her participation might help others. Her chief complaint was feeling emotionally numb ("I don't feel anything") and being haunted by intrusive memories. Surprised to learn that she was eligible for PTSD treatment as a military veteran, she initially expressed doubt that "this will really change anything."

Janine described multiple traumas. Her mother left the family when Janine was very young. Her father, a substance abuse counselor in a nontraditional program, sometimes brought patients home over the weekend, although this made Janine and her brother uneasy. When Janine was 9 years old and her father was not at home, one such patient sexually molested her. She told no one, but became sullen, angry, and withdrawn, fighting with her brother and receiving poor grades in school. When Janine reported the incident to her father at age 15, he did not believe her, saying she should be a "better person" and kinder to the less fortunate.

Janine joined the military at 18, working as a clerk for the Army National Guard. She deployed to Afghanistan when she was 22. One of her primary duties became processing paperwork of slain servicemembers. This involved reviewing the details of the cause of death (sometimes including pictures) and personal information, and coordinating handling and transportation of remains and personal effects. Janine found these tasks tremendously stressful and upsetting, but felt it was her duty to be "strong" and not show any strain or discomfort. She felt she had no business being too upset or distressed, as she had not experienced combat herself.

Upon entering treatment, Janine met full criteria for PTSD and major depressive disorder, with scores in the severe range: 42 on the Clinician-Administered PTSD Scale for DSM-5 (CAPS-5; Weathers et al., 2015) and 21 on the Hamilton Depression Rating Scale—17 (Ham-D-17; Hamilton, 1960). She suffered from depressed mood, anhedonia, nightmares, intrusive memories, feeling numb, feeling worthless, insomnia, trouble concentrating, and heightened startle reflex. She functioned at her work as an ophthalmologist's receptionist but tended to keep to herself and avoid conflict. She kept distance from family and friends. She described her relationship with her boyfriend as positive, but stated: "It's only a matter of time before he gets tired of me and leaves." Although her interviewer presented the rationale and therapeutic benefit of prolonged exposure, as well as its extensive research support, she preferred IPT, stating: "I already think about this enough." For a year following her military discharge at age 26, Janine had been in supportive psychotherapy, which she described as helpful but yielding little symptomatic improvement. Medical history was unremarkable. She did not take medications and in general was opposed to psychotropics.

Mental Status Examination

Janine, a composed, simply and neatly dressed woman, appeared to be roughly her stated age. Her speech and tone were normal, and eye contact was good. Her mood was depressed, with inappropriately bland affect. Although Janine was overtly friendly, she seemed guarded, and it was hard to connect to her personally. There was no evidence of thought disorder, hallucinations, or delusions, and she denied suicidal and homicidal ideation. Her sensorium was grossly clear.

Initial Sessions

The therapist elicited the interpersonal inventory over the first two sessions. He learned that Janine's father refused to talk about her mother or explain why she had left the family. Janine felt confused and hurt by this early loss, but she had no one with whom to discuss it. She reported having felt close to her brother, but she distanced herself from him after the sexual assault. Janine stated that although her father provided food and shelter, he was a very emotionally distant parent who often left her and her brother unattended. She never told him when she felt hurt, angry, or frightened, and she rarely cried. When Janine did ask for help or attention, he rebuffed or ridiculed her. Janine's expression and tone were notably bland and nonchalant in describing these painful experiences. The therapist pointed this out and asked why, for example, Janine smiled when she said that her father "couldn't be bothered" with checking on her when she injured her hand in an accident. She shrugged: "It's not like it really matters."

Janine described a series of friendships in her teens and young adult years that sounded shallow and lacked reciprocity. Rather, most relationships involved Janine helping and giving to everyone around her but never asking for anything for herself. She again shrugged this off: "I don't need much. I don't like asking people for things." A similar pattern appeared in romantic relationships. Janine stated that most men "got tired of me," which she blamed on long periods of feeling sad and withdrawn and "not wanting to be around people." Janine reported tolerating sex but not particularly enjoying it; she acquiesced to sexual advances from boyfriends, never initiating them. She found her relationship with her current boyfriend, Max, baffling, in that he seemed truly enamored of her and remained supportive and loving even when she was distant.

The therapist worked with Janine to lay the groundwork for treatment, emphasizing that PTSD and depression are medical illnesses and not her fault, and that her tendency to distance herself and withdraw was understandable in this symptomatic context. In Session 3, the therapist defined Janine's situation as a "role transition," explaining that trauma at a young age in an unsupportive environment had interrupted the development of her natural interpersonal trajectory, and that the trauma she experienced during military service had further affected her. In the formulation, the therapist stated:

"If I understand what you've told me, you've been through some terrible traumas that have left you emotionally numb, and now without knowing how you feel, it's hard to know whether or not you can trust other people. It's good you've come for help, and this treatment itself can be a role transition from feeling numb and withdrawn to using your emotions to understand and negotiate more comfortable interactions with other people. If you can handle your feelings and use them to handle your interactions, you're likely to feel better, and the PTSD and depression may well go away. I suggest we spend the remaining 11 weeks of treatment focusing on this pattern, understanding how your feelings and interpersonal relationships affect each other, and trying to use your feelings to change this so that you can feel better and recover your life."

Janine blithely accepted this pronouncement, but her tone and posture made clear that she doubted anything would change. The therapist validated her feelings and encouraged her to continue to "speak up" regarding any feelings concerning the treatment or the therapist.

Middle Sessions

In subsequent sessions, responding to the therapist's opening question, "How have things been since we last met?" Janine described "petty" interactions that occurred during the interval week, which the therapist was quick to help her link to mood. For example, in response to "My coworkers went to lunch today but didn't invite me," the therapist said, "I'm sorry to hear that. How did that make you feel?" Although Janine initially struggled to identify feelings, she eventually started to label reactions to these events, such as annoyance, irritation, and finally, anger. When the therapist asked if these feelings made sense, Janine dismissed them: "I suppose there really isn't any good reason to feel this way. I mean, I don't think anybody is really trying to upset me. It doesn't matter." The therapist challenged Janine by asking why her feelings did not seem to matter. She replied: "Other people have bigger problems and anyway, I can handle it."

In Session 5, the therapist challenged Janine further. He wondered aloud what would happen when Janine expressed feelings such as sadness or annoyance in childhood. Janine responded, "Nobody really cared." Noticing a slight catch in her voice, the therapist reflected that she sounded very sad, to which Janine responded, "I guess."

THERAPIST: (*gently incredulous*) You guess?!

JANINE: I suppose I could understand why it might sound sad to someone else.

THERAPIST: And how does it sound to you?

JANINE: I guess it sounds sad to me, too.

THERAPIST: Does it feel sad?

JANINE: I guess.

The therapist noted that Janine sounded sad, that it looked like there were tears in her eyes. Janine quickly brushed her eyes and tried to change the subject. The therapist, gentle but persistent, returned her focus to the feeling, then became quiet as Janine began to weep quietly. After maintaining a quiet sadness for some time, the therapist asked: "What was that like for you, to tell me about feeling sad and let me see it, and not chase it away?" Janine replied that it felt scary, but good. She seemed surprised. The therapist quietly pointed out that Janine seemed to feel worse after a disturbing event or in response to an interpersonal slight, which is a normal reaction, yet she tended to dismiss her feelings about it. But in fact, many things did bother her, and she seemed to feel better when she allowed herself to feel sad or upset, talk about it, and seek support, which again is a normal reaction. Janine nodded, again surprised. She offered, with a sad smile: "I guess I got used to not talking about these things, or pretending I didn't feel them. I never wanted to upset my Dad growing up, and now I just stay that way. It was the same in the military. I always needed to show I've got this under control."

In following weeks, patient and therapist focused on interpersonal interactions, at each point underscoring and validating Janine's sadness or anger, exploring options, then employing role play to encourage her to act on them. The therapist encouraged Janine to "live dangerously," reminding her that treatment was time-limited and provided a good opportunity to try doing things differently. In Session 7, Janine confronted Max about having forgotten an important date, but she felt abashed that he was hurt by her anger. In treatment, the therapist applauded her efforts and validated Janine's feelings of anger, guilt, and shame. He then asked: "What are your options?" Janine considered dropping the matter, breaking up with Max, and apologizing for her behavior. Ultimately, however, using role play with the therapist, she arrived at a script that captured her feelings and felt good to say: "I'm sorry that I came on so strong. But I also really need you to understand how upset I was. This matters to me." This interaction with Max was an enormous revelation to Janine: She learned she could get upset about something that mattered to her, express her feelings to another person, tolerate Max's initially poor reaction, and subsequently repair the damage, leaving the relationship stronger than before. This and similar interactions helped strengthen her relationship with Max and contributed to Janine's growing sense of confidence.

After this session, Janine showed a profound transformation. She became much more assertive at home and at work, and freer in expressing her feelings and needs. She began to reconnect with old friends and was surprised to learn that many had missed her and wondered why she had become so distant. She began explaining to friends, in small doses, what she had experienced in the military and how much it had upset her, and she was enormously gratified to receive support and encouragement. Janine spontaneously decided to tell Max about her childhood sexual assault and other painful details of her childhood. Max responded extremely positively and supportively, telling Janine how much it meant to him that she trusted him with this, and that it helped him understand her better. Janine finally began to let herself believe that Max truly loved her and intended to remain a constant in her life.

Final Sessions

In the final three sessions, the therapist worked with Janine to consolidate gains and encourage continued growth. Janine reported feeling much better and, indeed, her PTSD and depression symptoms had essentially remitted: PTSD symptoms declined to an 8 on the CAPS-5, considered subthreshold, and depressive severity decreased to 9 on the Ham-D, considered mild. Janine said she was sad to terminate the relationship with the therapist but was optimistic about the future. When the therapist asked what in therapy had been most helpful, she replied: "I never really fully believed that what I went through was traumatic. I mean, I understood that it was bad, but that's as far as it went. Hearing you call it traumatic, telling me it wasn't my fault, encouraging me to recognize that I was upset, and hurt, and afraid—I've never done that, no one has ever helped me do that." Once she understood her feelings and understood that they were legitimate, Janine explained, it became much more possible to talk to others about them and insist on being heard, and it was helpful to have a safe space to practice these conversations. Janine realized that it was okay for her to be upset, and that she could tolerate the upset of others as well. Finally, Janine said that she realized how important relationships were, and mourned how much she had missed by isolating and withdrawing from her friends due to the PTSD and depression. Now she felt she had people to reach out to when feeling sad or anxious. She looked forward to a much brighter future with Max. As a parting comment, just after she and her therapist shared an emotional good-bye, Janine said she intended to reconnect with her brother and have a long conversation about their childhood; in addition, after considerable debate, she decided she wanted to confront her father about her mother's absence, his treatment of her in childhood, and his role in and reaction to the sexual assault.

Commentary on the Case Example

Janine's story begins in a home devoid of warmth and support, and veiled in secrecy. Her mother's unexplained disappearance, her father's emotional distance and dismissal of her hurts and needs contributed to Janine's sense that her feelings (and by extension, she herself) did not matter. The sexual assault and its aftermath reinforced this sense. When Janine finally revealed what had happened to her, only to be dismissed, disbelieved, and told to "be a better person," she learned that her feelings were not just irrelevant but wrong and potentially harmful to others, that she could depend on no one, and that sharing her feelings and needs with others would only hurt her more.

Like many military veterans with histories of childhood trauma, these messages were compounded by further trauma exposure that occurred during Janine's service. Having learned that her own feelings were unimportant or wrong, and attempting to attain her father's value of "being kind to the less fortunate," Janine felt it was wrong to complain of any discomfort and that her duty was to tend to the needs of others. Janine thus became locked in a pattern in which her feelings were untrustworthy and she could expect no support from anyone, haunted as she was by the sense of being selfish and troublesome. She coped through emotional numbing and by always placing the needs of others above her own. This pattern kept Janine distant from potential supports throughout her life and made her more vulnerable to trauma in the military. The combination of suffering trauma, having her feelings invalidated, and lacking social support constituted an interpersonal setup for PTSD.

The therapist's first task was to explain that PTSD is a treatable medical condition and not her fault, that she had experienced trauma, and that her reaction to trauma was understandable, if no longer adaptive. The therapist framed how Janine was coping as a form of resilience, gently encouraging her to emerge from maladaptive patterns by understanding that her coping style was maintaining her PTSD and depression, that her feelings did matter, and that she could use them to make choices that were not influenced by PTSD. An IPT therapist sometimes presents this as "You are not a child anymore, with no control over your situation; as an adult, you now have many more options"; or in the case of veterans, "Your strategy made sense serving in the military, as being able to shut down your emotions may have helped you and those you served with survive some very difficult moments. But it's not working as well now, and in fact you're no longer in the military and this is now getting in your way."

Janine's initial reluctance to experience and display emotion—her shrugs and "I guess" responses—is typical in early sessions of IPT for PTSD. People who suffer from trauma often fear the strength of their emotions, feeling that too much sadness or anger might destroy themselves or others. This is especially true for veterans who have harmed others during military service, many of whom worry that feeling angry is "dangerous" and will lead to violence of some sort. In contrast to some other therapies, IPT does not label fear, anger, anxiety, and sadness as "negative"; its goal is not to reduce these emotions through cognitive restructuring. Instead, IPT normalizes these feelings and encourages their expression, as feelings provide valuable information and are critical to the formation of healthy relationships, and expressing them can relieve emotional pressure. IPT addresses this by encouraging emotional expression in the therapy room, and more importantly, in the patient's real-life interactions with others.

To help Janine accomplish these goals, the therapist worked in early sessions to build a warm and responsive relationship, accepting, without endorsing, her early guardedness and pessimism, and validating her sense of despair. This safe environment created sufficient trust for Janine to allow herself to cry in session, an emotionally vulnerable and frightening display she typically avoided. Whereas direct pleas to Janine to connect to her feelings and not allow herself or others to dismiss them fell short, these moments in which Janine experienced her emotions and allowed them to show were transformative. She learned through such experiences that her strong feelings might be uncomfortable but would ultimately pass, and that another human being could experience these feelings with her without rejecting or abandoning her, or putting her down. Furthermore, Janine began to transform in these moments from the "no emotions/no relationship/no self" approach to life she had established as a result of a childhood filled with abandonment, dismissal, betrayal, and sexual violence to an "emotions and relationships are positive/I deserve to be treated as a worthy person" perspective. This transformation likely reduces the avoidance, dysphoria, lack of trust, and hypervigilance symptoms of PTSD.

Although Janine's emotional display in session was important, IPT emphasizes the need for patients to take such risks in the outside world as well. Doing so helps the patient to build a sense of agency, environmental confidence, and capability rather than dependence on the therapist. The therapeutic relationship is viewed as a temporary partnership to help the patient transition to a healthier, more fulfilled future. This message may be especially important for military veterans, who often feel civilians cannot relate to their experience, that it is safe to talk only to other veterans or psychotherapists. Consequently, the therapist encouraged Janine to act on her feelings in her life outside of therapy, boosting motivation by leveraging the 14-week time limit. Rather than battle with patients over completion of homework, IPT uses the time limit to motivate patients to act, which ultimately serves development of self-efficacy. Janine's increased willingness to confront her boyfriend, coworkers, and others over the course of treatment is a classic example of how a patient may use the content and experiences of therapy sessions, as well as the therapeutic alliance itself, as a springboard to take emotional risks without being prescribed specific "assignments."

Janine's initial "failure" to evoke the desired response from Max is a common and expectable happenstance, and presents an opportunity for growth. An IPT therapist often prepares patients for a potential adverse response by stating: "This is a good time to try things out. If it goes well, great! If not, at least you've tried, and that gives us something to work on." The danger of a "failure" is that it will discourage the patient from trying again, as the patient might conclude that taking emotional risks is doomed to failure. This happened to Janine when her father dismissed her report of her assault. Regarding the circumstance with Max, the therapist provided positive feedback, encouragement, and sympathy, then helped Janine disentangle Max's rebuff like any other interpersonal episode: What were her feelings, did they make sense, and what were her options? Although not needed here, in circumstances in which a patient feels greatly discouraged or receives negative response to multiple attempts with the same individual, the therapist might point out that even if the patient does not achieve the desired response, it is better to say something: The patient will feel a sense of affirmation by having spoken up for him- or herself and less helpless. Doing so can help establish clarity in the relationship, and sometimes a person will hear a message and think twice about acting aversely again in the future. "Speaking up" also shifts blame from the patient to the offender.

If the patient is in a physically abusive relationship, the therapist should, of course, encourage the patient to make safe choices. In these instances, the concept of "speaking up" may mean setting limits in other ways, such as going to the police, refusing to acquiesce to unreasonable or humiliating demands, seeking social support, and so forth, rather than confronting someone who is violent and potentially dangerous. The point remains nonetheless the same: The patient will feel better and be better off when recognizing the validity of feelings and acting on them, even if the response is less than ideal.

Another point that arose in the interaction with Max was Janine's distress not only from her own feelings, but from how upset Max became. Many traumatized people focus more concern on the feelings of others than on their own, especially if they devalue their own self-worth. The military often reinforces this tendency in veterans, training them to support others and not be a "burden." IPT therapists encourage patients to endure not only their own strong emotions but also those of others. It was okay for Janine to say something that (inadvertently) hurt Max's feelings; sometimes one needs to say something that might hurt another person's feelings for one's own benefit and for the benefit of the relationship. In IPT parlance: "It's not good to be too selfish. But no one can be

selfless all the time, and a modicum of selfishness is healthy and self-protective."
And: "Feelings are powerful but not dangerous" (Markowitz, 2016).

By the end of treatment, Janine's symptoms and outlook on life had greatly improved, but important areas remained unresolved. Her relationship with her boyfriend had strengthened, but their future together remained uncertain, and some areas of their relationship functioning, such as their sexual intimacy, were not addressed in depth. This remains a challenge in IPT, as time-limited treatment can never address every problem. Nonetheless, Janine seemed to have developed the tools she needed to navigate her relationship with Max, which achieves the primary goal of treatment: empowering patients to solve their own problems rather than become overly reliant on the therapist or the treatment itself. Janine's willingness to reach out to friends and be more honest and demanding in her relationship with Max are extremely positive prognostic indications for the future. Although Janine declined this offer, some patients engage in maintenance treatment after completing IPT, with benefit (Miller et al., 2012; Weissman et al., 2018). As in other forms of IPT, the acute core treatment of IPT for PTSD itself is not typically extended, because this could undermine the motivation generated by the built-in time limit.

In the final session, Janine mentioned that she was considering confronting her father about the sexual assault. Although IPT does not encourage exposure to traumatic memories, IPT therapists have anecdotally noted that treated patients often do so on their own (Bleiberg & Markowitz, 2005; Markowitz, 2016). Janine's decisions to describe some of her experiences to her boyfriend and other friends, and later potentially to confront her father, came not from direct therapist encouragement but appeared a natural outgrowth of her growing self-confidence and bolstered ability to endure and even welcome feelings of anger, anxiety, and sadness in the service of herself and her relationships. In other words, the act of exposure itself is not key to IPT treatment, but it is an indirect consequence of this approach as part of recovery from PTSD. Ultimately, an IPT therapist might very well help a patient figure out how to confront someone responsible for or associated with the trauma (e.g., exploring the patient's feelings in the context of interactions with this person, asking if these feelings make sense to the patient, encouraging the patient to identify options for what the patient might say, and practicing via role play), but would not consider this necessarily critical, and would usually only do so if the patient expressly wished to or if there were a clear interpersonal reason related to the focus of treatment. Typically, the terror and intrusive nature of traumatic memories begins to lessen once the patient realizes that the associated feelings are tolerable, can be discussed, and need not be avoided, as evinced in Janine's case by her considerable reduction in symptom scores.

Conclusion

IPT for PTSD is a promising treatment for individuals with PTSD and complex trauma histories. Although exposure-based treatments for PTSD are well-supported by extant research, some patients refuse these treatments, drop out, or do not respond, and outcomes are poorer for those with complex trauma symptoms. IPT offers an advantage to such individuals by focusing on affect and effective communication of emotion in interpersonal relationships rather than the trauma narrative or anxious avoidance. IPT addresses the consequences of trauma, including several core features in complex forms of PTSD: social isolation and loss of trust in people, emotional numbness, mistrust of the environment, and reduced self-confidence and agency.

References

Alexander, F., & French, T. M. (1946). *Psychoanalytic therapy: Principles and application.* New York: Ronald Press.

American Psychological Association. (2017). Clinical practice guideline for the treatment of PTSD. Retrieved from *www.apa.org/ptsd-guideline/ptsd.pdf.*

Bateman, A., & Fonagy, P. (2004). *Psychotherapy for borderline personality disorder.* New York: Oxford University Press.

Bleiberg, K. L., & Markowitz, J. C. (2005). A pilot study of interpersonal psychotherapy for posttraumatic stress disorder. *American Journal of Psychiatry, 162*(1), 181–183.

Bowlby, J. (1973). *Attachment and loss.* New York: Basic Books. (Original work published 1969)

Bowlby, J. (1988). Developmental psychiatry comes of age. *American Journal of Psychiatry, 145*(1), 1–10.

Briere, J., & Spinazzola, J. (2005). Phenomenology and psychological assessment of complex posttraumatic states. *Journal of Traumatic Stress, 18*(5), 401–412.

Campanini, R. F., Schoedl, A. F., Pupo, M. C., Costa, A. C., Krupnick, J. L., & Mello, M. F. (2010). Efficacy of interpersonal therapy-group format adapted to post-traumatic stress disorder: An open-label add-on trial. *Depression and Anxiety, 27*(1), 72–77.

Carroll, K. M., Rounsaville, B. J., & Gawin, F. H. (1991). A comparative trial of psychotherapies for ambulatory cocaine abusers: Relapse prevention and interpersonal psychotherapy. *American Journal of Drug and Alcohol Abuse, 17*(3), 229–247.

Cloitre, M., Stovall-McClough, C., Zorbas, P., & Charuvastra, A. (2008). Attachment organization, emotion regulation, and expectations of support in a clinical sample of women with childhood abuse histories. *Journal of Traumatic Stress, 21*(3), 282–289.

Courtois, C. A., & Ford, J. D. (Eds.). (2009). *Treating complex traumatic stress disorders: An evidence-based guide.* New York: Guilford Press.

Cuijpers, P., Geraedts, A. S., van Oppen, P., Andersson, G., Markowitz, J. C., & van Straten, A. (2011). Interpersonal psychotherapy for depression: A meta-analysis. *American Journal of Psychiatry, 168*, 581–592.

Cusack, K., Jonas, D. E., Forneris, C. A., Wines, C., Sonis, J., Middleton, J. C., . . . Gaynes, B. N. (2016). Psychological treatments for adults with posttraumatic stress disorder: A systematic review and meta-analysis. *Clinical Psychology Review, 43*, 128–141.

Department of Veteran Affairs & Department of Defense. (2017). VA/DoD clinical practice guideline for the management of posttraumatic stress disorder and acute stress disorder. Retrieved from *www.tricare.mil.*

Foa, E. B. (2011). Prolonged exposure therapy: Past, present, and future. *Depression and Anxiety, 28*(12), 1043–1047.

Foa, E. B., Hembree, E. A., & Rothbaum, B. O. (2007). *Prolonged exposure therapy for PTSD: Emotional processing of traumatic experiences.* New York: Oxford University Press.

Ford, J. D., & Courtois, C. A. (2014). Complex PTSD, affect dysregulation, and borderline personality disorder. *Borderline Personality Disorder and Emotion Dysregulation, 1*(9).

Frank, J. (1971). Therapeutic factors in psychotherapy. *American Journal of Psychotherapy, 25*, 350–361.

Gerger, H., Munder, T., & Barth, J. (2014). Specific and nonspecific psychological interventions for PTSD Symptoms: A meta-analysis with problem complexity as a moderator. *Journal of Clinical Psychology, 70*(7), 601–615.

Guay, S., Billette, V., & Marchand, A. (2006). Exploring the links between posttraumatic stress disorder and social support: Processes and potential research avenues. *Journal of Traumatic Stress, 19*(3), 327–338.

Hamilton, M. (1960). A rating scale for depression. *Journal of Neurology, Neurosurgery, and Psychiatry, 23*(1), 56–62.

Imel, Z., Laska, K., Jakcupcak, M., & Simpson, T. L. (2013). Meta-analysis of dropout in treatments for post-traumatic stress disorder. *Journal of Consulting and Clinical Psychology, 81*(3), 394–404.

Institute of Medicine. (2014). *Treatment for posttraumatic stress disorder in military and veteran populations: Final assessment.* Washington, DC: National Academies Press.

Klerman, G. L., Weissman, M. M., Rounsaville, B. J., & Chevron, E. (1984). *Interpersonal psychotherapy of depression.* New York: Basic Books.

Krupnick, J. L., Green, B. L., Stockton, P., Miranda, J., Krause, E., & Mete, M. (2008). Group interpersonal psychotherapy for low-income women with posttraumatic stress disorder. *Psychotherapy Research, 18*(5), 497–507.

Lipsitz, J. D., & Markowitz, J. C. (2013). Mechanisms of change in interpersonal psychotherapy. *Clinical Psychology Review, 33*, 1143–1147.

Lipsitz, J., & Markowitz, J. C. (2016). Interpersonal theory. In J. C. Norcross, G. R. VanderBos, & D. K. Freedheim (Eds.), *APA handbook of clinical psychology* (Vol. 2, pp. 183–212). Washington, DC: American Psychological Association.

Markowitz, J. C. (2016). *Interpersonal psychotherapy for posttraumatic stress disorder.* New York: Oxford University Press.

Markowitz, J. C., Meehan, K. B., Petkova, E., Zhao, T., Meter, P. E., Neria, Y., . . . Nazia, Y. (2016). Treatment preferences of psychotherapy patients with chronic PTSD. *Journal of Clinical Psychiatry, 77*(3), 363–370.

Markowitz, J. C., Milrod, B., Bleiberg, K., & Marshall, R. D. (2009). Interpersonal factors in understanding and treating posttraumatic stress disorder. *Journal of Psychiatric Practice, 15*(2), 133–140.

Markowitz, J. C., Neria, Y., Lovell, K., VanMeter, P. E., & Petkova, E. (2017). History of sexual trauma moderates psychotherapy outcomes for posttraumatic stress disorder. *Depression and Anxiety, 34*(8), 692–700.

Markowitz, J. C., Petkova, E., Biyanova, T., Ding, K., Suh, E. J., & Neria, Y. (2015a). Exploring personality diagnosis stability following acute psychotherapy for chronic posttraumatic stress disorder. *Depression and Anxiety, 32*(12), 919–926.

Markowitz, J. C., Petkova, E., Neria, Y., Van Meter, P. E., Zhao, Y., Hembree, E., . . . Marshall, R. D. (2015b). Is exposure necessary?: A randomized clinical trial of interpersonal psychotherapy for PTSD. *American Journal of Psychiatry, 172*(5), 430–440.

Markowitz, J. C., & Swartz, H. A. (2007). Case formulation in interpersonal psychotherapy of depression. In T. D. Eels (Ed.), *Handbook of psychotherapy case formulation* (2nd ed., pp. 221–250). New York: Guilford Press.

Markowitz, J. C., & Weissman, M. M. (2012). Interpersonal psychotherapy: Past, present and future. *Clinical Psychology Psychotherapy, 19*(2), 99–105.

Miller, M. D., Frank, E., & Levenson, J. C. (2012). Maintenance interpersonal psychotherapy (IPT-M). In J. C. Markowitz & M. M. Weissman (Eds.), *Casebook of interpersonal psychotherapy* (pp. 343–364). New York: Oxford University Press.

Mufson, L., Dorta, K. P., Moreau, D., & Weissman, M. M. (2004). *Interpersonal psychotherapy for depressed adolescents.* New York: Guilford Press.

Murphy, R., Straebler, S., Basden, S., Cooper, Z., & Fairburn, C. G. (2012). Interpersonal psychotherapy for eating disorders. *Clinical Psychology and Psychotherapy, 19*(2), 150–158.

O'Hara, M. W., Stuart, S., Gorman, L. L., & Wenzel, A. (2000). Efficacy of interpersonal psychotherapy for postpartum depression. *Archives of General Psychiatry, 57*(11), 1039–1045.

Ozer, E. J., Best, S. R., Lipsey, T. L., & Weiss, D. S. (2003). Predictors of posttraumatic stress disorder and symptoms in adults: A meta-analysis. *Psychological Bulletin, 129*(1), 52–73.

Parsons, T. (1951). Illness and the role of the physician: A sociological perspective. *American Journal of Orthopsychiatry, 21,* 451–460.

Pietrzak, R. H., Johnson, D. C., Goldstein, M. B., Malley, J. C., Rivers, A. J., Morgan, C. A., & Southwick, S. M. (2010). Psychosocial buffers of traumatic stress, depressive symptoms, and psychosocial difficulties in veterans of Operations Enduring Freedom and Iraqi Freedom: The role of resilience, unit support, and postdeployment social support. *Journal of Affective Disorders, 120*(1–3), 188–192.

Reynolds, C. F., Frank, E., Perel, J. M., Imber, S. D., Cornes, C., Miller, M. D., . . . Kupfer, D. J. (1999). Nortriptyline and interpersonal psychotherapy as maintenance therapies for recurrent major depression: A randomized controlled trial in patients older than 59 years. *Journal of the American Medical Association, 281*(1), 39–45.

Rytwinski, N. K., Scur, M. D., Feeny, N. C., & Youngstrom, E. A. (2013). The co-occurrence of major depressive disorder among individuals with posttraumatic stress disorder: A meta-analysis. *Journal of Traumatic Stress, 26*(3), 299–309.

Steenkamp, M. M., Litz, B. T., Hoge, C. W., & Marmar, C. R. (2015). Psychotherapy for military-related PTSD. *Journal of the American Medical Association, 314*(5), 489–500.

van der Kolk, B. A. (2005). Developmental trauma disorder: Toward a rational diagnosis for children with complex trauma histories. *Psychiatric Annals, 35*(5), 401–408.

van der Kolk, B. A., Pelcovitz, D., Roth, S., Mandel, F. S., McFarlane, A. C., & Herman, J. L. (1996). Dissociation, somatization, and affect dysregulation: The complexity of adaptation of trauma. *American Journal of Psychiatry, 153*(7), 83–93.

Weathers, F. W., Blake, D. D., Schnurr, P. P., Kaloupek, D. G., Marx, B. P., & Keane, T. M. (2013). Clinician-Administered PTSD Scale for DSM-5 (CAPS-5). Available from *www.ptsd.va.gov.*

Weissman, M. M., Klerman, G. L., Prusoff, B. A., Sholomskas, D., & Padian, N. (1981). Depressed outpatients: Results one year after treatment with drugs and/or interpersonal psychotherapy. *Archives of General Psychiatry, 38*(1), 51–55.

Weissman, M. M., Markowitz, J. C., & Klerman, G. L. (2018). *The guide to interpersonal psychotherapy.* New York: Oxford University Press.

Wilfley, D. E., MacKenzie, K. R., Welch, R. R., Ayres, V. E., & Weissman, M. M. (2000). *Interpersoanl psychotherapy for groups.* New York: Basic Books.

CHAPTER 17

Cognitive-Behavioral Therapy

CHRISTIE JACKSON
KORE NISSENSON
MARYLENE CLOITRE

Cognitive-behavioral therapy (CBT) seeks to improve functioning and emotional well-being by identifying beliefs, feelings, and behaviors that are associated with psychological disturbance and revising them through critical analysis and experiential exploration in order to be consistent with desired outcomes and positive life goals (e.g., Dobson & Dozois, 2001). This approach to psychotherapy was in distinct contrast to the traditions that came before it, and expressed an optimistic philosophy about human nature that was consistent with the American pragmatism from which it emerged: that new ways of thinking, behaving, and feeling are possible and the client can effect change.

Advances in CBT research have traditionally emphasized symptom reduction or resolution, yet the evolution of CBT for complex traumatic stress disorders (CTSDs) has also involved attention to the dynamics of the therapeutic relationship, and such approaches are highlighted in this chapter. Interpersonal expectations and relational dynamics are inextricably woven into psychotherapeutic work, and this is particularly salient in the treatment of patients with CTSDs, as the "injury" for which they seek treatment is essentially an interpersonal one (i.e., experiencing abuse, neglect, or violence in critically important relationships). Effective CBTs for CTSDs include an approach that maintains the traditional view that interventions provide guidance and instruction to improve functioning (e.g., skills development, more adaptive cognitive appraisals of current conflicts). However, the interventions also provide a means for clients to shift their inner experience of themselves and sense of interpersonal relatedness.

Some CBTs explicitly articulate the goals and process of therapy as enhancement of self-regulation and secure attachment, as in skills training in affective and interpersonal regulation (STAIR) narrative therapy (Cloitre, Cohen, Ortigo, Jackson, & Koenan, 2019). Dialectical behavior therapy (DBT), a well-established CBT, emphasizes the client's experience of self as "authentic," a critical part of the process of acceptance and change (Linehan, 2018), through the therapist's validation of the client's difficulties in self-regulation as derived from an "invalidating" relational environment.

CBT therapists incorporate psychoeducation about the etiology of clients' symptoms, as well as the mechanisms of change. Identification of symptoms as resulting from adverse or traumatic events rather than from perceived character flaws can liberate the client from a burdensome and potentially paralyzing sense of shame. This point of view can engender a sense of hope and empowerment. In addition, psychoeducation about the mechanisms of change, such as explaining the rationale and behavioral principles involved in skills training or exposure exercises, can increase clients' sense of control and mastery over their symptoms and over their lives. Playing an active role in one's own recovery can be especially important for individuals with complex trauma histories as their symptoms can reduce the individual's autonomy and self-direction. The use of skills practice between sessions, including *in vivo* exposure exercises and practice of skills outside of session to promote treatment generalizability encourages the adoption of an active stance on the part of the client.

CBT is based on collaborative empiricism, whereby the client and therapist act as "co-investigators" to explicitly identify the goals for therapy and the means by which these goals will be reached. They explore the logic and experiential basis for the client's assumptions, beliefs, and behaviors. The therapist often prompts the client to identify ways in which thoughts limit flexible and healthy functioning, and together they develop potential alternatives. Behavioral exploration or tests of these proposed changes are implemented in a graduated (incremental) fashion, documented, and corrected to lead to the desired change. Repeated practice and elaboration of alternative thoughts, feelings, and behaviors promote the acquisition and consolidation of new skills and thinking strategies, as well as flexibility in their application.

Last, the fact that CBT is a relatively short-term therapy focused on the acquisition of skills may itself provide some benefit. The structured nature of the sessions and interventions seems to reduce clients' anxiety about working with their feelings and facilitates a sense of "containment of affect" and increased ability to tolerate often intense emotions, which is particularly beneficial for complex trauma survivors who have difficulties with inter- and intrapersonal boundaries. A structured approach to therapy models for clients that experiences, including feelings, can have finite beginnings and endings. In addition, explicitly shaping the parameters of therapy, setting goals, and outlining session agendas gives the client a clear idea of what to expect from the therapy.

Review of Research on CBT with CTSDs

CBTs for CTSDs have been largely adapted from cognitive-behavioral interventions for posttraumatic stress disorder (PTSD), including prolonged exposure (PE), cognitive processing therapy (CPT), eye movement desensitization and reprocessing (EMDR), and problem-solving or skills training therapies. These adaptations have involved the importation of interventions into a complex trauma therapeutic framework (e.g., Courtois & Ford, 2013) and the integration of CBT interventions related to other disorders, including those from DBT.

A recent meta-analysis identified 79 randomized controlled trials treating patient populations with a history of complex trauma (Coventry, 2018). This included studies of individuals who had experienced childhood abuse, domestic violence, war as a civilian and war as a refugee, as well as samples of combat veterans (many of whom experience repeated exposure to death and violence). The studies indicated that compared to wait list, CBTs were effective in reducing PTSD symptoms (re-experiencing, avoidance, and arousal), anxiety, and depression. Importantly, the findings indicated that, overall, multicomponent therapies were superior to single-component therapies for these symptoms. Multicomponent therapies include interventions or sets of interventions (*modules*) intended to address specific sets of symptoms. Such therapies might include, for example, social skills training *and* exposure or processing of traumatic memories *and* emotion regulation interventions. Symptoms specifically related to complex PTSD as recently defined (i.e., ICD-11 complex PTSD (Maercker et al., 2013), which includes problems in emotion regulation, negative self-concept, and interpersonal difficulties, were also assessed. Compared to wait-list control, negative self-concept improved in both single-component and multicomponent treatments; emotion regulation improved in only multicomponent therapies. There were so few studies that assessed interpersonal problems that no conclusion could be made about the potential benefits of CBTs for interpersonal functioning among complex trauma populations. Overall the results suggest that a multicomponent treatment approach may optimize outcomes for adults who have experienced complex traumas.

Below we identify important symptoms to target in the treatment of individuals with CTSDs. Given that research to date is suggesting the value of using a multicomponent approach to the treatment of CTSDs, we provide a case example of how a multicomponent trauma might work using the example of STAIR narrative therapy (Cloitre et al., 2010, 2019).

Clinical Application of CBT to CTSDs

Creating Safety

Behaviors such as self-harm and suicide attempts in individuals with CTSDs are often the result of feeling emotionally overwhelmed. One of the core components of treatment for CTSDs is focused breathing to help clients be present and calm in their bodies. In addition, fearful or negative appraisals of bodily sensations can be explored and tested in an experiential fashion. Anxiety management interventions use relaxation training for this purpose. Mindfulness (see Chapter 25), a core component of DBT, can help clients focus in the present moment purposefully and nonjudgmentally, and includes attention to bodily feelings. Emotion regulation skills can be used to aid clients in experiencing emotions while fully being present in their bodies.

Emotion Dysegulation and Dissociation

Emotion regulation refers to a broad range of abilities, including awareness of emotional states; identifying, differentiating, and describing feelings; self-soothing; tolerating negative states; and pursuing and heightening positive emotional states. CBT emotion regulation strategies include exposure to emotion-eliciting situations while being aware of both feelings and the situation, focused breathing, practiced naming and verbalization of feelings, and building of client self-efficacy in the ability to experience, manage, and even enjoy feelings.

Acceptance and exploration of frightening feelings is a core task of trauma-focused CBT and is viewed as a prerequisite to self-coherence and self-identity. Several CBTs extend emotion and interpersonal regulation strategies to address dissociation and to enhance a sense of positive self-identity. Feelings that are viewed as unacceptable or overwhelming, such as rage, shame, envy, fear, and sadness, may be avoided or defended against through radical means such as the "splitting off" of the feelings and the events that prompted them. This process takes place in the contexts of various interventions, such as the processing of traumatic memories, direct exploration of feelings and beliefs about the self, and exposure to difficult emotions such as shame.

Improving Sense of Self and Relationships

The potential role of disturbed attachment in the early life of many clients is a critical aspect of treatment work. The attachment frame addresses both sense of self and sense of self in relationships. Some, but not many, CBTs address this problem. STAIR narrative therapy is an example of a therapy that does explicitly draw the principles of attachment into the treatment. It explicitly introduces the concept of attachment to the client (*psychoeducation*), systematically explores the nature of the clients' caretaker relationships using Bowlby's (1988) "working models," and identifies templates for interpersonal relating based on early life experiences. STAIR narrative therapy uses the cognitive-behavioral construct of the "relationship model" to provide a frame for articulating specific expectations that the individual holds regarding relationships. *Relationship analysis* involves the examination of current interpersonal interactions with respect to basic beliefs about trust, intimacy, and fairness, in order to evaluate and enhance these beliefs and the person's flexibility in engaging in relationships.

Trauma Memory Processing

Trauma memory processing is a frequent component in many therapies for PTSD symptoms and complex PTSD symptoms. This work helps reduce clients' PTSD symptoms. Repeated exposure to traumatic memories through storytelling enables the client to confront fearful memories and develop a sense of control over them (Rothbaum & Foa, 1999). This process helps put their trauma memories into perspective as something that happened in the past and can no longer hurt them. Last, and perhaps most important, the work of "storytelling" helps a person develop a coherent sense of self by organizing the events in memory and creating meaning about the events to help create foundations for the person he or she plans or aspires to be.

Clinical Case Example

CBT treatment for CTSDs begins with an evaluation of the client's symptoms, particularly any threats to the client's safety, such as self-harm or substance use. In addition to identifying all symptoms and problematic behaviors, clear identification of strengths, including coping skills, is critical at the outset of CBT.

Creating Safety

Early sessions of CBT focus on psychoeducation and normalization about maladaptive coping behaviors, such as drinking, cutting, or dissociating. Clients are taught to identify and stop the spiral of reinforcement following these behaviors. These behaviors are understood as efforts intended to be adaptive (e.g., to reduce distress or regain feelings). The therapeutic goal is to replace them with strategies that promote health and have fewer negative consequences.

At this stage of therapy, it is of critical importance that the clinician work with the client to establish a safety plan. This should include a thorough assessment of any self-harm behaviors the client may engage in, and a plan for alternative, safe behaviors that may be utilized during times of distress. Together, client and therapist should determine what the client should do in emergency situations—call 911, go to the nearest emergency room, page the therapist, if available, and so forth. During this process, the therapist should determine his or her own limits of on-call availability and comfort level with various types of harmful behavior. Clients should commit to using skills to tolerate their suicidal, self-harm, or other destructive urges rather than engaging in the behavior. For example, the client may commit to replacing self-harm behavior and binging/purging with distress tolerance skills. The therapist should routinely monitor whether the client has engaged in any of these behaviors and reinforce the use of healthy coping skills. Work on reconstructing memories of traumatic experiences and other potentially distressing therapeutic tasks should be implemented only after the client has attained a sufficient period of stabilization and acquisition of emotion regulation skills.

Another important task in the early stages of CBT is to begin building the therapeutic alliance. In CBT, the alliance is based not only on the therapist's genuine concern for and willingness to work with the client toward achieving the client's goals, but also on describing clearly to the client how the therapy process enables the client to know that he or she is succeeding in accomplishing these goals. The therapist helps the client to formulate specific behavioral changes that operationalize the client's goals and describes how experimenting with new ways of thinking and new behavioral choices will be undertaken in the therapy.

Demonstrating to clients that change is possible and offering them a projected time frame for the course of therapy is an extremely effective way for therapists to instill hope. Moreover, the strength of the early therapeutic alliance in CBT is associated with clients' improved capacity to regulate negative mood states during the trauma memory reconstruction phase of therapy, and this enhances the overall success of treatment for clients with CTSDs (Cloitre, Stovall-McClough, Miranda, & Chemtob, 2004).

Sample Session on Establishing Client Safety

THERAPIST: So, your history includes pretty regular drinking, cutting, and dissociative behaviors.

CLIENT: Yeah, I feel really ashamed about that. It makes me feel really bad about myself, and then I end up doing even more of it!

THERAPIST: Believe it or not, that is not so unusual. Many clients with a history like yours engage in these behaviors as an effort to adapt and survive. So, for example, people who cut may do it in order to feel, or to feel a release from stress. People might engage in these behaviors to bring themselves into an emotional comfort zone that feels manageable. Cutting and drinking can be used to tamp down feelings that seem unacceptable, overwhelming, and maybe even scary. Our goal in this therapy is for you to get into an emotional comfort zone that you can live and function in without using strategies that have so many negative consequences. Another way for you to think about this is that you're trying to use rules that applied under extreme situations from the past in situations now that are very different. It's like you are applying rules from an Arctic survival guide to get through your daily life in a warm climate!

CLIENT: Hmm, I never thought about it that way. That would be great, but how can it really happen?

THERAPIST: Well, you already have some real strengths, including some healthy coping strategies. I'm here to help you increase the use of these and ultimately let go of the need for the others. The first priority in this treatment is always going to be your safety. So we need to figure out how to keep you safe, which means not engaging in dangerous drinking, cutting, or dissociative behaviors while you go through this treatment. Now let's develop a plan that we can both commit to. So, for example, do you think you can replace cutting and drinking with more adaptive behaviors, like talking with people whom you trust when you need help?

CLIENT: I can call my friend Cathy—I can rely on her. Sometimes writing in my diary helps, too. And instead of binge drinking I can binge clean!

THERAPIST: And don't forget about how you feel better after going for a walk or working out. I will also be teaching you focused breathing, a basic form of meditation to help feel "centered" and remain in the present. It is also a basic building block of various other emotion regulation strategies we will work on later.

Building Emotion Regulation and Interpersonal Skills

Skills development regarding emotion regulation and interpersonal efficacy begins as soon as safety is established and, indeed, can be part of maintaining and reinforcing safety. Emotion regulation skills development incorporates continued efforts to help the client recognize triggers for urges to self-harm and other maladaptive behaviors and to replace safety-interfering behaviors with more effective coping skills. Emotion regulation skills building includes exploration of the bases for habitual emotion regulation strategies and interpersonal tendencies in the context of early life experiences. It provides an opportunity for the client to expand on and enhance important life skills, with an emphasis on healthy emotional and interpersonal functioning. Last, work is intended to provide clients with sufficient security in their emotional experience and in their working relationship with the therapist to develop a sense of competence and confidence to confront and explore traumatic memories later in the treatment. Examples of introducing and applying interventions to enhance emotion and interpersonal regulation skills follow below.

Sample Session on Emotion Regulation

In this session, the client works with her therapist to identify the kinds of feelings she has, what she thinks about them, and how she manages them. Her emotion regulation strategies are understood in the context of her family history. This facilitates better understanding of her patterns of emotional reaction and emotion-driven behaviors. It also helps reduce feelings of shame and opens up curiosity about how feelings might be managed differently.

THERAPIST: How were emotions expressed in your family while you were growing up, and what kind of strategies did you learn? A lot of people manage their feelings based on strategies emerging from their family. Some families scream out their feelings, other families sweep them under the rug—how was it in your family?

CLIENT: It was never safe for me to have emotions. I would get hit. You never knew what type of mood my father was in when he walked in the door. He was a rage-aholic. And it terrified me!! I learned to be as invisible as I could. I've learned to keep my feelings to myself.

THERAPIST: So you learned that feelings were explosive and dangerous.

CLIENT: Yeah, I avoid them, because I was at the other end of the stick. I don't want to go there now.

THERAPIST: It makes sense that you would feel this way given the damage that you saw, caused by your father's rage. But, you're paying the price by cutting, drinking, and dissociating. Because you do have feelings, and they are very important. Feelings, both good and bad, give you information about a situation. For example, fear can help you know it's time to protect yourself. And feeling happiness reminds you that life is worth living. Feelings don't need to be so extreme or overwhelming. Feelings can exist at different levels of intensity. The first step in managing your emotions involves awareness of your emotions, including body sensations and thoughts and urges. This allows you to intervene sooner, so that your feelings can be more manageable and help you stay in that comfort zone we have been talking about. I'd like to ask you to keep track of your feelings over the next week. Here is a self-monitoring form. Let's do an example now. Can you think of a time in the past when you had an especially strong emotional reaction?

CLIENT: OK. Yesterday, I had to confront my roommate about not paying her share of the rent.

THERAPIST: OK, so let's put this down at the prompting event. What thoughts went through your mind when you had to confront her?

CLIENT: Umm, she's going to yell at me. She will hate me. She'll say why am I bothering her. And umm, I also feel like I should pay her half of the rent for her, because she's going through a tough time now financially.

THERAPIST: OK, good. What were you feeling in your body at the time?

CLIENT: What do you mean exactly?

THERAPIST: Well, what was your heart doing, was it pounding, or beating regularly?

CLIENT: Well, now that you mention it, my heart was racing. It was hard for me to breathe. I felt kind of nauseous.

THERAPIST: OK, very good. Let's put that down, too. And so now, what emotion do you think you were feeling? Here is a list of feelings to help you identify yours. Sometimes it's hard to put a name to your emotions. Like anything else, it's going to take some practice.

CLIENT: I felt afraid.

THERAPIST: Anything else?

CLIENT: Oh yeah, I think I was feeling ashamed, too.

THERAPIST: And how did you cope with those feelings?

CLIENT: I avoided my roommate. I closed my door and had three glasses of wine. Then I sent her an e-mail.

THERAPIST: OK, so that's very important to note. We'll come back to this later. We'll be talking about other ways to cope with these feelings next session. Let's end today by planning some specific ways you can practice identifying your feelings and associated thoughts during the next week. This will help us decide when and how you can apply some coping strategies that we'll discuss in our next session. What this will enable you to do is learn to *tolerate and accept* feelings rather than avoid them by drinking or dissociating.

Sample Session on Dissociation and Its Relationship to Emotion Regulation

In this session, dissociation is viewed as resulting from the client feeling overwhelmed by intense anger. Therapy focuses on helping the client resolve her fear of her own anger, in order to accept angry feelings (previously associated with danger) instead of dissociating.

THERAPIST: How did the self-monitoring forms go for you this past week?

CLIENT: Well, I didn't do it every day like you asked me to, but I have a few of them for you.

THERAPIST: OK, good. You managed to do it several times. Let's look over the ones you do have. I see it was your birthday. You wrote that you felt sad and empty on that day. Your thoughts were that you aren't worthy of other people's attention.

CLIENT: Yeah, if they really liked me, then they would have planned a surprise party for me.

THERAPIST: So let's talk about how you coped with the feelings of sadness and emptiness. I see that you found yourself on the subway in your pajamas. That sounds very scary.

CLIENT: It was terrifying! I had no idea where I was or how I got there. Especially since this hasn't happened to me in a long time.

THERAPIST: So often when people experience feelings that are overwhelming, they disconnect. This was a survival strategy that you adopted during the traumatic experiences of your childhood. Actually, those strategies were essential for you; they helped keep you alive. Now, however, this kind of dissociative behavior can be really dangerous, and in fact, is typically more harmful than helpful. As we've been discussing, awareness of your feelings is very important. People dissociate because they are afraid that if they feel their emotions, they will lose control. Ironically, dissociating strips you of control because you are not able to have choice over your emotions and behaviors and respond appropriately. So let's talk about how you might cope without dissociating, and let's review what happened before the subway event so we can identify experiences or situations that create a risk for you to dissociate. On the self-monitoring sheet you wrote that the prompting event was not having a surprise party on your birthday.

CLIENT: I was given gifts by my friends but really wanted a party. It just made me sad and angry, because I started thinking about all the things I didn't get as a kid.

THERAPIST: Your birthday elicited strong feelings, including anger. Feeling angry is incredibly scary for you, and it makes sense that you wouldn't want to feel anger and would try to avoid it. So we've learned that birthdays are emotionally risky for you and can lead to dissociation. Now that we're aware of this connection, what coping strategies could you use in the future to help regulate these feelings before they escalate?

CLIENT: Well, one thing I can do is engage in calming and self-soothing activities, like you showed me at the beginning of our work. Using the breathing on a regular basis really helps me to stay in the moment. Now that I know ahead of time how hard birthdays can be, I can use these skills to negotiate this really rough patch. I can tell myself it's a rough moment and won't last forever, I can rely on my friends, and I can write in my journal, which I did yesterday, because I was still upset about my birthday.

THERAPIST: That sounds like a terrific plan. That includes strategies to deal with how your body is feeling, what you are thinking, and the presence of friends as a resource. And don't forget that you can share your feelings with your boyfriend, since that's something we've been working on as well. You may recall that old relationship models such as "I cannot trust others enough to ask for help" are often activated when you experience strong emotions.

Sample Session on Interpersonal Skills

The idea of a relationship model is introduced to identify ways in which feelings from past interactions can influence current relationships. Good emotion regulation includes the ability to distinguish the presence of a feeling from the past that is interfering with current interpersonal goals. The therapist also works with the client to develop an alternative relationship model that is better suited to current circumstances and is consistent with the client's goals of establishing more positive trusting and stable relationships with friends.

THERAPIST: Let's go back to your very disappointing birthday. Let's see if some of your reactions, particularly those of disappointment, may have arisen from negative and deep-seated beliefs about yourself and others. Your reaction may be explained as a relationship model about your expectations regarding what you deserve from others.

CLIENT: What's a relationship model?

THERAPIST: A relationship model is a way of viewing the world. People have models for how they see themselves and how they expect other people to react to them. This is called a relationship model. These beliefs are based on early experiences in childhood with your primary caregivers. These models guide how we interact with other people and are "rules" for dealing with the world. Relationship models are often triggered when there is high affect. But what made you so angry?

CLIENT: Well, at the time I was thinking, "If I allow myself to expect certain things from my friends and they don't do it, then I feel rejected and invalidated."

THERAPIST: You noted that you sometimes think, "I don't deserve things. People don't feel like I'm worth it." I remember that you told me that your father used to say this to you when you were growing up. Given that, it makes sense that you would have these thoughts about yourself—like echoes of your father's hurtful words, and not necessarily what *you* really think. It also explains why you would feel sad and angry. The problem is, you are applying this rule from childhood in your life now, and this may not be true anymore. Your friends remembered your birthday. They may have gotten the manner of celebration wrong, but given everything you have said about them, the gifts and cards were intended to send the message "we appreciate you." Your expectation that others view you as "undeserving" may have colored your interpretation of your friends' actions. How might you think about this differently? Let's see if together we can find an alternative relationship model.

CLIENT: I can think they still care, and I can still reach out and communicate with them, even if I'm disappointed. I guess I can be pretty all-or-nothing, but I like this middle ground!

THERAPIST: That's perfect. So now when you notice that you are feeling like "I don't deserve things—people don't feel like I'm worth it," remind yourself that this is a relationship model from the past. What you just came up with, "I can think they still care, and I can reach out," is your new model that matches with people in your present life.

CLIENT: You know, this sounds good, but I can't really imagine doing anything to change how I deal with my friends. I can handle the idea that they intended well. But I can't imagine asking for what I really want, even if they were interested in hearing what I had to say.

THERAPIST: It's hard for you to believe that your friends would care about what you want. But that may be what they really feel. It may be hard for you to experience that, because you've had so little experience asking for what you wanted and getting a positive response. The action of "asking for something you want" has all but faded from your interpersonal repertoire. Why don't you just try finding the words and saying them out loud.

CLIENT: Just out loud?

THERAPIST: Yes. Imagine the situation. Pretend that I am your friend Barbara. Say out loud what you would want to communicate to her about your wish for a party.

CLIENT: Uhm, OK. How about "Barbara, I am thinking about my birthday and would really love to have a party. We've had parties for Bill and Sandra, and well, I'm guessing I feel I think it's my turn, now."

THERAPIST: Good. You came out and said want you wanted. Congratulations, I know that was hard. But I do think I detected uncertainty in your tone of voice. Also, why bring Bill and Sandra into this? You have a right to your own desires, and your friends care for you and clearly want to find ways to celebrate your birthday. Just ask. Let it come from a place of your own desires, and your (developing) belief that your friends know you, enjoy you, and have a positive interest in and a desire to respond to your wants and wishes.

CLIENT: OK. Here goes: "Barbara. You know what I was thinking? I would very much love a birthday party this year. It would thrill me if you could consider putting something together like that rather than all the gifts and such. What do you think of that?!"

THERAPIST: Congratulations. You got it out, straight from your heart's desire.

CLIENT: Just asking feels empowering. Saying what I feel and think out loud makes it all feel more real. And you know what? The here-and-now reality of my friendship with Barbara, not Barbara-as-my-father, is that she probably would say yes.

Trauma Memory Processing

In STAIR narrative therapy, a series of traumatic events are described with a beginning, middle, and end. Each story is viewed as a chapter in the client's autobiography. The client is the author of the story, with the goal ultimately of making meaning of the experience.

The stories are recorded, and often therapist and client listen to the recording together to appraise its meaning. As an initial part of the meaning-making work, the client names the various feelings experienced as he or she told the story (anger, fear, shame, sadness). This reinforces the integration of feelings that belong in the story. It is also an important emotion regulation exercise. The client becomes aware that these feelings are alive in him- or herself but they do not have to overwhelm him or her. This further reinforces in an experiential way that the client is not the same person as the one in the story, who understandably felt overwhelmed in past traumatic experiences but who can now look back at those experiences in a planful and effective manner.

Client and therapist identify relationship models that are embedded in the narrative. These are often transparent variations of models that the client earlier identified as operating in current relationships. This realization often is an important moment in therapy. It provides the client with an explanation for ongoing behaviors that often seem mysterious, peculiar, or at odds with current circumstances. It also begins to liberate the client from the models, as the discovery highlights that some very negative models are rooted in relational circumstances that no longer exist and are not necessary or even helpful in the present. Identifying the link between past experience and current behavior validates the reality of the trauma and its enduring impact on the client.

However, the simultaneous observation that the present is in many ways very unlike the past is critical. The environmental contingencies that created chronic fear, and absence of autonomy and self-direction, no longer exist. The interpersonal models that were once adaptive need no longer apply. Disentangling the past from the present is a critical task for clients with CTSDs, as it provides for the recognition that they have the opportunity to become active agents for change in their own behalf. This process contributes to organization of an autobiographical memory and from it an evolving sense of self living in the present and future.

Therapist and client work together to decide on the amount of material (number of events and level of details) that will be covered, the pace of telling of the story, and the emotional intensity that is expected to arise in any one narration. Therapist and client also identify several favored emotion regulation strategies that the client will use to manage the emotions that arise while doing the memory recollection task. This includes beginning with reminders of the client's present safety, ending with preferred grounding exercises and identifying emotion regulation strategies (e.g., breathing, self-talk) to implement as needed during the telling of the story. The story is told aloud by the client and recorded to provide an enduring record of the event and sometimes as a symbol of the process of "containing" the past. Once specifics of the task are agreed upon, the therapist guides the client through the process, gently lending structure and focus to the narrative work. The therapist also monitors the client's emotion state and offers encouragement. In this way, the therapist takes on the role of co-regulator in the emotional experience that emerges from the creation of the narrative.

Plans for listening to the recording at home are developed by client and therapist, and include details around time and location to ensure uninterrupted and comfortable conditions for the task. The importance of self-care strategies after listening to the recording is emphasized. This includes identification of the amount of time the client will listen to the recording and a plan for putting the recording away and going on to other activities. Structuring the task in this way helps clients to understand that their memories of traumatic experiences should not prevent them from having a life beyond their traumatic past experiences.

Sample Session on Trauma Memory Reconstruction

THERAPIST: As we discussed in our last session, today we begin putting together some of the stories from your childhood. By telling what's happened to you, you have the opportunity to put together the pieces of the trauma—your thoughts, feelings, and sensations related to the experience—that now disturb you in your nightmares and in intrusive memories. Making the fragments of your memory whole will reduce your trauma-related symptoms. While it may be painful and scary to confront your trauma memories, the reality is that you live with these experiences every day through reenactments, flashbacks, nightmares, and intrusive thoughts and images that are likely far more painful than the work we will do here.

    This is a safe place for you to do this work. I will be with you the entire time. We will go at your pace as we put together the memory. You will likely see that once we begin this work, you will be able to tolerate the feelings that these past events generate. And that will do something very important—to reduce the likelihood of you dissociating. You will become confident in your ability to feel, stay present, and manage these emotions. You won't have to check out anymore. This won't be only option when you are feeling these emotions.

CLIENT: This sounds good but hard to believe. How will this really change me?

THERAPIST: You will figure out more of who you are and more of who you can be in the future. And you will also realize that your trauma is in the past and can't hurt you anymore.

CLIENT: I've wanted to believe that for a long time, but the memories always seem to come back to haunt me. I can't seem to get them off my mind, especially when I really want to focus on something important like being close to someone or doing well at work. Replaying the memories seems like exactly the opposite of what I want to do, which is to get rid of them.

THERAPIST: It makes perfect sense that you want to put the memories out of your mind, and the truth is that the best way to put a memory away is to look at it carefully and not try to just avoid it. The harder you try to avoid a memory, the more it comes back and the more you want to check out. Does it make sense that dealing with a memory can put it to rest?

CLIENT: I guess so. I mean, it makes sense, I just don't know if I can do it.

THERAPIST: We'll do this very carefully, so that you are sure you can handle it every step of the way. So we will be using the most distressing memory that you think you can *tolerate* from the hierarchy that we put together last week. This would be the memory in which your father is chasing you with a bat in the woods. We are going to audiorecord your recollection of this memory for you to listen to at home. I will give you a recording log, so that you can note your levels of distress each time you listen.

Let's begin by you closing your eyes. The recorder is on. (*Pause*) Now, using the present tense, tell me about your father chasing you in the woods.

CLIENT: I come home from working my afterschool job and I am already so very tired. I can hear Mom and Dad yelling as I walk up into the yard.

THERAPIST: What are you wearing?

CLIENT: I have on my blue work smock and my favorite jeans. I think I'm wearing my Frankie Goes to Hollywood RELAX T-shirt.

THERAPIST: And what do you see and smell?

CLIENT: Well, I see the front of our metal mobile home. It has grey siding with blue trim. It has a wooden deck in the front, and there are two big windows. I think I can hear them yelling because a window is open. Oh, and I smell a woodsy smell. I am crushing pine needles underfoot. And I smell something greasy—I think somebody was frying chicken.

THERAPIST: And what happens next?

CLIENT: I go toward the house and I'm already feeling apprehensive. I sense trouble brewing. I see an eviction notice on the front door and I begin to panic. Not again!! We just moved in here.

I walk inside, hear the creak of the screen door. I take off my shoes and put them by the door like we always do. I put my head down and try to go in without being noticed. But then I decide to risk it and ask what we are going to do about the eviction notice. Dad screams at me that it's none of my f---ing business. All I do is cause trouble he says. I should have stayed at work! And I realize I should always keep my mouth shut. Why did I have to say anything!!!

THERAPIST: You're doing fine, what happens now?

CLIENT: I think about running into my bedroom, but Dad is blocking the doorway. And I know from experience that he can break the door down anyway. He is a very large man. Imposing shoulders. Booming voice. He's scowling at me. I can see his face so clearly. I just want to get out of there, just be invisible so he can't hurt me. (*Begins to cry.*)

THERAPIST: It's OK. Take a breath and keep going.

CLIENT: I figure out that I'll never make it all the way to my bedroom. I just stand there for a second. "This is all your fault!" screams my dad. Both our eyes lock onto a wooden bat standing in the corner. I know what's coming next, so I take off, running out the door. I can hear Dad close behind. Luckily, he's been drinking, so he's kind of stumbling around. But I know I better run fast to avoid getting beat. There were so many times he did this to me. It is so unfair!

THERAPIST: You're absolutely right. You did *not* deserve to be treated this way.

(*gently*) But now, I need you to stay focused and tell me the rest of what happens.

CLIENT: OK, well, I am running, running, running. I hide behind bushes and try to come out, but I'm afraid he's right there, so I just keep running and hiding. I think I ran for hours. I'm running so long I realize it has gotten dark. I am already so tired from school and work. And my stomach hurts because I'm hungry, but I'm afraid of being caught. So I'm just running and listening for him.

THERAPIST: And what are you feeling?

CLIENT: I am terrified! My heart is racing, I'm breathing fast, and my knees are aching. Wow, I didn't even realize that before.

THERAPIST: And what else are you feeling in your body?

CLIENT: Hmm, even though I'm hungry, I feel nauseous. Oh, wow, and now I remember that I had no shoes on! My feet are bloody and cut up. I am so sweaty. Finally, I risk it and go back to the house. The door is wide open, and my father is not there. I race down the hall to my bedroom and lock the door. That's it.

THERAPIST: OK, now I want you to open your eyes. Look at me. Look around the room and out the window. See that you're here with me now, and you're safe. Feel yourself in the chair, safe in my office.

CLIENT: (*Sighs, and looks around the room. Takes a deep breath.*)

THERAPIST: How do you see yourself in this story?

CLIENT: I should have known better than to come home then. My Dad was usually getting off work about then, and I should have hung around at work longer. I was so stupid.

THERAPIST: So this is similar to the relationship model we were formulating several sessions ago: "If I don't plan ahead, then bad things will happen."

CLIENT: Well, that's not exactly how I feel here. It's more like "If I don't plan for my safety, I'll always be in danger from others." I constantly need to protect myself from how other people might hurt me both physically and emotionally.

THERAPIST: That's quite a principle to live by. It makes sense to plan for safety, and to choose how and with whom you associate, but does it have to be in the forefront "constantly?"

CLIENT: But that's how I live.

THERAPIST: That must take a lot of your time and energy. Wouldn't it be easier if you didn't always have to constantly be on red alert for danger? You mentioned before that you're always all or nothing, but that you really prefer the middle ground in between. Is there a middle ground here, where you can be aware of safety but not "constantly" on guard?

CLIENT: I don't know how to do that.

THERAPIST: Well, one thing with trauma storytelling is that it reminds you that this event is in the past. And that you are at a distance from these experiences. They are memories, and only memories. And the more you practice talking about them, the more you will feel you own them, rather than having them own you. Also, one of the reasons we have been doing so many experiential exercises around positive experiences and self-soothing activities is to give you experiences to counter your belief that you are always in danger.

CLIENT: If I were to propose an alternative, so to speak, it would be "I can't always have a plan. There are other ways of being safe than predicting all the terrible things that can happen."

THERAPIST: Right, you've noticed that when you spend time talking with people and sharing your feelings, your view of the world changes, so you see that not everyone is dangerous and catastrophe isn't always around every corner. And that some people are good and kind. That sounds more like a livable middle ground. It requires you taking a risk, though, which means reaching out and spending time with people, talking with them and sharing your feelings.

Depending on others is scary for you, of course, but so far in your adult life, you've had experiences that tell you others can be there for you.

CLIENT: It's funny. This memory of me running, running, running, really contrasts with my other bad memory. The one where my father strapped me to a chair and was force-feeding me my birthday cake. There I couldn't move at all.

THERAPIST: It's so interesting that you can have these two very different and opposing bodily experiences—one where you are in flight and the other where you can't move. These are the two poles of the traumatized state. You have experienced both. Putting words to these experiences allows you to process the memory. In other words, creating this narrative enables you to make sense of these bodily experiences using words. Language helps you create a coherent story that then becomes less frightening. And, just like your level of distress related to the birthday cake memory decreased significantly after the exposure exercises, your level of distress related to this memory with your father will also decrease.

Sample Session Analyzing the Trauma Narrative and Discussing Its Implications

CLIENT: I listened to the recording every day this week and I brought in some relationship patterns worksheets to review with you.

THERAPIST: Great. I can see from your distress record that your distress levels related to this memory decreased a great deal since we met last time.

CLIENT: Yes, I feel much better about this memory, and about the things I've been through in general. I am realizing that I couldn't control what happened back then, but now I have more choice over my life. Although it's still a little scary. I know I don't need to spend all my time warding off danger. It really does make me sad, though, that I didn't get the kind of care and concern that my boyfriend got from his parents. I see what a different person I could have been.

THERAPIST: You have every right to feel that way, and now you are creating the kind of life you should have had and want still to have. It sounds like you also might have a healthy feeling of pride and self-esteem, proud of yourself for working so hard at letting yourself be close to people you choose. It's impressive that you've been working to implement the belief that it's not always dangerous to become close to someone. There are some wonderful benefits when you allow yourself to experience intimacy in a healthy way. This is illustrated in one of the relationship patterns worksheets you brought in, the one about your feelings with your boyfriend, and becoming closer to him.

CLIENT: It is so surprising that I can actually see myself settling down with him. If we have children, I know my parents won't be part of that; that still really hurts. But I'm learning to create my own family without them. I realize that there are some people, wonderful people, who care about me now. I am learning to be OK with who I am and what I have.

Commentary on the Case Examples

As indicated in the previous dialogue, the narrative work attends to sensory perceptions, feelings, bodily sensations, beliefs, and behaviors. Consequently, the memory that emerges from this process integrates all aspects of experience. Clients often express their surprise, relief, pleasure, and pride in having accomplished this task. The telling of the story is a creative act and, as such, enhances a sense of autonomy, independence, and self-determination. The dynamic and repeated process of telling and then listening to the story facilitates a sense of a self in time. The ability of clients to recognize the psychic and physical injuries imposed on them without being overwhelmed derives in part from viewing these events from the safety of the present, and from the safety of an emerging belief that the person listening to the story is not quite the same as the person the story is about. Clients note that doing the skills work has given them an inkling of their distance from these events: that they are not the same person as the person in the story.

Last, the presence of the therapist creates a context in which the work can be successfully done, and in which a type of "secure attachment" is experienced. The therapist does not attempt to replace or substitute for other caregivers from the client's life. Rather, the therapist serves as a guide in the therapeutic task of the narrative work. This includes providing structure in the task of telling the story and functioning as a co-regulator in the titration of the emotional intensity of the experience. The therapist gives comfort and encouragement at moments of both distress and success. In listening to the narrative, the therapist "sees" the client more completely than others might have in the past, both in the dark parts of his or her history as well as his or her success in emerging from those experiences. The therapist sustains engagement and interest in this task often over several sessions, repeatedly providing guidance, support and practical help, and in doing so conveys belief in the client's worth and even admiration for the client's capacities for development. The tasks of providing comfort, recognition, and perception of worth to the client are all tasks of the therapeutic caregiver that engender a feeling of security in the client and models a template or interpersonal model for future relationships.

Conclusion

CBT provides skills training that can address not only PTSD but also the emotion regulation and interpersonal disorganization characteristic of clients with complex trauma histories. Skills help clients prepare for and engage in trauma memory work, and they promote a sense of mastery in place of feeling "less than." CBT is an individualized, assessment-guided approach (Beck, 2011) that facilitates objective assessment of treatment progress and clients' engagement in therapy. Another strength of CBT is its efficacy with psychiatric conditions that often involve complex trauma, such as schizophrenia, bipolar disorder, eating disorders, and borderline personality disorder. CBT also can achieve positive outcomes with difficult disorders within a relatively short time period.

Finally, CBT recognizes the relation among thoughts, feelings, and behavior, and enables clients to modulate feelings by modifying thoughts and behavior. Thus, CBT models and CBT interventions have great potential to help the clinician engage in a flexible manner that can tailor the treatment plan to a wide range of clients with CTSDs.

References

Beck, J. S. (2011). *Cognitive behavior therapy: Basics and beyond*. New York: Guilford Press.

Bowlby, J. (1988). *A secure base*. New York: Basic Books.

Cloitre, M. C., Cohen, L. R., Ortigo, K., Jackson, C. L., & Koenen, K. C. (2019). *Treating survivors of childhood abuse: Psychotherapy for the interrupted life*. New York: Guilford Press.

Cloitre, M., Stovall-McClough, K. C., Miranda, R., & Chemtob, C. (2004). Therapeutic alliance, negative mood regulation, and treatment outcome in child abuse-related PTSD. *Journal of Consulting and Clinical Psychology, 72*, 411–416.

Cloitre, M., Stovall-McClough, K. C., Nooner, K., Zorbas, P., Cherry, S., Jackson, C. L., . . . Petkova, E. (2010). Treatment for PTSD related to childhood abuse: a randomized controlled trial. *American Journal of Psychiatry, 167*(8), 915–924.

Courtois, C. A., & Ford, J. D. (2013). *Treating complex trauma: A sequenced, relationship-based approach*. New York: Guilford Press.

Coventry, P. (2018, November). INterventions for Complex Traumatic Events (INCiTE): A systematic review and research prioritisation exercise. In M. Cloitre (Chair), *Symposium on Innovations in Complex Trauma Treatment: Trauma-Focused or Not?*. Annual conference of the International Society of Traumatic Stress Studies, Washington, DC.

Dobson, K. S., & Dozois, D. J. A. (2001). Historical and philosophical bases of the cognitive-behavioral therapies. In K. S. Dobson (Ed.), *Handbook of cognitive behavioral therapies* (pp. 3–39). New York: Guilford Press.

Linehan, M. M. (2018). *DBT skills training manual* (2nd ed.). New York: Guilford Press.

Maercker, A., Brewin, C. R., Bryant, R. A., Cloitre, M., Reed, G. M., van Ommeren, M., . . . Rousseau, C. (2013). Proposals for mental disorders specifically associated with stress in the International Classification of Diseases-11. *Lancet, 381*(9878), 1683–1685.

Rothbaum, B. O., & Foa, E. B. (1999). *Reclaiming your life after rape*. New York: Oxford University Press.

CHAPTER 18

Trauma Affect Regulation:
Guide for Education and Therapy

JULIAN D. FORD

Trauma Affect Regulation: Guide for Education and Therapy (TARGET©) is a manualized intervention that provides (1) a neurobiologically informed, strengths-based metamodel of how stress-related information is processed by the "learning brain" (Ford, 2009) and how this is altered when posttraumatic stress disorder (PTSD) and complex traumatic stress disorders (CTSDs) activate the "survival brain" (Ford, 2009), and (2) a practical algorithm (the "SOS" and "FREEDOM" sequences) for restoring the "learning brain" by intentionally engaging executive functions, self-reflective processing, and emotion regulation. This chapter describes the rationale for TARGET and its evidence base, followed by a description of how TARGET addresses CTSDs with case study example. Finally, TARGET's approach to guiding therapists in handling critical therapeutic dilemmas (e.g., severe dysregulation, dissociation, alexithymia, enmeshed relationships, ongoing victimization, addiction, self-harm) is discussed.

Clinical and Scientific Rationale for TARGET

TARGET originally was developed in order to make the two fundamental therapeutic mechanisms that are universal across multiple approaches to psychotherapy for PTSD/CTSDs (Schnyder et al., 2015) transparent and practically accessible for clients and therapists: *trauma processing* and *emotion regulation*. When TARGET was first formulated two decades ago, evidence-based therapies for PTSD typically required some form of therapist-guided recollection of memories of specific traumatic events (Ehlers et al., 2010). The goal of trauma memory processing is to break the vicious cycle in which avoidance of trauma memories paradoxically escalates rather than ameliorates hypervigilance/hyperarousal, trauma-infused emotions and beliefs, and ultimately intrusive reexperiencing of trauma memories themselves. However, many clients (and therapists) are hesitant or frankly unwilling to engage in explicit and intensive recollection and disclosure of traumatic memories. Despite the best intent and efforts of PTSD treatment developers to creatively adapt trauma memory processing therapies (Schnyder et al., 2015), at that time there was no systematic approach to ensure that clients were both motivated to undertake trauma memory processing and prepared to handle the emotion dysregulation that such processing can evoke. TARGET was developed in order to bridge the transition from Phase 1 alliance building and preparation to Phase 2 trauma processing of the CPTSD metamodel, as well as to consolidate and sustain the gains from Phases 1 and 2 in the survivor's ongoing day-to-day life (Phase 3).

TARGET's psychoeducation therefore was designed to enable clients (and therapists) to understand and mentalize (i.e., visualize the internal workings of) the networks within the brain that are responsible for stress reactivity and emotion dysregulation in PTSD and CTSDs. Clients are provided with pictures and a technically accurate but nontechnical description of how stress reactions involve an interaction of the stress/salience network (represented by the amygdala), the self-referential memory encoding/retrieval network (represented by the hippocampus), and the executive function network (represented by the prefrontal cortex). Additional pictures show how these neural interactions are altered in PTSD/CTSDs. With this framework, trauma processing can be understood as a logical way to return control to the executive network by activating the brain's "thinking center" and thus resetting the brain's "alarm" (i.e., the stress/salience network), so that it returns to its normal role as an alerting system rather than an emergency responder. This reframe of PTSD/CTSDs as a hyperactivated inner alarm and sidelined thinking center in the brain offers a technically accurate and intuitively appealing explanation of what is involved in trauma-focused therapy (i.e., reactivating the brain's thinking center and resetting the alarm).

TARGET draws on emotion regulation research to explain that the brain's thinking center is activated by deployment "of attentional processes that might allow individuals to disengage from rigid patterns of regulation . . . [so that,] rather than seeking to replace maladaptive strategies for adaptive strategies, emotion regulation interventions . . . help individuals . . . learn to implement strategies flexibly and appropriately . . . [which] is consistent with the concept of developing a mindful awareness" (Aldao & Nolen-Hoeksema, 2012, p. 498). In TARGET, mindful awareness/acceptance of emotions is described as occurring when the brain's thinking and memory systems are activated sufficiently to reset the brain's alarm, such that the amygdala alarm is no longer hijacking the memory and executive systems (Ford & Wortmann, 2013)—as depicted in a set of intuitively meaningful graphic illustrations (Figure 18.1).

normal stress

The brain and body working together

ALARM SYSTEM *(amygdala)*
- Sends warning signal of potential problem; wake-up message to pay attention
- Signals need for self-protection or focused attention

FILING CENTER *(hippocampus)*
- Retrieves information from memory
- Prepares for action using past experience

THINKING CENTER *(prefrontal cortex)*
- Uses information to think one thought at a time and problem solve
- Creates action plan; evaluates success; sets future goals and hopes

extreme stress

The ALARM takes control

ALARM SYSTEM *(amygdala)*
- Signals an emergency
- Goes on "red alert" to survive danger; overrides FILING and THINKING CENTERS

FILING CENTER *(hippocampus)*
- Slows down and becomes disorganized or shuts down entirely
- Fails to use incoming information or to retrieve information from memory

THINKING CENTER *(prefrontal cortex)*
- Shuts down the normal thinking and problem-solving processes
- Relies on automatic survival reactions and emotions (e.g., confused, overwhelmed, or trapped)

FIGURE 18.1. TARGET psychoeducation graphics explaining the brain's response to stress. Copyright © by the University of Connecticut. All rights reserved. Reprinted by permission.

In order to activate the brain's memory and thinking systems, and reset a hyperaroused alarm in the brain and body, TARGET provides a practical sequence of emotion regulation skills that is distilled from the empirical literature, which demonstrates that emotion regulation involves (1) awareness of bodily states, (2) inhibition of impulsive emotional reactions, (3) maintenance of bodily arousal within a window of tolerance (i.e., neither too intense nor numbed/dissociated), (4) tolerance of distress, (5) awareness of one's own emotion states, (6) translation of feelings into words, (7) making meaning of emotions, (8) intentional modulation of emotion states, (9) awareness of others' emotions states, (10) empathic validation of one's own and others' emotions, (11) expression of emotions in a personally and interpersonally meaningful manner, and (12) translation of emotions into self-enhancing prosocial goals. TARGET distills this complex array of skills/functions into a seven-step sequence for emotion regulation that is summarized by the acronym, FREEDOM. This sequence involves (1) choosing an adaptive Focal point (referred to as an orienting thought), (2) Recognizing triggers that set off the alarm, followed by reappraisal in four domains, including (3) Emotion awareness, (4) Evaluation (i.e., thoughts, beliefs), (5) Defining goals, (6) Option identification (i.e., plans, behaviors), and finally (7) Making a contribution, which involves taking responsibility for using the first six skills in the sequence, in order to make decisions and take actions that increase the safety of the individual and others, and that honor the individual's core values and life goals.

The reappraisal steps in the FREEDOM skills sequence are similar to but differ in important ways from the cognitive restructuring approach in cognitive-behavioral therapy (CBT). In CBT, emotions, thoughts, goals, and behaviors that are associated with symptoms are designated as maladaptive, and the goal is to eliminate them and replace them with adaptive alternatives. In TARGET, such emotions, thoughts, goals, and behavioral choices are designated as "reactive" rather than maladaptive, conceptualizing them as stress reactions that, despite being problematic in current daily life, originated to serve an adaptive purpose in situations in which survival was at risk (i.e., traumatic events). Because survival and safety are a priority for complex trauma survivors even when the current or imminent threat level is low, "reactive" emotions, thoughts, and behaviors are viewed as having potential value if they are recognized as a carryover from past traumas and valued as a reminder to verify that past or possible future traumatic threats either are not currently or imminently occurring, or are (or will be) effectively handled. An important added value of reactive emotions, thoughts, and behaviors is that they mobilize the individual's thinking center to anticipate and effectively respond to problems and take advantage of opportunities in daily life even if traumatic events are not a current or future survival threat.

Therefore, rather than attempting to eliminate or replace reactive emotions, thoughts, and behaviors, the goal in TARGET is to recognize and extract useful information from them. Rather than asking, "How can I eliminate or modify this maladaptive emotion, thought, or behavior?," in TARGET, the question is "How did this reactive emotion, thought, or behavior help me survive traumatic experience(s) in the past, and what can I learn from it that can help me be effective in my current life?" TARGET proposes that embedded within every reactive emotion, thought, or behavior, there are less obvious and more fundamental emotions, beliefs, and goals that are based on the person's core values, relational connections, and aspirations. Retrieving these "main" emotions, beliefs, and goals from the brain's memory center and holding them in awareness alongside the "reactive" emotions, thoughts, and behaviors that are dominant in PTSD and CTSDs, enables the individual to actually think reflectively rather than react reflexively. Intentionally comparing the "reactive" with the "main" thus engages the self-reflective functions that are a hallmark of true executive function—and provides a practical way to restore personal authority over memory and achieve meaning making (Harvey, 1996). This approach to activating executive appraisal and modulating alarm reactivity is consistent with neuroimaging research with survivors of maltreatment (Teicher & Samson, 2016). TARGET's approach to emotion regulation can be used to process either current-day sequelae of complex trauma (i.e., reframing symptoms as stress reactions, signaling that the inner alarm requires resetting) or trauma memories (i.e., reframing memory processing as enabling the thinking center to reset the inner alarm by intentionally accessing and reevaluating trauma memories).

TARGET thus potentially fills a gap in the PTSD/CTSD psychotherapy field by providing a transparent description of, and systematic practical skills set for enhancing, complex trauma survivors' ability to process trauma and regulate their emotions. Improvement in emotion dysregulation (e.g., reduced anger, shame, rumination, alexithymia, interpersonal enmeshment, or distrust) can be achieved in psychotherapies for a range of psychiatric and behavioral health disorders (Sloan et al., 2017), and specifically by CBTs for PTSD (Cahill, Rauch, Hembree, & Foa, 2003; Gallagher, 2017; Mitchell, Wells, Mendes, & Resick, 2012; Resick et al., 2008; Schnyder et al., 2015). Additionally, there is growing evidence that CBTs for PTSD enhance emotion regulation capacities (Cloitre et al., 2010; Hinton, Hofmann, Pollack, & Otto, 2009; Jerud, Zoellner, Pruitt, & Feeny, 2014). However, PTSD/CTSD therapies tend to explain how trauma processing works by invoking the rule of reducing avoidance or differentiating the past from the present, without explaining how or why this makes trauma memories less intrusive and emotionally distressing. They also tend to operationalize emotion regulation in the form of an array of coping skills for emotion awareness and expression, without explaining how find useful and tolerable meaning in distressing emotions and associated thoughts and behavior. By shedding light on the "black box" of trauma processing and emotion regulation, TARGET can help clients with PTSD and CTSD make an informed decision to engage in trauma-focused therapy, while providing a practical skills set for shifting from the survival brain to the learning brain.

The Evidence Base for TARGET
as a Treatment for PTSD/CTSDs

TARGET was developed and tested first as a group therapy for adults with psychiatric and/or substance abuse disorders comorbid with complex PTSD. In a randomized controlled trial (RCT) comparing outpatient group therapy with either PTSD psychoeducation or TARGET with adults in substance abuse treatment, TARGET was associated with significant reductions in trauma-related beliefs and symptoms, and with sustained sobriety-related self-efficacy (Frisman, Ford, Lin, Mallon, & Chang, 2008). A second RCT compared manualized supportive group therapy versus TARGET groups with incarcerated women with complex PTSD (Ford, Chang, Levine, & Zhang, 2013). Both therapies were associated with significant reductions in PTSD, depression, anxiety, and anger symptoms, and increased self-efficacy, with low dropout rates (<5%). However, TARGET groups were significantly more effective than supportive therapy in increasing a sense of forgiveness toward the self and trauma perpetrators, and was associated with greater reductions in trauma-related beliefs about the self and relationships, and increases in affect regulation capacities. Two quasi-experimental studies comparing TARGET groups with services as usual in juvenile justice residential settings demonstrated that TARGET was associated with significant reductions in dangerous incidents, coercive punishments (physical restraints, solitary confinement), recidivism, depression, and anxiety symptoms, and increased youth self-efficacy and engagement in rehabilitation (Ford & Hawke, 2012; Marrow, Knudsen, Olafson, & Bucher, 2012). In the latter two studies, TARGET also served as a total milieu intervention: All staff, teachers, and administrators were trained to utilize TARGET psychoeducation and skills in their day-to-day interactions with youth in the program.

TARGET also has been tested as a one-to-one psychotherapy for complex PTSD. An RCT compared TARGET and an evidence-based manualized social problem-solving therapy for PTSD (present-centered therapy [PCT]; Frost, Laska, & Wampold, 2014) with low-income mothers with complex trauma histories and severe PTSD symptoms who were caring for young children (Ford, Steinberg, & Zhang, 2011). TARGET was more effective than PCT in achieving sustained (at 3- and 6-month follow-up assessments) reductions in PTSD severity and enhanced affect regulation capacities, as well as reducing anxiety and trauma-related self-cognitions and blame, and increasing active coping and secure attachment working models. In a second RCT, TARGET was more effective than a manualized relational therapy in reducing juvenile justice-involved girls' PTSD (intrusive reexperiencing and avoidance) and anxiety symptoms, and improving posttraumatic cognitions and emotion regulation (Ford, Steinberg, Hawke, Levine, & Zhang, 2012). TARGET also reduced the girls' anger problems and increased their sense of hope, but less so than the relational therapy—suggesting the importance of including a relational focus in TARGET. A third RCT with military veterans with CPTSD (Ford, Grasso, Greene, Slivinsky, & DeViva, 2018a) demonstrated that TARGET resulted in comparable or superior reductions in PTSD and CPTSD symptoms, with substantially fewer dropouts, than prolonged exposure (PE).

Another example of a flexible application of TARGET comes from a recently completed study with college students who wanted to overcome clinically significant problem drinking (Ford, Grasso, Levine, & Tennen, 2018b). Abbreviated versions of TARGET psychoeducation about stress, trauma, and the brain, and TARGET modules teaching the FREEDOM emotion regulation skills, were incorporated into a therapist-delivered cognitive-behavioral intervention based on a curriculum on the Web. The TARGET modules were seamlessly added to the responsible drinking CBT protocol, keeping the amount of therapist contact time constant for the CBT-alone and CBT + TARGET conditions. Reductions in the frequency and severity of problem drinking were found for both treatment conditions, based on standardized questionnaire and daily self-report measures. The TARGET-enhanced CBT achieved greater reductions in days of drinking, days of heavy or problem drinking, and PTSD symptoms, and increases in emotion regulation than did CBT-alone. These findings suggest that TARGET can be successfully integrated with CBT protocols for problems frequently comorbid with PTSD, such as alcohol abuse.

Key Clinical Features of TARGET Relevant to CTSDs

TARGET facilitates client engagement in treatment by addressing the questions that lead people to seek help with PTSD/CTSD symptoms. Sample questions and answers include the following:

- **Q:** Why can't I make these terrible memories and dreams stop? **A:** The alarm in your brain is trying to protect you by signaling your brain's memory filing center to pull up those memories, so you'll be prepared if that kind of trauma ever happens again.

- **Q:** How does being tortured by horrible memories "protect" me? It just makes me feel tense and on edge all the time, so I can never relax or trust anyone. **A:** You're right, the memories don't actually protect you, and they do interfere with living your life today. Your brain's alarm isn't paying attention to the present, because it's gotten stuck in survival mode, reliving past traumas when you had to be on guard prepared for the worst. Now your brain's alarm needs to be reset so that it can help you be safe and ready to make the most of your life rather than being stuck in survival mode and keeping you on edge.

- **Q:** How do you reset an alarm that's been stuck in survival mode for years? **A:** That is a real challenge, but it's exactly what we're going to do in this therapy. The way to reset a stuck alarm is to activate and empower the thinking center in your brain, so that it sends the alarm a clear, consistent message that you are fully aware of the danger involved in the kinds of traumas you've experienced, and ready and able to draw on your core values and handle that or any other serious challenge to your (and your loved ones') safety or well-being.

- **Q:** I keep trying to tell myself that I'm safe now, that the trauma is over and isn't going to happen again, and that I need to stop being so tense and suspicious, and trust myself and people I know care about me, but I can't seem to get that message through to this thing you call the alarm in my brain. What am I doing wrong? Why can't I get over this? **A:** The reason is not anything wrong about you, it's because you've never had the one thing that every trauma survivor needs: a user's manual to the brain that shows the practical steps necessary to reset an alarm that is stuck in survival mode. If this were as simple as just flipping a switch in your brain to turn off the alarm, or telling yourself to get over it because that was then and this is now, you would have done it years ago. But the brain is like the engine in a car: It needs a tune-up if its accelerator—the alarm—has been pushed to the maximum and has gotten stuck. There's nothing wrong with the engine—that is, with your brain—it just needs a readjustment, and for that you need a manual, so that you understand how the different parts of the brain work and how to get them readjusted.

- **Q:** Do you actually have a user's manual for the brain? Isn't that something only a highly trained doctor or therapist can understand and use? **A:** I actually have a user's guide that takes all the technical facts and explains them in down-to-earth terms, so you can actually see how the brain handles stress, how its alarm gets stuck in survival mode when trauma occurs, and practical steps I can help you take to teach your brain how to reset its alarm.

TARGET also explicitly addresses the concerns that lead many clients to be reluctant or unwilling to engage in PTSD/CTSD therapy. Adapting a motivational enhancement framework, TARGET enables therapists to validate concerns about treatment and to join with each client in pursuing their personal goals. Clients' first priorities often focus on maintaining at least a basic degree of stability, safety, and harm reduction in their lives, including (1) not repeating past unsuccessful or even detrimental treatments, (2) not causing a worsening in the severity or impairment of PTSD/CTSD or related (e.g., substance use) symptoms, (3) not being deprived of or criticized/rejected for asserting their personal autonomy and authority over their own choices and decisions, (4) completing external requirements (e.g., formal mandates or sanctions imposed by legal, vocational, or educational authorities; informal expectations or conditions by significant others in key relationships) in order to restore or maintain important perogatives (e.g., return to work, regaining custody of children) and relationships (e.g., as an intimate partner or parent). In TARGET, these goals are validated as entirely legitimate expressions of self-protection that should be taken seriously in order to honor the input of the person's inner alarm based on past stressful or traumatic experiences. Preventing a reoccurrence of the toxic dynamics of traumatic or severely negatively stressful past experiences is a completely valid priority deserving respect.

- **Q:** I don't want to be in this therapy—nothing ever gets any better, I just have to deal with this myself and I wish you'd leave me alone. It makes me feel worse when I have to bring up things that I just want to forget. I'm only doing this because the judge and my parents tell me I have to, so why should I even listen to anything you have to say? **A:** You're absolutely right to point out these problems, so that we pay careful attention to not repeating past mistakes by other people who have let you down, misled you, or told you to do things that made it worse for you and not better. And I agree that nothing I can say will be of any value to you unless it helps you to prove to the judge and your parents that you should be able to get on with your life without them getting in your way—even if they and I really do want to help you, you need to be able to have the freedom to make your own decisions and not just have to do what others tell you that you have to do. So tell me, what do they want from you, and how is that getting in the way of what you want to do in your life? I may not have any better answers than you already have, but maybe there are ways I can help you to have the freedom you need to achieve your goals.

- **Q:** You don't know me and you don't know my life, so what can you possibly do to help me deal with problems that I've had all my life since the abuse? **A:** You're right, I don't know you or your life, and although I want to get to know whatever you're willing to share, I will never fully know what it's like to live in your shoes. The way I might be able to be of help to you is by sharing what I know about why abuse can have such a terrible ongoing impact and ways to overcome that which you may not have ever heard about. You probably know a lot about this, but did you know that the key to recovering from abuse is an area in the brain that is an alarm? Did you know that you have an alarm in your brain? And that it's there to protect you, but it can get stuck turned on really loud when a trauma such as abuse happens, and then it needs to be reset so it doesn't keep you on edge or angry or depressed or shut down all the time? Would you be interested in knowing more about this alarm and how you can use the rest of your brain to reset it?

TARGET's approach to reframing PTSD/CTSD symptoms as being due to the brain's alarm getting stuck in survival mode establishes a foundation for a mutually respectful collaboration by solving the mystery for the client of what's gone wrong and how together they can fix it. The therapist brings to this relationship the ability to translate complicated technical knowledge about how the brain is affected by trauma into practical explanations and action steps that are logical, meaningful, and useful. It is the client, however, and not the therapist, who ultimately has the personal expertise to determine how best to apply this knowledge to her or his own life. The therapist does not teach the knowledge and skills in order to correct "maladaptive" ways of thinking or behaving, but instead to provide the client with an understanding of how their adaptive personal strengths, abilities, and values were adaptively engaged to survive trauma and now can be drawn upon in order to adaptively reset the alarm in her or his brain from survival mode back into learning mode (Ford, 2009). The therapeutic alliance in TARGET is based on a shared commitment by therapist and client to empower the client with knowledge that gives a new meaning to trauma and traumatic stress symptoms. Trauma elicits an adaptive stress reaction in the brain and body that can become chronic symptoms if the brain's alarm is not reset. In order to reset the brain's alarm system, TARGET provides a practical set of skills that are steps to enable the brain's thinking center to take back control of the body and mind from the alarm. With the thinking center back in place as the executive in charge, survivors can once again draw on their full range of life experiences (including but not limited to trauma), values, and abilities.

Although affect dysregulation obviously is the core CTSD focus of TAR-GET, the intervention is designed to remediate each one of the CTSD and PTSD symptom domains: dysregulation of emotions, the body, attention and thinking, behavior, relationships, self-concept, and faith/spiritual beliefs.

Affect Dysregulation

The distressing emotions associated with PTSD (e.g., fear, anxiety, anger, guilt, shame, dysphoria) and the difficulties in modulating extremely intense or numbed/dissociated emotions involved in CTSDs are explained by TARGET as having the common denominator of survival-focused hyperactivity of the brain's alarm that is not being balanced by input from the brain's thinking center. The central thread running throughout all of TARGET's affect regulation protocol, the FREEDOM steps, therefore, is engaging the client in a self-reflective appraisal of the dialectical tension between (1) the self-protective but primarily negative valence "reactive" input from the brain's alarm and (2) the self-affirming and primarily positive valence "main" input (i.e., based on core values, hopes, and relationships) from the brain's thinking and memory centers. The goal is to restore and strengthen affect regulation by replacing avoidant hypervigilance (and its toxic manifestations in CTSDs (e.g., devaluation of self and relationships, dissociation) with mindful self-reflection, while preserving adaptive forms of safety-related vigilance.

Physiological Dysregulation

TARGET explains the physiological symptoms of PTSD (e.g., hyperarousal, startle responses, bodily distress triggered by trauma reminders) and CTSDs (e.g., somatoform illness, dissociation, or pain; stress-related exhaustion or exacerbation of physical illness) as bodily expressions of alarm/stress reactions involving avoidance or dissociation of emotions or beliefs. Physical symptoms are addressed primarily by promoting survivors' awareness and understanding of their body state. Body awareness is emphasized in the first part of the first FREEDOM steps (i.e., Focusing to activate the brain's thinking center; specifically, the first "S" in the SOS sequence, see below), as well as when the physical manifestations of emotions are identified in the FREEDOM Emotion recognition step.

Attentional and Cognitive Dysregulation

TARGET explains difficulties with attention or concentration as the result of the alarm prioritizing recognition of potential threats when stuck in survival mode. In order to enhance the client's ability to intentionally focus and sustain attention while experiencing threat-related vigilance, the Recognizing triggers FREEDOM step engages purposeful (rather than automatic and hypervigilant) scanning for cues or contexts that elicit alarm signals. In order to counteract the self-defeating effects of avoidance of trauma reminders, the FREEDOM steps focused on cognitions (i.e., Evaluating thoughts; Defining goals) begin with the identification of alarm-driven cognitions and a validation of their adaptive self-protective intent. Those "reactive" thoughts and goals then are reappraised by identifying associated "main" thoughts and goals (based on past experiences) that not only share the intent of affirming safety but also express the client's core values, aspirations, and relational connections. This mindful dialectical validation of both the "reactive" cognitions elicited by the alarm and the "main" cognitions based on memories of core values, hopes, achievements, and relationships is explained as a means of enabling the brain's thinking center to honor the self-protective input of the alarm, while also honoring the person's true self. When dissociative episodes interrupt sustained attention and cognition, this dialectical consideration of both the "reactive" and "main" thoughts and goals (and also emotions) provides a framework for identifying internal experiences that are lost or fragmented due either to having been too threatening to retrieve consciously (typically "reactive" cognitions or emotions) or invalidated by trauma (typically "main" cognitions or emotions).

Behavioral Dysregulation

The avoidant, interpersonally detached or conflictual, impulsive and potentially reckless, aggressive, and self-harming behaviors in PTSD and CTSDs are explained by TARGET as the downstream result of having a limited available set of behavioral Options due to the inner alarm becoming stuck in survival mode. Accessing "main" as well as "reactive" emotions, thoughts, and goals in the "EED" steps of the FREEDOM process primes the brain's memory center to retrieve memories associated with prosocial and self-affirming actions. Those memories may be of actions by the survivor themselves or actions by other persons that the survivor observed and admired. With these additional behavioral options now at the front of the memory queue, the survivor is now in a position to actually choose how to act rather than simply reacting. For example, when TARGET is conducted in juvenile or criminal justice settings, the youth and adults—staff as well as clients—often report that by using the FEEDOM skills, they are able to catch themselves and choose how to handle triggers that previously elicited what seemed to be automatic and uncontrollable anger and verbal or physical aggression. "In the past I would have lashed out without even thinking, and I felt I had to do that to stand up for myself, even though it always led to more trouble in the long run. Now I realize that's my alarm trying to defend me, and I know how to stop just long enough to actually think it through, so now I'm in control."

Relational Dysregulation

In addition to helping clients to recognize how their own alarm reactions can lead them to withdraw from, or become enmeshed or in conflict in their relationships, TARGET also facilitates empathic perspective taking by reframing relationship problems as a result of reactivity by the inner alarms of *all* of the persons in the relationship. TARGET enables survivors to recognize triggers in relationships and take responsibility for their own alarm reactions, as well as to recognize when and how the other person(s) are experiencing alarm reactions. With this knowledge, survivors are better able not to inadvertently trigger, or escalate, other persons' inner alarms as well. By accessing their "main" emotions, thoughts, and goals when interacting with another person, rather than reacting to triggers, they are able to avoid making demands, creating or intensifying conflicts, or withdrawing from relationships. This also helps survivors to remember that when others interact in ways that are problematic (e.g., criticism, blame, demands, withdrawal), they are having an alarm reaction, the survivor can help to deescalate by focusing on expressing "main" emotions, thoughts, and goals they share.

Self-Dysregulation

TARGET is designed to enable clients to reexamine and reappraise trauma-impacted and often negative self-perceptions by affirming (1) the adaptive nature (i.e., both self-protective, and protective of other persons' safety) of the alarm reactions that underlie their PTSD/CTSD symptoms, and (2) their capacity to draw on personal strengths (as represented by the "main" emotions, thoughts, goals, and behavioral options that can be accessed by activating their brain's thinking center).

Demoralization (Loss of Hope and Faith)

Making a contribution, the final FREEDOM step, reminds survivors that each of us makes the world a better place by recognizing our own (and others') alarm reactions and activating our thinking centers in order to reset the inner alarm. Much of the stress, distress, and even trauma that occurs in the world is the result of people either inadvertently or intentionally letting their inner alarm control their emotions, beliefs, goals, and actions. Each time a person takes responsibility by resetting their own inner alarm, and honoring their "main" emotions, beliefs, and goals, this brings some compassion and justice into the world and sets an example that others can follow.

TARGET begins with psychoeducation that explains PTSD symptoms—particularly the trauma-related development or alteration of how perceptual, affective, interpersonal, and self-related information is processed—as the result of a shift in the brain's stress response system. The primary implication of TARGET's metamodel of trauma-related alterations of stress reactivity in the brain is that recovery from CPTSD requires adjustments in cognitive processing that enable the brain's thinking center to be activated sufficiently to reset the traumatized brain's otherwise hyperactivated alarm. This view is consistent with the cognitive therapy emphasis on reappraisal, but it adds a crucial caveat: Trauma-related cognitions are viewed as alarm reactions that cannot be erased or nullified by logic, but that can be adapted to survivors' current circumstances if complemented by the "main" beliefs and goals that reflect their core values.

If PTSD is understood as a shift from a brain focused on *learning* to a brain (and body) focused on *survival* (Ford, 2009), survival-focused PTSD hypervigilance involves patterns of brain activation that facilitate rapid automatic adjustments to avert harm and stabilize arousal (e.g., brainstem, midbrain, amygdala, insula) instead of neural connections among areas of the brain that are involved in complex learning and cognition (e.g., anterior and posterior cingulate, insula, medial and dorsolateral prefrontal cortex, hippocampus) (Vermetten & Lanius, 2012). A survival-focused brain appears to automatically defend against external threats, but in so doing, it can overutilize crucial bodily systems that are essential both to prevent exhaustion, injury or illness—"allostasis" (Danese & McEwen, 2012)—and to develop and effectively activate complex cognitive information-processing capacities (Bluhm et al., 2012; Daniels et al., 2011).

In order to provide a nontechnical but scientifically based metamodel for therapists and clients, three interconnected brain areas and their functions are described in language and with graphics that are comprehensible at a fifth-grade reading level. First, the "alarm center" in the brain is the amygdala, which activates the body's peripheral autonomic nervous system and hormonal stress system. Second, the hippocampus is anatomically adjacent to the amygdala and functions as a "memory filing center" that serves as librarian or search engine for the storage and retrieval of memories and related experiential information. Third, the prefrontal cortex serves as the brain's integrative "thinking center," translating the input from the alarm and filing centers into conscious emotions, thoughts, goals, and behavioral choices. This biological model provides a transparent, down-to-earth, and destigmatizing explanation of how the brain shifts into survival mode when confronted by traumatic stressors and related adversity: The brain's alarm gets hyperactivated to signal that an emergency is occurring, and a burst of alarm signals flood the brain's filing center, creating an information overload, exceeding the filing center's processing capacities. As a result, trauma memories stored by the filing center tend to be intensely distressing and incomplete—often in the form of fragmented flashes of disorganized and disconnected bodily reactions and emotions dominated by a sense of shock, confusion, terror, horror, aloneness, and powerlessness. When reminders of traumatic events occur for a survivor, this sets off the alarm and leads the filing center to retrieve those disturbing and confusing memories (i.e., intrusive reexperiencing).

The TARGET metamodel explains how PTSD and CTSDs are the result of an adaptive survival reaction, the automatic self-protective attempt by the brain's alarm center to mobilize the body and brain in order to survive a traumatic threat. Under ordinary circumstances, the brain's alarm reacts to stressors (both challenges and opportunities) by signaling the filing center to store and retrieve relevant information as memories that, when accessed and transmitted to the thinking center, enable the individual to respond based on organized, contextually adaptive, and goal-directed cognitions. Not only does the thinking center's synthesis of information in the form of conscious emotions, beliefs, and goals facilitate planful effective action, but it also has a key adaptive benefit in terms of emotion regulation: Activation of the medial prefrontal cortex has an inhibitory effect of reducing amygdala activation (i.e., resetting the brain's alarm).

In PTSD, to the contrary, it appears that the brain's alarm center is stuck in survival mode, and the body is correspondingly stuck in a state of physiological and emotional hyperarousal—or the opposite pole of hypoarousal, dissociation, and profound emotional numbing (Lanius, Brand, Vermetten, Frewen, & Spiegel, 2012). In PTSD, the brain's filing center appears to have become primed by the ongoing emergency input from the alarm to access primarily survival/threat-related memories and information (i.e., intrusive reexperiencing). The brain's thinking center thus may be unable to activate sufficiently to retrieve appropriate memories from the filing center and use them to think clearly and reset the alarm.

TARGET engages therapist and client in learning a seven-step sequence for refocusing cognitively when experiencing alarm reactions that draws on but systematizes and makes transparent (and thus, feasible for frequent replication and practice *in vivo*) cognitive skills taught in CBT, mindfulness and meditative therapies, and experiential and psychodynamic psychotherapies. The skills sequence is summarized in the easily learned acronym, FREE-DOM:

- Focusing on one thought that you choose, based on your core values and self
- Recognizing micromomentary triggers for posttraumatic "alarm" reactions

- Distinguishing alarm-driven ("reactive") versus reflective ("main") Emotions
- Distinguishing alarm-driven ("reactive") versus reflective ("main") Evaluations
- Defining reflective ("main") goals distinct from alarm-driven ("reactive") goals
- Distinguishing alarm-driven ("reactive") versus reflective ("main") Options
- Making a positive contribution by using these steps to reset the brain's alarm

The seven-step sequence will be familiar to psychotherapists regardless of their specific theoretical orientation, because it employs a transtheoretical set of cognitive tactics to facilitate self-monitoring (i.e., the first and last—focusing and making a contribution—steps), nonavoidant experiential awareness (i.e., the recognizing triggers and emotion identification steps), behavior analytic chain analyses (i.e., the sequential link between triggers, emotions, thoughts [evaluations], goals, actions [options], and outcomes [making a contribution]), reappraisal (i.e., the emotions, evaluations, and goals steps), and problem solving (i.e., focusing, defining goals, selecting options, and outcomes [making a contribution] steps). The FREEDOM sequence also draws attention to the dialectical interplay among emotions, thoughts, goals, and choices that are alarm-based "reactive" versus those that are "reflective," based on the person's core beliefs, values, relational commitments, and sense of self (Linehan, 1993).

TARGET draws on two transtheoretical psychotherapy models to provide a practical guide for the client (and therapist) in using the cognitive emotion regulation tactic of planful refocusing (Min, Yu, Lee, & Chae, 2013) in psychotherapy for PTSD. First, Gendlin's focusing psychotherapy (an offshoot of Rogerian client-centered therapy and one of the key precursors to EEF (emotion awareness, evaluation of thoughts, focusing) and mindfulness-based psychotherapies) is used as an approach to enhancing clients' capacities for purposeful mental focusing by deliberately facilitating experiential awareness (Gendlin, 1982). In order to shift from survival-related reactivity to proactive engagement in goal-directed attention with mental acuity, mental focusing is operationalized in TARGET by dividing the FREEDOM skill of focusing into three substeps. A well-recognized mnemonic that connotes seeking help in the face of danger, SOS, is use to summarize the three substeps in a manner that was selected as likely to be learnable and memorable, because it is pedagogically "sticky" (i.e., simple, efficient, active, and linked to a network of associative connections that have a connotation of trauma and recovery) (Biggs & Tang, 2011; Taylor & Cranton, 2012):

- Slow down and Sweep your mind clear of all thoughts.
- Orient yourself by choosing one thought (using words, imagery, sound,

or any of the other five senses) that represents what is most important to you right now, based on what you value, believe in, and who you are as a person.

- Self-check by rating (on a scale from 1 to 10) your levels of (1) stress (from *none at all* to *worst ever*) and (2) personal control (from *none* to *most ever*)

The SOS mnemonic thus provides a generic protocol that can be individualized by and for each client, based on their preferred modalities and approaches for mentally focusing (Gendlin, 1982) on core beliefs, values, aptitudes, interests, and personality characteristics.

Second, Fonagy's mentalizing approach to psychodynamic psychotherapy (Allen, Fonagy, & Bateman, 2008) is used to enable the client to mentally visualize how and why PTSD symptoms occur as an automatic survival adaptation by the brain, and how key areas within the brain can be harnessed to reduce or manage CTSD and PTSD symptoms, thus freeing the brain from being hijacked by its own alarm and preventing the survivor from being trapped in survival mode. The metaphor of activating thinking and filing centers in the brain in order to counterbalance and reset a trauma-driven hyperactive alarm center is a practical tool for mentalizing, providing a picture that can be used to visualize how the brain changes in the process of recovering from complex trauma or PTSD/CTSDs. The FREEDOM steps are a map for applying this mental model to identify and unpack both trauma-related (alarm-based, "reactive") and self-congruent (thinking center-based, "main") emotions, thoughts, goals, and choices. In this way, mentalizing in TARGET provides the scaffolding for clients to mentally observe and modify the changes in the brain and in affective information processing that lead to PTSD and CTSDs.

The FREEDOM steps are learned and practiced incrementally through dialogue with a therapist or counselor, or in guided interactions in a therapy group or a milieu program. This involves the application of CBT techniques, including observational learning via modeling, opportunities for guided practice with coaching and self-monitoring, and individualized applications in the youth's natural environment to promote generalization and refine skills application. A structured FREEDOM practice exercise template is provided for the client to review recent or historical experiences either with the clinician or independently between or following therapy sessions. The practice exercise is designed to enable clients to distinguish "alarm reactions" from focused self-regulation and improve their ability to use their innate skills for focused self-regulation while experiencing PTSD symptoms. The goal is not to eliminate symptoms but to encourage mindful awareness and acceptance (Hayes, Luoma, Bond, Masuda, & Lillis, 2006) by self-monitoring them, recognizing their adaptive value, and drawing on core personal values and strengths to choose how to respond when they are triggered.

TARGET also has a creative arts activity designed to enhance positive and negative emotion recognition skills through the creation of personalized "lifelines" via collage, drawing, poetry, and writing. The lifeline provides a way to apply the SOS and FREEDOM steps to constructing a life narrative that includes traumatic and stressful events but does not involve repeated retelling of them. TARGET does not require trauma memory processing, but instead engages clients in a process of learning how to systematically reconstruct narratives describing current or past stressful events. The intervention's premise is that knowing how to reconstruct memories that are predominantly dysphoric, fragmented, and incomplete will make them more emotionally and cognitively coherent and complete. This in turn enhances the client's ability to regulate distressing emotions related either to past traumas or current stressful events. Thus, the FREEDOM sequence is compatible with trauma memory processing—in fact, it is designed to enhance clients' abilities to purposefully and mindfully engage in memory processing while also acquiring a transparent set of skills for independently reconstructing both implicit and explicit aspects of memories (of other traumatic events, or other important nontraumatic experiences) in a coherent narrative, while also enhancing self-awareness and emotion regulation.

Clinical Case Examples

To ensure that privacy and confidentiality are preserved, the name and personal details for this "client" have been disguised as a composite of several actual clients and their families.

Miriam, a 44-year-old woman, was psychiatrically hospitalized after an episode in which paramedics were called when she was wandering through a large store, disoriented and arguing with voices in her head. After she was medically and psychiatrically stabilized, and appeared fully oriented and competent, Miriam disclosed that she had been sexually molested by her stepfather between ages 8 and 12 years old. Her mother discovered the abuse when she came home early from work one day and found them in the couple's bed together. Miriam's mother told her husband to leave and find another place to live, and also angrily told Miriam, "You ruined my life, and we will never speak of this shameful thing again." Miriam believed this meant that she must never tell anyone, to spare her mother from further hurt and to hide her guilt and shame. From that point in her life to the present, more than thee decades later, Miriam heard voices in her head telling her she was "dirty and disgusting, and ruined everything good." As a teenager, she found that she could make the voices "shut up" by drinking until she passed out or by cutting herself, but over the years she increasingly found herself becoming lost and disoriented while having long debates with the voice at inconvenient times—as had happened in the incident preceding her hospitalization. She also told her inpatient psychiatrist, "I don't want to talk any more about the details. I'm only telling you this much because this is confidential, and I didn't want to lie when you asked me how the voices started."

When the inpatient team met with Miriam to discuss a discharge plan, they recommended that she begin therapy to deal with the past abuse. Miriam had avoided therapy, and said that she didn't want to "open up old wounds," especially at this vulnerable point in her life. Reluctantly, she agreed to meet with a therapist from the outpatient clinic before her discharge, to learn what therapy involved and whether it could help her without making things worse. The therapist explained that she respected Miriam's wish to not do anything that would interfere with her life and her peace of mind, particularly while she was recovering from a crisis and adapting to new medications. She also reassured Miriam that therapy was entirely her decision, and the purpose of their meeting was only to assist Miriam in making an informed choice.

THERAPIST: Your psychiatrist here told me that you gave him permission to share just a few things with me so you didn't have to tell your story all over again to me, is that right?

MIRIAM: (Nods yes.) So you know I don't want to dredge up what happened to me all over again. The voices start whenever something reminds me, and I don't shut out the memories. If you have to talk about bad memories in therapy, I'm not going to put myself through that.

THERAPIST: That makes sense. You don't want to do anything that starts the voices. Therapy should help you handle the voices and the memories, not make them worse. An important thing to know about the therapy we do is that it explains what's going on in your brain that brings on the bad memories and the voices—and how you can help your brain to stop doing that.

MIRIAM: So my brain is all messed up, that's why I feel so miserable and crazy? I have brain damage and I'm never going to be right in the head? That's what my mother used to say!

THERAPIST: This definitely is *not* brain damage, Miriam. You actually have a very strong and healthy brain, which is why you've been able to deal with the stress of the abuse and keep it all to yourself for all these years. I don't know many people who have your strength and resilience, but you're brain has been working overtime to keep you going, and that can be very exhausting.

MIRIAM: I feel tired all the time, but I can't let down my guard. So I never relax or really sleep.

THERAPIST: And there's a reason why you've been caught in this dilemma, but it's not something wrong with you. It's a change that happens in anyone's brain when they go through traumas like you did as a child. You didn't know it, but a part of your brain stepped up and helped you to get through the abuse. Did you know your brain has an alarm that's there to protect you?

MIRIAM: An alarm? In my brain? No, I didn't know that. That's weird. Like a fire alarm?

THERAPIST: Right. When there's an emergency—like when you were being abused—the alarm in our brain is like a fire alarm that signals our body to go into high stress mode, fight or flight. You know what that feels like? It's the body's automatic way to help us survive something awful.

MIRIAM: Yeah, I was definitely a total stress case when he started messing with me. I was so scared and confused, yuck! I hate to even think about it.

THERAPIST: We don't have to go back to that, and in therapy you won't have to talk about those specific memories unless you decide you want to deal with them, so that you can put them away and not have them turning your brain's alarm on all the time. Because that's what's happening. By trying to not think about the memories, you're unintentionally setting of your brain's alarm—when you shut out the memories temporarily, that leaves them in the back of your mind, so your brain never really knows the abuse is over and you're actually safe now. And that tells the alarm that it can't turn off, because it won't turn off until you know that you're safe. The alarm just wants to protect you, but it's gotten stuck turned on, and it needs to be reset!

MIRIAM: And the voices . . . are those this alarm trying to tell me something's still wrong? Why would my own brain treat me like that? That's really messed up!!

THERAPIST: That's a very important point. The voices may actually be a way your alarm is trying to tell you there's an emergency. But the message is getting mixed up, because you aren't really in danger now, because the abuse is over, but your alarm is stuck with the hurtful memory of your mother being angry and blaming you. So maybe the voices are your alarm's way of repeating what your mother said. I think your mother's alarm went off because she was shocked and upset, and then she couldn't help you see that you weren't to blame.

MIRIAM: I don't think she ever got over that, or ever forgave me. I feel so bad about that.

THERAPIST: I can see that you're a very caring and loyal person, Miriam, and you've carried this burden of grief and guilt with a lot of integrity for a long time. You've protected your mother by keeping all of this to yourself, which shows you have a lot of loyalty. Therapy could help you to continue to be loving and strong, and also to do something to put the abuse behind you: to reset that alarm in your brain so that it can keep you safe but not be a fire alarm with the angry voices.

MIRIAM: If therapy is that simple, how come nobody ever told me about this alarm before? Don't you need medications to turn down that alarm? If it's in the brain, what good is talking?

THERAPIST: The mental health field only recently learned how trauma can lead our brain's alarm to get stuck in emergency mode, and this has improved our therapies, so that a user's manual is provided on to manage and reset the body's alarm system. Medications can help to turn down the volume of the alarm, and the voices, too, but they don't reset the alarm. To do that, you need to activate another important area in the brain, the thinking center. Therapy can show you to activate the thinking center and reset the brain's alarm by developing the abilities you already have to think in a highly focused manner. Would you like to learn more about that?

Commentary on the Case Example

This vignette illustrates how TARGET enables therapists to explain the origin of PTSD/CTSDs in a destigmatizing manner as specific, logical, and empirically based changes in the brain and body's stress response system. This metamodel of PTSD/CTSDs offers a down-to-earth and strengths-based rationale for how and why therapy is of practical benefit. Miriam initially did not want to talk (or think) about memories of abuse, but as she learned and applied the FREE-DOM sequence to prepare for and handle *in vivo* daily life dilemmas in which intrusive memories and "the voices" were triggered, she felt increasingly confident that she could face and put to rest abuse memories: "I *hate* remembering what happened. I wish it would just go away or never happened. I never want to see him again, but I'm not scared to remember what happened."

Miriam was able to use the FREEDOM sequence as a structure to organize an oral narrative that included details of the abuse that were relevant to her.

"The trigger moment when my alarm was going off strongest was when he started to touch me. After that it seemed like my brain just shut down, but now I realize that my alarm was still protecting me and keeping me alive. And I remember I had one main thought that kept me going then and until the abuse was over—I saw my mom smiling and reaching out to hug me. I lost that thought when she got so angry and blamed me, but now I know she didn't hate me. It was her alarm doing the yelling. I can't change the hurt I felt then or the distance it created between my mom and me, but now I can think of her without hearing her—or the voices—yelling at me. And I can remember the times when I was younger, when I knew she loved me, before her alarm shut her down."

After 5 months of weekly (or in the final 6 weeks, twice monthly) psychotherapy, Miriam described PTSD/CTSD symptoms as mild or nonexistent, with one exception. She still felt intense, but manageable, distress when reminded of the abuse and her mother blaming her. In those instances of intrusive reexperiencing, Miriam was able to recognize her bodily, affective, and cognitive symptoms as signals from her brain's alarm, and to intentionally focus her mind (while picturing a powerful supercomputer as the thinking center in her brain) by orienting to a visual image of herself being held in a loving embrace (as a child by her mother, or as an adult by her primary intimate partner). Occasionally, she would "hear" what she had interpreted as an external "voice" blaming her, but she was able to accept this as a memory that her brain's alarm was using to prepare her for current life challenges—and to remember that she could indeed trust herself to handle those challenges rather than being drawn into an argument with herself. Miriam was surprised, and pleased, at her ability to be highly focused in important relationships, in her career, and in daily life: "I didn't believe my therapist when she told me, the first time we met, that I had a strong mind and could be highly focused. I saw myself as a scatterbrain, but I now know my brain was working overtime and I just needed a user's manual to get it on track."

The Dissemination Infrastructure for TARGET

TARGET has a dissemination infrastructure for exportation of the model to large organizations and service systems. TARGET has been implemented in several statewide behavioral health, juvenile, and adult criminal justice systems in the United States, and in multiprogram agencies and organizations in North America and Europe providing mental health, child welfare, juvenile justice, substance abuse treatment, and homelessness services. The University of Connecticut has copyrighted the TARGET model and licensed a small business (Advanced Trauma Solutions, Inc.; *www.advancedtrauma.com*) as the sole commercial distributor of the model. The implementation program involves an intensive organizational readiness assessment, multiday trainings for clinicians and staff who directly implement the intervention, overview presentations for all other agency/organization administrators and staff to support consistent implementation, and a multiyear protocol for quality assurance (including independent rating by the trainers of videotape recordings of TARGET sessions); ongoing consultation to ensure fidelity and enhance competence of implementation; assistance with implementation and analysis of data from outcome, alliance, and satisfaction measures; and a certification process for both TARGET providers and TARGET trainer/consultants. The implementation infrastructure and process was rated as 4.0 on a 4.0 scale by the Substance Abuse and Mental Health Services Administration (SAMHSA) National Registry of Evidence-Based Programs and Practices (see *www.nrepp.samhsa.gov*). Adaptations of the TARGET model are under development and disseminated on a limited pilot-test basis by the Center for Trauma Recovery and Juvenile Justice in the National Child Traumatic Stress Network (*www.nctsn.org*).

References

Aldao, A., & Nolen-Hoeksema, S. (2012). The influence of context on the implementation of adaptive emotion regulation strategies. *Behaviour Research and Therapy, 50*(7–8), 493–501.

Allen, J. G., Fonagy, P., & Bateman, A. (2008). *Mentalizing in clinical practice*. Washington, DC: American Psychiatric Press.

Biggs, J., & Tang, C. (2011). *Teaching for quality learning at university*. New York: McGraw-Hill.

Bluhm, R. L., Frewen, P. A., Coupland, N. C., Densmore, M., Schore, A. N., & Lanius, R. A. (2012). Neural correlates of self-reflection in post-traumatic stress disorder. *Acta Psychiatrica Scandinavica, 125*(3), 238–246.

Cahill, S. P., Rauch, S. A., Hembree, E. A., & Foa, E. B. (2003). Effect of cognitive behavioral treatment for PTSD on anger. *Journal of Cognitive Psychotherapy, 17*, 113–131.

Cloitre, M., Stovall-McClough, K. C., Nooner, K., Zorbas, P., Cherry, S., Jackson, C. L., . . . Petkova, E. (2010). Treatment for PTSD related to childhood abuse: A randomized controlled trial. *American Journal of Psychiatry, 167*(8), 915–924.

Danese, A., & McEwen, B. S. (2012). Adverse childhood experiences, allostasis, allostatic load, and age-related disease. *Physiology and Behavior, 106*(1), 29–39.

Daniels, J. K., Hegadoren, K., Coupland, N. J., Rowe, B. H., Neufeld, R. W., & Lanius, R. A. (2011). Cognitive distortions in an acutely traumatized sample: An investigation of predictive power and neural correlates. *Psychological Medicine, 41*(10), 2149–2157.

Ehlers, A., Bisson, J., Clark, D. M., Creamer, M., Pilling, S., Richards, D., . . . Yule, W. (2010). Do all psychological treatments really work the same in posttraumatic stress disorder? *Clinical Psychology Review, 30*(2), 269–276.

Ford, J. D. (2009). Neurobiological and developmental research: Clinical implications. In C. A. Courtois & J. D. Ford (Eds.), *Treating complex traumatic stress disorders: An evidence-based guide* (pp. 31–58). New York: Guilford Press.

Ford, J. D., Chang, R., Levine, J., & Zhang, W. (2013). Randomized clinical trial comparing affect regulation and supportive group therapies for victimization-related PTSD with incarcerated women. *Behavior Therapy, 44*(2), 262–276.

Ford, J. D., Grasso, D. J., Greene, C. A., Slivinsky, M., & DeViva, J. C. (2018a). Randomized clinical trial pilot study of prolonged exposure versus present centred affect regulation therapy for PTSD and anger problems with male military combat veterans. *Clinical Psychology and Psychotherapy, 25*(5), 641–649.

Ford, J. D., Grasso, D. J., Levine, J., & Tennen, H. (2018b). Emotion regulation enhancement of cognitive behavior therapy for college student problem drinkers: A pilot randomized controlled trial. *Journal of Child and Adolescent Substance Abuse, 27*(1), 47–58.

Ford, J. D., & Hawke, J. (2012). Trauma affect regulation psychoeducation group and milieu intervention outcomes in juvenile detention facilities. *Journal of Aggression, Maltreatment and Trauma, 21*(4), 365–384.

Ford, J. D., Steinberg, K. L., Hawke, J., Levine, J., & Zhang, W. (2012). Randomized trial comparison of emotion regulation and relational psychotherapies for PTSD with girls involved in delinquency. *Journal of Clinical Child Adolescent Psychology, 41*(1), 27–37.

Ford, J. D., Steinberg, K. L., & Zhang, W. (2011). A randomized clinical trial comparing affect regulation and social problem-solving psychotherapies for mothers with victimization-related PTSD. *Behavior Therapy, 42*(4), 560–578.

Ford, J. D., & Wortmann, J. (2013). *Hijacked by your brain*. Naperville, IL: Sourcebooks.

Frisman, L. K., Ford, J. D., Lin, H., Mallon, S., & Chang, R. (2008). Outcomes of trauma treatment using the TARGET model. *Journal of Groups in Addiction and Recovery, 3*, 285–303.

Frost, N. D., Laska, K. M., & Wampold, B. E. (2014). The evidence for present-centered therapy as a treatment for posttraumatic stress disorder. *Journal of Traumatic Stress, 27*(1), 1–8.

Gallagher, M. W. (2017). Transdiagnostic mechanisms of change and cognitive-behavioral treatments for PTSD. *Current Opinion in Psychology, 14*, 90–95.

Gendlin, E. T. (1982). *Focusing* (2nd ed.). New York: Bantam Books.

Harvey, M. (1996). An ecological view of psychological trauma and trauma recovery. *Journal of Traumatic Stress, 9*, 3–23.

Hayes, S. C., Luoma, J. B., Bond, F. W., Masuda, A., & Lillis, J. (2006). Acceptance and commitment therapy: Model, processes and outcomes. *Behaviour Research and Therapy*, *44*(1), 1–25.

Hinton, D. E., Hofmann, S. G., Pollack, M. H., & Otto, M. W. (2009). Mechanisms of effi-cacy of CBT for Cambodian refugees with PTSD: Improvement in emotion regulation and orthostatic blood pressure response. *CNS Neuroscience and Therapeutics, 15*(3), 255–263.

Jerud, A. B., Zoellner, L. A., Pruitt, L. D., & Feeny, N. C. (2014). Changes in emotion regulation in adults with and without a history of childhood abuse following post-traumatic stress disorder treatment. *Journal of Consulting and Clinical Psychology, 82*(4), 721–730.

Lanius, R. A., Brand, B., Vermetten, E., Frewen, P. A., & Spiegel, D. (2012). The dissocia-tive subtype of posttraumatic stress disorder: Rationale, clinical and neurobiological evidence, and implications. *Depression and Anxiety, 29*(8), 701–708.

Linehan, M. M. (1993). *Cognitive-behavioral treatment of borderline personality disorder*. New York: Guilford Press.

Marrow, M., Knudsen, K., Olafson, E., & Bucher, S. (2012). The value of implementing TARGET within a trauma-informed juvenile justice setting. *Journal of Child and Ado-lescent Trauma, 5*, 257–270.

Min, J. A., Yu, J. J., Lee, C. U., & Chae, J. H. (2013). Cognitive emotion regulation strategies contributing to resilience in patients with depression and/or anxiety disorders. *Compre-hensive Psychiatry, 54*(8), 1190–1197.

Mitchell, K. S., Wells, S. Y., Mendes, A., & Resick, P. A. (2012). Treatment improves symp-toms shared by PTSD and disordered eating. *Journal of Traumatic Stress, 25*(5), 535–542.

Resick, P. A., Galovski, T. E., Uhlmansiek, M. O., Scher, C. D., Clum, G. A., & Young-Xu, Y. (2008). A randomized clinical trial to dismantle components of cognitive processing therapy for posttraumatic stress disorder in female victims of interpersonal violence. *Journal of Consulting and Clinical Psychology, 76*(2), 243–258.

Schnyder, U., Ehlers, A., Elbert, T., Foa, E. B., Gersons, B. P., Resick, P. A., . . . Cloitre, M. (2015, August 14). Psychotherapies for PTSD: What do they have in common? *Euro-pean Journal of Psychotraumatology, 6*.

Sloan, E., Hall, K., Moulding, R., Bryce, S., Mildred, H., & Staiger, P. K. (2017). Emotion regulation as a transdiagnostic treatment construct across anxiety, depression, sub-stance, eating and borderline personality disorders: A systematic review. *Clinical Psy-chology Review, 57*, 141–163.

Taylor, E. W., & Cranton, P. (Eds.). (2012). *The handbook of transformative learning: The-ory, research, and practice*. San Francisco: Jossey-Bass.

Teicher, M. H., & Samson, J. A. (2016). Annual Research Review: Enduring neurobiological effects of childhood abuse and neglect. *Journal of Child Psychology and Psychiatry and Allied Disciplines, 57*(3), 241–266.

Vermetten, E., & Lanius, R. A. (2012). Biological and clinical framework for posttraumatic stress disorder. *Handbook of Clinical Neurology, 106*, 291–342.

PART III

GROUP/CONJOINT THERAPY MODELS

CHAPTER 19

Group Therapy

JULIAN D. FORD

Group therapy provides an interpersonal context of physical and emotional safety in which complex trauma survivors can "restore social connections while also addressing the deleterious impact of interpersonal trauma on [their] experience of self in relationships . . . [and] for repairing the cognitive schemas for safety, trust/dependency, independence, power, self-esteem, and intimacy that are often disrupted by psychological trauma" (Mendelsohn et al., 2011, p. 13). As a result, a variety of approaches to group therapy have been developed for adults with histories of many types of complex trauma, including childhood abuse, domestic or community violence, racial/ethnic or other identity-based (e.g., sexual orientation, gender, disability) violence, hate crimes, war, trafficking, terrorism, and genocide and torture.

Group therapies for posttraumatic stress disorder (PTSD) and complex traumatic stress disorders (CTSDs) also use a variety of therapeutic models. Trauma-focused group therapy models include cognitive-behavioral therapy (CBT)—with or without trauma memory processing (TMP), emotion regulation (ER), interpersonal psychotherapy (IPT), as well as psychodynamic, feminist, and relational/supportive therapeutic approaches. In this chapter, the clinical features and potential benefits of group therapy for CTSDs are described, and the growing scientific evidence base of research on group therapy for these conditions and comorbidities is reviewed. A composite sample of group therapy for women with CTSDs is presented to illustrate the role of psychoeducation, affect and interpersonal regulation skills, and TMP in such groups.

Clinical Considerations in Conducting Group Therapy for Traumatic Stress Disorders

Overview

Group therapies tend to be organized around a theme that is relevant to all group members. The theme may be relatively generic (e.g., education, support for recovery; building self-esteem; interpersonal assertiveness, overcoming addiction, anxiety or depression; anger management) or the group may be organized around a more specific theme or dilemma (e.g., understanding and recovering from sexual abuse or assault, intimate partner violence, combat or war trauma, or traumatic loss and bereavement; managing or preventing dissociation, self-harm, or suicidality, skills building). Several cross-cutting goals (Herman, Kallivayalil, & Members of the Victims of Violence Program, 2019; Mendelsohn et al., 2011) for trauma survivors in group therapy include the following:

1. Accurately assess, and take necessary steps to increase, personal safety.
2. Nonjudgmentally and accurately understand how trauma impacts the body, behavior, emotions, core beliefs, memory, relationships, and sense of self.
3. Develop skills for self-care and coping with stress and distress.
4. Develop skills in emotional regulation and other forms of self-control.
5. Develop a support network and feel less isolated and alone.
6. Develop skills for self-care and coping with stress and distress.
7. Overcome feelings of self-blame, shame, and being defective or damaged.
8. Develop self-compassion and pride to counter stigmatization and self-contempt.
9. Recognize and value emotions, and recover from intense or shutdown emotions.
10. Develop relationship skills to support finding, accepting, and creating safe, mutually respectful, and meaningful relationships.
11. Gain a sense of mastery and personal empowerment.
12. Safely and voluntarily recall memories of past traumas that continue to be troubling without being overwhelmed (i.e., regain mastery of one's own memory) (Harvey, 1996).
13. Reevaluate and affirm core beliefs and values about the world, the future, relationships, and oneself that are realistic and provide a genuine sense of hope.
14. Transfer the knowledge, skills, and sense of being cared for, worthy, and effective that were gained in group outside into daily life, relationships, and accomplishments.

Selection and Preparation of Group Members

Before beginning group therapy, each group member should be carefully selected and prepared. The primary contraindication for group participation for adult complex trauma survivors is psychological or behavioral instability that could put the individual, or other group members, at risk physically or psychosocially. Specific contraindications include (1) suicidal intent with a definite plan and means; (2) imminent risk of serious physical or emotional aggression toward others; (3) current substance abuse or dependence involving ongoing actual or potential uncontrolled use and for which the individual is not receiving treatment or is not in recovery; (4) severe dissociative fragmentation or flashbacks that require intensive acute therapeutic management; (5) incapacitating psychotic or manic symptoms for which the individual is not receiving treatment; (6) ongoing exposure to imminent severe physical harm; and (7) unwillingness or inability to make an informed consent (or when treatment is externally mandated, a meaningful assent) to participate in the group.

However, it is important to note that suicidal or aggressive ideation, or involvement in a potentially dangerous relationship or living situation do not automatically rule out group participation so long as there is no imminent risk of severe harm to self or others. Group therapy can provide a supportive relational context in which trauma survivors can take positive steps toward relinquishing such ideation and thereby increase their own and others' safety. Present-day danger requires careful assessment and planning, because positive changes that occur as a result of participating in group therapy (e.g., increased personal assertiveness; new recognition of the difference between healthy and unhealthy relationships) can inadvertently escalate conflicts in relationships outside the group and put the group member at increased risk of harm.

Intense emotional distress and dysregulation also does not automatically rule out group participation. Indeed this is a hallmark of CTSDs. However, participation is contraindicated if the prospective group member has extreme difficulties with rage or dependence that could harm, burden, or trigger intrusive reexperiencing of trauma memories by other group members (Cloitre & Koenen, 2001; Courtois, 2010). Co-occurring substance use disorders and PTSD or CTSDs also do not automatically rule out group therapy if the therapy explicitly addresses the link between those disorders (see Chapter 22) and the group member is receiving clinically indicated recovery supports or treatment (or both).

Trauma survivors with ongoing psychotic, manic, or dissociative symptoms also should not be ruled out if the group therapy has a "focus on improvement of interpersonal functioning . . . [and an] explicit treatment frame with set expectations and boundaries for the participants' actions inside and outside the group (e.g., limitations on discussion of trauma memories in group, no socializing between members outside the group)" (International Society for the Study of Trauma and Dissociation, 2011, p. 150). For example, group therapy has traditionally not been recommended as a primary treatment modality for dissociative identity disorder, especially in heterogeneous groups, because such patients "do poorly in generic therapy groups that include individuals with heterogeneous diagnoses and clinical problems . . . [due to] difficulty tolerating the strong affects elicited by . . . psychotherapy groups of those that encourage discussion, even in a limited way, of participants' traumatic experiences" (p. 149). That said, dissociative adults can be actively engaged in and benefit from group with the provision of education about dissociation and specialized guidelines and ground rules to manage and address it (Courtois, 2010; see also Chapter 6).

Careful selection requires a thorough individual intake interview with prospective group members by the group therapist(s) to ascertain readiness and willingness to participate in the group. In addition to assessing personal and treatment history (including ongoing individual treatment, if this is a requirement for group participation), as well as current life circumstances, the intake should include a careful review of the individual's experiences in groups in general and any past experience in group therapy. Potential triggers for severe adverse reactions (e.g., past episodes of acute suicidality, self-harm, aggression, relationship crises, decompensation, or addiction) should be carefully inquired about and discussed in order to determine whether either the planned group process or unplanned disclosures or actions by other group members pose a likely risk of serious destabilization. This is especially important if the group process will include required or optional disclosure and working through of traumatic experiences and memories. The possibility that group interactions could lead to transient but manageable distress should not rule out participation, because such reactions are expectable and their therapeutic resolution in group (with the support of other members as well as the therapist/therapists) is a benefit of group therapy.

Group Formats

Therapy groups differ from drop-in groups, with the latter requiring no preliminary intake assessment and primarily providing information and social support. Therapy group formats differ in whether enrollment is open or closed, with the latter using a "rolling admissions approach," in which new members may join at any session (unless the group has a ceiling for the number of members that has been reached). Closed groups have new members join only at designated starting points, based on the length of a predetermined "cycle" that is the preset number of sessions defined as constituting a full dose of group participation (with some groups offering the option of members repeating more than one "cycle of group sessions, and others limiting participation to one "cycle"). The length of a group therapy cycle varies from a few sessions (e.g., four to eight) for psychoeducational groups to, midrange (e.g., 10–30 sessions) for groups that usually have a specific therapeutic approach and curriculum, to long term (e.g., six to 12 months or open ended, with no fixed limit) for groups that tend to have a psychodynamic, interpersonal, experiential/existential, or feminist focus (see below). Most therapy groups limit the number of members to, at most, nine to 10, in order to permit all members to be actively involved. Most also are gender-specific (based on members' self-identified gender) with either biological and transgender males or females as participants. The duration of each group session also varies, typically 45–120 minutes. The frequency of sessions usually is either once or twice weekly. The group described below was midrange duration (i.e., 16-session cycles), with weekly 90-minute sessions once weekly and open admission, with a maximum of eight members at any time.

Engaging Group Members and Restoring or Sustaining Safety

The first priority for any therapy with trauma survivors is providing a sense of safety and hope, while identifying and proactively dealing with any current threats to their emotional and physical safety. This includes informing members about their rights and responsibilities as group participants, including how they and the group leader(s) will ensure that every member's confidentiality, identity, culture, and physical and emotional safety are respected, and any requirements for attendance, fees, and communication between group leader(s) and members' other therapists or health care providers (see Chapter 4 for a description of these practice management procedures).

Although information about trauma is often included in the brief introduction to the group during a first session, Herman and colleagues (2019) developed a more comprehensive approach for adult survivors of complex trauma. Their "Trauma Information Group" (TIG) has ground rules and basic principles that systematically address the preceding cross-cutting goals 1 to 11 in every group session. While the TIG is designed for adults "in early recovery," it is applicable to the engagement and safety phase of group therapy for any complex trauma survivor. Each TIG session begins with a check-in "about how [he or] she is doing or feels about being in the group session today" (p. 29). Such inquiry can be frightening or confusing for trauma survivors who have been exposed to emotional, physical, or sexual abuse, violence, or victimization when their honest self-disclosure led to retaliation, escalation, humiliation, or punishment. Group leaders therefore treat the check-in as a sensitive matter that helps them both assess and empathically understand members' traumatic stress reactions, while modeling a warm and supportive acceptance of whatever each is able to share—and never as a test or challenge, or as a superficial ritual or a coercive obligation or requirement to "open up" or "tell your story." After check-in, to further highlight the importance given to safety and self-care in the group—and to help group members develop or strengthen the ability to be aware of and regulate their bodies and emotions— many groups include a relaxation exercise based on either progressive muscle relaxation and breathing or basic yoga movements designed to gently enhance body awareness and a sense of calm.

Psychoeducation

Learning is an integral part of group therapy for PTSD and CTSDs. Although different group therapy models each have their own distinct ways of describing core concepts, the themes identified earlier represent the key psychoeducation topics across all complex trauma treatment models. Group leaders highlight key concepts and debunk common misconceptions in order to provide a foundation for hope and to reduce group members' sense of shame, stigma, and powerlessness. When conducted in a conversational manner that encourages discussion among group members as peer teachers and commentators rather than in a didactic teaching style, psychoeducation not only informs but also engages and empowers members by bringing concepts related to trauma and recovery in line with their personal knowledge and experiences. In each TIG session, members discuss, and apply to their own lives, one of the core trauma recovery themes, with the psychoeducation facilitated by handouts that summarize key points and pose self-reflection questions that elicit thoughtful introspection and personal sharing.

A closing individual check-out concludes each session, encouraging members to consider how to transfer what they learned in session to their daily lives. Here, group members' input is of particular importance, because feedback and modeling by peers is often of as much, if not more, value than that from leaders or informational handouts. The closing check-out also is designed to reinforce each member's sense of being appreciated and supported as a valued individual and contributor, and provides a check on immediate emotional and physical/relational safety (and an opportunity for leaders to intervene with immediate access to resources if anyone is unsafe).

Ground Rules

Another universal feature of group therapy for PTSD or CTSDs is a set of ground rules designed to ensure that every participant is safe (emotionally, as well as physically), respected, able to freely choose when and how to participate and self-disclose, and valued for their unique personal characteristics, history, strengths, and abilities. Ground rules are treated by the leaders as more than a formality or common courtesy: For members, being able to articulate and be supported by guidelines for how every person will treat and be treated by others is deeply meaningful, as it signifies that the abuse and other mistreatment they experienced are recognized as wrong and harmful and will be challenged if they occur in group. Ground rules typically are generated initially by either leaders or group members who are helped by the leaders to articulate the practical "dos and don'ts" that they require to feel safe, supported, and able to disclose more about themselves and their often painful experiences and emotions. Ground rules vary from group to group but usually include mutual respect, privacy and confidentiality, personal boundaries (e.g., setting limits on out-of-group contact, including personal, romantic/sexual, or business relationships; the sharing of phone numbers and e-mail addresses and whether contact between sessions is allowed; physical touching and personal space; and what each group member is willing to disclose), expectations for participation (e.g., regularity and timeliness of attendance, sharing the floor and permission to be a silent observer), and how disagreements or conflict will be handled. Ground rules are revisited at the start of each group session, and often are referred to during group interactions in order to underscore the commitment all members have made to ensuring that the group is safe, respectful, and empowering for all.

Stabilization

Present-focused therapeutic interventions focused on safety, engagement and psychoeducation can serve as a means of emotionally and behaviorally "stabilizing" dysregulated complex trauma survivors (Dorrepaal et al., 2012). As a counterpoint, some have argued that stabilization is unnecessary in therapy for complex trauma survivors and only serves to delay the delivery of the "active ingredients" of trauma-focused therapy—TMP and cognitive restructuring (CR) (De Jongh et al., 2016). However, when clients' PTSD or CTSD symptoms include severe problems with affective or interpersonal dysregulation, risky or impulsive behaviors, self-harm, suicidality, dissociative or psychotic crises, or ongoing revictimization, *stabilization is a necessity, not an option*: It is ethically and clinically essential in those circumstances that the group therapy includes careful monitoring of safety and proactive intervention to ensure that at-risk clients are engaged in treatment and equipped with the self-regulation skills necessary to have sufficient emotional and relational stability to effectively prevent or recover from serious harm in the group sessions as well as in their day-to-day lives.

Indeed, group therapy for complex trauma survivors has been found to be relatively ineffective when group members destabilize the group interaction with unmitigated conflict or extreme expressions of emotion dysregulation (Cloitre & Koenen, 2001). Initial selection procedures designed to identify prospective members who are at risk for extreme emotion dysregulation are important to minimize such occurrences, but when they occur, it is incumbent on group leaders to interact calmly but firmly to assist the dysregulated group member in regaining a modulated emotion state and to attend to all other members who are likely to be experiencing distress either vicariously as a sympathetic reaction, or directly if they have been challenged or verbally aggressed against by the dysregulated group member. In some cases, a time-out is called for, in which the dysregulated member steps out (usually with a group leader) to restabilize. The group leader explains to all group members that the time-out is done with the understanding that the group member will return to the group as soon as they feel able to work through the conflict in a thoughtful manner with the support of the leader and the entire group. This is done to prevent the dysregulated group member and all other group members (those indirectly, as well as directly, affected) from experiencing the incident as a repetition of past emotional or physical violence they may have experienced, and also to prevent an abrupt leave-taking by the dysregulated member from replicating their—or other group members'—past experiences of traumatic emotional cutoffs and rejection or abandonment.

Extreme dissociative states can precipitate similar crises in group therapy. Therapeutic crises that put the client's safety at risk (e.g., suicidality, impulsive, reckless or addictive behavior, revictimization) and potentially compromise the therapeutic alliance (e.g., severe dissociative episodes, explosive affective discharges) are not the norm for persons with CTSDs, but they can occur, especially in members diagnosed with dissociative identity disorder (Ford, 2017a; Ford & Courtois, 2014). However, when the CTSD-related dysregulation triggers or precipitates a crisis, timely deescalation and stabilization are essential. Therapeutic interventions that develop or strengthen mindfulness and affect regulation skills are useful for the amelioration of such crises (Ford, 2017b). Specific therapist skills for preventing and deescalating dissociative crises in group therapy include (Ford, Fallot, & Harris, 2009, p. 422):

> (1) knowing how to identify subtle, as well as obvious, instances of dissociative alterations in personality and awareness [see Chapter 6]; (2) skill in "grounding" participants when they or other group members are significantly dissociating (e.g., sensorimotor strategies [see Chapters 24–26]); and (3) the ability to "gently confront" dissociative defenses . . . and acknowledge rather than challenge dissociated parts of the self if these structural splits emerge (e.g., in the form of dissociative flashbacks or intrusive memories, as well as in more obvious [e.g., dissociative identity disorder "alters"] shifts in self-state [see Chapter 6]. . . .

Resilience Building

For many group therapy clients with PTSD or CTSDs, extreme crises are not an imminent concern, as many are able to cope resiliently, even despite severe symptoms, without formal stabilization intervention. In that case, psychoeducation and present-centered experiential/skills-focused interventions in group therapy can play a vital role by providing opportunities to learn, observe, and practice self-regulation and interpersonal skills that are alternatives to coping based on PTSD/CTSD-related avoidance, hypervigilance, hyper- or hypoarousal, or dissociation (Ford, 2017b). In contrast to dyadic psychotherapy or psychopharmacology, group therapy is inherently relational and interpersonal, providing not only a safe space for developing supportive relationships but also a laboratory in which each group member does not just imagine or talk about, but also empirically experiments with, ways of thinking, feeling, and interacting that are adaptive alternatives to PTSD- and CTSD-related symptoms (Johnson & Lubin, 2008; Mendelsohn et al., 2011).

Trauma Memory Processing

Psychoeducation, experiential activities, and associated peer-to-peer interaction in group therapy for PTSD and CTSDs also provide a valuable foundation for group sessions focused on trauma processing. TMP may be done using a CBT approach, as an intensive first-person or narrative retelling of a specific trauma memory, with or without cognitive restructuring (Ready, Vega, Worley, & Bradley, 2012). Alternatively, TMP may be done in a relational and testimonial manner, in which a group member discloses the trauma and describes its past and current impact on their life, including their emotions, self-concept, relationships, achievements, self-defined failures or disappointments, ability to function, health status, addictions, self-harm or suicidal crises, spirituality, and view of the future (Mendelsohn et al., 2011). Even when group therapy does not explicitly engage clients in formal TMP, these trauma-focused interventions can be woven into educational, skills-building, experiential, or peer support activities that ostensibly are purely present-centered. Trauma survivors consistently affirm the importance of being able to find "their voice" and tell their "story" in a respectful and validating peer group, as a source of both greater internal clarity, hope, and empowerment, and belongingness and worthiness to be accepted by other people (Fallot & Harris, 2002; Mendelsohn et al., 2011). As complex trauma survivors disclose currently troubling symptoms or describe troubling current or past events in group interaction, they often (and typically with, at most, partial awareness) are also recalling and even reliving past traumatic experiences. With skillful guidance from attuned group leaders, the group member who is processing trauma memories can reflect on the parallels between the current distress or challenge that they are describing and the psychophysiological reactions they are experiencing as they disclosed to the group, and the distress and reactions they experienced in past traumatic events. In this respect, the present-focused interactions in group therapy can serve as an opportunity for *in vivo* TMP and CR (Ford, 2018). The case vignette illustrates how *in vivo* TMP and CR can be done in present-focused group therapy with complex trauma survivors.

Therapeutic Approach

Group therapy may have an interpretive psychodynamic focus (Ogrodniczuk, Sochting, Piggott, & Piper, 2009) in which the leader helps members recognize and develop more authentic and self-affirming ways of handling core conflictual relationship themes (Leibovich, Nof, Auerbach-Barber, & Zilcha-Mano, 2018) . However, confrontational tactics in which group members are aggressively challenged to "face up to" psychic defenses such as denial, projection, suppression, rationalization, avoidance, and minimization, are not recommended due to the potential to replicate past abusive relational dynamics of devaluation and shaming. If a more empathic and supportive interpretive approach is used, however, it is important to note that group members without strong extragroup support systems or with limited emotion regulation abilities and self-efficacy may not benefit and may react adversely (Ogrodniczuk et al., 2009).

More typically, group therapies for CTSDs take a supportive relational approach in which group members are provided with validation for their feelings, assistance in reflecting on and reframing thoughts and beliefs (e.g., schemas about self and others), and in developing interpersonal skills and behavioral and relational choices that affirm their core values and do not reenact traumatic victimization or losses (Mendelsohn et al., 2011). Supportive group therapies for complex trauma survivors also may include CBT components such as cognitive restructuring, problem-solving skills, and behavioral activation (Johnson & Lubin, 2008). TMP also may be done if members are encouraged to share only as much as they feel ready to recall and disclose, and with careful attention by the therapist to helping members who have strong (and often subtle or disguised) reactions when listening to another member's trauma memory (Mendelsohn et al., 2011).

Expectable Group Dynamics

CTSDs develop in the context of traumatic experiences that often involve extremely adverse and toxic interpersonal dynamics—and those dynamics often are inadvertently elicited and reenacted in group therapy interactions. Group leaders are imbued with a status of (parental or other authority) that can trigger trust and control-related transference reactions by group members, such as suspiciousness, fear of punishment or exploitation, projective identification of hostility or dependency, or oppositionality and defiance. The group leader also is a caregiver, and this can elicit attachment-related transference reactions from group members (e.g., dependence, insecurity, and ambivalent alternation between idealization and detachment; expectancy of betrayal, abandonment, or exploitation; or projective identification of devaluation and rejection (Courtois, 2010). As described by Ford et al. (2009, p. 424), such emotionally and behaviorally extreme member–leader dynamics are "likely to be especially true for those participants who also long to be rescue by idealized, powerful individuals and relieved of the burden of responsibility of having been placed in parentified role in relationship to caregivers and other victims (e.g., their siblings), or those who never expect consistent support from others." These reenactments can include extreme states of dissociation (e.g., flashbacks, regression) and emotional numbing or explosiveness on the part of group member(s) who are triggered by their own memories or vicariously by the dysregulation of another group member. As a result, these complex trauma-related group dynamics can lead group members to play out their own, or other members' (or both), traumatic or other profoundly invalidating experiences in a potentially iatrogenic manner.

Therapeutic prevention of such wildfires or avalanches of trauma-related interpersonal dynamics in group therapy begins with careful monitoring of group members' often subtle early warning signs of reexperiencing, physical and emotional detachment, or dissociation. Early identification of potentially problematic reenactments also is facilitated by keeping in mind each individual member's unique complex trauma history and the traumagenic dynamics (Finkelhor & Browne, 1985) that were involved. When group members shift their physical or psychological state in ways that are consistent with reexperiencing their own traumagenic dynamics or becoming caught up in those of other members, group leaders supportively, nonjudgmentally, and empathically (Elliott, Bohart, Watson, & Murphy, 2018) acknowledge the relational difficulties that members are working through. This provides an opportunity for all of the group members to shift from reacting defensively to reflecting and reappraising the dynamics in the new context of a safe and supportive group and of their own personal growth and resources.

When trauma-related reenactments occur unexpectedly or escalate rapidly, the redirection, deescalation, and grounding interventions described earlier can restore the group members' present-focused awareness and sense of safety and security. It is important for leaders to rapidly assess and therapeutically intervene with every group member, and not just with those who are most obviously dysregulated. Members who appear relatively unaffected may be highly affected but either intentionally or involuntarily experiencing avoidant, detached, dissociative adaptations consistent with how they survived complex trauma in the past. Even if group members are able to cope and modulate their reactions to other members' reenactment of traumatic interpersonal dynamics, it is important for them—and for the entire group—that the therapist clearly communicate the equal value of every member, and no member's safety and well-being is overlooked simply because they are not the "squeaky wheel." For many complex trauma survivors, being resilient in the face of adversity led to either neglect or parentification, and group therapy is an opportunity to acknowledge and correct that tragic misalignment.

Finally, the group leader typically is emotionally impacted as well by group dynamics. In addition to the potentially distressing impact of being the focus of members' intense (positive or negative) transference reactions, the traumatic origins or associations of those group dynamics can lead to strong secondary traumatic stress reactions by group leaders (Sprang, Ford, Kerig, & Bride, 2018). That combination, in turn, can lead to countertransference reactions on the part of the group leader that must be managed (Hayes, Gelso, Goldberg, & Kivlighan, 2018) with awareness and emotional modulation, in order to maintain a consistent therapeutic stance of empathy and a reflective awareness of the nature of the group members' intra- and interpersonal dynamics. The affect regulation and mindfulness skills that are integral to many approaches to group therapy for CTSDs are essential for the therapist to practice as well.

Research Evidence on Outcomes of Group Therapy for Traumatic Stress Disorders

A meta-analysis of 16 randomized clinical trials (RCTs) of group therapy with adults with trauma histories who were diagnosed with PTSD found evidence of greater improvement in PTSD and related symptoms following group therapy than for wait-list controls, but no evidence that trauma-focused group therapy had superior outcomes when compared to alternative active treatments (Sloan, Feinstein, Gallagher, Beck, & Keane, 2013). Seven of the studies included TMP, and nine did not. Dropout rates were slightly lower for non-TMP than for TMP group therapies (i.e., 0–47%, median 25% vs. 0–52%, median = 34%). Improvement in PTSD symptoms was somewhat greater for non-TMP than for TMP group therapies when compared to wait list (i.e., $d = 0.58$–0.91 vs. 0.31–0.69), but TMP group therapies were slightly more efficacious than non-TMP group therapies when compared to an active control treatment (i.e., median $d = 0.14$ vs. 0.04). Although complex trauma history and CTSD symptoms were not formally assessed in those studies, the outcomes were more favorable when participants predominantly had single-incident or adulthood-only trauma histories and less positive when participants had histories of childhood sexual abuse or military combat trauma.

A more recent meta-analysis identified 36 RCTs of group therapy for CTSD, 10 studies with TMP group therapies, and 26 with trauma-focused group therapies that did not involve TMP (Mahoney, Karatzias, & Hutton, 2018). Participants were predominantly adult women with histories of childhood abuse or intimate partner violence. Similar to the findings of the Sloan et al. (2013) meta-analysis, trauma-focused group therapies achieved greater improvements in PTSD symptoms than did wait-list control conditions or treatment as usual (TAU) but were not superior to active non-trauma-focused group therapies. The trauma-focused group therapies had comparable benefits in improving PTSD and dissociation symptoms, regardless of whether TMP was included. However, trauma-focused group therapy yielded the best outcomes for depression and psychological distress if TMP was *not* included. Thus, psychoeducation and skills for affect and interpersonal regulation may be of particular value in group therapy for adults with CTSDs (Mahoney et al., 2018, p. 317), consistent with findings for the full range of therapeutic interventions for individuals with complex trauma histories (Ford, 2017a, 2017b).

Group Therapy for Survivors of Childhood Sexual Abuse

More than 20 studies have evaluated variants of group therapy with women survivors of childhood sexual abuse (CSA). Four studies included both individual and group therapy. A 10-session relationally focused supportive therapy was associated with reductions in PTSD, general psychiatric, and dissociative symptoms, and improvement in global functioning, when delivered either in a group or one-to-one format. However, half of the women sought additional treatment during 12-month posttreatment follow-up, which suggests the need for a longer or alternative therapeutic approach (Stalker & Fry, 1999). An adaptation of the cognitive processing therapy approach to TMP for CSA that combined 17 group therapy sessions and 10 one-to-one therapy sessions resulted in greater reductions in PTSD symptoms and a 93% recovery rate among treatment completers (vs. no change on average and a 26% recovery rate for the wait list) (Chard, 2005). Dropout rate was low in the combined group and one-to-one therapy (i.e., 17%).

The latter findings are consistent with preliminary evidence that a 12-session (Sutherland et al., 2012) or 16-session (Ready et al., 2008) group therapy that combined the prolonged exposure approach to TMP with stress management skills was well accepted (with 0–3% dropouts) and associated with large reductions in PTSD symptoms when tested with male military veterans. An earlier study with male military veterans had found no incremental benefit when group therapy utilizing prolonged exposure was compared to an interpersonal skills group therapy that did not include TMP, and a higher dropout rate in the prolonged exposure group therapy condition (Schnurr et al., 2003). A study with women CSA survivors directly compared 24 sessions of a "present-focused" affect/interpersonal skills group versus a "trauma-focused" group utilizing an approach to TMP that combined prolonged exposure and narrative processing (Classen et al., 2011). Dropout rates were comparable for both group therapies and for a treatment-as-usual cohort provided with an individual case manager (i.e., 22–24%). Compared to case management, the group therapies resulted in greater reductions in PTSD, depression, and CTSD symptoms (i.e., dissociation symptoms; blame or vindictiveness toward abuse perpetrators; interpersonal, sexual, and self/identity problems) but no incremental benefit in HIV risk behaviors (which improved in all cohorts). The present-focused group was more effective than the TMP group in reducing HIV risk behaviors, but the TMP group yielded greater reductions in anger. Overall, these findings suggest that TMP can be safely and potentially beneficially conducted in group therapy with women or men with severe PTSD due to CSA. However, cognitive processing, stress management, and affect/interpersonal regulation skills may provide a viable alternative approach, or a stabilizing addition to TMP, when CTSD symptoms are a focus of therapy.

Two other studies tested group therapies explicitly designed to address CTSD symptoms along with adjunctive one-to-one TAU. The therapies were similar to the present-focused intervention tested by Classen et al. (2011), including an extensive array of stabilizing and affect/interpersonal self-regulation skills. A 15-session affect management group combined with TAU (one-to-one therapy and pharmacotherapy) resulted in greater reductions in PTSD and dissociative symptoms and more than twice the rate of recovery among treatment completers (87% vs. 41%) than TAU with no group therapy (Zlotnick et al., 1997). A 20-session group therapy that taught affect regulation, cognitive reappraisal, anger management, body/sexual awareness, and interpersonal skills, when combined with TAU (i.e., one-to-one therapy and medication management), was not clearly superior to TAU alone in reducing PTSD and CTSD symptoms but resulted in twice the recovery rate for PTSD (i.e., 55% vs. 24%) and a 50% greater recovery rate for PCTSD (i.e., 74% vs. 50%) among treatment completers (Dorrepaal et al., 2012). Notably, and in contrast to an earlier report (Cloitre & Koenen, 2001), women diagnosed with borderline personality disorder were more likely to complete group therapy than other participants (i.e., 95% vs. 66%; Dorrepaal et al., 2012). Thus, group therapy focused on self-regulation skills relevant to CTSD symptoms may complement or enhance the benefits of one-to-one therapy for women with CSA histories (see also Chapter 18).

Other studies have evaluated lengthier group therapies for women with CSA histories. A 24-session psychodynamic/interpersonal group therapy resulted in reductions in depression, anxiety, and general psychiatric symptoms, but a small effect size compared to previous group therapy evaluations and no improvement in interpersonal function (Calvert, Kellett, & Hagan, 2015). A long-term (46-session) and short-term (22-session) version of psychodynamic, family systems, and TMP group therapy each were associated with reductions in general psychiatric symptoms and an increased sense of personal coherence (Lundqvist, Svedin, Hansson, & Broman, 2006). A psychodynamic/interpersonal group therapy conducted weekly for 46 weeks and a systemic solution-focused group therapy conducted twice weekly for 34 sessions were associated with comparable improvements at a 1-year follow-up, although the systemic group therapy had evidence of more rapid reductions in general psychiatric symptoms and psychosocial gains (Elkjaer, Kristensen, Mortensen, Poulsen, & Lau, 2014). Whether, and for whom, the more enduring support provided by longer-term group therapies may be beneficial or even necessary to enable women with CSA histories and CTSD symptoms to achieve recovery beyond the 3- to 12-month follow-ups reported in these studies is an important unanswered question.

Group Therapy for Other Subpopulations with Complex Trauma Histories

Women who have experienced intimate partner violence often have histories of abuse or victimization and CTSD symptoms. An eight-session social support group with women in a domestic violence shelter resulted in greater reductions in psychological distress and health care utilization than services as usual (Constantino, Kim, & Crane, 2005). Another study provided eight-session group therapies to women survivors of intimate partner violence who shared a base of psychoeducation and stress, affect, and interpersonal regulation skills, but differed by using prolonged exposure TMP or teaching present-focused communication skills (Crespo & Arinero, 2010). Comparable reductions in PTSD, anxiety, and depression symptoms were maintained at a 12-month follow-up for each group therapy. A third study with women survivors of intimate partner violence, Kelly and Garland (2016) found that an eight-session, trauma-informed mindfulness group therapy was associated with greater reductions in PTSD and depressive symptoms, and anxious and avoidant attachment style than a wait-list control condition. A novel combination of separate group therapy for women survivors of intimate partner violence and their 6- to 12-year-old children with conjoint multifamily group therapy compared goal-oriented and emotion-focused approaches to improving coping skills and relationships in five sessions (McWhirter, 2011). Both group therapies were associated with reductions in depression, alcohol use, and family conflict, and improved social support, with the goal-oriented group showing the strongest effect for reduced family conflict and the emotion-focused group, for social support.

Incarcerated women are frequently complex trauma survivors, including but not limited to CSA. Several group therapy models have been evaluated in prison settings with women complex trauma survivors. Incarcerated women with CSA histories receiving a 16-session affect management skills group (which also included a single session in which memory narratives of childhood sexual abuse were written) reported reductions in CTSD and general psychiatric symptoms—although the gains were no greater than those reported by wait-list controls (Cole, Sarlund-Heinrich, & Brown, 2007). An emotion regulation group therapy that included intensive TMP was associated with improvements in PTSD and depression symptoms, and reduced interpersonal problems compared to TAU—although 45% of the group participants dropped out, compared to 28% of the controls (Bradley & Follingstad, 2003). Two RCTs evaluated group therapies that provided trauma-focused emotion and interpersonal regulation skills but did not include TMP. A group therapy for co-occurring PTSD and substance use disorders (Seeking Safety) in addition to mandatory TAU was associated with reductions in PTSD and general psychiatric symptoms, with the latter continuing to improve over a 6-month follow-up period (Zlotnick, Johnson, & Najavits, 2009). In the second study, a 12-session group therapy using a sequential set of trauma-focused self-regulation skills (Trauma Affect Regulation: Guide for Education and Therapy [TARGET]; see Chapter 18) was compared to a relational-focused group therapy with incarcerated women with complex trauma histories (i.e., abuse and violence exposure in childhood [50–65%] and adulthood [67–82%]). Both therapies were associated with reductions in PTSD, CTSD, dissociative, and general psychiatric symptoms, and improvements in emotion regulation and self-efficacy (Ford, Chang, Levine, & Zhang, 2013). In that study, TARGET resulted in greater increases in forgiveness of perpetrators than the relational group therapy (cf. Classen et al.'s [2011] vindictiveness finding).

Clinical Case Example

This vignette is based on a composite of groups conducted at a university-based outpatient psychiatry clinic for women in recovery from a combination of CSA and emotional abuse/neglect, and adult intimate partner violence.

Group members were diagnosed with PTSD- and CTSD-related problems (i.e., dissociation, depression, emotion dysregulation, bulimia, substance abuse, treatment-refractory medical conditions [e.g., obesity, chronic pain]). Groups meet weekly for 90 minutes, led by a female social worker, psychologist, or psychiatric nurse. Enrollment was done on a rolling basis: New members join as slots open when members feel ready to graduate. The vignette begins as two new members, "C" and "L," join the group.

Early Phase of Group Work: Psychoeducation, Engagement, and Therapeutic Alliance

GROUP LEADER: I'd like to welcome two new members, C. and L. Let's go around and do first-name introductions. . . . Now, could you fill in C and L on the ground rules the group has set in order to make sure that this group is a safe and supportive place for everyone?

S: Yeah, confidentiality, what's said in the group stays in the group, that's number 1.

Y: We treat each other with respect, no bad mouthing or put downs or behind the back.

H: We're here to deal with our trauma, not for small talk or chitchat, to face it and take strength from how we've overcome it, even if it still bites us when triggers happen time to time.

M: But you don't have to share anything private unless you want to. Nothing's required except to pay attention, be a good listener and be supportive— unless you feel ready to share . . .

GROUP LEADER: I think the group also decided that personal boundaries should always be respected.

R: Right, no physical touching except to be supportive *and* you ask first and get a definite OK. And no personal relationships between members, or gossip or secrets, outside of group.

GROUP LEADER: C and L, how do those guidelines sound? Anything you'd add? These ground rules belong to the group—they're created by group members not me, although I fully support them.

L: That's new to me. I'm used to other people making the rules, but I like this better!

Comment

The statement that the group members create and own the ground rules is a way of acknowledging members' autonomy in making their own choices. Note how each group member's choice of and way of describing a rule provides a behavioral sample that can help the leader to recognize and work with each person's unique personality, strengths, and goals.

GROUP LEADER: [After explaining the check-in as an opportunity to share current or past experiences that the members feel are relevant to their recovery and goals for therapy, and facilitating a round-robin check-in, the leader continues orienting new members and supporting all members' therapeutic processing by focusing on members' understand of a core theme for the group.] Since this group is about recovering from trauma, it might be helpful to our new members if we revisit a key question. Let's talk about what the term *trauma* really means.

H: Any kind of abuse. . . . Or getting used by someone like a pimp or a john . . .

R: Stuff that is so awful you never get over it and can never get it out of your mind . . .

Y: Seeing someone murdered or die of an OD [overdose] . . .

S: Times when you're sure you're gonna die, or wish you could just die and end it all . . .

C: I've been through a lot of that, but if that's just your life then is it really trauma?

GROUP LEADER: That's a really important question. If trauma is a threat to your survival or your life as you knew it, or to that of people you care about or know—like abuse or violence or being exploited—does it stop affecting you if it becomes your everyday life and you can't escape?

S: That's what I used to think, you know, that I got so used to trauma happening all the time that it didn't bother me anymore, like whatever, no big deal, just the way it is.

L: So now you just don't care anymore, you give up? I can't see how that's better.

S: No, I *do* care, I never gave up! It's just that I got so I couldn't feel anything anymore. I didn't *want* to feel anything, because it just hurt too much and I couldn't let that make me weak. So what I'm saying, I *thought* nothing bothered me, but then something minor would happen. Like some fool getting in my space when I'm in a store. I would lose it and start beating on them or screaming at them to stop messing with me. I really thought I was a crazy person, because I'd go from ice cold and numbed out to losing it so bad that I could kill them over nothing.

GROUP LEADER: (*noting that as S becomes more animated, other group members are pulling back or starting to become visibly physically activated*) So S, you just described perfectly how having to deal with trauma could put any of us so deep into survival mode that we either shut down and go numb, or escalate and fight back, even when that's not how we really want to live—because it's not really living, it's just surviving—trying to do anything to stop the pain or not be messed with. You couldn't see that, and no one can really see it when they're that deep into trauma—until you find someplace and some people, like in this group, where you can get off the trauma-go-round just enough to be able to see that there's more to your life, and to you, than just surviving.

H: Yeah, that's for sure true for me. I thought I knew the score, but I didn't know nothing except how to run over here or hide over there, and even so I'd still get whacked by my old man just like I got beat by my so-called father, and a stepfather after that, when I was a kid . . .

R: But you kept finding ways to escape. You ran away from your abusive parents and you left that wife beater. You *did* know something, and you were strong enough and smart enough to find what's better, even if you had to go through being an addict while you were getting out.

H: Drugs were my escape, which made me a target for abusers. Drugs helped me survive, but they almost killed me, too. I didn't know it then, but I wanted something better even if I never quite got to it. I wanted peace of mind, and I was like a pit bull who wouldn't let go 'til I got it.

S: It's a good thing you are so stubborn, even if you can bite sometimes when you're holding on to that hope (*smiling and laughing*). You give us old b_____s hope, too!

GROUP LEADER: Maybe that's the flip side of trauma. You do what you have to, to survive, but you don't stop there. You hold on or fight for the hopes that give your life meaning. Doesn't solve every problem or make every dream come true, but living your truth is really living and not just surviving stuck on the trauma treadmill. What is your truth, that thing that makes your life real?

M: I wasn't going to say nothing, if all we're gonna talk about is trauma. But I can relate to truth. The truth I live for is love for my children and my grandchildren. They give me hope. I messed up my own life, but I won't let that happen to them. Their lives are my truth.

C: I never thought loving my children was anything special, but I see that in how you shine when you talk about loving yours. I want that! I lost two children to drugs, so I failed them. What difference does me loving them make if they're dead?

GROUP LEADER: Did they know you loved them when they were alive? (*C nods reluctantly.*) And now you remember them with love, even though it hurts. Keeping love alive in spite of trauma takes a lot of courage and strength. Maybe that makes a difference to others in your life now.

M: It makes a difference to me, knowing that gives me strength to not give up on love.

Y: It does for me, too. I don't have children, but I have parents. They give me strength with their love. Even when we're not getting along, which is usually because of something I did, they love me and believe in me, the way you do for your children. Sometimes I get so mad that I never want to have anything to do with them, but they never give up on me. They are my truth.

L: I wish I had parents, but I never did. Mine gave me up real young. I lived in foster homes and never felt like I belonged—so I kept running away and getting put in juvie. I see now that I was smart, not stupid and stubborn like they said. I didn't have love, so mind was my truth. I saw things for what they are and made stories in my mind that gave me something to live for. Now I write stories for kids and young adults, and when I read to them I see their eyes light up.

H: I never knew you were a writer, too! Stories like you write, that's what gave me hope growing up. I lived for the books that took me away from my miserable real life. Thank you.

GROUP LEADER: Going through trauma is not just about surviving, it's also about keeping your hopes alive, even though trauma can seem to kill those hopes. So, facing the memories of trauma, which each of you is doing in your own individual way, is not being stuck in survival mode. It's how you look in the mirror and see that you're more than just a survivor—you're living your truth. You can see how other members of the group have been courageous and strong, and kept their hopes alive by living their truth, but look around you and see how they see that in you, too. You empower others to do the same and they empower you, if you let them.

Comment

This section illustrates a therapeutic transition from recalling and describing the survival adaptations that had become second nature during prolonged or repeated exposure to complex interpersonal traumas, to reflecting on their capacity to shift out of survival mode by recognizing the hopes and truth that makes it possible to envision a life that has meaning. While the hopes may be unfulfilled or hard to sustain, they are not mere fantasies of a trauma-free life, but instead are a statement of what group members were—and still are—striving to achieve or experience that affirm their integrity and worth in spite of their traumas and disappointments. This shift involves facing the reality of trauma, while also validating the ability to persevere in the quest to find the meaning and purpose in their lives that ultimately provides a sense of peace.

Survivors of complex trauma often feel unable to feel self-compassion due to experiences in which they were blamed or shamed (e.g., emotional abuse), betrayed or exploited, or blamed themselves for having harmed or failed to protect others (e.g., moral injury) (Au et al., 2017). The interpersonal dynamics in group therapy can elicit intense reexperiencing and reenactment of those complex relational dilemmas (Grossmark, 2007). As the following session transcript illustrates, managing such reenactments can be necessary not only when a group engages in formal trauma memory processing but also when spontaneous trauma memory reexperiencing occurs. Managing reenactments

is crucial to maintaining emotional safety and for therapeutic trauma processing by all group members, including those who are observers.

GROUP LEADER: How is the theme of today's session, self-compassion, relevant
in your lives?

L: I didn't know you could have compassion for yourself, and that it's not the
same as self-pity. I hate it when anyone comes across as "poor me," but I
secretly did that all the time.

R: Self-compassion is just basic human kindness, not whining or self-pity.

L: I get that now, but I never got that—or saw anyone get it, actually—growing
up.

M: It's safer to blame yourself than to be compassionate. Any sign of self-
compassion and my husband would laugh at me and humiliate me. But
if I beat myself up, then he leaves me alone, because I've done the job for
him. Self-compassion sounds great, but it gets you hurt.

S: You sound just like my mother. My father would fly into a rage at the slight-
est thing. She'd just look away and pretend nothing was happening. Worse
yet, she'd apologize and agree with him just to placate him. When my ex
put me down, I stood up to him, even if it meant going toe-to-toe and
taking a beating—which often happened. I refuse to be a passive victim
like you!

M: I guess I'm not strong like you. I get scared and give in. You're right, I'm
a mess.

C: That's not right. Being scared and doing what you have to do to survive
doesn't mean you're giving in or that you're a mess. I remember how you
talked about loving your children and how you've dedicated yourself to
making their lives safe and successful. That's strength, not fighting with
an abuser. It takes strength to pick your fights, that's smart not passive.

GROUP LEADER: I appreciate how you're reminding M, and all of us, that feeling scared and doing what's necessary to survive, takes strength, C. And
that you're not just surviving as a passive victim, M, you're living your
truth by dedicating yourself to your love for your children. That's a way of
standing up for yourself, and standing up against anyone who is abusive,
without getting caught in the trap that abusers set by picking fights and
being disrespectful. You hold your head high and don't get dragged down
to that level. That can be scary but it keeps you true to yourself. And that's
the key to self-compassion, being true to yourself and your deepest values,
so you can show yourself the respect and human kindness, as R said, that
you deserve.

S, I hear that you felt you had to stand up for yourself, and that you
had the courage to do it even if it was dangerous, but I think you weren't
looking for a fight—that's what your father and your ex were looking for.
And that like your mother, you refused to sink to that level. She did it in

her way and you did it in your way. At the time, that probably seemed like she was giving up and not protecting herself, or you. But maybe we could look at whether she might have been *actively* doing what M is describing, protecting you out of love and showing you a different way of standing up to an abuser, with kindness and nonviolence. Maybe that's not true, but I think you've said in past sessions that you got your strength from your mother—you called it being "stubborn," but I think you meant strength—and not from angry people like your father.

S: I think you're giving my mother, and me, too much credit. You always find a way to be kind and turn everything around to be supportive, Doc. I can't do that, I just get angry and say stuff that I think I mean at the time, but it comes out harsh and not kind like you.

GROUP LEADER: For a person who sees herself as just an angry survivor, you have a keen eye for kindness, S. In my experience, a person has to have a true inner kindness, and a lot of strength, to recognize and appreciate kindness in someone else. But you can hide that kindness if you want, although I don't think you're hiding it very well from the group right now. And watch out, (*smiles gently*) you might just be having a kindness moment and apologizing to M for being a bit harsh and forgetting how strong she is with her ability to love those who she cares for.

Comment

A profound sense of abandonment by a passive mother and betrayal by an abusive father, then by a violent husband can be seen in S's reaction to M as being "a passive victim." In psychodynamic terms, S was identifying with an aggressor (her father and ex-husband), projecting her sense of powerless submission onto M, and idealizing the group leader as the exemplar of kindness and authority. Such intense and chaotic transference reenactments can derail the classic progression of group process by introducing a threat to the emotional safety and mutual respect (Courtois, 2010; Cloitre & Koenen, 2001). However, when addressed with humility and kindness by the group leader, and a careful reframing that underscores the resilience and wisdom of both directly and indirectly involved group members, reenactments can be opportunities for therapeutic reflection, the restoration of safety and mutual respect, and gradual reparation of deep psychic wounds (Whewell, Lingam, & Childton, 2004).

Conclusion

Although the case vignette illustrated a therapy group for women, many of the highlighted issues and principles also apply to group therapy for men with such histories. For examples of group work with men with complex trauma histories, the TIG manual provides an adaptation for male survivors (Herman et al., 2019, pp. 89–96), and other resources are available (Ford & Stewart, 1999; Friedman, 1994; Masten, Kochman, Hansen, & Sikkema, 2007).

As the composite case transcript illustrates, a variety of therapeutic approaches can be integrated seamlessly in group therapy for CTSDs. There is no inherent contradiction between cognitive-behavioral, interpersonal, affect regulation, psychodynamic, mindfulness, experiential, or other therapeutic models when they are used in response to the historical (e.g., complex trauma and traumagenic dynamics) or current (e.g., relational or self-esteem difficulties) concerns and goals expressed by group therapy participants. TMP is an essential focus for group leaders whether formal TMP is conducted or it is in response to spontaneous disclosures or reenactments of trauma memories by group members. When trauma processing occurs, by prescription or spontaneously, core psychoeducational concepts and emotion regulation and communication skills provide a framework for the therapist to use to balance encouraging nonavoidant experiencing with reframing to support members' self-compassion and recognition of their deeper values and personal strengths. The group context extends these therapeutic processes into the relational realm by embedding them in peer-to-peer interactions in which conflict and reenactments can occur but, unlike traumatic experiences, ruptures are repaired, respect and trust are restored. Thus, group therapy can provide adults with complex trauma histories a unique, firsthand experience of gaining mastery of the memories and symptoms that have caused them great pain and impairment, while simultaneously being able both to give and receive compassion and recognition of personal worth, and resilience in relationships that are grounded in honesty, mutual respect, shared responsibility, and healthy boundaries.

References

Au, T. M., Sauer-Zavala, S., King, M. W., Petrocchi, N., Barlow, D. H., & Litz, B. T. (2017). Compassion-based therapy for trauma-related shame and posttraumatic stress: Initial evaluation using a multiple baseline design. *Behavior Therapy, 48*(2), 207–221.

Bradley, R. G., & Follingstad, D. R. (2003). Group therapy for incarcerated women who experienced interpersonal violence: A pilot study. *Journal of Traumatic Stress, 16*(4), 337–340.

Calvert, R., Kellett, S., & Hagan, T. (2015). Group cognitive analytic therapy for female survivors of childhood sexual abuse. *British Journal of Clinical Psychology, 54*(4), 391–413.

Chard, K. M. (2005). An evaluation of cognitive processing therapy for the treatment of posttraumatic stress disorder related to childhood sexual abuse. *Journal of Consulting Clinical Psychology, 73*(5), 965–971.

Classen, C., Palesh, O. G., Cavanaugh, C., Koopman, C., Kaupp, J., Kraemer, H., . . . Spiegel, D. (2011). A comparison of trauma-focused and present-focused group therapy for survivors of childhood sexual abuse: A randomized controlled trial. *Psychological Trauma, 3*, 84–93.

Cloitre, M., & Koenen, K. C. (2001). The impact of borderline personality disorder on process group outcome among women with posttraumatic stress disorder related to childhood abuse. *International Journal of Group Psychotherapy, 51*(3), 379–398.

Cole, K. L., Sarlund-Heinrich, P., & Brown, L. (2007). Developing and assessing effectiveness of a time-limited therapy group for incarcerated women survivors of childhood sexual abuse. *Journal of Trauma and Dissociation, 8*(2), 97–121.

Constantino, R., Kim, Y., & Crane, P. A. (2005). Effects of a social support intervention on health outcomes in residents of a domestic violence shelter: A pilot study. *Issues in Mental Health Nursing, 26*(6), 575–590.

Courtois, C. A. (2010). *Healing the incest wound* (2nd ed.). New York: Norton.

Crespo, M., & Arinero, M. (2010). Assessment of the efficacy of a psychological treatment for women victims of violence by their intimate male partner. *Spanish Journal of Psychology, 13*(2), 849–863.

De Jongh, A., Resick, P. A., Zoellner, L. A., van Minnen, A., Lee, C. W., Monson, C. M., . . . Bicanic, I. A. (2016). Critical analysis of the current treatment guidelines for complex PTSD in adults. *Depression and Anxiety, 33*(5), 359–369.

Dorrepaal, E., Thomaes, K., Smit, J. H., van Balkom, A. J., Veltman, D. J., Hoogendoorn, A. W., & Draijer, N. (2012). Stabilizing group treatment for complex posttraumatic stress disorder related to child abuse based on psychoeducation and cognitive behavioural therapy: A multisite randomized controlled trial. *Psychotherapy and Psychosomatics, 81*(4), 217–225.

Elkjaer, H., Kristensen, E., Mortensen, E. L., Poulsen, S., & Lau, M. (2014). Analytic versus systemic group therapy for women with a history of child sexual abuse: 1-year follow-up of a randomized controlled trial. *Psychology and Psychotherapy, 87*(2), 191–208.

Elliott, R., Bohart, A. C., Watson, J. C., & Murphy, D. (2018). Therapist empathy and client outcome: An updated meta-analysis. *Psychotherapy, 55*(4), 399–410.

Fallot, R. D., & Harris, M. (2002). The Trauma Recovery and Empowerment Model (TREM): Conceptual and practical issues in a group intervention for women. *Community Mental Health Journal, 38*(6), 475–485.

Finkelhor, D., & Browne, A. (1985). The traumatic impact of child sexual abuse: A conceptualization. *American Journal of Orthopsychiatry, 55*(4), 530–541.

Ford, J. D. (2017a). Complex trauma and complex PTSD. In J. Cook, S. Gold, & C. Dalenberg (Eds.), *Handbook of trauma psychology* (Vol. 1, pp. 322–349). Washington, DC: American Psychological Association.

Ford, J. D. (2017b). Emotion regulation and skills-based interventions. In J. Cook, S. Gold, & C. Dalenberg (Eds.), *Handbook of trauma psychology* (Vol. 2, pp. 227–252). Washington, DC: American Psychological Association.

Ford, J. D. (2018). Trauma memory processing in PTSD psychotherapy: A unifying framework. *Journal of Traumatic Stress, 31,* 933–942.

Ford, J. D., Chang, R., Levine, J., & Zhang, W. (2013). Randomized clinical trial comparing affect regulation and supportive group therapies for victimization-related PTSD with incarcerated women. *Behavior Therapy, 44*(2), 262–276.

Ford, J. D., & Courtois, C. A. (2014, July 9). Complex PTSD, affect dysregulation, and borderline personality disorder. *Borderline Personality Disorder and Emotion Dysregulation, 1.* [Epub ahead of print]

Ford, J. D., Fallot, R., & Harris, M. (2009). Group therapy. In C. A. Courtois & J. D. Ford (Eds.), *Treating complex traumatic stress disorders: An evidence-based guide* (pp. 415–440). New York: Guilford Press.

Ford, J. D., & Stewart, J. (1999). Group psychotherapy for war-related PTSD with military veterans. In B. H. Young & D. D. Blake (Eds.), *Approaches to group psychotherapy with PTSD* (pp. 75–100). San Francisco: Taylor & Francis.

Friedman, R. M. (1994). Psychodynamic group therapy for male survivors of sexual abuse. *Group, 18*(4), 225–234.

Grossmark, R. (2008). The edge of chaos: Enactment, disruption, and emergence in group psychotherapy. *Psychoanalytic Dialogues, 17*(4), 479–499.

Harvey, M. (1996). An ecological view of psychological trauma and trauma recovery. *Journal of Traumatic Stress, 9,* 3–23.

Hayes, J. A., Gelso, C. J., Goldberg, S., & Kivlighan, D. M. (2018). Countertransference management and effective psychotherapy: Meta-analytic findings. *Psychotherapy, 55*(4), 496–507.

Herman, J. L., Kallivayalil, D., & Members of the Victims of Violence Program. (2019). *Group trauma treatment in early recovery: Promoting safety and self-care.* New York: Guilford Press.

International Society for the Study of Trauma and Dissociation. (2011). Guidelines for treating dissociative identity disorder in adults. *Journal of Trauma and Dissociation, 12*(2), 115–187.

Johnson, D. R., & Lubin, H. (2008). *Trauma-centered group psychotherapy for women: A clinician's manual.* New York: Routledge.

Kelly, A., & Garland, E. L. (2016). Trauma-informed mindfulness-based stress reduction for female survivors of interpersonal violence: Results from a Stage I RCT. *Journal of Clinical Psychology, 72*(4), 311–328.

Leibovich, L., Nof, A., Auerbach-Barber, S., & Zilcha-Mano, S. (2018). A practical clinical suggestion for strengthening the alliance based on a supportive-expressive framework. *Psychotherapy, 55*(3), 231–240.

Lundqvist, G., Svedin, C. G., Hansson, K., & Broman, I. (2006). Group therapy for women sexually abused as children: Mental health before and after group therapy. *Journal of Interpersonal Violence, 21*(12), 1665–1677.

Mahoney, A., Karatzias, T., & Hutton, P. (2018). A systematic review and meta-analysis of group treatments for adults with symptoms associated with complex post-traumatic stress disorder. *Journal of Affective Disorders, 243*, 305–321.

Masten, J., Kochman, A., Hansen, N. B., & Sikkema, K. J. (2007). A short-term group treatment model for gay male survivors of childhood sexual abuse living with HIV/AIDS. *International Journal of Group Psychotherapy, 57*(4), 475–496.

McWhirter, P. T. (2011). Differential therapeutic outcomes of community-based group interventions for women and children exposed to intimate partner violence. *Journal of Interpersonal Violence, 26*(12), 2457–2482.

Mendelsohn, M., Herman, J. L., Schatzow, E., Coco, M., Kallivayalil, D., & Levitan, J. (2011). *The trauma recovery group: A guide for practitioners.* New York: Guilford Press.

Ogrodniczuk, J. S., Sochting, I., Piggott, N., & Piper, W. E. (2009). Integrated group therapy for a heterogeneous outpatient sample. *Journal of Nervous and Mental Disease, 197*(11), 862–864.

Ready, D. J., Thomas, K. R., Worley, V., Backscheider, A. G., Harvey, L. A., Baltzell, D., & Rothbaum, B. O. (2008). A field test of group based exposure therapy with 102 veterans with war-related posttraumatic stress disorder. *Journal of Traumatic Stress, 21*(2), 150–157.

Ready, D. J., Vega, E. M., Worley, V., & Bradley, B. (2012). Combining group-based exposure therapy with prolonged exposure to treat U.S. Vietnam veterans with PTSD: A case study. *Journal of Traumatic Stress, 25*(5), 574–577.

Schnurr, P. P., Friedman, M. J., Foy, D. W., Shea, M. T., Hsieh, F. Y., Lavori, P. W., . . . Bernardy, N. C. (2003). Randomized trial of trauma-focused group therapy for posttraumatic stress disorder: Results from a department of veterans affairs cooperative study. *Archives of General Psychiatry, 60*(5), 481–489.

Sloan, D. M., Feinstein, B. A., Gallagher, M. W., Beck, J. G., & Keane, T. M. (2013). Efficacy of group treatment for posttraumatic stress disorder symptoms: A meta-analysis. *Psychological Trauma, 5*(2), 176–183.

Sprang, G., Ford, J. D., Kerig, P. K., & Bride, B. (2018). Defining secondary traumatic stress and developing targeted assessments and interventions: Lessons learned from research and leading experts. *Traumatology, 25*(2), 72–81.

Stalker, C. A., & Fry, R. (1999). A comparison of short-term group and individual therapy for sexually abused women. *Canadian Journal of Psychiatry, 44*(2), 168–174.

Sutherland, R. J., Mott, J. M., Lanier, S. H., Williams, W., Ready, D. J., & Teng, E. J. (2012). A pilot study of a 12-week model of group-based exposure therapy for veterans with PTSD. *Journal of Traumatic Stress, 25*(2), 150–156.

Whewell, P., Lingam, R., & Childton, R. (2004). Reflective borderline group therapy: The patient's experience of being borderline. *Psychoanalytic Psychotherapy, 18,* 324–345.

Zlotnick, C., Johnson, J., & Najavits, L. M. (2009). Randomized controlled pilot study of cognitive-behavioral therapy in a sample of incarcerated women with substance use disorder and PTSD. *Behavior Therapy, 40*(4), 325–336.

Zlotnick, C., Shea, T. M., Rosen, K., Simpson, E., Mulrenin, K., Begin, A., & Pearlstein, T. (1997). An affect-management group for women with posttraumatic stress disorder and histories of childhood sexual abuse. *Journal of Traumatic Stress, 10*(3), 425–436.

CHAPTER 20

Dual-Trauma Attachment-Based Couple Therapy

PAMELA C. ALEXANDER

A variety of psychotherapy approaches have been developed for couples in which one of the partners has a history of complex trauma (Clulow, 2007; Johnson, 2002, 2004; Miehls & Basham, 2013; Monson & Fredman, 2012). However, little has been written about couples in which *both* partners have such a history, even though dual-trauma couples are both common and seriously troubled. This chapter is focused on the application of emotionally focused therapy (EFT) to dual-trauma couples, with particular emphasis on the incorporation of what is known about disorganized attachment—a body of research that has received less than optimal attention in couple therapy interventions.

Many individuals with a history of complex trauma are fortunate enough to be in a relationship with a supportive partner who does not have his or her own history of trauma. This partner may experience stress, confusion, and even vicarious trauma as a function of living with a survivor who has a history of complex trauma (MacIntosh & Johnson, 2008). However, research on assortative mating finds that survivors of complex trauma are actually more likely to have partners with their own history of abuse and unresolved trauma, even in studies that control for convergence over time (van IJzendoorn & Bakermans-Kranenburg, 1996; Whisman, 2014). Therefore, dual-trauma couples are more prevalent than would be expected by chance.

Partners in dual-trauma couples may experience empathy for each other as a function of similar experiences. Nonetheless, they are also frequently at increased risk for problematic outcomes, including intimate partner violence (IPV) and other significant conflict management difficulties, suggesting that these couples deserve more attention in the clinical literature (Alexander, 2014; Creasey, 2002).

EFT Approaches to Trauma

The most well-known approach to working with couples is EFT (Johnson, 2004), which is an experiential and systemic therapy based on attachment theory. It purports that unmet attachment needs (e.g., closeness and comfort) lead to self-defeating behaviors that result in negative interactional cycles. Typically, one partner's strategy to engage the other (albeit through behaviors perceived by the other partner as criticism) is matched by the other partner's attempt to reduce or avoid conflict (albeit through behaviors perceived by the first partner as stonewalling and withdrawal). Thus, one partner's pursuit leads to the other partner's withdrawal, leading to the first partner's further attempts at pursuit, and so on. The goals of EFT include increasing the couples' awareness of and changing their negative cycle, while helping them establish a secure emotional connection, so that partners become a "secure base" and "safe haven" for each other, using attachment theory terms. The focus is on facilitating and highlighting expressions of vulnerability and longing rather than arriving at solutions to specific problems. Research demonstrates the effectiveness of EFT, with 70–73% of couples treated using EFT recovering from relationship distress and 86–90% experiencing significant increases in relationship satisfaction (Johnson, 2004). Furthermore, the effects appear to be stable over time (Halchuk, Makinen, & Johnson, 2010).

EFT is also helpful for couples in which one partner has a history of trauma, leading to reductions in posttraumatic stress disorder (PTSD) symptoms and higher relationship satisfaction (Dalton, Greenman, Classen, & Johnson, 2013; Johnson & Courtois, 2009; MacIntosh & Johnson, 2008). The specific goals in using EFT with couples with a trauma history include regulating affect, facilitating the sharing of vulnerable feelings, creating new meaning, and integrating a revised, more empathic view of self and other for each member of the couple (Rheem & Campbell, 2018). In this way, the relationship becomes a source of protection and comfort and the partner helps to co-regulate the trauma survivor's feelings of helplessness, anger, fear, and shame.

EFT has relied primarily on the personality/social psychology body of attachment research, with its use of self-report measures of "attachment styles" of conscious, potentially inaccurate self-descriptions of behavior and experiences (Bartholomew & Shaver, 1998). In contrast, the Adult Attachment Interview (AAI; Main & Goldwyn, 1998), used by the developmental psychology field to assess adult attachment, focuses on unconscious defensive "states of mind regarding attachment" of which respondents are frequently unaware. Not surprisingly, the measures are not equivalent, with the AAI more predictive of proactive emotion regulation in marital interactions than are self-report attachment measures (Bouthillier, Julien, Dube, Belanger, & Hamelin, 2002). The distinction between the two types of assessment is especially pertinent to the population of individuals who have experienced childhood trauma; that is, given that complex trauma arises primarily out of experiences in childhood (often originating in preverbal or preoperational developmental periods), attachment difficulties in adulthood often are not consciously articulated or understood. Thus, it is important to incorporate what is known about the dynamics of parent–child attachment relationships and how the experience of trauma in early development manifests itself in adult couple relationships (Alexander, 2015). After an overview of organized attachment categories, the following discussion focuses on disorganized attachment as a model of complex trauma and its implications for subsequent symptoms as they occur in couple relationships, whether one or both partners have been traumatized. It also focuses on strategies for intervention in such couple dynamics.

Attachment Behaviors in Children and Adults: Organized Strategies

Attachment theory is based on the assumption that there is an underlying biologically based bond that assures the proximity of the child to the caregiver, especially under conditions of stress (Bowlby, 1969/1982). Attachment behaviors reflect a survival-driven strategy that operates implicitly outside of the child's awareness for maintaining this connection. Consequently, both children and adults will do whatever is necessary, including distorting their feelings and thoughts, in order to ensure access to their attachment figure(s).

There are four recognized categories of attachment behavior in children based on carefully coded behavioral reactions of the child to the caregiver in the Strange Situation, a research protocol consisting of a series of separations and reunions between the child and the caregiver (Ainsworth, Blehar, Waters, & Wall, 1978). Categories of attachment in adults are conceptually similar to these categories in childhood and are based on responses to the AAI (Main & Goldwyn, 1998).

Three of these attachment categories are considered to be "organized" or systematic learned but implicit strategies on the part of the child that are often lifelong, and may be observed in differing degrees in individuals with a history of complex trauma. *Secure attachment* in children, associated with the parent's warmth, attunement, accessibility, and responsiveness, is characterized by the child's use of the parent as a secure base from which to explore and as a safe haven to which to return under conditions of threat. The secure child internalizes this experience, is able to self-soothe, and develops a sense of self-confidence, social competence, and trust in others. Secure adults typically value attachment relationships, tend to experience less depression and better mood, and are able to resolve conflict with partners without too much distress (Alexander, 2015).

Avoidant attachment is associated with the adult primary caregiver's rejection, nonresponse, and insensitivity to the child, particularly when the child is upset or needy. In order to maintain a connection to the parent, the avoidant child learns to cope by deactivating the attachment needs that seem to drive the parent away (Izard & Kobak, 1991). Since emotions or needs have not been recognized or responded to by the caregiver, the child fails to learn how to recognize and modulate emotions. Adults with dismissing or avoidant attachment minimize the importance of attachment relationships, self-report little distress and, like the avoidant child, use the strategies of extreme self-reliance, emotional inhibition, and interpersonal withdrawal during stressful interactions with a partner.

Anxious–ambivalent attachment in a child is associated with the parent's inconsistent behavior, vacillating from neglect to overprotectiveness or intrusiveness. As a consequence, the anxious–ambivalent child is needy, demanding, fussy, and unable to be soothed or to use the inconsistent parent as a secure and reliable base. Adults who are similarly preoccupied with and dissatisfied by their partners, whom they perceive as inaccessible, often exhibit intense and volatile emotions, and tend to equate conflict and expressions of anger with intimacy and closeness (Pietromonaco & Barrett, 1997).

As stated previously, any of these three organized attachment strategies may be seen in individuals with a history of complex trauma, although the two insecure attachment categories predominate over secure attachment in survivors of trauma (Bakermans-Kranenburg & van IJzendoorn, 2009). *Disorganized attachment* is particularly relevant to the experience of complex trauma and is therefore described in more detail and provides the basis for the rest of this chapter. However, because disorganized attachment is typically coded along with one of the underlying organized attachment strategies, all of these attachment categories are relevant in working with dual-trauma couples.

Disorganized Attachment and Complex Trauma Symptoms

The category of disorganized attachment was developed when the three organized strategies described earlier did not seem to capture the behavior in the Strange Situation of children with a known history of trauma associated with that parent. These children exhibit odd contradictory approach–avoidant behavior when reunited with this parent in the Strange Situation, such as approaching the parent with their head averted or exhibiting freezing or dissociative/trance-like behavior in the presence of the parent or asking to be picked up, then heaving themselves out of the parent's arms (Main & Solomon, 1990). In essence, they seem to lack a consistent strategy for accessing and connecting to their attachment figure.

Studies of parents of children who are disorganized in their attachment have shown that they are more likely to be unresolved regarding their own history of trauma or loss (Hesse & Main, 2006). These parents have been characterized as either hostile (displaying a mix of rejecting and attention-seeking behaviors) or as helpless–fearful (displaying fearfulness, withdrawal, and inhibition) in their interactions with their children (Lyons-Ruth, Melnick, Bronfman, Sherry, & Llanas, 2004). Certain common outcomes of disorganized attachment have been observed, potentially leading to serious problems over the lifespan and especially within the context of intimate or parenting relationships in adulthood (Alexander, 2015). The following interrelated clinical features and intergenerational patterns of engagement of children who are disorganized in their attachment or adults who are unresolved in their attachment are frequently seen in the interactions of dual-trauma couples and comprise the primary targets for intervention.

Approach–Avoidance

On the one hand, the seemingly contradictory behavior of the child with disorganized attachment may be understandable and even functional as a reaction to a hostile or fearful caregiver. On the other hand, an unresolved adult's lack of a fairly consistent strategy for pursuing attachment needs causes confusion, mistrust, and helplessness in the partner. Obviously, this confusion and absence of safety are magnified when both members of a couple are unresolved in their attachment and engage in this contradictory behavior with each other. Thus, although the typical pursue–withdraw cycle observed by EFT therapists may be challenging in its own right, the much more complicated negative cycle of the dual-trauma couple will be even more difficult to identify and map out as both individuals fluctuate between approaching and avoiding each other in often confusing and contradictory ways.

Dissociation and Parent–Child Role Reversal

Not only is a parent's dissociation the best predictor of a child's disorganized attachment (Abrams, Rifkin, & Hesse, 2006), but such disorganized attachment in childhood also puts the individual at risk for severe dissociative symptoms in childhood, adolescence, and adulthood. For example, in a longitudinal study in which Ogawa, Sroufe, Weinfield, Carlson, and Egeland (1997) controlled for intervening exposure to trauma, disorganized attachment in infancy predicted dissociation at age 19. The underlying mechanism for this intergenerational effect appears to be parent–child role reversal (Lyons-Ruth et al., 2004). Namely, Liotti (1992) described how the child's very presence triggers the attachment-related anxieties of the parent who has his or her own history of unresolved trauma or loss. The parent then looks to the child to allay the parent's fears. Being faced with the parent's abandonment of the caregiving role and with the impossible expectation of parenting one's own parent, the child often reacts with fear, leading the child to seek comfort from the attachment figure who is the very source of the distress. As a result, especially if the child has no other viable source of comfort, the child may develop multiple incompatible models of the parent and the self, leading to the development of dissociation, up to and including dissociative disorders and dissociative identity disorder (DID).

While a partner's dissociation and inconsistency are disconcerting for a nontraumatized partner, it can be terrifying to a partner who him- or herself is similarly dissociative and relationally disorganized. It reenacts the adult's experience as a child, when his or her parent suddenly became inaccessible or inexplicably angry and expected the child to somehow intuitively take over the parenting and caregiving role. As such, an individual's dissociation will also trigger the partner's fears and his or her own dissociative response. The therapist needs to be alert for this reciprocal triggering of dissociation and even the emergence of different self-states during the session.

Controlling Behavior

Children who are disorganized in their attachment and who experience the parent–child role reversal described earlier typically begin to engage in controlling behavior in latency age, when their cognitive development allows them to attempt to manage the parent's anxiety with either punitive/domineering or caregiving control. Punitively controlling children tend to issue harsh commands, verbal threats, and even physical aggression toward the parent who appears intimidated, withdrawn and stressed by the child (Moss, Cyr, & Dubois-Comtois, 2004; Moss, Bureau, St-Laurent, & Tarabulsy, 2011). In contrast, caregiving controlling children exhibit their parent–child role reversal through attempts to helpfully and protectively structure the interactions with their passive, disengaged, and disinvested parent (Moss et al., 2004, 2011).

Retrospective and longitudinal studies highlight the correlation between controlling behavior in childhood and diagnoses of borderline personality disorder in adolescence and adulthood (Lyons-Ruth, Melnick, Patrick, & Hobson, 2007; Lyons-Ruth, Bureau, Holmes, Easterbrooks, & Brooks, 2013). In another study, adolescents who were characterized as either domineering/punitive or as caregiving/controlling in their interactions with their parents were dissociative and in abusive relationships with their romantic partners (Obsuth, Hennighausen, Brumariu, & Lyons-Ruth, 2014). Finally, the connection between complex trauma and controlling behavior was noted in a study of partners engaging in a conflict management task (Creasey, 2002). Not only did individuals who were unresolved regarding trauma (as assessed by the AAI) display more domineering behavior, but couples with two unresolved individuals also displayed the most negative behaviors of all. Thus, the controlling behavior and accompanying emotional dysregulation of children with disorganized attachment frequently translate into long-term negative outcomes for dual-trauma couples.

Reflective Functioning and Emotion Dysregulation

That emotional dysregulation is prevalent in individuals with a history of complex trauma and disorganized attachment is widely accepted (Schore, 2013).

The model of reflective functioning posits that the development of the infant's right hemisphere is dependent on the mother's (or other caregiver's) accurate reading of the infant's facial cues (Fonagy, Target, & Gergely, 2000), and that through the mother's verbal and nonverbal mirroring, validating, and labeling of these cues, the child is taught to identify feelings. But, importantly, the mother then expresses a different set of emotions when she calms and soothes the child. In other words, the mother shifts from mirroring the child's distress to displaying her own emotion regulation. In this way, the child not only learns to identify and regulate his- or her own emotions but also learns that these emotions are distinct from those of the mother. Thus, the child's developing sense of self and capacity for emotion regulation are dependent on the mother's ability to identify and regulate her own emotional state.

Unfortunately, a mother's ability to engage in this process of reflective functioning with her child may be seriously compromised by her unresolved history of trauma or loss. Thus, reflective functioning can be undermined in several ways (Fonagy & Target, 1997). The mother may fail to mirror the child's facial expressions due to the need to avoid her own discomfort or traumatic memories that are triggered by the child's distress. Alternatively, the parent may be so preoccupied with her own traumatic memories that she may express them, and in the process amplify and heighten the child's distress, failing to soothe the child and precluding the child from differentiating his or her own feelings from those of the parent.

The long-term implications of this disrupted reflective functioning are significant for dual-trauma couples. The inability to identify and regulate one's own emotions is clearly a problem in and of itself. Furthermore, the inability to recognize that one's partner's needs are distinct from one's own and not an indictment of one's deficiencies can lead to a projection of one's own needs and a misinterpretation of the partner's needs. As a result, therapists need to help partners identify and reflect on their unacknowledged feelings—that is, to understand that their inner thoughts about their partner are not necessarily true (Clulow, 2007). Furthermore, while individuals or couples who are dismissing in their attachment may require more validation, individuals or couples who are preoccupied or unresolved in their attachment may require more emphasis on boundaries of thoughts and feelings (Clulow, 2007). In this way, partners become more able to seek and provide a secure base and safe haven for each other.

Goals of Treatment with Dual-Trauma Couples

Assessment

Given the potentially severe range of issues and the complexity that may be present in the interactions of dual-trauma couples, a thorough assessment of each partner is mandatory before the start of treatment. For example, when one individual is referred to treatment due to a history of trauma or behavior consistent with such a history (e.g., emotional lability, IPV), it is essential to assess both partners for a trauma history and for aggressive behavior (see Chapter 5). When IPV is disclosed or suspected, this poses a dilemma. Generally, EFT is not advised when ongoing risk is high and safety cannot be assured given that revealing vulnerabilities during the course of treatment may in itself increase anxieties that could trigger aggression. On the other hand, not seeing dual-trauma couples with a less severe risk of violence is problematic, because such a policy can deny help to couples who desperately need it and whose conflict may escalate without intervention. The AAI is typically administered in individual sessions with each partner. This provides clients with the privacy to disclose any relationship violence, as well as any history that is not directly pertinent to their current relationship. Clients are strongly encouraged and helped to disclose to their partner any ongoing affairs or addictions as a basis for establishing the trust and transparency necessary for treatment to be effective.

Whenever possible, the use of the full AAI protocol in the assessment is advised, since characteristics of the family of origin that are unearthed in this instrument can prove invaluable both to inform the treatment plan and to explicitly refer to throughout the course of treatment. Steele and Steele (2008) described several ways in which administering the AAI to each partner prior to therapy can be helpful. First, it highlights the assumption that current interactions with one's partner result in part from dynamics experienced in one's family of origin. Second, it provides a systematic way of identifying histories of trauma. Third, it serves as a basis for gathering important information about the defensive processes of attachment described earlier. It also assesses the existence of disorganized attachment dynamics that may be present even in the absence of overt abuse—most notably, parent–child role reversal, given its prominence in the development of dissociation and controlling behavior. Responses to the question "Why do you think your parents behaved the way they did during your childhood?" can provide an indication of a client's ability to engage in reflective functioning.

Partly as a function of responses on the AAI and assessment of risk for IPV, ancillary individual therapy may be warranted for either or both partners. This is often recommended, since attachment issues associated with the original trauma will certainly be triggered by couple interactions, although that decision should be based in part on the degree of the clients' resolution of the trauma. In other words, each partner must be able to sufficiently tolerate (often through the scaffolding of support provided in individual therapy) the emotions that will inevitably arise in couple therapy, without resorting to violence or other destructive behavior. Similarly, both partners need to have some awareness of how their early experiences in childhood affect their role in current intimate relationships. (Reciprocally, participation in individual or group therapy often triggers reactions in couples, which suggests that focusing on trauma experiences in the family of origin without exploring the impact of both the trauma and its resolution on current attachment relationships may seriously compromise the benefits of the individual or group therapy and may actually adversely affect the current relationship; Follette, Alexander, & Follette, 1991).

Alliance and Engagement in Treatment

A good therapeutic alliance is essential, of course, to therapy with all clients. While it is even more important for successful therapy with traumatized clients (Dalton et al., 2013), it is particularly relevant to therapy with dual-trauma couples. It is also likely harder to achieve with these couples, because both partners have experienced the dangers and disappointments of trusting attachment figures in the past, mistrust that they might project onto the therapist and onto one another.

The therapist must therefore pay close attention to potential traumatic transference, as well as countertransference, reactions (Alexander & Anderson, 1994). For example, the common countertransference reactions of defensiveness and power struggles in working with a client who is dismissing in attachment can be remedied with a stance of curiosity and centeredness, as well as an awareness of the painful rejection and lack of validation associated with avoidant attachment in childhood. The frequent countertransference feelings of suffocation in reaction to the client with preoccupied attachment potentially leads the therapist to alternate between excessive caregiving, then retreat and detachment that is then followed by reengagement out of guilt. Needless to say, the therapist of this client needs to be clear and comfortable about boundaries, power and responsibility, alert to the client's high-risk behavior but still having a healthy dose of humility about what a therapist can and cannot control. Finally, therapists working with clients with a history of disorganized attachment often feel overwhelmed, exhausted, overresponsible, and occasionally manipulated. These therapists need to remind themselves and the clients of the past function of their behavior and the resultant slow nature of the development of trust with the therapist and with the partner. The therapist's personal reactions to a client can also be used as hypotheses about the partner's potential reactions.

For all of these couples, safety (both physical and psychological) is of paramount importance, requiring ongoing monitoring both individually and by reviewing the impact of previous sessions during the intervening week. Psychological safety also suggests the need to proceed very slowly in order to avoid the potential for these dual-trauma couples to very rapidly trigger each other or decompensate, personally or as a couple. The dual-trauma couple needs to be assured that the therapist knows what to expect and is able to communicate his or her hypotheses about treatment and their dynamics with some degree of confidence.

Negative Cycle

As mentioned previously, one important goal of EFT is to identify the negative cycles in which couples find themselves, and in which they become stuck. As seen in the approach–avoidant behavior of the disorganized child, the negative cycle of the dual-trauma couple will often be much more complicated, with a seemingly random switching of roles (sometimes related to the switching associated with DID). Therefore, tracking the cycle will need to occur much more slowly and systematically, with little expectation that the typical pursue–withdraw cycle is in play. By commenting on the negative cycle when it occurs, the therapist reminds the couple that neither partner is to blame, that instead the behavior of each is an understandable and predictable response given the existence of this cycle. A reminder such as this settles the partners and reinforces the reflective functioning of each by making distinctions between each other's assumptions and behaviors. It also sets the stage for the disclosure of underlying feelings of longing for each other, through which their needs for secure attachment will emerge.

Emotion Regulation

Individuals with complex trauma often experience primitive fears and shame in reaction to their partners' expression of needs and concerns (MacIntosh, 2013). Given that these fears and behaviors may feel both irrational and baffling to each partner, another way of providing a sense of emotional security and safety is to repeatedly refer back to each partner's family-of-origin experience in order to explore their bases and how, as a child, each partner managed to cope and adapt to the dysfunction in the family. Similar to a parent engaging in reflective functioning with a child, the therapist validates, normalizes, and legitimizes fears, shame, and other core emotions as understandable reactions to previous and highly adverse experiences. The therapist then provides the emotion regulation often lacking in the couple by attending to and inquiring about each partner's emotional state—in essence, by co-regulating the couple's affect in the room until the partners are gradually able to engage in new ways of responding to each other. The therapist also works to prevent clients from staying stuck in memories and interactional patterns from the family of origin by contrasting and differentiating the past from the present. This process demonstrates to them how each can grow and how their growth can make great differences in their interactions and in their relational satisfaction. In this way, pride can replace shame, and hope for a better future can replace helplessness and despair.

Dissociation and Reflective Functioning

The stage is set for dissociation when the child is put in the impossible situation of seeing him- or herself as the cause of the parent's anxiety (leading to a deep sense of shame and confusion) and also as somehow responsible for controlling the parent's anxiety. From the framework of reflective functioning, the abused and neglected child's healthy identity as a unique and independent being is derailed, as is the ability to rely on an attachment figure for comfort and solace. Instead, relationships are seen as dangerous, partly because they represent this undifferentiated sense of self and other. Similar to the concept of the "drama triangle" (Karpman 1968), divisions occur between different relational dyads (e.g., me as victim/you as perpetrator vs. me as rescuer/you as victim vs. me as perpetrator/you as victim) rather than between different individuals (me vs. you). These roles are often embodied in dual-trauma couples when one partner experiences or expresses a feeling and the other is perceived as experiencing its counterpart rather than having his or her own response. This pattern can lead to the need of one partner to control his or her own fears or behaviors by controlling those of the partner, in the process creating a dysfunctional interactional cycle of stereotyped roles. Thus, one goal of treatment is to encourage differentiation of one partner from the other, while respecting the legitimacy of the feelings and expectations of each.

Trauma Memories

From an attachment perspective, trauma memories reside not in discrete historical events but instead in the context of relationships (Alexander, 2015). The complex trauma was not only the physical, sexual, or emotional abuse but also the relationship in which the abuse occurred, as well as the relationship that allowed the abuse to occur and/or that failed to provide intervention, protection, or recovery. Trauma memories (which might be explicit, but more often are implicit and nonverbal) may occur experientially and continuously in current relationships, especially under conditions of distress or abandonment risk. The therapist's task is not so much to prepare the client to disclose the memories as to try to catch up and make sense of the constant acting out of the memories between the partners—in essence, to jump on board a runaway train in an attempt to slow it down rather than to prepare to board the train in the station. With dual-trauma couples, the train already has left the station.

Clinical Case Example

The following case description is based on a composite of several dual-trauma couples.

Steve was in a role-reversing relationship with his mother, who was a trauma survivor herself. She was both emotionally rejecting and very dependent on him. Steve's father was a minister and leader of the community but also a closet alcoholic. When he was drunk, Steve's father would beat him severely "for his own good." By the time he reached adolescence, Steve would fight back, but his mother would side with her husband.

Mary similarly grew up in a highly conflictual household. Her father was physically abusive of her and her mother. Her mother was clearly terrified of him and was often "not there." As the marital conflict worsened, Mary's mother started making frequent trips to her own parents, who lived in another state, leaving Mary alone with her father. When Mary was around 12, her father began sexually abusing her but would then appear to feel guilty and become extremely physically abusive. Mary described sitting very still, waiting for his rage to subside.

Steve and Mary's negative cycle can be described as the following: Mary becomes anxious about something extraneous to their relationship, such as her job, leading to Steve's attempts to reassure her. Mary feels invalidated when she perceives that Steve apparently does not understand the seriousness of her concerns. She then tries even harder to persuade Steve as to the basis of her anxiety. Steve feels guilty about her distress, feels inadequate at helping her, appears somewhat sullen and retreats to his cellphone. Mary feels even more alone and becomes more persistent, to the point of threatening divorce when pursuing a conversation with him. Eventually, she triggers his anxiety with these threats. Steve reaches out to her in his anxiety, but Mary becomes angry about his sudden accessibility and so withdraws. Thus, both exhibit aspects of the approach–avoidant behavior seen in children with disorganized attachment. What is more, both partners at times show difficulty in reflective functioning (i.e., in differentiating their own feelings and anxiety from that of each other). While much about their cycle is characteristic of couples without trauma histories, Mary experiences Steve's withdrawal as reminiscent of her mother's actual dissociation and leave-taking, triggering a truly disorienting traumatic response for her based on the mother's past actual abandonment.

Neither of them reports any violence within the relationship; however, in their attempts to control their own anxieties, they often exhibit caregiving control over each other—frequently referring to each other's "mental health issues." Unfortunately, this projection of their own anxieties leads them to avoid asking each other directly about what they need. They also each experience labeling by their partner as shaming and intrusive—much like what each of them experienced in their respective families of origin.

The following transcripts (of Sessions 20 and 22 respectively) depict some of the dynamics discussed earlier.

Session 20

THERAPIST: When Steve doesn't express his feelings, it's tough for you. Can you explain why?

MARY: I feel alone, because I don't know what's happening. I feel anxious and unsafe, like when my mom left me alone with my dad whenever things got bad.

THERAPIST: So she couldn't protect you from your father.

MARY: No, she couldn't or wouldn't. I think she was just as afraid of him as I was.

THERAPIST: So it was constant anxiety?

MARY: Yes, it was like a vacuum and very confusing.

THERAPIST: I want to bring that up to date in terms of how that affects your reaction to Steve being silent. What does that feel like to you?

MARY: (*long pause*) I get really scared and confused.

THERAPIST: As if he's drifting away or not there?

MARY: Yes. I'm even afraid to tell him about it because whenever I do, he gets more angry and more withdrawn.

THERAPIST: So even letting him know about your feelings feels a little risky.

MARY: Because he'll give me the silent treatment when we get home.

THERAPIST: Let's get his permission to ask him about that here.

MARY: OK, I guess. (*to Steve*) I want to talk about my reaction to you but I'm afraid you won't like it.

STEVE: Well, that's what we're paying the therapist for—to help us talk.

THERAPIST: (*to Steve*) So you're saying that you're willing to listen? Even if it feels uncomfortable to you, too?

STEVE: Yes.

THERAPIST: So when Steve goes silent, it feels like he's getting ready to go away and leave you in a dangerous place.

MARY: (*long pause*) I don't know if I thought of it that way before.

THERAPIST: But is that the feeling associated with it?

MARY: Yeah.

THERAPIST: You really miss him when he stops talking.

MARY: Yeah.

THERAPIST: That's the part of you that wants him to come back and reengage. (*to Steve*) Did you know that she felt that way?

STEVE: No, she just always seems angry with me.

THERAPIST: (*to Mary*) You're actually struggling with the fear that he's like your mom?

MARY: Steve often says he'll have to think about whatever we're talking about and then never gets back to me.

THERAPIST: Like your mom?

MARY: Yes. He just leaves me high and dry.

STEVE: My initial reaction is one of defensiveness. [classic negative shutdown cycle]

THERAPIST: But sometimes you'll bring it back up?

STEVE: Yes.

THERAPIST: And that's the part of you that is changing?

STEVE: I think so.

MARY: He thinks I'm unreasonable about wanting him to return to the topic, and that's not true.

THERAPIST: You're saying, "I don't care how long it takes—I just need to be part of the process."

MARY: Yes.

THERAPIST: Can you tell him that?

MARY: (*pause; nervous laughter*)

THERAPIST: I sense a lot of sadness there. It's not so much the embarrassment of saying it on cue but the sadness below it.

MARY: Yes.

THERAPIST: Can you tell him about that?

MARY: (*to Steve*) (*long pause*) It makes me really sad when I don't feel like you're there, and I worry that you will leave me.

STEVE: (*pause; then becomes teary*)

THERAPIST: In some ways, that's different from her talking about her anxiety, isn't it?

STEVE: Yes. I'm numb to hearing about her anxiety, because I hear about it so often. This is different. I can understand it better.

THERAPIST: Yes, with her anxiety, there's more of a demand that you're supposed to fix it. While sadness is simply an expression of her vulnerability and her willingness to be vulnerable with you. That's a real gift, isn't it?

STEVE: Yes.

THERAPIST: Her trusting you with her sadness is a lot more meaningful right now than her telling you about her anxiety.

Session 22

THERAPIST: (*to Steve*) When we last spoke, we were talking about how you'd always had the sense that Mary would not rely on you. For example, in dealing with finances?

STEVE: She doesn't believe I can take care of her, that I'm trustworthy and that I'll stay around.

THERAPIST: That you're not going anywhere?

STEVE: Yes. I don't take it personally that it's something about me. She doesn't trust anybody.

THERAPIST: But there's a difference between her not trusting anybody and her not trusting you, because you're the most important person in her life. To that degree it's very personal. What's that like for you?

STEVE: It makes me crazy that she doesn't believe or trust me. I fluctuate between getting angry about it and actually wanting to escape.

THERAPIST: A feeling that there's nothing you can possibly do to convince her. And what happens when you feel frustrated like that?

STEVE: I feel totally helpless. Like I have to work twice as hard.

THERAPIST: To prove to her . . .

STEVE: Yes, because she doesn't trust that I'm going to do my part. I think that's when she gets more anxious because she thinks she has to do it all.

THERAPIST: And when she feels that she needs to do it all, how does that affect you?

STEVE: It makes me anxious myself.

THERAPIST: Because the feeling is what? That maybe she's right—that you can't do it?

STEVE: Yes. I second guess myself.

THERAPIST: That must feel awful. And then that's when you withdraw?

STEVE: Yes.

THERAPIST: Can you explain that to her?

STEVE: (*to Mary*) I worry that I can't live up to your expectations of me.

MARY: I don't expect you to do it on your own—I want us to talk about our finances together and figure things out together.

THERAPIST: (*to Mary*) Because when he withdraws, that's when you're more likely to feel alone? And the more you feel alone, the less you trust him?

MARY: (*nods*)

THERAPIST: (*to Steve*) It sounds like a big deal. What would happen if she saw your frustration and hurt for not trusting you? What keeps you from letting her see your hurt?

STEVE: My upbringing.

THERAPIST: Which is that you don't have a right to be hurt?

STEVE: There's no space for expressing my feelings. It's very hard for me.

THERAPIST: Tell me about your experience in your family of origin growing up that makes expressing hurt taboo? Scary for you?

STEVE: Emotions were not expressed in my family. If you were upset, it was glazed over with "You're fine. Everything's OK." I would be told, "That's not how you feel."

THERAPIST: So, now as an adult, part of you even has a hard time recognizing when you're upset or hurt. Right?

STEVE: Yes, it's hard for me sometimes. Not being able to figure out what I'm feeling.

THERAPIST: (*to Mary*) What's it like for you when he expresses his frustration and hurt? How does it feel?

MARY: It's painful—it makes me sad—but it doesn't scare me. I'm sure I get defensive but it's different than him being withdrawn. It's easier for me to understand. It's the absence that is . . .

THERAPIST: . . . terrifying.

MARY: Yes, it is.

THERAPIST: Because it brings forth memories of your mom?

MARY: Yes, when she left me alone with my dad.

THERAPIST: So if Steve expresses his anger, it doesn't scare you like when your dad got angry?

MARY: No. It would probably wake me up. To see how my inability to trust him—and that Steve's response is to doubt himself and then retreat into himself—it's a very different thing. When we've talked about it before, it was just about trusting in an abstract way.

THERAPIST: So can you tell him how his confronting you when you don't trust him would be OK with you and maybe even welcome at times. Can you explain that to him?

MARY: (*to Steve*) I'm OK with you being upset with me. I'm not going to love you any differently. I may get defensive, but it doesn't mean you're not right.

Commentary on the Case Example

Given limitations of space, these transcripts portray therapeutic interactions that are more condensed than is sometimes the case for couples at an earlier stage of treatment, when the intervention may need to be painstakingly slow. The first transcript focuses on Mary's reactions to Steve based on her perceptions of his similarity to her mother. Although sexual abuse by her father certainly complicated her sexual relationship with Steve (and was explored in other sessions), it was his withdrawal that most triggered her anxiety regarding his availability.

Mary sends Steve very mixed messages regarding her dependence on him and simultaneously her suspicion that he cannot (or will not) meet her needs. Thus, her expressed anxiety leaves him confused and undermines his natural tendency toward benevolent control of the attachment relationship. Her ambivalence also triggers his memories of frustration and helplessness when his mother would confide in him about his father but then continue to side with his father, even after episodes when his father was abusive and violent (these memories of his mother were explored in other sessions).

Steve initially dismisses Mary's mistrust of him as characteristic of her relationships in general. However, it was important to personalize her mistrust in order to touch his hurt stemming from this distance. The therapist highlights for both of them how Steve's withdrawal from Mary due to his sense of powerlessness at reassuring her leads to her increased anxiety and continued mistrust—in essence, their negative cycle. Frequent short references to their respective families of origin reassure them that their own behavior is not crazy and that their partner's behavior is not vindictive. But then the therapist tries to come back to their current relationship to avoid overanalysis of the past. Slowly, very gradually, they begin to differentiate the past from the present.

Conclusion

Most couple therapists at some time see dual-trauma couples. EFT is particularly relevant to these couples given its emphasis on insecure attachment relationships and the underlying co-dysregulation of emotions that is associated with a history of trauma (Johnson, 2002). In this chapter I make the case that the use of EFT with these couples can become even richer by incorporating what the field of developmental psychology teaches about trauma and disorganized attachment. Close attention to the clients' experiences in childhood can provide a road map for helping the partners make sense of their very strong, primal reactions to each other. Reciprocally, creating secure attachment relationships in the present—especially with one's partner—can contribute to the resolution of complex trauma. This interactional focus in the context of treatment that is deliberately supportive sets the stage for relational growth in both parties and in their relationship to one another.

References

Abrams, K. Y., Rifkin, A., & Hesse, E. (2006). Examining the role of parental frightened/frightening subtypes in predicting disorganized attachment within a brief observational procedure. *Development and Psychopathology, 18,* 345–361.

Ainsworth, M. D. S., Blehar, M. C., Waters, E., & Wall, S. (1978). *Patterns of attachment: A psychological study of the Strange Situation.* Oxford, UK: Erlbaum.

Alexander, P. C. (2014). Dual-trauma couples and intimate partner violence. *Psychological Trauma, 6,* 224–231.

Alexander, P. C. (2015). *Intergenerational cycles of trauma and violence: An attachment and family systems perspective.* New York: Norton.

Alexander, P. C., & Anderson, C. L. (1994). An attachment approach to psychotherapy with the incest survivor. *Psychotherapy: Theory, Research, Practice, Training, 31,* 665–675.

Bakermans-Kranenburg, M. J., & van IJzendoorn, M. H. (2009). The first 10,000 adult attachment interviews: Distributions of adult attachment representations in clinical and non-clinical groups. *Attachment and Human Development, 13,* 253–269.

Bartholomew, K., & Shaver, P. R. (1998). Methods of assessing adult attachment. In J. A. Simpson & W. S. Rholes (Eds.), *Attachment theory and close relationships* (pp. 25–45). New York: Guilford Press.

Bouthillier, D., Julien, D., Dube, M., Belanger, I., & Hamelin, M. (2002). Predictive validity of adult attachment measures in relation to emotion regulation behaviors in marital interactions. *Journal of Adult Development, 9,* 291–305.

Bowlby, J. (1982). *Attachment and loss: Vol. 1. Attachment.* New York: Basic Books. (Original work published 1969)

Clulow, C. (2007). John Bowlby and couple psychotherapy. *Attachment and Human Development, 9,* 343–353.

Creasey, G. (2002). Associations between working models of attachment and conflict management behavior in romantic couples. *Journal of Counseling Psychology, 49*, 365–375.

Dalton, E. J., Greenman, P. S., Classen, C. C., & Johnson, S. M. (2013). Nurturing connections in the aftermath of childhood trauma: A randomized controlled trial of emotionally focused couple therapy for female survivors of childhood abuse. *Couple and
Family Psychology: Research and Practice, 2*, 209–221.

Follette, V. M., Alexander, P. C., & Follette, W. C. (1991). Individual predictors of outcome
in group treatment for incest victims. *Journal of Consulting and Clinical Psychology,
59*, 150–155.

Fonagy, P., & Target, M. (1997). Attachment and reflective function: Their role in self-
organization. *Development and Psychopathology, 9*, 679–700.

Fonagy, P., Target, M., & Gergely, G. (2000). Attachment and borderline personality disorder: A theory and some evidence. *Psychiatric Clinics of North America, 23*, 103–122.

Halchuk, R. E., Makinen, J., & Johnson, S. M. (2010). Resolving attachment injuries in couples using emotionally focused therapy. *Journal of Couple and Relationship Therapy,
9*, 31–47.

Hesse, E., & Main, M. (2006). Frightened, threatening and dissociative parental behavior in
low-risk samples. *Development and Psychopathology, 18*, 309–343.

Izard, C., & Kobak, R. (1991). Emotion system functioning and emotion regulation. In J.
Garber & K. Dodge (Eds.), *The development of affect regulation* (pp. 303–321). Cambridge, UK: Cambridge University Press.

Johnson, S. M. (2002). *Emotionally focused couple therapy with trauma survivors: Strengthening attachment bonds.* New York: Guilford Press.

Johnson, S. M. (2004). *The practice of emotionally focused couple therapy: Creating connection.* New York: Brunner/Routledge.

Johnson, S. M., & Courtois, C. A. (2009). Couple therapy. In C. A. Courtois & J. D. Ford
(Eds.), *Treating complex traumatic stress disorders: An evidence-based guide* (pp. 371–
390). New York: Guilford Press.

Karpman, S. (1968). Fairy tales and script drama analysis. *Transactional Analysis Bulletin,
7*, 39–43.

Liotti, G. (1992). Disorganized/disoriented attachment in the etiology of the dissociative
disorders. *Dissociation, 5*, 196–204.

Lyons-Ruth, K., Bureau, J.-F., Holmes, B., Easterbrooks, A., & Brooks, N. H. (2013).
Borderline symptoms and suicidality/self-injury in late adolescence: Prospectively
observed relationship correlates in infancy and childhood. *Psychiatry Research, 206*,
273–281.

Lyons-Ruth, K., Melnick, S., Bronfman, E., Sherry, S., & Llanas, L. (2004). Hostile–helpless relational models and disorganized attachment patterns between parents and their
young children. In L. Atkinson & S. Goldberg (Eds.), *Attachment issues in psychopathology and intervention* (pp. 65–94). Mahwah, NJ: Erlbaum.

Lyons-Ruth, K., Melnick, S., Patrick, M., & Hobson, R. P. (2007). A controlled study of
hostile-helpless states of mind among borderline and dysthymic women. *Attachment
and Human Behavior, 9*, 1–16.

MacIntosh, H. B. (2013). Mentalizing: An exploration of its potential contribution to understanding the challenges faced by childhood sexual abuse survivors in couple therapy.
Couple and Family Psychoanalysis, 3, 188–207.

MacIntosh, H. B., & Johnson, S. (2008). Emotionally focused therapy for couples and childhood sexual abuse survivors. *Journal of Marital and Family Therapy, 34*, 298–315.

Main, M., & Goldwyn, R. (1998). *Adult attachment scoring and classification system, Version 6.3.* Unpublished manuscript, University of California, Berkeley, CA.

Main, M., & Solomon, J. (1990). Procedures for identifying infants as disorganized/disori-
ented during the Ainsworth Strange Situation. In M. T. Greenberg, D. Cicchetti, & E.
M. Cummings (Eds.), *Attachment in the preschool years: Theory, research, and intervention* (pp. 121–160). Chicago: University of Chicago Press.

Miehls, D., & Basham, K. (2013). Object relations couple therapy with trauma survivors.

In D. Catherall (Ed.), *Handbook of stress, trauma, and the family* (pp. 473–491). New York: Routledge/Taylor & Francis Group.

Monson, C. M., & Fredman, S. J. (2012). *Cognitive-behavioral conjoint therapy for PTSD: Harnessing the healing power of relationships.* New York: Guilford Press.

Moss, E., Bureau, J.-F., St-Laurent, D., & Tarabulsy, G. M. (2011). Understanding disorganized attachment at preschool and school age: Examining divergent pathways of disorganized and controlling children. In J. Solomon & C. George (Eds.), *Disorganized attachment and caregiving* (pp. 52–79). New York: Guilford Press.

Moss, E., Cyr, C., & Dubois-Comtois, K. (2004). Attachment at early school age and developmental risk. *Developmental Psychology, 40,* 519–532.

Obsuth, I., Hennighausen, K., Brumariu, L. E., & Lyons-Ruth, K. (2014). Disorganized behavior in adolescent-parent interaction: Relations to attachment state of mind, partner abuse, and psychopathology. *Child Development, 85,* 370–387.

Ogawa, J., Sroufe, A., Weinfield, N., Carlson, E., & Egeland, B. (1997). Development and the fragmented self: Longitudinal study of dissociative symptomatology in a non-clinical sample. *Development and Psychopathology, 9,* 855–879.

Pietromonaco, P. R., & Barrett, L. (1997). Working models of attachment and daily social interactions. *Journal of Personality and Social Psychology, 73,* 1409–1423.

Rheem, K., & Campbell, T. L. (2018). Emotionally focused couple therapy and trauma. In J. L. Lebow, A. Chambers, & D. C. Breulin (Eds.), *Encyclopedia of couple and family therapy* (pp. 1–5). Basel, Switzerland: Springer International.

Schore, A. N. (2013). Relational trauma, brain development, and dissociation. In J. D. Ford & C. A. Courtois (Eds.), *Treating complex traumatic stress disorders in children and adolescents: Scientific foundations and therapeutic models* (pp. 3–23). New York: Guilford Press.

Steele, H., & Steele, M. (2008). Ten clinical uses of the Adult Attachment Interview. In H. Steele & M. Steele (Eds.), *Clinical applications of the Adult Attachment Interview* (pp. 3–30). New York: Guilford Press.

van IJzendoorn, M. H., & Bakermans-Kranenburg, M. J. (1996). Attachment representations in mothers, fathers, adolescents, and clinical groups: A meta-analytic search for normative data. *Journal of Consulting and Clinical Psychology, 64,* 8–21.

Whisman, M. A. (2014). Dyadic perspectives in trauma and marital adjustment. *Psychological Trauma, 6,* 207–215.

CHAPTER 21

Family Systems Therapy

JULIAN D. FORD

F amily systems therapy addresses the impact of exposure to complex trauma and its aftermath on all members of families and their relationships with one another. The experience of living with complex traumatic stress disorders (CTSDs) is transmitted into family relationships in many subtle as well as obvious ways. Whether only one or a few members are survivors of or direct witnesses to complex trauma, or an entire family, their community, nation, or culture is exposed, the impact of complex traumatic stress reactions reverberates across relationships and can fundamentally alter the life and health of everyone in a family. As the Prince of Verona poignantly exclaimed, upon learning of the deaths of Romeo and Juliet (Act 5, Scene 3):

> See what a scourge is laid upon your hate,
> That heaven finds means to kill your joys with love!
> And I, for winking at your discords, too
> Have lost a brace of kinsmen. All are punished.

This chapter extends a prior survey of the field (Ford & Saltzman, 2009) in a discussion of the profound effects on families of intra- and extrafamilial complex trauma, followed by a review of foundational concepts of family systems theory as applied to families impacted by CTSDs. Conceptual and clinical models of family systems therapy for posttraumatic stress disorder (PTSD) and their research evidence bases are discussed, emphasizing approaches that address CTSDs. The chapter concludes with a composite case vignette illustrating family systems interventions, including illustrative samples of the therapeutic interaction, with a family that comprises parents who are both adult survivors of childhood sexual and emotional abuse/neglect, and who have engaged in intimate partner violence with each other that is currently impacting their own children and threatening the integrity of their marriage and the entire family.

Complex Trauma and Family Systems

Families can be affected by complex trauma in two essentially different ways. *Intrafamilial* complex trauma results from all forms of abuse, violence, exploitation, neglect, or other forms of victimization that members of the biological or extended family (or those in close relationship with them who function in a family role, i.e., mother's boyfriend, father's best friend, who is accepted as an uncle) perpetrate upon one another. *Extrafamilial* complex trauma involves experiences of abuse, violence, or victimization perpetrated by persons or institutions outside the family. Each form of complex trauma can profoundly injure and destabilize not only direct and indirect victims but also the entire family; however, the dynamics of each type of trauma and its effects differ in important ways that must be understood in treatment.

Intrafamilial complex trauma represents a failure on the part of what should be core and essential functions of families—protection of members and maintenance of their emotional and physical security—and is an essential betrayal of trust for all members of the family. Incest, a particularly insidious and corrosive type of intrafamilial complex trauma, is both a violation and a betrayal by one or more family members who have the power to force (whether by overt coercion and physical injury or threat, or by more deceptive forms of grooming and seduction) another family member—usually an accessible, dependent, and vulnerable child or early adolescent—to engage in sexual contact (Courtois, 2016). It creates rivalries and conflicts within the family, and its occurrence is maintained by denial and injunctions to silence and secrecy. It can occur within the immediate or more extended family and can be transmitted intergenerationally. Physical and emotional abuse and neglect (Ragavan et al., 2018; Teicher & Samson, 2016), often within the context of intimate partner or domestic violence (Bacchus, Ranganathan, Watts, & Devries, 2018; Vu, Jouriles, McDonald, & Rosenfield, 2016), are additional types of intrafamilial complex trauma that often co-occur with one another, as well as with incest and other forms of child abuse.

Any one of these types of intrafamilial traumatic exposure can alter the course of a victimized child's development, with especially extensive and profoundly adverse effects if the child's primary caregiving bond and sense of attachment security have already been or are then directly or indirectly undermined or shattered (Spinazzola, van der Kolk, & Ford, 2018), as especially occurs in incest (Courtois, 2010). Such attachment trauma, along with the abuse, makes these victims vulnerable to revictimization over the entire life course (Courtois, 2010). Intrafamilial complex trauma also can adversely alter the mental and physical health and subsequent development of adults who are victimized directly (e.g., survivors of intimate partner violence) or indirectly (e.g., adults whose spouse/partner or other relative has abused their child[ren] but who themselves are nonoffenders (Boeckel, Blasco-Ros, Grassi-Oliveira, & Martinez, 2014).

Treatment of Intrafamilial Complex Trauma

Intrafamilial complex trauma and its adverse effects have many layers that must be carefully unraveled and dealt with when and if family therapy is undertaken. The treatment of incestuous and otherwise abusive families was first formally developed in the 1980s, when the extent of incestuous abuse began to be identified (Courtois, 2010). It requires a sophisticated understanding of the negative dynamics that undergird the incestuous interactions within these families and that are reinforced by denial. Specialized training is required, as the treatment usually unfolds in stepwise fashion, after the safety of the victim is ensured: individual therapy of the perpetrator (which may be court-mandated when criminal charges have been brought) and other family members, then therapy in dyads (including the victim–perpetrator and victim–nonoffending parent and victim–sibling(s), once the victim has been empowered and safety is ensured), then therapy involving the parents and child–victim, and ultimately conjoint therapy with the entire family.

It is often the case that victimized family members are not only directly harmed by the abuse, violence, or nonprotection/intervention but subsequently are also subjected to the additional stigma of being blamed or scapegoated as if they are responsible for the trauma, a typical dynamic in an incestuous or otherwise abusive family. For example, a physically abused child or battered adult might be accused by the perpetrator of "making me beat you" or "needing to be taught a lesson." Or a sexually abused child or sexually assaulted adult partner might be told by the perpetrator or other family members—or even by people or institutions in the community outside the family—"You asked for it"; "You were seductive and irresistible"; "You're destroying this family by talking about/reporting it"; "You're lying, that can't be true"; or "No one's going to believe you." In family therapy, victim-blaming must be challenged in a manner that both supports the victimized family member and shifts the responsibility for the trauma entirely from the victim to the perpetrator (Madanes, 1980), a task that is not easily accomplished, since these families are often organized around defensiveness, denial, and scapegoating of the victim, especially one who "breaks ranks" by breaking silence and disclosing abuse. These abuses might also be related to substance abuse disorders and addictions in the perpetrator or other family members that can also facilitate the occurrence of abuse and denial. Without effective intervention, abusive/incestuous families tend to return to their known interactional patterns without change, and abuse may resume or even worsen when a perpetrator or others play out their rage at having been found out. As a result, all family members must be helped to recognize and heal from the psychological injury that they and their relationships have experienced and, most important, the ongoing safety of all family members must be emphasized. The case vignette at the close of this chapter illustrates aspects of this crucial and delicate intervention in family therapy involving complex intrafamilial trauma.

The case vignette also shows the dilemmas involved when intrafamilial complex trauma involves intergenerational experiences and dynamics that become normative and facilitate its occurrence and become methods of transmission of across generations. When parents have experienced complex trauma as children in their own families of origin, the survival coping and adaptations that they developed as children can profoundly affect their selection of partner/spouse(s) in adulthood—tragically often leading them to be revictimized by intimate partner physical, sexual, or emotional violence, and infrequently, the incestuous abuse of their own children. Moreover, their children then grow up with their own traumatic sense of harm, or threat, either through direct experience or by having witnessed domestic abuse and violence (Assink et al., 2018). A detailed discussion of the dynamics of intergenerational transmission can be found in Courtois (2010). Even when the parents are not embroiled in violence or abuse, their own childhood trauma can have lasting adverse developmental effects (Spinazzola et al., 2018) that may predispose them to inadvertently be neglectful (Mulder, Kuiper, van der Put, Stams, & Assink, 2018), unable to bond with and emotionally unresponsive (Schechter et al., 2015; van Ee, Kleber, & Jongmans, 2016), or harsh (Grasso et al., 2016) in parenting their children (Zvara, Mills-Koonce, Appleyard Carmody, Cox, & Family Life Project Key Investigators, 2015). These findings parallel findings from attachment studies that parents of children with insecure and especially disorganized/dissociative attachment styles often have unresolved trauma and loss in their own histories that is passed on or "transmitted" through their parenting (Granqvist et al., 2017). Furthermore, when abuse, conflict, and emotional enmeshment/intrusion or detachment are transmitted across generations in this manner, children are at risk for the additional trauma of being victimized by and victimizers of their own siblings (Tucker, Finkelhor, Turner, & Shattuck, 2014), as well as other peers (i.e., cousins, classmates, playmates).

In family therapy, members can begin to recognize and understand how intrafamilial complex trauma can lead to lifelong patterns of survival coping and to the exposure of subsequent generations of children in the family to further trauma—and also to the transmission of trauma-related survival coping and its adverse effects across several generations. Multigenerationally traumatized families often are extremely isolated, harboring painful and debilitating secrets, while keeping up appearances as a happy and intact family (sometimes called "perfect families" due to their superficial success in self-presentation) in order to prevent the outside world from discovering the hidden shame and turmoil within. Intervening therapeutically with such internally traumatized and traumatizing families requires helping all of the family members to take the courageous and often painful step of accepting external help and revealing the secrets in order to restore appropriate internal boundaries that maintain the safety and health of every family member. As these families are often highly mistrustful of outsiders and fearful of both judgment and criminal charges, informed consent and treaters who can maintain a nonjudgmental stance (and who themselves receive the support of ongoing consultation with a treatment team) are essential to the success of treatment. Acceptance and support from the outside can be a starting point for an empathic and nonjudgmental reevaluation by adult caregivers of how engaging in chronic survival coping has led them to treat their children, partners, and themselves in ways that have not only caused harm but also violate their own values and hurt those they love. That reexamination can provide their children with a new role model and a basis for restoring trust and security, which is a crucial first step toward breaking the intergenerational cycle of complex trauma by changing long-standing patterns of behavior and sustaining dynamics that are the artifacts of—and tragically, often the perpetuation and repetition of—intrafamilial complex trauma.

When complex intrafamilial trauma occurs across generations, it is not only detrimental patterns of behavior (i.e., survival coping) and interaction (i.e., conflict, neglect, abuse) that may be transmitted intergenerationally. As noted earlier, children's fundamental sense of security in their relational bond with parents or other primary caregivers can be compromised (i.e., insecure or disorganized attachment) when either they (Byun, Brumariu, & Lyons-Ruth, 2016; Granqvist et al., 2017; van Hoof, van Lang, Speekenbrink, van IJzendoorn, & Vermeiren, 2015) or their primary caregiver (Bailey, Tarabulsy, Moran, Pederson, & Bento, 2017; Berthelot et al., 2015; Bosquet Enlow, Egeland, Carlson, Blood, & Wright, 2014; Khan & Renk, 2018) have been exposed to intrafamilial complex trauma in childhood. Children of parents who were exposed to complex intrafamilial trauma in their own childhoods are at risk for developing a disorganized pattern of attachment as early as infancy, and those early life attachment problems put them at risk for severe problems with dissociation, stress reactivity, disruptive behavior, and emotion dysregulation later in childhood, as well as adolescence and adulthood (Bosquet Enlow et al., 2014; Lyons-Ruth, Pechtel, Yoon, Anderson, & Teicher, 2016).

Therapy with families in which there are intergenerational patterns of intrafamilial complex trauma therefore must also carefully identify and provide reparative interventions to address intergenerational patterns of impaired relational attachment. This involves empathically helping parents with complex trauma histories to understand and resolve feelings of insecurity and confusion that originated in relational or attachment trauma with their own caregivers. Then parents can reexamine their current caregiving and other close personal relationships more realistically and with self-compassion, which is the essential foundation for subsequently reexamining and changing how they engage in their intimate partner relationship and how they co-parent their children. This in turn can enable the parent(s), with therapeutic guidance, to care for their children in a responsive and consistent manner so as to foster a sense of secure attachment to their children, crucial to the success of trauma-focused therapy for complexly traumatized (or vicariously traumatized) children (Lieberman & Van Horn, 2008).

The result is not always a "happy ending" for everyone in the family, because it is not always possible, even with the best evidence-based approaches to family therapy and trauma-focused therapy, for families with deeply ingrained patterns of survival coping, severely disorganized attachment relationships and schemas, and skewed boundaries and dynamics to break the vicious cycle of cumulative victimization and revictimization. Family members who have perpetrated complex trauma by victimizing their children, partner, or other family members, and who were likely victimized in some way earlier in their life (Godbout et al., 2019), often have difficulty accepting responsibility for and changing themselves and their actions. Careful and specialized assessment of the perpetrator is needed, as some are pedophiles, while others are not, and still others serially abuse both inside and outside of the family. The possibility of rehabilitation of pedophilic offenders is the subject of considerable debate in the criminal justice and mental health communities, as is the possibility of safe family reunification in these cases.

Couples in which both partners have experienced intrafamilial complex trauma in childhood often find themselves enmeshed in love-hate relationships that re-enact each partner's earlier traumatic dilemmas in a manner that can be very difficult to disentangle (Johnson & Courtois, 2009; see also Chapter 20). Victimized adult or adolescent family members may decide to leave (e.g., divorce) or greatly reduce contact with an abusive partner, parent, or sibling, and while this can be a positive step toward restoring safety and healthy relational boundaries, such decisions bring with them a high degree of stress and often a deep sense of loss for all family members. Family therapy involving the aftermath (or continuation) of intrafamilial complex trauma thus may need to focus on supporting family members who are undergoing major life changes and experiencing not only the aftereffects of trauma but also painful emotional losses.

One other point of complication must be highlighted. Many types of intrafamilial violence and sexual and other forms of child abuse are illegal, and reporting to authorities following disclosure is mandated in many, if not most, jurisdictions. Therapists must be aware of these reporting laws and provide clients with informed consent at the start of the assessment process. In some cases, reporting results in criminal charges, a step that can torpedo the treatment. Additionally, treatment can be court-mandated as part of an offender's sentence, as part of or in lieu of a jail sentence. In such a situation, the therapist must be cognizant of these legal complexities and be prepared to comply with them. It is not unusual for a family member (or members) to try to coerce the therapist not to report when mandated to do so or otherwise to compromise the therapist in a desperate attempt to maintain the status quo.

Family Therapy for Extrafamilial Complex Trauma

Family therapy can be of major benefit with families in which one or more members have been exposed to complex trauma outside the family. Such extrafamilial traumas include abuse, assault, or other forms of victimization or exploitation by trusted adults outside the nuclear family (e.g., other relatives, clergy, teachers, coaches, employers, or coworkers) or by strangers (e.g., community or war violence, sexual assault or exploitation, immigration-related violence). This can occur whether the trauma has been disclosed or not—the behavioral and other changes may be obvious, although the cause is not known. In these families, members who have not been directly traumatized often have difficulty understanding and knowing how to respond to and accommodate changes in traumatized family members' behavior and mental and emotional state (e.g., "I don't know what happened to the affectionate and open child/spouse I used to know—now they are so angry, tense, and closed-off that I can't seem to get through to them and nothing I do seems to make it any better"; "They came back from the deployment a different person"). Psychoeducation can help all of the family members understand how trauma triggers posttraumatic reactions (i.e., changes in emotions, beliefs, and behavior) that can become chronic survival coping mechanisms. This can serve as the starting point for therapy sessions to reduce the sense of confusion, estrangement, and hopelessness that often permeates the family in response to the changes members observe and experience. Although the case vignette focuses on intrafamilial complex trauma, it illustrates how this type of restoration of direct and empathic communication among family members can be focused on restoring the affection, hope, trust, and cohesion in a family that is crucial to all members' ability to recover from the cascading impact of complex trauma.

From this brief review, it is apparent that therapy with families whose members are affected by complex trauma requires an understanding on the part of the therapist of the often complicated and variable (and highly individual) ways in which each family member has been influenced and how this has altered (or adversely defined) the nature of the communication and relationships within the family. The impact of complex trauma may have been transmitted not only from the parents to their children but also across multiple and between generations. Therefore, the overarching goal of family therapy in its aftermath is to assist all members of the current family to recognize and nonjudgmentally understand how trauma has led to their family member(s)' adaptations in behavior, beliefs, and relationships that might have been necessary for survival but that need to be—and can be—replaced with alternatives that restore family relationships. It is also geared toward identifying and eliciting individual and family strengths and resources, and in reinforcing the significance of physical and emotional support to the healing process. Family therapy does not replace trauma-focused therapy, but it is a potential source of support for trauma survivor family members as they engage in trauma-focused therapy and other recovery efforts, and for others in the family as they vicariously go through the recovery process. With this framework, we now turn to a closer examination of essential concepts in family systems therapy.

Foundational Concepts of Family Systems Theory

The focus in family therapy is on *communication*, the fundamental process that drives all human relationships, including activities and outcomes both within a family and between the family members and outside social systems. Communication occurs on both an *explicit* (i.e., messages that are overtly acknowledged by the sender) and *implicit* (i.e., messages that are sent in a manner, or have content, that is opaque—unacknowledged or disguised by the sender) level. Communication also can be *validating* (i.e., respectful and affirming of the identity and worth of the recipient) and *coherent* (i.e., internally consistent, accurate, and meaningful to the recipient), or, alternatively, *coercive* (i.e., controlling, demanding, intrusive, exploitive, threatening, blaming, or devaluing) and *confusing* (i.e., fragmented, deceptive, disconnected, overgeneral, conflicted and inconsistent, filled with unverified assumptions masquerading as facts, or based on mind reading). In family therapy, explicit forms of communication that are validating and coherent are modeled by the therapist as they guide the family in recognizing and relinquishing implicit (and also explicit) communications that are coercive and confusing. This shift in communication style can be extremely difficult to accomplish, but it is of critical importance. Families with complex trauma histories often have hidden secrets in a maze of implicit communications that make up deeply ingrained (often intergenerational) patterns of survival coping and disorganized attachment that extend to all relationships.

Several family characteristics must be considered when intervening with a trauma-impacted family to help family members establish healthier communication and relationships. Also, note that these families may have intergenerational addictions, and the characteristics discussed below are often found in these families as well. All families have *boundaries*: *Internal boundaries* define family membership and relationships between members, and how emotionally close or distant they can be with one another. Boundaries can be too rigid, leading to too much distance or detachment, or too permeable, leading to enmeshment and intrusion. In contrast, *external boundaries*, as the name implies, separate and differentiate the family and its members from outsiders. They can be overly rigid and keep a family isolated from "outsiders," which in turn can lead to missed opportunities for social support and overreliance and enmeshment of family members one with the other. The functioning of the family may have historically been impacted by intergenerational or other forms of intra- or extrafamilial trauma or by trauma that is more current and attenuated. Such trauma-impacted family systems tend to have boundaries that are unstable and unreliable. They may be so open that members feel insecure, as if they do not really belong or matter. These families tend to be detached, neglectful, and unable (or unwilling) to protect their members. Members paradoxically may also be unable to maintain their personal privacy and safety. When boundaries are too rigid and closed, members may be unable to feel close to anyone, whether inside or outside, yet they might also feel smothered and entrapped in the family.

In trauma- and addiction-impacted families there also tend to be *family rules* (i.e., implicit expectations about how people should act) that perpetuate both survival coping (e.g., "In our family, you always have to watch out so that no one takes advantage of you") and disorganized attachment (e.g., "You'll only get hurt if you let yourself care about someone"). The *family roles* in trauma-impacted families also tend to emphasize survival and emotional detachment (e.g., the selfless and victimized caretaker, the dominant and controlling authority, the stigmatized scapegoat, the needy and helpless invalid) and role reversal (e.g., the child(ren) caretake and "parent" their parents, and may be responsible for raising and protecting their siblings). Finally, trauma-impacted families often include *coalitions* that divide family members against each other, such as a *triangle,* in which two members use a third member as the intermediary in a conflict (e.g., a father and daughter each complain about the other to their wife/mother instead of working out their conflict directly together) or an *intergenerational coalition,* in which two members of different generations act as if they have a relationship that is more intimate than is appropriate (e.g., a father and daughter acting as partners and as though the mother is the child).

Family patterns of communication often are profoundly altered by PTSD and CTSDs. PTSD's intrusive reexperiencing, avoidance, and hypervigilance symptoms can lead to implicit communications by trauma survivors that are extremely confusing for other family members (e.g., "Why is he always on edge and distant with me? Doesn't he still love me?"; "He's normal and loving one minute, then angry and critical the next") and at times coercive (e.g., "She watches me like a hawk, always looking to tell me what to do and what I'm doing wrong"; "He's always trying to control me and the kids"). The negative emotion states in PTSD and emotion dysregulation in CTSDs convey both explicit and implicit messages to other family members that are invalidating (e.g., "He's always irritable, and if I do something that upsets him he'll explode and then just shut me out for days at a time"; "The kid's being rambunctious and normal kids really bother him, so he lashes out at them"), and often laced with mixed messages and mind reading ("One minute she's relaxed and happy, then without any warning she's convinced that I'm going to leave her and she does things that make me question why I stay") and hypervigilance ("He's always on guard and doesn't trust anybody, including family members"; "He has these nightmares and wakes up like someone is attacking him. I'm afraid to be in bed with him when he's like that"; "He has guns in the house and that scares me. One time, he threatened to shoot himself, and another, to shoot all of us. And this was when he was drinking"). Dissociative symptoms can lead family members to feel confused and emotionally cut off (e.g., "She just seems to go away, like she's not really here and doesn't even know who I am"; "He seems numb and like he's very detached and indifferent") or distrustful and fearful (e.g., "He becomes a completely different person, someone who just wants to use other people or doesn't care who he hurts in order to get his way, including me").

The reckless, aggressive, and self-harming behaviors that can occur in PTSD and CTSDs introduce additional coercion and confusion into family relationships and communication. Family members often feel pressured into placating, rescuing, or watching helplessly when another family member persistently takes extreme risks, is verbally or physically assaultive, or directly or indirectly harms themselves or others. These behaviors, and the apparent absence of self-control and concern for their own and others' safety and well-being, can be deeply frightening and also confusing for other family members (e.g., "I don't know how I can stand by and watch her hurt herself and other people, but I can't find a way to get through to her when she's out of control"). PTSD and CTSDs can lead a family member to adopt a variety of problematic stances in family relationships, including interacting in a manner that others experience as hostile and aggressive, helpless and dependent, controlling and demanding, or withdrawing and distancing—and often a combination of several of these invalidating, coercive, and confusing modes of communication.

Family dynamics are profoundly influenced by these PTSD/CTSD-related patterns of communication (in addition to or absent from addictions). Family rules tend to emphasize maintaining a hypervigilant preparedness for overwhelming survival threats—or alternatively, an avoidant, emotionally numbed, or dissociated detachment and lack of awareness of realistic safety concerns. Family roles can become correspondingly limited to those that have a focus on detecting and surviving—or paradoxically, recklessly "bringing on" or submitting to—harm and threats (e.g., the Drama Triangle of victim, persecutor, and rescuer or enabler). When impacted by PTSD or CTSDs, the myths that create a historical context for the family tend to be based on traumatic victimization, isolation or dependency, survival or death, victory or defeat, and vigilance or obliviousness to danger. In a trauma-infused context, family members often seek refuge and solace in coalitions borne of a sense of desperation and necessity, leading to a blurring of boundaries between generations and the formation of problematic intergenerational coalitions (e.g., a mother and son join together emotionally to defend themselves against the CTSD/alcohol-fueled outbursts by a spouse/father) and triangles (e.g., a husband and wife who independently confide in a teenage daughter in order to complain about the other spouse, in large part in reaction to the wife, who is a survivor of childhood sexual abuse, having become increasingly avoidant of intimacy).

As a result of this wide array of potential adverse alterations in communication and family dynamics related to complex trauma history and PTSD/CTSD symptoms, the family system's equilibrium often is compromised. Homeostasis may be disrupted by problems in communication related to a survivor member's distress (e.g., the entire family may become stuck in a state of hypervigilance and avoidance). This can lead to allostasis (i.e., breakdown in the family system) in the form of overt or thinly disguised conflict among family members. For example, family conflict may ensue if some members feel sympathetic toward and attempt to support a survivor member who angrily challenges other members for denying or minimizing the impact of past abuse. Alternatively, in the family just described, triangles may emerge, with the survivor and sympathetic members joining together to blame others for being uncaring or disloyal, while other members form coalitions to defend themselves and blame the others for being "enablers" of the survivor as a helpless victim.

PTSD and CTSD symptoms may also lead to volatile destabilization of family communication and dynamics. Extreme forms of either intense aggressive/intrusive or shutdown detached/disengaged communication may emerge when family members become distressed, frustrated, or exhausted emotionally in response to a survivor member's extreme emotional or behavioral instability. For example, families experiencing persistent crises related to a survivor member's repeated and intractable medical illnesses, addictions, self-harm, or suicidality may develop correspondingly severe and persistent crises in communicating with the survivor or one another (e.g., lashing out verbally, making threats, cutting off communication, scapegoating the survivor, goading the person to "get it over with"). Family dynamics become severely dysregulated as members attempt to adapt their relationships within and outside the family (i.e., *morphogenesis*) in order to accommodate a survivor's PTSD and CTSD symptoms. For example, family members who traditionally have valued kindness and respect in relationships may find themselves struggling not to become distrustful, bitter, or intolerant toward one another and outsiders when a survivor member's symptoms elicit those attitudes. As a result, members of a family that was formerly accepting and cohesive may find themselves drawn increasingly into conflict and volatility in their relationships inside and outside the family.

On the other hand, the inadvertent influence of a member experiencing PTSD/CTSDs may lead a family system to become frozen in a highly dysfunctional state of static equilibrium and shutdown (Madanes & Haley, 1977). Hypervigilance and emotional disconnection or dissociation may become the organizing principle not only for the member experiencing PTSD or CTSDs but also the entire family. This often occurs gradually and subtly, as if by osmosis, as family members find themselves experiencing a contagious sense of hypervigilance and detachment/dissociation that is consistent with the phenomenon of secondary traumatic stress (Sprang, Ford, Kerig, & Bride, 2018). The resultant "new normal" for the entire family thus may be organized around implicit rules (e.g., "Us against the world"; "Every person for themselves"; "Nobody understands—or can understand—what we are going through"), roles (e.g., helpless victim, angry protector, passive observer), communication patterns (e.g., "Don't ask, don't tell, don't feel"), and relational dynamics (e.g., "Keep secrets at all costs"; "Never let anyone get close") that are rigid and self-defeating—mirroring the survivor member's symptoms.

Family Systems Therapy for PTSD and CTSDs

Family systems therapy is designed to achieve several goals that are directly relevant to recovery from PTSD and CTSDs (Catherall, 1998; Figley, 1989). This includes restoring adaptive intra- and extrafamilial communication (i.e., *homeostasis*) that has been disrupted or altered in reaction to a family member's PTSD or CTSD symptoms. It also includes transforming trauma-infused family dynamics (i.e., rules, roles, myths, and rituals) and restoring the integrity of relational boundaries that have become rigid or otherwise compromised (e.g., triangles, intergenerational coalitions, enmeshed relationships); decreasing aggressive behavior toward self, family members, or others; and addressing addictions and fostering recovery by developing or strengthening adaptive relational patterns (i.e., *morphogenesis*).

Family therapy was provided to military veterans in the Vietnam era in order to assist all members in understanding the nature and severity of the traumatic experiences and aftereffects on the survivor member. This was done in order to "detoxify" the traumatic experiences in several ways (Rosenheck & Thomson, 1986, p. 559). These include facilitating a careful discussion of the military veteran's traumatic experiences with other family members, separate from the veteran, prior to conjoint family sessions in which current relational issues were discussed with the entire family. The goal was to enhance family members' empathy for the veteran while also therapeutically mitigating the adverse vicarious impact on them as they learned about the veteran member's traumas and its consequences. By informing family members, while simultaneously protecting them from experiencing overwhelming sympathetic distress or horror, they were able to understand their veteran's trauma-related reactions without negative judgment. This preparatory work with family members also reduced the military veteran family member's sense of emotional disconnection by ensuring that past traumatic experiences were not kept secret, and that other family members understood that those experiences were a legitimate source of distress—without burdening the veteran with the responsibility of explaining or justifying the experiences and their impact. As a result, neither the veteran nor others in the family had to deal with an overwhelming disclosure but could focus instead on supporting one another in reconnection and recovery.

Family systems therapy is designed to provide a safe place for family members to learn how exposure to traumatic stressors impacts the survivor(s) and, in turn, their loved ones, so as to reduce the stigma, guilt and shame, and confusion that can affect every person in a family (Catherall, 1998). This form of therapy also offers a unique opportunity for family members to share their questions, experiences, and feelings related to past traumatic experiences and ongoing traumatic stress reactions with therapeutic guidance. This is crucial in assisting family members to learn to accurately and sensitively communicate with other family members, whether they are on the expressing or the receiving end of the communication. Effective communication is a foundation for not only emotional support, intimacy, and affection between family members but also active problem solving and conflict resolution among them.

When one or more family members are experiencing complex traumatic stress reactions that originated years or even decades earlier as a result of exposure to childhood complex traumas (e.g., childhood abuse or victimization by family, peer, or community violence), family systems therapy can assist the survivor(s) to therapeutically process trauma memories (Ford, 2018) with the support of other family members (Basham, 2004). This may be done in several formats, depending on the type of trauma, the preferences of the survivor(s) and other family members, the nature and strength of their relationships with one another, and the training of the therapist. Conjoint sessions in which several family members participate simultaneously can provide a safe place for survivors to explain how they are working through trauma memories in separate one-to-one therapy sessions and reduce other family members' anxieties about the process and their survivor member's safety and ability to benefit from it. Conjoint family sessions, usually only with adult family members (e.g., couples or adult siblings) and not children, also can be a setting in which survivors actually engage in trauma memory processing in the presence of carefully selected family members who are prepared to be supportive. Either way, family therapy provides a tangible way for complex trauma survivors to break the vicious cycle of secrecy, avoidance, shame and guilt, emotional dysregulation, dissociation, and relational detachment/isolation in CTSDs with the support of other members, and to ensure that this process benefits healing—and is not emotionally overwhelming for—all involved.

Family systems therapy also can address difficulties with parenting that may result from PTSD or CTSD symptoms in an adult or child family member (or both) (Gewirtz, Forgatch, & Wieling, 2008). When traumatic stress symptoms interfere with a parent's emotional availability and responsiveness to their child(ren), family therapy provides opportunities for therapist-guided parent–child interactions in the sessions with therapeutic preparation, modeling, and feedback (usually undertaken after the adult has been stabilized and supported to some degree). Child victims may also need a period of stabilization and trauma processing prior to being able to work productively within the family context. An additional benefit of family therapy is that it can assist with access to social support and other resources (e.g., from neighbors and community members, or educational, governmental, or religious organizations or family/parent support programs). With traumatized children, it is often advisable to involve as many of their extrafamilial social systems as possible in their treatment (Saxe, Ellis, & Brown, 2015).

The Evidence Base for Family Systems Therapy with PTSD and CTSDs

Family systems therapies have been tested for PTSD prevention and treatment primarily with families in which a young child and parent have been exposed to domestic violence (Lieberman, Ghosh Ippen, & Van Horn, 2006; Toth, Rogosch, Manly, & Cicchetti, 2006), or with a school-age child who is experiencing internalizing or externalizing problems after having been exposed to family or community sexual or physical abuse (King et al., 2000; Sheinberg & True, 2008) or violence (Berkowitz, Stover, & Marans, 2011). A family systems approach to treatment focused on improving parenting skills and providing parents with social–emotional support with children who have experienced maltreatment was found to improve positive therapeutic outcomes (van der Put, Assink, Gubbels, & Boekhout van Solinge, 2018).

Family systems therapies have shown evidence of effectiveness in treating adolescents with substance use disorders, conduct/disruptive behavior disorders, affective disorders, and eating disorders (Hartnett, Carr, Hamilton, & O'Reilly, 2017; Jewell, Blessitt, Stewart, Simic, & Eisler, 2016; Sprenkle, 2012; van der Pol et al., 2017). Although these youths' trauma histories and PTSD or CTSD symptoms have not been reported in family system therapy studies with troubled adolescents, clinical epidemiological data suggest that a majority of them have trauma histories and are experiencing PTSD/CTSD symptoms in addition to their identified behavioral health problems (Cuevas, Finkelhor, Ormrod, & Turner, 2009; Ford, Wasser, & Connor, 2011).

Another subgroup of potentially trauma-exposed youth, adolescents who had recovered from cancer and children who are newly diagnosed with cancer, received a 1-day, four-session family-based program, the Surviving Cancer Competently Intervention Program (SCCIP) with their families. SSCIP was found to be associated with reductions in adolescent cancer survivors' PTSD hyperarousal symptoms and their fathers' (but not their mothers') PTSD reexperiencing and hyperarousal (but not avoidance and emotional numbing) symptoms (Kazak et al., 2004).

One component, family psychoeducation, when delivered as a freestanding intervention, has been found to additionally benefit adults with a variety of conditions, including psychiatric disorders, serious mental illness (e.g., schizophrenia, bipolar disorder), and substance use disorders (Bressi, Manenti, Frongia, Porcellana, & Invernizzi, 2008; Cai, Zhu, Zhang, Wang, & Zhang, 2015; Gottlieb, Mueser, & Glynn, 2012; Lucksted, McFarlane, Downing, & Dixon, 2012; Miklowitz & Chung, 2016; Weisman de Mamani, Weintraub, Gurak, & Maura, 2014). Cultural adaptations of family psychoeducation have shown promise with Pacific Island military veterans (Whealin et al., 2017), Rwandan families with children affected by HIV (Betancourt et al., 2017), and families of patients with severe mental illness in Iran, Mexico, and Viet Nam (Dominguez-Martinez et al., 2017; Mirsepassi, Tabatabaee, Sharifi, & Mottaghipour, 2018; Ngoc, Weiss, & Trung, 2016). However, there is very limited evidence that conjoint family systems therapies, over and above the contributions of family psychoeducation, are effective with adults, except in engaging adult substance users in treatment (Sprenkle, 2012). An exception is that behavioral couple therapies have shown evidence of efficacy in reducing depression and substance misuse, conflictual communication, and relational dissatisfaction in adult couples with depression or a substance use disorders (Sprenkle, 2012). However, behavioral couple therapy was not found to enhance the outcome of one-to-one prolonged exposure therapy for PTSD with military veterans (Glynn et al., 1999).

Since PTSD and CTSDs in an adult family member not only affects the couple but also parenting and the relationships with the couple's children, as well as the children's sibling relationships and other intra- and intergenerational relationships (Gerlock, Grimesey, & Sayre, 2014; Paley, Lester, & Mogil, 2013), adult partners of survivor family members may play an important role in either buffering (preventing) or inadvertently increasing the transmission of post-traumatic stress to the next generation (i.e., children) (Bachem, Levin, Zhou, Zerach, & Solomon, 2018; Bair-Merritt, Mandal, Epstein, Werlinich, & Kerrigan, 2014; Sherman, Larsen, Straits-Troster, Erbes, & Tassey, 2015). Harsh or emotionally abusive parenting is associated with more severe PTSD and CTSD symptoms in children who experienced multiple types of victimization (Turner et al., 2012) and with more severe disruptive behavior problems in young children exposed to their parents' intimate partner violence (Grasso et al., 2016). On the other hand, nurturing and responsive parenting is associated with lower levels of PTSD/CTSD symptoms in victimized children (Turner et al., 2012) and with positive co-regulation and competence among children coping with family homelessness (Herbers, Cutuli, Supkoff, Narayan, & Masten, 2014).

PTSD specifically was found to be associated with lower levels of empathic concern and perspective taking among mothers (Parlar et al., 2014), and maternal PTSD symptom severity was shown to be related to emotion and behavioral regulation problems in their infant children at ages 6 months and 13 months (Bosquet Enlow et al., 2011). Similarly, military fathers' PTSD symptoms were associated with their children's behavioral and emotional problems (as reported by both parents), and worsening paternal PTSD symptoms were associated with worsening emotional and behavioral problems by their children over time (Parsons et al., 2018). Among families exposed to war and poverty in the Middle East, children who had more severe and persistent PTSD symptoms during the subsequent year were more likely than less symptomatic or more resilient children to have fathers who had insecure relational attachment styles (Punamaki, Palosaari, Diab, Peltonen, & Qouta, 2015). Thus, both maternal and paternal PTSD and CTSD difficulties are associated with their children's emotional and behavioral difficulties. The potentially complex interplay of maternal and paternal PTSD symptoms, parenting behaviors, and child psychosocial problems was highlighted by results of a study with families in which the father had been deployed to a combat zone (Snyder et al., 2016). PTSD symptoms of both the father and the mother were reciprocally associated with their 4- to 13-year-old children's internalizing and externalizing behaviors in what was described as a cascade of interlinked adult and child problems; importantly, this study showed that coercive parenting behavior was associated with an escalation of this negative cascade, while positive engagement between the two parents was associated with lower levels of child internalizing problems.

Unfortunately, few studies have investigated the efficacy of conjoint family systems therapy when an adult family member has experienced trauma or is experiencing PTSD. Quasi-experimental effectiveness studies of conjoint family systems therapy have been conducted with military veterans experiencing psychosocial impairment due either to exposure to potentially traumatic war-zone stressors (Ford et al., 1997) or stressful non-war-zone deployments and prolonged separation from their families (Ford et al., 1998). War-zone deployed military veterans who received brief (i.e., one to five sessions) family systems therapy showed clinically significant and sustained (at a 6-week follow-up) reductions in PTSD and psychiatric symptoms, and improvements in family functioning as compared to a cohort of non-treatment-seeking war-zone deployed veterans; therapy was delivered on an individual, couple, or conjoint family basis, with no differences between those formats on any outcome (Ford et al., 1997). In a parallel study with non-war-zone deployed military veterans, family therapy was associated with reductions in psychological distress and improvements in family functioning and marital satisfaction at the conclusion of therapy and at 6-week follow-up (Ford et al., 1998).

A manualized, eight-session therapy, Families OverComing Under Stress (FOCUS), was developed for military families in order to provide psychoeducation about PTSD, identify family communication patterns and relational dynamics, support open and effective communication and coping/resilience skills, and create a shared family narrative of traumatic or stressful experiences and their impact on every family member (Saltzman, 2016). When FOCUS was provided to more than 2,500 military families, parent subjects reported reduced depression, anxiety, and PTSD symptoms at the conclusion of treatment and at 1-month and 6-month follow-up. By their own report and their parents' observations, participating children were less anxious and displayed fewer behavioral problems and more prosocial behaviors. Parents also reported reductions in problematic family dynamics following treatment (Lester et al., 2016).

At its start, FOCUS is delivered in three parent-only sessions, two children-only sessions, and sessions to teach each generation separately and in age-appropriate ways about PTSD symptoms and coping/resilience skills. The development of a life narrative is also introduced. It is a timeline showing stressful events not limited to traumatic stressors (e.g., difficult separations, deaths and losses, problems in relationships, work, or school), but also including key life transitions and positive events and accomplishments. The final three sessions engage the entire family in co-creating a shared narrative that emphasizes the members' resilience and the family's ability to support and value every member while achieving shared and individual goals. FOCUS is designed to assist parents in "maintaining clear leadership" and the entire family in "maintaining clear . . . boundaries and roles" (Saltzman, 2016, p, 657).

Clinical Case Example

The following case example involves a family that is a masked composite of several distressed families. It involves two parents who both experienced developmental trauma in childhood (including sexual, physical, and emotional abuse; betrayal; and violence by primary caregivers), traumatic intimate partner violence in their relationship as adolescents and as adults; and severe undetected and untreated CTSD symptoms that have contributed to problems with substance abuse, sexual identity confusion, verbal and physical relational aggression, and depression. A focus on CTSDs as a shared dilemma for both adults as a couple and as parents (and thus for the entire family) provides a framework for meaningful individual engagement in trauma-focused one-to-one treatment for the mitigation of past adverse effects, in order to prevent continued intergenerational transmission to their adolescent daughter and son.

The Parents

Leon and Carol, both African Americans, met when they were kids. Both experienced multiple adversities in their childhoods. Each had a parent addicted to alcohol and drugs (in Carol's case, both parents), and as children, witnessed violence, poverty, racism, drug use and abuse, and experienced the deaths of family members and peers. They started dating in high school. Leon fell "head over heels" in love, but Carol was uncomfortable with getting emotionally intimate. She had never told anyone, but she had been sexually abused by her maternal grandfather from ages 7–12 when she had "special" visits at her grandparents. When Leon and Carol were seniors, they started to have sex, and Carol got pregnant. Leon was happy that they could start a family together, but Carol felt ashamed and disgusted at the thought of being pregnant, so she decided to have an abortion, which she did, without consulting Leon. When he learned, he was livid, slapped her across the face, and said he was done with the relationship. He relented after a week of stony silence, and they both promised to make the relationship work. Initially, when feeling emotionally wounded, Carol lashed out verbally and Leon, physically, but ultimately both used verbal and physical aggression on one another. Shortly before high school graduation, Carol broke up with Leon.

Leon went into the military and Carol, to college. For years, each lived separate lives that had similar patterns of distinctly different public and private sides. Outwardly popular socially and successful in launching their careers (Carol as an intensive care nurse, and Leon as a noncommissioned officer, then in biotechnology sales), both secretively drank to the point of blackout several times a week. Neither married, and 15 years after graduation, they met at a high school reunion and "fell back in love." Both felt guilt for having hurt the other and, as they had both matured and been successful, believed they would never hurt each other again.

The Family

The couple married after living together for a year, and had a daughter, Jasmine, and a son, Leshawn. Leon was away a lot on sales trips, making Carol the primary parent while she worked as an on-call nurse in a local hospital. Leshawn and Jasmine were very competitive and often had verbal spats that Carol found upsetting, but Leon wrote it off as "kids being kids." Leshawn was shy and a good student ("a real nerd," according to Jasmine), and Jasmine, a star athlete, was socially very popular ("a Facebook queen" according to Leshawn). While maintaining a public image as a happy couple, Carol and Leon became estranged emotionally, largely due to being apart so much and having fewer shared interests and ways to enjoy being together. Most evenings were spent apart or alone together, drinking alcohol—while their children were busy with school or athletic activities. Periodically, when Leon's work was stressful, he came home late and intoxicated. In this state, he would yell at Carol seemingly for no reason—yelling which she returned in kind, as she had often been drinking as well. On several occasions, these yelling episodes escalated into physical pushing, slapping, and smashed walls and furniture, leaving the children upset, confused, and fearful of future recurrences.

The Crisis

When Leshawn was 15 and Jasmine, 17, Leon came home early from a canceled trip to find Carol drinking and wearing his clothes. Shocked, he angrily demanded to know "What the hell is going on?" Feeling guilty and defensive, Carol replied angrily, saying that "someone in this family needs to wear the pants, since you won't." Leon became enraged and grabbed Carol's hair from the back, dragging her screaming onto the couch; she was terrified that he had lost control and might kill her. Fortunately, the children were not at home, and Carol fled to the house of a neighbor, who, having heard the yelling and seeing Carol shaking and sobbing, called the police. When Leshawn and Jasmine returned home later, they found the police talking to their father, and no sign of their mother. A Child Protective Services crisis worker arrived soon afterwards and reassured them that their mother was safe next door. After talking with Leon, and then with Carol and conducting a violence risk assessment and learning there had been no previous reports of violence to the authorities, the crisis worker met with the whole family. Both parents indicated their willingness to take immediate steps to stop the conflict, to keep their family together, and to make their home safe for their children. They indicated their willingness to engage in family therapy. Leshawn and Jasmine said they wanted to stay at home rather than going to a respite or foster home, as they believed their parents' promise to stop fighting and get help immediately.

Initial Evaluation

Leon and Carol met the next day with a therapist with expertise in crisis family therapy and trauma recovery. After meeting with the parents, first separately and then together, the therapist determined that concurrent couple therapy with Leon and Carol, as well as conjoint family therapy with the parents and both children, would be important not only to help the children but also to get and keep both parents engaged in individual therapy, and skills-based and support groups focused on addiction recovery and anger management.

Couple Therapy: Early Sessions

When asked why they thought they were in therapy and what they wanted to accomplish, Leon acknowledged a problem with drinking and anger. Carol said that she wanted them both to stop keeping secrets and living like stranger roommates. Leon replied that the only secret was that Carol was gay and did not really want an intimate relationship with him. The therapist challenged him gently, saying that it sounded like Carol did want a meaningful relationship with him, but she had some serious questions about herself with which to contend.

CAROL: I don't know who I am or what I want, I've used drinking and putting on a happy face to hide who I am, even myself, for so long. I know I love you, Leon, but now I'm losing you all over again. I can't be with anyone, truly, unless I get serious in understanding me.

LEON: So now you're going to dress like a man and find your true love with a woman. I don't want anything to do with that, it's not right. What's this gonna do to our children?

CAROL: We're already hurting out children when we act like we don't care about anything, including each other, and just drink ourselves into oblivion. And they're terrified every time we get violent. That's what hurts them, not my being honest.

LEON: This is what you call honesty? Ruining our relationship and our family because you dress like a man and don't want to be with a real man? No wonder I drink!

THERAPIST: I see how much you each care about this relationship and each other, but there are obvious issues and obstacles. (*Leon scoffs.*) Yes, I can see how confusing this is for you, Leon, and for both of you. But you're both saying that you don't want to lose what is at the heart of your relationship and your family. Carol, I hear you saying that your relationship has gotten watered down by the drinking violence, and could be lost forever if you don't both put aside the pretenses and find a way to get honest and open up to each other.

CAROL: That's right, and even though I make it sound like Leon is the bad guy, that's just not true. He's been my rock while I've been fighting with ghosts from the past. It's not fair to him that I blame him, but I don't know how I can stop if I keep lying to myself. I don't know why I want to wear his clothes. I don't feel any attraction to women; in fact, Leon's the only one I want to be with physically. But it seems like he's always somewhere else even when we're together, and that makes me feel so lonely that I just grab for anything to get some comfort.

LEON: So now you're going to throw it all away, and me, too? That's worse than any beating I ever had, even when I was getting whupped and beat down by my old man as a kid.

CAROL: Well, when I was a child, I didn't get beaten but I got something worse. My body got taken and used. For as long as I can remember, even when I was just a kid, I always felt like something was off. I hated the frilly dresses that my parents wanted me to wear, because they just reminded me of how my grandmother and grandfather would dress me up on "special" visits, but that was just a lie they told so he could molest me. For years, I cried in secret every time I returned from seeing them, and then I cried almost every night until I found out when I was 12 that drinking could blot out the memories. I pretended I was a boy, even made up a boy's name to call myself, just so maybe I wouldn't have to have any more "visits."

THERAPIST: You're both making some very important points, which might sound unrelated, but I think actually are at the heart of the matter. Each of you has bad memories that you've been able to keep at bay by shutting them out with drinking and anger. You've kept them locked away even if it meant giving up feeling close to each other. Therapy can help you safely face those memories and put them where they belong, in the past, so that you don't keep reliving them. While you each do that, together we can clear away all the emotional fog that those memories have created, to give you a chance to decide what really is your truth and how to live it together.

Family Therapy

Therapy continued with conjoint sessions with all family members.

LEON: I want to start by saying to all of you that I am really sorry that I let my anger get the better of me, and I know this is not the first time—but I'm going to do everything I can to make it last. I know I hurt and scared your mom, and I know that I've made you scared that I was going to do something terrible to her, but I never want to hurt or scare her or either of you.

JASMINE: Well you had a right to be angry this time, Dad. I can't believe she could be so twisted. That's not what a real woman would do, and not the kind of mother I want.

LESHAWN: That's just cold. I feel sorry for her having to put up with his drinking and his yelling and smashing things all the time. That makes me depressed, and I don't have to put up with it most of the time, because I can just leave. She has to stay and deal with his drinking and his meanness every day and be waiting for it to start all over again every night.

JASMINE: Yeah, little brother, you're sooo depressed that you probably still wet the bed every night. You can't blame him. You're too old to still be whining and crying like a baby.

LEON: That's what I'm saying (*turning to Carol*), you always act like you have to defend him. That just makes him weak. Now *you* want to be the man—how's he gonna become a man?

LESHAWN: Yeah, a man like you, who drinks too much? Is that how I'm supposed to be a man? (*turning to Jasmine*) Or I should have a nasty mouth like you, always taking his side against her, when she's the one who's always there for us? (*Carol nods and puts her hand on his knee.*)

JASMINE: Always there for us, huh? Not for me. I can't have a mother who goes around in men's clothes. It's disgusting. I'm supposed to go shopping for clothes with a woman who dresses like a man? My friends will laugh at me, they'll drop me like a dirty penny; everyone will laugh at me because my mother is a freak.

CAROL: Jasmine, I know this is hard for you and your father. I'm not gonna do anything to embarrass you. I just need to stop pretending everything is fine when I know the drinking and the fighting isn't. And I don't understand why I dress in men's clothes sometimes. I've got to get to the bottom of this for me and for all of us.

THERAPIST: Jasmine, you're right to say that you need a mother you can be proud of. Leshawn, I think you're saying the same thing to your father about how important he is to you as a role model. What's happening here is not that your mother is suddenly changing or going away, but she is trying to sort things out. In many ways, the clothes and are a symptom of secrets from the past playing out in the present. Your parents, like their parents before them, managed their hurt and confusion with solitary and often secret drinking that later led to conflict and unhappiness, even violence. That can happen when good people are carrying around a heavy load from past, things that should never have happened to them. But now, instead of keeping secrets like the clothes, the drinking, or the anger and violence, we can talk about what's really going on and try to heal the hurt. Does that make sense? (*Carol nods and looks at Leon; Leshawn looks inquiringly at the therapist; Leon and Jasmine look puzzled, then sigh deeply.*)

LEON: I don't see why we have to talk about all this, especially in front of our children. This shouldn't involve them. It's between their mother and me." (*Jasmine nods pointedly.*)

THERAPIST: You're absolutely right, Dad. There are things that you and your wife need to talk about together in your couple sessions and separately, in individual therapy, that are private for you as adults, and Jasmine and Leshawn shouldn't hear. They're young adults and they need to focus on their own lives without being burdened by their parents' problems. But they need to know that you are dealing with that adult business in a way that supports this family as a unit, and that they can trust you to be there for them and to be role models—that they can be proud of and draw on. So, when I say that we can talk honestly with no more secrets, this means that parents deal with the private adult matters apart from the young adults, but the whole family deals openly with various issues that affect them all.

LESHAWN: (*looking at his father*) If we're gonna work this out together, I have something to say. I'm not gonna keep pretending everything is all right when it's not. I'm not weak and I don't keep secrets. I keep my mouth shut unless I have something to say that's true and shows respect. I don't care what clothes anyone wears (*looking at Carol*), or whether they're popular and have all the right friends (*looking at Jasmine*), if they're truthful and show respect (*looking again at Leon*).

THERAPIST: How's that sound as a place to start? Truth and respect. Each of the adults in this family have made a commitment to work on their own issues, in therapy both separately and together. In these family sessions, we can work on making the changes that you all agree will restore your relationships with each other. I recognize that each of you has said and done things that have communicated disrespect and caused hurt. We can work together to figure out how you can live more honestly without giving up your hopes and love and respect for one another. It's hard work, but it's the best way to be sure you can count on one another and that you're wearing the right clothes on the inside of yourself as well as on the outside.

Commentary on the Case Example

This case illustrates how family systems therapy approaches complex trauma histories with PTSD and CTSD symptoms in both spouses and assists them to recognize how the unresolved past plays out in current relationships, indicating a need to change how they communicate with one another and with their children. By helping the couple and their children speak about emotions, fears, and hopes, along with unspoken issues (e.g., parents' drinking and violence, parents' emotional detachment from one another, father's absence, mother's choice of dress when at home and drinking, parents' histories of abuse and neglect), the therapy revealed a number of family secrets and rules (e.g., "If you try to be true to yourself you'll ruin the family"; "Keep your problems to yourself"; "You can't rely on anyone in this family") and two problematic coalitions (i.e., father and daughter; mother and son). These secrets, rules, and coalitions appeared to be the result of traumatic circumstances and experiences that carried over from the parents' childhoods into their couple relationship, their parenting, and into the next generation as their children now are adopting survival coping to deal with the effects of complex intrafamilial trauma and the confusion and insecurity it has caused. In a conversational manner, the therapist first talked with the family about childhood trauma and its immediate and long-term/intergenerational effects. Without going into a lot of detail, the children were given information about trauma in their parents' backgrounds and how it could relate to their present drinking and behavior with one another and with them. They learned that behaviors that once might have helped to cope with trauma can later become problematic, if the trauma effects persist and are not directly addressed or resolved. The therapist then laid out a treatment plan of individual, addictions, couple, group, and family sessions to help the couple and the family to reconnect. The need for safety of all members in the family was emphasized as the first priority. The therapist consistently modeled ways to shift out of crisis/survival mode and to reaffirm deep emotional bonds. These included empathizing with each member's sense of hurt, betrayal, shame, disappointment, sadness, and fear (of past and present traumatic harm/violation/exploitation/conflict and abandonment/loss); validating each member's core values and goals; highlighting the contribution each makes to the entire family; reframing anger and conflict as an expression of motivation and determination to change maladaptive ways of ways of thinking and behaving; reorienting to the present context when memories of anger, hopelessness, or detachment lead to conflict or dissociation; constructively and supportively challenging family members who are dysregulated to refocus on their core values; clarifying how family secrets, rules, and coalitions create barriers that separate and isolate family members and reduce their privacy, trust, and autonomy; identifying and restructuring intergenerational coalitions so that the children were not parentified; and acknowledging hurt but refocusing on family members' sense of determination to find a shared path forward.

Conclusion

Well-established therapeutic principles and practices for family systems therapy have great potential applicability for CTSDs. Careful attention to family dynamics is essential in all cases, but especially when the multilayered impact of intrafamilial trauma (e.g., incest, multigenerational family violence) is involved. Family systems therapy may also contribute to the secondary prevention of PTSD/CTSDs by enabling family members (especially children) who are affected by direct or vicarious trauma to not "play it forward" with their own children. Formalization and systematic evaluation of CTSD-focused family systems therapy protocols thus is an important next step in the evolution of CTSD treatments over the next decade.

References

Assink, M., Spruit, A., Schuts, M., Lindauer, R., van der Put, C. E., & Stams, G. J. M. (2018). The intergenerational transmission of child maltreatment: A three-level meta-analysis. *Child Abuse and Neglect, 84*, 131–145.

Bacchus, L. J., Ranganathan, M., Watts, C., & Devries, K. (2018). Recent intimate partner violence against women and health: A systematic review and meta-analysis of cohort studies. *BMJ Open, 8*(7), e019995.

Bachem, R., Levin, Y., Zhou, X., Zerach, G., & Solomon, Z. (2018). The role of parental posttraumatic stress, marital adjustment, and dyadic self-disclosure in intergenerational transmission of trauma: A family system approach. *Journal of Marital and Family Therapy, 44*(3), 543–555.

Bailey, H. N., Tarabulsy, G. M., Moran, G., Pederson, D. R., & Bento, S. (2017). New insight on intergenerational attachment from a relationship-based analysis. *Development and Psychopathology, 29*(2), 433–448.

Bair-Merritt, M. H., Mandal, M., Epstein, N. B., Werlinich, C. A., & Kerrigan, D. (2014). The context of violent disagreements between parents: A qualitative analysis from parents' reports. *BMC Public Health, 14*, 1324.

Basham, K. (2004). Transforming the legacies of childhood trauma in couple and family therapy. *Social Work in Health Care, 39*(3–4), 263–285.

Berkowitz, S. J., Stover, C. S., & Marans, S. R. (2011). The Child and Family Traumatic Stress Intervention: Secondary prevention for youth at risk of developing PTSD. *Journal of Child Psychology and Psychiatry and Allied Disciplines, 52*(6), 676–685.

Berthelot, N., Ensink, K., Bernazzani, O., Normandin, L., Luyten, P., & Fonagy, P. (2015). Intergenerational transmission of attachment in abused and neglected mothers: The role of trauma-specific reflective functioning. *Infant Mental Health Journal, 36*(2), 200–212.

Betancourt, T. S., Ng, L. C., Kirk, C. M., Brennan, R. T., Beardslee, W. R., Stulac, S., . . . Sezibera, V. (2017). Family-based promotion of mental health in children affected by HIV: A pilot randomized controlled trial. *Journal of Child Psychology and Psychiatry, 58*(8), 922–930.

Boeckel, M. G., Blasco-Ros, C., Grassi-Oliveira, R., & Martinez, M. (2014). Child abuse in the context of intimate partner violence against women: The impact of women's depressive and posttraumatic stress symptoms on maternal behavior. *Journal of Interpersonal Violence, 29*(7), 1201–1227.

Bosquet Enlow, M., Egeland, B., Carlson, E., Blood, E., & Wright, R. J. (2014). Mother–infant attachment and the intergenerational transmission of posttraumatic stress disorder. *Development and Psychopathology, 26*(1), 41–65.

Bosquet Enlow, M., Kitts, R. L., Blood, E., Bizarro, A., Hofmeister, M., & Wright, R. J. (2011). Maternal posttraumatic stress symptoms and infant emotional reactivity and emotion regulation. *Infant Behavior and Development, 34*(4), 487–503.

Bressi, C., Manenti, S., Frongia, P., Porcellana, M., & Invernizzi, G. (2008). Systemic family therapy in schizophrenia: A randomized clinical trial of effectiveness. *Psychotherapy and Psychosomatics, 77*(1), 43–49.

Byun, S., Brumariu, L. E., & Lyons-Ruth, K. (2016). Disorganized attachment in young adulthood as a partial mediator of relations between severity of childhood abuse and dissociation. *Journal of Trauma and Dissociation, 17*(4), 460–479.

Cai, J., Zhu, Y., Zhang, W., Wang, Y., & Zhang, C. (2015). Comprehensive family therapy: An effective approach for cognitive rehabilitation in schizophrenia. *Neuropsychiatric Disease and Treatment, 11*, 1247–1253.

Catherall, D. R. (Ed.). (1998). *Treating traumatized families.* Boca Raton, FL: CRC Press.

Courtois, C. A. (2010). *Healing the incest wound: Adult survivors in therapy* (2nd ed.). New York: Norton.

Cuevas, C. A., Finkelhor, D., Ormrod, R., & Turner, H. (2009). Psychiatric diagnosis as a risk marker for victimization in a national sample of children. *Journal of Interpersonal Violence, 24*(4), 636–652.

Dominguez-Martinez, T., Rascon-Gasca, M. L., Alcantara-Chabelas, H., Garcia-Silberman, S., Casanova-Rodas, L., & Lopez-Jimenez, J. L. (2017). Effects of family-to-family psychoeducation among relatives of patients with severe mental disorders in Mexico City. *Psychiatric Services, 68*(4), 415–418.

Figley, C. R. (1989). *Helping traumatized families.* San Francisco: Jossey-Bass.

Ford, J. D. (2018). Trauma memory processing in PTSD psychotherapy: A unifying framework. *Journal of Traumatic Stress, 31*, 933–942.

Ford, J. D., Chandler, P., Thacker, B., Greaves, D., Shaw, D., Sennhauser, S., & Schwartz, L. (1998). Family systems therapy after Operation Desert Storm with European-theater veterans. *Journal of Marital Family Therapy, 24*(2), 243–250.

Ford, J. D., Greaves, D., Chandler, P., Thacker, B., Shaw, D., Sennhauser, S., & Schwartz, L. (1997). Time-limited psychotherapy with Operation Desert Storm veterans. *Journal of Traumatic Stress, 10*(4), 655–664.

Ford, J. D., & Saltzman, W. (2009). Family systems therapy. In C. A. Courtois & J. D. Ford (Eds.), *Treating complex traumatic stress disorders: An evidence-based guide* (pp. 391–414). New York: Guilford Press.

Ford, J. D., Wasser, T., & Connor, D. F. (2011). Identifying and determining the symptom severity associated with polyvictimization among psychiatrically impaired children in the outpatient setting. *Child Maltreatment, 16*(3), 216–226.

Gerlock, A. A., Grimesey, J., & Sayre, G. (2014). Military-related posttraumatic stress disorder and intimate relationship behaviors: A developing dyadic relationship model. *Journal of Marital and Family Therapy, 40*(3), 344–356.

Gewirtz, A., Forgatch, M., & Wieling, E. (2008). Parenting practices as potential mechanisms for child adjustment following mass trauma. *Journal of Marital and Family Therapy, 34*(2), 177–192.

Glynn, S. M., Eth, S., Randolph, E. T., Foy, D. W., Urbaitis, M., Boxer, L., . . . Crothers, J. (1999). A test of behavioral family therapy to augment exposure for combat-related posttraumatic stress disorder. *Journal of Consulting and Clinical Psychology, 67*(2), 243–251.

Godbout, N., Vaillancourt-Morel, M. P., Bigras, N., Briere, J., Hebert, M., Runtz, M., & Sabourin, S. (2019). Intimate partner violence in male survivors of child maltreatment: A meta-analysis. *Trauma, Violence, and Abuse, 20,* 99–113.

Gottlieb, J. D., Mueser, K. T., & Glynn, S. M. (2012). Family therapy for schizophrenia: Co-occurring psychotic and substance use disorders. *Journal of Clinical Psychology, 68*(5), 490–501.

Granqvist, P., Sroufe, L. A., Dozier, M., Hesse, E., Steele, M., van IJzendoorn, M., . . . Duschinsky, R. (2017). Disorganized attachment in infancy: A review of the phenomenon and its implications for clinicians and policy-makers. *Attachment and Human Development, 19*(6), 534–558.

Grasso, D. J., Henry, D., Kestler, J., Nieto, R., Wakschlag, L. S., & Briggs-Gowan, M. J. (2016). Harsh parenting as a potential mediator of the association between intimate partner violence and child disruptive behavior in families with young children. *Journal of Interpersonal Violence, 31*(11), 2102–2126.

Hartnett, D., Carr, A., Hamilton, E., & O'Reilly, G. (2017). The effectiveness of functional family therapy for adolescent behavioral and substance misuse problems: A meta-analysis. *Family Process, 56*(3), 607–619.

Herbers, J. E., Cutuli, J. J., Supkoff, L. M., Narayan, A. J., & Masten, A. S. (2014). Parenting and coregulation: Adaptive systems for competence in children experiencing homelessness. *American Journal of Orthopsychiatry, 84*(4), 420–430.

Jewell, T., Blessitt, E., Stewart, C., Simic, M., & Eisler, I. (2016). Family therapy for child and adolescent eating disorders: A critical review. *Family Process, 55*(3), 577–594.

Johnson, S. B., & Courtois, C. A. (2009). Couple therapy. In C. A. Courtois & J. D. Ford (Eds.), *Treating complex traumatic stress disorders* (pp. 371–390). New York: Guilford Press.

Kazak, A. E., Alderfer, M. A., Streisand, R., Simms, S., Rourke, M. T., Barakat, L. P., . . . Cnaan, A. (2004). Treatment of posttraumatic stress symptoms in adolescent survivors of childhood cancer and their families: A randomized clinical trial. *Journal of Family Psychology, 18*(3), 493–504.

Khan, M., & Renk, K. (2018). Understanding the pathways between mothers' childhood maltreatment experiences and patterns of insecure attachment with young children via symptoms of depression. *Child Psychiatry Human Development, 49*(6), 928–940.

King, N. J., Tonge, B. J., Mullen, P., Myerson, N., Heyne, D., Rollings, S., . . . Ollendick, T.

H. (2000). Treating sexually abused children with posttraumatic stress symptoms: A randomized clinical trial. *Journal of the American Academy of Child and Adolescent Psychiatry, 39*(11), 1347–1355.

Lester, P., Liang, L. J., Milburn, N., Mogil, C., Woodward, K., Nash, W., . . . Saltzman, W. (2016). Evaluation of a family-centered preventive intervention for military families: Parent and child longitudinal outcomes. *Journal of the American Academy of Child and Adolescent Psychiatry, 55*(1), 14–24.

Lieberman, A. F., Ghosh Ippen, C., & Van Horn, P. (2006). Child–parent psychotherapy: 6-Month follow-up of a randomized controlled trial. *Journal of the American Academy of Child and Adolescent Psychiatry, 45*(8), 913–918.

Lieberman, A. F., & Van Horn, P. (2008). *Psychotherapy with infants and young children: Repairing the effects of stress and trauma on early attachment.* New York: Guilford Press.

Lucksted, A., McFarlane, W., Downing, D., & Dixon, L. (2012). Recent developments in family psychoeducation as an evidence-based practice. *Journal of Marital Family Therapy, 38*(1), 101–121.

Lyons-Ruth, K., Pechtel, P., Yoon, S. A., Anderson, C. M., & Teicher, M. H. (2016). Disorganized attachment in infancy predicts greater amygdala volume in adulthood. *Behavior and Brain Research, 308*, 83–93.

Madanes, C. (1980). Protection, paradox, and pretending. *Family Process, 19*(1), 73–85.

Madanes, C., & Haley, J. (1977). Dimensions of family therapy. *Journal of Nervous and Mental Disease, 165*(2), 88–98.

Miklowitz, D. J., & Chung, B. (2016). Family-focused therapy for bipolar disorder: Reflections on 30 years of research. *Family Process, 55*(3), 483–499.

Mirsepassi, Z., Tabatabaee, M., Sharifi, V., & Mottaghipour, Y. (2018). Patient and family psychoeducation: Service development and implementation in a center in Iran. *International Journal of Social Psychiatry, 64*(1), 73–79.

Mulder, T. M., Kuiper, K. C., van der Put, C. E., Stams, G. J. M., & Assink, M. (2018). Risk factors for child neglect: A meta-analytic review. *Child Abuse and Neglect, 77*, 198–210.

Ngoc, T. N., Weiss, B., & Trung, L. T. (2016). Effects of the family schizophrenia psychoeducation program for individuals with recent onset schizophrenia in Viet Nam. *Asian Journal of Psychiatry, 22*, 162–166.

Paley, B., Lester, P., & Mogil, C. (2013). Family systems and ecological perspectives on the impact of deployment on military families. *Clinical Child and Family Psychology Review, 16*(3), 245–265.

Parlar, M., Frewen, P., Nazarov, A., Oremus, C., MacQueen, G., Lanius, R., & McKinnon, M. C. (2014). Alterations in empathic responding among women with posttraumatic stress disorder associated with childhood trauma. *Brain and Behavior, 4*(3), 381–389.

Parsons, A., Knopp, K., Rhoades, G. K., Allen, E. S., Markman, H. J., & Stanley, S. M. (2018). Associations of Army fathers' PTSD symptoms and child functioning: Within- and between-family effects. *Family Process, 57*(4), 915–926.

Punamaki, R. L., Palosaari, E., Diab, M., Peltonen, K., & Qouta, S. R. (2015). Trajectories of posttraumatic stress symptoms (PTSS) after major war among Palestinian children: Trauma, family- and child-related predictors. *Journal of Affective Disorders, 172*, 133–140.

Ragavan, M. I., Thomas, K. A., Fulambarker, A., Zaricor, J., Goodman, L. A., & Bair-Merritt, M. H. (2018, December 3). Exploring the needs and lived experiences of racial and ethnic minority domestic violence survivors through community-based participatory research: A systematic review. *Trauma, Violence, and Abuse.* [Epub ahead of print]

Rosenheck, R., & Thomson, J. (1986). "Detoxification" of Vietnam War trauma: A combined family–individual approach. *Family Process, 25*(4), 559–570.

Saltzman, W. R. (2016). The FOCUS family resilience program. *Family Process, 55*(4), 647–659.

Saxe, G., Ellis, B. H., & Brown, A. B. (2015). *Trauma systems therapy for children and teens* (2nd ed.). New York: Guilford Press.

Schechter, D. S., Suardi, F., Manini, A., Cordero, M. I., Rossignol, A. S., Merminod, G., . . . Serpa, S. R. (2015). How do maternal PTSD and alexithymia interact to impact maternal behavior? *Child Psychiatry and Human Development, 46*(3), 406–417.

Sheinberg, M., & True, F. (2008). Treating family relational trauma: A recursive process using a decision dialogue. *Family Process, 47*(2), 173–195.

Sherman, M. D., Larsen, J., Straits-Troster, K., Erbes, C., & Tassey, J. (2015). Veteran–child communication about parental PTSD: A mixed methods pilot study. *Journal of Family Psychology, 29*(4), 595–603.

Snyder, J., Gewirtz, A., Schrepferman, L., Gird, S. R., Quattlebaum, J., Pauldine, M. R., . . . Hayes, C. (2016). Parent–child relationship quality and family transmission of parent posttraumatic stress disorder symptoms and child externalizing and internalizing symptoms following fathers' exposure to combat trauma. *Development and Psychopathology, 28*(4, Pt. 1), 947–969.

Spinazzola, J., van der Kolk, B., & Ford, J. D. (2018). When nowhere is safe: Trauma history antecedents of posttraumatic stress disorder and developmental trauma disorder in childhood. *Journal of Traumatic Stress, 31*(5), 631–642.

Sprang, G., Ford, J. D., Kerig, P. K., & Bride, B. (2018). Defining secondary traumatic stress and developing targeted assessments and interventions: Lessons learned from research and leading experts. *Traumatology, 25*(2), 72–81.

Sprenkle, D. H. (2012). Intervention research in couple and family therapy: A methodological and substantive review and an introduction to the special issue. *Journal of Marital Family Therapy, 38*(1), 3–29.

Teicher, M. H., & Samson, J. A. (2016). Annual Research Review: Enduring neurobiological effects of childhood abuse and neglect. *Journal of Child Psychology and Psychiatry and Allied Disciplines, 57*(3), 241–266.

Toth, S. L., Rogosch, F. A., Manly, J. T., & Cicchetti, D. (2006). The efficacy of toddler–parent psychotherapy to reorganize attachment in the young offspring of mothers with major depressive disorder: A randomized preventive trial [see comment]. *Journal of Consulting and Clinical Psychology, 74*(6), 1006–1016.

Tucker, C. J., Finkelhor, D., Turner, H., & Shattuck, A. M. (2014). Family dynamics and young children's sibling victimization. *Journal of Family Psychology, 28*(5), 625–633.

Turner, H. A., Finkelhor, D., Ormrod, R., Hamby, S., Leeb, R. T., Mercy, J. A., & Holt, M. (2012). Family context, victimization, and child trauma symptoms: Variations in safe, stable, and nurturing relationships during early and middle childhood. *American Journal of Orthopsychiatry, 82*(2), 209–219.

van der Pol, T. M., Hoeve, M., Noom, M. J., Stams, G., Doreleijers, T. A. H., van Domburgh, L., & Vermeiren, R. (2017). Research Review: The effectiveness of multidimensional family therapy in treating adolescents with multiple behavior problems—a meta-analysis. *Journal of Child Psychology and Psychiatry, 58*(5), 532–545.

van der Put, C. E., Assink, M., Gubbels, J., & Boekhout van Solinge, N. F. (2018). Identifying effective components of child maltreatment interventions: A meta-analysis. *Clinical Child and Family Psychology Review, 21*(2), 171–202.

van Ee, E., Kleber, R. J., & Jongmans, M. J. (2016). Relational patterns between caregivers with PTSD and their nonexposed children: A review. *Trauma, Violence, and Abuse, 17*(2), 186–203.

van Hoof, M. J., van Lang, N. D., Speekenbrink, S., van IJzendoorn, M. H., & Vermeiren, R. R. (2015). Adult Attachment Interview differentiates adolescents with childhood sexual abuse from those with clinical depression and non-clinical controls. *Attachment and Human Development, 17*(4), 354–375.

Vu, N. L., Jouriles, E. N., McDonald, R., & Rosenfield, D. (2016). Children's exposure to intimate partner violence: A meta-analysis of longitudinal associations with child adjustment problems. *Clinical Psychology Review, 46*, 25–33.

Weisman de Mamani, A., Weintraub, M. J., Gurak, K., & Maura, J. (2014). A randomized clinical trial to test the efficacy of a family-focused, culturally informed therapy for schizophrenia. *Journal of Family Psychology, 28*(6), 800–810.

Whealin, J. M., Yoneda, A. C., Nelson, D., Hilmes, T. S., Kawasaki, M. M., & Yan, O. H. (2017). A culturally adapted family intervention for rural Pacific Island veterans with PTSD. *Psychological Services, 14*(3), 295–306.

Zvara, B. J., Mills-Koonce, W. R., Appleyard Carmody, K., Cox, M., & Family Life Project Key Investigators. (2015). Childhood sexual trauma and subsequent parenting beliefs and behaviors. *Child Abuse and Neglect, 44,* 87–97.

CHAPTER 22

Complex Trauma and Addiction Treatment

DENISE HIEN
LISA CAREN LITT
TERESA LÓPEZ-CASTRO
LESIA M. RUGLASS

Substance-related and other addictive disorders are recognized as common consequences of early childhood abuse and neglect. Among those seeking treatment for substance use disorders (SUDs), current rates of trauma-related disorders, such as posttraumatic stress disorder (PTSD), range from 25 to 42% and, specifically among women, can be as high as 30–59% (Hien, Litt, Cohen, Miele, & Campbell, 2009). Lifetime rates of PTSD in these populations are estimated to range from 36 to 50% (Dworkin, Wanklyn, Stasiewicz, & Coffey, 2018). Less is known about rates of SUDs and other addictive disorders in those diagnosed with complex traumatic stress disorders (CTSDs), due to the lack of a formal diagnosis in DSM-5, but clinical reports suggest that for many individuals with core emotion regulation deficits, interpersonal difficulties and multiple psychiatric comorbidities (e.g., depression and anxiety), substance-related and addictive disorders (e.g., gambling disorder) present unique clinical challenges during treatment.

Consequences of co-occurring CTSDs and SUDs in traumatized individuals include more severe and multiple types of symptomatology (e.g., comorbid mood, anxiety, eating, and personality disorders), bingeing or polysubstance use, use of substances with greater addiction potential (i.e., opioids, stimulants), self-harming behaviors, suicidal ideation, early treatment dropout, and increased chances of relapse compared with nontraumatized counterparts (Hien et al., 2009). Thus, common problems associated with CTSDs are often a centerpiece of the treatment of addictive disorders. Likewise, the compulsive use of substances presents challenges for the clinician and treatment program helping clients with CTSDs.

We present in this chapter an *integrative treatment framework* for working with clients who have CTSDs and problems with substances that range from substance misuse to diagnosable SUDs. We focus on substance-related rather than behavioral addictions (e.g., gambling, gaming, and other compulsive behaviors), although many of the principles and intervention approaches may be tailored to such conditions. We provide a conceptualization for employing evidence-based approaches that treat addictions and CTSDs, highlighting key features necessary for successfully addressing addictions in survivors of complex psychological trauma. We conclude with a case description to illustrate some of the likely clinical issues that emerge while working with this population and the integrative strategies shown to effectively address such challenges. This *integrative treatment framework* and our clinical example are derived from over 20 years of experience conducting research and providing successful treatment for diverse populations.

Clinical Rationale and Evidence Base
for the Integrative Treatment Framework

Decades of research indicate that the development and maintenance of SUDs among those with CTSDs are driven by a number of underlying and shared neurobiological mechanisms, including genetic factors, circuitry in the reward and noradrenergic systems, hypothalamic–pituitary–adrenal (HPA) axis dysregulation, and structural deficits in several brain regions (especially the amygdala, hippocampus, and anterior cingulate) (Norman et al., 2012). These findings support the likelihood of multidetermined, overlapping causal pathways that originate after early, prolonged childhood abuse. In the clinical realm, the *self-medication* hypothesis (Khantzian, 2013) provides an understanding of how the dynamic relationship between CTSDs and addiction may manifest in an individual's life. A client may use a psychoactive substance in an attempt to dampen painful feelings, to reduce (or paradoxically, to increase) emotional numbing and dissociation, or to gain a sense of personal control and sustain hypervigilance in the face of disparate psychological states and symptoms. Though substance use may effectively diminish symptoms and immediate distress in the short term, developing a reliance on a substance typically leads to poor outcomes in the long term—often including an exacerbation of the very symptoms that substance use is intended to reduce.

Of importance, the body of empirical treatment studies relevant to CTSDs has been conducted with individuals diagnosed with PTSD and comorbid SUD (PTSD + SUD), but not specifically with CTSDs. Despite this limitation, we stress that the majority of patients with PTSD + SUD are exposed to and suffering from the consequences of complex psychological trauma. One review (Najavits & Hien, 2013) points to the relevance of many clinical and open trials for PTSD + SUD to guide treatment recommendations for CTSDs, demonstrating that, across the board, these treatments impact the hallmark clinical challenges of CTSDs linked to mood and anxiety issues, chronic emotional dysregulation, and attachment disturbances. Also critical to note is that treatment advances for these overlapping problems have been hampered by the historical segregation of addiction services from mental health care. Unfortunately, treating each condition separately, or significantly postponing the treatment of one condition to address the other, often leads to a worsening of symptoms or treatment dropout (Najavits, Hyman, Ruglass, Hien, & Read, 2017). In contrast, from an integrative approach, client and therapist focus on trauma *and* substance misuse simultaneously, or in alternating short time frames (several sessions of one type of intervention followed by another), rather than delaying treatment of one set of problems until the other is resolved. Built on 20 years of clinical trials, the evidence base provides compelling support for combined treatment of both conditions, rather than a siloed approach (Roberts, Roberts, Jones, & Bisson, 2015).

An *integrative treatment framework* provides a conceptual umbrella for a range of approaches that recognize the interconnectedness of trauma and SUDs and require flexible, client-specific, and client-driven care. Optimal care is provided in a context wherein the primacy of promoting a secure attachment within the therapy is respected as the essential foundation for all other therapeutic work (including trauma processing). The stage model of trauma recovery (Herman, 1997) provides a valuable guide for the application of our framework. Integrated models for PTSD + SUD typically fall into the Stage 1 (safety and stabilization) and Stage 2 (trauma memory processing) categories. Stage 1 approaches, often called *present-focused,* typically do not focus on direct processing of traumatic memories and for this reason have been referred to as "integrated, non-trauma-focused" treatments (Roberts et al., 2015). Present-focused PTSD + SUD models include psychoeducation on the links between traumatic stress symptoms and problematic substance use, cognitive restructuring, and the development of coping skills for relapse and affect management. In turn, Stage 2 PTSD + SUD approaches are often termed *past-focused* and center on the processing of relevant trauma memories—typically through narrative work or imaginal exposure—and thereby are also referred to as "integrated, trauma-focused" treatments. Like Stage 1 treatments, these approaches combine psychoeducation linking trauma-related problems to substance use and coping skills for relapse prevention and psychological well-being. Integrated approaches for PTSD + SUDs, whether largely focusing on stabilization or trauma memory processing, devote some attention to the task of reintegration, with a particular focus on the delicate process of cultivating social networks supportive of both their CTSD and SUD recoveries. This reconnection may not be a discrete and final stage, however, as clients are typically working to reestablish connection throughout treatment. Herman (1992, p. 155) herself cautioned that these conceptual "stages" are more flexible than linear: The terminology suggests "a convenient fiction . . . an attempt to impose simplicity and order upon a process that is inherently turbulent and complex." This is especially true for clients with CTSD and SUDs, whose progress may realistically involve movement back and forth between stages to attain the milestones of stabilization, processing, and reconnection.

Both systematic reviews and meta-analyses have examined a growing number of evidence-based interventions reflecting Stage 1 and 2 approaches for PTSD+SUD (Roberts et al., 2015; van Dam, Vedel, Ehring, & Emmelkamp, 2012). On balance, they provide strong evidence for the treatment utility of cognitive behavioral techniques, including psychoeducation, cognitive behavioral coping skills, and trauma processing, for comorbid PTSD and addictions. In addition to demonstrating that trauma-focused treatments can be used safely among those substance-related problems, outcome studies suggest that ameliorating PTSD symptoms is a critical pathway to recovery from addictions. This has liberated clinicians to target symptoms of traumatic stress with clients who would not previously have been offered this opportunity for fear of jeopardizing their progress in SUD recovery. Indeed, some research suggests that until PTSD and/or the traumatic memories are addressed, many clients *may not* discontinue or reduce their substance use (Roberts et al., 2015).

Promoting Engagement and Alliance in the Integrative Treatment Framework

Treatment engagement constitutes a major challenge in the care of individuals with CTSDs and SUDs, with many clients declining to engage in either or both PTSD and SUD treatment, or dropping out and/or attending only a small number of available treatment sessions. Attrition is magnified among racial/ethnic minorities and other vulnerable subgroups (e.g., lesbian, gay, bisexual, transgender, and gender nonconforming) for various reasons, including stigma, clinician conscious/unconscious bias, and cultural attitudes and beliefs that may contribute to discomfort with asking for or receiving mental health services. Lack of engagement and early treatment attrition are likely contributors to the persistence or worsening of symptoms in this population. Cognizant of these challenges, the *integrative treatment framework* assumes an inherently harm reduction-oriented stance that is culturally sensitive to the needs of diverse populations. Harm reduction approaches seek to lessen the harmful consequences of using substances or other problematic behavior, without demanding a commitment to abstinence or behavioral change as a precursor to treatment. For those with CTSDs, a goal of treatment may include abstinence, but at a pace of the client's choosing, with controlled or moderate use as a more immediate goal. The flexibility of harm reduction may more fruitfully allow for the integration of trauma services at any stage of SUD recovery, whereas an abstinence-only or abstinence-first approach may make it difficult to effectively or safely treat severe PTSD or CTSD symptoms with individuals who are not willing or ready to seek SUD treatment if abstinence is a requirement.

To further facilitate and sustain client engagement and retention, integrated models typically incorporate *motivational interviewing* (MI; Miller & Rollnick, 2012) or *motivational enhancement therapy* (MET) strategies early and throughout treatment (Lenz, Rosenbaum, & Sheperis, 2016). MI/MET strategies dovetail with the transtheoretical model of how people change (Prochaska, DiClemente, & Norcross, 1993), which recognizes that people go through a series of stages as they embark and proceed through change and recovery processes. To be effective, intervention strategies must be tailored to the individual's specific stage of change (i.e., precontemplation, contemplation, preparation, action, or maintenance). For instance, collaborative inquiry can enhance motivation and commitment to change, particularly among those in the precontemplation or contemplation stages. In line with a harm reduction stance, MI skills provide guidance for clinicians to listen to and reflect back the issues about which clients are most concerned, in order to help them identify goals for themselves.

Among those grappling with substance misuse in the context of a CTSD, there are significant obstacles that may make it difficult to establish and sustain a therapeutic relationship and require heightened sensitivity and focus on the part of therapist. Intimacy in relationships may feel threatening (Hien et al., 2009). Likewise, clients with long-term, chronic substance use may have neurobiological and psychological alterations—as a consequence of the toxic effects of the substance—that contribute to social deficits and alliance-building challenges (Flückiger et al., 2013). Furthermore, those who are in the early stages of change (i.e., precontemplation and contemplation) regarding their pattern of use may be ambivalent about reducing or giving up a substance, particularly if it is a means of self-medication of painful memories/emotions.

The widespread stigmatization of the "addict" may additionally complicate the clinician's efforts to develop and maintain the therapeutic alliance. Being mindful of the likelihood of enactments (particularly around ongoing substance use or splitting among a clinical team), working from an empathic, nonjudgmental, and nonconfrontational stance is critical in building trust and collaboration throughout the treatment process.

The potential of the individual relationship and common factors in the efficacy of all forms of psychotherapy have been empirically demonstrated. "Common factors" or elements of the therapy relationship, now known as evidence-based relationship variables (EBRs), contribute to the success of treatment as much as the technique used (Norcross, 2011). This may be even more the case with individuals who have suffered chronic interpersonal trauma and lack of response or assistance that creates additional betrayal trauma (Freyd, 1996). "Relational healing for relational trauma" is the mantra of many who work with the complex problems that result from complex trauma (Ford & Courtois, 2009; Kinsler, 2017). Finally, therapist-initiated discussions around the role of race/ethnicity, sexual orientation, gender identity, and other possible dimensions of difference in the therapeutic process may help to mitigate any perceived negative consequences of mismatch between clients and providers.

Primary Clinical Targets and Techniques
in the Integrative Treatment Framework

In addition to targeting the classic symptoms of PTSD (i.e., intrusion, avoidance, alterations in mood and cognition, and hyperarousal), integrated treatment models address CTSD symptoms such as problems in emotion regulation
and disturbances in interpersonal relationships (e.g., interpersonal mistrust,
harmful relationships) and self-identity, dissociation, and self-harm. Many of
these have relevant targets for SUDs (e.g., Concurrent Treatment of PTSD and
Substance Use Disorders Using Prolonged Exposure [COPE]: Back et al., 2014;
Seeking Safety: Najavits, 2002; Trauma Affect Regulation: Guide for Education and Therapy [TARGET]: Ford, 2015; Eye Movement Desensitization and
Reprocessing (EMDR) Therapy and Stages of Change: Abel & O'Brien, 2015).

Prior to presentation of specific skills building activities, therapists share
knowledge about the possible impact of complex psychological trauma,
including difficulties in emotion regulation, interpersonal trust, identity and
self-esteem, substance misuse, and other common problems that trauma survivors experience. *Psychoeducation* links clients' current difficulties in managing
fear, anger, and sadness to their trauma histories, which can help to reduce
tendencies towards shame and self-blame (Hien et al., 2009). The functional
relationship between CTSD symptoms and substance use is collaboratively
identified with the client; for instance, how substances may be a way to deal
with stressful interpersonal situations or to manage or avoid painful thoughts,
feelings, and memories. Clients learn how substance use can be triggered by
various trauma-related reactions and, as a consequence, may prevent healing
from the psychological and relational wounds and injuries caused by exposure
to complex psychological traumas. Information is provided on the array of
possible strategies to manage emotional pain in lieu of substance misuse (Back
et al., 2014; Najavits, 2002). Communicating to clients that these skills can
still be learned often inspires hope and motivation.

Many evidence-based, integrated treatment models (e.g., cognitive-
behavioral therapy [CBT] for PTSD: McGovern et al., 2009; COPE: Back et
al., 2014; Seeking Safety: Najavits, 2002) employ *skills training* that focuses
on building coping strategies to reduce or abstain from substances, manage
overwhelming emotions/behaviors (e.g., self-harm), increase daily life structure, enhance self-care, and improve interpersonal relationships. Clients are
also provided with strategies to identify and change maladaptive thinking patterns that have helped perpetuate symptoms and distress (Hien et al., 2009).

Depending on the treatment approach, clients are taught relapse prevention (RP) skills (Carroll, 1998), such as identifying high-risk situations that
trigger substance use; managing thoughts/beliefs that set the client up for substance use; learning how to refuse substances in high-risk interpersonal contexts; and learning how to cope with cravings and urges to use (Back et al.,
2014; Najavits, 2002). Skills such as *urge surfing*, a mindful approach to noticing distress in the body by "riding the wave" of feeling, help clients feel more

in control of their cravings and urges to use. RP strategies have proven to be an effective resource as clients learn to approach their substance use differently and have been shown to improve comorbid psychiatric symptoms as well. Notably, RP have been shown to reduce trauma symptoms of reexperiencing, hyperarousal, and avoidance, even though RP skills do not specifically address these PTSD symptoms (Hien et al., 2009).

Clients are also taught behavioral *techniques to decrease distress, dissociation, and physiological arousal* (e.g., breathing retraining, relaxation exercises, mindfulness practices). These include increasing emotional awareness by learning how to label, identify, and differentiate emotional states; assisting clients with accepting and trusting their own feelings; and learning distress tolerance strategies. A client's reliance on dissociation as a defense mechanism, while also common, can be identified and addressed with these behavioral approaches. These are powerful tools to manage both complex traumatic stress responses and triggers to use substances.

Integrated treatment models also teach skills in *how to develop more adaptive interpersonal relationships*. Relationship issues specific to this population (e.g., difficulty trusting others, problems in managing conflict, substance use as a substitute for intimacy) are typically oriented toward helping clients develop communication skills and a healthy support network. Clients benefit from attention to establishing safe and appropriate boundaries in their relationships, with a focus on relational patterns that reflect boundaries that may be too permeable, leaving clients persistently vulnerable to exploitation or temptation to use substances, or by contrast, boundaries drawn too tightly, causing clients to lead solitary, isolated lives.

When treating PTSD and SUDs from an integrated treatment framework, the intervention techniques, sequence, and pacing must be personalized to the client and rooted in a thorough, holistic assessment and a multidisciplinary, coordinated care approach. Optimal care for CTSDs and co-occurring SUDs requires a collaborative provider team that spans psychology, social work, psychiatry, and other allied health professions. For example, coordinating pharmaco- and psychotherapies is crucial given evidence from PTSD + SUD trials that medication combined with present- and past-focused integrated therapies have an additive effect to help reduce symptoms (Hien, Levin, Papini, Rug*lass, & López-Castro, 2015). We provide an example of the application of a client-tailored, integrated assessment and treatment plan in the following clinical case example. Many clients experience substantial reduction in CTSD and SUD symptoms from present-focused interventions and skills building.

However, past-focused trauma-processing work often is additionally beneficial, and *in some cases necessary,* for recovery. All integrated treatment models recognize how traumatic memories/reactions may trigger thoughts about and cravings to use substances and, conversely, how substances may be used to actively avoid facing the trauma memories and related stimuli through dissociative mechanisms. However, models that include past-focused components, such as COPE or prolonged exposure (PE) alone, seek to help clients emotionally process their traumatic memories to help them step out of this conundrum. As clients develop a greater sense of control over their trauma memories, they also gain an enhanced sense of competence to manage their emotional experiences. Throughout the trauma processing sessions, integrated treatment models allow time in each session for check-in's regarding substance-use-related triggers, cravings, and skills review. The COPE treatment model, for example, enables clients to engage in imaginal and *in vivo* exposures and attends to substance use by integrating RP techniques throughout the treatment.

Timing and preparation for past-focused work with this co-occurring group are crucial and raise various critical questions. Where substance use and affect dysregulation are concerned, a key clinical assessment is whether the client is stable enough to begin trauma processing. Working within the "therapeutic window" (Briere & Scott, 2006) is often cited as an important guiding principle with survivors of complex psychological trauma who also misuse substances. Additionally, since the establishment of safety may be an ongoing process, when can the clinician feel confident that the client can safely work within his or her therapeutic window? How traumatic stress symptoms and substance use influence each other in the course of treatment often leads to a related consideration and question: If a client continues to use substances over the course of treatment, does that preclude the use of trauma-focused treatments that are potentially emotionally activating? At these clinical junctures, it is important to consider the client-specific relevance of the body of research indicating that past-focused approaches *can be used effectively* with many substance-using individuals without greater risk of destabilization, treatment dropout, or risk of relapse (e.g., Roberts et al., 2015).

Another critical factor informing the timing of past-focused processing relates to the role of substances in clients' lives other than for their psychoactive purpose. If clients are also engaged in risky, potentially retraumatizing, or retriggering behavior for survival (e.g., selling drugs, or trading sex for drugs or money), then helping clients to achieve greater stability in this psychosocial sphere may be an important precursor to undertaking trauma processing work. Similarly, any other aspects of a client's life that pose current violence, risk, or danger may need to be addressed before work that focuses on any past trauma. Finally, in answering these questions, the *integrative treatment framework* adopts harm reduction's commitment to being client-centered; decisions to proceed with past-focused work should be consistently informed and guided by client interest.

Clinical Case Example

Sarah is a case composite, drawn from our work at the Women's Health Project (WHP), a treatment center in New York City dedicated to providing integrated services to clients with histories of both trauma and substance misuse. A 35-year-old single woman when she sought treatment at WHP, Sarah received services over the span of 3 years for depression, anxiety, alcohol use, binge eating, and troubled relationships. Sarah felt that some of her struggles related to her history of childhood physical and sexual abuse. At the time of her intake, Sarah was severely depressed and reported sleeping 13 hours per day, weight gain, difficulty concentrating, and recurrent passive suicidal ideation ("I wish I were dead"), without active suicidal plan or intent. Sarah reported that leaving her apartment had become increasingly harder after a series of panic attacks at the local grocery store and subway station. Two months earlier, she had visited a nearby medical clinic for an evaluation and received a prescription for escitalopram oxalate (brand name, Lexapro). Sarah began taking the antidepressant but was unsure whether it was helping her. She struggled to understand how she felt and to notice changes. Sarah also felt uncomfortable discussing this with her doctor and did not return for refill or follow-up appointments.

Sarah would drink one to three bottles of wine daily, which she would consume alone in her apartment over the course of the day. This pattern of drinking evolved over time, with Sarah initially engaging in binge drinking as a young adult but gradually shifting to more consistent drinking in her 20s and 30s "just to get through" her day. In the previous month, Sarah was also smoking cannabis, "three or four puffs" in preparation for leaving her apartment, which usually occurred every few days. Both Sarah's drinking and depressive episodes appeared to have worsened following the end of a period of relative stability and sobriety. Two years earlier, Sarah underwent inpatient alcohol detoxification, followed by a 20-day inpatient rehabilitation program. Upon discharge, she regularly attended group and individual therapy through the program's outpatient clinic. Upon the breakup of a 6-month romantic relationship, however, Sarah reported that she began drinking a glass of wine nightly and smoking cannabis on occasion, while continuing to receive outpatient services. Her drinking and cannabis use had increased over the course of the last 3 months. Sarah left her alcohol treatment program and grew progressively depressed, anxious, emotionally dysregulated, and isolated.

Sarah reported a chaotic home environment when she was a child, characterized by screaming and fighting between her parents, and at times violence by both parents, directed at Sarah and her two siblings. Sarah's father died in a car accident when she was 9, and Sarah's mother remarried when Sarah was 11, further adding to a sense of instability at home. Soon after, Sarah's stepfather began to sexually abuse her. The abuse continued until she began to develop physically in high school, at which time the abuse ceased. Sarah had not told anyone about the abuse, out of fear of being disbelieved or being punished. After leaving for college, Sarah became estranged from her family and reported little social support. She acknowledged that these traumatic experiences had bothered her throughout her life, but she had avoided delving into them in any of her prior treatments.

When asked about her drinking history, Sarah described that she first experimented with drinking in high school, immediately enjoying the sensation of being intoxicated. Through her late adolescence, she experimented with cannabis and cocaine but reported that alcohol was, by far, her preferred substance. Alcohol quickly provided a means of feeling unburdened by the distress she felt at home and enabled her to fit in socially as a "wild and fun" teen. Sarah reported a family history of alcohol use disorder; her mother died at the age of 52 from liver cirrhosis, and an older sister was a heavy drinker with various lifetime treatment episodes. As a teenager, Sarah also found herself binge eating on a weekly basis, which led to weight gain and an accompanying preoccupation with her body. She acquired a self-loathing and worry about her physical appearance that has continued to the present. Sarah reported one suicide attempt, consuming 10 acetaminophen pills at the age of 19 with the intention of killing herself. She did not require medical care and told no one of the suicide attempt, but shortly thereafter, she withdrew from college. Sarah attempted reenrollment several times, but during each instance felt unable to manage the combination of academic demands and full-time work, leaving before the end of the semester. Additionally, she worked as a temporary office administrator but has not been employed for the past 6 months, nor did she apply for unemployment benefits. At the outset of treatment, Sarah was in jeopardy of losing her apartment.

Sarah reported a number of brief, intense, and high-conflict romantic relationships and a history of unprotected sex while intoxicated. While these encounters were ostensibly consensual, Sarah indicated that in several instances she did not recall what had happened. At other times, she tearfully reported that she had not wanted to engage in some sexual activity that felt forced upon her while intoxicated. Sarah noted that she had particular difficulty asserting herself in sexual relationships and often felt she was subjected to acts in which she felt demeaned, yet powerless to resist.

Commentary on the Case Example

Integrative Assessment and Treatment Planning

Sarah's case highlights the importance of attending to the role of substances during the assessment of a client who has been traumatized. Clinicians often do not fully assess their clients' use and misuse of substances or the history of addiction in their families of origin. However, the initial and ongoing assessment of substance use enables the provider to begin to understand the adaptive function that substances play for a client (and what substances are used for what purposes), as well as the severity of the substance use over time and currently. In Sarah's case, the comorbidity between traumatic stress and substance misuse is evident. Alcohol quickly became a "solution" for managing Sarah's distress as a teen. As a response to feeling emotionally dysregulated, her compulsive overeating, or bingeing, may have served a similar role. Over time, these solutions became problematic, as Sarah's alcohol use pervaded her life and also left her vulnerable to subsequent victimization and trauma. Likewise, her bingeing may have served a momentary role in relieving distress, but it also added to her mounting self-disgust.

The trajectory of Sarah's alcohol use, and her struggle to control or reduce it, provides an important perspective on the central features of her presenting concerns. The intensity of a client's substance misuse factors prominently in developing an initial treatment plan—particularly regarding level of care—and substance use and mental health treatment goals, including whether a Stage 1 or Stage 2 approach might be appropriate. Standardized substance use screening measures (e.g., Alcohol Use Disorders Identification Test [AUDIT] or Drug Abuse Screening Test [DAST]; for review, see Donovan & Marlatt, 2005) or other structured self-report or clinician-guided questionnaires (e.g., Washton & Zweben, 2006) may be helpful to identify the breadth and depth of a client's substance use in a systematic fashion. The assessment should involve consideration of whether it is possible to work with someone on an outpatient basis, or whether physiological dependence will require detoxification and/or medication to assist with recovery and maintenance. This was an important consideration regarding Sarah's treatment, as the level of her alcohol use indicated that Sarah might not safely be able to reduce or discontinue her alcohol use without medical supervision at some point.

Sarah's treatment needs were addressed jointly with members of her interdisciplinary treatment team. Her treatment plan targeted her drinking and cannabis use, depression, disordered eating, trauma history, psychosocial functioning, and housing instability. The team actively sought Sarah's input on what treatment goals to prioritize. Sarah agreed to work on decreasing her drinking and monitoring her cannabis use. She concurred with the team's assessment that a goal of moderate drinking would likely be unrealistic given her personal and family history of alcohol use disorder. However, Sarah would not commit to abstaining until the severity of her depression abated substantially. The treatment team took a harm reduction approach, supporting Sarah's decision not to eliminate alcohol immediately and working with Sarah to shore up her motivation to follow through with a plan to reenter detoxification if needed, whenever she was ready. The team introduced Sarah to RP skills to help her identify and cope with her specific triggers for drinking, to be able to refuse offers that would put her at increased risk of drinking, and to find alternative pleasant and soothing activities.

The team also highlighted the possibility that Sarah's depression might be exacerbated by her drinking, and that some mood improvement might only be evident once she discontinued her drinking. Sarah and her team agreed that tracking her cannabis use during the initial months of treatment would be the first step in evaluating its role in her mood and functioning. Sarah was seen by the staff psychiatrist, who prescribed an antidepressant and naltrexone for alcohol cravings. To help Sarah feel a greater sense of self-efficacy, the team encouraged Sarah to discuss her feelings and questions about the medication or any side effects she might have rather than discontinuing the medications on her own.

Sarah's psychosocial treatment consisted of weekly individual therapy; an integrated, present-focused women's group (Seeking Safety); and an additional emotion regulation group. Her individual therapy began with a focus on coping skills training and cognitive restructuring in the substance use area, building interpersonal support and safety, and exploring the impact of her trauma history on her drinking, binge eating, depression, and anxiety. Individual and group therapy also worked to expand Sarah's tolerance of distress and to promote strategies to regulate negative emotions, focusing specifically on the connections between her feelings and her patterns of eating, and alcohol and cannabis use. Sarah also met with a social worker to apply for rent payment assistance and to see whether she qualified for entitlement benefits. Notably, Sarah's case demonstrates the benefits of working as part of a multidisciplinary team. For solo practitioners, clients like Sarah require a "virtual team" of linked clinicians and programs who are willing to collaborate on client care in order to provide the necessary range of services.

Integrative Treatment: Harm Reduction and Engagement

An integrative treatment plan is not a one-size-fits-all endeavor. Sarah presented to treatment for a number of concerns—of which alcohol use was only one, and not even her primary, concern. To Sarah, her depressed mood and relationship issues were most pressing. In many mental health settings, however, Sarah might be discouraged or even dissuaded from pursuing psychotherapy for these concerns until she was "clean" from substances. Rather than being treated, she might be funneled into a stand-alone substance abuse setting to treat her substance problems first. Once there, Sarah might be required to commit to abstinence from all substances in order to stay in the program, regardless of whether she was interested in or ready for this step. Moreover, in that setting, she might not have a chance to effectively address the other mental health issues for which she primarily sought treatment. Unfortunately, this dilemma has prevented many clients from obtaining effective treatment for their specific needs. For many individuals, the outcome has been treatment dropout rather than effective engagement. Attempts to compel clients to change their substance use without addressing some of the underlying concerns, such as the use of substances to self-medicate dysregulated emotion or triggers related to traumatic stress, often end in treatment failure.

Sarah's treatment team sought to be sensitive to this by working from a harm reduction perspective and encouraging Sarah to work toward her goals for substance reduction at her own pace, while also helping to provide the skills and support that would help her to successfully make changes in her drinking pattern when she was ready. It was likely that Sarah was in the precontemplation/contemplation stage of change regarding her substance use; she realized that she needed help with her alcohol use, but it was not her reason for seeking treatment, nor was she sure how she wanted to approach it. MI strategies were used with Sarah to sensitively and nonjudgmentally explore the impact of her alcohol and cannabis use on her life, to identify goals that were realistic for her, and to help her progress through her ambivalence toward action and maintenance phases of her recovery. Sarah decided to continue using alcohol and cannabis while working on her trauma-related symptoms. Her team was mindful of collaboratively monitoring her substance intake weekly and having conversations around reducing any harmful consequences of her use. With time, Sarah agreed to complete abstinence from alcohol after receiving inpatient treatment (see below). Similarly, the team encouraged Sarah to monitor her cannabis use but did not press her to identify cannabis as a problem. Sarah's cannabis use remained mild and did not seem to create any additional risk factors. Sarah continued to use cannabis even after her subsequent alcohol detoxification.

Session Transcript from an Early Individual Therapy Session

In this early session, the clinician and Sarah began to lay the groundwork for collaborative decisions about Sarah's treatment, honoring the fears and worries that arose because of dogmatic and judgmental past treatment experiences. The clinician provided a framework for developing tools to manage some of Sarah's symptoms and substance misuse, and addressed Sarah's concerns about whether she would need to talk about her traumatic past. Of central concern to the clinician was remaining attuned to emergent themes of trust and safety.

SARAH: I feel like drinking and smoking are the two things that keep me together. Without them, I can't make it through the day without breaking down in tears or snapping at someone. They're my lifelines.

THERAPIST: What do you notice makes you want to take the day's first drink or smoke?

SARAH: I don't really notice most of the time. I just do it. I avoid noticing. (*long pause*) I guess I notice wanting to run far, far away. When I last tried to quit drinking—I'm so fat, I had to do something—I couldn't bear going outside and talking to people or even thinking about being on the street or in the train. I stayed at home and cried. Smoking weed helped, but even when I did make it out of the house, I was so irritated and overwhelmed. When I told the counselor that I hadn't had a drink in more than a week, she couldn't see past the fact that my pee tested for marijuana. I felt humiliated and so broken. I said, "Screw this," and walked out.

THERAPIST: Learning to cope can feel so overwhelming, especially when you feel like you didn't have the chance to learn how. (*pause*) There *are* tools that can help, and we *can* learn them when we're given the chance and support. The drinking and the smoking—I think they are two ways you've been trying to handle it all, trying to stay ahead of everything that's been worrying, scaring, chasing after you. Over time, they work so well you don't notice what's behind them anymore. But I hear you when you say that it's taking its toll. The first part of our work together will be about learning to feel safe in this world—safe *and* competent—so that more options feel available to you, more than drinking and smoking.

SARAH: I can't even imagine.

THERAPIST: It's unimaginable now, that makes sense. Testing things out in here with me will be really important in helping you imagine what it might be like out there in the world. I'll help you learn how to recognize the feelings and the thoughts that trigger that instinct to run. We'll practice how to soothe yourself, how to respond, and what seems to work best and when. Feeling safe with me will be part of our work, too. Being able to talk about your drinking and smoking with me will be hard sometimes, I guess, but crucial. Sharing with me when you're worried about what I might think will give us the opportunity to practice understanding and managing those worries.

SARAH: And what about the stuff with my stepdad? When will we get to him? I know that he's somewhere in all of this, but I can't stand the thought of letting him get any closer.

THERAPIST: You mean talking about your memories of what happened? (*Sarah nods, gaze averted.*) We won't talk about it until you're ready—and it's really important for you to know talking about your memories is not a given for you to feel better. What do you make of that?

SARAH: I don't know. A part of me wants to talk about him, and another part doesn't.

THERAPIST: Yes, that makes sense, and we'll want to make sure to build room for both parts. Can I share with you some of my experiences? (*Sara nods, eye contact regained.*) "Trauma processing"—that's what we call the specific kind of focus on the memories—can be really helpful. For many clients I've worked with, this has resulted in a great amount of positive change, of regained and new strength, *without* the memories ever being front and center.

SARAH: I can totally see myself getting into this thing where unless I do it all, I'll feel like I failed.

THERAPIST: That's such a key observation about yourself. We'll be talking quite a lot about how what you've experienced shapes how the world feels to you and how you feel about yourself. And that may not involve specific memories. Like, for instance, I hear a little bit in what you just said—correct me if I'm wrong—that you *must* submit totally to this therapy. One of the things we'll be working on is getting to feel in control, instead of feeling coerced, or sometimes, like you don't know what to do unless someone else tells you. How does that sound to you?

SARAH: I like that. But it also sounds scary.

THERAPIST: Too scary?

SARAH: No, just scary-new.

THERAPIST: OK. Can we make an agreement to check-in and see how it's going between us as we move forward? There may be a time when you decide that you would like to talk about what happened with your stepdad. Now and later, we can talk about what goes into making that decision, and about how to do so that in safe and structured way.

SARAH: Yeah, I'd like that.

Commentary and Treatment Progress

Collaborative Therapeutic Process

In this dialogue, the clinician listened carefully to how Sarah described her experience, learning about past treatment failures and the expectations about being shamed and coerced to accept treatment goals that were not her own. The clinician did not try to railroad Sarah into "admitting" that she had a substance use problem. Instead, she spoke about Sarah's goals for herself and the challenges Sarah anticipated if and when she changed her drinking. This dialogue reflected a nonjudgmental, harm reduction stance as the clinician and Sarah collaborated on her recovery process. To help Sarah with her worries about not being able to tolerate the feelings of distress that she anticipated without alcohol, the clinician introduced the idea of developing coping skills. She also assured Sarah that if they were going to discuss the details of her past trauma, they would do so when Sarah was ready, and with a structure that would help to make that manageable. In this and other areas, the clinician acknowledged and validated Sarah's feelings and her ambivalence. Sarah was able to feel heard, and she experienced the clinician as working with her and for her, as someone she could potentially trust.

Safety and Stabilization

The team felt that providing Sarah with Stage 1 skills was important in helping to better regulate her emotions and to have psychoeducation around the relationship between her traumatic stress and her substance misuse. This rationale was discussed with Sarah as part of her treatment planning. Through her individual and group work, Sarah was taught affect management skills (e.g., distress tolerance and affect regulation, mindfulness skills, grounding skills, breathing retraining, and progressive muscle relaxation skills, as well as RP skills). Sarah experienced significant relief through this psychoeducation and skills building process, allowing for widening of "the therapeutic window" and Sarah's ability to tolerate a broader range of emotion. This proved useful for her substance use and binge eating, and her overall ability to tolerate distress. Through learning and implementing these skills, Sarah also reported feeling more empowered. Because Sarah often struggled with trusting authority and easily felt disempowered, this was a significant development.

Trauma Processing

Once Sarah's mood began to stabilize and she found herself gaining confidence in her relationships and less likely to turn to food or alcohol to manage distress, Sarah and her individual therapist began to consider trauma processing work to address some of the salient memories from her abusive childhood. Fortunately, Sarah was not currently engaged in any dangerous situations, and helping her to obtain entitlements added to her level of safety and stability. Sarah had avoided talking about her traumatic memories, but in talking with her therapist, she began to feel that she would like to work through them. Using the past-focused framework of COPE, Sarah continued to develop RP skills while undertaking prolonged exposure (PE) to address several memories of childhood sexual abuse. After understanding its rationale and procedures, Sarah began the processing, which lasted eight sessions, mixed with RP and attention to her continued use of alcohol and cannabis during this time. Sarah identified two salient memories of abuse by her stepdad. While difficult to go through, PE provided Sarah with additional relief related to her traumatic past. She was able to speak about these memories without becoming overwhelmed and expressed a notable improvement in her negative self-concept and the guilt and shame she had carried at having "allowed" the abuse to happen.

Sarah's Ongoing SUD Recovery

The stabilization and processing work provided Sarah with the confidence to ultimately abstain from drinking. It had been clear for a while that Sarah would struggle to effectively moderate her drinking, but she had not been ready to stop drinking. Skills building and trauma processing helped move Sarah along the stages of change. Having sought treatment in more of a contemplation stage, Sarah had progressed through preparation and fully entered into an action stage during her Stage 1 and Stage 2 work. Sarah had been attending to her substance use through the implementation of RP skills, and monitoring and making changes to her alcohol intake. Following PE, Sarah completed a brief inpatient detoxification to safely discontinue her alcohol use and agreed to a regimen of disulfiram and naltrexone to help maintain sobriety upon discharge. Sarah returned to work with her WHP team after discharge. She also began to attend 12-step groups for additional support throughout the week. Clients often benefit from other supports for their recovery, and clinicians can help to coordinate care with additional specialized SUD treatment or self-help groups in the community that can bolster a client's stability. These were important additions for the maintenance stage of Sarah's recovery.

This process of connecting to supports within the community was also an integral part of Sarah's Stage 3 work. Throughout treatment, Sarah addressed some of the impediments to forming healthy relationships, working through her difficulties trusting others, and developing skills to create safe boundaries and avoid interpersonal red flags. Sarah was also able to enroll in a back-to-work training program for individuals in recovery. Sarah was optimistic that she would be able to find and sustain work following the completion of this program. Helping Sarah to reintegrate back into social and vocational settings was an important part of the process of solidifying her gains and helping Sarah to feel more functional and independent. The therapist helped Sarah gradually talk about how drinking had seemed like a way to escape from the bad memories (and related feelings, especially shame, and difficulties with trust), and that over time that link was important as a motivator for Sarah to choose to do PE.

Conclusion

Our delineation of an integrative treatment framework and composite case encompassing a personalized, comprehensive care model demonstrates various approaches that can be flexibly applied to treat individuals struggling with CTSDs and addictions of all kinds. We have highlighted a number of evidence-based models that have been used either concurrently, or in sequence, to successfully help clients with the collection of interrelated problems associated with substance misuse, emotional dysregulation, interpersonal conflicts, and other sequalae of complex psychological trauma. As addiction and mental health treatment silos gradually give way, each has something to offer the other in the treatment of these clients, particularly through their integration.

Working with clients with comorbid CTSDs and SUDs can be emotionally challenging for providers, who are at enhanced risk of experiencing burnout, vicarious traumatization, or compassion fatigue. Education and training of therapists is very important in this regard. Specialized training in many of the evidence-based treatments is critical, in order to apply them as developed and with fidelity. Supervision and consultation are also recommended, in addition to the engagement of self-care strategies and social support systems in order to reduce the deleterious impact of the work on treatment providers. For solo practitioners, without the benefit of an in-house treatment team, we recommend ongoing consultation with a seasoned provider or peer who can provide much needed support when dealing with highly distressed clients. Despite the often overwhelming number of fronts that therapists and clients must contend with when addictions are added to the clinical mix, applying the evidence-based approaches of an *integrative treatment framework* can help bring clarity, containment, and transformation for those who have often lived without such hope.

References

Abel, N. J., & O'Brien, J. M. (2015). *Treating addictions with EMDR therapy and the stages of change*. New York: Springer.
Back, S. E., Foa, E. B., Killeen, T. K., Mills, K. L., Teesson, M., Cotton, B. D., . . . Brady, K. T. (2014). *Concurrent treatment of PTSD and substance use disorders using prolonged exposure (COPE): Therapist guide*. New York: Oxford University Press.

Briere, J., & Scott, C. (2006). *Principles of trauma therapy: A guide to symptoms, evaluation, and treatment.* Thousand Oaks, CA: SAGE.

Carroll, K. M. (1998). *A cognitive behavioral approach: Treating cocaine addiction* (Vol. 1). Rockville, MD: National Institute on Drug Abuse.

Donovan, D. M., & Marlatt, G. A. (Eds.). (2005). *Assessment of addictive behaviors* (2nd ed.). New York: Guilford Press.

Dworkin, E. R., Wanklyn, S., Stasiewicz, P. R., & Coffey, S. F. (2018). PTSD symptom presentation among people with alcohol and drug use disorders: Comparisons by substance of abuse. *Addictive Behaviors, 76,* 188–194.

Flückiger, C., Del Re, A. C., Horvath, A. O., Symonds, D., Ackert, M., & Wampold, B. E. (2013). Substance use disorders and racial/ethnic minorities matter: A meta-analytic examination of the relation between alliance and outcome. *Journal of Counseling Psychology, 60*(4), 610–616.

Ford, J. D. (2015). An affective cognitive neuroscience-based approach to PTSD psychotherapy: The TARGET model. *Journal of Cognitive Psychotherapy, 29*(1), 69–91.

Ford, J. D., & Courtois, C. A. (2009). Defining and understanding complex trauma and complex traumatic stress disorders. In C. A. Courtois & J. D. Ford (Eds.), *Treating complex traumatic stress disorders: An evidence-based guide* (pp. 13–30). New York: Guilford Press.

Freyd, J. J. (1996). *Betrayal trauma: The logic of forgetting childhood abuse.* Cambridge, MA: Harvard University Press.

Herman, J. L. (1992). *Trauma and recovery: The aftermath of violence—from domestic abuse to political terror.* New York: Basic Books.

Herman, J. L. (1997). *Trauma and recovery. The aftermath of violence—from domestic abuse to political terror.* New York: Basic Books.

Hien, D. A., Levin, F. R., Papini, S., Ruglass, L. M., & Lopez-Castro, T. (2015). Enhancing the effects of cognitive behavioral therapy for PTSD and alcohol use disorders with antidepressant medication: A randomized clinical trial. *Drug and Alcohol Dependence, 146,* e142.

Hien, D. A., Litt, L. C., Cohen, L. R., Miele, G. M., & Campbell, A. (2009). *Trauma services for women in substance abuse treatment: An integrated approach.* Washington, DC: American Psychological Association.

Khantzian, E. J. (2013). Addiction as a self-regulation disorder and the role of self-medication. *Addiction, 108*(4), 668–669.

Kinsler, P. J. (2017). *Complex psychological trauma: The centrality of relationship.* New York: Routledge.

Lenz, A. S., Rosenbaum, L., & Sheperis, D. (2016). Meta-analysis of randomized controlled trials of motivational enhancement therapy for reducing substance use. *Journal of Addictions and Offender Counseling, 37*(2), 66–86.

McGovern, M. P., Lambert-Harris, C., Acquilano, S., Xie, H., Alterman, A. I., & Weiss, R. D. (2009). A cognitive behavioral therapy for co-occurring substance use and posttraumatic stress disorders. *Addictive Behaviors, 34*(10), 892–897.

Miller, W. R., & Rollnick, S. (2012). *Motivational interviewing: Helping people change* (3rd ed.). New York: Guilford Press.

Najavits, L. M. (2002). *Seeking Safety: A treatment manual for PTSD and substance abuse.* New York: Guilford Press.

Najavits, L. M., & Hien, D. (2013). Helping vulnerable populations: A comprehensive review of the treatment outcome literature on substance use disorder and PTSD. *Journal of Clinical Psychology, 69*(5), 433–479.

Najavits, L. M., Hyman, S. M., Ruglass, L. M., Hien, D. A., & Read, J. P. (2017). Substance use disorder and trauma. In S. N. Gold (Ed.), *APA handbook of trauma psychology: Foundations in knowledge* (Vol. 1, pp. 195–213). Washington, DC: American Psychological Association.

Norcross, J. C. (2011). *Psychotherapy relationships that work: Evidence-based responsiveness* (2nd ed.). New York: Oxford University Press.

Norman, S. B., Myers, U. S., Wilkins, K. C., Goldsmith, A. A., Hristova, V., Huang, Z., . . . Robinson, S. K. (2012). Review of biological mechanisms and pharmacological treatments of comorbid PTSD and substance use disorder. *Neuropharmacology, 62*(2), 542–551.

Prochaska, J. O., DiClemente, C. C., & Norcross, J. C. (1992). In search of how people change: Applications to addictive behaviors. *American Psychologist, 47*(9), 1102–1114.

Roberts, N. P., Roberts, P. A., Jones, N., & Bisson, J. I. (2015). Psychological interventions for post-traumatic stress disorder and comorbid substance use disorder: A systematic review and meta-analysis. *Clinical Psychology Review, 38,* 25–38.

van Dam, D., Vedel, E., Ehring, T., & Emmelkamp, P. M. G. (2012). Psychological treatments for concurrent posttraumatic stress disorder and substance use disorder: A systematic review. *Clinical Psychology Review, 32,* 202–214.

Washton, A. M., & Zweben, J. E. (2006). *Treating alcohol and drug problems in psychotherapy practice: Doing what works.* New York: Guilford Press.

PART IV

EMERGING PSYCHOTHERAPY MODELS

CHAPTER 23

Sensorimotor Psychotherapy

PAT OGDEN

Trauma first and foremost affects the body. Under threat, prefrontal cortical activity in the brain is inhibited, and animal defensive instincts are catalyzed (see Chapter 1). The trademark symptoms of posttraumatic stress disorder (PTSD)—intrusive reexperiencing and numbing/avoidance—reflect the body's efforts to survive in a threatening environment. Although the symptom presentation associated with complex traumatic stress disorders (CTSDs), such as difficulties with affect regulation, disorganized and insecure attachment patterns, dissociation, disorders of the self, and relationship struggles (Ford, Courtois, Steele, van der Hart, & Nijenhuis, 2005) have psychological components, they are fundamentally rooted in the body's patterns of dysregulated arousal and unfettered instinctive defense mechanisms common to all mammals. When threatened, sympathetic nervous system arousal mobilizes defensive instincts. Crying out to secure the protection of an attachment figure is the infant's first line of defense, followed by those that mobilize the body to flee or fight as motor capacities mature. When these active attempts to get help, fight back, or escape are unsuccessful, the body becomes immobilized either by "freezing"—hyperarousal coupled with cessation of movement—or shutting down—a feigned death response driven by dorsal vagal hypoarousal. Each defense is accompanied by emotions such as terror, panic, despair, or rage that further arouse and sustain the corresponding defense (Janet, 1925). Long after the traumatic event(s) is over, if unprocessed and unresolved, elements of these defenses continue in distorted and altered forms (Herman, 1992). An overwhelming cascade of disturbances in autonomic arousal, sensation, perception, movement, and emotions associated with animal defenses replays endlessly in the body, complicating traditional treatment of trauma-related disorders (see Chapter 6).

The symptoms associated with reliving—unbidden movements, pain, sensory distortions, autonomic dysregulation causing increased heart rate, tension, and constricted breathing—as well as those associated with shutdown and avoidance—numbing, depersonalization, immobilization, and loss of pain perception—are baffling and distressing to clients and clinicians alike. Language may prove inadequate to address these symptoms for several reasons. Since the verbal retelling of past trauma can stimulate dysregulation and somatoform symptoms, talking about what happened is challenging at best for most survivors. Traumatic memories can be split off from conscious awareness, stored as sensory perceptions and behavioral reenactments, as Janet (1925) suggested long ago. Words may be unavailable due to the recurring sense of impending danger, referred to as "speechless terror." Thus, a therapist's exclusive reliance on the "talking cure" might limit clinical efficacy.

Nonetheless, most treatment approaches for trauma-related disorders focus primarily on the client's words, emphasizing the role of the verbal narrative, emotional expression, and meaning making. They lack the theoretical foundations and interventions to directly address the physiological and somatic alterations that perpetuate the symptoms of complex trauma. Cognitive-behavioral therapies may assist the client in addressing problematic thoughts and beliefs, and in learning relaxation skills to address states of hyperarousal, but they do not directly remediate the somatoform symptoms associated with these trauma-related disorders. Experiential psychotherapies (see Chapters 24 and 26) help clients become more aware of the bodily changes and sensations associated with certain emotional states. Yet while therapists may notice the appearance and even the movements of the client's body, they fail to utilize straightforward physical interventions that are specifically designed to recalibrate a dysregulated physiology and change the muscular, postural, and movement patterns that underlie symptoms.

Treatment of complex trauma is not easy, and therapists of all persuasions are often mystified and frustrated by the limitations of existing modalities to resolve their clients' symptoms. When somatoform symptoms are not addressed by explicit attention to the body, somatic and physiological propensities can maintain and even exacerbate psychological symptoms despite otherwise adequate treatment. An approach that facilitates awareness of body-based symptoms, appreciates their adaptive functions, then modifies or metabolizes them can provide significant guidance for therapeutic intervention and ultimately healing.

Evolution of Sensorimotor Psychotherapy

Sensorimotor psychotherapy (SP), which I developed in the 1970s and 1980s as a body-oriented talking therapy, has evolved into a comprehensive psychotherapy model, with interventions designed to treat the effects of PTSD and CTSDs, as well as attachment failures and developmental disturbances (Ogden

& Minton, 2000; Ogden, Minton, & Pain, 2006; Ogden & Fisher, 2015). Ron Kurtz, a body psychotherapist, inspired the foundations of SP in the 1970s with his conviction that mindful awareness of the internal organization of experience holds more promise for healing than does conversation. Patterns of nonconscious organization rather than conscious thought drive behavior, and mindfulness facilitates awareness of implicit patterns, whereas conversation engages them. Kurtz's (1990) emphasis on tracking the body for signs of early attachment imprints, and using mindfulness to discover and change the organization of experience are hallmarks of SP. In addition, several physical disciplines influenced the direct body-oriented interventions of SP: yoga, dance, continuum movement, rolf movement, Reichian bodywork, and most importantly, structural integration (Rolf, 1977), with its emphasis on the natural alignment of the spine and an expanded movement vocabulary. Studies of fundamental neurological movements also contributed to SP's evolution (Banbridge-Cohen, 1993; Aposhyan, 2004).

Starting in the 1990s, additional influences advanced SP's conceptualization of complex trauma and refinement of treatment interventions: The infant research of Tronick (2009) and Beebe (2006) on prelinguistic forms of communication has highlighted the significance of early movement sequences; Schore's (2011) assertion that the right brain "implicit self" is dominant for human behavior and his emphasis on the psychobiological underpinnings of affect regulation have expanded SP's emphasis on attunement and interactive regulation. Bromberg's (2006) articulation of "not-me" self-states has clarified how the therapist's and clients unsymbolized implicit processes interact, highlighting the importance of relationally negotiating therapeutic enactments. Porges (2011) described the autonomic nervous system's hierarchical reaction to safety, danger, and life threat, contributing to the focus in SP on the social engagement system, regulation of physiological arousal, and inhibition of animal defenses. His conceptualization of "faulty neuroception" as "an inability to detect accurately whether the environment is safe or another person is trustworthy" (2011, p. 17) has impacted the way SP conceptualizes trauma-related triggering. The pioneering perspectives of Janet (1925), Nijenhuis (2006), van der Hart, Nijenhuis, and Steele (2006) and Steele and van der Hart (see Chapter 6) on structural dissociation and the somatoform nature of trauma symptoms have profoundly impacted our understanding and treatment of trauma-related disorders.

In addition to Kurtz's (1990) emphasis on mindfulness as a route to reveal the organization of experience, the research and writings of LeDoux (2002) and Siegel (2007) have clarified the role of mindfulness to regulate arousal and expand integrative capacity, reflected in the central role of mindfulness in SP treatment. Frewen and Lanius (2015) suggest that mindfulness exercises may increase awareness of both emotion and the body, and thus support reintegration of the self, especially for those with dissociative symptoms. Zerubavel and Messman-Moore (2015) suggest that using mindfulness can help clients stay in the here and now and increase their ability to predict dissociative processes and thus have more control over them. They also assert that mindfulness may decrease problematic absorption by increasing the ability to control attention and reduce fragmentation. Although mindfulness meditation is not formally taught in SP, the method's use of relational mindfulness may foster similar gains.

Although, currently, no definitive formal research findings validate the efficacy of SP, two pilot studies report promising findings in reducing symptoms of CTSDs and PTSD. Langmuir, Kirsh, and Classen (2011) taught somatic resources for stabilization (grounding, orienting, boundaries and movement) to women who had suffered chronic interpersonal trauma in a group setting. Outcome assessments following this 20-session group therapy revealed increases in participants' capacity to regulate arousal and reduce trauma-related symptoms. Another pilot study assessed the effect of SP interventions for a severely and chronically traumatized population (Gene-Cos, Fisher, Ogden, & Cantrell, 2016). In a 12-week group therapy structure, the researchers used SP stabilization skills to regulate biphasic patterns and symptoms of hyper- and hypoarousal. Statistically significant changes in pretreatment scores on measures of PTSD symptoms, depression, overall health, and social functioning were demonstrated.

Features of SP for the Treatment of Complex Trauma

SP integrates top-down "talk therapy" interventions with bottom-up somatic attention. Features of this method for complex trauma treatment include the emphasis on mindful awareness of the body-based organization of experience rather than the verbal narrative; the use of body-oriented interventions through a focus on the body's posture, movement, and sensation in relationship to cognitions and emotions; the role of direct physical interventions to address the repetitive, unbidden physical sensations, movement inhibitions, and somatosensory intrusions of trauma, dysregulated emotions and other trauma-related symptomatology; addressing trauma-related parts of the self as reflected and sustained in physical patterns; and employing a phase-oriented treatment approach to provide overall structure to clinical practice.

Embedded Relational Mindfulness

Rather than prioritizing insight or analysis, SP emphasizes teaching clients to become mindful of their internal organization of experience—how the body's sensation and movement interacts with thoughts and emotions. Internal reactions to stimuli happen rapidly and often unconsciously, and when they are distorted by implicit memories of the past or negative expectations of the future, observing them through mindful attention can lessen their negative impact. However, mindfulness is not practiced through solitary structured meditation exercises; rather SP's "embedded relational mindfulness" is uniquely integrated into what transpires moment to moment between therapist and client (Ogden et al., 2006; Ogden, 2014).

Through embedded relational mindfulness, clients become aware of their present-moment internal experience in the context of an attuned therapeutic dyad instead of facing it alone, becoming immersed in it, or tuning it out. They learn to mindfully identify the five basic "building blocks" of here-and-now experience that comprise their internal reactions: thoughts, emotions, and internally generated sensory perceptions (e.g., images, movements, and sensations), and describe these elements to the therapist. Building blocks associated with trauma exert a profound influence on the client's experience but typically remain just outside of conscious awareness. Triggered clients report disturbing alterations in the five building blocks, sometimes not realizing that these reactions do not pertain to current reality but to traumatic reminders and triggers. Mindfulness brings conscious attention to them, so that they can be addressed directly. For example, hyperarousal can be observed to have several components: physical or attentional constriction, shallow breathing, increased heart rate, images related to past trauma, panic, and thoughts such as "I'm a failure." Identifying the components of alterations and symptoms can prevent identifying with them and provide information to regulate arousal somatically. A critical set of relational mindfulness skills is used to facilitate awareness of the organization of experience (Ogden et al., 2006; Ogden, 2014). First, the therapist observes and empathically attunes to both the client's words and physical reactions, then verbally calls attention to particular elements of present-moment experience through a "contact" statement: "It seems your shoulders and arms tighten up when you talk about the rape" or "You have the thought that he had the right to abuse you." This attunement, with its encouragement for clients to pay close attention to reactions that are usually automatic and unnoticed, as well as verbalize what they notice, can be inherently regulating. Therapists use mindfulness questions and experiments to help clients become aware of the relationship of the body's movement, autonomic reactivity, and posture to thoughts, beliefs, and emotions. For example, when a self-attribution (e.g., "I'm a bad person") surfaces, the therapist might ask, "What happens right now when you have this thought?" or "How does that thought affect your body's sensations, posture, autonomic arousal, and movement?" These skills of tracking present experience, naming it, and asking mindfulness questions assist clients in becoming aware of their present moment internal experience.

Many clients with CTSDs have difficulty naming the elements of present experience for a variety of reasons: Certain elements are experienced as threatening; attention may be constantly changing, or the internal experience itself changes rapidly. Since the body is the seat of distressing symptoms, and emotions are often out of control, awareness of emotion and body sensation may be triggering. Frewen and Lanius (2015) note that although mindfulness can be useful in PTSD treatment, clients can be triggered by its use. SP uses the concept of "directed mindfulness," which purposely focuses mindful attention on one or more building blocks considered important to therapeutic goals (Ogden et al., 2006; Ogden, 2009). For example, if dysregulated, clients are directed to become mindful of internal experiences that are regulating for them—peripheral sensations in the arms, legs or back, pleasant sensations or images, calm emotions, and more neutral thoughts. The goal is to bring arousal into a window of tolerance (Siegel, 2007)—an optimal zone of arousal in between hyper- or hypoarousal.

Concurrent Bottom–Up and Top-Down Interventions

SP relies on the body as a source of information, target for treatment intervention, and avenue of psychotherapeutic change. Symptoms are often impervious to "top-down" resolution via insight or even through emotional expression. Using bottom-up interventions allows clients to experience a somatic sense of growing mastery over these deeply ingrained disturbing neurobiological and procedural patterns of arousal and defense. MacLean (1985) depicts these two directions of processing with his triune brain metaphor, which explains that the human brain can be divided into three "brains": reptilian, the seat of survival instincts; mammalian, the seat of subjective emotions; and neocortex, the seat of declarative knowledge and thought. SP employs both a top-down approach by targeting insight and cognitive meaning making and a bottom-up approach by targeting the arousal and instinctive defensive movements.

For clients to feel safe in their bodies, arousal must be regulated. Perry (2009, p. 252) suggests that to foster regulation of arousal, "the idea is to start with the lowest (in the brain) undeveloped/abnormally functioning set of problems and move sequentially up the brain as improvements are seen" by using somatic interventions. In SP, therapists guide clients to become mindfully aware of the relationship between bodily signs of dysregulation such as tightness in the chest or shallow breathing, and thoughts such as "I'm never safe" and emotions such as panic. Once they become aware of these signs, they can experiment with actions, or "somatic resources," such as aligning the spine, grounding through the legs, regulated breathing, self-touch actions (e.g., placing one's hand on the heart) that are regulating. Gradually, clients learn to draw upon the body as a resource to mitigate the dysregulated arousal driving their symptoms.

Clients with CTSDs are often phobic of their bodies, regarding the body as repulsive, terrifying, the enemy, and "not-me." They may be numb, disconnected, and disregard their bodies by neglecting rudimentary self-care. They may feel a hatred of their physical self for betraying them in some way (e.g., having an erection or orgasm during sexual abuse; freeze or collapse responses) or being the site of pain and abuse. Self-harm, extreme risk taking, and neglect are often prevalent. These negative attitudes are exacerbated by debilitating somatoform symptoms and intense dysregulation. Vehement emotions and distorted trauma-related beliefs are coupled with body sensations, confirming that the body is not "safe" and that being aware of it will only make things worse. To address this, clients learn how to "uncouple" the sensations of the body from thoughts, narrative content, and emotions. In doing so, they find the sensations less threatening and more acceptable. For example, when a client reports a tingling sensation accompanied by hyperarousal, terror, and intrusive images, the therapist might suggest focusing exclusively on the body, putting the panic and images aside, until the sensation settles. Or the therapist may suggest pushing the feet against the floor and focusing all attention on that action. Helping clients learn to limit the amount and kind of information they are aware of promotes regulation and provides a valuable tool for setting internal stops and boundaries.

In addition to learning somatic resources that regulate arousal, clients learn to regulate actions. Mobilizing defenses (a cry for help, fight and flight) give way to immobilizing ones (freeze and feigned death) when active defenses are overwhelmed, unavailable, or ineffective. Attempts to utilize them can incite the perpetrator to violence or provoke punishment. By instinct, immobilized defenses are employed to ensure the best possible outcome for the victim. With repeated iterations, as is the case of clients with inescapable chronic trauma exposures, immobilization can become habitual, turning into default responses in the face of perceived, as well as active, threat. This response can be frightening for clients and those around them, including the therapist. However, because they are instincts, the impulses to actively defend remain as urges within the body long after the original trauma is over (Levine, 1997; Ogden & Minton, 2000; Ogden et al., 2006). These impulses—striking out, pushing away, hitting, kicking, raising an arm in self-protection, fleeing, crying for help—are "actions that wanted to happen" and can be directly reinstated in the therapy hour. Signs of defensive responses arise as subtle involuntary actions, or "preparatory" movements, that are dependent on the planned or voluntary motor movement for the form they take (Bouisset, 1991). These insipient movements emerge spontaneously in therapy as tension, such as tension in the legs (readiness to flee), or actions such as lifting the fingers or beginning to form a fist (readiness to fight), or a reach of the hand (a cry for help). SP emphasizes noticing preparatory movements and capitalizing on their therapeutic potential. Once the therapist tracks and contacts a preparatory movement (e.g., lifting the fingers), the client is asked to slowly and mindfully follow the movement the body "wants" to make, executing the action indicated by its preparation (e.g., a pushing motion). Doing so generates a feeling of mastery rather than discharge, a sense of being able to protect oneself. It contradicts powerlessness, helplessness, and immobilization, and finishes the action.

Movement interventions take place in the context of a resonant responsive therapeutic relationship that strengthens the client's ability to collaborate, engage, and to find the courage to execute new actions that might have been dangerous or futile in the past but can engender competence and mastery in the present. If these same interventions were employed as a rote physical exercise, rather than emerging organically within in intersubjective relational context, they would not have the same therapeutic advantage. Similar to a caregiver with a child, an attuned intersubjectivity in SP requires right brain to right brain communications (Schore & Schore, 2008) via implicit means—prosody, degree of empathy, body language, facial expression, proximity, eye contact, and seriousness versus playfulness to up- or down-regulate the client as needed, in the process minimizing distress and maximizing pleasurable states.

Dissociation and the Body

SP draws on the structural dissociation theory (Chapter 6) to understand and treat complex dissociative aspects of complex trauma and CTSDs. This theory clarifies that after repeated trauma, one part of the self remains fixated on *animal defense systems* (cry for help, fight, flight, freeze and shutdown/feign death), while another part(s), associated with *daily life systems* (attachment, exploration, sociability, sexuality, play, etc.) tries to keep the implicit traumatic memories sequestered to carry on with the normal life activities. However, these avoidance strategies are unsuccessful when traumatic reminders trigger animal defensive responses and extremes of arousal. The structural dissociation model helps clients and therapists alike make sense of unintegrated parts of the self related to reactions to complex trauma.

The expression *part of the self* is a metaphor used to describe the lack of integration between the systems of daily life and those of defense. As Bromberg (2011, p. 15) asserts, each part of the self "holds a relatively non-negotiable affective 'truth' that is supported by its self-selected array of 'evidence' designed to bolster its own insulated version of reality." These "truths" are reflected in the body. SP pays attention to the manifestations of parts of the self that are visible in the procedural and regulatory tendencies (Ogden & Fisher, 2014, 2015; Fisher, 2017). Clients learn to recognize the physical signs that indicate certain parts with their associated emotions and agenda are being activated and thus increase awareness of the elements of present experience that might precipitate the full emergence of a part. For example, low arousal, a slumped posture, blank expression, and loss of muscle tone are often connected with a feigned death/shutdown response. High arousal, darting eyes, and tense arms may indicate a "fight part," while tension or movement in the legs might indicate a "flight part." A "freeze part" might be reflected in constriction, lifted shoulders, and wide eyes combined with stillness. Parts rooted in daily life may demonstrate less tension, more movement, with midlevel arousal. Therapists observe the physical indictors of various parts of clients, cultivate curiosity about them, and explore the use of movement to regulate dysregulated parts and increase communication among them. As clients learn to mindfully observe and describe the various parts, they develop mindfulness of two or more parts simultaneously—a skill that is particularly important in the treatment of dissociative disorders, as it promotes integration (Ogden & Fisher, 2015). Therapists convey to clients that each part has a function, and the behaviors related to each pertain to implicit memories and attempts to ensure survival. With this viewpoint, clients become more accepting of and curious about internal parts, regulatory resources needed for each part can be developed, and eventually implicit trauma memories of each part can be processed.

Phase-Oriented Treatment

SP adapts the phase-oriented approach pioneered by Janet (1925) to provide a general hierarchical structure for treatment. Phase 1 is focused on regulating arousal, behavior, and emotion, developing somatic resources; Phase 2 is focused on reprocessing traumatic memory, completing or regulating defensive responses, and recalibrating a dysregulated nervous system; and Phase 3 attends to the relational effects of attachment failures, proximity-seeking actions, and other movements that support overall success in life. Therapists often share this three-phase model with clients to communicate that a series of steps exist that are designed to gradually resolve the effects of the past, so that they understand that the first task of therapy is to increase safety and stabilize dysregulated arousal that leads to maladaptive behavior. The three phases are fluid rather than rigidly sequential. Once stabilization goals are met in Phase 1, work on traumatic memories in Phase 2 can catalyze dysregulation and decompensation, necessitating a return to Phase 1 to rework and strengthen resources. Therapists adapt phase-oriented treatment moment by moment to respond appropriately to the needs of each client.

Clinical Case Example

Jamie, a single, cisgender, African American woman in her mid-30s, grew up in a working-class community in a large city in the midwestern United States. Raised by a single mother, Jamie is an only child, a college graduate, and holds a position as a hotel receptionist. She has a heterosexual sexual orientation and is in a new relationship with a man 9 years her senior. Jamie has completed several years of conventional therapy, but her symptoms have not resolved. At the invitation of her therapist to discuss perceptions about beginning a cross-racial therapy, Jamie expressed that her therapist, a white, cisgender, 52-year-old woman of middle-class socioeconomic status, does not have firsthand knowledge of what it is like to be a person of color and grow up marginalized. She seemed reassured when her therapist agreed, acknowledged her own white privilege, and brought up the power differential and the privilege/oppression dynamics inherent in their relationship. Jamie concurred with her therapist that it would be important that they continue to openly address these issues, and together they agreed to check in regularly about what might be needed to make cross-racial therapy work. They also discussed the implicit and explicit racism, and her therapist asked Jamie about the role of racism and oppression in her life. She reported numerous incidents of racial harassment and trauma, including a white child refusing to sit next to her in elementary school; being given menial tasks in her workplace (e.g., sweeping the floor); being followed by clerks in stores; witnessing incidents of police brutality toward people of color in her community and in the media; being called demeaning racial slurs; and being forced to perform oral sex at knifepoint by a white boy. Additionally, Jamie reported being sexually abused by her mother's boyfriend, also white. What follows are brief excerpts of Jamie's therapy at various phases of treatment.

Phase 1 Treatment

Mapping Parts

Jamie expressed being distraught and confused by her sharply discordant thoughts, feelings, and behaviors. Psychoeducation was used to help her understand that these dramatic shifts can be the result of different internal parts coming forward and "taking over." Her therapist clarified that the use of "parts" terminology does not indicate a real split of the self into separate "people," but describes the internal systems of defense against threat, as well as engagement in daily life. Jamie's therapist suggested that they might map parts by writing or drawing a representation of her internal system on paper, and identifying the behaviors, thoughts, emotions, memories, and especially physical components, associated with each part. Note that this exercise is adjusted depending on the client's regulatory capacity and ability to identify parts rather than identify with them. Mapping delineates parts rooted in defense, and identifies daily life part(s) that can best communicate with defensive parts and regulate their dysregulated arousal (Ogden & Fisher, 2014, 2015; Fisher, 2017). Although some clients do not resonate with the term *parts*, many find that mapping their dissociative system leads to understanding and relief, because it can elucidate the logic of an internal system and even provide hope of integration.

Jamie and her therapist began by identifying the "daily life part of her" that could go to work and relate to her friends. She agreed to try to keep this part of her present in the therapy hour and become aware of the disruptive defense parts, rather than identify with them. Jamie described several "defensive parts": a part associated with a fight defense that turned her anger toward herself, reflected in a familiar pattern of tension in her jaw, arms, and hands; a cry-for-help part that came forward in Jamie as a sensation of panic in her chest when her boyfriend was upset with her; a flight part connected with addictions, precipitated by a jittery feeling in her body, especially her lower extremities; and a freeze part reflected in overall constriction and high anxiety. She also identified a shutdown, feigned death part, apparent in numbness and a collapsed posture, that experienced disabling self-loathing and shame. Jamie began to understand that the implicit memories of each defensive part fueled thoughts, feelings, and actions that interfered with daily life tasks, like getting to work on time, self-care, and socializing. Jamie said that she sometimes "couldn't get herself back" when the defensive parts emerged.

Strengthening the Daily Life Part

At the onset of therapy, interventions were geared toward strengthening the daily life part, with the intention of improving Jamie's overall functioning and stabilizing arousal. Her therapist suggested that maybe they could find out about this part by remembering a recent event during which Jamie felt competent and good about herself.

JAMIE: But I never feel good about myself.

THERAPIST: Maybe there was a time when you felt less bad.

JAMIE: Hmmm—last month, I brought cookies to a party at work. My boss liked them.

THERAPIST: OK, that's a good example! Let's pause right there for a moment, if that's OK? Can you recall the moment in that memory when you knew your boss liked your cookies?

JAMIE: He was smiling at me and eating my cookies.

THERAPIST: So let's stay with seeing him smile—can you see his face in your mind's eye? (*Jamie smiles slightly.*) It makes you smile, too, huh?

JAMIE: (*Nods.*) He looked like he was proud of me. Most of the time I'm nothing to be proud of at all. (*Her smile changes to a frown, and her posture begins to slump.*)

THERAPIST: I understand it's hard when you feel you're nothing to be proud of. But I wonder if, just for a moment, we can inhibit that impulse to collapse and keep seeing his face and smile . . . stay with the good feeling, then maybe we'll look at the parts of you that feel bad.

[Asking Jamie to stay with the positive feelings and inhibit awareness of the elements that counter them strengthens the daily life part and teaches Jamie internal boundaries, so that she does not have to "give in" to the negative thoughts and emotions of dysregulated or self-disparaging parts when they threaten to emerge.]

JAMIE: (*straightening her spine*) OK, it does feel kind of good.

THERAPIST: Sense your body . . . it seems that maybe your shoulders are a bit squarer and your spine lengthens a bit.

JAMIE: I sit a little taller.

THERAPIST: Wonderful that you can be aware of that. See if you can stay right with seeing that image of your boss's smile, that good feeling, and sitting a little taller. . . . Don't let your mind go anywhere else for right now. I wonder if this tells you something about yourself . . .

JAMIE: That I must be all right.

THERAPIST: Yes, that's right. You are all right.

JAMIE: But I'm anxious. I feel exposed. (*Her posture slumps.*)

[Jamie explained that she had tried to be invisible at school and on the streets to avoid racial harassment. Since actions, like sitting taller, can be adversarial or threatening to other parts of the self, it is important to find a way to integrate rather than override them.]

THERAPIST: So, there's a part of you that's scared. Where do you sense that in your body?

JAMIE: In my stomach.

THERAPIST: So let's try this: What happens in your stomach if you sit tall? (*Both sit more upright.*)

JAMIE: I get anxious in my stomach.

THERAPIST: What happens to the anxiety if you slump again? (*Demonstrates Jamie's slumped posture.*)

JAMIE: It goes away.

THERAPIST: So no wonder you want to slump—the anxiety goes away. Hmmmm. I have an idea: If you just place your hands over your stomach (*demonstrating*) to connect with that anxious part and just straighten your posture a little. What happens to the anxiety?

JAMIE: (*sitting taller*) That's better. I feel safe, and I feel warm.

[Jamie had discovered two somatic resources: one, the upright posture that strengthened her daily life part, and two, the self-touch that protected the anxious part, which together helped to integrate these two parts. Her homework was to practice these actions in her daily life to help her daily life part stay present, and soothe the anxiety. Her therapist pointed out that Jamie was in control and could decide when and how to practice these resources, so that she used them in ways that best helped her feel empowered and safe.]

Regulating Arousal

JAMIE: (*angrily*) I just hate myself! I spent most of the weekend drinking and could barely go to work on Monday. I just wish this would end! I'm such a failure! What is wrong with me?

[Jamie does not have access to the capacities of her daily life part as she interprets her actions as evidence that something is terribly wrong with her in the present. It appears that her fight part is hostile to the part of her that escapes through alcohol.]

THERAPIST: So there's a part of you here that hates yourself right now. And your arousal seems outside the window. Is that true?

JAMIE: Yes, I'm so angry I'm shaking inside!

THERAPIST: OK, remember, we agreed that if your arousal gets too high, we'll pause and help that arousal return to the window . . . and then we can look at these patterns, OK? Can you tell me how you experience that anger and arousal in your body?

JAMIE: My whole upper body is tight . . . my heart is pounding. My jaw hurts it's so tight. I just want to kill myself.

THERAPIST: It looks like all your energy is moving upwards. I wonder if you can sense your legs?

JAMIE: I don't feel my legs.

THERAPIST: Maybe we should focus on feeling your legs. . . . Let's just put the anger aside for now, and just sense your legs. . . . Maybe you could push them into the floor and notice what happens inside—would that be OK?

JAMIE: Well, that's kind of hard to do right now . . .

THERAPIST: I know it's not easy. Let's do it together, both of us press our feet into the floor. . . . What happens, Jamie? Maybe you notice the tension changes, or your breathing deepens, or your jaw starts to relax—or maybe nothing changes . . . just notice whatever happens . . .

[Offering a menu helps to direct mindful attention, doing the action together promotes collaboration and social engagement, and grounding helps Jamie be in the here and now.]

JAMIE: Well, things do seem to relax a little . . .

THERAPIST: Great, just stay with that relaxation. How do you sense it?

JAMIE: The tension is draining out of my arms . . . my jaw lets go a little.

THERAPIST: OK, so just sense that. How's the pounding in your heart?

JAMIE: A little better.

THERAPIST: Let's think about this for a moment. It seems that you wanted some relief, so your flight part took over and led you to drink. Is that right?

JAMIE: Yes, I guess so. . . . I just needed to feel better.

THERAPIST: Maybe together we could find out what could help that flight part. Do you remember what was going on before you started drinking?

JAMIE: I felt good when I got home from work, and I was just watching TV. Then Jerome [boyfriend] called and canceled Saturday plans. I got upset; I drove him away . . . this panic in my chest [an indicator of the cry for help part] . . . I don't matter to anyone . . . it's always going to be like this . . . things never change . . .

THERAPIST: Hmmm. So that part of you that feels hopeless and alone is up. . . . It makes sense that you just wanted to get away by drinking. I wonder what you're feeling in your body as we talk about this?

JAMIE: I feel this panic . . . I'm not breathing . . . and tight, my body is tight . . .

THERAPIST: Where do you feel the tightness?

JAMIE: All over. I feel stuck. My legs are really tight.

THERAPIST: I wonder if you would be willing to try something? (*Jamie nods.*) Let's stand up together for a moment. Maybe we can walk a little and notice that our legs could carry us away from certain things in the room and toward others (*Jamie looks skeptical.*) Let's just try it. What happens if together if we just take one step . . .

JAMIE: I feel like I have to fight the feeling that nothing's going to help . . . why bother . . . what good will this do? (*However, she takes a step and her therapist mirrors the action.*)

THERAPIST: What happens as we both take a step?

JAMIE: It's OK . . .

THERAPIST: Let's continue just walking slowly—sense the movement in your legs . . . that your legs can carry you through space, away from things and toward other things or people. . . . What happens?

[Jamie's comfort doing the action and ability to remain relationally engaged are supported by her therapist walking with her around the room, rather than asking Jamie to do it alone.]

JAMIE: It's good to feel the movement . . . there's strength in my legs.

THERAPIST: Take your time to feel that your legs are strong and can move. Can that part that feels so alone sense this movement?

JAMIE: It's better when I move. . . . My chest feels better . . . (*Takes a visible breath.*)

[After taking several steps, Jamie's arousal settles, and she begins to make sense of her addiction and anticipate more adaptive options for the future.]

JAMIE: That's a lot. I can't quite sort it out. . . . But maybe when I drink, I really feel helpless and panicky . . . trapped like I don't have any options. . . . I don't want to go down [into panic and then depression]. . . . So I drink, which doesn't help.

THERAPIST: Maybe next time you feel the impulse to drink you could do something more physically active.

JAMIE: Yeah, maybe I'll go for a run instead.

THERAPIST: That's a great idea to try! Before we close, I wonder if we can check in with that angry fight part you came in with today.

JAMIE: Not so angry. That part is disgusted when I'm weak.

THERAPIST: Maybe now that part understands the other parts better. All these parts are trying to help you in their own way. They're survival resources, and now you're finding other resources to use, too.

[The experience of walking was a simple action that provided an experience, rather than a concept, of being able to move, an action that she could not execute when past trauma occurred. Reinstating the felt sense of a flight response helped alleviate the panic and threat of shut down that precipitated her drinking.]

Phase 2 Treatment

Once Jamie had developed sufficient resources in Phase 1 to be able to better regulate, she was ready to revisit a childhood memory when she was sexually assaulted at age 11. In preparation to address this trauma, contextualizing it as racialized gender violence that occurred within a historical and socio-cultural context, helped Jamie feel "seen." Together Jaimie and her therapist acknowledged that the history of sexual violence perpetrated on many African American women and girls in the United States is often bypassed, and is linked to the centuries of mental and physical domination and exploitation of people of color. Memory work is approached by helping clients become aware of how elements of experience—sensations, movements, perceptions, emotions and thoughts—are "organized" in mind and body in relation to the memory, with the intention of recalibrating the nervous system and promoting flexibility among defensive responses through bottom-up interventions. Memory work is conducted in a stepwise manner, pausing to work somatically when the body is affected by the telling (e.g., when arousal becomes dysregulated, or when physical impulses or changes emerge).

JAMIE: I can remember bits and pieces of what happened—life was never the same—I wanted to die. (*Her body is tight and her voice is shaky and constricted.*)

THERAPIST: I want to hear what happened, but I notice your arousal seems to be escalating. We don't want to go beyond what your body can handle. . . . How about we pause for a moment and just notice what's happening in your body—let's put the emotions and content aside for now.

[To continue to talk about content when clients are already hyper-aroused can cause arousal to continue to escalate and exacerbate dissociation, leading to reenactment instead of integration.]

JAMIE: I'm starting to feel really scared . . .

THERAPIST: Can you just focus on your body? Sense the scared feeling as body sensation—what does fear feel like in your body?"

[When clients experience the sensation of their arousal approaching the upper limits of the window of tolerance, it is important to put memory content aside, so that arousal does not continue to escalate. Mindful attention is then directed exclusively to following and describing the body sensation as it changes, until arousal settles.]

JAMIE: It's in my spine—there's a weird feeling . . .

THERAPIST: So just sense that weird feeling—as long as you're comfortable. What is the quality of it? Is it tingling or a buzzy feeling, or maybe jumpy or electric?

[Offering a "menu" of sensation vocabulary helped direct Jamie's mindfulness exclusively on sensation, rather than using emotion vocabulary such as scared, ashamed, panicked, or anxious. Doing so facilitates bottom-up processing.]

JAMIE: It's sort of tingling . . .

THERAPIST: Just stay with the tingling. What happens next?

JAMIE: It's kind of vibrating now . . . it's moving up my spine . . . into my arms.

THERAPIST: Just follow the movement of that vibration with your awareness— see what happens next. . . . Maybe the tingling changes, gets stronger or weaker . . .

JAMIE: It feels like the it is moving up into my shoulders. Now it's going down my arms, out my fingertips (*Takes a deep breath.*) It's settling down.

[As Jamie was describing the progression of these sensations, she noticed that, gradually, the sensations settled, trembling abated, and arousal returned to her window of tolerance. This helped her develop confidence in her body's natural ability to process and resolve hyperarousal.]

THERAPIST: Do you feel that it's right to go back to the memory?

JAMIE: OK. It was awful. I was walking home and this boy was on the corner. He was watching me with a weird look. I was scared about what was going to happen. (*Her body seems to be tightening and her eyes widen in fear.*)

THERAPIST: Let's pause again for a moment and see what is going on in your body.

JAMIE: My stomach is clenching. (*Puts her hands on her stomach.*)

THERAPIST: Just sense your hands coming to your body—what's that like?

JAMIE: My hands feel warm. I want to press in.

THERAPIST: So let your hands press in and feel that warmth. What happens to the clenching?

JAMIE: It's starting to let go. (*Takes a breath.*)

THERAPIST: OK, feel it letting go. . . . Take your time to sense the letting go before we continue.

[Jamie is learning to track the initial signs or dysregulation, then to intervene before arousal becomes overwhelming. She learns that she can either follow her sensation with awareness until it settles or use a somatic resource (hands on her belly) to calm her arousal.]

JAMIE: The boy came toward me and he had a knife. (*softly*) He calls me a little black slut. (*Her body starts to curl.*) I want to collapse and curl up . . . I'm so ashamed. . . . Why did I let that happen?

THERAPIST: So there's shame, too, huh. . . . Let's take our time here. . . . It seems when you hear the words he said, you just want to collapse and curl up (*Jamie nods.*) Let's try something. If you're willing, just let yourself hear those words that the boy says—stay sensitive to your body. . . . Do you notice anything besides that impulse to curl up?

[Directing Jamie's mindful attention to a "sliver" of memory—the words the boy said—rather than discussing the event in detail, creates an opportunity to discover whether an active defense that Jamie could not execute at the time of the event is available.]

JAMIE: There's a little tension . . .

THERAPIST: Tension is usually a precursor to movement. . . . If your body could move, what action would it want to make?

JAMIE: I feel like I want to strike out! It coming up strong—feels explosive, like out of control . . . (*Her arousal is escalating.*)

THERAPIST: OK, let's go slow here, because I don't think we want an explosion. Can you tell how your body wants to strike out? Do you want to push away, or hit out, or . . . ?

JAMIE: I wish I could have pushed him away! But I couldn't do it! (*Her fingers lift slightly in what appears to be a preparatory movement of pushing.*)

THERAPIST: Of course not, you were too small. He was much bigger. You couldn't do it then, but you can do it now. Do you sense your fingers lifting? (*Jamie nods.*) Maybe you can sense that lifting and see if there is a movement your arms or hands want to make.

JAMIE: I just want to push him off me!

THERAPIST: Just sense your body, put that memory aside for now, and feel the impulse in your body. See what happens if you just slowly follow that impulse right now and push against the pillow. (*Holds pillow up for Jamie to push against.*) But let's do it in slow motion . . . and tell me what you notice.

[Executing a defensive action slowly in relationship, with mindfulness, and verbally reporting internal experience facilitates integration rather than abreaction. The impulse to push emerged as Jamie focused attention on a sliver of memory—the words—not as an idea or concept. As she began to push, Jamie sensed the powerful instinctive nature of this defensive impulse.]

JAMIE: (*pushing against the pillow*) It feels good—but it's such a powerful feeling! I'm afraid. . . . His eyes are so mean! This could get out of control. . . . Rage is coming up . . .

    [Jamie is struggling to separate past from present, regulate her arousal, and manage triggering stimuli. Her therapist encourages her to focus exclusively on the body, which reduces the struggle. Additionally, since trauma-related default action tendencies are formed from cumulative traumas, the impulses that emerge do not necessarily pertain to a specific memory. Although content of a single incident is used to catalyze truncated animal defensive impulses, putting the memory aside ensures that the impulses emerge from the body rather than from ideas or fears about the potential effects of an action executed in relation to a specific incident.]

THERAPIST: Let's just drop that image now and only sense your body. . . . Focus on the good feeling in your body—and push in a way that feels right to all parts of you. Can you tell me what you notice?

JAMIE: (*Takes a breath, and pushes differently, a little slower and more regulated.*) This is better.

THERAPIST: Great, see if you can push in a way that is right for those different parts—the angry part, the scared part . . .

JAMIE: It's OK for them. Feels kind of good. I feel in control, not scared.

THERAPIST: Push for as long as you want . . . and tell me what happens, just on a body level.

JAMIE: There was surge of energy. It sort of starts in my jaw and shoulders and comes into my arms and hands. My jaw is starting to relax . . . (*Ceases pushing.*)

THERAPIST: It feels complete, huh? (*Jamie nods.*) So, just sense the aftermath of all that pushing.

JAMIE: It feels relaxed. It feels good that the angry part did not get out of hand. I got a little scared. Well, I got pretty scared.

    [For memory work to be successful, somatic and sensory elements of the memory must be stimulated in an appropriate, state-specific reexperiencing, which provides the opportunity for dysregulated arousal to be regulated, and emergent preparatory actions to be completed. Instead of only discussing the memory content, the somatosensory effects of the trauma are addressed.]

Phase 3 Treatment

In Phase 3, the therapeutic focus shifts to overcoming core phobias of normal life, change, connection, and intimacy. SP emphasizes changing cognitive distortions, their corresponding physical habits, and expressing attachment-related emotions within the context of an attuned therapeutic relationship. Jamie's complex trauma symptoms were complicated further by living in two "different worlds." She said that sometimes she did not know who she was, because she acted and talked so differently with people of color than she did with whites. She expressed a pervasive sense of disconnection and lack of safety, saying that no one ever really wanted to connect with her. In this excerpt, proximity-seeking actions are used to explore these issues.

THERAPIST: Maybe we can use our relationship to explore the lack of connection that you experience. (*Jamie nods.*) Let's notice what happens when I make this movement. (*reaches out her hand in a proximity-seeking action toward Jamie.*)

JAMIE: (*very still and flat voice tone*) Nothing happens really. It's fine.

THERAPIST: You seem still—what are you sensing?

JAMIE: (*Looks away.*)

THERAPIST: Can you say what's going on? (*pause, during which Jamie is silent*) So I reached out and you seem to get still. Seems like a different part of you has emerged? (*still no response*) Maybe it's hard to talk . . .

JAMIE: I don't know what's going on.

THERAPIST: (*after a pause*) It seems that when I reached out to you, something changed. (*pause*) Maybe you're feeling distrustful in our relationship.

JAMIE: Maybe . . .

THERAPIST: Can you tell me?

JAMIE: (*after a pause, with eyes averted*) Everyone wants something from me.

THERAPIST: Maybe when I reached out, it seemed that I wanted something from you.

JAMIE: (*squirming and clearly uncomfortable*) White people usually do.

THERAPIST: I know a lot of white people have wanted something from you and even hurt you. It makes sense you think I want something, too. I'm not aware of that in myself. But let me think about that for a moment. . . . (*Jamie looks toward the therapist for the first time.*) I can sense that there is a feeling in me that I want you to feel better, more connected. I guess I did want you to respond when I reached out.

JAMIE: See, you do want something from me, too.

THERAPIST: In a way, I do. You're right. I appreciate your helping me see that.

[Jamie and her therapist talked about her history of being abused by whites and the privilege/oppression dynamics in cross-racial interactions, including theirs. The therapist disclosed that her desire to "make it better," in part came from her own sense of "white guilt" for the way her race treats people of color. Jamie said she was relieved that they could talk about this, and the therapist thanked her for the opportunity. After the discussion, they decided to try the experiment of the therapist reaching out a second time.]

JAMIE: My heart beats faster. I can feel my muscles tighten up. . . . I can still here those words in my head, "What do you want from me?"

THERAPIST: Ah, there is a part of you that still feels I would only want to connect because I want something from you.

JAMIE: (*sadly*) Yes, there's that part of me, even though we talked about it . . .

[A brief conversations ensued about white people's lack of boundaries with black bodies, such as strangers touching Jamie's hair. Her therapist validated the wisdom of Jamie's suspicion as a protector part.]

THERAPIST: It's a habit, isn't it—it's how you've protected yourself (*Jamie nods and appears sad.*) You seem a little sad . . . (*Jamie nods.*) Stay with that sadness, if you're willing. . . . What do you notice in your body?

JAMIE: I sort of pull in . . .

THERAPIST: Sense your body pulling in. . . . Are there thoughts, images, or emotions that go with it?

[Up until this point, Jamie's therapy has focused on resolving trauma symptoms and integrating parts through bottom-up interventions. Now, since Jamie has developed sufficient integrative capacity and a wider window of tolerance, the therapist can to begin to direct mindful attention to emotional and cognitive, as well as physical, elements.]

JAMIE: (*after a pause*) So many memories—this woman who wouldn't sit by me on the subway, this guy looking at me with this hateful look, the time my boss wouldn't give me time off when he gave the white girl time off (*Puts her head in her hands.*) and then there's that time I told my mom about her boyfriend coming into my room. She just yelled at me for being disrespectful! I feel so worthless . . . (*Begins to weep.*)

THERAPIST: (*Ceases reaching out, since emotions and memories are coming up.*) So painful . . . you only wanted her help . . .

JAMIE: (*crying*) I can't ever tell anyone anything—they use it to hurt me.

THERAPIST: (*empathically*) It just didn't work, did it? . . .

[As Jamie's sobs subsided, she and her therapist discussed her mother's actions within a larger context of African American parents who often taught their children to be silent in the face of abuse by whites, for fear of retaliation. Jamie said that her mother's seemingly unsupportive attitude was intended to help her develop the strength and resilience she would need to navigate in a racist society. Realizing her mother had suffered in similar ways, Jamie experienced a softening and a felt sense of connection with her mother. Yet she also sensed the emotional pain of her internalized message, and so the work with the memory resumed.]

THERAPIST: Can you sense or see that young girl in this memory?

JAMIE: I see her—she stuck in shock when my mom yells . . .

THERAPIST: And your body seems to tighten up right now as you remember—and curl in . . . (*Jamie nods.*) Just stay with this girl you were . . . so shocked. . . . I wonder what this experience with her mom is telling her about herself that make tighten up and curl in. . . . See if you can sense it . . .

JAMIE: That my only value is to serve others (*crying*).

THERAPIST: Oh, what a terrible message for this child—so painful. . . . (*Jamie cries in earnest for a few moments, and the therapist makes empathic sounds until Jamie's sobs subside and her body relaxes.*) I wonder if you still sense that child . . .

JAMIE: I can see her. She is not in shock any more.

THERAPIST: Can she sense us both with her?

JAMIE: (*Nods.*)

THERAPIST: Maybe her experience with us is telling her something different.

JAMIE: (*quietly*) Maybe that she does have value . . .

THERAPIST: That's right. She does have value. She can feel that now, right?

JAMIE: Yeah. I feel her here (*Points to her heart.*)

THERAPIST: OK, maybe you can put a hand on your heart, symbolically to connect with her. (*Slowly, tenderly demonstrates the action, and Jamie mirrors it.*)

THERAPIST: What happens?

JAMIE: It feels good—my body relaxes. I can sit up straighter.

THERAPIST: Great. I wonder if we should come back to that gesture I made and see if anything has changed? (*Jamie nods.*) Let's see what happens this time when I reach out (*slowly extending her hand*) . . .

JAMIE: It's different . . . not so scary . . . I can look at you. You don't seem to want anything from me. I sort of want to reach back, but I don't quite feel safe . . . still apprehensive . . .

THERAPIST: Perhaps it would help if you made a boundary with your hands. (*Holds both hands up in a "stop" gesture, demonstrating the boundary to Jamie physically.*)

JAMIE: (*Puts her hands up*) But then I'm just alone! That's how it's always been—no connection. (*Tears up.*)

THERAPIST: OK, so, it doesn't feel safe to reach out, but you're all alone if you have a boundary. (*Jamie nods.*) Let's try both at once and see what happens . . . (*Models putting up one hand in a "stop" gesture and reaching out with the other.*)

JAMIE: (*mirroring the action*) This feels better. Wow, I never thought of that . . . I can have both . . . (*Jamie sits taller, makes direct eye contact, and breathes easily, embodying changes in procedural habits of tension, constrained breath, slumping, and avoiding eye contact.*)

THERAPIST: So, just *enjoy* that feeling! When you have a boundary, it feels safer to have connection . . . and your body changes, too. . . . You're sitting taller, making eye contact, more relaxed (*Jamie is embodying changes in procedural habits of tension, slumped posture, and avoiding eye contact.*)

JAMIE: (*laughing and tearful*) I feel like I just landed in my body! It only took me 35 years to find out I can have a boundary! That girl thought she just had to give in to what others wanted. I'm kind of in awe of this!

[a few moments later]

THERAPIST: Let's come back to you and me. How do you feel with me right now?

JAMIE: Good. Really good.

Conclusion

As therapists listen attentively to clients' verbal narratives, they carefully observe the patterns of organization, particularly of the body, understanding that these habits are the legacy of trauma and attachment failures that drive symptoms. Neither insight nor understanding can replace discovering these automatic reactions, interrupting them, and exploring alternative empowering actions that were impossible at the time of the original event(s). Although body awareness is helpful, it is not enough; therapists must employ body-based interventions capable of resolving somatoform symptoms on the somatic level. Bottom-up interventions that install somatic resources, facilitate completing truncated mobilizing defensive actions, regulate out-of-control arousal, and track the disturbing sensations of the body until these sensations settle, lead to a profound trust in the body as a resource and a somatic sense of mastery.

Clients become comfortable with a somatic approach as interventions are uniquely tailored to their therapeutic goals and needs. For example, when clients are hesitant or phobic of working with the body, the therapist seeks to discover the cause to provide effective psychoeducation, so that clients can benefit from SP. Knowing that even the word *body* may trigger shame or alarm, the therapist may use other words, such as *activation, experience,* or *movement,* that are acceptable to the client. Interventions are designed to help clients mindfully observe, then transform these patterns.

Integration takes place as here-and-now connections are made on cognitive, emotional, and especially somatic levels, and are cumulative over time. As integrative capacity expands, strong emotions and painful limiting beliefs are identified, experienced. and integrated, along with the procedural tendencies that have sustained them. Adaptive and integrated actions take place when physical patterns that are the legacy of trauma and attachment failures are challenged. Clients develop a bodily felt sense of not only safety but also an expectation that the rich, fulfilling life that was previously only a dream is now a real possibility.

Acknowledgment

The author wishes to thank Sherri Taylor, PsyD, for her contributions to this chapter.

References

Aposhyan, S. (2004). *Bodymind psychotherapy: Principles, techniques and practical applications*. New York: Norton.

Bainbridge-Cohen, B. (1993). *Sensing, feeling, and action*. Northampton, MA: Contact Editions.

Beebe, B. (2006). Co-constructing mother–infant distress in face-to-face interactions: Contributions of microanalysis. *Infant Observation, 9*(2), 151–164.

Bouisset, S. (1991). Relationship between postural support and intentional movement: Biomechanical approach. *Archives Internationales de Physiologie, de Biochimie et de Piophysique, 99*, A77–A92.

Bromberg, P. M. (2006). *Awakening the dreamer: Clinical journeys*. Mahwah, NJ: Analytic Press.

Bromberg, P. M. (2011). *The shadow of the tsunami and the growth of the relational mind*. New York: Routledge.

Fisher, J. (2017). *Healing the fragmented selves of trauma survivors: Overcoming internal self-alienation*. New York: Routledge.

Ford, J. D., Courtois, C. A., Steele, K., van der Hart, O., & Nijenhuis, E. R. (2005). Treatment of complex posttraumatic self-dysregulation. *Journal of Traumatic Stress, 18*(5), 437–447.

Frewen, P., & Lanius, R. (2015). *Healing the traumatized self: Consciousness, neuroscience, treatment*. New York: Norton.

Gene-Cos, N., Fisher, J., Ogden, P., & Cantrell, A. (2016). Sensorimotor psychotherapy group therapy in the treatment of complex PTSD. *Annals of Psychiatry and Mental Health, 4*, 1080–1087.

Herman, J. (1992). *Trauma and recovery*. New York: Basic Books.

Janet, P. (1925). *Principles of psychotherapy*. London: Allen & Unwin.

Kurtz, R. (1990). *Body-centered psychotherapy: The Hakomi method*. Mendocino, CA: LifeRhythm.

Langmuir, J., Kirsh, S. G., & Classen, C. C. (2011). A pilot study of body-oriented group psychotherapy: Adapting sensorimotor psychotherapy for group treatment of trauma. *Psychological Trauma: Theory, Research, Practice, and Policy, 4*(2), 214–220.

LeDoux, J. (2002). *The synaptic self*. New York: Viking.

Levine, P. A. (1997). *Waking the tiger: Healing trauma*. Berkeley, CA: North Atlantic Books.

MacLean, P. D. (1985). Brain evolution relating to family, play, and the separation call. *Archives of General Psychiatry, 42*(4), 405–417.

Nijenhuis, E. R. S. (2006). *Somatoform dissociation*. Assen, the Netherlands: Van Gorcum.

Ogden, P. (2009). Emotion, mindfulness, and movement: Expanding the regulatory boundaries of the window of tolerance. In D. Fosha, D. Siegel, & M. Solomon (Eds.), *The healing power of emotion* (pp. 204–231). New York: Norton.

Ogden, P. (2014). Embedded relational mindfulness: A sensorimotor perspective on the treatment of trauma. In V. Folette, J. Briere, D. Rozelle, J. Hopper, & D. Rome (Eds.), *Mindfulness-oriented interventions for trauma: Integrating contemplative practices* (pp. 227–239). New York: Guilford Press.

Ogden, P., & Fisher, J. (2014). Integrating body and mind: Sensorimotor psychotherapy and treatment of dissociation, defense, and dysregulation. In U. Lanius, S. Paulsen, & F. Corrigan (Eds.), *Neurobiology and treatment of traumatic dissociation: Towards an embodied self* (pp. 399–422). New York: Springer.

Ogden, P., & Fisher, J. (2015). *Sensorimotor psychotherapy: Interventions for trauma and attachment*. New York: Norton.

Ogden, P., & Minton, K. (2000). Sensorimotor psychotherapy: One method for processing traumatic memory. *Traumatology, 6*(3), 149–173.

Ogden, P., Minton, K., & Pain, C. (2006). *Trauma and the body: A sensorimotor approach to psychotherapy*. New York: Norton.

Perry, B. D. (2009). Examining child maltreatment through a neurodevelopmental lens. *Journal of Loss and Trauma, 14*, 240–255.

Porges, S. W. (2011). *The polyvagal theory: Neurophysiological foundations of emotions, attachment, communication, and self-regulation*. New York: Norton.

Rolf, I. P. (1977). *Rolfing: The integration of human structures*. Santa Monica, CA: Dennis-Landman.

Schore, A. N. (2011). *The science of the art of psychotherapy*. New York: Norton.

Schore, A. N., & Schore, J. R. (2008). Modern attachment theory: The central role of affect regulation in development and treatment. *Clinical Social Work, 36*, 9–20.

Siegel, D. J. (2007). *The mindful brain: Reflection and attunement in the cultivation of well-being*. New York: Norton.

Tronick, E. Z. (2009). Multilevel meaning making and dyadic expansion of consciousness theory: The emotional and the polymorphic and polysemic flow of meaning. In D. Fosha, D. J. Siegel, & M. Solomon (Eds.), *The healing power of emotion: Affective neuroscience, development and clinical practice* (pp. 86–111). New York: Norton.

Zerubavel, N., & Messman-Moore, T. L. (2015). Staying present: Incorporating mindfulness into therapy for dissociation. *Mindfulness, 6*, 303–314.

CHAPTER 24

Experiential Approaches

JANINA FISHER

Without a clear chronological record of what happened, and vulnerable to the uninvited activation of trauma-related feeling and body sensations, chronically traumatized individuals are often left with a legacy of symptoms and reactions, with no coherent autobiographical context that identifies them as personal memories (van der Kolk, 2014). These individuals often have generalized complaints of depression, free-floating anxiety, shame, low self-esteem, loneliness and alienation, absent or conflicted relationships, problems with anger, and impulsivity or acting out. They may also be troubled by chronic expectations of danger: intrusive anxiety and dread, social phobia, hypervigilance ("eyes in the back of my head"), a conviction that the worst is about to happen, fears of abandonment, or agoraphobia. Or they come to therapy as a last resort, because they are fighting a losing battle against addiction, self-harming impulses, eating disorders, or a longing or even determination to die. Often, they can tell us very little about what evokes the self-destructive impulses other than that it confirms their worst fears about themselves: "I do it to punish myself"; "I hate myself"; "I don't deserve to live"; "I'm disgusting—I wish I were dead." They sometimes sense that there is a connection to the traumatic past but struggle with how that could be so and how to approach the trauma and make those connections. This is especially the case given that they may not want to think about what happened, experience any of its aversive emotional responses, or they may recall very little of the chronological events. Thus, they are alienated from a childhood past that belongs to them but that once overwhelmed their fragile coping capacities and threatened their existence.

In this chapter, I describe how alienation from one's own past experiences evolves as an adaptation necessary to survive complex trauma intact. This dissociative disconnection or fragmentation has profound implications for the development of a core self, leading to discontinuities in identity and often a rejection of the past or aspects of the individual's self. Straightforward therapeutic interventions focused on self-compassion and self-esteem are often frustrated by this disowning of the trauma and rejection of the traumatized child to whom it happened. Using an approach that combines mindful awareness with visualization and somatic techniques for evoking and befriending the individual's disowned child selves, I describe in this chapter how the therapist can help survivors of complex trauma to befriend these wounded aspects of self, evoke warm acceptance and compassion for the child who survived the traumatic past, and experience the sense of wholeness and belonging for which they have longed.

Alienation from Self

In the face of abuse and trauma (especially when repeated, chronic, and progressive over time), children need psychological distance from what is happening to avoid being overwhelmed and to survive in a way that leaves them psychologically intact (Fisher, 2017b, 2017c). Preserving some modicum of self-esteem and hope for the future requires victims to disconnect from the abusive experiences, doubt their recollection, and disown the "bad [victim] child" to whom it happened as "not me." By holding out some sense of themselves as "good," disconnected from the mistreatment, abused children capitalize on the human brain's innate capacity for dissociative splitting or compartmentalization. Dissociation is an ingenious and adaptive survival strategy—but one with a steep price. To ensure that the rejected "not-me" child is kept out of consciousness and to enforce the split requires that survivors rely on dissociative disconnection, denial, and/or self-hatred. In the end, they survive the abuse and betrayal and the failure of safety at the cost of disowning themselves (see Chapter 6).

Aware that their self-presentation and ability to function are only one piece of who they really are, they now feel fraudulent, like imposters, especially in the domains of their existence in which they function normally. Struggling to stay away from the "bad" and painful side and identifying with the "good," they have a felt sense of "faking it," "pretending," or of being what others want them to be rather than who they really are. For some, this conviction of fraudulence engenders resentment; for others, shame and self-doubt. Often, there is a loss of motivation to function, because being able to "keep on" feels like fakery.

As children abused early in life continue to grow through latency into adolescence (during which time the abuse and trauma may continue or even worsen) and subsequently into adulthood, this splitting of the self supports another important aspect of surviving trauma: mastering normal developmental tasks, such as learning in school, developing peer relationships, finding interests on which to focus; developing a purpose, a career, and sense of competence; and eventually developing intimate relationships and families of their own (Fisher, 2017a). The "good" part of the child (now an adult) engages in normal life activity and tasks, while that "not-me" part of the child continues to bear the emotional and physical imprint of the past, continuously scanning for signs of danger, and bracing for the next set of threats and abandonments (see discussion of the "learning brain" and the "survival brain" in Chapter 2). Due to the nature of traumatic memory, what can be "recalled" after trauma tends to appear in the form of intrusive images, emotions, and physical reactions that occur out of context and spontaneously, without warning, often in response to cues or triggers that are not consciously available to the individual (van der Kolk, 2014). To make the situation more complicated, neither the "me" nor the "not-me" self is likely to have well-developed chronological memories of the traumatic events that could provide a context for self-understanding. Some survivors of complex trauma cannot reliably access a sequence of narrative memories that make a clear-cut case for what happened "beyond a reasonable doubt" (Williams, 1994, 1995). However, even when memory is fairly intact, it is often still avoided and kept sequestered from everyday functioning, maintaining the internal split.

The Legacy of Traumatic Attachment

Human beings have a brain and body specialized for a host of functions, from attention and concentration to regulating heart rate and respiration, empathizing with others, storing accumulated knowledge, and instinctively fighting and fleeing in the face of danger. We fight with different parts of our bodies than those areas of the body that help us flee: for example, we instinctively smile when we see a baby but would have trouble smiling at someone threatening to rob us. We can more easily comply if we feel shame, but if we feel anger, it is harder to submit because our bodies tense, fists clench, and jaws tighten (Ogden, Minton, & Pain, 2006). The human brain is organized structurally and functionally. Brain activity is automatically inhibited in some areas when other areas become more active—and vice versa (Siegel, 2006). For instance, in the context of danger, activity in the prefrontal cortex is instinctively inhibited, and more primitive, survival-focused areas in the brain, such as the amygdala, are highly activated, presumably so that instinctive self-protective reactions automatically override thinking in favor of acting (LeDoux, 2002). When threatened, we act first and put words to what we did later.

Attachment research has also contributed to the literature supporting the concept of an innate tendency to compartmentalize under stress. In longitudinal studies of attachment behavior (Lyons-Ruth, Dutra, Schuder, & Bianchi, 2006; Solomon & Siegel, 2003; Solomon & George, 2011), researchers have demonstrated that children with "disorganized attachment" status at age 1 are significantly more likely to exhibit dissociative symptoms by age 19 and/or to be diagnosed with borderline personality disorder (BPD)/complex PTSD or dissociative identity disorder (DID) in adulthood. Since disorganized attachment status is highly correlated with abuse or maltreatment (especially ongoing chronic abuse and polyvictimization), we can hypothesize that dissociation is not only common but also adaptive whenever the child's source of safety is simultaneously the source of danger. When parents' abusive behavior repeatedly alternates with more nonabusive interactions, their child's instinctual tendencies are put in direct conflict. Innately, the need for attachment drives children to seek proximity to the attachment figure when distressed, but when the parent is the source of that distress due to threat, violence, and abuse, animal defense survival responses are simultaneously activated, and the child is caught in an irresolvable double bind (Spiegel, 1994; van der Hart, Niijenhuis, & Steele, 2006). This apparently contradictory behavior is observed in disorganized children and later in adolescents and adults. Although labeled "disorganized" for obvious reasons, researchers have stressed that this is an organized strategy developed by the child in response to a "frightened or frightening" attachment environment. Liotti (2011) hypothesized that dissociative splitting is necessitated by the child's internal struggle with these two intense instinctual emotional and physical drives, and the very different internal working models of attachment that result: Is it safe to approach? Or is it safer to avoid?

The structural dissociation theory of van der Hart et al. (2006) offers an explanatory model for trauma-related splitting of the personality based on "fault lines" created by the compartmentalized structure of the human brain (see Chapter 6). In a traumatizing environment, the left brain-mediated apparently normal or "going on with normal life" self of the child (the "learning brain") carries on (going to school, engaging in peer relationships and activities, reading, exploring nature, etc.), while "emotional parts" (driven by the "survival brain"), serving the animal defense functions of fight, flight, freeze (or fear) or collapse/submit are simultaneously braced to be mobilized in the face of the next anticipated threat or danger. Thus, in this public versus private self-presentation, we can see the origins of the sense of a fake or fraudulent self that develops in the context of chronic complex trauma. For normal development to proceed despite the abnormal environment requires a split between the "going on with normal life" part of the child, while surviving in a dangerous world requires instinctive defensive responses split off from each other and from the "normal life" self, and operating automatically to anticipate and defend against potential threat.

By the time an individual with complex trauma and consequent patterns of disorganized attachment comes to therapy, the emotional part's mistrust of others (including the therapist), overwhelming and unstable emotions, incapacitating depression or anxiety, impulsive risk taking, and self-destructive behavior have themselves become problems. The presenting complaints of many clients are indicative of being flooded by these primitive feelings and physiological reactions related to autonomic hyperarousal. Another group of clients with complex trauma have developed patterns of chronic hypoarousal, disconnection, and numbing, often leading to chronic depression or depersonalization. Although some of these clients in both groups may present with diagnosable dissociative disorders (DDs), many more come to therapy with trauma-related symptoms that initially appear straightforward, such as complex traumatic stress disorders (CTSDs), anxiety and mood disorders, or personality disorders.

Advantages of Working with a Parts Model

A *parts perspective* offers some new possibilities for addressing the challenges of CTSDs (Fisher, 2017c). First and foremost, therapeutic approaches centered on working with the symptoms as manifestations of parts invite the therapist to incorporate mindfulness-based practices early in treatment (Fisher, 2017c; Schwartz, 2001; Shapiro, 2018). The intense autonomic dysregulation (or hyperarousal) associated with unresolved trauma often makes "getting in touch with emotions" overwhelming, which can then lead to acting out to discharge the tension or a plunge into autonomic hypoarousal (i.e., numbing, dissociation, and disconnectedness). In either case, the client's initial levels of anxiety, depression, and impulsive behavior tend to be exacerbated. Helping clients to "notice" their emotional distress as communications from "parts" rather than as "feelings" generally results in decreased dysregulation and overwhelm. Mindful and slowed down observation of present-moment experience (thought by thought, feeling by feeling) teaches the client about *dual awareness,* the ability to be connected to the emotional or somatic experience while also observing it with interest and curiosity, a valuable skill to develop (Ogden & Fisher, 2015). Research shows that mindful consciousness is associated with increased activity in the medial prefrontal cortex, counteracting the prefrontal inhibition associated with trauma responses, and decreased activity in the amygdala, the brain's fear and alarm center, resulting in decreased traumatic activation and distress (Creswell, Way, Eisenberger, & Lieberman, 2007).

Second, a parts approach allows individuals to titrate emotions or memories so that they can be better tolerated. While one part holds the intense emotion, the client might notice that other parts are calm, curious, or even disconnected. If a part is remembering something alarming or devastating, other parts can be asked to offer support, validation, or comfort. As meditation practice and clinical hypnosis attest, the human brain is capable of holding multiple states of consciousness "in mind" simultaneously, and this ability has important therapeutic uses on which the therapist can capitalize. For example, in eating disorders treatment and addiction recovery programs, externalization techniques have been shown to be helpful in decreasing overidentification with the symptoms and mobilizing that part of the individual ready for recovery. In the "Ed" model (Madigan & Goldner, 1998), the use of parts language is used to help anorexic clients to shift from identifying with their eating-disordered behavior to being in relationship to the symptoms held by "Ed" (i.e., their eating disordered part), increasing their ability to perceive the eating disorder as "other." Similarly, relating to shame as the emotional reaction of part that is ashamed, anger as the expression of an angry part, and loneliness as the feeling memory of an abandoned child all help trauma clients to better tolerate their trauma-related emotions and implicit memories (Fisher, 2017b, 2017c).

Overcoming Alienation from Self

In today's trauma treatment world, there are many technical approaches to resolving traumatic experiences. We can choose to treat implicit memory or explicit recall of events; we can focus on either the memories of victimization or the memories of ingenious survival. We can focus on memories held by parts or address unresolved cognitive schemas; we can focus on the body's incomplete defensive actions (Ogden & Fisher, 2016; Levine, 2015) or on procedural memory for habitual actions and reactions (Ogden & Fisher, 2015). We can intentionally focus on recalling a traumatic event by acknowledging it, generalizing from it, desensitizing the responses evoked by it, and/or by observing how the event continues to exert its effects through pathogenic kernels that may or may not have any obvious connection to any narrative (van der Hart et al., 2006).

In the model of treatment described here, traumatic experiences are resolved by overcoming self-alienation, cultivating self-compassion, and using visualized and imaginative experiences to repair emotional injuries. The focus is on present time: on how parts carry their implicit memories into the here and now, distorting the client's perception of present experience. Before we can address the events of the past, we have to address their effects in the present (van der Kolk, 2014), first by differentiating the parts, so that dissociative displacement or dual awareness can be utilized as a therapeutic intervention, then by building internal communication and collaboration. It is the ability to "befriend our inner selves" that facilitates resolution of experiences of abuse and attachment failure (i.e., the ability to soothe the distress of traumatized parts and to provide imaginatively or hypnotically the "missing experiences"; Kurtz, 1990) needed to heal each part's unresolved traumatic responses. Paradoxically, this process of differentiating parts and attending to each individually is an integrative one (Siegel, 2010). Each time the client makes a cognitive, imaginative, or affective connection to a "part" holding a particular memory or emotion, he or she is simultaneously reversing years of avoidance, disconnection, and self-alienation, and increasing the capacity for self-acceptance, integration, and wholeness.

Symptoms as Communications from Parts

In structural dissociation theory, each trauma-related part embodies a different survival strategy or animal defense response, resulting in different signs and symptoms (van der Hart et al., 2006) connected to each. To help clients differentiate their emotional responses and relate to them as communications from trauma-related parts requires some practice and psychoeducation (Fisher, 2010). Understanding the emotions, sensations, beliefs, instincts, and perspective of each type of part aids individuals in identifying it and eventually working with the parts. Assuming that each part embodies an animal defense also helps in narrowing down the possible projections onto the parts by clients, based on whether they have identified with the part or disowned it.

A "fight part," on the one hand, is assumed to be related to the animal defense of fight, indicating that it has a propensity to anger as an emotion, a connection to aggressive or violent impulses, hypervigilance or mistrust of other human beings, and autonomic hyperarousal. A "submit" part, on the other hand, is likely to exhibit hypoarousal responses: slowed thinking and reaction time; feelings of depression and shame; a collapsed body; beliefs in one's inadequacy, fault, hopelessness, or helplessness. (Often, clients who present with chronic depression turn out to have a depressed "submit" part inaccessible to treatment.) The "freeze" part is characterized by fear, paralysis, speechless terror, and anticipation of attack. These parts tend to be younger, even preverbal, as do the "attachment cry" or "attach" parts. "Attachment cry" parts are characterized by fear of abandonment, idealization of others, and strong needs for proximity, often leading mental health professionals to diagnose them as having dependence disorders or BPD. On the one hand, "attach" parts can become overly dependent on the therapist or manifest severe separation anxiety between sessions. A "flight" part, on the other hand, distances in relationships, even from the therapist, and is associated with behaviors that help clients "flee" from traumatic memories and intense emotions, such as eating disorders, substance abuse, and addictive behavior. However, suicidality and self-harm are more likely to be associated with the fight part, rather than the flight part, because both require a level of aggression that is only consistent with the body's fight response.

Understanding the animal defenses of each part usually helps clients more easily identify, as well as accept, the emotions, actions, and reactions associated with different parts. With some psychoeducation, most clients are able to recognize the parts with which they frequently struggle or that "highjack" their attempts to be stable or dominate their way of being. Whether the client suffers from complex PTSD or has a DD (dissociative disorder not otherwise specified [DDNOS] or DID), whether the parts are experienced as feeling or behavioral states or have names and separate identities, the approach is the same. A psychoeducational understanding of the model paves the way for mindful awareness of the moment-by-moment thoughts, feelings, impulses, and beliefs of the parts as they are stimulated by trauma-related triggers or by the emotions and reactions of other parts. Only when the parts are differentiated and linked (Siegel, 2010) to the roles they played in helping the client to survive can individuals feel a sense of being "whole" and "safe."

Working "Beyond Words"

However, the experience of feeling "whole" or "safe" is not a verbal experience. It is a "felt sense" (Gendlin, 1981), reflecting the fact that attachment experiences, good or bad, occur preverbally, long before the development of the capacity for language. The formation of secure attachment in childhood always begins from the "bottom up," starting with the way infants' bodies are held, reached for, stimulated, rocked, fed, soothed, or gazed upon (Ogden et al., 2006). Attachment bonds develop organically through the repetition of small somatic transactions over weeks, months, and years between infant/toddler and parent/primary caregiver. When parents reach out their arms and say "Up?" babies and toddlers reach up in response—not in reaction to the word but to the gesture. The arms are a potent conveyer of safety, insecurity, *or* threat in childhood. Whether and how parents reach out—whether their arms are limp, tense, halfheartedly offered, or used to intimidate—conveys the quality of parents' attachment bonds (Ogden & Fisher, 2015; Ogden et al., 2006).

Inviting Parts "Here" Instead of "Going There"

In contrast to early models of trauma treatment, the focus of internal attachment work is being "here," not "there." Rather than revisiting the early traumatic experiences, attention stays focused on helping the "normal life self" to "stay present in the present" and to contribute to repairing the damage left by the past through the provision of crucial "missing experiences" (Kurtz, 1990; Ogden & Fisher, 2015). Complex trauma involves not only harmful, inappropriate experiences but also a lack or loss of positive experiences that are just as crucial for children to feel safe. The provision of a missing experience, of course, does not involve the actual past event. There is no way to turn back time and provide the holding and attention an infant should have had. There is no way for a 5-year-old part to go back to the first day of school and have someone there to hold his or her hand. But the therapist can help the client make an emotional, physically felt connection to that 5-year-old self, then imaginatively create a felt sense of the emotional and somatic experience the child should have had: the sensation of someone bigger next to him or her; a big, comforting hand taking the little hand; feeling the warmth and solidity of a caring adult presence. With the therapist's help in supporting dual awareness and differentiation of child and adult, each connects viscerally and emotionally to the experience of the other and mirrors it back. Each mentalizes the other: What is it like for the client's "normal life self" to feel the hurting little boy or girl next to him or her? What happens for the little boy or girl when the grownup self feels the hurt and reaches for the child's hand in support? How does that little hand feel in the client's big hand? What happens when the child hears him or her talk about how good it feels to feel close to the little boy or girl?

Clinical Case Example

Marjorie (a composite of several individual clients) was quiet and thoughtful as she said to her therapist, "You know, I used to think I was the wrong child born into a good family, the right family—I thought the problem was that I was 'wrong.' Now [*lifting her head and meeting her therapist's gaze*], I know that I was a right child born into the wrong family. They did not know how to care for a child, and they made me feel it was about me."

That feeling of being "the right child" was a missing experience for Marjorie all through her childhood, but as she took it in as her child part's feeling, she felt how "wrong" her family of origin was for a child like her. Her belief that she didn't belong no longer felt so true.

MARJORIE: Of course, I didn't belong! Thank God. Those were not people I would want to belong to. [Holding that present-moment perspective, Marjorie then included her parts.] The parts belong with me now—I'm the right family for them, just like I'm the right family for my own kids.

THERAPIST: Can you connect to the part who has always had that inner feeling of wrongness and not belonging? Can you feel her here with you right now?

MARJORIE: She's there—still feeling sick about herself . . .

THERAPIST: Ask her if she'd be willing to show you a picture of the home and family where she doesn't belong . . .

MARJORIE: There's an image coming up: It's the apartment where I grew up—not much furniture, very bare—I just hear the sound of my grandmother's oxygen tank. She's little, like kindergarten age, and there's no one to welcome her home from school. She's lonely, but she's also relieved: "If I'm just alone with my grandmother, I won't get hurt."

THERAPIST: Let her know that you understand how she feels—in that home, it was better to be lonely than scared and hurt.

MARJORIE: It was . . . (*sadly*)

THERAPIST: How do you feel toward her as you see that "home" she has to live in?

MARJORIE: It breaks my heart . . .

THERAPIST: And what's that like for her to hear you say that it makes you sad to see her sad?

MARJORIE: It feels strange but good-strange—no one ever knew she was sad. No one seemed to care. She imagined that her grandmother cared, and that helped.

THERAPIST: Now ask her if she'd like to see a different picture? Would she like to see where you live?

MARJORIE: She's curious—I'm showing her a family photograph with my hus-

band and kids and me out on the deck—you can see the geraniums in
bloom and the trees in back, and the sun is shining . . .

THERAPIST: What's that like for her to see *your* home? Does she like it?

MARJORIE: She's interested but a little confused about who "these people" (my
husband and kids) are. . . . I'm explaining to her that this is my family and
it could be her family, too, if she likes it here. (*smiling at the little part's
delight*) She says she likes the red flowers and the sun on her face. I'm telling her that she can stay here if she wants. . . . She's saying, "Really????"
like I just invited her to Disneyland! (*Laughs, enjoying this moment with
her little part.*)

THERAPIST: Such a tender moment: Notice that feeling of her innocence and
delight. This little girl takes nothing for granted, does she? (*Deliberately
directs her attention to the positive feelings being shared between the little
girl and adult, so they can amplify each other's pleasurable experience.*)

MARJORIE: I can feel her holding my hand very tightly—she'd like to stay here,
but she's afraid "those people," meaning my family, won't like it. And if
they don't like it, they'll be mean to her.

THERAPIST: Of course, she'd be a little afraid to trust this—the people she knew
didn't need much of an excuse to reject her.

MARJORIE: It's so sad—how do I tell her that no one will hurt her here? She'll
never believe me . . .

THERAPIST: Tell her with your arms, your feelings, your body—she won't believe
the words, but she might believe how it feels. Can you see her?

MARJORIE: She's pulling at my hand—she wants me to go to the far side of
the deck, away from my husband and kids. She looks scared to go near
them—it's just so sad—she thinks they would hurt her, and she's not taking any chances.

THERAPIST: What's your impulse, Marjorie? Just see her frightened eyes and
little face, and do whatever your motherly instincts tell you to do . . .

MARJORIE: I just picked her up, and I'm holding her in my arms . . . (*Takes a
cushion and holds it tenderly.*) "I'm here with you—no one can hurt you
now" . . . (*Tears come up.*) "You can come here and see the red flowers
whenever you want—I'll be here."

The key to the emotional connection between Marjorie and the little girl
she once was is the evocation of a multisensory experience: seeing the child's
face, reexperiencing the sense of loneliness, feeling the child's hand in hers,
sensing an impulse to reach out and hold her, hearing the tenderness in Marjorie's voice, the exchanging of images, the color of the red flowers, the emotions
of grief, and the physical sense of relief. Each of these sensory components is, in
and of itself, nonthreatening, and the emotions of sadness and grief are muted
by the warm, comforting feelings growing between adult and child. Alienation

from her child part no longer feels imperative in these moments: There are no overwhelming emotions or horrifying images from which distance is needed. If there had been, it would have been a more difficult session, but many of the same multisensory elements could have modulated the distress, for example, images of "here" to balance traumatic images, or more focus on Marjorie's comforting presence and connection to the child.

Touching moments of heart-to-heart connection between a small child part and a compassionate adult self are important, but to facilitate the shift from internal alienation to "earned secure" attachment requires repetition. Repair of traumatic attachment requires repeated emotional connection to the parts, creating moments of repair and attunement, deepening the bond between child and adult selves, then integrating the experience by evoking it again and again. In the 1980s and 1990s, we believed that the intensity of the emotional experience in response to a traumatic memory would result in a transformative shift. Now, informed by neuroscience research, we know that neural plasticity or actual brain change is best facilitated by intensive repetition of new patterns of action and reaction (Schwartz & Begley, 2002).

Rupture and Repair of Internal Attachment Relationships

Experiential healing involves a different focus to the therapy that goes beyond the traditional ingredients associated with trauma treatment, namely, stabilization and memory processing. Without efforts to repair internal emotional ruptures related to avoided and unprocessed trauma responses, to bring solace to parts in distress, and to combat self-alienation and self-loathing with internal attachment bonding, many traumatized clients encounter difficulty feeling whole, safe, and welcome despite good memory processing work. Deeply felt self-acceptance and self-compassion can only develop when young, wounded parts experience the safety of a here-and-now adult's unconditional attachment to them, when they can sense the presence of a caring protector and advocate. Because clients may be focused on the most current crisis or problem, the therapist must shoulder responsibility for keeping in mind the ultimate purpose of the work: "repairing" the implicit memories of early attachment rupture that are being communicated by the parts' feelings of shame, fear, sadness, anger, or other emotional pain. Although each client and each part is unique, and each manifestation of internal self-alienation is subtly different, the building blocks of attachment repair remain the same:

• As the client reports emotional distress, negative thoughts, or physical reactions to a trigger, *the therapist asks the client to recognize these symptoms as communications from a part*: "There's a part of you that's really overwhelmed by shame, huh? Can you feel her here with you now?" The therapist first helps the client mindfully differentiate the traumatized child part from the adult observer, then poses questions that evoke a felt sense of the child part in such a way that the client spontaneously feels interest in that part and can respond empathically to the question, "And how do you feel toward this part now?" (Schwartz, 2001). If the answer isn't mindful or compassionate, the therapist assumes that another part is intruding that also needs to be named and welcomed.

• *Elicit a felt sense of each part,* not an intellectual interpretation: "Notice how she speaks to you through feelings or words or physical sensations—that's her way of communicating—let her know you're listening—you want to know what she's trying to tell you. And if you're not sure what she's saying, just ask her . . . "

• *Place greater emphasis on the togetherness of adult client and child* than on the content of their conversation: "What's it like for that child to feel you here with him? To feel your interest and concern?" Questions such as these help clients notice the effect of their attention, words, and concern on that part, to realize the impact their compassion has on the parts. "It's very special for him, huh? And how does it feel to sense how much your interest means to him?" The therapist takes advantage of opportunities to bring to the attention of the "normal life part" how pleasurable mutuality in attachment feels. As attuned parents know, the warm and loving feelings are their reward for taking the time to meet a child's needs, the "payoff" that fuels greater efforts to be attuned and responsive.

• *Encourage inner reciprocal communication.* "Ask her: Can she feel you there with her now? Good, she can—that's great. Let her know that we're both listening, and we want to understand how upset she is." Make sure "inner communication" is not a guess or intellectualized interpretation: "Don't try to think about what she would answer—ask her and then just listen inside. You might hear words, feel an emotion or a physical sensation, get an image or memory"; "He's giving you a picture of his room . . . maybe he's trying to say that he's upset about something that happened there." The therapist guides the client's "Normal Life self" to interpret the child's nonverbal communications and then ask for correction: "Did I get that right? I really want to understand."

• *Cultivate trust.* "Let her know you understand completely: She *wants* to trust you but it's hard—she's been hurt so much. Communicate to her that you know—really, really know—why she'd be afraid to trust you. Because you do know. You remember what it was like in that home." The therapist needs to capitalize on these moments of emotional recognition and use them to deepen the sense of connection: "What's it like for her to sense that you 'get' it? Does she like it when you understand? When you believe her?"

• *Use what doesn't work as an attachment-building moment.* Repairs are even more powerful when they follow from what goes wrong relationally.

"He's retreating, huh? He's so afraid of being hurt that he's backing away from what he most wants. Let him know that's OK—you understand why he's doing that, right? See what it's like if you reassure him that you won't go away? You'll stay right here, and he can take all the time he needs to be sure he can trust you." Feeling the importance of the moment, the therapist speaks for the child and guides the adult to an attuned response. The therapist conveys the wish to help the client gain confidence in interpreting the child's signals and responding empathically—not as a technique, but because the child parts have been waiting and hoping that someone would hear them and come to their aid.

• *Each response by a part becomes another chance for repair* facilitated by the therapist's guidance: "So she's telling you that she wants to believe you 'get it,' but she's afraid you'll just take advantage of her trust—as they all did. . . . Do you get that, too? Let her know with your feelings and your body that you completely understand why she expects people to use her instead of help her . . . " No therapist can turn back the clock and prevent heartbreaking, horrifying events from having taken place, but we can help clients and their parts to experience how the visualized moments of safety, care, or heartfelt connection in present time can build warm, nourishing implicit memories side by side with the old memories of abandonment and abuse, and, in the process, create internal change.

• *Insist on responsibility and accountability.* The "internal community of parts" has often unconsciously re-created the hostile environment of the client's family of origin: The "normal life self" is likely to have neglected the victimized, hurt (usually younger) parts, may have blamed them for causing the abuse and believed they "deserved" additional mistreatment by parts hostile to vulnerability. When parts say to the "normal life self," "I don't trust you because you only care about going on without us" or "How can I trust you when you've never listened? You never even seemed to care what I felt," the therapist must encourage the client to connect to that complaint: "Do you think there's some truth to what this part is saying? Is he right that you didn't want to listen, didn't want to care? If so, let him know that in your need to forget the abuse and be normal, you cut him off. Let him hold you accountable. . . . He deserves that."

• *Use the mistakes and empathic failures in the service of repair.* "What's it like for him to have you take responsibility? To hear you say that you realize you have been pushing him away?" "Yes, you can feel him relaxing just a little bit when you acknowledge the truth . . . Not many grownups ever did that, huh?"

• *Maximize the moments of attunement,* so they are experienced physically and emotionally: "If this little girl were standing in front of you right this minute looking lost and afraid. . . . Can you see her? Notice: What's your impulse? Reach out to her? Take her hand? Or pick her up and hold her?"; "Feel what that's like to have this little boy in your arms? To feel his hand in yours? Is it a good feeling? Take in the warmth of his body and the feeling of holding him safely. . . . Ask him if he would feel less scared if you did this every time he got afraid?"

• *Avoid the tendency to shift away from emotional connection to a part* to habitual, insight-oriented discussion. In this experiential approach, it is the therapist's job to remind clients that there is a child right there, listening to every word spoken, who needs to know he or she will not be forgotten again: "As we are talking, check in with that little boy and see how he's doing now. He needs to feel that he won't be forgotten this time, and the only way he'll know is to make sure you don't forget him. Remember that children learn what they live. You can say you won't forget him—now you'll have to live your life without forgetting him. It may be hard, but you can't break a promise to a child—every safe, caring parent knows that . . . "

When these steps are repeated over and over again, the "normal life self" feels increasingly differentiated from the trauma-driven emotional parts but also, paradoxically, feels more integrated, stable, and centered. As the distressing feelings are noticed as communications from hurt children and adolescents, and as blame and alienation from these internal parts get resolved though understanding them as ingenious survivors of abuse, the "normal life self" generally feels more spontaneously caring and compassionate toward them. The young parts in turn increasingly feel "held" by someone older and wiser. Each feels needed and wanted, just as parents and children in a secure attachment relationship feel. "Earned secure attachment" (Roisman, Padron, Sroufe, & Egeland, 2002) bestows on the human mind and body the same qualities and resources as secure attachment in childhood: an ability to empathize, to tolerate closeness and distance, to give and receive, to see the shades of grey, and the capacity to tolerate hurt and disappointment.

When a wounded child part is evoked imaginatively or visually, and the client helped to access empathy for the young girl or boy he or she once was, both have an experience that was absent in the client's early life. The adult client feels the sadness or courage or vulnerability of the young child part, and compassion for that child elicits his or her loving gaze and shining eyes. There is a visceral sense of holding by the adult and the felt experience of being held in the children/adolescents, creating the building blocks of secure attachment. As the client connects to the imagined and felt sense of the child, the physical sensation of holding becomes an emotional state of feeling close and warm, the felt sense of "being with" and "being connected" versus being alone and lonely. There is mutual attunement between a compassionate adult and the child self who longed for moments of caring but instead suffered abuse, abandonment, humiliation, and rejection. In human beings, imagined or visualized experiences can evoke the same somatic sensations as an actual event and stimulate the activity of motor "mirror neurons" (Iacoboni et al., 2005) responsible for impulses to reach out, hold, and comfort the visualized young child.

Conclusions

The components and techniques that comprise this approach have in most cases been validated in clinical practice. Visualization techniques and guided imagery have a long and honorable history in the mental health world (Arbuthnott, Arbuthnott, & Rossiter, 2001). The only concerns raised about their use have been about the potential risk that these approaches modify how memories are encoded and recalled (Arbuthnott et al., 2001). But unless the client is undertaking legal proceedings (which would rule out many trauma treatment approaches), the purpose of trauma processing models has always been to facilitate a healing conclusion to the memories of traumatic events. A restructuring or reconsolidation of traumatic memory (Ecker & Ticic, 2012) has historically been the goal of trauma treatment. When questions are raised about the impact of the approach on accuracy of recall, clinicians are usually advised to warn their clients about these concerns.

Working in present-moment time is also a component of many other models, including sensorimotor psychotherapy (Ogden et al., 2006), somatic experiencing (Levine, 2015), internal family systems (Schwartz, 2001), and other mindfulness-based approaches. The two latter methods, somatic experiencing and internal family systems, are supported by research results attesting to their efficacy. Babette Rothschild (2017) makes a strong argument that a focus on present experience is necessary in trauma work:

> Truth be told, the past is stable. What happened, happened. No matter what we do in therapy . . . , no one can change history. How it is remembered, how it is reported, how it is felt or interpreted, how we regard it, and different viewpoints can all change, but the facts of the past are permanent. We cannot change the past, no matter how hard we try or how good our tools. . . . The good news is, we can change the *effect* the past continues to have on ourselves and our clients now and in the future. (Rothschild, 2017, p. 13)

Although this parts-based, attachment-focused experiential model is based on theoretical findings from research in multiple fields of study (i.e., attachment research, neuroscience research, relational psychotherapy, somatic treatment), as of yet, no formal effectiveness research has been conducted. A pilot study implemented the model under the name of trauma-informed stabilization treatment (TIST; Fisher, 2017b) with a group of hospitalized patients ages 19–25, who reported a childhood history of trauma and presented with a high-risk status. Unlike studies that exclude subjects with suicidal behavior, self-harm, violent, or aggressive behavior toward others, comorbid conditions, and dissociative symptoms, the pilot study focused on the *treatment of patients with these issues,* with the goal of reducing the patients' level of risk and returning them to the community. According to anecdotal reports by the clinical staff members who delivered the services and statistical data collected on incidents of self-injurious behavior, this approach yielded positive results for most of the very severely symptomatic patients who participated, many of whom had been chronically hospitalized, sometimes for years (Fisher, 2017b). Clearly, more research looking at treatment effectiveness in comparison to a wait list or other alternative treatment condition is needed to support this model. At the same time, the principles and techniques described here are noninvasive, within the capacity of even very low-functioning clients, and pose little to no risk. As the pilot study suggests, this approach may alleviate severe symptomatology and high-risk behavior, and bring a positive resolution to clients suffering the long-term effects of complex trauma. As Ecker and Ticic (2012, p. 6) remind us, "Emotional memory converts the past into an expectation of the future, without our awareness, and that is both a blessing and a curse. It is a blessing because we rely daily on emotional implicit memory to navigate us. . . . Yet our emotional implicit memory is also a curse because it makes the worst experiences in our past persist as felt emotional realities in the present and in our present sense of the future."

For those worst experiences to feel part of a long-ago past, not a life-long stigma to be avoided with shame, the survivor of complex trauma has to "reconsolidate" the memory, so that it becomes an aspect of the healing process, not a reopening of old wounds. Traumatic memory can be resolved in many different ways. Ecker and Ticic (2012) argue the importance of therapeutic facilitation of positive experiences and feeling states that directly contradict the terror or shame associated with memories of complex trauma. Only in the face of somatically and emotionally felt safety and connection to present time can survivors of complex trauma firmly believe that "it" is over and they are safe at last.

References

Arbuthnott, K. D., Arbuthnott, D. W., & Rossiter, L. (2001). Guided imagery and memory: Implications for psychotherapists. *Journal of Counseling Psychology, 48*(2), 123–132.

Creswell, J. D., Way, B. M., Eisenberger, N. I., & Lieberman, M. D. (2007). Neural correlates of dispositional mindfulness during affect labeling. *Psychosomatic Medicine, 69*, 560–565.

Ecker, B., & Ticic, R. (2012). *Unlocking the emotional brain: Eliminating symptoms at their root using memory reconsolidation.* New York: Routledge.

Fisher, J. (2010). *Psychoeducational aids for treating psychological trauma.* Cambridge, MA: Kendall Press.

Fisher, J. (2017a). *Healing the fragmented selves of trauma survivors.* New York: Routledge/Taylor & Francis.

Fisher, J. (2017b). Trauma-informed stabilisation treatment: A new approach to treating unsafe behaviour. *Australian Psychologist, 3*(1), 55–62.

Fisher, J. (2017c). Twenty-five years of trauma treatment: What have we learned? *ATTACHMENT: New Directions in Psychotherapy and Relational Psychoanalysis, 11*, 273–289.

Gendlin, E. T. (1981). *Focusing.* New York: Random House.

Grigsby, J., & Stevens, D. (2002). Memory, neurodynamics, and human relationships. *Psychiatry, 65*(1), 13–34.

Iacoboni, M., Molnar-Szakacs, I., Gallese, V., Buccino, G., Maziotta, J. C., & Rizzolatti, G.

(2005). Grasping the intentions of others with one's own mirror neuron system. *PLOS Biology, 3*(3), e79.

Kurtz, R. (1990). *Body-centered psychotherapy: The Hakomi method*. Mendocino, CA: LifeRhythm.

LeDoux, J. E. (2002). *The synaptic self: How our brains become who we are*. New York: Viking Press.

Levine, P. (2015). *Trauma and memory: Brain and body in search of the living past: A practical guide for understanding and working with traumatic memory*. Berkeley, CA: North Atlantic Books.

Liotti, G. (2011). Attachment disorganization and the controlling strategies: An illustration of the contributions of attachment theory to developmental psychopathology and to psychotherapy integration. *Journal of Psychotherapy Integration, 21*(3), 232–252.

Lyons-Ruth, K., Dutra, L., Schuder, M. R., & Bianchi, I. (2006). From infant attachment disorganization to adult dissociation: Relational adaptations or traumatic experiences? *Psychiatric Clinics of North America, 29*(1), 63–86.

Madigan, S. P., & Goldner, E. M. (1998). A narrative approach to anorexia: Discourse, reflexivity, and questions. In M. Hoyt (Ed.), *The handbook of constructive therapies: Innovative approaches from leading practitioners*. San Francisco: Jossey-Bass.

Ogden, P., & Fisher, J. (2015). *Sensorimotor psychotherapy: Interventions for trauma and attachment*. New York: Norton.

Ogden, P., Minton, K., & Pain, C. (2006). *Trauma and the body: A sensorimotor approach to psychotherapy*. New York: Norton.

Roisman, G. I., Padron, E., Sroufe, L. A., & Egeland, B. (2002). Earned-secure attachment status in retrospect and prospect. *Child Development, 73*(4), 1204–1219.

Rothschild, B. (2017). *The body remembers: Vol. II. Revolutionizing trauma treatment*. New York: Norton.

Schwartz, J., & Begley, S. (2002). *The mind and the brain: Neuralplasticity and the power of mental force*. New York: HarperCollins.

Schwartz, R. (2001). *Introduction to the internal family systems model*. Oak Park, IL: Trailhead.

Shapiro, F. (2018). *Eye movement de-sensitization and re-processing (EMDR) therapy: Basic principles, protocols and procedures* (3rd ed.). New York: Guilford Press.

Siegel, D. J. (2006). An interpersonal neurobiology approach to psychotherapy. *Psychiatric Annals, 36*(4) 248–256.

Siegel, D. J. (2010). *The neurobiology of "we."* Keynote address, Psychotherapy Networker Symposium, Washington, DC.

Solomon, J., & George, C. (Eds.). (2011). *Disorganized attachment and caregiving*. New York: Guilford Press.

Solomon, M. F., & Siegel, D. J. (Eds.). (2003). *Healing trauma: Attachment, mind, body and brain*. New York: Norton.

Spiegel, D. (1994). *Dissociation, mind, and culture*. New York: American Psychiatric Publishing.

van der Hart, O., Nijenhuis, E. R. S., & Steele, K. (2006). *The haunted self: Structural dissociation and the treatment of chronic traumatization*. New York: Norton.

van der Kolk, B. A. (2014). *The body keeps the score: Brain, mind and body in the treatment of trauma*. New York: Viking Press.

Williams, L. M. (1994). Recall of childhood trauma: A prospective study of women's recollections of sexual abuse. *Journal of Consulting and Clinical Psychology, 62*(6), 1167–1176.

Williams, L. M. (1995). Recovered memories of abuse in woman with documented child sexual victimization histories. *Journal of Traumatic Stress, 8*, 649–674.

CHAPTER 25

Mindfulness Approaches

BARBARA L. NILES
SARAH KRILL WILLISTON
DEANNA L. MORI

Mindfulness is becoming increasingly popular and has gained attention across different areas of mental health treatment, with many individuals actively practicing mindfulness or seeking it out for its benefits. In this chapter we first offer a definition of mindfulness and describe mindfulness-based and mind–body treatments. We discuss how these treatments may be integrated into psychotherapies and review the research on mindfulness treatments for posttraumatic stress disorder (PTSD). We then consider possible mechanisms by which mindfulness interventions and practices may alleviate complex traumatic stress disorder (CTSD) symptoms. Finally, we offer case studies to illustrate how mindfulness interventions may be used in the treatment of CTSDs.

What Is Mindfulness?

Mindfulness has its roots in Buddhist philosophy, culture, and practice (Thera, 1962). It has emerged within the Western medical and psychological community over the last 40 years (Kabat-Zinn, 2005; Fields, 1992), and has been adapted and applied in a range of secular contexts to enhance wellness and reduce disease among a variety of psychiatric and medical populations (Grossman, Niemann, Schmidt, & Wallach, 2004; Shapiro & Carlson, 2017). *Mindfulness* can be described as "an openhearted, moment-to-moment, nonjudgmental awareness" (Kabat-Zinn, 2005, p. 24). While there is debate on the precise underlying nature of the construct of mindfulness, a common operational description in Western psychology involves five core psychological processes: (1) observation of personal experiences in the present moment, (2) describing and labeling those experiences, (3) responding nonreactively, (4) nonjudgmental acceptance of the present-moment experiences, and (5) and acting with awareness within the present moment (Baer, Smith, Hopkins, Krietemeyer, & Toney, 2006; Bishop et al., 2004). By maintaining awareness in the present moment, with a nonreactive and nonjudgmental stance, individuals may have greater agency and ability to move away from reactive, unhelpful habitual responses and instead choose more intentional ways of responding that promote both their physical and psychological health.

The Evolution of Mindfulness-Based Therapies

Mindfulness-based treatment emerged in Western medicine initially as an alternative treatment for individuals with medical comorbidities that had not responded to more traditional medical interventions. One of the most popular and well-researched mindfulness programs is mindfulness-based stress reduction (MBSR; Kabat-Zinn, 1993). MBSR is an 8-week, intensive mindfulness practice in a variety of forms, such as seated meditations and mindful body movement. Since the late 1970s, MBSR has continued to be studied and has shown a variety of positive health benefits, such as reduced physical pain and increased relaxation (Grossman et al., 2004; Gotink et al., 2015). Furthermore, mindfulness has been integrated into a variety of psychological treatments in what is now referred to as the "third wave" of behavior therapies. The third wave includes acceptance and commitment therapy (ACT; Hayes, Strosahl, & Wilson, 1999), dialectical behavior therapy (DBT; Linehan, 1993), mindfulness-based cognitive therapy (MBCT; Segal, Williams, & Teasdale, 2013), acceptance-based behavior therapy (Roemer & Orsillo, 2014), among many other treatments (see Kahl, Winter, & Schwieger, 2012, for a review and summary of other third-wave therapies). These therapies share theoretical foundations and techniques with "traditional" cognitive-behavioral treatments, such as the emphasis on learning history; the reciprocal connection among thoughts, feelings, and behaviors; and a focus on enacting behavioral changes. However, there are two notable distinctions. First, third-wave interventions are primarily focused on addressing an individual's *relationship to* his or her internal experiences, rather than targeting change in the *content of* those experiences, and support the individual's to cultivation of a relationship with his or her internal experiences marked by acceptance and compassion rather than self-invalidation and self-criticism. This relationship to internal experiences is often referred to as "decentered" or "defused" (Hayes, 2004). Second, third-wave therapies encourage engagement in meaningful actions to increase quality of life and personal growth rather than focusing on symptom reduction (Hayes, 2004; Hayes et al., 1999). From this framework, mindfulness skills (present-moment awareness of thoughts, feelings, reactions, urges), help individuals clarify personally held values, and specific actions they can take to act in line with those values (Michelson, Lee, Orsillo, & Roemer, 2011).

In addition to third-wave psychotherapies, mindfulness has also been a central component of mind–body therapies that integrate mindfulness practices with promotion of physical health. Tai chi, yoga, and other wellness interventions, such as the Veterans Affairs "Whole Health" initiative (Department of Veterans Affairs, 2017) are primary examples of mind–body therapies. They are attracting interest in the Western psychological and medical community to address a variety of physical and psychological health concerns. For example, tai chi, an ancient Chinese exercise that encourages mindful awareness of the present moment via diaphragmatic breathing and slow, graceful movements (Lan, Lai, & Chen, 2002), has been shown to address symptoms of pain and depression, and to improve both physical function and psychological well-being (Wang et al., 2010a, 2010b; Wang, Collet, & Lau, 2004).

As is evident, mindfulness has been integrated into a diverse range of clinical practices for a wide array of physical and psychological problems. For our purpose in this chapter, we use *mindfulness-based interventions and practices* as an umbrella term to include (1) programs such as MBSR and other mindfulness classes that directly seek to improve mindfulness skills to enhance quality of life, (2) third-wave psychotherapies that employ mindfulness as a foundational component and hypothesized mechanism of change to reduce psychological distress, and (3) mind–body therapies that utilize mindful awareness as a central component to practices aimed at enhancing mental and physical health (e.g., tai chi, yoga, and wellness interventions). We conceptualize these interventions and practices to be complementary to other directive trauma-focused treatments, such as prolonged exposure (Foa, Hembree, & Rothbaum, 2007) or cognitive processing therapy (Resick, Monson, & Chard, 2017), and to other therapies for trauma as well (see other chapters in this text on various other treatment models). We illustrate how mindfulness-based interventions and practices can be meaningfully utilized before, during, following, and/or instead of engagement with trauma-focused and present-focused mental health treatments.

How Is Mindfulness Integrated into Psychotherapies?

While the overall function of mindfulness is to cultivate compassionate, present-moment awareness, the form mindfulness practice takes varies within the interventions and practices considered in this chapter. First, mindfulness practices can vary by their level of formality. Guided meditations led by a therapist would be considered a formal practice. Within yoga or tai chi, formal practice would be mindful engagement in a specific physical posture, or series of postures, and noticing the physical sensations in the body as one breathes into a pose. However, mindfulness may also take a more informal, unguided form, and involve bringing mindful attention to ongoing daily tasks, such as mindfully washing the dishes or mindfully walking through the grocery store. Often mindfulness takes on both "formal" and "informal" practice forms, and there is a dearth of research on the differences between these two styles of practice or the clinical utility of one over the other (Morgan, Graham, Hayes-Skelton, Orsillo, & Roemer, 2014).

In addition, mindfulness-based treatments vary in the amount of focus they place on explicitly drawing mindful awareness to thoughts and feelings. For example, within many third-wave therapies such as DBT and ACT, the focus of mindful awareness is often on uncomfortable emotional experiences or unwanted thoughts, and on bringing curiosity, compassion, and acceptance to them. However, within practices such as tai chi and yoga, mindfulness is integrated physically, with careful, compassionate attention directed to the placement of the body into specific, graceful, slow postures, and with less explicit discussion about states of mind or specific thoughts and feelings.

Furthermore, mindfulness practices vary in their scope of present-moment awareness. Some mindfulness practices emphasize focused, compassionate, and curious attention to a single particular object, experience, or word, such as the practice of mantram repetition, which focuses sustained attention on a single, spiritual word (Bormann, Thorp, Wetherell, Golshan, & Lang, 2013). Other types of mindfulness practices are focused on broadening awareness. For example, loving-kindness meditation, which stems from Buddhist tradition, involves wishing safety, health, and peace first toward oneself, then toward a loved other, then a "difficult" person in one's life, and then the whole world (Dalai Lama, 2001). This sequence broadens attention beyond self-focused, critical thoughts, and draws forth positive feelings for self, others, and the world. Loving-kindness meditation has recently been integrated into a variety of treatments for individuals exposed to complex trauma, though empirical evidence is still being collected on its efficacy (Kearney et al., 2013; Litz & Carney, 2018).

Another example of broadening awareness is the "3-minute breathing space" meditation, integrated into a variety of third-wave therapies. This practice is relatively brief and encourages individuals to first broadly notice their holistic experiences in the present moment (including thoughts, feelings, urges, physical sensations) without trying to change them. Individuals are then asked to shift attention specifically to the breath, and finally to shift attention to the body as a whole, and to notice any specific sensations that arise. This meditation teaches the skill of broadening, and intentionally shifting attention can be a useful skill for individuals caught in ruminative, anxious, and self-critical thoughts (Segal et al., 2013). For individuals with CTSDs practicing mindfulness, both intentional narrowing and broadening of attention can be therapeutic and used for different purposes. For example, mindful grounding skills may prevent dissociation by focusing attention narrowly on a specific, physical object. Mindful broadening of attention and compassionate awareness may be helpful when one is immersed in a spiral of self-critical thoughts.

Review of the Evidence

The positive focus of mindfulness-based interventions and practices on improving health and quality of life may appeal to individuals with complex and long-standing responses to trauma. In fact, surveys indicate that many traumatized individuals seek and receive mindfulness and mind–body therapies to address symptoms: 20% of those diagnosed with PTSD and approximately 50% of U.S. veterans and military personnel use complementary and integrative modalities (Bystritsky et al., 2012; Davis, Mulvaney-Day, Larson, Hoover, & Mauch, 2014; Libby, Pilver, & Desai, 2013; Taylor, Hoggatt, & Kligler, 2019). Over 75% of specialized PTSD treatment programs in the Veterans Health Administration offer mindfulness treatments (Libby, Pilver, & Desai, 2012).

Over the past decade, as interest in mindfulness approaches has continued to grow, research to support the use of mindfulness-based approaches to address PTSD and CTSDs has advanced considerably. For example, in a non-randomized study to address symptoms of CPTSD, Kimbrough, Magyari, Langenberg, Chesney, and Berman (2010) offered an 8-week MBSR program to adult survivors of childhood sexual abuse. This early and influential study was the first to demonstrate that this treatment was not only safe and feasible for this population with complex needs, but also efficacious in reducing PTSD, depression, and anxiety symptoms. Notably, the participants were highly compliant with both class attendance and home practice, and the significant reductions in symptoms were maintained through the 24-week follow-up.

There are now several high-quality randomized controlled trials (RCTs) that support mindfulness interventions and practices. Davis et al. (2018) studied 214 veterans with PTSD and found no significant differences between MBSR and present-centered therapy (PCT) on clinician-assessed PTSD symptoms. However, both groups evidenced significant improvements in PTSD symptoms. In addition, veterans' self-reports of PTSD symptoms at posttreatment were significantly lower for the MBSR group. Although MBSR was not shown to be a superior treatment in this study, it is notable that the effects were similar to those of a more traditional therapy for veterans with PTSD.

Mantram repetition treatment has been evaluated in several studies, the largest and most rigorous of which was a recent RCT that compared mantram repetition to PCT with 173 veterans with military-related PTSD (Bormann et al., 2018). Mantram repetition teaches participants to intentionally slow down thoughts and to practice "one-pointed attention." Individuals selected a personalized *mantram,* a word or phrase with a spiritual meaning, to repeat silently. Initially participants practiced in nonstressful situations and at bedtime. Over time, participants were encouraged to repeat the mantram to help regulate emotions and to calm behavior before and during stressful or triggering events. In comparison to PCT, participants in the mantram repetition condition had significantly greater improvements in clinician-assessed PTSD and insomnia at both posttreatment and at the 2-month follow-up. In addition, significantly more participants in the mantram condition experienced sufficient symptom reductions to drop below the threshold for PTSD diagnosis—59% in the mantram repetition condition compared to 40% in the PCT condition.

In another recent RCT with 203 veterans, Nidich and colleagues (2018) compared three 12-week interventions: transcendental meditation (TM), prolonged exposure, and a health education control. TM is a specific type of silent meditation that is similar to mantram repetition in that it involves repetition of a sound (in TM called a *mantra*) to facilitate meditation. The results suggest that TM was equally effective (not inferior) to prolonged exposure, and both conditions were superior to health education on the primary outcome of clinician-assessed PTSD.

In terms of mind–body therapies using movement, several RCTs have examined yoga and support its use in the treatment of PTSD, though there have not yet been any published RCTs of tai chi for PTSD. In the largest yoga study to date, van der Kolk and colleagues (2014) compared a 10-week trauma-informed yoga intervention to a health education control group. The yoga group exhibited larger decreases in clinician-assessed PTSD than the health education group, with a moderate between-group effect size. A significantly higher proportion of participants in the yoga group (53%) fell below the diagnostic cutoff for PTSD diagnosis after treatment than those in the control group (21%).

Many of the trials of mindfulness-based practices are small and suffer from important methodological weaknesses (Niles et al., 2018), and there are no published RCTs of tai chi. However, many of these treatments have strong research support in areas that are relevant to CTSDs, such as psychological well-being, depression, and chronic pain. For example, there is accumulating evidence that tai chi is associated with improved psychological well-being and reductions in mood disturbances (e.g., Wang et al., 2010a). Furthermore, it is encouraging that increasing numbers of RCTs and larger, more rigorous studies are regularly added to the growing research base. Overall, the evidence base to support mindfulness-based interventions and practices for PTSD is promising.

It is important to note that many empirical questions remain about the most effective ways to teach mindfulness skills to those experiencing the additional symptoms associated with complex PTSD. It is likely that there are specific modifications and modes of instruction and practice that can enhance the efficacy of mindfulness when working with complex trauma survivors (Treleaven, 2018), and this is an area in which ongoing study is needed. Based on the available research and our own experience, we offer suggestions on how these mindfulness-based practices can be meaningfully integrated into the treatment of CTSDs.

How Might Mindfulness-Based Interventions and Practices Alleviate Complex PTSD Symptoms?

Mindfulness practices enhance several skills that may help alleviate CTSD symptoms, and these skills fall into three loose categories: *attentional focus, reduced physiological arousal,* and *emotion regulation.* Although these skills are multifaceted and interrelate with one another, we highlight the distinct ways these skills may function in alleviating CTSD symptoms.

First, related to *attentional focus,* regular mindfulness practice creates a greater nonjudgmental awareness and acceptance of internal states, and requires a willingness to attend to the present moment (e.g., Walser & Westrup, 2007). In this way, mindfulness practice directly counteracts a core maintaining factor of PTSD: experiential and behavioral avoidance (Foa, Riggs, Massie, & Yarczower, 1995). Mindfulness training encourages individuals to observe rather than push away whatever arises in a given moment, including trauma-related memories, thoughts, feelings, and physical sensations. Directing attention to notice intrusive trauma images is the first step of mindful engagement. Conscious awareness then allows the opportunity to make skillful choices about how to respond to the experience.

Rather than continuing to devote emotional and physiological energy to avoiding and controlling upsetting experiences, mindfulness training encourages individuals to recognize the inherent transient nature of thoughts, emotions, urges, and physical sensations. Individuals are encouraged to step back from being immersed in aversive feelings and to notice that although feelings may be intense, they dissipate over time. Mindfulness practice therefore may increase the ability to attend to thoughts, emotions, and sensations as they arise, and to tolerate distressing internal experiences by observing their transient nature.

Awareness of sensations in the body, or *interoceptive awareness,* may also serve indirectly as exposure to uncomfortable physical sensations (e.g., chest tightness). Increased tolerance of these sensations may then facilitate less avoidance and greater engagement in meaningful actions. For example, an individual who is able notice and accept feeling overheated and sweatiness in his or her palms while attending a large social function may be more likely to continue to attend family parties even in the face of that physical discomfort. Through mindful awareness, individuals with CTSDs may become more willing to confront trauma-related external and internal triggers that arise for them, including cognitions, emotions, and body sensations, as well as people, places, and activities that had previously been avoided (Carlin & Ahrens, 2014; Follette & Vijay, 2009), and this willingness to engage in the present moment more fully may promote recovery and resilience.

Mindfulness practices also can foster attentional flexibility and augment short-term coping strategies. Correlational research has shown that mindfulness training is associated with the ability to sustain attention, to purposefully switch attention, and to selectively direct attention from one stimulus to another (Jha, Krompinter, & Baime, 2007). *Mindful distraction,* or *grounding* (Batten, Orsillo, & Walser, 2005) can be used to help an individual cope with intense emotions or memories in the present moment. Shifting attention and concentrating on one specific object or experience (e.g., focusing on one's breath or listening to ambient sounds) while engaging in mindful grounding is an example of *concentrative attention* (Jha et al., 2007). For example, if a powerful trauma-related emotion is triggered by a video shown in a classroom setting, it may be adaptive for an individual with complex PTSD to utilize grounding skills (e.g., attending to the sensations of feet on the floor, rhythmic breathing, and the pencil in one's hand) to prevent hyper- or hypoarousal or dissociation, then refocus on classroom activities once the intensity of the reaction has subsided. Later, when free from classroom demands, this individual may choose to direct attention to processing the trauma-related memory and emotion, perhaps in a supportive context (e.g., on the phone with a friend, speaking with a therapist).

In addition to increased focused attention, mindfulness practice has been shown to increase *receptive attentional skill* (Jha et al., 2007), which is the ability to maintain attention that includes the "whole field of awareness." For example, an individual may be able to notice not only the sadness associated with a trauma memory but also sensory experiences in the moment (e.g., the smell of coffee and sounds in the room) and other distinct emotions (e.g., appreciating for support from a caring friend). Thus, with increased mindfulness training, individuals might be able to better differentiate how and where to focus their attention, broaden their attention and perspective on a difficult situation or circumstance, and gain wisdom and knowledge about when to apply short-term coping strategies (e.g., grounding) and longer-term strategies (e.g., emotional processing).

Second, mindfulness practices may enhance skills that diminish symptoms of CTSD by *reducing physiological arousal* and stress reactivity (e.g., Brown & Ryan, 2003; Delizonna, Williams, & Langer, 2009; Kim, Schneider, Kravitz, Mermier, & Burge, 2013). Mindfulness enhances interoceptive awareness as individuals learn to attend to bodily cues (e.g., breathing rate, muscle tension). This provides individuals with the ability to self-regulate in a more adaptive manner (e.g., Brown & Ryan, 2003). For example, when engaging mindfully, an individual may notice early indicators of stress, such as shoulders tightening and heart rate increasing, and apply adaptive coping strategies such as diaphragmatic breathing, grounding, or seeking social support. In this manner, mindfulness practice might have a beneficial effect on symptoms of PTSD-related hyperarousal, such as sleep difficulty, exaggerated startle responses, and difficulty concentrating. Indeed, mindfulness practice has been associated with more adaptive sleep functioning (Howell, Digdon, & Buro, 2010).

In addition, mindfulness practices may serve to interrupt the reciprocal relationship between hyperarousal and reexperiencing symptoms, whereby increased hyperarousal leads to increased reexperiencing symptoms, which lead to increased hyperarousal (Doron-LaMarca et al., 2015) and may then result in hypoarousal and dissociation. For example, the slow deliberate movements of tai chi and the focus on rhythmic breathing may lead to calming of the sympathetic nervous system and indirectly reduce the intensity of intrusive symptoms before they trigger other psychophysiological responses.

The final set of skills that mindfulness practices enhance is *emotion regulation*. Mindful awareness may promote the ability to identify and describe emotional experiences (Frewen, Dozois, Neufeld, & Lanius, 2012). This is particularly important due to the pronounced difficulties that individuals with CTSDs have in identifying, feeling, and describing emotions (Zlotnick, Mattia, & Zimmerman, 2001). For example, when confronted with a trauma-related memory, an individual may be able to label the feeling of fear after noticing body reactions (e.g., clenched teeth, increased heart rate, sweating), and become aware of thoughts that "something bad is going to happen." With regular mindfulness practice, individuals learn to notice and identify such feelings and related physical sensations and cognitions, which may allow them to then make deliberate choices about how to respond to them.

Responding to powerful emotions with awareness and intention rather than impulsivity is another emotion regulation skill that mindfulness practice enhances (Lu & Huffman, 2017; Peters, Erisman, Upton, Baer, & Roemer, 2011). For example, a survivor of complex trauma may choose to ask for a time-out in a triggering discussion with a partner rather than engage in harmful and hurtful externalizing behaviors. In this way, mindfulness skills may create space for individuals to choose their behavioral responses when experiencing very strong emotions and to identify ways to act that are consistent with their values and goals, rather than be controlled by their emotional experiences.

Mindfulness skills may also help reduce the intensity and duration of emotions that often result from thinking habits that are unduly critical and self-invalidating (e.g., shame and guilt, also referred to as *secondary emotions*; Goldsmith et al., 2014; Keng & Tan, 2018). Individuals may be able to notice their unhelpful thoughts, which will allow them to disengage from them. In this way, an individual may be able to engage in active coping with primary emotions, such as fear and sadness, rather than become overwhelmed by shame as a result of self-critical and self-invalidating thoughts (Goldsmith et al., 2014; Held, Owens, Monroe, & Chard, 2017; Roemer & Orsillo, 2014). For example, an individual who often is overwhelmed by shame for avoiding an important family event may be better able to notice thoughts such as "I always let my family down" or "I never can get myself together." Rather than getting caught up in a cycle of self-directed negative thoughts and increasing shame and guilt, the individual may be able to step back and notice feelings of fear that were triggered by a trauma reminder and that preceded self-critical thoughts and shame. Attending to and labeling the primary emotion of fear then allows the individual to decide how to respond to it (e.g., accept the emotion of fear and choose to focus on self-care or engage in valued action and use grounding skills to help him or her attend the family event). Increased emotional awareness, intentional action in the face of strong emotions, and reduced engagement with secondary emotions work in concert to contribute to improved emotion regulation.

Clinical Case Examples

We selected three distinct case examples to illustrate the ways mindfulness-based interventions and practices can be used to treat CTSDs. Each case is a composite of several cases, and specific personal details were altered to ensure privacy. We chose these cases because they highlight the different forms that mindfulness-based treatments can take, as well as the how the acquisition of distinct mindfulness skills (e.g., awareness, nonreactivity, nonjudgment) address particular symptoms of CTSD (e.g., chronic anger, self-harming behaviors, emotion dysregulation, avoidance, hyperarousal). We also chose these cases because they represent three different ways mindfulness-based treatments can be used in a larger treatment plan: as a complement to individual trauma-focused treatment, integrated into individual psychotherapy, and as a mind–body treatment to maintain gains and improve physical health following individual trauma-focused psychotherapy.

Jason

Jason, a 66-year-old, divorced, black male Army veteran, presented for a mindfulness-based wellness group. Jason had a history of childhood physical and emotional abuse by his father, witnessing race-related community violence as an adolescent, and combat-related trauma when he served in Vietnam as an 18-year-old infantryman and was diagnosed with PTSD and several comorbid health problems, such as diabetes and hypertension. He had recently initiated cognitive processing therapy (CPT) with an individual therapist, who referred him to the mindfulness-based wellness group. His hope in attending this group was that it would provide additional skills and supportive relationships to help him better engage in CPT and cope with the intensity of trauma-focused individual psychotherapy.

This mindfulness-based wellness group included four veterans and met twice weekly for 12 weeks, for a total of 24 group sessions. Each session included a brief, formal mindfulness practice, followed by discussions about health and individualized coaching to identify personally meaningful, specific, and attainable health-related goals. Session content also focused on monitoring progress and addressing barriers to achieve specific health goals. This group was based on the VA Whole Health model, which defines health broadly; therefore, sessions focused on health-related goals in different areas of life, including physical, social, emotional, and spiritual health. This program did not focused on disclosing or processing traumatic memories. Patients who began to talk about details of a trauma were gently redirected to connect back to the present moment. In addition, wellness facilitators coordinated with Jason's CPT therapist and were aware that Jason had decided to focus first on his combat trauma, then on his childhood abuse in CPT.

Within the wellness group, Jason reported that his primary concerns were related to the impact that complex PTSD had on his life. These included chronic difficulty managing intense emotions (i.e., anger) and hyperarousal symptoms (i.e., difficulty sleeping, heightened startle responses). He also reported behavioral habits (i.e., overeating and hours of TV watching) that functioned to help him avoid unwanted internal experiences and had a negative impact on his physical health. He stated he had few friends, no sense of community, and was estranged from his family. He attributed all these problems with his health and social functioning to the effects of having felt unsafe, devalued, and unable to trust from childhood through early adulthood.

Jason presented to the group initially distrustful of providers and generally concerned about his privacy and documentation of what was discussed in group sessions. Facilitators met with him privately, carefully explained how his privacy would be protected and the purpose of the documentation, and repeatedly validated his concerns about privacy and documentation in order to communicate understanding and respect. After that meeting, Jason was much more open and willing to participate fully in the group. Despite being new to mindfulness practice and his initial distrust of the group format and facilitators, Jason was receptive to psychoeducation about mindfulness, and was willing to try practices both in and out of session. In the early weeks of this group, his goals centered around increasing mindfulness practice out of session. He was particularly drawn to informal mindfulness practices, such as mindful walking. He did not find seated meditation helpful and noted that it was a time when intrusive symptoms tended to increase. Facilitators reinforced his awareness of what types of practices worked best for him and encouraged Jason to continue with those that were helpful.

Three dimensions of mindfulness practice, or mindfulness skills, that appeared to be most helpful for Jason were (1) developing present-moment awareness, (2) cultivating a nonjudgmental stance toward internal experiences, and (3) skillful action in the face of strong emotions. Jason first developed the skill to notice moments when his mind wandered to past traumatic experiences or imagined future threats, and he learned to gently reorient his attention to the present moment using brief mindfulness focusing strategies, such as grounding. He shared that he would mindfully notice the feeling of his feet on the floor, or the colors in the scenery around him, to ground himself in the present. He also gained skill at nonjudgmentally noticing the habits of his mind and behavior. For example, he noticed that he tended to ruminate over past experiences in which people violated his trust. Then, when caught in a cycle of rumination, he noticed that he was more likely to engage in aggressive behaviors or poor self-care (e.g., select unhealthy foods, remain sedentary for longer periods of time). Here, Jason developed a nonjudgmental awareness of these patterns, which in turn helped him identify what behaviors he could modify to act more in line with his personal goals and values.

By the end of the group, Jason was walking over 5 miles daily and had made major dietary changes. He had lost enough weight (over 20 pounds) to meet his weight loss goal for the first time in over 10 years. Furthermore, when he did choose to eat sugary foods, he reported he did so mindfully and with increased enjoyment. He also began to reach out to friends and scheduled regular walks with them. He was an excellent group participant, was supportive of other members, and encouraged their health-related goals. Upon completing CPT, he spoke of how his mindfulness skills facilitated his engagement in the therapy. Specifically, he reported being more aware of his thoughts or "stuck points" and becoming less reactive and fearful of the thoughts and feelings themselves. By the end of both treatments, his self-report was no longer reflective of a diagnosis of PTSD, and he had a clinically meaningful reduction in other symptoms.

Mark

Mark, a 32-year-old, single, white, male veteran, worked as an emergency medical technician (EMT). He was exposed to early childhood emotional and physical neglect. In addition, he described frequent exposure to traumatic events while serving in Afghanistan, such as being hit by improvised explosive devices (IEDs), exposure to civilian casualties, and cleaning up human remains. He reported continued exposure to human injury and death in his civilian job as an emergency responder. In terms of CTSD symptoms, Mark reported feeling depressed, empty, and angry through adolescence. Following his military deployment, he noticed reexperiencing symptoms such as thoughts, memories, and nightmares about Afghanistan that were worse after exposure to trauma while working as an EMT. Fire and explosions, severe human injuries, and the smell of burnt flesh or hair all triggered him to recall events from the war zone. In addition to pronounced intrusive symptoms, Mark also continued to suffer from strong and persistent negative affect. He reported that he felt angry and guilty most of the time while he was awake and would often engage in unhealthy risk-taking behaviors to try to distract himself from his negative feelings (e.g., driving far above the speed limit without a seat belt, binge drinking, and provoking others into physical altercations).

Mark received 10 sessions of mindfulness-based psychotherapy. The initial phase of treatment focused on providing psychoeducation about PTSD symptoms and the role of experiential and behavioral avoidance in maintaining symptoms. Next, psychoeducation about mindfulness and valued actions were introduced to address strong habits of avoidance that are predominant in life with PTSD. Each session included mindfulness practice, discussion of reactions to practice, and applications to current life circumstances, and concluded with out-of-session mindfulness practice suggestions and self-monitoring forms to track experiences with and reactions to mindfulness practice.

At the beginning of treatment, Mark believed that if he allowed himself to think about the traumas he had experienced, he would be permanently overwhelmed by emotion. He was particularly concerned about being able to continue to function at work, where he was continually exposed to devastating life events. He began with focusing mindfulness exercises, such as mindfulness of the breath, sounds, and physical sensations, that drew attention to a specific experience in the present moment. These skills helped him develop grounding skills when triggered and increased his sense of self-efficacy to cope with emotions in the present moment. He then worked up to more complicated exercises that drew mindful awareness of complex emotions and thoughts. Mark learned that thoughts and emotions naturally shift and change, and that feelings, by their nature, are fleeting and not dangerous. This awareness allowed Mark to reduce his use of thought suppression and emotional avoidance, and to gain self-efficacy to manage his internal experiences. This helped Mark to shift away from a life focused on avoiding trauma-related memories, feelings, and thoughts, to a rich engagement in experiences and an increase in valued behaviors. He gained increased insight into the function of his risky behaviors and began to identify alternative ways to cope that did not put himself or others at risk of harm. These included strategies such as journal writing, intense physical exercise, and discussions with his therapist. Mark began to feel increased positive emotions and reduced anger and guilt.

This case study also illustrates the use of formal versus informal mindfulness practice. Early in treatment, Mark's therapist led him in formal, guided mindfulness exercises and until Session 6, Mark also engaged in formal mindfulness practice between sessions. In Mark's practice of formal mindfulness, he intentionally practiced and developed mindfulness skills. Discussing his experiences with formal practice in therapy sessions provided Mark an opportunity to bring to the surface the challenges he encountered and allowed his therapist to offer suggestions. For example, when Mark reported that he used "mindful distraction" whenever he felt sadness, the therapist suggested that Mark try balancing his grounding skills with practice noticing difficult emotions and acceptance of them. After Session 6, Mark rarely engaged in formal mindfulness practice. Since Mark chose to stop his formal practice and showed evidence that he was using mindfulness skills daily in an informal manner, his therapist did not push him to continue formal practice. Mark talked about his use of grounding, mindful breathing, and noticing his physical responses without judgment. He discussed with his therapist when and how he used these skills and in what ways they were helpful or not. The therapist reflected that use of these skills allowed Mark to change his pattern of avoidance and extreme reactivity to thoughts and emotions about distressing events. Although the therapist felt that Mark would benefit from continued formal practice, she supported Mark's choice to practice only informal use of mindfulness skills. This led to Mark's feeling of agency to choose how he conducted his practice and increased his efficacy in managing his symptoms. Furthermore, this support seemed to enhance the therapeutic relationship.

At the end of treatment, Mark had experienced clinically significant improvements in PTSD symptom severity, depression, and alcohol use. These gains were maintained in a 3-month follow-up assessment. Importantly, Mark also reported an increase in subjective quality of life, increased hopefulness about his future, and stronger relationships with his peers.

Tanya

Tanya, a 49-year-old Latina woman, signed up to participate in a 12-week tai chi group program that was offered through an outpatient PTSD clinic to help her cope more effectively with her symptoms of PTSD and comorbid chronic pain, while also improving her physical fitness. Tanya's PTSD was related to her history of childhood and adult sexual trauma. She was distrustful of men, struggled with feelings of anger, and had a sense of shame and vulnerability about her body. She had also experienced race-related discrimination, which contributed to a general attitude of guardedness. Tanya had already received exposure-based treatment for her PTSD and had successfully obtained some positive results, and she hoped that participation in tai chi would give her additional skills to help her cope adaptively.

In the twice-weekly groups, each 1-hour session started with warm-up stretches. The participants then mindfully practiced tai chi postures, movements, and sequences, and ended with a warm-down and meditation, either seated or standing. The instructor was trained to be sensitive to the preferences of individuals with PTSD, in order to increase their sense of control and self-efficacy. For example, many of the participants chose to stand at the back of the room rather than at the front, near the instructor. Although in other tai chi classes, the instructor might have encouraged group participants to move forward or spread out more, he did not do so in this group. He was also highly responsive to participant feedback and modified or avoided exercises or terminology that made participants feel uncomfortable or vulnerable. For example, he encouraged participants to choose whether to keep their eyes open during the sitting meditation.

As there were only two female participants in the group, a decision was made to have a female mental health clinician participate in the class to increase the women's sense of safety. Nonetheless, Tanya always chose a spot in the back of the room, against the wall, with a good view of the door, and she appeared quite uncomfortable at times during the first several sessions. The only person in the room who could see her doing the exercises was the instructor, who was facing the group.

Having ready access to a mental health clinician, each group meeting proved to be helpful, giving Tanya an opportunity to provide feedback about the class in a timely manner. Before class, during one of the early sessions of the program, Tanya reported to the clinician that she was very uneasy with some of the warm-up exercises that made her feel vulnerable, such as forward bends and standing pelvic tilts. The clinician gave her permission to engage in the exercises only as she felt comfortable, and the instructor also modified some of the exercises Tanya found most difficult. Tanya's feedback and observations made by both the mental health clinician and tai chi instructor allowed other adaptations in the class. Specifically, Tanya expressed frustration when she was encouraged to "feel limp" and reported that she did not like to do that. In response, the instructor instead spoke of "releasing stress," since Tanya appeared motivated to feel powerful rather than "limp."

Tanya grew more comfortable as time progressed. The instructor's respect and responsiveness to her feedback helped her to build trust. She had a strong appreciation for the fact that the movements in tai chi are derived from the martial arts, and she would often ask the instructor to directly explain the connection or describe how each movement prepares a person to make a powerful move. Tanya was able to immerse herself in the exercises, and practicing mindfulness through strong movements was empowering to her. Gradually, she appeared more physically and mentally relaxed, and less guarded. Her interactions with both the group leader and other class members became more trusting, relaxed, and friendly. Toward the end of the 12 weeks, after developing a strong sense of mastery in her ability to carry out the tai chi forms, Tanya moved to the front of the room during classes, with her back to the other participants and the door.

After this group ended, Tanya decided to incorporate regular tai chi practice in to her life to help her maintain the sense of balance and empowerment she had achieved. In addition to doing regular home practice, she found other tai chi classes she could attend and continued to go twice each week. At a 3-month follow-up, Tanya reported that although she had tried other types of mindfulness practices in the past, mindfully focusing on powerful body movements came more naturally to her, and she connected with the feeling that she was doing something that made her feel strong and positive about her body, while also feeling mentally calm and in control. In addition, she enjoyed attending the classes, as she found that sharing this experience with others, and learning from others, enhanced her ability to feel connected to people in a positive way.

Conclusions

The use of and interest in mindfulness approaches with individuals who have CTSDs has grown rapidly. We have provided in this chapter an overview of how mindfulness-based interventions and practices address the specific symptoms associated with trauma exposure and complement more traditional treatments for CTSDs. While there are many forms of mindfulness practice, some defining characteristics that are found across all are the encouragement of present-moment awareness, nonjudgmental acceptance, and attentional focus, in the service of intentional action.

As is evident in this review and case examples, there is an inherent flexibility in mindfulness approaches that allows them to be tailored to the interests and needs of the client. For example, some practices, such as tai chi, are more physical in nature and require a focus on body movements. These types of physical practices offer a good alternative for individuals who find it challenging to maintain the cognitive focus required in other types of mindfulness practices. Furthermore, a clinician can tailor recommendations for mindfulness practice based on the client's symptoms and preferences. For instance, an individual who tends to use dissociation to cope in stressful experiences might be encouraged to develop mindful grounding skills. Another individual, more prone to cycles of ruminative, self-critical thoughts, may be encouraged to develop skills of nonreactivity to thoughts and emotions.

As noted in the case examples, mindfulness-based strategies are also flexible, in that they can be used before, during, or after trauma-focused treatment to enhance coping, improve quality of life, and support trauma memory processing. Furthermore, for the sizable number of individuals who do not want to receive more traditional trauma-focused or other forms of individual psychotherapy, mindfulness and health promotion approaches provide an alternative that may be more appealing and flexible, and less stigmatizing.

Although there is a growing literature on mindfulness-based therapies, there is still much to learn about how these therapies can be used most effectively to address the symptoms associated with CTSDs. More rigorous research is needed using RCT methodology to further evaluate how these treatments work, and for whom, and under what conditions (e.g., duration of sessions, types of mindfulness instruction, group or individual modality). While we have offered some hypotheses on the mechanisms underlying how mindfulness practices can specifically address symptoms of PTSD and CTSDs, based on prior research and our clinical experiences, there is a need to examine these further empirically. The importance of continued research notwithstanding, mindfulness-based treatments for CTSD offer a flexible, clinically effective, and appealing approach to recovery that can help clients heal from their trauma and rebuild their lives with intention and confidence.

References

Baer, R. A., Smith, G. T., Hopkins, J., Krietemeyer, J., & Toney, L. (2006). Using self-report assessment methods to explore facets of mindfulness. *Assessment, 13*(1), 27–45.

Batten, S. V., Orsillo, S. M., & Walser, R. D. (2005). Acceptance and mindfulness-based approaches to the treatment of posttraumatic stress disorder. In S. M. Orsillo & L. Roemer (Eds.), *Acceptance and mindfulness-based approaches to anxiety: Conceptualization and treatment* (pp. 241–269). New York: Springer Science + Business Media.

Bishop, S. R., Lau, M., Shapiro, S., Carlson, L., Anderson, N. D., Carmody, J., . . . Devins, G. (2004). Mindfulness: A proposed operational definition. *Clinical Psychology: Science and Practice, 11*(3), 230–241.

Bormann, J. E., Thorp, S., Smith, E., Glickman, M., Beck, D., Plumb, D., . . . Elwy, R. (2018). Individual treatment of posttraumatic stress disorder using mantram repetition: A randomized clinical trial. *American Journal of Psychiatry, 175*(10), 979–988.

Bormann, J. E., Thorp, S. R., Wetherell, J. L., Golshan, S., & Lang, A. J. (2013). Meditation-based mantram intervention for veterans with posttraumatic stress disorder: A randomized trial. *Psychological Trauma: Theory, Research, Practice, and Policy, 5*(3), 259–267.

Brown, K. W., & Ryan, R. M. (2003). The benefits of being present: Mindfulness and its role in psychological well-being. *Journal of Personality and Social Psychology, 84*, 822–848.

Bystritsky, A., Hovav, S., Sherbourne, C., Stein, M. B., Rose, R. D., Campbell-Sills, L., . . . Roy-Byrne, P. P. (2012). Use of complementary and alternative medicine in a large sample of anxiety patients. *Psychosomatics, 53*(3), 266–272.

Carlin, E. A., & Ahrens, A. H. (2014). The effects of mindfulness and fear-inducing stimuli on avoidance behavior. *Mindfulness, 5*(3), 276–281.

Dalai Lama. (2001). *An open heart: Practicing compassion in everyday life.* Boston: Little, Brown.

Davis, L., Whetsell, C., Hamner, M., Carmody, J., Rothbaum, B., Allen, R., . . . Bremmer, D. (2018, September 13). A multisite randomized control trial of mindfulness-based stress reduction in the treatment of post-traumatic stress disorder. *Psychiatric Research and Clinical Practice.* [Epub ahead of print]

Davis, M. T., Mulvaney-Day, N., Larson, M. J., Hoover, R., & Mauch, D. (2014). Complementary and alternative medicine among veterans and military personnel: A synthesis of population surveys. *Medical Care, 52,* S83–S90.

Delizonna, L. L., Williams, R. P., & Langer, E. J. (2009). The effect of mindfulness on heart rate control. *Journal of Adult Development, 16,* 61–65.

Department of Veterans Affairs. (2017). Whole Health for life. Retrieved from *www.va.gov/patientcenteredcare/explore/about-whole-health.asp.*

Doron-LaMarca, S., Niles, B. L., King, D. W., King, L. A., Pless Kaiser, A., & Lyons, M. J. (2015). Temporal associations among chronic PTSD symptoms in US combat veterans. *Journal of Traumatic Stress, 28*(5), 410–417.

Fields, R. (1992). *How the swans came to the lake: A narrative history of Buddhism in America.* Boston: Shambhala.

Foa, E. B., Hembree, E. A., & Rothbaum, B. O. (2007). *Prolonged exposure therapy for PTSD: Emotional processing of traumatic experiences: Therapist guide.* New York: Oxford University Press.

Foa, E. B., Riggs, D. S., Massie, E. D., & Yarczower, M. (1995). The impact of fear activation and anger on the efficacy of exposure treatment for posttraumatic stress disorder. *Behavior Therapy, 26*(3), 487–499.

Follette, V. M., & Vijay, A. (2009). Mindfulness for trauma and posttraumatic stress disorder. In F. Didonna (Ed.), *Clinical handbook of mindfulness* (pp. 299–317). New York: Springer Science + Business Media.

Frewen, P. A., Dozois, D. J. A., Neufeld, R. W. J., & Lanius, R. A. (2012). Disturbances of emotional awareness and expression in posttraumatic stress disorder: Meta-mood, emotion regulation, mindfulness, and interference of emotional expressiveness. *Psychological Trauma: Theory, Research, Practice, and Policy, 4*(2), 152–161.

Goldsmith, R. E., Gerhart, J. I., Chesney, S. A., Burns, J. W., Kleinman, B., & Hood, M. M. (2014). Mindfulness-based stress reduction for posttraumatic stress symptoms: Building acceptance and decreasing shame. *Journal of Evidence-Based Complementary and Alternative Medicine, 19*(4), 227–234.

Gotink, R. A., Chu, P., Busschbach, J. J. V., Benson, H., Fricchione, G. L., & Hunink, M .G. M. (2015). Standardised mindfulness-based interventions in healthcare: An overview of systematic reviews and meta-analyses of RCTs. *PLOS ONE 10*(4), e0124344.

Grossman, P., Niemann, L., Schmidt, S., & Walach, H. (2004). Mindfulness-based stress reduction and health benefits: A meta-analysis. *Journal of Psychosomatic Research, 57*(1), 35–43.

Hayes, S. C. (2004). Acceptance and commitment therapy, relational frame theory, and the third wave of behavioral and cognitive therapies. *Behavior Therapy, 35*(4), 639–665.

Hayes, S. C., Strosahl, K. D., & Wilson, K. G. (1999). *Acceptance and commitment therapy: An experiential approach to behavior change.* New York: Guilford Press.

Held, P., Owens, G. P., Monroe, J. R., & Chard, K. M. (2017). Increased mindfulness skills as predictors of reduced trauma-related guilt in treatment-seeking veterans. *Journal of Traumatic Stress, 30*(4), 425–431.

Howell, A. J., Digdon, N. L., & Buro, K. (2010). Mindfulness predicts sleep-related self-regulation and well-being. *Personality and Individual Differences, 48*(4), 419–424.

Jha, A. P., Krompinger, J., & Baime, M. J. (2007). Mindfulness training modifies subsystems of attention. *Cognitive, Affective and Behavioral Neuroscience, 7*(2), 109–119.

Kabat-Zinn, J. (1993). Mindfulness meditation: Health benefits of an ancient Buddhist practice. In D. Goleman & J. Gurin (Eds.), *Mind/body medicine* (pp. 259–275). Yonkers, NY: Consumer Reports Books.

Kabat-Zinn, J. (2005). *Coming to our senses: Healing ourselves and the world through mindfulness.* New York: Hyperion.

Kahl, K. G., Winter, L., & Schweiger, U. (2012). The third wave of cognitive behavioural therapies: What is new and what is effective? *Current Opinion in Psychiatry, 25*(6), 522–528.

Kearney, D. J., Malte, C. A., McManus, C., Martinez, M. E., Felleman, B., & Simpson, T. L. (2013). Loving-kindness meditation for posttraumatic stress disorder: A pilot study. *Journal of Traumatic Stress, 26*(4), 426–434.

Keng, S.-L., & Tan, H. H. (2018). Effects of brief mindfulness and loving-kindness meditation inductions on emotional and behavioral responses to social rejection among individuals with high borderline personality traits. *Behaviour Research and Therapy, 100*, 44–53.

Kim, S. H., Schneider, S. M., Kravitz, L., Mermier, C., & Burge, M. R. (2013). Mind–body practices for posttraumatic stress disorder. *Journal of Investigative Medicine, 61*(5), 827–834.

Kimbrough, E., Magyari, T., Langenberg, P., Chesney, M., & Berman, B. (2010). Mindfulness intervention for child abuse survivors. *Journal of Clinical Psychology, 66*(1), 17–33.

Lan, C., Lai, J. S., & Chen, S. Y. (2002). Tai chi chuan: An ancient wisdom on exercise and health promotion. *Sports Medicine, 32*(4), 217–224.

Libby, D. J., Pilver, C. E., & Desai, R. (2012). Complementary and alternative medicine in VA specialized PTSD treatment programs. *Psychiatric Services, 63*(11), 1134–1136.

Libby, D. J., Pilver, C. E., & Desai, R. (2013). Complementary and alternative medicine use among individuals with posttraumatic stress disorder. *Psychological Trauma: Theory, Research, Practice, and Policy, 5*(3), 277–285.

Linehan, M. M. (1993). *Skills training manual for treating borderline personality disorder.* New York: Guilford Press.

Litz, B., & Carney, J. R. (2018). Employing loving-kindness meditation to promote self- and other-compassion among war veterans with posttraumatic stress disorder. *Spirituality in Clinical Practice, 5*(3), 201–211.

Lu, J., & Huffman, K. (2017). A meta-analysis of correlations between trait mindfulness and impulsivity: Implications for counseling. *International Journal for the Advancement of Counselling, 39*(4), 345–359.

Michelson, S. E., Lee, J. K., Orsillo, S. M., & Roemer, L. (2011). The role of values-consistent behavior in generalized anxiety disorder. *Depression and Anxiety, 28*(5), 358–366.

Morgan, L. P. K., Graham, J. R., Hayes-Skelton, S. A., Orsillo, S. M., & Roemer, L. (2014). Relationships between amount of post-intervention mindfulness practice and follow-up outcome variables in an acceptance-based behavior therapy for generalized anxiety disorder: The importance of informal practice. *Journal of Contextual Behavioral Science, 3*(3), 173–178.

Nidich, S., Mills, P. J., Rainforth, M., Heppner, P., Schneider, R. H., Rosenthal, N. E., . . . Rutledge, T. (2018). Non-trauma-focused meditation versus exposure therapy in veterans with post-traumatic stress disorder: A randomised controlled trial. *Lancet Psychiatry, 5*(12), 975–986.

Niles, B. L., Mori, D. L., Polizzi, C., Pless Kaiser, A., Weinstein, E. S., Gershkovich, M., & Wang, C. (2018). A systematic review of randomized trials of mind–body interventions for PTSD. *Journal of Clinical Psychology, 74*(9), 1485–1508.

Peters, J. R., Erisman, S. M., Upton, B. T., Baer, R. A., & Roemer, L. (2011). A preliminary investigation of the relationships between dispositional mindfulness and impulsivity. *Mindfulness, 2*(4), 228–235.

Resick, P. A., Monson, C. M., & Chard, K. M. (2017). *Cognitive processing therapy for PTSD: A comprehensive manual.* New York: Guilford Press.

Roemer, L., & Orsillo, S. M. (2014). An acceptance-based behavioral therapy for generalized anxiety disorder. In D. H. Barlow (Ed.), *Clinical handbook of psychological disorders: A step-by-step treatment manual* (5th ed., pp. 206–236). New York: Guilford Press.

Segal, Z. V., Williams, J. M. G., & Teasdale, J. D. (2013). *Mindfulness-based cognitive therapy for depression* (2nd ed.). New York: Guilford Press.

Shapiro, S. L., & Carlson, L. E. (2017). Mindfulness-based interventions in mental health populations. In *The art and science of mindfulness: Integrating mindfulness into psychology and the helping professions* (2nd ed., pp. 69–80). Washington, DC: American Psychological Association.

Taylor, S. L., Hoggatt, K., & Kligler, B. (2019). Complementary and integrated health approaches: What do veterans use and want? *Journal of General Internal Medicine, 34*(7), 1192–1199.

Thera, N. (1962). *The heart of Buddhist meditation.* New York: Weiser.

Treleaven, D. A. (2018). *Trauma-sensitive mindfulness: Practices for safe and transformative healing.* New York: Norton.

van der Kolk, B. A., Stone, L., West, J., Rhodes, A., Emerson, D., Suvak, M., & Spinazzola, J. (2014). Yoga as an adjunctive treatment for posttraumatic stress disorder: A randomized controlled trial. *Journal of Clinical Psychiatry, 75*(6), e559–e565.

Walser, R. D., & Westrup, D. (2007). *Acceptance and commitment therapy for the treatment of post-traumatic stress disorder and trauma-related problems: A practitioner's guide to using mindfulness and acceptance strategies.* Oakland, CA: New Harbinger.

Wang, C., Bannuru, R., Ramel, J., Kupelnick, B., Scott, T., & Schmid, C. H. (2010a). Tai Chi on psychological well-being: Systematic review and meta-analysis. *BMC Complementary and Alternative Medicine, 10,* 23.

Wang, C., Collet, J. P., & Lau, J. (2004). The effect of tai chi on health outcomes in chronic conditions: A systematic review. *Archives of Internal Medicine, 164,* 493–501.

Wang, C., Schmid, C. H., Rones, R., Kalish, R., Yinh, J., Goldenberg, D. L., . . . McAlindon, T. (2010b). A randomized trial of tai chi for fibromyalgia. *New England Journal of Medicine, 363*(8), 743–754.

Zlotnick, C., Mattia, J. I., & Zimmerman, M. (2001). The relationship between posttraumatic stress disorder, childhood trauma and alexithymia in an outpatient sample. *Journal of Traumatic Stress, 14*(1), 177–188.

CHAPTER 26

Complementary Healing Therapies

STEFANIE F. SMITH
JULIAN D. FORD

Alongside the recent advances in understanding the mechanisms and consequences of complex trauma (see Chapter 2), several new or adapted therapies for complex traumatic stress disorders (CTSDs) have been developed to complement talk-based therapies (Wahbeh, Senders, Neuendorf, & Cayton, 2014). These complementary healing therapies explicitly target the whole body, consistent with the integrative perspective articulated by van der Kolk et al. (2016) that, in the aftermath of psychological trauma, "the body keeps the score." Rather than viewing the mind and conscious thinking as the central locus of the self, which is a foundational theme in the dualistic mind–body framework of Western cultures, complementary healing therapies take a view more consistent with Eastern cultures and view the body as the center of a person's being (and the mind and conscious thought as a secondary derivative rather than the driving force). CTSD symptoms are understood as expressions of injury or imbalance in the body—which may result from emotional or spiritual harm, as well as physical injury or illness.

From this viewpoint, therapy for CTSDs requires restoring the body's health and integrity in addition to mental ideas or insights (see Chapter 2). Several therapeutic models described in this book take a similar approach to that of the complementary healing therapies. These include interventions that are grounded in talk-based psychotherapy but focus on enhancing conscious awareness of the body's expression of trauma-related psychic injuries or coping adaptations (see Chapter 23), or that include body awareness as a channel for accessing and understanding trauma-related emotion dysregulation (see Chapters 12–15, 17–18). They also include adaptations of meditative and mindfulness practices to CTSD treatment (see Chapter 25). In this chapter, we expand this array of body-focused therapies for CTSDs by considering interventions that are intended to alter body functions directly, or indirectly through movement, without relying on verbally mediated talk or self-reflection as the driver.

There are two principal reasons to consider complementary healing therapies for the treatment of CTSDs. In the first place, complementary healing therapies directly involve the body and somatic responses as important sources of information in the treatment, based on research findings that trauma is most often encoded implicitly and somatosensorily (i.e., a "bottom-up" rather than "top-down" approach to understanding the impact of complex trauma) (Akiki, Averill, & Abdallah, 2017; Lamb, Porges, Lewis, & Williamson, 2017) and target the neurophysiological changes that develop due to traumatization and can have long-lasting (and most often implicit) impact (Abdallah, Southwick, & Krystal, 2017; Lanius & Olff, 2017). In addition to the extensive alterations in brain structure and function that have been found to be sequelae of complex trauma (Teicher & Samson, 2016), an array of adverse (McEwen, 2017) physiological changes in stress-sensitive body systems have also been discovered. Most notably, the body's autonomic nervous system (ANS) exhibits dysregulation (Felmingham, Rennie, Gordon, & Bryant, 2012; Thome et al., 2017) in both the arousal-inducing sympathetic branch (Dieleman et al., 2015; Freed & D'Andrea, 2015; McLaughlin, Sheridan, Alves, & Mendes, 2014b; Naegeli et al., 2018) and the arousal-inhibiting parasympathetic/vagal branch (Chou, La Marca, Steptoe, & Brewin, 2018; D'Andrea et al., 2013; McLaughlin, Alves, & Sheridan, 2014a; Rabellino et al., 2017; Ulmer, Hall, Dennis, Beckham, & Germain, 2018). Relatedly, the stress hormone system involving the hypothalamus–pituitary–adrenal (HPA) axis and the expression and reactivity of the modulating hormone cortisol also becomes dysregulated (Carvalho Fernando et al., 2012; Flandreau, Ressler, Owens, & Nemeroff, 2012; Houtepen et al., 2016; Keeshin, Strawn, Out, Granger, & Putnam, 2014; Morris, Abelson, Mielock, & Rao, 2017; Sriram, Rodriguez-Fernandez, & Doyle, 2012; Sumner, McLaughlin, Walsh, Sheridan, & Koenen, 2014; D. A. Young, Inslicht, Metzler, Neylan, & Ross, 2018a). In combination with brain system alterations, these physiological alterations can lead to deficits in body awareness, or *interoception* (Lanius, Frewen, Tursich, Jetly, & McKinnon, 2015; Mallorqui-Bague, Bulbena, Pailhez, Garfinkel, & Critchley, 2016; Nicholson et al., 2016b). Diminished bodily self-awareness, a hallmark symptom of CTSDs, can create a vicious cycle in which interoceptive unawareness leads to unfettered escalation of bodily dysregulation and increasingly severe (but often unrecognized or even somatically dissociated; see Chapter 6) breakdown in bodily systems and associated physical illness and psychic distress (van der Kolk, 2014).

A second rationale for complementary healing therapies for CTSDs is to address the needs of those not responding to the available trauma-focused talk therapy practices (often labeled as "top-down" approaches) (Metcalf et al., 2016). Practitioners and researchers have proposed that complementary healing therapies offer innovative treatment methods and interventions (Ley, Rato

Barrio, & Koch, 2018; van der Kolk et al., 2016) for the half or more of recipients of current evidence-based therapies for PTSD and CTSDs who do not benefit or continue to have residual symptoms (Bisson, Roberts, Andrew, Cooper, & Lewis, 2013; Mahoney, Karatzias, & Hutton, 2019; Morina, Koerssen, & Pollet, 2016). Complementary healing therapies also provide a potential approach to increase accessibility and acceptability, culturally and financially, of treatment for CTSDs. Complementary therapies may be culturally syntonic for some clients, who are not familiar or comfortable with talk psychotherapy, thus increasing the reach and cultural humility of providers (Chapter 7). Furthermore, many of the adjunctive alternative interventions are techniques that can be practiced on an individual basis, with no financial outlay and within one's natural environment, thus keeping costs lower and making stigma-free access more available than with conventional clinical interventions.

There is a nascent but growing body of research supporting the use of complementary healing therapies for PTSD, notably for combat-related trauma (Wahbeh et al., 2014), including randomized clinical trial (RCT) investigations that support the efficacy of yoga, acupuncture, neurofeedback, transcranial magnetic stimulation, and Japanese herbal medicines (see *www.istss.org/ treating-trauma/new-istss-guidelines.aspx*). What follows is a description and review of available evidence for the effectiveness of these and other promising complementary healing therapies for adult survivors of complex trauma.

Yoga

Trauma-sensitive yoga is an approach to the meditative movement practices of yoga that has been modified for use with trauma survivors and is led by specially trained instructors. Modifications include an invitational approach rather than a directive or prescriptive one, small class sizes (e.g., six or fewer participants), a focus on body sensations rather than asking participants to clear their mind or focus on thoughts, fewer or no physical adjustments or assists of participants' posture/movement by the leader, use of a gentle and slow pace, less focus on the spiritual aspect, and being conducted in a trauma-informed space (e.g., where participants can see the door and the teacher, no visible yoga straps, adequate lighting and no darkness, and informing students before each change). The objective of trauma-sensitive yoga is to enhance clients' sense of body awareness, embodiment, choice, and empowerment, along with health-related benefits, such as increased flexibility and strength. Emotions and memories (including trauma memories) are not inquired about or discussed in trauma-sensitive yoga.

There are several features of a yoga practice that may serve as mechanisms of action to help with the CTSD symptoms, including mindfulness meditation (see Chapter 25), breath work, and physical postures. Yogic breath work involves controlling the depth and rate of breathing. Research indicates that breath work can improve emotional regulation (Arch & Craske, 2006), modulate the sympathetic nervous system, decrease arousal, and improve parasympathetically mediated heart rate variability (Brown & Gerberg, 2009), and reduce sympathetic nervous system activation, muscle tension, and blood pressure (Emerson, Sharma, Chaudhry, & Turner, 2009). Yoga physical postures are carefully designed alignments of the body in poses intended to provide a present-moment somatic focal point that feels safe to trauma survivors, who are often overwhelmed by body sensations. Thus, yoga poses may be beneficial in dealing with hyperarousal and increasing attention, emotional awareness, and affect tolerance (Salmon, Lush, Jablonski, & Sephton, 2009; van der Kolk et al., 2014, 2016).

Furthermore, particular yoga poses and movement may enhance physiological self-regulation. Neurologically, the use of oppositional and bilateral balancing poses may help stimulate the corpus callosum, which has been implicated in the difficulty with hemispheric integration associated with PTSD (Saar-Ashkenazy et al., 2014). The combination of both stimulating and sitting postures can encourage balance in the nervous system. For example, yoga postures practice may increase brain levels of an inhibitory neuropeptide (gamma-aminobutyric acid [GABA]), which tend to be low in PTSD (Streeter et al., 2007). Salmon et al. (2009) suggested that the repetitiveness of yoga may retrain the rhythmicity of biological functions that can be disrupted due to traumatic stress. This impact may be increased when yoga is practiced in groups: When rhythmic movement is done with others, it may also spark a feeling of connection as the participants become "united by external rhythmic elements in synchronous movement" (Berrol, 1992).

One study has shown promising results for trauma-sensitive yoga with adults who have complex trauma histories. The largest study to date found evidence of greater effect sizes in reductions in PTSD and depression symptoms for women with interpersonal trauma histories and treatment-resistant PTSD who also participated in a 10-week yoga group, when compared to those who participated in a supportive health education group (van der Kolk et al., 2014). Although there was no difference in PTSD symptoms between the groups 1.5 years later, women who continued to practice yoga frequently showed the greatest long-term symptom reductions (Rhodes, Spinazzola, & van der Kolk, 2016). A 12-session yoga group with women similarly resulted in small to moderate reductions in PTSD and anxiety symptoms compared to a self-monitoring control condition (Mitchell et al., 2014).

Additionally, two RCTs with male military veterans showed similarly mixed but promising results—although participants did not all have complex trauma histories. A 10-week group retained fewer than one-third of enrollees but showed modest reductions in PTSD symptoms compared to a wait-list period (but not compared to a self-monitoring condition) (Reinhardt et al., 2018). A breath-work focused yoga intervention resulted in large effect-size reductions in PTSD and anxiety symptoms and physical assessments of startle response an respiration rate (versus no change by a wait-list group) that were maintained at a 1-year follow-up (Seppala et al., 2014).

Overall, yoga has promise as an adjunctive intervention in combination with other evidence-based treatments for PTSD, and women (and possibly also men) with CTSDs. Trauma-sensitive yoga, which has not been tested as a stand-alone intervention with adults with trauma histories, may complement trauma-focused therapies by helping adults with CTSDs to enhance their body awareness, physical and mental well-being, and ability to regulate a range of emotions.

Acupuncture

Acupuncture refers to a group of therapies in which needles are placed into chosen points in subcutaneous tissue for a given period of time and are manipulated to obtain the sensation of *de qi,* a fullness or heaviness and warmth, but not pain. Depending on the practitioner's theoretical orientation, the goal of acupuncture is to either move vital energy around the body to restore balance between body systems, or to directly impact neural pathways. Neurologically, effective acupuncture stimulates A-delta fibers in the skin or muscle, which terminate in the spinal cord (and therefore may influence nervous system activity in the peripheral body and in the brain).

Acupuncture can be applied either manually or electronically. In electroacupuncture (EA), the needles are attached to a device that generates continuous electric pulses using small clips, with frequency and intensity of the impulse varied, depending on the condition being treated. EA uses two needles at a time, so that the impulses can pass from one to the other. Several pairs of needles can be stimulated simultaneously, usually for no more than 30 minutes at a time. With EA, the practitioner does not have to be as precise with the insertion of needles, because the current delivered through the needle stimulates a larger area than the needle itself. A similar technique called *transcutaneous electrical nerve stimulation,* or TENS, uses electrodes that are taped to the surface of the skin instead of inserted needles.

The use of acupuncture has a long history and some efficacy studies have examined the treatment of clinical symptoms that are commonly experienced by complex trauma survivors, including anxiety, depression, and insomnia (Eich, Kihlstrom, Bower, Forgas, & Niedenthal, 2000; Spence et al., 2004; Wang, Hu, Wang, Pang, & Zhang, 2012). Brain imaging demonstrates that acupuncture impacts extensive central neurological responses encompassing the amygdala, hippocampus, hypothalamus, cerebellum, basal ganglia, anterior cingulate, insula, and other limbic structures (Hollifield, 2011; Napadow et al., 2005). The response appears to be a lowering of sympathetic nervous system activity (Hui et al., 2000; Middlekauff, Yu, & Hui, 2001), although some acupuncture sites may lead to increased arousal (Mori et al., 2010). Acupuncture can alter neurotransmitter systems that affect bodily opioid systems (Hollifield, 2011), which may be important when addiction co-occurs with CTSDs (see Chapter 22).

Despite acupuncture's long history of use, its application to traumatic stress disorders is fairly limited. Only one study has tested acupuncture with complex trauma survivors (Hollifield, Sinclair-Lian, Warner, & Hammerschlag, 2007). This RCT compared acupuncture to cognitive-behavioral therapy (CBT) and a wait-list control. Both CBT and acupuncture were associated with reduced PTSD symptoms, depression and anxiety symptoms, and daily functioning when compared to the wait-list control, with gains for acupuncture maintained on all outcomes at a 3-month follow-up. A meta-analysis including seven RCTs examining acupuncture's outcomes with adults with varied trauma histories found evidence of moderate reductions in PTSD symptoms that were maintained at follow-up, and moderate reductions in depressive symptoms at follow-up but not immediately after intervention (Grant et al., 2018). However, there was no evidence of reductions in anxiety symptoms or sleep problems, and methodological problems with the research studies limited confidence in their findings. Thus, while acupuncture may have comparable benefits to CBT for adults with complex trauma histories for the reduction of PTSD and depressive symptoms, its impact on the broader range of CTSD symptoms is less promising and in need of more extensive research.

Energy Psychology: Tapping/Acupoints

Energy psychology is a clinical and self-help modality that links psychological and physiological stressors with disturbances within the energy fields of the body (typically referred to as *acupuncture meridians*), in conjunction with cognitive protocols that allow for therapeutic shifts in targeted emotions, behaviors, and cognitions (Mason, 2012). These energy fields in the body are described in Chinese as *chi,* in Japanese as *ki,* in Indian as *prana,* and by Hippocrates as *vismedicatrix naturae* (Gallo, 2000). Energy psychology theory suggests that psychological problems reflect disturbed bioenergy patterns within the body's neurobiological systems that regulate cognitive–behavioral–emotional patterns (Oschman, 2000a, 2000b).

Although there are many variations of energy psychology, the most well-known and frequently utilized protocols combine the stimulation of acupuncture points (*acupoints*), by tapping on, holding, or massaging them, with mental reflection on a targeted psychological issue. The stimulation of acupoints in psychotherapy, through tapping instead of needles, was first formulated as thought field therapy (TFT) in the 1970s (Callahan, 1995). More recently, adaptations of TFT have emerged, including emotional freedom techniques (EFT; Craig, 2011). In an RCT with military veterans diagnosed with PTSD, 80–90% of EFT completers no longer met criteria for PTSD at 3- and 6-month follow-ups (Church et al., 2013).

TFT combines the manual stimulation in individualized sequences of acupuncture treatment (or *meridian points*) with reflection on targeted symptoms and traumatic memories (Feinstein, 2008). EFT also utilizes tapping of a precise sequence of meridian points, called an *algorithm,* paired with verbalized, positive self-affirmations (Gilomen & Lee, 2015), with a single protocol sequence regardless of presenting concern. Although this has not been scientifically verified, somatic activation of acupoints is hypothesized to alter limbic brain structure activity, thereby reducing hyperarousal and creating a new association to the memory of a less aroused emotional state (Feinstein, 2008; Panda, 2014). It is possible that other therapeutic components (e.g., affirmations, expectancies) and not the tapping on meridian points produce the reduction in emotional distress; however, a meta-analysis concluded that tapping acupoints was specifically associated with reduced PTSD, depression, and anxiety symptoms (Church, Stapleton, Yang, & Gallo, 2018), and a systematic review revealed that tapping of the meridian points led to more positive results than tapping sham points (Tan, Suen, Wang, & Molassiotis, 2015).

Neurobiochemical effects of acupoint stimulation have also been identified, with levels of neurotransmitters, endorphins, and cortisol affected by tapping (Church, Yount, & Brooks, 2012; Ruden, 2005). Three investigations have demonstrated changes in brain wave patterns following acupoint treatments (Diepold & Goldstein, 2009; Lambrou, Pratt, Chevalier, & Archives, 2003; Swingle, Pulos, & Swingle, 2004). More in line with the healing traditions from which tapping originates, such as acupuncture, stimulating a well-selected set of acupoints may shift bioenergy fields and restore balance that has been disrupted by exposure to traumatic stressors and subsequent traumatic stress reactions. Consistent with energy systems theory, research has identified anatomical and physiological evidence of the hypothesized meridian system in what has been described as a primo vascular system (PVS), which incorporates the body's nervous, cardiovascular, immune, and hormonal systems (Stefanov et al., 2013).

Tapping is an efficient intervention that requires no special equipment and/or setting. However, although several RCTs have produced consistently strong outcomes with military veterans, genocide survivors, and mixed trauma populations (Church et al., 2018), it is not clear that a single (or a defined set of) replicable intervention(s) has actually been evaluated under the rubric of tapping, TFT, and EFT. In addition the brevity of these interventions (i.e., typically one to six sessions), and the fact that most outcome studies involved a combination of tapping and other ongoing therapeutic interventions and supports, suggest that tapping/acupoint interventions are largely applicable for CTSDs as an adjunctive rather than a stand-alone therapy.

Transcranial Magnetic Stimulation

Lasting changes in cortical activity and plasticity have been detected following the use of transcranial magnetic stimulation (TMS; Philip et al., 2018). Repetitive transcranial magnetic stimulation (rTMS) is a treatment modality that involves applying rapidly alternating magnetic fields to the scalp to induce small, focal electrical currents in the superficial cortex (Rowny & Lisanby, 2008). Animal models of the stress response suggest that perhaps the impact of rTMS is due to its ability to effect changes within the HPA axis, as well as dopaminergic and serotonergic systems of the brain (Ipser, Pillay, Stein, & van Honk, 2007).

In 2008, the U.S. Food and Drug Administration (FDA) approved rTMS as a treatment for unipolar major depression, but it has not yet approved it for PTSD, thereby limiting the research on its effectiveness for complex trauma. A meta-analysis of 11 RCTs comparing rTMS to sham controls (i.e., application of similar electrodes without actual TMS) concluded that both high-frequency and low-frequency rTMS resulted in reduced PTSD and depression symptoms with mixed trauma populations (Yan, Xie, Zheng, Zou, & Wang, 2017). High-frequency rTMS produced the strongest overall results for PTSD symptoms, demonstrating reductions in each of the DSM-IV PTSD symptom domains, as well as anxiety and depression symptoms. An earlier meta-analysis identified two studies of particular relevance to CTSDs, showing a positive response to rTMS in the form of reductions in affective impulsivity by patients with borderline personality disorder symptoms and reductions in emotion regulation difficulties in patients with complex trauma histories and eating disorders (Berlim, van den Eynde, Tovar-Perdomo, & Daskalakis, 2014).

rTMS can be used to target focal brain areas involved in PTSD and CTSDs (Philip et al., 2018), including the medial prefrontal, insular, and anterior cingulate cortex, orbitofrontal cortex, dorsolateral prefrontal cortex, ventromedial prefrontal cortex, hippocampus, thalamus, and the stress hormone system (HPA axis). The most consistent and strongest improvements in PTSD appear to be achieved when rTMS has targeted the right hemisphere, particularly the amygdala and the insular cortex and striatum (Karsen, Watts, & Holtzheimer, 2014). The application of rTMS following a single session of exposure therapy (i.e., repetitively reading a client-constructed script describing a traumatic event) was found to produce greater reductions in PTSD intrusive reexperiencing and trauma-related autonomic arousal (i.e., heart rate), than either rTMS or exposure therapy alone—suggesting that rTMS may be a helpful adjunct to trauma memory processing therapy (Isserles et al., 2013). However, precisely when (e.g., before, during, or after trauma memory processing), how (i.e., high vs. low frequency; right vs. left hemisphere; specific brain areas or combinations thereof), and with what approaches to verbal psychotherapy (e.g., exposure, cognitive processing, affect regulation) rTMS is safest and most effective with different clinical populations and forms of CTSDs remains to be scientifically and clinically verified (Pradhan, D'Amico, Makani, & Parikh, 2016). Caution is warranted, however, given a case study report of mania induced by TMS in a client with PTSD (of unknown CTSD status, but with a complex chronic clinical presentation consistent with CTSD; Gijsman, 2005).

Neurofeedback

EEG neurofeedback (NF) training utilizes neuroimaging to provide visual and/or auditory feedback on patterns of brain activation that is designed to facilitate a reduction physiological arousal level and an increase in the stability and flexibility of brain activity associated with self-regulation (Gruzelier, 2009). The EEG signal is obtained by placing sensors on a person's scalp, then detected neuronal activity at that specific placement is shown to the individual through a game or image on a computer screen. In response to this information, shifts in the EEG signal to more optimal states tend to occur spontaneously, accompanied by an increased sense of calm and focused attention (Marzbani, Marateb, & Mansourian, 2016). As brain activity becomes regulated through NF, neurophysiological and behavioral changes that occur are specific to the brain region or network targeted by NF (Scheinost et al., 2013; Shibata, Watanabe, Sasaki, & Kawato, 2011; Zhang, Yao, Zhang, Long, & Zhao, 2013). Therefore, in addition to EEG NF, real-time functional magnetic resonance imaging (fMRI) NF (rt-fMRI-NF) was developed as a means of targeting not only specific frequencies of brain neural activity but also specific sites in the brain (Thibault, MacPherson, Lifshitz, Roth, & Raz, 2018; Zotev et al., 2018).

Three decades ago, a pioneering study demonstrated that EEG NF of slow-wave (alpha and theta) frequency bands was associated with reductions in male military veterans' PTSD symptoms (Peniston & Kulkosky, 1991). Since then, NF has been tested extensively with a wide range of psychiatric (e.g., depression, autism, attention deficit hyperactivity disorder, eating disorders) (K. D. Young et al., 2018) and medical (e.g., chronic illness, chronic pain, traumatic brain injury, cancer-related fatigue, stroke; Blaskovits, Tyerman, & Luctkar-Flude, 2017; Renton, Tibbles, & Topolovec-Vranic, 2017) disorders, and as an approach to optimizing learning, mood, and performance in healthy persons (Gruzelier, 2014; Mirifar, Beckmann, & Ehrlenspiel, 2017). However, studies on NF with PTSD are sparse, with only one RCT with patients with chronic PTSD (van der Kolk et al., 2016). In that study, adults with extensive chronic trauma histories consistent with complex trauma received either mental health treatment as usual (TAU) or 12 weeks of twice-weekly EEG NF. In addition to reductions in PTSD symptoms and remission from the PTSD diagnosis (by 73% of NF recipients vs. 32% of TAU recipients), NF was associated with improvements in affect regulation, affect stability, and tension reduction behaviors—all hallmarks of CTSDs. Other clinical studies of adults with complex trauma histories also have shown improved affect regulation, increased calm, and reduction in PTSD symptoms across different durations and frequencies of NF sessions (Fisher, Lanius, & Frewen, 2016; Gapen et al., 2016; Kluetsch et al., 2014), typically with NF as an adjunct to trauma-focused therapy.

Although the precise mechanisms by which NF may reduce CTSD symptoms are not yet established, brief sessions of EEG NF targeting cortical alpha wave oscillations have been shown to alter connectivity within brain networks associated with stress and self-regulation (Kluetsch et al., 2014; Ros, Baars,

Lanius, & Vuilleumier, 2014), while also shifting the functional connectivity of the amygdala "from areas implicated in defensive, emotional, and fear processing/memory retrieval . . . to prefrontal areas implicated in emotion regulation/ modulation. . . . with . . . reduced arousal [and] greater resting alpha synchronization" (p. 506), which was accompanied by reduced PTSD symptoms (Nicholson et al., 2016a). A study providing three sessions of rt-fMRI-NF to patients with mixed trauma histories and diagnosed with PTSD demonstrated reductions in amygdala activation that were accompanied by increased activation in the PFC, anterior cingulate, and insula areas associated with emotion regulation that were inversely correlated with dissociative symptoms (Nicholson et al., 2017). Another rt-fMRI-NF study with military veterans diagnosed with PTSD similarly demonstrated increases in connectivity between the PFC and the amygdala, but also in connectivity between midbrain areas associated with fear and dysphoria and PFC and anterior cingulate cortex areas associate with emotion regulation (Misaki et al., 2018). These findings are consistent with the view that CTSDs involve a shift from the "learning brain" to a "survival brain" (see Chapter 2). Thus, despite the limited evidence base, NF appears to be a promising adjunctive intervention that may enhance the treatment of CTSDs. NF's side effects, optimal frequency or duration of sessions, target-specific and generalized effects on brain activity, and specific mechanisms of action, all remain to be determined empirically.

Animal-Assisted Interventions

The International Association of Human–Animal Interaction Organizations (Jegatheesan et al., 2014) defines *animal-assisted intervention* (A-AI) as a "goal-oriented and structured intervention that intentionally includes or incorporates animals in health, education and human service . . . for the purpose of therapeutic gains in humans" (p. 5). A-AI encompasses targeted therapeutic interventions with animals (animal-assisted therapy), less structured enrichment activities with animals (animal-assisted activities), and the provision of trained animals to assist with daily life activities (service or assistance animals). Animal-assisted therapy (Levinson, 1969) is a goal-oriented, planned, and structured therapeutic intervention that focuses on enhancing physical, cognitive, behavioral, and/or social–emotional functioning of the human recipient and is usually delivered by professionals with specialized training and expertise (Balluerka, Muela, Amiano, & Caldentey, 2014; Bass, Duchowny, & Llabre, 2009; Dietz, Davis, & Pennings, 2012; Kamioka et al., 2014). The animals most often used in A-AI are horses and dogs.

Animals may play several roles in PTSD and CTSD treatment. For example, the presence of an animal can be grounding, either as a reminder that past danger is no longer present (Yount, Ritchie, Laurent, Chumley, & Olmert, 2013) or as a secure context for mindful experiences in the present (Parish-Plass, 2008). The presence of an animal can also counter emotional and physical numbing by eliciting positive emotions and warmth (O'Haire, 2013). Animals also can be social facilitators that connect people (Wood, Giles-Corti, & Bulsara, 2005) and reduce loneliness (Banks & Banks, 2002). The concept of the human–animal bond has been proposed to explain the impact of animal-assisted therapy (Katcher, 2000). This parallels the concept of co-regulation in attachment-focused therapy (Yorke, 2010). Neurobiologically, the human–animal interaction bond may regulate cortisol (Yorke, 2010) and increase oxytocin, endorphin, and serotonin levels (Beetz, Uvnas-Moberg, Julius, & Kotrschal, 2012).

Equine-assisted therapies include equine-assisted or equine-facilitated psy-chotherapy and therapeutic riding. Both involve a mental health professional working with (or as) a certified equine specialist and involve equine activi-ties such as handling, grooming, ongoing riding, driving, and vaulting. How the client interacts with the horse provides content for therapeutic dialogue with the mental health professional. Equine-assisted therapies take place in accredited riding centers, where participants attend weekly sessions, usually for 6–8 weeks, during which they work on individually determined goals with their riding team. Sessions are individually tailored to each rider because of the diverse needs of participants involved. In equine therapy, clients learn to be present, clear, and consistent in order to communicate effectively with the horse. This can serve as a grounding experience, which is especially helpful with dissociation and emotional dysregulation.

Working with horses provides clients numerous opportunities to practice self-monitoring of emotional and physiological arousal levels (Shambo, Seely, & Vonderfecht, 2010).The physical benefits of therapeutic horse riding include sitting posture, postural balance, and improved balance and gait, all aspects of the vestibular and proprioception systems that impact attention and emotional regulation—thus adding a sensorimotor component, along with the poten-tial benefits of increased attachment security, self-efficacy, and social support. Equine therapy takes clients out of the common routine of talk therapy into a new sensory-based experience that can offer new ways to resolve distress and to engage in emotionally arousing and multisensory experiences (Mandrell, 2006). The emotional and sensory experiences involved in interacting with horses may enhance mind–body feedback (Mandrell, 2006). Equine therapy also can be a culturally responsive intervention (e.g., with Native American and Native Alaskan populations; Chalmers & Dell, 2011; Goodkind, LaNoue, Lee, Freeland, & Freund, 2012).

Although efficacy studies of A-AI now offer support for its mental health benefits with children and adults (Hoagwood, Acri, Morrissey, & Peth-Pierce, 2017), few studies have been done with adults with complex trauma histo-ries. All involve equine-facilitated psychotherapy that did not include riding and was delivered by a mental health professional. Across four studies, which collected quantitative and qualitative data, reductions were found in PTSD symptoms, depression, anxiety, and dissociation, as well as increases in self-awareness, self-efficacy, empowerment, and mindfulness (Earles, Vernon, & Yetz, 2015; Meinersmann, Bradberry, & Roberts, 2008; Schroeder & Stroud, 2015; Shambo et al., 2010). However, the studies had small sample sizes (varying from four to 16 subjects), were not RCTs, and provided insufficient detail about the specific therapeutic techniques to allow for replication. A-AI, therefore, represents a promising but largely untested potential adjunct to trauma-focused psychotherapy for CTSDs.

Exercise

Exercise, the structured and repeated physical activity with a specific objective such as the improvement or maintenance of fitness, physical performance, and health, can take four forms according to the American College of Sports Medicine (Garber et al., 2011): (1) cardiorespiratory, aerobic endurance; (2) resistance, muscular strength, endurance; (3) flexibility, coordination, and relaxation; and (4) neuromotor exercise training or functional fitness training (balance, coordination, gait, agility, and proprioceptive). Aerobic exercise includes jogging, brisk walking, bicycling, aerobic dancing, cross-country skiing, and swimming. Nonaerobic exercise does not systematically increase respiratory function, but instead focuses on muscular endurance, body composition, flexibility, coordination and/or relaxation (e.g., weight-training, yoga, and isometrics). Exercise has been shown to enhance the outcomes of therapy for depression, anxiety, and stress-related problems, with improvements across a variety of other psychological dimensions, including cognitive functioning, self-concept, and self-esteem (Fernandes, Arida, & Gomez-Pinilla, 2017) and sleep (Brand et al., 2010).

Physiologically, exercise, especially aerobic exercise, may impact several of the body systems that are altered in CTSDs, including hippocampal volume and plasticity (Firth et al., 2018), vagal tone (Dale et al., 2009), heart rate variability (Sandercock, Bromley, & Brodie, 2005), the sympathetic nervous system (Dale et al., 2009), HPA-axis response (Campeau et al., 2010; Nyhuis, Masini, Sasse, Day, & Campeau, 2010), endogenous opioid activity (Anderson & Shivakumar, 2013), and levels of mood-related neurochemicals such as dopamine, endorphins, serotonin, and norepinephrine (Bassuk, Church, & Manson, 2013; Lin & Kuo, 2013). Exercise can mimic the fight–flight response and may therefore be used to train the body to better recover from extreme hyper- or hypoarousal states (Dale et al., 2009). Exercise also may produce bodily sensations (e.g., increased heart rate, muscle tension or pain, sweating or shortness of breath) that are associated traumatic stress reactions, allowing for interoceptive exposure that may provide anxiolytic effects by demonstrating the nonthreatening nature of these bodily sensations and reducing anxiety sensitivity (Asmundson et al., 2013; Ley, Rato Barrio, & Koch, 2018). Exercise may also enhance the sense of mastery (Buckworth & Dishman, 2002) and the ability to cope with feared or unpleasant sensations (Asmundson et al., 2013; Ley et al., 2018). Use of exercise to enhance interoceptive bodily awareness can shift the perceptive focus away from thinking about body sensations toward simply feeling them, potentially reducing rumination and associated arousal

(Farb et al., 2015). This in turn may increase the ability to down-regulate hyperarousal, thus leading to a sense of mastery.

Although clinicians and researchers in the field of traumatic stress often recommend physical exercise as an adjunct to trauma-focused psychotherapy, there are few empirical studies of exercise's effects with trauma survivors. Studies with military veterans with PTSD using aerobic and nonaerobic exercise have produced mixed findings, with one study reporting no improvement in PTSD but improved sleep (Bosch, Weaver, Neylan, Herbst, & McCaslin, 2017), while others have reported reductions in PTSD (Goldstein et al., 2018; Rosenbaum et al., 2016) and improved quality of life and mind-set (Mehling et al., 2018). Two studies with adolescents with complex trauma histories have reported reductions in PTSD symptoms (Diaz & Motta, 2008; Newman & Motta, 2007). Two studies with adults with complex trauma histories reported decreased PTSD symptoms after participants engaged in aerobic exercise for 2 weeks (six sessions) or 1 week (Fetzner & Asmundson, 2015) or 10 weeks (Manger & Motta, 2005) for 20–30 minutes per session. In these studies, exercise was an adjunct to other therapeutic services, not a freestanding intervention.

Conclusion

Complementary healing therapies show promise but have yet to be established as evidence-based treatments for PTSD or CTSDs. The strongest evidence of efficacy with PTSD and CTSDs is found for yoga, acupuncture, NF, and TMS, although each of these interventions—and other promising ones, such as A-AI and exercise—seems best utilized as an adjunct to evidence-based verbal psychotherapies such as those described in other chapters in this book. However, complementary healing therapies should not be viewed as merely secondary adjuncts to verbal psychotherapy, because they address physical, affective, behavioral, relational, and spiritual aspects of both traumatic stress and resilience that often are not considered in verbal psychotherapies. Therefore, complementary healing therapies (and similar multimodal approaches; see Chapters 23–25) deserve careful consideration by clinicians and researchers who seek to advance the still emergent field of CTSD treatment—and to broaden and enhance the quality of the lives of individuals who are recovering from complex trauma.

References

Abdallah, C. G., Southwick, S. M., & Krystal, J. H. (2017). Neurobiology of posttraumatic stress disorder (PTSD): A path from novel pathophysiology to innovative therapeutics. *Neuroscience Letters, 649,* 130–132.

Akiki, T. J., Averill, C. L., & Abdallah, C. G. (2017). A network-based neurobiological model of PTSD: Evidence from structural and functional neuroimaging studies. *Current Psychiatry Reports, 19*(11), 81.

Anderson, E., & Shivakumar, G. (2013). Effects of exercise and physical activity on anxiety. *Frontiers in Psychiatry, 4,* 27.

Arch, J. J., & Craske, M. G. (2006). Mechanisms of mindfulness: Emotion regulation following a focused breathing induction. *Behaviour Research and Therapy, 44*(12), 1849–1858.

Asmundson, G. J., Fetzner, M. G., Deboer, L. B., Powers, M. B., Otto, M. W., & Smits, J. A. (2013). Let's get physical: A contemporary review of the anxiolytic effects of exercise for anxiety and its disorders. *Depression and Anxiety, 30*(4), 362–373.

Balluerka, N., Muela, A., Amiano, N., & Caldentey, M. A. (2014). Influence of animal-assisted therapy (AAT) on the attachment representations of youth in residential care. *Children and Youth Services Review, 42,* 103–109.

Banks, M. R., & Banks, W. A. (2002). The effects of animal-assisted therapy on loneliness in an elderly population in long-term care facilities. *Journals of Gerontology A: Biological Sciences and Medical Sciences, 57*(7), M428–M432.

Bass, M. M., Duchowny, C. A., & Llabre, M. M. (2009). The effect of therapeutic horseback riding on social functioning in children with autism. *Journal of Autism and Developmental Disorders, 39*(9), 1261–1267.

Bassuk, S. S., Church, T. S., & Manson, J. E. (2013). Why exercise works magic. *Scientific American, 309*(2), 74–79.

Beetz, A., Uvnas-Moberg, K., Julius, H., & Kotrschal, K. (2012). Psychosocial and psychophysiological effects of human–animal interactions: The possible role of oxytocin. *Frontiers in Psychology, 3,* 234.

Berlim, M. T., van den Eynde, F., Tovar-Perdomo, S., & Daskalakis, Z. J. (2014). Response, remission and drop-out rates following high-frequency repetitive transcranial magnetic stimulation (rTMS) for treating major depression: A systematic review and meta-analysis of randomized, double-blind and sham-controlled trials. *Psychological Medicine, 44*(2), 225–239.

Berrol, C. F. (1992). The neurophysiologic basis of the mind–body connection in dance/movement therapy. *American Journal of Dance Therapy, 14*(1), 19–29.

Bisson, J. I., Roberts, N. P., Andrew, M., Cooper, R., & Lewis, C. (2013). Psychological therapies for chronic post-traumatic stress disorder (PTSD) in adults. *Cochrane Database of Systematic Reviews, 12,* CD003388.

Blaskovits, F., Tyerman, J., & Luctkar-Flude, M. (2017). Effectiveness of neurofeedback therapy for anxiety and stress in adults living with a chronic illness: A systematic review protocol. *JBI Database of Systematic Reviews and Implementation Reports, 15*(7), 1765–1769.

Bosch, J., Weaver, T. L., Neylan, T. C., Herbst, E., & McCaslin, S. E. (2017). Impact of engagement in exercise on sleep quality among veterans with posttraumatic stress disorder symptoms. *Military Medicine, 182*(9), e1745–e1750.

Brand, S., Gerber, M., Beck, J., Hatzinger, M., Puhse, U., & Holsboer-Trachsler, E. (2010). High exercise levels are related to favorable sleep patterns and psychological functioning in adolescents: A comparison of athletes and controls. *Journal of Adolescent Health, 46*(2), 133–141.

Brown, R. P., & Gerbarg, P. L. (2009). Yoga breathing, meditation, and longevity. *Annals of the New York Academy of Sciences, 1172*(1), 54–62.

Buckworth, J., & Dishman, R. (2002). Determinants of exercise and physical activity. In J. Buckworth & R. Dishman (Eds.), *Exercise psychology* (pp. 191–209). Champaign, IL: Human Kinetics.

Callahan, R. J. (1995). A thought field therapy (TFT) algorithm for trauma. *Traumatology, 1*(1), 7–13.

Campeau, S., Nyhuis, T. J., Sasse, S. K., Kryskow, E. M., Herlihy, L., Masini, C. V., . . . Day, H. E. (2010). Hypothalamic pituitary adrenal axis responses to low-intensity stressors are reduced after voluntary wheel running in rats. *Journal of Neuroendocrinology, 22*(8), 872–888.

Carvalho Fernando, S., Beblo, T., Schlosser, N., Terfehr, K., Otte, C., Lowe, B., . . . Wingenfeld, K. (2012). Associations of childhood trauma with hypothalamic–pituitary–adrenal function in borderline personality disorder and major depression. *Psychoneuroendocrinology, 37*(10), 1659–1668.

Chalmers, D., & Dell, C. A. (2011). Equine-assisted therapy with First Nations youth in residential treatment for volatile substance misuse: Building an empirical knowledge base. *Journal of Native Studies Review, 20*(1), 59–87.

Chou, C. Y., La Marca, R., Steptoe, A., & Brewin, C. R. (2018). Cardiovascular and psychological responses to voluntary recall of trauma in posttraumatic stress disorder. *European Journal of Psychotraumatology, 9*(1), 1472988.

Church, D., Hawk, C., Brooks, A. J., Toukolehto, O., Wren, M., Dinter, I., & Stein, P. (2013). Psychological trauma symptom improvement in veterans using emotional freedom techniques: A randomized controlled trial. *Journal of Nervous and Mental Disease, 201*(2), 153–160.

Church, D., Stapleton, P., Yang, A., & Gallo, F. (2018). Is tapping on acupuncture points an active ingredient in emotional freedom techniques?: A systematic review and meta-analysis of comparative studies. *Journal of Nervous and Mental Disease, 206*(10), 783–793.

Church, D., Yount, G., & Brooks, A. J. (2012). The effect of emotional freedom techniques on stress biochemistry: A randomized controlled trial. *Journal of Nervous and Mental Disease, 200*(10), 891–896.

Craig, G. (2011). *The EFT manual.* Santa Rosa, CA: Energy Psychology Press.

Dale, L. P., Carroll, L. E., Galen, G., Hayes, J. A., Webb, K. W., & Porges, S. W. (2009). Abuse history is related to autonomic regulation to mild exercise and psychological wellbeing. *Journal of Applied Psychophysiology Biofeedback, 34*(4), 299–308.

D'Andrea, W., Pole, N., DePierro, J., Freed, S., & Wallace, D. B. (2013). Heterogeneity of defensive responses after exposure to trauma: Blunted autonomic reactivity in response to startling sounds. *International Journal of Psychophysiology, 90*(1), 80–89.

Diaz, A. B., & Motta, R. (2008). The effects of an aerobic exercise program on posttraumatic stress disorder symptom severity in adolescents. *International Journal of Emergency Mental Health and Human Resilience, 10*(1), 49–59.

Dieleman, G. C., Huizink, A. C., Tulen, J. H., Utens, E. M., Creemers, H. E., van der Ende, J., & Verhulst, F. C. (2015). Alterations in HPA-axis and autonomic nervous system functioning in childhood anxiety disorders point to a chronic stress hypothesis. *Psychoneuroendocrinology, 51,* 135–150.

Diepold, J. H., & Goldstein, D. M. (2009). Thought field therapy and QEEG changes in the treatment of trauma: A case study. *Traumatology, 15*(1), 85–93.

Dietz, T. J., Davis, D., & Pennings, J. (2012). Evaluating animal-assisted therapy in group treatment for child sexual abuse. *Journal of Child Sexual Abuse, 21*(6), 665–683.

Earles, J. L., Vernon, L. L., & Yetz, J. P. (2015). Equine-assisted therapy for anxiety and posttraumatic stress symptoms. *Journal of Traumatic Stress, 28*(2), 149–152.

Eich, E., Kihlstrom, J. F., Bower, G. H., Forgas, J. P., & Niedenthal, P. M. (2000). *Cognition and emotion.* New York: Oxford University Press.

Emerson, D., Sharma, R., Chaudhry, S., & Turner, J. (2009). Trauma-sensitive yoga: Principles, practice, and research. *International Journal of Yoga Therapy, 19*(1), 123–128.

Farb, N., Daubenmier, J., Price, C. J., Gard, T., Kerr, C., Dunn, B. D., . . . Mehling, W. E. (2015). Interoception, contemplative practice, and health. *Frontiers in Psychology, 6,* 763.

Feinstein, D. (2008). Energy psychology in disaster relief. *Traumatology, 14*(1), 127–139.

Felmingham, K. L., Rennie, C., Gordon, E., & Bryant, R. A. (2012). Autonomic and cortical reactivity in acute and chronic posttraumatic stress. *Biological Psychology, 90*(3), 224–227.

Fernandes, J., Arida, R. M., & Gomez-Pinilla, F. (2017). Physical exercise as an epigenetic modulator of brain plasticity and cognition. *Neuroscience and Biobehavioral Reviews, 80,* 443–456.

Fetzner, M. G., & Asmundson, G. J. (2015). Aerobic exercise reduces symptoms of post-traumatic stress disorder: A randomized controlled trial. *Cognitive Behaviour Therapy,* *44*(4), 301–313.

Firth, J., Stubbs, B., Vancampfort, D., Schuch, F., Lagopoulos, J., Rosenbaum, S., & Ward, P. B. (2018). Effect of aerobic exercise on hippocampal volume in humans: A systematic review and meta-analysis. *NeuroImage, 166,* 230–238.

Fisher, S. F., Lanius, R. A., & Frewen, P. A. (2016). EEG neurofeedback as adjunct to psychotherapy for complex developmental trauma-related disorders: Case study and treatment rationale. *Traumatology, 22*(4), 255–260.

Flandreau, E. I., Ressler, K. J., Owens, M. J., & Nemeroff, C. B. (2012). Chronic overexpression of corticotropin-releasing factor from the central amygdala produces HPA axis hyperactivity and behavioral anxiety associated with gene-expression changes in the hippocampus and paraventricular nucleus of the hypothalamus. *Psychoneuroendocrinology, 37,* 27–38.

Freed, S., & D'Andrea, W. (2015). Autonomic arousal and emotion in victims of interpersonal violence: Shame proneness but not anxiety predicts vagal tone. *Journal of Trauma and Dissociation, 16*(4), 367–383.

Gallo, F. P. (2000). *Energy diagnostic and treatment methods.* New York: Norton.

Gapen, M., van der Kolk, B. A., Hamlin, E., Hirshberg, L., Suvak, M., & Spinazzola, J. (2016). A pilot study of neurofeedback for chronic PTSD. *Applied Psychophysiology and Biofeedback, 41*(3), 251–261.

Garber, C. E., Blissmer, B., Deschenes, M. R., Franklin, B. A., Lamonte, M. J., Lee, I. M., . . . Swain, D. P. (2011). American College of Sports Medicine position stand: Quantity and quality of exercise for developing and maintaining cardiorespiratory, musculoskeletal, and neuromotor fitness in apparently healthy adults: Guidance for prescribing exercise. *Medicine and Science in Sports and Exercise, 43*(7), 1334–1359.

Gijsman, H. J. (2005). Mania after transcranial magnetic stimulation in PTSD. *American Journal of Psychiatry, 162*(2), 398–400.

Gilomen, S. A., & Lee, C. W. (2015). The efficacy of acupoint stimulation in the treatment of psychological distress: A meta-analysis. *Journal of Behavior Therapy and Experimental Psychiatry, 48,* 140–148.

Goldstein, L. A., Mehling, W. E., Metzler, T. J., Cohen, B. E., Barnes, D. E., Choucroun, G. J., . . . Neylan, T. C. (2018). Veterans Group Exercise: A randomized pilot trial of an integrative exercise program for veterans with posttraumatic stress. *Journal of Affective Disorders, 227,* 345–352.

Goodkind, J., LaNoue, M., Lee, C., Freeland, L., & Freund, R. (2012). Feasibility, acceptability, and initial findings from a community-based cultural mental health intervention for American Indian youth and their families. *Journal of Community Psychology,* *40*(4), 381–405.

Grant, S., Colaiaco, B., Motala, A., Shanman, R., Sorbero, M., & Hempel, S. (2018). Acupuncture for the treatment of adults with posttraumatic stress disorder: A systematic review and meta-analysis. *Journal of Trauma and Dissociation, 19*(1), 39–58.

Gruzelier, J. (2009). A theory of alpha/theta neurofeedback, creative performance enhancement, long distance functional connectivity and psychological integration. *Cognitive Processing, 10*(Suppl. 1), S101–S109.

Gruzelier, J. H. (2014). EEG-neurofeedback for optimising performance: I. A review of cognitive and affective outcome in healthy participants. *Neuroscience and Biobehavioral Reviews, 44,* 124–141.

Hampson, M., Scheinost, D., Qiu, M., Bhawnani, J., Lacadie, C. M., Leckman, J. F., . . . Papademetris, X. (2011). Biofeedback of real-time functional magnetic resonance imaging data from the supplementary motor area reduces functional connectivity to subcortical regions. *Brain Connectivity, 1*(1), 91–98.

Hoagwood, K. E., Acri, M., Morrissey, M., & Peth-Pierce, R. (2017). Animal-assisted therapies for youth with or at risk for mental health problems: A systematic review. *Applied Developmental Science, 21*(1), 1–13.

Hollifield, M. (2011). Acupuncture for posttraumatic stress disorder: Conceptual, clinical, and biological data support further research. *CNS Neuroscience and Therapeutics, 17*(6), 769–779.

Hollifield, M., Sinclair-Lian, N., Warner, T. D., & Hammerschlag, R. (2007). Acupuncture for posttraumatic stress disorder: A randomized controlled pilot trial. *Journal of Nervous and Mental Disease, 195*(6), 504–513.

Houtepen, L. C., Vinkers, C. H., Carrillo-Roa, T., Hiemstra, M., van Lier, P. A., Meeus, W., . . . Boks, M. P. (2016). Genome-wide DNA methylation levels and altered cortisol stress reactivity following childhood trauma in humans. *Nature Communications, 7,* 10967.

Hui, K. K., Liu, J., Makris, N., Gollub, R. L., Chen, A. J., Moore, C. I., . . . Kwong, K. K. (2000). Acupuncture modulates the limbic system and subcortical gray structures of the human brain: Evidence from fMRI studies in normal subjects. *Human Brain Mapping, 9*(1), 13–25.

Ipser, J. C., Pillay, N. S., Stein, D. J., & van Honk, J. (2007). Transcranial magnetic stimulation for post-traumatic stress disorder. *Cochrane Database of Systematic Reviews, 4,* CD006824.

Isserles, M., Shalev, A. Y., Roth, Y., Peri, T., Kutz, I., Zlotnick, E., & Zangen, A. (2013). Effectiveness of deep transcranial magnetic stimulation combined with a brief exposure procedure in post-traumatic stress disorder—a pilot study. *Brain Stimulation, 6*(3), 377–383.

Jegatheesan, B., Beetz, A., Choi, G., Dudzik, C., Fine, A., & Garcia, R. (2014). *IAHAIO White Paper: The IAHAIO definitions for animal assisted intervention and animal assisted activity and guidelines for wellness of animals involved* [Final report]. Seattle, WA: International Association of Human–Animal Interaction Associations.

Kamioka, H., Okada, S., Tsutani, K., Park, H., Okuizumi, H., Handa, S., . . . Mutoh, Y. (2014). Effectiveness of animal-assisted therapy: A systematic review of randomized controlled trials. *Complementary Therapies in Medicine, 22*(2), 371–390.

Karsen, E. F., Watts, B. V., & Holtzheimer, P. E. (2014). Review of the effectiveness of transcranial magnetic stimulation for post-traumatic stress disorder. *Brain Stimulation, 7*(2), 151–157.

Katcher, A. H. (2000). The future of educational research on the animal–human bond and animal-assisted therapy. In A. Fine (Ed.), *Handbook on animal-assisted therapy* (pp. 486–469). New York: Academic Press.

Keeshin, B. R., Strawn, J. R., Out, D., Granger, D. A., & Putnam, F. W. (2014). Cortisol awakening response in adolescents with acute sexual abuse related posttraumatic stress disorder. *Depression and Anxiety, 31*(2), 107–114.

Kluetsch, R. C., Ros, T., Theberge, J., Frewen, P. A., Calhoun, V. D., Schmahl, C., . . . Lanius, R. A. (2014). Plastic modulation of PTSD resting-state networks and subjective wellbeing by EEG neurofeedback. *Acta Psychiatrica Scandinavica, 130*(2), 123–136.

Lamb, D. G., Porges, E. C., Lewis, G. F., & Williamson, J. B. (2017). Non-invasive vagal nerve stimulation effects on hyperarousal and autonomic state in patients with posttraumatic stress disorder and history of mild traumatic brain injury: Preliminary evidence. *Frontiers in Medicine (Lausanne), 4,* 124.

Lambrou, P., Pratt, G., Chevalier, G. J. S. E., & Archives, E. M. J. (2003). Physiological and psychological effects of a mind/body therapy on claustrophobia. *Subtle Energies and Energy Medicine, 14*(3), 239–251.

Lanius, R. A., Frewen, P. A., Tursich, M., Jetly, R., & McKinnon, M. C. (2015). Restoring large-scale brain networks in PTSD and related disorders: A proposal for neuroscientifically informed treatment interventions. *European Journal of Psychotraumatology, 6,* 27313.

Lanius, R., & Olff, M. (2017). The neurobiology of PTSD. *European Journal of Psychotraumatology, 8*(1), 1314165.

Levinson, B. M. (1969). *Pet-oriented child psychology.* Springfield, IL: Charles C Thomas.

Ley, C., Rato Barrio, M., & Koch, A. (2018). "In the sport I am here": Therapeutic processes and health effects of sport and exercise on PTSD. *Qualitative Health Research, 28*(3), 491–507.

Lin, T. W., & Kuo, Y. M. (2013). Exercise benefits brain function: The monoamine connection. *Brain Sciences, 3*(1), 39–53.

Mahoney, A., Karatzias, T., & Hutton, P. (2019). A systematic review and meta-analysis of group treatments for adults with symptoms associated with complex post-traumatic stress disorder. *Journal of Affective Disorders, 243,* 305–321.

Mallorqui-Bague, N., Bulbena, A., Pailhez, G., Garfinkel, S. N., & Critchley, H. D. (2016). Mind–body interactions in anxiety and somatic symptoms. *Harvard Review of Psychiatry, 24*(1), 53–60.

Mandrell, P. J. (2006). *Introduction to equine-assisted psychotherapy.* Maitland, FL: Xulon Press.

Manger, T. A., & Motta, R. W. (2005). The impact of an exercise program on posttraumatic stress disorder, anxiety, and depression. *International Journal of Emergency Mental Health and Human Resilience, 7*(1), 49–57.

Marzbani, H., Marateb, H. R., & Mansourian, M. (2016). Neurofeedback: A comprehensive review on system design, methodology and clinical applications. *Basic and Clinical Neuroscience, 7*(2), 143–158.

Mason, E. (2012). Energy psychology and psychotherapy: A study of the use of energy psychology in psychotherapy practice. *Counselling and Psychotherapy Research, 12*(3), 224–232.

McEwen, B. S. (2017). Allostasis and the epigenetics of brain and body health over the life course: The brain on stress. *JAMA Psychiatry, 74*(6), 551–552.

McEwen, B. S., Bowles, N. P., Gray, J. D., Hill, M. N., Hunter, R. G., Karatsoreos, I. N., & Nasca, C. (2015). Mechanisms of stress in the brain. *Nature Neuroscience, 18*(10), 1353–1363.

McLaughlin, K. A., Alves, S., & Sheridan, M. A. (2014). Vagal regulation and internalizing psychopathology among adolescents exposed to childhood adversity. *Developmental Psychobiology, 56*(5), 1036–1051.

McLaughlin, K. A., Sheridan, M. A., Alves, S., & Mendes, W. B. (2014). Child maltreatment and autonomic nervous system reactivity: Identifying dysregulated stress reactivity patterns by using the biopsychosocial model of challenge and threat. *Psychosomatic Medicine, 76*(7), 538–546.

Mehling, W. E., Chesney, M. A., Metzler, T. J., Goldstein, L. A., Maguen, S., Geronimo, C., . . . Neylan, T. C. (2018). A 12-week integrative exercise program improves self-reported mindfulness and interoceptive awareness in war veterans with posttraumatic stress symptoms. *Journal of Clinical Psychology, 74*(4), 554–565.

Meinersmann, K. M., Bradberry, J., & Roberts, F. B. (2008). Equine-facilitated psychotherapy with adult female survivors of abuse. *Journal of Psychosocial Nursing and Mental Health Services, 46*(12), 36–42.

Metcalf, O., Varker, T., Forbes, D., Phelps, A., Dell, L., DiBattista, A., . . . O'Donnell, M. (2016). Efficacy of fifteen emerging interventions for the treatment of posttraumatic stress disorder: A systematic review. *Journal of Traumatic Stress, 29*(1), 88–92.

Middlekauff, H. R., Yu, J. L., & Hui, K. (2001). Acupuncture effects on reflex responses to mental stress in humans. *American Journal of Physiology: Regulatory, Integrative and Comparative Physiology, 280*(5), R1462–R1468.

Mirifar, A., Beckmann, J., & Ehrlenspiel, F. (2017). Neurofeedback as supplementary training for optimizing athletes' performance: A systematic review with implications for future research. *Neuroscience and Biobehavioral Reviews, 75,* 419–432.

Misaki, M., Phillips, R., Zotev, V., Wong, C. K., Wurfel, B. E., Krueger, F., . . . Bodurka, J. (2018). Real-time fMRI amygdala neurofeedback positive emotional training normalized resting-state functional connectivity in combat veterans with and without PTSD: A connectome-wide investigation. *NeuroImage: Clinical, 20,* 543–555.

Mitchell, K. S., Dick, A. M., DiMartino, D. M., Smith, B. N., Niles, B., Koenen, K. C., & Street, A. (2014). A pilot study of a randomized controlled trial of yoga as an intervention for PTSD symptoms in women. *Journal of Traumatic Stress, 27*(2), 121–128.

Mori, H., Tanaka, T. H., Kuge, H., Taniwaki, E., Sasaki, K., Yamashita, K., . . . Kikuchi, Y. (2010). Is there any difference in human pupillary reaction when different acupuncture points are stimulated? *Acupuncture in Medicine, 28*(1), 21–24.

Morina, N., Koerssen, R., & Pollet, T. V. (2016). Interventions for children and adolescents with posttraumatic stress disorder: A meta-analysis of comparative outcome studies. *Clinical Psychology Review, 47,* 41–54.

Morris, M. C., Abelson, J. L., Mielock, A. S., & Rao, U. (2017). Psychobiology of cumulative trauma: Hair cortisol as a risk marker for stress exposure in women. *Stress, 20*(4), 350–354.

Naegeli, C., Zeffiro, T., Piccirelli, M., Jaillard, A., Weilenmann, A., Hassanpour, K., . . . Mueller-Pfeiffer, C. (2018). Locus coeruleus activity mediates hyperresponsiveness in posttraumatic stress disorder. *Biological Psychiatry, 83*(3), 254–262.

Napadow, V., Makris, N., Liu, J., Kettner, N. W., Kwong, K. K., & Hui, K. K. (2005). Effects of electroacupuncture versus manual acupuncture on the human brain as measured by fMRI. *Human Brain Mapping, 24*(3), 193–205.

Newman, C. L., & Motta, R. W. (2007). The effects of aerobic exercise on childhood PTSD, anxiety, and depression. *International Journal of Emergency Mental Health and Human Resilience, 9*(2), 133–158.

Nicholson, A. A., Rabellino, D., Densmore, M., Frewen, P. A., Paret, C., Kluetsch, R., . . . Lanius, R. A. (2017). The neurobiology of emotion regulation in posttraumatic stress disorder: Amygdala downregulation via real-time fMRI neurofeedback. *Human Brain Mapping, 38*(1), 541–560.

Nicholson, A. A., Ros, T., Frewen, P. A., Densmore, M., Theberge, J., Kluetsch, R. C., . . . Lanius, R. A. (2016a). Alpha oscillation neurofeedback modulates amygdala complex connectivity and arousal in posttraumatic stress disorder. *NeuroImage: Clinical, 12,* 506–516.

Nicholson, A. A., Sapru, I., Densmore, M., Frewen, P. A., Neufeld, R. W., Theberge, J., . . . Lanius, R. A. (2016b). Unique insula subregion resting-state functional connectivity with amygdala complexes in posttraumatic stress disorder and its dissociative subtype. *Psychiatry Research, 250,* 61–72.

Nyhuis, T. J., Masini, C. V., Sasse, S. K., Day, H. E., & Campeau, S. (2010). Physical activity, but not environmental complexity, facilitates HPA axis response habituation to repeated audiogenic stress despite neurotrophin mRNA regulation in both conditions. *Journal of Brain Research, 1362,* 68–77.

O'Haire, M. E. (2013). Animal-assisted intervention for autism spectrum disorder: A systematic literature review. *Journal of Autism and Developmental Disorders, 43*(7), 1606–1622.

Oschman, J. L. (2000a). The electromagnetic environment: Implications for bodywork: Part 1. Environmental energies. *Journal of Bodywork Movement Therapies, 4*(1), 56–67.

Oschman, J. L. (2000b). The electromagnetic environment: Implications for bodywork: Part 2. Biological effects. *Journal of Bodywork Movement Therapies, 4*(2), 137–150.

Panda, S. (2014). Stress and health: Symptoms and techniques of psychotherapeutic management. *Indian Journal of Positive Psychology, 5*(4), 516.

Parish-Plass, N. (2008). Animal-assisted therapy with children suffering from insecure attachment due to abuse and neglect: A method to lower the risk of intergenerational transmission of abuse? *Journal of Clinical Child Psychology, 13*(1), 7–30.

Peniston, E. G., & Kulkosky, P. J. (1991). Alpha–theta brainwave neuro-feedback therapy for Vietnam veterans with combat-related post-traumatic stress disorder. *Medical Psychotherapy, 4,* 47–60.

Philip, N. S., Barredo, J., van 't Wout-Frank, M., Tyrka, A. R., Price, L. H., & Carpenter, L.

L. (2018). Network mechanisms of clinical response to transcranial magnetic stimulation in posttraumatic stress disorder and major depressive disorder. *Biological Psychiatry, 83*(3), 263–272.

Pradhan, B., D'Amico, J. K., Makani, R., & Parikh, T. (2016). Nonconventional Interventions for chronic post-traumatic stress disorder (PTSD): Ketamine, repetitive trans-cranial magnetic stimulation (RTMS) and alternative approaches. *Journal of Trauma and Dissociation, 17*(1), 35–54.

Rabellino, D., D'Andrea, W., Siegle, G., Frewen, P. A., Minshew, R., Densmore, M., . . . Lanius, R. A. (2017). Neural correlates of heart rate variability in PTSD during sub- and supraliminal processing of trauma-related cues. *Human Brain Mapping, 38*(10), 4898–4907.

Reinhardt, K. M., Noggle Taylor, J. J., Johnston, J., Zameer, A., Cheema, S., & Khalsa, S. B. S. (2018). Kripalu yoga for military veterans with PTSD: A randomized trial. *Journal of Clinical Psychology, 74*(1), 93–108.

Renton, T., Tibbles, A., & Topolovec-Vranic, J. (2017). Neurofeedback as a form of cognitive rehabilitation therapy following stroke: A systematic review. *PLOS ONE, 12*(5), e0177290.

Rhodes, A., Spinazzola, J., & van der Kolk, B. (2016). Yoga for adult women with chronic PTSD: A long-term follow-up study. *Journal of Alternative Complementary Medicine, 22*(3), 189–196.

Ros, T., Baars, B. J., Lanius, R. A., & Vuilleumier, P. (2014). Tuning pathological brain oscillations with neurofeedback: A systems neuroscience framework. *Frontiers in Human Neuroscience, 8,* 1008.

Rosenbaum, S., Tiedemann, A., Stanton, R., Parker, A., Waterreus, A., Curtis, J., & Ward, P. B. (2016). Implementing evidence-based physical activity interventions for people with mental illness: An Australian perspective. *Australasian Psychiatry, 24*(1), 49–54.

Rowny, S., & Lisanby, S. H. (2008). Brain stimulation in psychiatry. In A. Tasman, J. Kay, J. A. Lieberman, M. B. First, & M. Maj (Eds.), *Psychiatry* (3rd ed., pp. 2354–2371). New York: Wiley-Blackwell.

Ruden, R. A. (2005). A neurological basis for the observed peripheral sensory modulation of emotional responses. *Traumatology, 11*(3), 145–158.

Saar-Ashkenazy, R., Cohen, J. E., Guez, J., Gasho, C., Shelef, I., Friedman, A., & Shalev, H. (2014). Reduced corpus-callosum volume in posttraumatic stress disorder highlights the importance of interhemispheric connectivity for associative memory. *Journal of Traumatic Stress, 27*(1), 18–26.

Salmon, P., Lush, E., Jablonski, M., & Sephton, S. E. (2009). Yoga and mindfulness: Clinical aspects of an ancient mind/body practice. *Journal of Cognitive Behavioral Practice, 16*(1), 59–72.

Sandercock, G. R., Bromley, P. D., & Brodie, D. A. (2005). The reliability of short-term measurements of heart rate variability. *International Journal of Cardiology, 103*(3), 238–247.

Scheinost, D., Stoica, T., Saksa, J., Papademetris, X., Constable, R., Pittenger, C., & Hampson, M. (2013). Orbitofrontal cortex neurofeedback produces lasting changes in contamination anxiety and resting-state connectivity. *Translational Psychiatry, 3*(4), e250.

Schroeder, K., & Stroud, D. (2015). Equine-facilitated group work for women survivors of interpersonal violence. *Journal for Specialists in Group Work, 40*(4), 365–386.

Seppala, E. M., Nitschke, J. B., Tudorascu, D. L., Hayes, A., Goldstein, M. R., Nguyen, D. T., . . . Davidson, R. J. (2014). Breathing-based meditation decreases posttraumatic stress disorder symptoms in U.S. military veterans: A randomized controlled longitudinal study. *Journal of Traumatic Stress, 27*(4), 397–405.

Shambo, L., Seely, S., & Vonderfecht, H. (2010). A pilot study on equine-facilitated psychotherapy for trauma-related disorders. *Scientific Educational Journal of Therapeutic Riding, 16,* 11–23.

Shibata, K., Watanabe, T., Sasaki, Y., & Kawato, M. (2011). Perceptual learning incepted by decoded fMRI neurofeedback without stimulus presentation. *Science, 334*(6061), 1413–1415.

Spence, D. W., Kayumov, L., Chen, A., Lowe, A., Jain, U., Katzman, M. A., . . . Shapiro, C. M. (2004). Acupuncture increases nocturnal melatonin secretion and reduces insomnia and anxiety: A preliminary report. *Journal of Neuropsychiatry and Clinial Neurosciences, 16*(1), 19–28.

Sriram, K., Rodriguez-Fernandez, M., & Doyle, F. J., III. (2012). Modeling cortisol dynamics in the neuro-endocrine axis distinguishes normal, depression, and post-traumatic stress disorder (PTSD) in humans. *PLOS Computational Biology, 8*(2), e1002379.

Stefanov, M., Potroz, M., Kim, J., Lim, J., Cha, R., & Nam, M.-H. (2013). The primo vascular system as a new anatomical system. *Journal of Acupuncture and Meridian Studies, 6*(6), 331–338.

Streeter, C. C., Jensen, J. E., Perlmutter, R. M., Cabral, H. J., Tian, H., Terhune, D. B., . . . Renshaw, P. F. (2007). Yoga Asana sessions increase brain GABA levels: A pilot study. *Journal of Alternative and Complementary Medicine, 13*(4), 419–426.

Sumner, J. A., McLaughlin, K. A., Walsh, K., Sheridan, M. A., & Koenen, K. C. (2014). CRHR1 genotype and history of maltreatment predict cortisol reactivity to stress in adolescents. *Psychoneuroendocrinology, 43*, 71–80.

Swingle, P. G., Pulos, L., & Swingle, M. K. (2004). Neurophysiological indicators of EFT treatment of post-traumatic stress. *Subtle Energies and Energy Medicine Journal, 15*(1), 75–86.

Tan, J.-Y., Suen, L. K., Wang, T., & Molassiotis, A. (2015). Sham acupressure controls used in randomized controlled trials: A systematic review and critique. *PLOS ONE, 10*(7), e0132989.

Teicher, M. H., & Samson, J. A. (2016). Annual Research Review: Enduring neurobiological effects of childhood abuse and neglect. *Journal of Child Psychology and Psychiatry and Allied Disciplines, 57*(3), 241–266.

Thibault, R. T., MacPherson, A., Lifshitz, M., Roth, R. R., & Raz, A. (2018). Neurofeedback with fMRI: A critical systematic review. *NeuroImage, 172*, 786–807.

Thome, J., Densmore, M., Frewen, P. A., McKinnon, M. C., Theberge, J., Nicholson, A. A., . . . Lanius, R. A. (2017). Desynchronization of autonomic response and central autonomic network connectivity in posttraumatic stress disorder. *Human Brain Mapping, 38*(1), 27–40.

Ulmer, C. S., Hall, M. H., Dennis, P. A., Beckham, J. C., & Germain, A. (2018). Posttraumatic stress disorder diagnosis is associated with reduced parasympathetic activity during sleep in US veterans and military service members of the Iraq and Afghanistan wars. *Sleep, 41*(12), 12.

van der Kolk, B. (2014). *The body keeps the score: Brain, mind, and body in the healing of trauma.* New York: Viking Penguin.

van der Kolk, B. A., Hodgdon, H., Gapen, M., Musicaro, R., Suvak, M. K., Hamlin, E., & Spinazzola, J. (2016). A randomized controlled study of neurofeedback for chronic PTSD. *PLOS ONE, 11*(12), e0166752.

van der Kolk, B. A., Stone, L., West, J., Rhodes, A., Emerson, D., Suvak, M., & Spinazzola, J. (2014). Yoga as an adjunctive treatment for posttraumatic stress disorder: A randomized controlled trial. *Journal of Clinical Psychiatry, 75*(6), e559–e565.

Wahbeh, H., Senders, A., Neuendorf, R., & Cayton, J. (2014). Complementary and alternative medicine for posttraumatic stress disorder symptoms: A systematic review. *Journal of Evidence-Based Complementary and Alternative Medicine, 19*(3), 161–175.

Wang, Y., Hu, Y. P., Wang, W. C., Pang, R. Z., & Zhang, A. R. (2012). Clinical studies on treatment of earthquake-caused posttraumatic stress disorder using electroacupuncture. *Evidence-Based Complementary and Alternative Medicine, 2012*, 1–7.

Wood, L., Giles-Corti, B., & Bulsara, M. (2005). The pet connection: Pets as a conduit for social capital? *Social Science and Medicine, 61*(6), 1159–1173.

Yan, T., Xie, Q., Zheng, Z., Zou, K., & Wang, L. (2017). Different frequency repetitive transcranial magnetic stimulation (rTMS) for posttraumatic stress disorder (PTSD): A systematic review and meta-analysis. *Journal of Psychiatric Research, 89,* 125–135.

Yorke, J. (2010). The significance of human–animal relationships as modulators of trauma effects in children: A developmental neurobiological perspective. *Early Child Development and Care, 180*(5), 559–570.

Young, D. A., Inslicht, S. S., Metzler, T. J., Neylan, T. C., & Ross, J. A. (2018). The effects of early trauma and the FKBP5 gene on PTSD and the HPA axis in a clinical sample of Gulf War veterans. *Psychiatry Research, 270,* 961–966.

Young, K. D., Zotev, V., Phillips, R., Misaki, M., Drevets, W. C., & Bodurka, J. (2018). Amygdala real-time functional magnetic resonance imaging neurofeedback for major depressive disorder: A review. *Psychiatry and Clinical Neurosciences, 72*(7), 466–481.

Yount, R., Ritchie, E. C., Laurent, M. S., Chumley, P., & Olmert, M. D. (2013). The role of service dog training in the treatment of combat-related PTSD. *Psychiatric Annals, 43*(6), 292–295.

Zhang, G., Yao, L., Zhang, H., Long, Z., & Zhao, X. (2013). Improved working memory performance through self-regulation of dorsal lateral prefrontal cortex activation using real-time fMRI. *PLOS ONE, 8*(8), e73735.

Zotev, V., Phillips, R., Misaki, M., Wong, C. K., Wurfel, B. E., Krueger, F., . . . Bodurka, J. (2018). Real-time fMRI neurofeedback training of the amygdala activity with simultaneous EEG in veterans with combat-related PTSD. *NeuroImage: Clinical, 19,* 106–121.

Epilogue

Overview and Future Directions in Treatment for Complex Traumatic Stress Disorders

JULIAN D. FORD
CHRISTINE A. COURTOIS

This book has addressed two fundamental questions that confront every helping professional, researcher, or advocate who works with people who have experienced psychological trauma.

1. Do some trauma survivors have complex trauma histories and correspondingly complex reactions that go beyond (although often include) the symptoms of posttraumatic stress disorder (PTSD) or other psychiatric or behavioral health disorders (i.e., complex traumatic stress disorders [CTSDs])?
2. Do the therapeutic services that are provided to complex trauma survivors need to be adapted in order to effectively help them to recover from these complex reactions?

We believe that, based on the insights provided by this book's authors, *the answer to both questions is a resounding "yes!"* In this Epilogue, we summarize why this is the case.

Despite arguments to the contrary (Resick et al., 2012), CTSDs (including, but not limited to, complex PTSD) are real, distinct, and make a difference in how clinicians approach treatment and how scientists do research (Bryant, 2012; Herman, 2012). We are encouraged by the World Health Organization's decision in the *International Classification of Diseases,* 11th Revision

(ICD-11), to formally distinguish complex PTSD from PTSD based on research showing that dysregulation of affect, disorders of the self, and interpersonal difficulties represent a distinct clinical syndrome (Karatzias et al., 2017; Shevlin et al., 2017). A careful read of each chapter in this book, however, makes it clear that the domain of CTSDs is much broader than the three domains and six symptoms that define complex PTSD in ICD-11. We conclude the book by summarizing several key points that we hope readers will find useful in their professional work and personal life.

- **Complex trauma is *interpersonal* and ongoing, not a single-incident or *impersonal* traumatic event (although victim/survivors may have also experienced impersonal trauma).** Instead, complex trauma involves traumatic stressors that are *emotional in both occurrence and intent*. Complex trauma involves violations of the fundamental social contract that obligates people to protect and not harm one another. Complex trauma also tends to involve victims who are dependent on caregivers and still maturing, or who possess less power and resources than perpetrators—for example, maltreatment of children by parents/primary caretakers or significant others who coerce, manipulate, entrap, exploit/abuse, reject/abandon, or fail to care for and protect them.

- **CT fundamentally alters a traumatized child's development and effects the entire lifecourse, and it can undermine adults' previous development.** The developmental compromise associated with complex trauma fundamentally involves essential capacities for *self-regulation* (Ford, Courtois, Steele, van der Hart, & Nijenhuis, 2005). Complex trauma, by virtue of its disruption of ongoing psychophysiological development in a relational context of ongoing or intermittent betrayal, misuse, uncertainty, and danger, can undermine the victim's core identity and sense of personal safety and secure attachment to others (see Chapters 2, 20, 23, and 24). Children experiencing complex trauma often fail to receive the attention, attunement, and experiences of co-regulation from their caregivers that provide a foundation for the self-regulation of their physical, emotional, and mental capacities (see Chapters 2, 6, and 18). Moreover, the adaptations developed in repeated traumatic interactions (whether chronic or intermittent) tend to develop into chronic approach–avoidance reactions in close relationships (i.e., insecure and disorganized attachment working models; see Chapters 6 and 20). As a further result of chronic dysregulation, the child's biological capacity to approach life in an unfettered way that enables ongoing curiosity, increased understanding, and personal growth, along with mutual, satisfactory relationships and the ability to be intimate with others (i.e., the "learning brain"; see Chapter 2) may be replaced by a preoccupation with anticipating and avoiding perceived threat and danger (i.e., hypervigilance and the "survival brain"; see Chapter 2). The result can be a vicious cycle of escalating dysregulation that often becomes overwhelming, leading to a profound emotional shutdown and hopelessness, or to a fundamental fragmentation of the person's sense of self (i.e., structural dissociation; see Chapter

6). In adolescence and adulthood, the impairments in self-regulation associated with complex trauma (which, other than dissociation, are the central features of the revised complex PTSD diagnosis in ICD-11; Shevlin et al., 2018) lead to major difficulties with emotional instability and the organization of the core self or identity (see Chapters 6, 15, 18, and 23–26), self-harm and suicidality, addictions (Chapter 22), somatic disorders (Chapter 23), and conflicted and (re)victimizing relationships (Chapters 16, 17, and 20–24).

- **The long-term adverse sequelae of complex trauma are CTSDs.** Due to their inherent complexity, CTSDs are difficult to accurately define, assess, and diagnose. Over the past decade, evidence has accumulated that distinguishes CTSDs from PTSD, as well as other psychiatric and personality or disruptive behavior disorders in adults (Böttche et al., 2018; Brewin et al., 2017; Karatzias et al., 2017; Murphy, Elklit, Dokkedahl, & Shevlin, 2018a) and children (Murphy et al., 2018b; Sachser, Keller, & Goldbeck, 2017; van der Kolk, Ford, & Spinazzola, 2019). With the advent of new conceptual frameworks such as ICD-11's complex PTSD (Karatzias et al., 2017) and developmental trauma disorder (DTD; Ford, Spinazzola, van der Kolk, & Grasso, 2018), there has been a corresponding increase in psychometric and epidemiological research on CTSDs and in the array of validated assessment measures for CTSDs (see Chapter 5).

- **No two persons with a CTSD have exactly the same symptoms.** Each CTSD symptom can take many forms and may have highly variable degrees of intensity, duration, modes, and timing of expression. For example, the CTSD feature of "emotion dysregulation" might include (but not be limited to) any or all the following: (1) extremely intense states of negative emotion (which could involve many different emotion states); (2) extreme numbing or absence of negative or positive emotions (or both), known as *alexithymia*; and (3) difficulty in recovering from extreme emotion states (which could take the form of physiological distress, diffuse or specific emotional distress, behavioral reactivity, impulsivity, risk taking, self-harm, aggressiveness, or withdrawal, interpersonal conflict, dependency, avoidance, or ambivalence) (see Chapters 15 and 17–21). What is crucial is to identify specific CTSD symptoms that are causing distress or functional impairment, and to provide treatment that directly targets those and any closely related symptoms that may be contributing to or exacerbating them.

- **It is important not to limit treatment for CTSDs to interventions that are efficacious for PTSD.** Other innovative therapies (Chapters 19–26) show promise in treating CTSDs. As noted in a recent editorial (Hoge & Chard, 2018), a range of trauma-focused treatments have been found to be effective for the symptoms of PTSD, but "the jury is still out" regarding other techniques that may be equally effective but await validation. A recent systematic review identified 15 evolving therapies and reported preliminary research support for some (Metcalf et al., 2016), including the somatosensory (Chapter 23), mindfulness (Chapter 25), and complementary healing (Chapter 26) modalities described in this book.

- **Psychoeducation is a crucial component in treatment across all therapy models for CTSDs.** Psychoeducation for clients with complex trauma histories provides an opportunity to inform them about the treatment process, their rights, and their mutual responsibilities with the therapist (see Chapter 4), and also is a crucial context and foundation for all subsequent therapeutic interactions and interventions. At a minimum, this involves providing a review of the nature of trauma and complex trauma, the symptoms of PTSD and CTSDs, including how these often go unrecognized as to their origin and are disconnected from lived experience as a result. Most psychotherapy models for CTSDs go further, providing psychoeducation that explains how CTSD symptoms are self-protective adaptations that occur as a healthy attempt to cope with and survive the harm caused by complex trauma, including the impact on the *body* (see Chapters 2, 18, 23, 24, and 26), for example, by describing how the body's innate stress response and the brain's alarm, memory, and executive processing centers shift into survival mode and can stay stuck in that mode if not reset (see Chapters 2 and 18). Psychoeducation also addresses the impact of CT on the self (see Chapters 12–15, 17, 18, and 23–26), for example, explaining how complex trauma can cause a child's emerging self to fixate or to fragment, leading to overwhelming feelings of fear, existential angst, and lack of meaning (see Chapters 6, 24, and 25). The impact of complex trauma on current relationships and the benefits of social support are other focal themes for psychoeducation (see Chapters 12, 14, and 17–21). A fourth psychoeducational focus involves the core beliefs and assumptions that are implanted or altered by the traumagenic dynamics of complex trauma (see Chapters 10–14 and 17–18).

- **Effective therapy for all types of trauma-related disorders, especially CTSDs, requires a solid and reliable relationship, and a collaborative therapeutic alliance** (Ellis, Simiola, Brown, Courtois, & Cook, 2018). Several key elements that have been empirically demonstrated to foster both a therapeutic alliance and positive psychotherapy outcomes are explicitly addressed by each therapy model described in this book (see Chapters 9–26): (1) nonjudgmental positive regard (Farber, Suzuki, & Lynch, 2018), (2) empathic (Elliott, Bohart, Watson, & Murphy, 2018) and genuine (Kolden, Wang, Austin, Chang, & Klein, 2018) validation of clients' feelings and beliefs in light of their unique life experiences (Goodwin, Coyne, & Constantino, 2018), (3) sensitivity to multicultural and other issues of diversity (Anderson, Bautista, & Hope, 2019; Davis et al., 2018), and (4) a clear, persuasive rationale for why the treatment process is a credible means of achieving the client's personal goals (Constantino, Coyne, Boswell, Iles, & Visla, 2018). Additionally, CTSD treatment can involve complex and intense countertransference reactions (Hayes, Gelso,

Goldberg, & Kivlighan, 2018) (see Chapters 3, 4, 6). Clients' disclosures of complex trauma histories and CTSD symptoms do not, in and of themselves, cause injury to therapists—instead, therapists are affected due to their caring and humanity, essential elements of effective therapy. However, vicarious exposure to clients' emotionally evocative complex trauma memories and resultant self-protective (but inadvertently hurtful or invalidating to others, as well as to the clients themselves) trauma-related adaptations, can trigger *adversarial* countertransference reactions by the therapist (Winnicott, 1949) (e.g., anger, hostility, blame, contempt, disappointment, disapproval, disgust, devaluation, indifference, and detachment). These reactions are not conventionally appropriate for a putatively caring and understanding therapist to have, yet they are understandable from the nonpathologizing perspective that therapists are human, too, and secondary traumatic stress reactions are parallel self-protective adaptations to those of the traumatized client (Sprang, Ford, Kerig, & Bride, 2019).

• **Many clients with CTSDs have remarkable innate resilience and strength, and some have supportive and healing relationships, but most have experienced decades of severe personal, familial, relational, and occupational/ socioeconomic distress and impairment.** In view of this, the therapy models in this book are designed to prevent clients from experiencing destabilization or worsening of symptoms or impairment that compromise their safety or basic functioning. In different ways, each therapy model also helps clients to be aware of and nonjudgmentally accepting of emotional distress, in order to escape the classic posttraumatic vicious cycle of avoidance that leads to escalating distress. Emotion acceptance is emphasized as a way to prevent extreme intrusive memories and hypervigilance (Chapters 15–18 and 23–26), dissociation (Chapters 6 and 23–24), or addiction (Chapter 22), as well as to foster positive change (Chapters 25–26). Attention to skills for emotion regulation (see Chapters 12–15, 17–18, and 20–25), somatic self-regulation (see Chapters 23, 24, and 26), interpersonal self-regulation (Chapters 12, 15–17, and 18–21), and cognitive self-regulation (Chapters 10–14, 17–18) also is emphasized across most CTSD treatment models. Client self-regulation is not simply a preparatory task, but is crucial to sustain throughout the entire therapy process and beyond. Optimally, it is modeled by and practiced with the therapist over the entire course of treatment and approached as a lifelong goal that extends to every aspect of the client's life for the rest of their lives.

• **Trauma memory processing (TMP) plays an important role in CTSD treatment and is a multifaceted process** (Ford, 2018). Systematic approaches to TMP were formalized in the 1980s and 1990s in pioneering therapies for PTSD such as prolonged exposure (Chapter 9), cognitive therapy (Chapter 10), cognitive processing therapy (Chapter 11), brief eclectic psychotherapy for PTSD (Chapter 12), eye movement desensitization and reprocessing therapy (Chapter 13), and narrative exposure therapy (Chapter 14). As is evident in the thoughtful guidance provided in those chapters for the application of each of these therapy models for those with CTSD symptoms, engaging the client as a fully informed and consenting partner who participates actively in doing the work and who learns to titrate the intensity and pacing of memory processing is a *sine qua non*. This is true for all clients but it has special significance when clients have endured coercion, exploitation, entrapment, rejection, or abandonment during or in the aftermath of complex trauma (see Chapters 3, 4, and 7).

In addition, trauma-focused therapies actively engage the client and therapist in a shared search for the personal meaning that complex trauma experiences had—and continue to have—for each unique client (Harvey, 1996). "Processing" trauma memories is a form of self-reflection, an examination of not only what happened but of how the event(s) altered the client's ways of feeling, perceiving, thinking, and relating to self and other human beings and the world—including core beliefs (Chapters 10–15, 17–26), emotion states (Chapters 12–15, 17–21, 23–26), body states (Chapters 2, 23, 24, and 26), relationship patterns and personal and interpersonal loss (Chapters 12, 14–17, and 20–24), and self-concept or identity (Chapters 6, 12–21, and 23–26). It is also geared to the identification of subcortical and somatically encoded implicit memory as well as cognitively based explicit memory (Chapter 2).

TMP is not necessarily limited to intensive recall of specific trauma memories. Indeed, the therapy models in this book emphasize the importance of *in vivo* recognition and reflection on daily life reminders (triggers or cues) of traumatic events, a key component of present-focused therapies for PTSD and CTSDs (Ford, 2018), as well as imaginal recall of trauma memories (see Chapters 9–19 and 22–24). In addition, some therapy models explicitly engage the client in the creation of a narrative not just of trauma memories but of their entire life and all formative experiences that the client considers important (see Chapters 12, 14, and 17–26). Somatosensory, energy, and experiential approaches focus on the client's experiencing and making changes that break the pattern of helplessness and reactivity through internally derived and body-based resources.

- **The exploration and construction of a life narrative is a central feature in CTSD treatments that do not formally require TMP but instead focus on helping clients to process the impact that traumatic experiences have had, and continue to have, in daily life.** Clients who are extremely phobic of trauma memories (Chapter 6), or who prefer for any reason not to repeatedly recall trauma memories, may be more willing to discuss aspects of their trauma and its impact and more likely to stick with therapy rather than dropping out (Ford, 2017), if given permission not to do intensive imaginal TMP and instead are provided with therapy focused on present-day concerns and experiences and learning tools for self-reflection and experiencing in the moment (person-centered and present-centered treatment). Beginning with trauma-focused and present-centered therapy can open the door to engaging in TMP for reluctant clients: knowing they are not required to do TMP can show clients that they are full partners in choices about their treatment, and not subject to the coercion that so often occurs in complex trauma.

A hallmark of CTSDs is a pervasive sense on the part of survivors that traumatic events define who they are, what their lives have been, and what they will be going forward. Discovering meaning and a coherent path and set of goals in life is often a major revelation for complex trauma survivors who may have long been entrapped in survival mode thinking and functioning, and never had a life narrative with flow and connection. A life narrative providing evidence of not only trauma but also courage, determination, integrity, talent, intelligence—and the capacity to both be cared about and caring of others—offers a basis for envisioning a safer and better future. Creating a life narrative also can help clients to recognize and grieve—rather than attempting to forget, minimize, or deny—important life interruptions and losses that otherwise might lead to the complications of unresolved bereavement (Eisma & Lenferink, 2018; Robinaugh, Millner, & McNally, 2016).

• **Complex trauma frays, strains, severs, breaks, and even destroys crucial social bonds and interferes with the development of healthy and sustaining relationships.** Several therapy models described in this book specifically emphasize assisting clients in recognizing how complex trauma has shaped their core relational beliefs, fears, expectations, hopes, and styles, as well as their behavioral engagement in (or disengagement from) relationships, including therapy (see Chapters 6, 12, 14–21, and 24). The emotion-focused therapy for trauma (Chapter 15), interpersonal psychotherapy (Chapter 16), and family systems (Chapters 20–21) models particularly emphasize examining past and current relationships that involved or were affected by complex trauma. Other therapy models teach or support the use of behavioral and cognitive skills for interpersonal effectiveness (Chapters 15–19 and 21). Across the therapy models, the troubled and often extremely traumatic relational history of clients with CTSDs is explicitly recognized and addressed by encouraging—or systematically assisting (Chapters 10–21)—clients to challenge overly restrictive beliefs about other people that may interfere with relationships with others and the teaching of self-affirming approaches and skills for engaging in healthy relationships. Also important with regard to relationships of clients with complex trauma histories is to restore (or develop anew) the capacity to engage in relationships on a genuinely reciprocal and appropriately intimate basis (i.e., neither ambivalently avoidant and detached, nor self-diminishing/ overly compliant, demanding, or enmeshed). Avoidance and detachment are self-protective reactions when complex trauma has altered or toxified key relationships, and are interpersonal expressions of the shift to a "survival brain" (see Chapter 2) rather than readily modifiable conscious choices or preferences. Thus, therapeutic repair of the relational harm done by complex trauma is critical and involves helping survivors to mindfully recognize (Chapters 4 and 25) many of the relational difficulties as survival tactics from the past that can be modified in different conditions. They can learn to intentionally choose how they will engage in current-day relationships, rather than relying reflexively on those relational survival tactics and attachment styles based on the past (Chapters 15–18, 20, and 21). In terms of attachment theory, the change from insecure/disorganized attachment styles to a more secure style (often described as *earned security*) is facilitated by the relationship with the therapist (and other healthy friends, family members, and intimates) who are attuned to the individual, attentive/curious, interactive, and responsive (Chapters 4, 6–7, 20, and 23–24).

- **Ultimately, trauma-related dysregulation in the bodily, affective, cognitive, and relational domains undermine the development and preservation of a healthy sense of self.** The personal and relational manifestation of a damaged self requires careful therapeutic assessment, in order not to assume that any single (or combined) form of self-disturbance characterizes each survivor of complex trauma. Assessment tools for self-disturbances are available but, as described in Chapter 5, most have relatively limited evidence of accuracy in detecting the more nuanced forms of damage to the self with complex trauma survivors specifically. Careful and empathic clinical engagement and observation therefore are essential for the therapist to accurately determine the exact nature of each client's sense of self and identity.

Complex trauma also often disconnects survivors from their culture and community (Summerfield, 2017), both in mass or historical traumas, such as genocide, war, pervasive racism, or institutional victimization (Goldsmith, Martin, & Smith, 2014; Kirmayer, Gone, & Moses, 2014; Nutton & Fast, 2015), and in more private traumas, such as sexual or emotional abuse, or family violence in which survivors are deliberately degraded and isolated by perpetrators (often family members or other intimates) or are again betrayed or stigmatized following a disclosure. Culture-bound definitions of what constitutes a psychiatric syndrome and culturally specific idioms of distress (Kohrt et al., 2014), along with injunctions against "airing one's dirty laundry" and bringing shame to one's group, can amplify these ill effects or prevent complex trauma survivors from being accurately assessed or from seeking or receiving effective therapy or other recovery services (de Jong, Komproe, Spinazzola, van der Kolk, & Van Ommeren, 2005).

Several populations whose members are at risk for complex trauma and CTSDs have distinctive life contexts that require sensitivity and affirmative collaboration for recovery and healing to occur (see Chapter 7). These include, but are not limited to (1) male survivors of sexual abuse; (2) children and adults who have been trafficked; (3) child and adult survivors of ethnic violence (including sexual enslavement/human trafficking and child soldiers); (4) LGBTQ youth and adults; (5) populations that have experienced historical culturally based colonialism trauma and continuing racial discrimination, including forced removal from families and placement in residential schools, and genocide; (6) homeless and chronically impoverished and displaced children, adults, and families; (7) victims of clergy abuse; (8) victims of cultic groups, often led by a charismatic but toxic narcissist; (9) children and adults with physical and mental disabilities; (10) asylum-seeking immigrant/refugees (including children forcibly separated from adult caregivers); and (11) victims of sexual harassment and abuse in fiduciary relationships (including therapy) and organizations.

- **An ultimate challenge for therapists is to use the reflective processing practices and self-regulation skills—the same ones they offer to clients—to be fully present emotionally, cognitively, and physically in assisting the client in treatment.** Ongoing attention to one's own emotional and physical health, and to approaching the work with an inner sense of attachment security is essential in order to engage *reflectively* and *not reflexively* over the course of the often lengthy therapeutic engagement with each unique client. This exceedingly delicate and demanding challenge must be met in order to be able to effectively engage in relational repair with the client when CTSDs lead to ruptures, impasses, misunderstandings, or even therapeutic mistakes in the therapy process. It is difficult to bear witness to complex trauma and its impact. The repercussions on helpers are now well recognized as secondary traumatic stress (Sprang et al., 2019) and vicarious traumatization (see Chapters 4 and 8). Clients with a complex trauma history often come to therapy with an unstated (and often unrecognized) hope that the therapist somehow can provide emotional stability and psychological tools that will transform inchoate distress into a knowable and solvable set of challenges (see Chapter 4). There also is the wish that the therapist has some "magic" that no one else has, or has been willing to share, to make life seem livable and worth living—and the fear that there is no such magic or anyone generous enough to bestow it. While therapists have no such magic, when they bring a high level of trauma-specific competence and a dedication to maintaining their own self-regulation to the therapy, they can offer clients both an immediate role model and a highly attuned therapeutic guide.

Thus, the CTSD psychotherapy models described in this book offer, and recommend, follow-up supervision/consultation and certification by their providers. Organizations such as the International and European Societies for Traumatic Stress Studies, the International and European Societies for the Study of Trauma and Dissociation, other traumatic stress societies in Asia, Australia, and North and South America, the Trauma Psychology Division (56) of the American Psychological Association, the National Child Traumatic Stress Network, the Academy on Violence and Abuse, the American Professional Society on the Abuse of Children, and the National Center for PTSD, among others, offer professionals a wealth of educational and professional practice through their websites, resource centers, and journals. We strongly suggest that all therapists avail themselves of these resources, in order to heed Courtois's elaboration of the Hippocratic oath: not only "Do No Harm," but "Do No *More* Harm" to clients with trauma histories (Courtois & Ford, 2013), so that the traumatic injuries they have already sustained in their lives are healed, and never disregarded, or compounded, by their treatment.

References

Anderson, K. N., Bautista, C. L., & Hope, D. A. (2019). Therapeutic alliance, cultural competence and minority status in premature termination of psychotherapy. *American Journal of Orthopsychiatry, 89*(1), 104–114.

Böttche, M., Ehring, T., Kruger-Gottschalk, A., Rau, H., Schafer, I., Schellong, J., . . . Knaevelsrud, C. (2018). Testing the ICD-11 proposal for complex PTSD in trauma-exposed adults: Factor structure and symptom profiles. *European Journal of Psychotraumatology, 9*(1), 1512264.

Brewin, C. R., Cloitre, M., Hyland, P., Shevlin, M., Maercker, A., Bryant, R. A., . . . Reed, G. M. (2017). A review of current evidence regarding the ICD-11 proposals for diagnosing PTSD and complex PTSD. *Clinical Psychology Review, 58*, 1–15.

Bryant, R. A. (2012). Simplifying complex PTSD: Comment on Resick et al. (2012). *Journal of Traumatic Stress, 25*(3), 252–253; discussion 253–260.

Constantino, M. J., Coyne, A. E., Boswell, J. F., Iles, B. R., & Visla, A. (2018). A meta-analysis of the association between patients' early perception of treatment credibility and their posttreatment outcomes. *Psychotherapy, 55*(4), 486–495.

Courtois, C. A., & Ford, J. D. (2013). *Treating complex trauma: A sequenced relationship-based approach.* New York: Guilford Press.

Davis, D. E., DeBlaere, C., Owen, J., Hook, J. N., Rivera, D. P., Choe, E., . . . Placeres, V. (2018). The multicultural orientation framework: A narrative review. *Psychotherapy (Chicago), 55*(1), 89–100.

de Jong, J., Komproe, I. H., Spinazzola, J., van der Kolk, B. A., & Van Ommeren, M. H. (2005). DESNOS in three postconflict settings: Assessing cross-cultural construct equivalence. *Journal of Traumatic Stress, 18*(1), 13–21.

Eisma, M. C., & Lenferink, L. I. M. (2018). Response to: Prolonged grief disorder for ICD-11: The primacy of clinical utility and international applicability. *European Journal of Psychotraumatology, 9*(1), 1512249.

Elliott, R., Bohart, A. C., Watson, J. C., & Murphy, D. (2018). Therapist empathy and client outcome: An updated meta-analysis. *Psychotherapy, 55*(4), 399–410.

Ellis, A. E., Simiola, V., Brown, L., Courtois, C., & Cook, J. M. (2018). The role of evidence-based therapy relationships on treatment outcome for adults with trauma: A systematic review. *Journal of Trauma and Dissociation, 19*(2), 185–213.

Farber, B. A., Suzuki, J. Y., & Lynch, D. A. (2018). Positive regard and psychotherapy outcome: A meta-analytic review. *Psychotherapy, 55*(4), 411–423.

Ford, J. D. (2017). Emotion regulation and skills-based interventions. In J. Cook, S. Gold, & C. Dalenberg (Eds.), *Handbook of trauma psychology* (Vol. 2, pp. 227–252). Washington, DC: American Psychological Association.

Ford, J. D. (2018). Trauma memory processing in PTSD psychotherapy: A unifying framework. *Journal of Traumatic Stress, 31*, 933–942.

Ford, J. D., Courtois, C. A., Steele, K., van der Hart, O., & Nijenhuis, E. R. (2005). Treatment of complex posttraumatic self-dysregulation. *Journal of Traumatic Stress, 18*(5), 437–447.

Ford, J. D., Spinazzola, J., van der Kolk, B., & Grasso, D. (2018). Toward an empirically based developmental trauma disorder diagnosis for children: Factor structure, item characteristics, reliability, and validity of the Developmental Trauma Disorder Semi-Structured Interview (DTD-SI). *Journal of Clinical Psychiatry, 79*(5), e1–e9.

Goldsmith, R. E., Martin, C. G., & Smith, C. P. (2014). Systemic trauma. *Journal of Trauma and Dissociation, 15*(2), 117–132.

Goodwin, B. J., Coyne, A. E., & Constantino, M. J. (2018). Extending the context-responsive psychotherapy integration framework to cultural processes in psychotherapy. *Psychotherapy (Chicago), 55*(1), 3–8.

Harvey, M. (1996). An ecological view of psychological trauma and trauma recovery. *Journal of Traumatic Stress, 9*, 3–23.

Hayes, J. A., Gelso, C. J., Goldberg, S., & Kivlighan, D. M. (2018). Countertransference management and effective psychotherapy: Meta-analytic findings. *Psychotherapy,* 55(4), 496–507.

Herman, J. L. (2012). CPTSD is a distinct entity: Comment on Resick et al. (2012). *Journal of Traumatic Stress, 25*(3), 256–257.

Hoge, C. W., & Chard, K. M. (2018). A window into the evolution of trauma-focused psychotherapies for posttraumatic stress disorder. *Journal of the American Medical Association, 319*(4), 343–345.

Karatzias, T., Cloitre, M., Maercker, A., Kazlauskas, E., Shevlin, M., Hyland, P., . . . Brewin, C. R. (2017). PTSD and Complex PTSD: ICD-11 updates on concept and measurement in the UK, USA, Germany and Lithuania. *European Journal of Psychotraumatology, 8*(Suppl. 7), 1418103.

Kirmayer, L. J., Gone, J. P., & Moses, J. (2014). Rethinking historical trauma. *Transcultural Psychiatry, 51*(3), 299–319.

Kohrt, B. A., Rasmussen, A., Kaiser, B. N., Haroz, E. E., Maharjan, S. M., Mutamba, B. B., . . . Hinton, D. E. (2014). Cultural concepts of distress and psychiatric disorders: Literature review and research recommendations for global mental health epidemiology. *International Journal of Epidemiology, 43*(2), 365–406.

Kolden, G. G., Wang, C. C., Austin, S. B., Chang, Y., & Klein, M. H. (2018). Congruence/genuineness: A meta-analysis. *Psychotherapy (Chicago), 55*(4), 424–433.

Metcalf, O., Varker, T., Forbes, D., Phelps, A., Dell, L., DiBattista, A., . . . O'Donnell, M. (2016). Efficacy of fifteen emerging interventions for the treatment of posttraumatic stress disorder: A systematic review. *Journal of Traumatic Stress, 29*(1), 88–92.

Murphy, S., Elklit, A., Dokkedahl, S., & Shevlin, M. (2018a). Testing competing factor models of the latent structure of post-traumatic stress disorder and complex post-traumatic stress disorder according to ICD-11. *European Journal of Psychotraumatology, 9*(1), 1457393.

Murphy, S., Hansen, M., Elklit, A., Yong Chen, Y., Raudzah Ghazali, S., & Shevlin, M. (2018b). Alternative models of DSM-5 PTSD: Examining diagnostic implications. *Psychiatry Research, 262,* 378–383.

Nutton, J., & Fast, E. (2015). Historical trauma, substance use, and Indigenous peoples: Seven generations of harm from a "Big Event." *Substance Use and Misuse, 50*(7), 839–847.

Resick, P. A., Bovin, M. J., Calloway, A. L., Dick, A. M., King, M. W., Mitchell, K. S., . . . Wolf, E. J. (2012). A critical evaluation of the complex PTSD literature: Implications for DSM-5. *Journal of Traumatic Stress, 25*(3), 241–251.

Robinaugh, D. J., Millner, A. J., & McNally, R. J. (2016). Identifying highly influential nodes in the complicated grief network. *Journal of Abnormal Psychology, 125*(6), 747–757.

Sachser, C., Keller, F., & Goldbeck, L. (2017). Complex PTSD as proposed for ICD-11: Validation of a new disorder in children and adolescents and their response to trauma-focused cognitive behavioral therapy. *Journal of Child Psychology and Psychiatry, 58*(2), 160–168.

Shevlin, M., Hyland, P., Karatzias, T., Fyvie, C., Roberts, N., Bisson, J. I., . . . Cloitre, M. (2017). Alternative models of disorders of traumatic stress based on the new ICD-11 proposals. *Acta Psychiatrica Scandinavica, 135*(5), 419–428.

Shevlin, M., Hyland, P., Roberts, N. P., Bisson, J. I., Brewin, C. R., & Cloitre, M. (2018). A psychometric assessment of disturbances in self-organization symptom indicators for ICD-11 complex PTSD using the International Trauma Questionnaire. *European Journal of Psychotraumatology, 9*(1), 1419749.

Sprang, G., Ford, J. D., Kerig, P. K., & Bride, B. (2019). Defining secondary traumatic stress and developing targeted assessments and interventions: Lessons learned from research and leading experts. *Traumatology, 25*(2), 72–81.

Summerfield, D. (2017). Culture and PTSD: Trauma in global and historical perspective. *British Journal of Psychiatry, 210*(3), 234.

van der Kolk, B., Ford, J. D., & Spinazzola, J. (2019). Comorbidity of developmental trauma disorder and posttraumatic stress disorder: Findings from the DTD field trial. *European Journal of Psychotraumatology, 10*(1), 1562841.

Winnicott, D. W. (1949). Hate in the counter-transference. *International Journal of Psychoanalysis, 30,* 69–74.

Afterword

BESSEL A. VAN DER KOLK

Over the past two decades, vast amounts of knowledge have accumulated about what we call "complex trauma," a psychiatric condition that officially does not exist, but which possibly constitutes the most common set of psychological problems to drive human beings into psychiatric care. In some respects, we have emerged from the Dark Ages. Back in 1974, when I was studying for my Board examinations, Freedman and Kaplan's *Comprehensive Textbook of Psychiatry* still stated that "incest is extremely rarely, and does not occur in more than 1 out of 1.1 million people" (Henderson, 1975, p. 1536). Over 30 years ago, this leading textbook of psychiatry still made what is now clearly known to be an egregious misstatement of the issue:

There is little agreement about the role of . . . incest as a source of serious subsequent psychopathology. The father–daughter liaison satisfies instinctual drives in a setting where mutual alliance with an omnipotent adult condones the transgression. . . . The act offers an opportunity to test in reality an infantile fantasy whose consequences are found to be gratifying and pleasurable. . . . Such incestuous activity diminishes the subject's chance of psychosis and allows for a better adjustment to the external world. . . . The vast majority of them were none the worse for the experience.

A host of information over the past three decades has shown how wrong Henderson was about aftereffects of childhood trauma: During the 1970s, case reports of sexual abuse and incest started to appear in the medical literature, and today we know that, each year, about 3 million children in the United States are reported to Child Protective Services for child abuse and neglect. Childhood sexual abuse and other forms of maltreatment are now known to consistently lead to severe problems with self-regulation, ranging from psychological and behavioral problems, such as extreme fluctuations of anger and anxiety, to impaired immunological functioning and changes in coordination, balance, and cognitive development. Though it is difficult to come up with exact figures, a national survey concluded that more than 1 in 4 girls and 1 in 20 boys in the United States had been sexually abused or assaulted by age 17 (Finkelhor, Shattuck, Turner, & Hamby, 2014), and comparable rates have been reported in Europe but rates are much higher (approaching or exceeding 1 in 3 girls) in Africa, Asia, and Central America (Singh, Parsekar, & Nair, 2014). Numerous epidemiological studies have shown how early adverse experiences increase the individual's chances to grow up depressed, hooked on alcohol and drugs, engaged in self-destructive activities, suffering from numerous medical illnesses, and with deeply unsatisfactory interpersonal relationships.

In reaction to abuse and neglect, the brain is programmed to adapt in a state of defensive adaptation, which enhances survival in a world of constant danger, but often at significant cost. Being dependent on hostile or severely misattuned caregivers may interfere with the necessary developmental capacities to become a focused, thoughtful, and well-regulated human being. Early exposure to danger molds mind and brain to make a person more irritable, impulsive, suspicious, and compelled to engage in fight-or-flight reactions (Heim, 2018; Teicher & Sampson, 2016).

We slowly are learning that how we understand trauma is much like the proverbial blind men giving their opinions about the true nature of an elephant: whether they focus on the tusks, trunks, ears, or tail, different wise men will make very different observations and come to vastly different conclusions. Psychologists, by virtue of the training, are conditioned to frame the issue in terms of abnormal behaviors, issues that should be resolved by talking about what happened in order to gain a deeper understanding and insight about oneself, in the context of a warm and supportive relationship. Psychopharmacologists are likely to conceptualize complex trauma in terms of abnormalities in the brain's dopamine and serotonin systems, to be resolved by the administration of substances (i.e., drugs) that will supposedly correct these chemical abnormalities, while neuroscientists are likely to focus on overactive fear detection systems and defective neural pathways. It does not stop there: Occupational therapists might readily observe serious sensory integration abnormalities (Reynolds et al., 2017); yoga teachers and martial artists are likely to observe awkward body movements and difficulties being physically attuned to one's body sensations and movements (Cramer, Anheyer, Saha, & Dobos, 2018). Neurofeedback practitioners might focus on abnormal neural connectivity between different parts of the brain (Panisch & Hai, 2018), while sensorimotor therapists would focus on body awareness; those trained in internal family systems therapy correctly point out how trauma causes people to develop extreme mental and physiological states, in which different internal managers and firefighters dictate radically different behaviors over time, which results in starkly different mental states and presentations under different circumstances (Schwartz, 1994). People familiar with the polyvagal theory are likely to focus on how trauma interferes with the development of the capacity to feel physically safe, and being able to filter relevant from irrelevant stimuli (Porges & Dana, 2018).

It is important to realize that all these observations are potentially valid, and all may need to be addressed in order to come to a full resolution. As time goes on, it is likely that a whole range of additional perspectives will emerge—after all, this whole field is only about three decades old, and look how many different perspectives have developed in such a short period of time. The sad issue is that therapists have a tendency to identify themselves with the latest technique that they have learned rather than with a comprehensive assessment of all the problems that need to be assessed. Of course, having a deeply flawed diagnostic framework, such as DSM-5 currently, is a major impediment to clinicians thoroughly evaluating the entire range of issues to be addressed with every particular traumatized individual they encounter.

Over the past few decades we have learned a great deal about brain development and how exploration and play in the context of secure attachment promote intelligence, collaboration, curiosity, and mental flexibility. In contrast, fear interferes with self-regulation, imagination, and empathy for self and others. Since the central nervous system matures in a use-dependent fashion (Perry, 2002), the brain areas that are most intensely stimulated in a growing child develop most vigorously: Safe children develop imagination, play, and curiosity, while terrified children cultivate strong alarm systems, defensive postures, and warning signals.

Play and exploration are critical prerequisites for optimal brain development in both humans and animals (Panksepp, 1998). Being raised in a safe context promotes the development of executive functioning, which includes learning to anticipate the feelings and reactions of the people around you, as well as developing the capacity to modulate your impulses. As they mature, children progressively become less reactive, less impulsive, and more "thoughtful" as they make increasingly complex appraisals of the world around them. Eventually, well-developed brains contain minds that can make decisions that incorporate a variety of points of view—an internal representation of themselves within the continuity of past and future, and the capacity to imagine a variety of different outcomes, depending on what action they decide to take.

Since the time of Hughlings Jackson (1958), it has been known that fear, danger, and other forms of excessive arousal deactivate higher brain areas that promote a flexible response to the environment. Stress, fear, and uncertainty stimulate abnormal autonomic nervous system activity of the brainstem (Porges & Dana, 2018), while predictable, attuned rhythmical interactions with caregivers, teachers, and classmates stimulate the development of brain areas related to safety, play, and exploration.

If children are well cared for, they learn how to deal with frustration with active assistance from caregiving adults, who help them modulate their arousal levels—by defining the problem, showing them how to do things, taking over when they cannot do the task themselves, and holding and rocking them when they are distressed. By means of attunement and mirroring by caregivers, children gradually learn to deal with frustrations and disappointments without kicking, screaming, or otherwise taking their misery out on those around them. Secure children also learn to deal with aggravation without feeling that this is proof that they are evil, inadequate, or doomed. Persistent fear activates primitive self-preservation systems in the brain at the expense of those involved in play and exploration. This interferes with learning to regulate arousal. Arousal modulation is essential for being able to imagine a variety of options and for feeling empathy for oneself and for others.

It is a sad reality that as our society in general and our profession in particular have become more and more technically proficient and knowledgeable about brain development, we often seem to lose track of the context in which human beings develop and thrive. Science has clearly supported what most human beings instinctively know: that secure attachment bonds are essential for the proper development of optimal cognitive and interpersonal functioning (e.g., Lyons-Ruth, Riley, Patrick, & Hobson, 2019).

Remarkably, even though research has shown that the majority of psychiatric inpatients have histories of having been molested, abused, or abandoned by a caregiver, and even though the consequences of adverse childhood experiences constitute the single largest public health problem in the United States (Fellitti et al., 1998) and, likely, worldwide, there is enormous resistance to place the care and feeding of developing human beings where it belongs: at the forefront of our attention. There continues to be vastly more funding for studying the genetic components of mental illness, and for relatively obscure disorders such as obsessive–compulsive disorder, than for preventing and treating the long-term effects of child abuse and neglect (van der Kolk, Crozier, & Hopper, 2001; Teicher & Sampson, 2016; Putnam, 2003).

Child abuse and neglect are tragically common. Despite the fact that research has repeatedly demonstrated that human beings who are exposed to betrayal, abandonment, and abuse by their caretakers suffer from vastly more complex psychobiological disturbances than human beings who are victims of earthquakes and motor vehicle accidents (van der Kolk, Roth, Pelcovitz, Sunday, & Spinazzola, 2005), our diagnostic system continues to lump all trauma-related symptomatology under the category of "posttraumatic stress disorder" (PTSD). Clinicians have always dealt with patients with complex trauma histories. For more than a century, people like Pierre Janet, Morton Prince, Sandor Ferenczi, and Leonard Shengold have provided us with luminous case descriptions and treatment reports about these patients. Reading them can be as fresh and illuminating as the best work of our contemporaries. However, what is new is the contribution by the brain sciences to a more precise understanding of the nature of the damage caused by chronic developmental trauma. The evolving knowledge about the biological underpinnings of the injuries caused by child maltreatment also invites us to explore, and to possibly radically expand, treatment directions for the future.

In the 1980s, Arthur Green and Dorothy Otnow Lewis wrote the first papers documenting that many abused children showed evidence of neurological damage, even when there were no reports of head injury (Teicher, Tomoda, & Andersen, 2006). In a study by Robert Davies and colleagues of 22 sexually abused patients, 77% had abnormal brain waves and 36% had seizures (Ito, Teicher, Glod, & Ackerman, 1998). This was the first concrete evidence that human abuse and neglect affect the development of vulnerable brain regions. Subsequent research has shown that when traumatized individuals are reminded of traumatic experiences, there is increased activation in brain regions that support intense emotions and decreased activation in brain regions involved in (1) the integration of sensory input with motor output, (2) the modulation of physiological arousal, and (3) the capacity to communicate experience in words (Rauch et al., 1996). The research by Martin Teicher, Michael DeBellis, Ruth Lanius, Christine Heim, Paul Plotsky, and many others has begun to delineate a constellation of brain abnormalities associated with childhood abuse. The results are quite consistent across studies: When a person is in a persistent low-level fear state, the primary areas of the brain that are processing information develop differently. Frightened people are dominated by subcortical and limbic activity. As a result, they tend to base their appraisal of what is happening on nonverbal information such as facial expressions, gestures, and arousal states.

Alarm states erase people's sense of time: In brain scans, one can observe decreased activation of these cortical areas when subjects are exposed to reminders of their traumatic experiences (Hopper, Frewen, van der Kolk, & Lanius, 2007; Lanius, Williamson, & Densmore, 2001). Cut adrift from internal regulating capabilities of the cortex, the brainstem acts reflexively, impulsively, and aggressively to any perceived threat. In alarm states, contemplation of the consequences of one's behavior is almost impossible. Because the brain areas responsible for executive functioning go offline under threat, frightened people lose touch with the flow of time and the knowledge that every sensation has a beginning, middle, and end—they get stuck in a terrifying, seemingly never-ending present. As a result, they are desperate for immediate relief, and delayed gratification is difficult, if not impossible.

The documentation of these abnormalities goes a long way in explaining why traumatized individuals usually have little idea what upsets them so much, and so little control over their reactions. One needs a well-functioning left prefrontal cortex to know one's feelings and grasp the effects of one's actions. Not really knowing what one feels and having no idea how one's actions affect other people go hand in hand with blowing up in response to minor provocations, with automatically freezing when frustrated, and with feeling helpless in the face of trivial challenges. To observers who do not understand that reminders of the past activate terror-inducing physical sensations, these emotional reactions appear bizarre, and the behavior reprehensible and in need of control and suppression.

The foundation of self-experience is grounded in the capacity to identify and utilize physical sensations (Damasio, 1999). When infants have upsetting sensations, they use their facial expressions, body movements, and vocal cords to ensure that their caregivers stop what they are doing and do whatever it takes to change the way the infants feel. Most caregiving interactions are able to change children's sensations and restore their inner balance. When moving and crying fail to elicit a caring response, children change their strategy. Crittenden (1998) and Fosha (2003) have described three ways in which children learn to cope with consistently unresponsive caregivers. One is "feeling but not dealing": getting stuck on a continuous alarm or defeat response that does not significantly change even when people around them seem to respond appropriately. No amount of care seems to be able to provide a sense of safety and comfort. These children seem to be stuck in a continuous state of alarm, which becomes independent from actual threat. The second adaptation is "dealing but not feeling": coping by shutting down. When this occurs, the children continue to be able to function despite inadequate caregiving by learning to ignore physical sensations and warning signs. They develop "alexithymia," in which they are plagued by unpleasant physical sensations that are disconnected from emotional experience. Emotions lose their function as warning signals. These individuals cannot use their feelings to adjust how they relate to other people and are prone to respond to stress with physical problems. The third form of coping has been called "neither feeling nor dealing," the sort of disorganized response that is most common in abused and neglected children who end up in residential treatment centers and chronic psychiatric care.

When parents and children can freely use language to communicate what they see and hear, and when children are encouraged to name and reflect on all aspects of reality, they learn to name what they see and articulate what they need. However, when reality is terrifying and experience is denied, children have trouble putting their inner world into communicable language. As Bowlby (1990) said, "What cannot be communicated to the (m)other cannot be communicated to the self" (p. 61). Research shows that lack of verbal interaction with caregivers, or the deliberate denial of certain aspects of reality, leads to decreased intelligence, decreased school performance, loss of focus, and increased dissociation (Pollak, Cicchetti, & Klorman, 1998). Traumatized individuals have more selective development of nonverbal cognitive capacities. People raised in the vortex of violence have learned that nonverbal information is more critical for survival than words.

Implications for Clinical Assessment and Treatment

Over the past two decades, there have been significant advances in the assessment and treatment of complexly traumatized people. Many of these have their foundation in the increased understanding of how trauma affects the developing brain and self-perception. Contemporary neuroscience research suggests that effective treatment needs to involve (1) learning to modulate arousal,

(2) learning to tolerate feelings and sensations by increasing the capacity for interoception, and (3) learning that after confrontation with physical helplessness, it is essential to engage in taking effective action.

Describing traumatic experiences in conventional verbal therapy runs the risk of activating implicit memory systems, that is, trauma-related physical sensations and physiological hyper- or hypoarousal. The very act of talking about one's traumatic experiences can make trauma victims feel hyperaroused, terrified, and unsafe. These reactions can aggravate posttraumatic helplessness, fear, shame, and rage. In order to avoid this situation, chronically traumatized individuals are prone to seek a supportive therapeutic relationship in which the therapist becomes a refuge from a life of anxiety and ineffectiveness rather than someone to help them process the imprints of their traumatic experiences. Learning to autonomously modulate one's arousal level is essential for overcoming the passivity and dependency associated with a fear of reliving the trauma.

Most clinicians agree that being able to regulate affective arousal is critical to being able to tolerate effective trauma-processing therapy. In recent years, there has been an increasing awareness that people have built-in ways of regulating themselves. Interestingly, there is little in the Western tradition that cultivates this inborn capacity—there always has been a tendency to believe that one can lead "a better life through chemistry." In Western cultures, alcohol traditionally has served as the primary way of dealing with excessive arousal and fear. During the past century, alcohol was gradually condemned as a way of coping, and psychopharmacological agents were increasingly substituted to help disturbed people "get a grip." However, in other, largely non-Western cultures, there are long traditions of cultivating the capacity to regulate one's physiological system. Examples are chi qong and tai chi in China, yoga in India, and drumming in Africa. All of these self-regulatory practices involve the activation of the 10th cranial nerve, the vagus nerve, which, as Darwin (1872/1898) already pointed out in *The Expression of the Emotions in Man and Animals*, is the principal pathway to emotion regulation between brain and body.

Contemporary research is beginning to support the notion that breathing, moving, chanting, tapping acupressure points, and engaging in rhythmical activities with other human beings can have a profound effect on physiological arousal systems. Clinicians are gradually learning that bodily sensations that have become dulled by avoidance of painful stimuli need to be reawakened and activated in order to help clients regain a sense of pleasure and engagement. Our initial studies utilizing yoga for complex trauma have been very promising (van der Kolk, 2006), and we are hopeful that this work will be just the beginning of the exploration of effective body-based self-regulatory practices.

Interoceptive, body-oriented therapies can directly deal with a core clinical issue in PTSD: Traumatized individuals are prone to experience the present with physical sensations and emotions that are associated with their traumatic past, and to act accordingly. For therapy to be effective, it is useful to focus on the patient's physical self-experience and increase his or her self-awareness rather than to focus exclusively on the meaning that people make of their experience—their narrative of the past. If past experience is embodied in current physiological states, and action tendencies and the trauma is reenacted in breath, gestures, sensory perceptions, movement, emotion, and thought, therapy may be most effective if it facilitates self-awareness and self-regulation. Once patients become aware of their sensations and action tendencies, they can set about discovering new ways of orienting themselves to their surroundings and exploring novel ways of engaging with potential sources of mastery and pleasure.

One of the most robust findings of the neuroimaging studies of PTSD is that, under stress, the higher brain areas involved in "executive functioning"—planning for the future, anticipating the consequences of one's actions, and inhibiting inappropriate responses—become less active. In particular, a well-functioning medial prefrontal cortex is essential to the extinction of conditioned fear responses (Morgan, Romanski, & LeDoux, 1993), by suppressing the stress response mediated by the hypothalamic–pituitary–adrenal axis. The fact that the medial prefrontal cortex, the brain region most implicated in interoceptive awareness, can directly influence emotional arousal has enormous clinical significance, since it suggests that the practice of mindfulness can enhance control over emotions.

Maybe one of the most profound lessons of the last 50 years has been that trauma that once was outside, and played itself out in a social setting, becomes lodged within people's internal experiences, in the very sinew and muscles of their organism. Deeply learning to tolerate, approach, befriend, and nurture one's deepest sensations and emotions becomes the greatest task of therapy. Clinical experience shows that traumatized individuals, as a rule, have great difficulty attending to their inner sensations and perceptions—when asked to focus on internal sensations, they tend to feel overwhelmed, or they deny having an inner sense of self. When they try to meditate, they often report becoming overwhelmed by being confronted with residues of trauma-related perceptions, sensations, and emotions; feeling disgusted with themselves, helpless, or panicked; or experiencing trauma-related images and physical sensations. Trauma victims tend to have a negative body image—as far as they are concerned, the less attention they pay to their bodies, and thereby their internal sensations, the better. Yet one cannot learn to take care of oneself without being in touch with the demands and requirements of one's physical self. In the field of traumatic stress disorders treatment, a consensus is emerging that, in order to keep old trauma from intruding into current experience, patients need to deal with the internal residues of the past. Neurobiologically speaking, they need to activate their medial prefrontal cortex, insula, and anterior cingulate by learning to tolerate orienting and focusing their attention on their internal experience, while interweaving and conjoining cognitive, emotional, and sensorimotor elements of their traumatic experience.

Traumatized individuals need to learn that it is safe to have feelings and sensations. If they learn to attend to inner experience, then they become aware that bodily experience never remains static. Unlike at the moment of a trauma, when everything seems to freeze in time, physical sensations and emotions are in a constant state of flux. Traumatized persons need to learn to tell the difference between a sensation and an emotion (How do you know you are angry/afraid? Where do you feel that in your body? Do you notice any impulses in your body to move in some way right now?). Once they realize that their internal sensations continuously shift and change, particularly if they learn to develop a certain degree of control over their physiological states by breathing and movement, they viscerally discover that remembering the past does not inevitably result in overwhelming emotions.

Lazar and colleagues (2005) at the Massachusetts General Hospital completed a functional magnetic resonance imaging study of 20 people engaged in meditation that involved sustained mindful attention to internal and external sensory stimuli and nonjudgmental awareness of present-moment stimuli without cognitive elaboration. They found that brain regions associated with attention, interoception, and sensory processing, including the prefrontal cortex and right anterior insula, were thicker in meditation participants than in matched controls. It has been proposed that by becoming increasingly more aware of sensory stimuli during formal practice, meditation practitioners gradually increase their capacity to navigate potentially stressful encounters that arise throughout the day. Lazar and colleagues' study lends support to the notion that treatment of traumatic stress may need to include becoming mindful, that is, learning to become a careful observer of the ebb and flow of internal experience, and noticing whatever thoughts, feelings, body sensations, and impulses emerge. In order to deal with the past, it is helpful for traumatized people to learn to activate their capacity for introspection and develop a deep curiosity about their internal experience. This is necessary in order for them to identify their physical sensations and to translate their emotions and sensations into communicable language—understandable, most of all, to themselves.

After having been traumatized, people often lose the effective use of fight-or-flight defenses and respond to perceived threat with immobilization. Attention to inner experience can help them to reorient themselves to the present by learning to attend to nontraumatic stimuli. According to LeDoux and Gorman (2001, p. 1954):

> By engaging these alternative pathways, passive fear responding is replaced with an active coping strategy. This diversion of information flow away from the central nucleus to the basal nucleus, and the learning that takes place, does not occur if the rat remains passive. It requires that the rat take action. It is "learning by doing," a process in which the success in terminating the conditioned stimulus reinforces the action taken.

The implications of this research are clear: Traumatized individuals need to engage in action that is pleasurable and effective, particularly in response to situations where in the past they were helpless and defeated. In our trauma center, we have a very active theater program for chronically traumatized adolescents that now has officially been declared an "evidence-based treatment," and we collaborate with programs such as Impact/Model Mugging to help traumatized people regain a sense of pleasure and competence as they take affective action (Kisiel et al., 2005; Macy et al., 2004).

We have rediscovered that traumatic memories are fragmented. Trauma is not primarily remembered as a story, but is stored in mind and brain as images, sounds, smells, physical sensations, and enactments. Our research showed that talking about traumatic events does not necessarily allow mind and brain to integrate the dissociated images and sensations into a coherent whole. Techniques other than figuring out, talking, and understanding have proven to be enormously helpful in the integration of these fragments of the traumatic past. In the early years of psychiatry, clinicians primarily used hypnosis for this purpose, but as yet we have no research to show how effective hypnosis was in accomplishing this.

Of course, one of the greatest challenges is that complex trauma is a condition that does not exist as a formally acknowledged disorder within the mental health field—with the partial exception of the European guidebook to medical diagnoses, the *International Classification of Diseases,* which includes a diagnosis of "enduring personality change after catastrophic experience" (F62.0). Despite valiant efforts to integrate complex types of diagnosis in DSM-IV (and attempts to do this again for DSM-5 under the rubric "developmental trauma disorder" [van der Kolk, 2005]), these patients do not have a diagnostic home; therefore, there is no real possibility that organized psychiatry and psychology can study people with complex trauma in a coherent fashion. As long as the various symptoms from which traumatized individuals suffer are relegated to seemingly disconnected diagnoses such as PTSD, attention-deficit/hyperactivity disorder (ADHD), bipolar illness, attachment disturbances, borderline personality disorder, and depression, it will be very difficult to systematically and scientifically study the full range of possible interventions to help human beings with complex trauma histories gain control over their lives.

Clinicians attempting to describe and understand the problems confronting patients who have complex trauma histories have had to go beyond the standard interview measures and diagnostic categories provided by the psychiatry profession. There is a remarkable array of psychometrically robust assessment measures that can help in this endeavor, as Briere and Spinazzola have thoroughly summarized in Chapter 5, on assessment of complex trauma sequelae. There also are frameworks for conceptualizing and developing treatment goals for complex traumatic stress disorders, as illustrated in the book's chapters on developmental neurobiology (Chapter 2) and emerging practice guidelines (Chapters 1 and 3).

It is ironic that, despite the fact that people with complex trauma histories probably make up the bulk of patients seen in mental health centers, they remain nameless and homeless. In the age of the genome project and highly evolved epidemiological methods and neuroimaging techniques, the treatment of chronically traumatized individuals fundamentally continues to play itself out on a village level of oral traditions and anecdotes. The profound clinical wisdom that results from intimate therapeutic interaction with chronically traumatized people continues to be largely anecdotal, and transmitted in supervision sessions, small conferences, and informal discussions among colleagues. Because dissociation is of little interest to mainstream psychology and psychiatry, it is not being studied systematically. Because affect regulation and its vicissitudes are not central to our scientific work, it is relegated to yoga studios, martial arts classes, and meditation centers. Because self-hatred and disgust are not understood as developmental inevitabilities after abuse and neglect, they are relegated to the realm of religion rather than the realm of science.

References

Bowlby, J. (1990). *The making and breaking of affectional bonds.* Boston: Routledge.

Cramer, H., Anheyer, D., Saha, F. J., & Dobos, G. (2018). Yoga for posttraumatic stress disorder—a systematic review and meta-analysis. *BMC Psychiatry, 18,* Article 72.

Crittenden, P. M. (1998). The developmental consequences of childhod sexual abuse. In P. K. Trickett & C. J. Schellenback (Eds.), *Violence against children in the family and the community* (pp. 11–38). Washington, DC: American Psychological Association.

Damasio, A. R. (1999). *The feeling of what happens: Body and emotion in the making on consciousness.* New York: Harcourt Brace.

Darwin, C. (1898). *The expression of the emotions in man and animals.* London: Greenwood Press. (Original work published 1872)

Felitti, V. J., Anda, R. F., Nordenberg, D., Williamson, D. F., Spitz, A. M., Edwards, V., . . . Marks, J. S. (1998). The relationship of adult health status to childhood abuse and household dysfunction. *American Journal of Preventive Medicine, 14,* 245–258.

Finkelhor, D., Turner, H. A., Shattuck, A., & Hamby, S. L. (2013). Violence, crime, and abuse exposure in a national sample of children and youth: An update. *Journal of American Medical Association Pediatrics, 167*(7), 614–621.

Fosha, D. (2003). Dyadic regulation and experiential work with emotion and relatedness in trauma and disorganized attachment. In M. F. Solomon & D. J. Siegel (Eds.), *Healing trauma: Attachment, mind, body, and brain* (pp. 221–281). New York: Norton.

Heim, C. (2018). Psychobiological consequences of child maltreatment. In J. G. Noll & I. Shalev (Eds.), *The biology of early life stress* (pp. 15–30). Cham, Switzerland: Springer.

Henderson, D. J. (1975). Incest. In A. M. Freedman, H. I. Kaplan, & B. J. Sadock (Eds.), *Comprehensive textbook of psychiatry* (Vol. 2, 2nd ed., p. 1536). Baltimore: Williams & Wilkins.

Hopper, J. H., Frewen, P., van der Kolk, B. A., & Lanius, R. A. (2007). Neural correlates of reexperiencing, avoidance, and dissociation in PTSD: Symptom dimensions and emotion dysregulation in responses to script-driven trauma imagery. *Journal of Traumatic Stress, 20,* 713–725.

Ito, Y., Teicher, M. H., Glod, C. A., & Ackerman, E. (1998). Preliminary evidence for aberrant cortical development in abused children: A quantitative EEG study. *Journal of Neuropsychiatry and Clinical Neuroscience, 10,* 298–307.

Jackson, J. H. (1958). Evolution and dissolution of the nervous system. In J. Taylor (Ed.), *Selected writings of John Hughlings Jackson* (pp. 45–118). London: Stapes Press.

Kisiel, C., Blaustein, M., Spinazzola, J., Swift, C., Zucker, M., & van der Kolk, B. A. (2005). Evaluation of a theater based youth violence prevention program for elementary school children. *Journal of School Violence, 5*(2), 19–36.

Lanius, R. A., Williamson, M., & Densmore, D. (2001). Neural correlates of traumatic memories in posttraumatic stress disorder: A functional MRI investigation. *American Journal of Psychiatry, 158*, 1920–1922.

Lazar, S., Kerr, C., Wasserman, R., Gray, J., Greve, D., & Treadway, M. (2005). Meditation experience is associated with increased cortical thickness. *NeuroReport, 16*, 1893–1897.

LeDoux, J. E., & Gorman. J. M. (2001). A call to action: Overcoming anxiety through active coping. *American Journal of Psychiatry, 158*, 1953–1955.

Lyons-Ruth, K., Riley, C., Patrick, M. P. H., & Hobson, R. P. (2019). Disinhibited attachment behavior among infants of mothers with borderline personality disorder, depression, and no diagnosis. *Personality Disorders, 10*(2), 163–172.

Macy, R. D., Behar, L., & Paulson, R., Delman, R., Schmid, L., & Smith, S. F. (2004). Community-based, acute posttraumatic stress management: A description and evaluation of a psychosocial–intervention continuum. *Harvard Review of Psychiatry, 12*, 217–228.

Morgan, M. A., Romanski, L. M., & LeDoux, J. E. (1993). Extinction of emotional learning: Contribution of medial prefrontal cortex. *Neuroscience Letters, 163*, 109–113.

Panisch, L. S., & Hai, A. H. (2018, January 1). The effectiveness of using neurofeedback in the treatment of post-traumatic stress disorder: A systematic review. *Trauma, Violence, and Abuse.* [Epub ahead of print]

Panksepp, J. (1998). *Affective neuroscience: The foundations of human and animal emotions.* New York: Oxford University Press.

Perry, B. D. (2002). The neurodevelopmental impact of violence in childhood. In D. H. Schetky & E. P. Benedek (Eds.), *Principles and practices of child and adolescent forensic psychiatry* (pp. 221–238). Washington, DC: American Psychiatric Publishing.

Pollak, S., Cicchetti, D., & Klorman, R. (1998). Stress, memory, and emotion: Developmental considerations from the study of child maltreatment. *Development and Psychopathology, 10*, 811–828.

Porges, S. W., & Dana, D. A. (2018). *Clinical applications of the polyvagal theory: The emergence of polyvagal-informed therapies* (Norton Series on Interpersonal Neurobiology). New York: Norton.

Putnam, F. W. (2003). Ten-year research update review: Child sexual abuse. *Journal of the American Academy of Child and Adolescent Psychiatry, 42*, 231–240.

Rauch, S., van der Kolk, B. A., Fisler, R., Alpert, N., Orr, S., Savage, C., . . . Pitman, R. K. (1996). Symptom provocation study using positron emission tomography and script driven imagery. *Archives of General Psychiatry, 53*, 380–387.

Reynolds, S., Glennon, T. J., Ausderau, K., Bendixen, R. M., Kuhaneck, H. M., Pfeiffer, B., . . . Bodison, S. C. (2017). Using a multifaceted approach to working with children who have differences in sensory processing and integration. *American Journal of Occupational Therapy, 71*(2), 7102360010p1–7102360010p10.

Schwartz, R. (1994). *The internal family systems model.* New York: Guilford Press.

Singh, M. M., Parsekar, S. S., & Nair, S. N. (2014). An epidemiological overview of child sexual abuse. *Journal of Family Medicine and Primary Care, 3*(4), 430.

Teicher, M. H., & Samson, J. A. (2016). Annual Research Review: Enduring neurobiological effects of childhood abuse and neglect. *Journal of Child Psychology and Psychiatry, 57*, 241–266.

Teicher, M. H., Tomoda, A., & Andersen, S. L. (2006). Neurobiological consequences of early stress and childhood maltreatment: Are results from human and animal studies comparable? *Annals of the New York Academy of Sciences, 1071*, 313–323.

van der Kolk, B. A. (2005). Developmental trauma disorder: Toward a rational diagnosis for children with complex trauma histories. *Psychiatric Annals, 35*, 401–408.

van der Kolk, B. A. (2006). Clinical implications of neuroscience research in PTSD. *Annals of the New York Academy of Sciences, 1071,* 277–293.

van der Kolk, B. A., Crozier, J., & Hopper, J. (2001). Child abuse in America: Prevalence, costs, consequences and intervention. *Journal of Aggression, Maltreatment and Trauma, 4,* 9–31.

van der Kolk, B. A., Roth, S., Pelcovitz, D., Sunday, S., & Spinazzola, J. (2005). Disorders of extreme stress: The empirical foundation of a complex adaptation to trauma. *Journal of Traumatic Stress, 18,* 389–399.

Index

Note. *f* following a page number indicates a figure.